THE RISE OF CIVILIZATION

THE RISE OF CIVILIZATION

From Early Farmers to Urban Society in the Ancient Near East

Charles L. Redman

State University of New York
Binghamton

W. H. FREEMAN AND COMPANY
San Francisco

Library of Congress Cataloging in Publication Data

Redman, Charles L.
  The rise of civilization.

  Bibliography: p.
  Includes index.
  1.   Near East—Civilization.   I.   Title.
DS57.R4   939   78–1493
ISBN 0–7167–0056–5
ISBN 0–7167–0055–7 pbk.

Printed in the United States of America

9   8   7   6   5   4   3   2

TO MY FAMILY

PREFACE

There are many compelling reasons for studying the past. Not only is it mysterious and distant, but it is the key to unlocking our origins. Few subjects are as exciting or as interesting as the rise of civilization. Men and women equipped with only simple tools faced the challenge of nature and molded out of a simple beginning a complex society. Their achievements include technical and engineering feats that amaze the experts, economic and industrial innovations that reshaped the world, and artistic and literary accomplishments that are as thrilling today as they were five thousand years ago. The period from 8000 to 2000 B.C., during which agriculture and urban life were introduced in the Near East, was a time of intense creativity and change. The events that took place then are certainly both fascinating to learn about and worthy of serious investigation.

The subject of this book is the rise of civilization in the ancient Near East. Although civilizations emerged in other regions of the world, current information leads to the conclusion that food production and urban society were achieved in the Near East at least as early as they were in any other region of the world, and perhaps even earlier than anywhere else. Even if a new discovery were to reveal that these accomplishments happened earlier in another region, that would not detract from the seminal effect that Near Eastern developments had on the formation of Western Civilization.

I have attempted to write this book so that it satisfies several goals. It is intended primarily for students of archeology, anthropology, and ancient history. It can be used as a basic textbook for courses on the rise of civilization, the Neolithic, or Near Eastern archeology. It is also designed to be a supplementary text or case study for general introductory courses in archeology.

Although I have attempted to present the material in this book objectively, the organization, selection of materials, and balance are affected by my own view of archeology. Hence, it is important for the reader to know what my perspective is. Essentially, I am a positivist and a pragmatist, and I view archeology from these perspectives. I believe that the important processes of the past can be known from the existing material remains, but at the same time I recognize that archeologists have yet to develop many of the techniques necessary for measuring phenomena of interest. Nevertheless, it seems unnecessary to wait until the potential of archeological research has been realized before writing this synthesis. The current state of knowledge is subject to change, and I expect that enormous strides will be taken during the next decades to fill out aspects of the picture that are now only speculative.

The book is organized according to developmental stages rather than strict regionalism or chronological periods. Many sections contain new syntheses for which cultural variables rather than site-by-site analyses are the bases. For each stage of development a few key sites are selected and described in detail as case studies with supporting photographic documentation. The intention is to combine broad coverage with in-depth treatment of existing empirical evidence and current hypotheses on important innovations. Hypotheses are presented as if they were completely developed positions and in some cases as if they were in direct opposition to each other. This is more than is meant by some of their proponents who view their proposals as loosely worked out ideas that they put forth for discussion and not as their final conclusions. I have attempted to be true to their ideas and integrate them in a meaningful fashion. I apologize for any misrepresentations.

There are many people and institutions that have made it possible for me to write this book and to all of them I owe a debt of gratitude. My own interest in the Near East can be traced to my family's influence and predates my career in archeology. I have been most fortunate in teachers, colleagues, and fieldwork, and have benefited greatly by working in the Near East with Linda Braidwood, Halet Çambel, Bruce Howe, Barbara Lawrence, Arthur Jelinek, Hans Nissen, Jean Perrot, Charles Reed, Robert Stewart, Willem van Zeist, Anita Walker, Richard Watson, Gladys Weinberg, Saul Weinberg, and Gary Wright. In addition, Robert McC. Adams, Robert J. Braidwood, and Patty Jo Watson have profoundly influenced my thinking and work by encouraging, advising, criticizing, and being the all-round good friends that every young professional hopes to have.

Field opportunities have been made available to me through a variety of funding institutions, including the National Science Foundation, Ford Foundation, and the Smithsonian Institution. The project that enabled me to collaborate with many of the scholars mentioned above is the Joint Prehistoric Project of the Universities of Istanbul and Chicago directed by Halet Çambel and Robert J. Braidwood. For that opportunity I am indeed grateful.

Many people have helped with various aspects of preparing this manuscript. The staff of W. H. Freeman and Company have been of great assistance, especially John H. Staples. Many others have generously allowed me to use photographs and line drawings in this text. Parts or all of the book were read and constructively commented on by Robert McC. Adams, Robert J. Braidwood, J. Desmond Clark, Jack Harlan, Patty Jo Watson, Richard A. Watson, and Herbert E. Wright. To all of them and to other colleagues I am indebted for many of the ideas expressed here, although they should not be held responsible for any of the shortcomings.

January 1978   *Charles L. Redman*

CONTENTS

THE RISE OF CIVILIZATION

1

PERSPECTIVE ON THE PAST

The Agricultural and Urban Transformations as they occurred in the ancient Near East are among the truly significant milestones in the history of humankind. The social changes that these processes fostered influenced all aspects of society and formed the structure out of which today's world has emerged.

The Near East has been selected as the geographical setting in which to examine the rise of civilization because changes took place there at a very early date, perhaps earlier than anywhere else in the world. In addition to this temporal priority, the history and prehistory of the Near East directly affected the emergence and growth of Western civilization.

To fully understand the material presented in this book, it is necessary to become acquainted both with its organization and with the intellectual perspective from which it was written. The subject matter of this book is cultural change, and the approach taken herein is that change is a gradual cumulative phenomenon but has aspects that are more rapid and sometimes affected by the behavior of individuals.

The presentation of information on the rise of civilization is designed to put the reader in the position of a researcher. Background information on environmental variables and earlier cultural developments are described first.

Hypotheses to explain the cultural transformations, along with special techniques available to the researcher, are presented next. Finally, information about selected sites and regions is presented from which generalizations can be made concerning overall empirical patterns. In this way, hypotheses are portrayed not as the logical conclusions to be drawn from the data, but as trial formulations combining the researcher's ideas, previous formulations, and available information. An hypothesis is, as is this entire volume, the starting point for research, not the final result of a completed investigation.

Human beings are a strongly introspective species, seeking to explain not only their own complexities, but those of the cultures in which they live. It is only by having a thorough knowledge of the past that we can begin to understand our present condition. Questions regarding the origin and development of modern social institutions and everyday lifeways fascinate scholar and layman alike. Why did our ancestors give up their natural existence as hunters and gatherers? What made them join together to live communally, foreshadowing the densely packed cities that characterize most regions of the modern world? When did people gain the upper hand in their efforts to control the environment? What is it that makes civilization civilized? How did the diverse elements that we think of as characteristic of civilization—for better or worse—combine into something so universally appealing to human nature that it was quickly adopted by people in all corners of the earth? These questions—and countless more—bear close examination in order to understand the processes and events that have shaped the human career (Figure 1-1).

Surveying the long sweep of history, we can identify four fundamental transformations in the human condition. The most recent transformation —well documented and analyzed by historians—is the Industrial Revolution of the nineteenth century. The earliest transformation—the least well understood—was the emergence of anatomically and intellectually modern hominids sometime during the Upper Pleistocene (c. 100,000–10,000 B.C.). I have termed this series of changes the Paleolithic Transformation. It was marked by the development of adaptive mechanisms for recognizing potentials within the environment and for organizing efficiently to exploit them. Utilizing their distinct physical, intellectual, and organizational capabilities, hominids set themselves apart from the remainder of the animal kingdom. Increasingly, with the development of cultural inventory, human beings were to play the pivotal role in their collective destiny.

By using the term transformation, I intend to emphasize that the character, appearance, and organization of the societies changed fundamentally. A transformation affects all aspects of a society, both the interrelationships of its constituents and their relationship to the biophysical environment and to other human groups. Although a transformation may be stimulated by inventions or by alterations in a single element or activity, the interdependence of all factors within a functioning society leads to changes in other elements or activities. Hence, even though the initial changes in the Industrial Revolution may have been due to several interrelated discoveries involving energy and mechanics, the ultimate effect was a restructuring of organization and values that permeated all aspects of human life. I believe that the same can be said of the earlier transformations, although evidence for many changes remains speculative.

The Agricultural Transformation (c. 8500–6500 B.C.) was the second major transformation in the human condition and is the subject of the first half of this book. Successful domestication of plants and animals ultimately allowed a larger, more secure food supply. General population growth and increasing numbers of permanent communities accompanied the introduction of agriculture (Figures 1-2 and 1-3, pages 4 and 5). For as long as people had inhabited the earth they had adapted by living successfully within the bounds defined by the natural system, but with agriculture they began to affect their environment to a greater extent than ever before: they cleared forests, introduced alien species of plants and animals, and irreversibly altered the natural ecosystem of many regions. Although human success—as measured in terms of population growth—was considerable, in many areas of the world, this success has produced unfortunate side effects; alterations initiated by prehistoric farmers started a process of degradation that has left vast stretches of land unusable.

The Agricultural Transformation was not solely in subsistence and settlement, but, unquestionably, these two aspects of prehistoric societies are easily recognizable and have been the subjects of extensive studies (G. Wright 1969; Flannery 1973; Reed, ed. 1977). Archeologists have a tendency to consider changes in subsistence activities in terms of

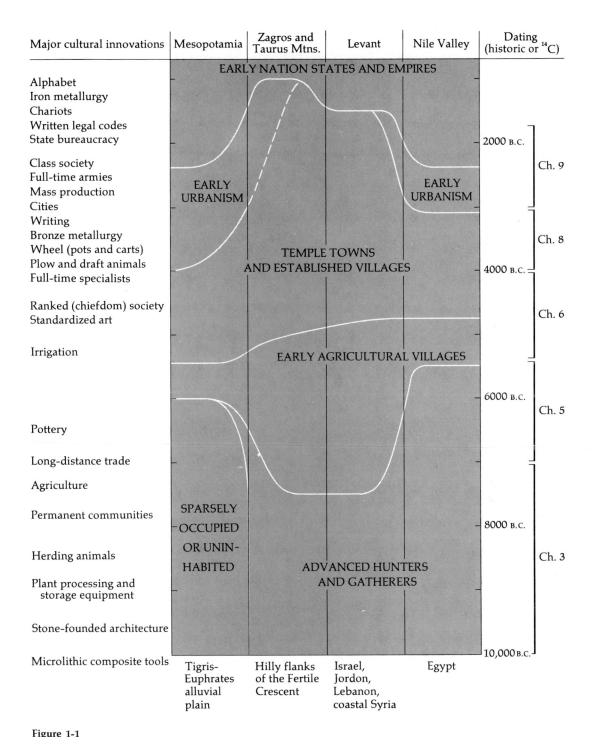

Figure 1-1
Correlation of chronology (^{14}C half-life = 5,570 years), community development, and cultural innovations in the four subregions of the Near East. The chapters in which they are discussed in this book are given at the right.

The following text appears within the figure:

Major cultural innovations	Mesopotamia	Zagros and Taurus Mtns.	Levant	Nile Valley	Dating (historic or ^{14}C)

EARLY NATION STATES AND EMPIRES

Alphabet
Iron metallurgy
Chariots
Written legal codes
State bureaucracy

2000 B.C. — Ch. 9

Class society
Full-time armies
Mass production
Cities

EARLY URBANISM   EARLY URBANISM

Writing
Bronze metallurgy
Wheel (pots and carts)
Plow and draft animals
Full-time specialists

TEMPLE TOWNS AND ESTABLISHED VILLAGES

Ch. 8

4000 B.C.

Ranked (chiefdom) society
Standardized art

Ch. 6

Irrigation

EARLY AGRICULTURAL VILLAGES

6000 B.C. — Ch. 5

Pottery

Long-distance trade

Agriculture

Permanent communities

SPARSELY OCCUPIED OR UNINHABITED

8000 B.C.

Herding animals

Ch. 3

Plant processing and storage equipment

ADVANCED HUNTERS AND GATHERERS

Stone-founded architecture

Microlithic composite tools

10,000 B.C.

| Tigris-Euphrates alluvial plain | Hilly flanks of the Fertile Crescent | Israel, Jordon, Lebanon, coastal Syria | Egypt |

Figure 1-2
Modern village of Ekinciler in the foothills of the Taurus Mountains in
southeastern Anatolia. The village is built on the mound of an ancient
community, continuing the slow accretion that has formed the mounds of
the Near East. (Photograph from the Joint Prehistoric Project of the Universities of Istanbul and Chicago.)

the major technological innovations that helped
make them possible. Of equal, or probably greater,
importance, however, were the organizational
changes that accompanied each of the four major
transformations (Smith 1972a). The particular tools
or facilities that signify a transformation were definitely important at the time, but their role was
transitory because they were rapidly replaced; in
some parts of the world they may never even have
been introduced. The organizational changes, on
the other hand, were so fundamental that their
structure continued throughout subsequent millenia and many of their effects are visible today.

The Agricultural Transformation was a metamorphosis in which almost every aspect of society
was altered. Food production and storage stimulated specialization of activities that furthered the
already emerging division of labor in hunting and
gathering societies. The larger, permanent communities supported by agriculture required new
forms of organization, both social and political.
Family structure and the roles and status of women
were radically altered by the rapidly changing lifestyle engendered by domestication. With perma-

nent facilities, such as houses, heavy artifacts, and
agricultural fields, came the concept of property;
eventually access to these productive goods was
restricted to selected segments of the society.
Changes in world view, moral values, and self-
image most certainly accompanied the material
innovations that archeologists have already noted.
Hence, the Agricultural Transformation included
an entire constellation of economic, organizational,
and moral changes that led to a new stage in the
human career. Village agricultural society is important for us to understand both because a large
part of the world is still at this level and because it
formed the necessary foundation for the emergence of urban civilization.

The third transformation, the subject of the
second half of this book, has been called the Urban
Revolution (Childe 1936). The overt manifestations
of this transformation were ancient cities and states
with all of their civilizational attributes. The emergence of urbanism was not simply an increase in
the size of settlements; it also included fundamental changes in the nature of interactions between
people and in community structure (Adams 1966a).

Figure 1-3
Modern village in the Zagros Mountains of Iran. The stone, mud, and
timber construction is similar to that used in prehistoric villages that were
located nearby.

Processes and institutions that were initiated
by this transformation have continued to evolve,
forming the basic structure of contemporary society. Today most of us live in urban societies,
of which many elements of organization were
first developed five thousand years ago in lowland
Mesopotamia (Figure 1-4, page 6).

Countless innovations, such as writing, ethics,
written legal codes, the wheel, the plow, metallurgy, mathematics, and engineering principles,
that are commonplace in our modern world were
first manifested in the cities of Sumer (Kramer
1959). But, the most significant developments
were those of organization. Social stratification
with differentiated access to strategic sources became the primary structure within a community.
Hierarchical political authority and administrative
systems often utilizing written legal codes emerged
as organizational mechanisms. Craft specialization,
mass-production industries, and large-scale trade
characterized the economy. Organized warfare in
the form of both massive defensive works and
long-distance offensive campaigns played an increasing role in the survival of cultures.

In general, the essential effect of the Urban
Transformation was the change in scale and the
complexity of societal organization that it heralded.
Quantitative growth in community size led to more
than quantitative changes in organizational mechanisms. The emergence of entirely new forms of
integrating institutions distinguishes the Urban
Transformation as one of the few fundamental
achievements in human history.

Geographic Focus

It is possible to study the introduction of agriculture and the emergence of urban life in many
regions of the world. From each region studied, a
great deal could be learned concerning the factors
that favored settled life and increasing organizational complexity. However, there are only a few
regions in which agriculture and urban communities developed with very little external influence.
These so-called pristine regions promise to yield
information on the internal growth of complex
society rather than on the secondary effects pro-

Figure 1-4
Aerial view of the modern city of Erbil in northern Iraq. The almost continuous occupation of this spot for several thousand years has created a high mound of cultural debris. The buildings inside the city walls are tightly clustered along narrow and twisting alleyways. Although there are marked differences, the visual image of this walled city is reminiscent of the early cities of Mesopotamia. (Photograph from Aerofilms Ltd. Copyright reserved.)

duced by external factors on cultures that had several options open to them. The contrast between pristine and secondary agricultural or urban societies is useful because the stimuli and processes contributing to the development of pristine societies were different from those of societies developing near more advanced civilizations. The ethnohistoric record is replete with examples of simple societies that became agriculturalist or urban under the direct influence of other civilizations, but according to Morton Fried (1967) and others the pristine civilizations are limited to Mesopotamia, India, China, Mesoamerica, and the Central Andes. It has been argued that even India and China were strongly influenced by the earlier Mesopotamian civilization (Wheeler 1968).

Current archeological evidence indicates that there is no region where either agriculture or urbanism developed earlier than in the Near East, although new discoveries in southeast Asia or elsewhere may eventually demonstrate that this is not the case. Nevertheless, it will remain unquestioned that the early developments in the Near East

had a greater effect on the nature of Western civilization than analogous developments anywhere else in the world. Direct historical connections link the later, historic empires and peoples of the Near East with the early Mediterranean civilizations of Greece and Rome that are acknowledged in many respects to be ancestral to European civilization. The Greeks and Romans were influenced by their Near Eastern predecessors' writing, ethics, science, engineering, art, mythology, architecture, and political administration.

The systemic perspective used throughout this book does not rely on the distinction between pristine and secondary development, though it was a factor in selecting the Near East as the region to be examined. No settlement, let alone civilization, developed in total isolation from foreign influences. The civilizational process itself is the evolution of a set of interacting components of a continually growing system. Even in the Mesopotamian example, of which there is no question of preceding civilizations, the influence of populations located on the fringes of Mesopotamia was of crucial significance. Secondary urbanization is thus redefined here to refer to only those societies that urbanized under the *direct* guidance or threat of foreign civilizations. This was common in the growth and spread of later civilizations.

All civilization does not stem from the Near East; however, the seminal importance of early developments in this region should not be minimized. Hence, it is the twofold aspect of its pristine nature on the one hand and relevance to subsequent civilizations on the other that have led so many scholars—including myself—to study the prehistoric and early historic societies of the ancient Near East. The complexity of the civilizational process and abundance of detailed information are too great to give equal coverage to all localities within the Near East. Therefore, I have chosen not to recount a history of the totality of the ancient Near East, but to present information on important cultural developments in the order of their occurrence in that particular region of the world. The focus is on what I consider to be areas containing evidence for the earliest developments of each crucial stage. Most of the data has been selected from sites about which a substantial amount of material has been published or that are known to me firsthand.

The environmental and cultural backgrounds of the various subregions of the Near East are presented in Chapters 2 and 3. An understanding of the ecological and human conditions of the entire Near East at the end of the Pleistocene (c. 8000 B.C.) enhances our understanding of why cultures in certain localities quickly began to develop, adopting new subsistence and organizational strategies.

Treatment of the Agricultural Transformation is limited geographically to two crucial subregions—the Levant and the Taurus-Zagros mountain arc. Emphasis is on what the various known sites have in common, as well as on the differences between them. These regions have been intensively investigated by archeologists because they are centers of early and somewhat unusual developments.

The geographic focus of this book is even more restricted in the discussion of the rise of cities. Developments in lowland Mesopotamia are described in detail, whereas the treatment of synchro-

nous developments in Egypt is mainly for the purpose of relating them to the Sumerian example and contrasting them with it. For each developmental stage, discussion is limited to settlements that are thought to have been the most advanced in the region (to a large extent, our knowledge reflects the biases of past archeologists). In a complete study, an emphasis on large, advanced settlements must be balanced by an even-handed treatment of the entire settlement system in each region and of the interactions of advanced regions with those not having equally complex communities. Past archeological biases and a lack of data preclude an exhaustive evaluation or reanalysis at this time. However, it would be counterproductive to avoid a synthetic approach because the data base is not "complete": trial formulations, which help to focus thinking and redirect future investigations, are at the core of scientific progress.

Intellectual Perspective

Cultural Change

It has frequently been suggested that the greatest contribution archeology can make to general social science is through studies of cultural change that span a great many years. In no other discipline does investigation penetrate time so deeply; nor do other disciplines have the diversity of societies available for examination. In addition, many of the events that occurred in the past are no longer occurring, such as the initial introduction of agriculture and urbanism. Although understanding the functioning of a prehistoric society at a particular time is important, knowing how such societies changed through time is also essential.

The usual response of archeologists to questions about cultural change has been the formulation of a chronology—a series of periods. This approach is a manifestation of the physical structure of our data—stratigraphically superimposed deposits—and a conceptual persepctive that emphasizes categorization. However, upon closer inspection the suggested neat boundaries between chronological

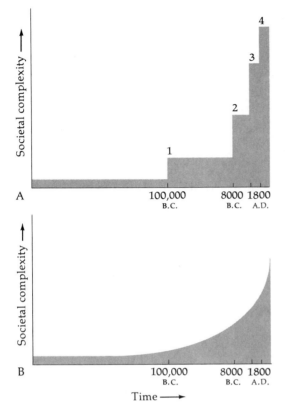

Figure 1-5
Alternative heuristic models for the nature of cultural transformations: (A) a steplike function that implies discontinuous rapid changes; (B) a ramplike function that represents slow cumulative growth.

periods or spatially separate cultures are not as distinct as implied. Cultures are made up of interrelated subsystems in which the members of the society participate. These subsystems may change at somewhat different rates, consequently blurring the boundaries between distinct periods. Changes taking place in each subsystem and in the total society would be better conceptualized as a series of continuous trajectories with varying rates of change. A trajectory could indicate that the cultural change is either a slow continuous process or a series of rapid innovations, the former alternative being depicted as a "ramp" and the latter as a "step" mode of change (Figure 1-5). Both models

are oversimplifications, the process for a cultural change being a combination of both ramps and steplike changes and differing for each subsystem within the transformation (Braidwood and Willey 1962). The choice of which paradigm more closely approximates the reality of the situation directly affects the intellectual approach taken by scientists, as well as the organization of this book.

A ramp model implies a gradual change, without major discontinuities caused by people or their inventions, whereas a step model implies major advances taking place in brief periods, followed by relative stability. Both paradigms are employed in this book for different aspects of the two transformations investigated. In general, I believe that major changes took place slowly, perhaps without the participants recognizing that significant changes were happening. Environmental, cultural, and sociological factors exerted a constant selective pressure favoring certain directions of development that are obvious in viewing many generations at a time. I also believe that alterations in each of the constituent subsystems of the societies undergoing change were gradual. This is emphasized by the fact that, in a long-range view of a process covering a long span of time, we are as yet unable to discern short periods of years.

The step paradigm, on the other hand, has greater significance if either the Agricultural or the Urban Transformation is viewed as a whole. In terms of the length of human history, the major transformations seem to have been few indeed and relatively restricted in duration. Compared with the two or more million years during which human beings were hunters and gatherers, the two thousand years required to accomplish the introduction of agriculture in many areas of the Near East seems instantaneous. Following the introduction of agriculture, there seems to have been a two-thousand-year period of consolidation and improvement in agricultural life, but it is difficult to judge whether this period of relative stability is a result of current archeological interpretations or is what in fact happened. After this two-thousand-year period, there was another short period of rapid innovation—the Urban Transformation. In

Stage 1   Stage 2   Stage 3   Stage 4   Stage 5   Stage 6   Stage 7

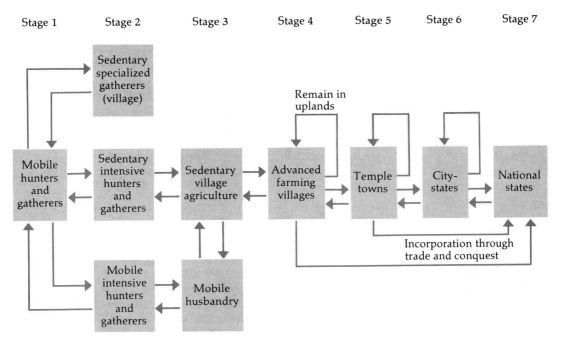

Figure 1-6
Seven developmental stages of subsistence-settlement development in the
Near East. (See Figures 4-6 and 7-1 and accompanying text for expanded
discussion.)

the course of a thousand years, cities became the centers of settlement and hierarchical administrative organizations emerged. The reason that these major transformations seem to have taken place in a steplike fashion is that they represent wholistic changes involving a constellation of subsystems and factors that may have been changing more slowly. Although individual activities may change in a slow continuous fashion, thresholds are reached that accelerate the interactions between variables, prompting additional changes. Hence, it is the interrelatedness of many aspects of these two transformations that accounts for their magnitude and apparent rapidity.

It is necessary to adopt a temporal framework for examining archeological data, with respect to both change and synchronic structure. One way of doing this is to classify information into chronological periods as the primary analytical units. Although this is frequently done by archeologists,

chronological precision is often insufficient for making inferences about contemporaneity, and the interpretations tend to be lists of artifact types rather than analyses of societal functioning. An alternative method is to view the archeological evidence as a series of developmental stages. These stages can be defined on the basis of subsistence pursuits, community organization, or some other criterion selected by the investigator (Figure 1-6). Although this method also is arbitrary and selective, it does focus the analysis on elements of the society's functioning that are of prime interest. In this book, data about sites are presented in terms of the periods reported by the excavators, whereas the interpretive models and the overall organization of chapters are cast in terms of developmental stages. Hence, the reader is given the chronological information for evaluating the developmental stages as defined herein.

The Agricultural and Urban transformations can

be divided into a series of alternative subsistence-settlement systems in which the ancient communities participated (Figure 1-6). To understand why particular changes occurred requires a description of the systems. However, even a complete description of these systems in their chronological order is not to be confused with an explanation of why a transformation occurred. Of ultimate interest are the cultural processes that caused these settlements to take the form they did. Hence, it is important to delineate not only the products of the processes (successive subsistence-settlement systems), but also the relationships of the variables involved, for these relationships constitute the process itself. Our goal is to examine each occurrence of a particular development and attempt to identify the general variables that were instrumental in causing it. Variables that are crucial in one transformation should be investigated in other transformations, keeping in mind the different systemic context within which they occur. By recognizing the cultural variables that are of recurrent importance and explaining their interrelationships, it should be possible to construct laws useful in explaining other specific instances of change throughout the world.

An *evolutionary perspective* is utilized to integrate the material from the long period spanning the rise of civilization in the Near East. Two interpretive assumptions are necessary to be able to investigate the causes of cultural change from an evolutionary perspective: (1) human behavior is adaptive and (2) successive forms of a community are related by culture and tradition. Hence, continuity through long periods can be traced to learning patterns and cultural mechanisms for transmitting information, whereas changing societal forms are related to what the participants view as adaptive strategies. Adaptive strategy does not imply that people always attempted to maximize their short-term options but that in the long run they behaved in an economic manner. Adaptive behavior depends partly on cultural constructs because the alternatives perceived by the decision-maker are affected by cultural values. Nevertheless, most decisions are those that are favorable in light of socioenviron-

mental opportunities, and persistently deviant cultures or people usually fail.

Two processes combine to determine cultural continuity and evolutionary change: *variety generation* and *variety selection* (Plog 1974b). Variety is continually being generated by every human population. Most people know a variety of ways of accomplishing the same end (yet choose to use only one method). Potential sources of variety include contact with others, individual invention, and mislearning. The general tendency observed among human groups is toward increasing variation in cultural inventories and concepts. For example, variety generation in terms of cultural inventory could be the several different ways of making and decorating ceramic vessels used for water storage; in terms of cultural concepts and strategies, it could be several different methods for procuring and preparing a particular food.

Variety selection is the process by which members of a society use only a limited number of the variations potentially available. In a society in which the selection procedures are generally agreed upon by its members, a modal pattern of preferred behavior is produced. Among the pressures that affect the selective patterns of a human group are environment, available technology, and cultural beliefs. The high productivity of certain choices makes them desirable components of patterns and they are adopted by new societies rapidly, whereas other, less-productive choices are not selected. There is a range of choices, especially in terms of subsistence strategies, that are not productive under normal conditions but prove to be invaluable during periods of severe need. Societies that retain these choices as known strategies, although not employing them regularly, will often survive under conditions fatal to groups who restrict their options more rigorously.

In a stable environment (both social and biophysical), the results of variety generation and selection reinforce the stable situation within culturally defined limits. In a changing environment, the variety generating and selecting mechanisms available to a human group are crucial to their evolutionary change and even their survival.

The evolutionary process is both specific and general (Sahlins and Service 1960). Specific evolution is based on the principle that lifeways tend inevitably toward diversification in the absence of strong selective (centralizing) pressures. Separate populations differentiate themselves economically, adjusting to the exploitation of their particular environments. Social groups often distinguish themselves from other groups in terms of cultural equipment and symbolism. The study of specific evolutionary developments includes following the sequence of changes within an individual group or a small region, emphasizing the historic relations of successive communities. Specific evolution includes specialization leading to multilinear paths of change. In an extreme situation, a culture may overspecialize in order to adapt to a particular environmental condition, but most overspecialized societies are not successful for long periods. The ability to remain structurally flexible is a very important characteristic for human groups. Situations and resources change and, if a community is too tightly tied to a specific lifeway, then it may not be able to cope with change. Hence, a major accomplishment of societies within the Near East is that they were able to recognize the resources available and adapt their organization to the changing opportunities that the environment and technology made possible.

General evolution emphasizes stages of development and the transformations between them. The study of general evolution requires an analysis of the similarities between disparate situations. Such an analysis includes the examination of problems of organization, complexity, and energy utilization. Whereas the specific historical sequence of events and settlements is the primary evidence for a specific evolutionary perspective, that of general evolution is the level of adaptation and organization taken as a whole. The duality that is explicit in the concept of evolution should be viewed as different perspectives on processes that contain elements of both. A productive approach is to delineate which observable traits and developments relate to a specific situation and which are elements of more general developmental significance.

Throughout this book an attempt is made to differentiate between significant regularities and the complexity and range of cultural variation indicated in the archeological record at each level of development.

Interpretive Frameworks

The methods of collecting and analyzing archeological data, as well as presenting the information, are closely tied to the interpretive framework used by the researcher. In this book, a systemic view of culture is adhered to for selecting and integrating information. The essential components of a systemic view of culture include the propositions that (1) culture is not shared but participated in differentially by its members; (2) culture is multivariate, comprising interrelated subsystems; and (3) the archeologists's knowledge of past cultures must be gained from information that can be obtained from material remains (Binford 1965; Struever 1971; Watson, LeBlanc, and Redman 1971). There are several methodological implications in these propositions, the most important being that a single "typical" example does not yield sufficient information on past behavior; it is the range of variation among members of a system and their interrelationships that allow an adequate understanding of past societies.

Acceptance of the systemic view of culture has led many archeologists to an interest in the principles of *systems theory*. Although the adoption of systems theory has not revolutionized archeological research, it has contributed in three ways to archeological investigations by supplying (1) a theoretical perspective; (2) a body of concepts; and (3) systems models for forming hypotheses and for interpretive purposes (Watson, LeBlanc, Redman 1971; Plog 1975). The overall theoretical perspective advocated by system theorists posits that there are systemic relationships so basic that they occur in many different living and nonliving entities. This position requires an initial wholistic approach to examining a system with an emphasis on the interrelatedness of its parts. Some archeologists have attempted to go beyond using this perspective to interpret past societies, suggesting that archeological remains themselves and the concepts used for categorizing them could be profitably viewed in a systemic context (Clarke 1968; Schiffer 1976). These innovative approaches are in their infancy but have already begun to help organize archeological interpretations into more realistic and inclusive propositions.

As in the current archeological literature, systemic concepts are used in many of the discussions in this book. The primary purpose in incorporating such terminology as *positive-feedback relationships* is to ask old questions in new ways that then channel energies in what are considered by many archeologists to be more productive avenues than those followed in the past. Systemic concepts, like the overall theoretical perspective, lead to a greater concern with variability and interrelatedness in the organization of societies. In some respects, negative feedback (a mechanism for damping deviation) and positive feedback (one for amplifying deviation) are not new concepts to the social scientists, but they have been put into a more readily usable form by the systems theorists. More complex systems concepts such as the segregation and linearization of hierarchical systems have been used to attempt to explain the rise of state administration without relying primarily on what have formerly been considered "prime movers," such as irrigation or warfare (Flannery 1972; Chapter 7 of this book).

Systems models have been used for a variety of purposes in archeology. They enable researchers to organize large quantities of data, to assess whether the suggested interrelationships of variables are logical and complete, and, by conducting a simulation analysis, to determine under what conditions the posited results would occur. So far, systems models have supplied no easy answers to archeologists; however, they have created frameworks within which to specify interrelationships in behavioral systems to help focus hypotheses and future research on questions of importance. To explain the appearance of new phenomena or changes in existing systems, it is necessary to outline in an explicit fashion the existence and inter-

relationships of relevant variables and stimuli (Hill 1971). The suggested relationships of variables and their products should be subsumed under confirmed general relationships deriving from social sciences. Because a codified body of such relationships or laws does not exist in a usable form, assertions on the nature and outcome of specific relationships are described in terms of logic and the inferences drawn from archeological, historical, and ethnographical investigations.

Three sets of factors are interrelated in the systems models presented in Chapters 4 and 7 to illuminate the processes by which agriculture was introduced and urbanism emerged:

1   Positive-feedback cycles between variables that promote change
2   Environmental or cultural stimuli (or both) that set up and initiate the positive-feedback relationships
3   Stabilizing and regulating mechanisms that emerge to control and integrate the changes that have taken place

From an effective systems model, a researcher should be able to infer the course of developments, given the preceding situation, the initial stimuli, and the potential feedback relationships. An adequate explanation requires a thorough understanding of the phenomenon, including answers to the questions of how and why a particular process occurred. This seemingly deterministic approach might seem unrealistic to some social scientists, but it should not. I acknowledge that prehistoric communities were composed of people who made decisions for which the bases were both rational and apparently irrational. With the emergence of an administrative elite composed of a small proportion of the population, the decisions and goals of a few may have influenced particular events of widespread significance. However, I do not interpret this as a reason for eschewing what has recently been termed a "gradualist-systemic approach." To the contrary, the positive-feedback relationships posited in Chapters 4 and 7 rely on the motivation of people to improve their own lives. This is particularly necessary in evaluating methods by which the emerging elite fostered situations and institutions that increased their growing control. In dealing with large population aggregates and long spans of time, individual goals and aspirations can be adequately accounted for in statistical, cumulative, behaviorist terms. Apparently unpredictable actions of a single person may cause minor perturbations in the course of development, but unless such actions are undertaken by many other members of a community and incorporated into on-going feedback relationships, they will not be of long-term, major significance. When a single person or a group made decisions in accordance with the interrelationships outlined in the systems models portrayed in Figures 4-6 and 7-6, they were more successful than those who acted otherwise. Not all communities nor all individual members of them behaved as suggested in these models, but those who did were at an advantage and, hence, there was a selective pressure for the suggested decisions and goals.

The introduction of agriculture and the process of urbanization were not linear arrangements in which one factor caused a change in a second factor, which caused a change in a third, and so on. Rather, these transformations should be conceptualized as a series of interacting incremental processes that were triggered by favorable ecological and cultural conditions and increased in a series of mutually reinforcing interactions. Development comprised several positive-feedback interrelationships. These feedback relationships did not function with little noticeable change for long periods followed by sudden metamorphosis. Rather, each development started slowly and increased by small increments, at an irregular pace determined by a series of factors. Although the changes occurring in a single human generation may have seemed minor to the participants, the cumulative effect was enormous.

Although systems theory, with its concepts and modelling procedures, supplies an interpretive structure in which to work, it is an *ecological approach* that gives interpretive substance to this framework. The close interdependence of human society in its biophysical environment is one of the underlying themes of this book. A major body of information gained from the study of cultural history concerns the alternative ways societies have adapted to their environments for hundreds of thousands of years in diverse habitats throughout the world. Although the transformations that constitute the rise of civilization were largely cultural, it is impossible to separate them from their environmental settings. The recognition of people as an integral part of nature has stimulated the growth of a new field of inquiry—human ecology (Bates 1953; Vayda and Rappaport 1968; Margalef 1968; Netting 1971). Human ecology is the study of the relationship of human beings to other organisms and to their physical surroundings. Some ecologists suggest that it is more useful to regard ecology as a pervasive point of view rather than as a special subject matter (Bates 1953:701). Persons using this ecological perspective view culture against an environmental background and emphasize the systemic nature of the interdependence of human beings with their surroundings. Culture is seen as one subsystem of the more general natural ecosystem. Culture in its technological, organizational, and ideational form acts as a buffer between the human group and its environment. To understand the developmental processes of cultural systems, the interactive relationships within the total ecosystem must be investigated. The effect of applying this perspective within a systems framework is to shift major research efforts away from an emphasis on cultural entities in isolation toward a concern with interrelationships. Artifacts, subsistence strategies, and social organizations should not be considered in isolation, but should be viewed in relation to one another, and to the general ecosystem of humans and nature. The ecological approach is well suited for archeologists because it relies on categories of data including topography, flora, fauna, and natural resources that are fairly easy to recognize in the archeological record.

An ecological approach should not be confused with classical theories of environmental determinism. Instead of suggesting one-to-one correlations between certain environments and respective cultural forms, ecological archeologists stress the interpenetration and interdependence of culture and environment. The complexity of the environmental situations and the detail of society's diverse adaptations to them are emphasized, together with the dynamic aspects of subsistence and other adaptive systems. An ecological approach has made workable and scientifically productive the old assumption that the environment has a strong influence on human lifeways.

Use of an ecological approach relies on the acceptance of several assumptions about culture and environment (Sanders and Price 1968):

1 Each biophysical environment presents particular obstacles to human use, generating varied human responses. These responses may be technological, organizational, ideational, or physiological.
2 There is an almost unlimited number of possible ways, but a limited number of probable ones in which a society can adapt to a given environment. Although there are exceptions, at a general level societies in similar environments tend to adapt in similar ways; in different environments, in different ways.
3 Human culture is, in an ecological sense, a means by which human beings compete and integrate with animals, plants, and other human beings within a particular physical setting. Almost all aspects of culture have positive or negative adaptive importance, but the effect of each human response must be evaluated in the context of the specific conditions available to the community (see Figures 4-6 and 4-7).

One method of conceptualizing the relationship between a community and its biophysical surroundings is to use the notion of an ecological niche, as employed by animal ecologists. An *ecological niche* is defined in cultural terms as the position of a human group in the total environmental system, the group's relationships to resources and competitors (Barth 1956:1079). Cultures are thought to participate in different aspects of general ecosystems, and to relate to each other and to their surroundings in differing ways. Ecological niches are not to be confused with environmental zones nor

with the simple geographic location of settlements. Environmental zones delineate the different regions occupied by distinctive arrays of plants and animals, and each is characterized by a particular topography, climate, and soil.

The ecological niche that a society occupies is not a part of a geographic region but is a position within a complex of relationships. The ecological niche is limited by the environmental zones available, each with its characteristic resources, but is most dependent on the specific range of those resources the society chooses to utilize. The natural environment is perceived and mediated by cultural ideas. A potential resource does not become a resource until it is recognized and exploited. Thus, niches are selectively occupied by a society and include the procurement systems of the society, plus its other relations with plants, animals, and human neighbors. Consequently, two societies can exist side by side in the same environmental zone or habitat and occupy different ecological niches. An example of this situation in both the ancient and the contemporary Near East is the coexistence of sedentary farmers and semisedentary pastoralists, whose herds feed on the stubble in farmers' fields and the unoccupied tracts of land in the vicinity (Barth 1961).

Framework of Presentation

The organization of the information presented in this book is related to the nature of the transformations being examined, the availability of evidence, and my perspective on archeological problem-solving. The arrangement of the chapters parallels the four steps in archeological problem-solving:

1 Background information is presented to familiarize the reader with the dimensions of the problem to be investigated. This includes both environmental and cultural information.
2 Current hypotheses about the transformation are discussed. These alternative formulations communicate the intellectual milieu within which

research is conducted and puts the data into a meaningful framework.

3 Methods, problems, and resources relevant to the transformation are introduced. These are the tools available to archeologists and the particular circumstances of research.

4 Data are presented from key sites and other sources. Information about settlements, subsistence resources, technology, and other activities are outlined from selected archeological sites, with brief descriptions of additional sites, to indicate the range of variation. The dual purpose is to present a description of the cultural historical sequence of events and to supply data for evaluating alternative hypotheses for each transformation.

Hypotheses and methods are presented before the description of available evidence because, to present data first, would imply that the hypotheses are logically reached by synthesizing the data. This is not the case in archeology nor any other discipline. Hypotheses are trial formulations derived from a complex combination of insight, intuition, and previously collected data. They should not be presented as conclusions but as starting points, informing the reader of reasonable alternative constructs and enabling him to view the data as test material for evaluating which of the mentioned theories are most strongly supported by the evidence. Hence data presented in Chapter 5 are relevant to the hypotheses in Chapter 4, just as the information in Chapters 8 and 9 illuminate the hypotheses in Chapter 7. Like a researcher, the reader is given background, hypotheses, and data to digest.

The data presented for each level of development are related to the nature of the archeological remains, as well as what the excavator has chosen to publish. The limitations of past work and the biases of investigators leave their imprint on my analysis. Several general limitations affect all materials: archeological periods are defined on the basis of diagnostic artifacts and any radioisotope or historic dating available. Hence, most periods are not of comparable length nor geographic scope and do not necessarily reflect individual societies. Dating becomes more accurate and periods shorter as the civilizations under study become closer in time to those that achieved literacy.

The nature of the remains, and consequently the descriptions of the sites, varies greatly from one level of development to the next. An attempt has been made to present comparable information for each level of development from each site, but categories of the material inventory, as well as the perspectives of the excavators, cause radical differences in the data published about each level. For the prefarming Pleistocene settlements described in Chapter 3, types of stone tools, radiocarbon dates, location of site, and animal resources consumed are the major categories of evidence. For early villages, this evidence is extended to include house form, specialized activities, plants consumed, and occasional regional settlement patterns. With early civilization, the research focus shifts from specifics of stratigraphy, subsistence, and house form to more general questions of government, religion, and economy. This is facilitated by the availability of written sources on which to base inferences. However, the early stages of urbanism lie between the two extremes. There are neither complete written sources nor the detailed studies characteristic of early village archeological research. Fortunately, recent regional settlement pattern studies and stratigraphic excavations have supplemented the scanty archeological data on early urbanism.

Although aspects of the data from different periods may be difficult to integrate and there may be other methods for presenting this information, I believe that an up-to-date synthesis, such as is attempted in this book, is overdue. Rather than waiting for the last spadeful of dirt to be excavated or for a total renovation of our existing information base, I have moved ahead with what is available in order to communicate to the reader the state of our knowledge on the exciting and seminal issues of past social development.

2

THE ENVIRONMENTAL BACKGROUND

Nature Sets the Stage

*The environmental conditions in the Near East afforded the
ecological background for the introduction of agriculture and the
growth of urban society; hence, a knowledge of these conditions is
essential to understanding the changes that took place. The
Near East is a region of great diversity dominated by hilly and
mountainous areas in the north and vast stretches of semiarid and
desert areas in the south. The climate is governed by a
regime of winter rainfall and summer drought, with seasonal
and geographical extremes in temperature and precipitation.
The topographic diversity and the distribution of
rainfall, soil, and plant communities of the Near East lead to the
logical conclusion that the area can be organized into a series
of environmental zones. Eight zones that characterize the
environmental features directly related to this study are described
in this chapter. Certain landforms and climatic conditions
enhance the growth of certain species of plants, which in turn
support certain animals, including human beings. In addition to
the characteristics of each environmental zone, the proximity of one
to another affects human utilization of the countryside. To
emphasize both content and juxtaposition of natural settings,
these environmental zones are presented as they would
be encountered in traveling across the Near East twice, first from
southeast to northwest and then from southwest to northeast.*

To understand the fundamental transformations in the rise of civilization requires knowledge of the ecological milieu in which they took place because, though the transformations themselves were largely cultural, they cannot be separated from their environmental settings. Human beings are an integral part of ecosystems composed of landforms, climate, plants, and animals. The environment of any particular region offers possibilities and limitations for human adaptation, and the manner in which human beings adapt in turn affects the natural surroundings. To adapt more effectively, they have developed culture, which in various forms acts as a mediator between the human group and its surroundings. With the aid of cultural agencies, human beings have become highly efficient at protecting themselves, securing food, and transmitting critical information about the environment—basic goals of any organism but especially well developed by human beings. The introduction of agriculture and the emergence of urban life are important adaptive strategies utilized by societies in the Near East to cope more effectively with their environment. To understand these processes, other aspects of human behavior, or the evolution of any culture, we must examine the ecological setting in question and the way human groups adapted to it.

The environmental information in this chapter is intended to facilitate the reader's understanding of the processes that were a part of the rise of civilization. One section contains a brief description of the major environmental factors that affected human habitation of the Near East, including general patterns of topography, hyrology, climate, soils, and vegetation. This is followed by a detailed description of what I define as the eight major environmental zones in the Near East (Figure 2-4). They are discussed in the order in which they would be encountered in two journeys (transects) covering the length and breadth of greater Mesopotamia (Figures 2-5 and 2-15). In the course of these journeys, the juxtaposition of zones and the conditions prevailing in each one are emphasized.

Society and Nature

The close interdependence of human society and its physical environment is one of the underlying themes of this book, as it is of all works on the evolution of culture. The study of cultural history yields information about the different ways in which societies have adapted to their environments through hundreds of thousands of years in diverse habitats throughout the world. In recent years, people have recognized both the seriousness of the effects that human activities have had on the global environment and the necessity for maintaining a worldwide ecological balance. Although industrialization and population growth have tremendously hastened degradation, it was during the transformations described in this book that human beings began to alter their surroundings in irreparable ways. Throughout the Near East there is ample evidence of how societies have produced in the past 10,000 years, as a by-product of intensive use and mismanagement, an environment that is far more hostile to human habitation than that which existed when the first farmers occupied the land. There are lessons—relevant today—to be learned from the past successes and failures of the relationships between human beings and nature. Ecological relationships can be studied in many parts of the world, but the Near East offers one of the longest, best-documented, and most diverse sets of data.

The extinction, or near extinction, of many species of animals, from lions to onagers, is an obvious result of human activities, but of even greater seriousness is the effect of the introduction and intensive practice of agriculture in large areas of the Near East. Vast stretches of foothills and mountains have been denuded of the woodlands by the cutting of timber for building and fuel, and enormous areas of grassland have been robbed of their herbaceous cover by poor farming practices and overgrazing by animals. Soil was left unprotected, leading to widespread erosion on steep slopes. The soil that is necessary for plant growth and animal subsistence cannot be replaced quickly. A visit to the foothill regions of the Near East, location of many of the earliest farming villages in the world, is sobering. We know from the archeological record that—besides growing grain and legume crops—these early villagers collected acorns, almonds, pistachios, and other plant foods, and they hunted such wild animals as deer, pigs, and aurochs. Today these areas are barren of animal life and treeless; yet the climate has not materially changed in the past eight thousand years. Human society has altered the landscape.

A striking example of such alteration is the heartland of Mesopotamian civilization where, in the lower reaches of the valley of the Tigris and Euphrates rivers, people first lived in cities and organized themselves into a complex society. Dense populations were supported by a very successful agricultural system. Today, in the shadow of many of the important ancient cities, there is not a single modern settlement. Much of Sumer today is a desert. Parts of the cradle of civilization are now desolate wastelands where only occasional goat herders or camel drivers pass with their animals. What happened, and continues to happen, is that the soil became salinized because of over-irrigation and inadequate drainage. Little can grow in areas where the salt content of the soil and ground water is so high that the surface is white from salt encrustation. Salinization is not only a recent phenomenon; it was a major problem in early historic times and a good deal of effort was made to ameliorate its effects. In different periods of history, people were more successful in retarding and correcting salinization than we are today.

Understanding the relationships between environments and cultural systems requires the examination of certain physical variables. Primary among them is the topography of a region. It has been demonstrated for several societies that landform was the single most important variable in the selection of a location for habitation by prehistoric peoples (Plog 1968; Redman 1974b). Topography was an important factor in evaluating a location's defendability; it also affected the establishment of overland routes for trade and communications.

Regional and local landforms not only affect the climate of an area, but also the nature of the soils that form there. The climate of an area is also affected by such factors as the proximity of a large body of water, a dry continental area, or a barrier of mountains. The combination of a region's topography and the effects of its surroundings determines weather patterns and, hence, the potential for plant and animal life. The location of water sources and the accessibility of ground water are of fundamental importance for the human inhabitants of a region, and mineral resources such as flints, obsidian, copper, gold, or bitumen also can be of major importance in the development of communities. All of these factors are interrelated and directly influence, although they do not totally determine, the course of cultural evolution in any particular geographic region.

In the Near East, certain plants and animals are indigenous to certain locations and terrain. Their distribution directly affects the types of settlements that can develop (see Chapter 4). The juxtaposition of different environmental zones offers diverse possibilities for local development. The environmental diversity within a region is a crucial variable for many cultural developments, and it can be due to changes in elevation within short distances or to resources that influence horizontal patterns (river valleys). It is important to note whether the occupants of an area specialize to take advantage of a limited range of available zones and resources or adapt to a wider spectrum of potential resources. The resource procurement strategy is to be determined, in part, by a variety of cultural factors, but the geographic situation influences the potential choices.

In a region such as the Nile Valley, the river and topography are a unifying force reflected in the political organization of the civilization that developed there. However, regions like the Levant, which is isolated and topographically dissected within, remained for most of their history politically fragmented. At each stage of the rise of civilization, one aspect of the environment may have influenced the course of human events more than any other, but it is clear that, at all stages, human beings and their environment were closely interrelated.

General Environmental Factors in the Near East

The amount of detail about the environment that is required for an archeological investigation depends on the purpose of the research. If regions of a continent or of different continents are being compared, vast areas can be treated as if they were homogeneous. Although such a "coarse grain" view of the environment can be useful for investigating certain types of large-scale problems related to the general workings of cultural systems integrated throughout entire regions, it obscures diversity—knowledge of which is important for an understanding of the processes that occurred in the Near East. If the goal is to understand the subsistence activities of a single community or of a group of settlements within a small area, then a "fine grain" perspective is required. For such a perspective, it is necessary to establish the alternative sources of food, their distributions, and their seasonal availability—a study referred to as a site catchment analysis (Higgs and Vita-Finzi 1972).

Landforms

Although there is great diversity in the physical terrain of different areas of the Near East, it is useful as a first approximation to divide this region into two major landform zones. The first zone is defined by the major mountain ranges—the Pontic and Taurus of Anatolia and the Zagros and Elburz of Iran—running across the northern half of the Near East (Figure 2-1, page 20). Many peaks are at higher elevations than the 2,000-meter tree line (especially in eastern Anatolia and northern Iran). Many alluvial valleys are interspersed among these mountains, and there are two major upland plateaus. The Anatolian plateau is surrounded by the Pontic and Taurus, and the Iranian plateau by the Zagros, Elburz, and other mountains in the east. Both plateaus are at elevations ranging from 500 to 1,500 meters and are generally dry.

The second major landform zone of the Near East comprises the southern hills and plains; its diverse topography ranges from alluvial plains to rolling hills and low mountains at elevations from sea level to 1,000 meters (Figure 2-1). Geologically, this zone is composed of horizontal sedimentary rocks—moderately warped, somewhat eroded, and dissected—overlying an ancient substratum. The major feature of this zone is the broad valley of the Tigris and Euphrates rivers. This depression occupies a tectonically unstable trough formed during the Pliocene by compressional movements of the earth's crust, forcing the Iranian plateau closer to the central platform of Arabia. The land between these plateaus was compressed, downwarped, and folded by inward pressure. The effect of this compression is evident in the parallel-fold ridges of the Zagros Mountains that border the Mesopotamian Plain (see Figure 2-1). The plain itself was depressed and began to fill with the erosion products of the surrounding mountain ridges of both the Zagros and Taurus ranges. Hence, the folded terrain near the center of the depression was covered with alluvial sediment and is now a very flat plain. To the north and east of the Mesopotamian Plain, the folds are higher and emerge above the level of the plain as parallel ridges, each being higher than the last until they can be considered mountains.

The Levant is a zone of junction where relatively recent sediments are folded onto the buckled and broken edge of the Arabian platform (Fisher 1963:396). Fracturing in a generally north–south direction, with minor cross-faults at intervals, has given rise to a series of detached upland masses separated from each other by small lowland areas arranged in a roughly rectangular pattern. This terrain was effective in limiting the development of politically unified states in the Levant and has also been a long-time refuge for religious and ethnic minority groups. The mountain ranges, especially in the north, are an effective barrier to movement inland from the narrow and broken coastal plain. Settlement in the hilly country is restricted to valley floors. Because of lower rainfall further inland in the Syrian desert, communities had to be located on rivers or near springs. These factors,

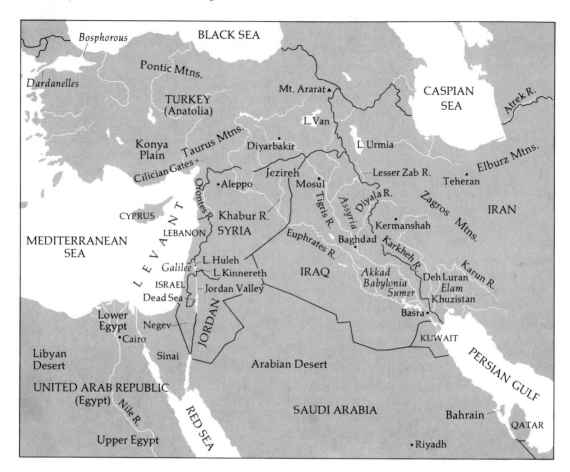

Figure 2-1
Map of the Near East identifying major regions and bodies of water.

among others, favored the growth of city-states rather than unified empires.

An area of the Levant of great archeological and geological interest is the Jordan Rift Valley. As the northern end of a major rift system that can be traced all the way to South Africa, the Jordan Rift Valley extends 400 kilometers north from the head of the Gulf of Akaba. The Jordan Rift varies in width from 3 to 25 kilometers; its lowest point, the surface of the Dead Sea, is 395 meters below sea level. The environmental diversity resulting from this irregular terrain and the archeological

sites in the Jordan Rift Valley are discussed in detail below.

Climate

Many physical conditions are related to the type of climate of a given region. Latitude, topography, neighboring landforms, and local floral conditions have their effect on temperature and precipitation. There are several general principles that both help to explain climatic patterns in the Near East and are applicable to the rest of the world.

A basic pattern for the temperature of a given region is that it is highest near the equator (to the south in the Near East) and becomes progressively lower as the distance from the equator increases. However, if latitude were the only variable affecting temperature, then similar temperatures would be expected in places with the same latitude. Elevation causing air masses to rise and fall also affects local temperature. Air coming to a landmass from over a body of water will cool as it goes up over a mountain range and drop most of its moisture as rain. (Air cools at a constant rate as it rises in elevation—approximately 1°C per 100 meters—but, after it has dropped most of its moisture, it cools more slowly—approximately 0.6°C per 100 meters.) When the air has passed over the peaks of the mountain range, it is relatively dry and heats up quickly as it descends into interior regions (warming approximately 1°C per 100 meters). Hence, air that is over a continental region blocked from the sea by a mountain range is warmer than that over a region that is not blocked from the sea, even though latitude and elevation are the same for both regions. Much of the Near East is blocked in the north and west by major mountain ranges that cause the prevailing westerly and northerly winds to lose their moisture in the coastal uplands and to increase their temperature by the time they reach the interior lowlands.

A regional feature of the Near East is its proximity to wide expanses of desert, from which intensly hot, dry air may be drawn. If a strong wind blows off the desert, it can raise the temperature by as much as 15° to 20°C within a few hours and lower the relative humidity to less than 10 percent (Fisher 1963:46). Driving sand and dust frequently accompany such bursts of desert air and are major causes of crop destruction on the fringes of desert areas. These wind storms occur chiefly in autumn and spring because at these seasons the desert heats up more rapidly than do the cooler northern areas and creates a pressure gradient.

Two major characteristics of Near Eastern climate in the lowlands are high temperatures in the summer and a broad temperature range, both annually and diurnally. A clear sky is an important factor responsible for intense heating, which is also promoted by the absence of soil and vegetation. Another factor affecting temperature is the mountainous coastline, which restricts the tempering effect of the sea to a narrow strip. Although the summers are hot in most parts of the Near East, the winters are usually quite cool or even cold. Snow falls in many places and only southern Arabia is entirely free from snowfall.

The distribution of rainfall in the Near East is largely controlled by topography and the disposition of land and sea in relation to rain-bearing winds (Figure 2-2, page 22). The Near East is predominantly a continental area, certain regions of which are affected by the proximity of small bodies of water. Its continental aspect is emphasized by the presence of high coastal mountain ranges. A rule of thumb for most regions is that the occurrence of rain is proportional to the length of coastline, especially westward-facing coastline (Figure 2-2). Moist winds frequently break through the coastal chain in Syria—through the Syrian Saddle—to contribute moisture to the Taurus and Zagros mountains and foothills. The amount of precipitation varies greatly from year to year, which makes average annual rainfall figures very misleading. For example, in a twenty-year period, the average annual precipitation was 139 millimeters at Baghdad, but it varied from as little as 72 millimeters to as much as 316 millimeters (Adams 1965:4). Few regions outside of the highlands have a stable annual rainfall. Factors affecting the usable proportion of the precipitation are season of rainfall, intensity of rainfall, and permeability of soil. Rainfall evaporates least during the winter when temperatures are lowest. Intense rainstorms lead to runoff that is either lost or feeds rivers or springs. If the combination of factors is favorable, considerably less rainfall is necessary for dry farming than would be required in other circumstances.

One of the overriding features of the Mediterranean climate regime of important regions of the Near East affecting the development of agricultural society is the winter rainfall regime. Most precipitation, and almost all usable rainfall, occurs in the winter months at the middle and lower elevations.

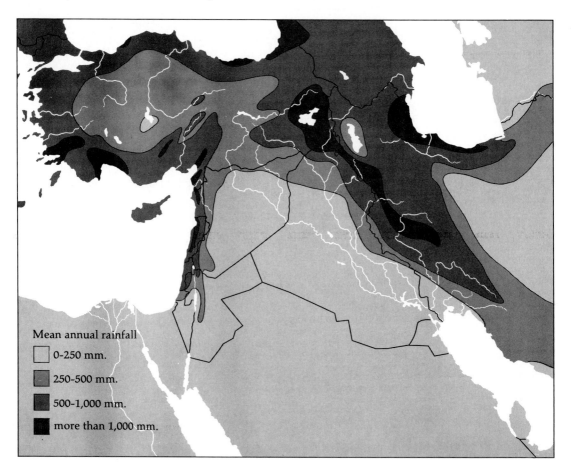

Figure 2-2
Annual precipitation in the Near East.

It is thought that early agriculturalists in the Near East cultivated their crops only in winter, on land that is located at the middle of the range of elevations (see Chapters 4 and 5 for details). Plants like barley, wheat, peas, lentils, flax, chickpeas, and vetch were originally adapted to a winter growing season; they were planted sometime between October and December and harvested between April and June, the exact dates varying according to region. These crops could be grown in the summer only in areas that were cool or at a high elevation because they cannot tolerate hot, humid conditions. Thus, the climatic characteristics, together with those of the crops themselves, determined the location and activities of early villagers. They also affected early irrigated farming in the Nile and Mesopotamian river valleys: the flooding of the Nile in late summer and early fall was ideal for crops grown in the winter, but the flooding of the Tigris and Euphrates in the late spring had to be controlled rather than allowed to flood the fields freely. A more detailed description of the regimes of these rivers is presented later in this chapter.

The suitability of a particular location for habitation depends on a series of interrelated variables. Great diversity in climate and in the agricultural potential of land can exist within a small area. Many of the variables are natural factors, but

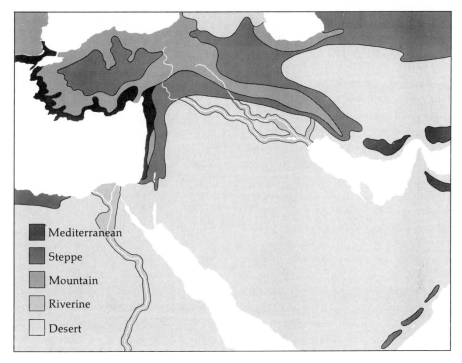

Figure 2-3
Natural vegetation zones of the Near East.

others are related to conditions created by human beings, who may have altered the long-term trends of Near Eastern climate by disturbing the ecosystem. Because the relationships between radiation, temperature, humidity, precipitation, and wind may be altered by interference with any one of them, completely new local climates may be introduced by irrigation or by dry-farming practices. Causing closely packed vegetation to become scattered by plowing, clearing, overgrazing, or fallowing may produce changes in the soil structure and climate.

Despite the deleterious effects of certain natural features of the Near Eastern climate, both in the past and at present, the average conditions for much of the region closely approach the optimum for animal and plant life. Prolonged cold and extreme heat are restricted to limited areas. The benefits of warm, sunny summers and cool, damp winters combined with the topographic and hy-

drologic aspects of the Near East have proved to be favorable for the rise of the world's first civilizations.

Vegetation

The distribution of the natural vegetation is of prime importance for human habitation of the Near East because all food—both animal and vegetable—ultimately derives from plant material.

The physiographical variation of landforms in the Near East and neighboring regions has created a mosaic of climatic variation across Southwest Asia. Minor variations in relief, altitude, aspect, and humidity have far-reaching consequences for vegetation, and hence, for animals and people. There is a close causal relationship between the landforms, soil, and climate of a locality and the vegetation it supports. The similarity in the distributions presented in Figures 2-1, 2-2, and 2-3 attest to the directness of the correlation between these phenomena. The regional variation in the distribution of natural vegetation is due to five principal factors.

First, climate determines the amount of sunlight and moisture available to plants and thus limits the species of plants that can grow in a particular location. The number of days without frost and the length of growing season before the temperature becomes too high are crucial to certain species. Severe or repeated frosts set northern limits on the cultivation of many species: an ecological limit for the distribution of a large variety of plant species is 30 days of frost annually (Butzer 1965:11). Throughout much of the Near East tree growth is impeded by severe drought. In areas having rain primarily in summer, the boundary between steppe and woodland is near the 500-millimeter precipitation line, and trees do not grow in areas with less precipitation. However, in areas having normal soil and winter rains, the boundary is at about 300 millimeters of annual rainfall, because of the diminished evaporation of winter rainfall. Although the exact figure varies with specific conditions, 300 millimeters of precipitation is approximately the minimum amount required for dry farming in the Near East.

The second factor affecting natural vegetation is the local topography. The topography is important to temperature, hydrology, precipitation, sunlight, soil, and wind. Locations within a few hundred meters of each other may support significantly different vegetation because of underground water sources or because of different exposures to sunlight and wind. These factors were surely important in determining favorable locations for prehistoric communities.

The third factor affecting vegetation is the soil. The type of soil in an area is related to topography, climate, type of bedrock, and the length of time the soil has been forming. In general, the soils of the Near East form slowly, often in thin or scanty layers, and contain few usable minerals. Organic material is scarce because the intense summer heat readily oxidizes that present in the soil. Soil formation is complex and in the Near East has led to a

variety of soil types ranging from the heavily saline deposits of arid regions to the leached acidic soils of the higher mountain zones. The soils of the desert and arid regions are more accurately described as rock rubble, with little true soil development. In the semiarid regions, the brown steppe soils can be agriculturally productive if adequately watered. In the higher rainfall areas of the foothills, soil forms from limestone bedrock known as terra-rosa. The high iron content together with the low humus content are responsible for its red color. Terra-rosa soil is good for the cultivation of cereals, and if it is thick enough fruit trees can be grown in it (Fischer 1963:73). A major disadvantage of terra-rosa soil is its susceptibility to erosion, which makes terracing necessary if there is any topographic relief. Soil that is left exposed on a slope quickly erodes and it takes a long time for it to reform. Large areas of the Near East consist of alluvial basins containing soils that are a result of slope erosion and are quite unconnected with any local climatic regime. In contrast to the generally light soils formed by surface weathering, alluvial soils have a high clay content. Soils with a high clay content do not give up water easily and increase the problems of drought, whereas very sandy, light soils do not hold moisture well. Hence, the composition of the soil has the effect of modifying the rainfall pattern—that is, some soils make available water accessible to plants, whereas others withhold it. Because of periodic flooding, certain alluvial soils contain a proportion of humus derived from the aquatic vegetation of the river banks. These soils can be very beneficial for cultivation, especially of shallow-rooted crops instead of deep-rooted trees. Heavy soils also require different cultivation techniques from those used on the lighter soils of the drier regions.

The fourth factor affecting natural vegetation is the distribution of phytogeographical regions—that is, where parent plants came from. The distribution of plants is closely related to climatic and other factors, but it also is a result of migrations of plants from one area to another. The natural habitats of the wild progenitors of early domesticated plants are outlined in Chapter 4.

The fifth and final factor affecting natural vegetation is the effect of human activity on the natural system. People affect their surroundings in many ways: in the Near East, for example, deforestation of many woodland areas was a result not only of the clearing and cultivation necessary for agriculture, but also of collecting fuel, making charcoal, and cutting timber for the construction of buildings. The deforestation of a woodland often leads to the replacement of the natural tree cover with hardier types of trees and bushes previously adapted to drier areas with poorer soil. In many areas of the Near East, a second stage of degradation was caused by human activities, resulting in further impoverishment by creating a steppelike shrub vegetation devoid of perennial grasses and restricted to several thorny species of plants that are able to resist the effects of overgrazing.

It is possible to classify the distribution of natural vegetation in the Near East into five general zones (Fisher 1963:80–84) (Figure 2-3).

1 *Mediterranean vegetation* is confined to the wetter parts of the Mediterranean coastal area and adjacent mountain flanks. It consists of open woodlands of evergreen oak with areas of subtropical pine and wild olive trees. Walnut and poplar trees are found in damper places, and introduced cacti grow luxuriantly. Today, because of deforestation, most areas of Mediterranean vegetation contain a somewhat impoverished set of plants including stunted oaks, pistachios, and many shrubs.

2 *Steppe vegetation* is caused by great seasonal variation of temperature and generally low rainfall. On the flanks of mountains there is open, savanna vegetation with scattered juniper and smaller bushes, but in regions of true steppe, consisting of various species of grasses, herbs, and low shrubs, trees are absent. The appearance of a steppe landscape differs greatly from summer to winter: in the late winter and early spring, many species of flowers and grasses grow rapidly, but they shrivel or are completely burned or grazed off during the rest of the year. The contrast between the summer

barrenness and the luxuriant early spring vegetation is striking, and even a small climatic fluctuation can greatly affect plant growth and, hence, the inhabitants who depend on it. It can prompt major movements of the primarily pastoral peoples who occupy this type of terrain.

3 *Mountain vegetation* is related to elevation and rainfall. Evergreen oaks predominate on the lower slopes, whereas deciduous oaks, cedar, maple, juniper, pine, or fir are found higher up, depending on the area. On the damp northern slopes of the Elburz and Pontic mountains, there are temperate deciduous and coniferous trees, as well as a dense undergrowth of shrubs and vines in some areas. At elevations higher than 2,000 meters in eastern Anatolia and northwestern Iran, there are areas of alpine vegetation reminiscent of the Swiss Alps.

4 *Riverine vegetation* is present in the lower courses of the Tigris-Euphrates Valley and consists of scattered willow, poplar, alder, and tamarisk. The abundant date palm, which is tolerant of excessive water and salinity, was introduced into this region. The thick undergrowth in deltaic regions is composed of aquatic grasses, papyrus, lotus, and reeds that can attain a height of 7 meters.

5 *Desert vegetation* is extremely adaptive to dry or saline conditions. Many desert plants complete their growing cycle within a few weeks after the end of the winter rains. Throughout the spring an extraordinary variety and abundance of flowering grasses can be seen that last only a few days before drying up under the increasing heat.

The natural vegetation of a region is indicative of the agricultural potential of the area. The plants grown by early farmers could survive only in certain regions. This limited the distribution of early farming villages. As strains of plants and animals improved and new technologies were developed, farming villages spread to other zones. Given adequate plants and techniques, the potential for plant growth in these new areas—especially in the alluvial lowlands—was significantly higher than it had been in the original farming center.

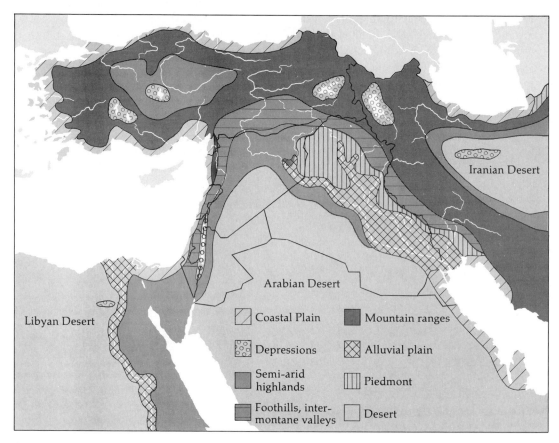

Figure 2-4
Major environmental zones of the Near East.

Environmental Zones of the Near East

An effective method of gaining an appreciation for the diversity of environmental settings in the Near East is to live there and travel extensively, observing both the ecological settings and the manner in which people have adapted to them today. It would be necessary to visit each region repeatedly because of the extreme seasonal variation in climate. A practical alternative to this method is a description of the characteristics of eight major types of environmental zones as they would be encountered in two journeys across the length and breadth of the Near East. The reason for using a journey as a vehicle of presentation is to emphasize the juxtapositions of these zones, as well as their characteristics, in order to know the environmental alternatives that were available to the prehistoric inhabitants of the Near East.

Although classifying the environment of the Near East into eight types of zones tends to oversimply its diversity, such classification affords a comprehensive view of the region, especially if the variables that affected the major developmental processes are taken into consideration. The zones listed below are illustrated in Figure 2-4.

1 Coastal plains
2 Alluvial plains
3 Piedmont
4 Semiarid highlands
5 Foothills and intermontane valleys
6 Mountain ranges
7 Depressions
8 Deserts

The most important criterion for defining these zones is their topographic composition, although climatic regime, natural vegetation, and local resources must also be considered.* Each zone can be subdivided into smaller environments (which is done in subsequent chapters in discussing important archeological sites). Further, the major environmental zones can be correlated with the distributions of different settlement types, which testifies to the value of an ecological perspective.

Southeast to Northwest Journey

The first journey is from the Persian Gulf to the Black Sea. We travel from southeast to northwest through the Tigris-Euphrates Valley to a point beyond the headwaters of the two rivers—a route similar to the ancient Persian road that stretched from Susa in southwest Iran to Sardis in western Anatolia. Our journey takes us from the hot, lowland area of Mesopotamia, through reasonably temperate foothill country, up into the cooler mountain region of the north (Figure 2-5, pages 28 and 29), allowing us to see the climatic and vegetative differences in the environmental zones of the Near East. Each zone has its own set of natural resources and potential adaptations. The ancient inhabitants of the Near East learned to recognize and exploit these potentials, and they settled with varying density in all eight environmental zones. The diverse adaptations stimulated by this set of environments created an interaction of human

*Further information on the environment of the Near East can be obtained by referring to general textbooks in geography (Fisher 1963, 1968; Cressey 1960) and the many books describing the geographic conditions of individual countries.

groups that led to what has come to be called civilization.

Persian Gulf Coastal Plains

We begin at the shores surrounding the Persian Gulf, an area predominantly hot and arid. On the Iranian side to the east, there is a narrow coastal plain and the Zagros Mountains come very close to the shore. Except in occasional ports such as contemporary Bandar Abbas and Bushire, there is sparse human occupation. The western, or Arabian, side of the gulf is lower in elevation, with the Arabian desert gently sloping upward from the broad coastal plain. There is virtually no rainfall or freshwater anywhere in this region, and so permanent settlement is restricted to locations at which there are underground springs, or oases. The most striking of these spots is the island of Bahrain, especially its northern coast. Many springs are located there, fed by distant underground sources (perhaps in the mountains of southwest Arabia). The entire Persian Gulf coastlands have been inadequately explored archeologically, but it is evident that they were occupied in prehistoric and early historic times and may have played an important role in the rise of civilization. This seems to be especially true of Bahrain and the nearby Saudi Arabian coastal plain (Bibby 1969; al-Masry 1973).

Mesopotamian Alluvial Plain

Continuing our journey, we come to the head of the Persian Gulf where the mouth of the conjoined Tigris and Euphrates rivers is located. These rivers, as well as the Karun River of Iran, join about 80 kilometers from the coast and form a single stream, the Shatt al 'Arab, which carries their waters into the Persian Gulf. All of the land in the lower reaches of the three rivers is extremely flat and low-lying. The slope of the plain averages 10 centimeters per kilometer (1:10,000) all the way to Baghdad and is as little as 2 centimeters per kilometer in the lower reaches of the plain. Consequently, the boundaries between areas of water and areas of dry land are unstable and not clearly defined. The rivers periodically overflow their

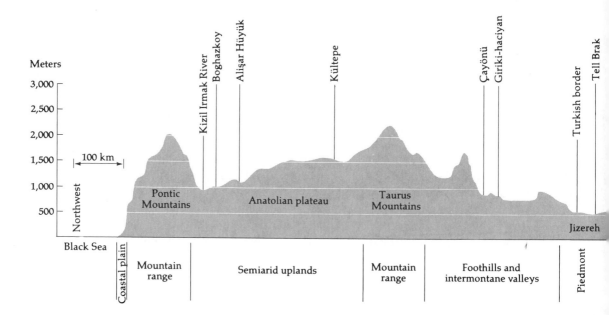

Figure 2-5
Altitudinal cross section of the Near East from southeast to northwest.

banks and flood the surrounding areas, resulting in great expanses of marshes and swamps. Semipermanent lakes carry much of the water from the Tigris and Euphrates rivers to the Shatt al 'Arab. Because of the bifurcating pattern of the lower Tigris and Euphrates rivers and the intense heat of this region, a significant proportion of their water evaporates before they enter the Persian Gulf. In fact, the water level of the Shatt al 'Arab is less affected by the annual flooding of the Tigris and Euphrates rivers than it is by the tides of the Persian Gulf. These tides cause the Shatt al 'Arab to back up at its mouth, resulting in its rising and falling as much as 1 or 2 meters twice daily. The vegetation in the area is generally that of a marshland with the exception that both banks of the Shatt al 'Arab are now lined with groves of date palm.

As we move northward up the Tigris-Euphrates Valley past the city of Basra, the rivers separate and the extent of marshland and semipermanent lakes

diminishes. The gradient of the land is very slight in the lower courses of the river, but upstream the gradient perceptibly increases and the aspect of the land changes accordingly. There is no distinct boundary between marshland and drier alluvial plain, but more effective levee formation by the rivers characterizes the plain. Because most of the water in the extreme south is backed up into swamps and lakes, it does not move fast enough to carry coarse sediments. Farther north, up the river valley, the water moves swiftly enough to carry tremendous amounts of sediments both in suspension and in solution, especially during the flood season. The rivers overflow their banks when the water in them rises because of the melting of snow or the spring rainfall in the mountainous headwater regions. As the rivers overflow their banks, the velocity of the water decreases and sediments are deposited, the coarser particles being deposited first and the finer silts later. This leads

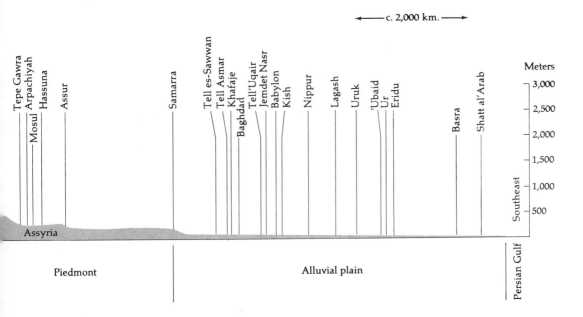

to the formation of natural levees of coarse materials adjacent to the banks of the rivers (Figure 2-6, page 30). Each time the river floods, the levees increase in size. The tops of the levees and their back slopes are favorable locations for human settlement and agriculture because they are raised above the plain and well drained. Farther from the rivers, the flood waters may settle into depressions where they eventually evaporate, leaving their mineral contents in the soil.

Because of the dryness of the climate and high clay content, the soil of Mesopotamia is hard and nearly impenetrable. Consequently, when the rivers overflow their banks the water is prone to runoff instead of being absorbed. This increases the destructiveness of the floods and diminishes their agricultural value.

Salinization of the soil is the most pressing agricultural problem in contemporary Mesopotamia, and from historic and archeological evidence it was a major problem for the early civilizations as well. There are three methods for controlling soil salinity from irrigation water: (1) constructing extensive networks of drainage ditches to carry away the water before it evaporates, (2) pumping groundwater out of the soil through specially made wells, and (3) flushing the soil with excess irrigation water after digging deep drains. Salinization has resulted in the abandonment of large parts of southern Mesopotamia, and the lack of vegetation has allowed the encroachment of desert sands into areas that were once fertile farmlands (Figure 2-7, page 30). The inhabitants of lower Mesopotamia have always had to fight this battle against salinization and the advance of the desert. The boundary between cultivatable land and desert is constantly shifting. Today the desert seems to be advancing in certain areas of lower Mesopotamia, but there have been many periods in history when the occupants of this region successfully pushed back the

Figure 2-6
Aerial view of the Tigris River near Baghdad during high flooding. Note that the intensively cultivated levees near the river bank are above the flood waters. (Photograph from Aerofilms Ltd. Copyright reserved.)

Figure 2-7
Region near the ancient site of Nippur in central Babylonia where salinization has become so severe that salt has reached the surface.

desert and were able to reclaim lost agricultural land by draining water off irrigated land before it evaporated and restoring vegetative ground cover.

The Mesopotamian Plain has a climate with two distinct seasons: a dry and intensely hot summer, lasting from May to October, and a relatively cold, damp winter from December to March (spring and autumn are short seasons). At the site of Babylon, temperatures in August may be as high as 50°C in the shade and between 70° and 80°C in the sun. During the summer, a hot and dry northwesterly wind blows constantly. This wind can be destructive because it often is so strong that it carries sand and silt that it has stripped from the desert, which

makes it look like thick fog that is painful to walk through. The fine dust passes through every hole and slit in even the best-built houses, fills in archeological ruins, and forms sand dunes. The temperature in summer does not significantly vary from the north to the south of the Mesopotamian Plain, but in winter it varies a great deal. In general, winter temperatures are lower than would be expected, the north often being from 5° to 10°C cooler than the south. January is the coldest month, with the lowest temperatures being 0°C at Basra and −11°C at Mosul. Rain falls almost exclusively in the winter and is almost entirely from the moist air from the Mediterranean. Late January and early

Figure 2-8
Canal irrigation of date-palm orchard near Euphrates River in what was
southern Sumer. (Photograph from the Prehistoric Project of The Oriental
Institute, The University of Chicago.)

February is the wettest time of the year, and normally there is no rainfall between the end of May and the end of September. Throughout most of Mesopotamia annual precipitation does not exceed 150 millimeters.

The general climatic regime of summer is unbearably hot, with no rain, and clear skies. The winter is a succession of clear balmy days, cool drizzly nights, brief violent rainstorms, and occasional dust storms.

In continuing our journey northward out of the marshlands and into the drier alluvial plain, we enter what was ancient Sumer (Figure 2-1). The homeland of the earliest known civilization, Sumer is located between the Tigris and Euphrates rivers in their lower courses. This part of the flood plain is characterized by the bifurcation of the major rivers into many smaller streams that criss-cross the flood plain (Figure 2-8). The abundance of naturally formed minor streams simplified the problem of bringing irrigation water to the farmland: because the land is extremely flat, large areas could be irrigated without the construction of major canals. However, the flatness of the land prevented runoff, a situation that increased the rate of salinization.

The area north of Sumer, but south of Baghdad, was known as Akkad in earliest historic times; later both Akkad and Sumer were called Babylonia (Figure 2-1). During the period of Sumerian civilization, Akkad farmland seems to have been less intensively cultivated than that of Sumer, and large areas were used for grazing. After the salinization of the Sumerian farmlands, Akkad became the heart of early civilization and was intensively cultivated (refer to Figures 2-9 and 2-10 on the next page).

Figure 2-9
Surface-level archeological site in central Babylonia in a region that is now largely desert.

Figure 2-10
Date-palm orchards bounding the Euphrates River at the ancient site of Babylon, in foreground. (Photograph from Aerofilms Ltd. Copyright reserved.)

Hypotheses on the formation of lower Mesopotamia

There has been a fair amount of controversy about the location of the ancient shoreline of the Persian Gulf and the nature of the lowlands adjacent to it. Ancient inhabitants of lower Mesopotamia referred to the cities of Ur and Eridu as seaports (see Figure 8-2 on page 247 for location). Archeologists who did not find archeological sites farther south than these two cities assumed that the area was under water in early historic times. Proponents of this view adhered to de Morgan's postulation of about 1900 that, in relatively recent geological times (c. 10,000 to 5000 B.C.), the shoreline of the head of the Persian Gulf lay much farther to the northwest in approximately the region of modern Baghdad (de Morgan 1905). The four rivers—Euphrates, Tigris, Karun, and Karkheh—entered the gulf by separate and distinct mouths. Because the Karun and Karkheh were swifter than the larger Euphrates and Tigris rivers, they tended to carry proportionally more sediment. Slow deposition of this sediment formed a delta southward across the Persian Gulf, enclosing the part of the gulf to the north as a lake, which then became a marsh. Sediments from the Euphrates and Tigris then filled up the marsh. This process, according to de Morgan, implies a southeastward creep of the coastline forming the head of the Persian Gulf.

In 1952, Lees and Falcon advanced a different explanation. They suggested that lower Mesopotamia and the Persion Gulf together are an area of subsidence. The marshlands of lower Iraq are the result of a delicate balance between the deposition of silt from the Tigris and Euphrates—which by itself would rapidly raise the level of the land—and the sinking of the underlying strata, presumably under the weight of accumulating deposits from the two rivers. Various types of geological data on the rate of accumulation and the nature of deposits in lower Mesopotamia seem to demonstrate the validity of this explanation.

On the basis of the newer hypothesis, archeologists were quick to reinterpret their data on the location of seaports, suggesting that boats probably came up the Euphrates and that, because the southern swampland was not suitable for cities, the ancients would have considered it to be part of the sea.

The idea that parts of the Mesopotamian Plain are continually sinking or being compressed under the weight of deposited sediments has an important implication for the land surface level during early historic times. Many archeological sites have been excavated to depths below the level of the contemporary plain. The usual assumption is that the depth of sterile soil (i.e., land surface before first human occupation) in an archeological site indicates the elevation of the plain at the time of first occupation. This depth can be as much as 10 meters, as is the case at Tell Asmar, northeast of Baghdad, where sterile soil was found that far below the level of the present plain. Adams has calculated that this depth suggests that the level of the plain at least in the Diyala region rose an average of 20 centimeters per century (1965:10). He cautions that the weight of the overlying archeological deposits could have increased the rate of subsidence and that it is important to know whether the early community was founded on a river levee or in a depression farther away from the river and to have information on the amount of aeolian erosion in the vicinity. Evidence from the Warka vicinity indicates less alluvial buildup, perhaps as little as 2 or 3 meters (Adams and Nissen 1972).

Piedmont

The piedmont is a zone of flat to rolling topography stretching from a lowland plain to the foot of a mountain range. North of Baghdad, the elevation of the Mesopotamian Plain increases rapidly, with natural terracing on the banks of the rivers (Figure 2-6). The water level of the Tigris River is 10 meters below the plain at the modern city of Samarra, and so simple irrigation techniques are no longer usable. The Assyrian Highlands, comprising successively higher ridges oriented northwest to southeast, extend from the Tigris River toward the northeast. Tributaries of the Tigris River have broken through the ridges, creating gaps or gorges and giving the whole region of Assyria a dissected appearance. The region is not affected by the problem of salinization, but neither does it benefit from the ease of irrigation that characterized Sumer and Akkad. However, it receives enough rainfall, between 300 and 500 millimeters annually, to support grassland vegetation and marginal cultivation. The Assyrian Highlands are part of the piedmont environmental zone. They were the center of major Mesopotamian civilizations during the first and second millennia B.C.

In summary, the Mesopotamian Plain is a vast, flat expanse that is 250 kilometers wide and 650 kilometers long. Marshes and swamps predominate in the southernmost part but, as the elevation of the land gradually increases upstream from the marshes and swamps, more land can be cultivated, though conditions promote salinization. Farther north, the elevation of the land continues to increase relative to that of the river until it reaches a point (close to Baghdad) at which it is no longer possible to irrigate by simple techniques, because the river level is more than 10 meters below the plain. Farming or herding in the piedmont zone is limited to areas having rainfall. Even farther north, the problem of salinization diminishes as the amount of rainfall increases. With the passage of time, the centers of early civilizations were located farther and farther to the north along the river. Salinization was undoubtedly a major reason for this northward shift.

Semiarid Uplands

Following the course of the Euphrates up from the junction of the alluvial plain and the Assyrian Highlands our journey takes us to the Jezireh (Figures 2-1 and 2-5). The Jezireh is located between the Tigris and Euphrates rivers with the first fold ranges of Anatolia as its northern boundary. The Jezireh consists of an undulating plain, or low plateau, from 150 to 300 meters above sea level, with a number of small enclosed basins from which there are no drainage outlets. For the most part, there is insufficient rainfall for agriculture, except in the north where the climate is affected by the nearby Taurus Mountains of Anatolia. This area maintains steppelike grassland vegetation and can be considered to be in the semiarid upland environmental zone (Figure 2-4). Throughout history, a major route of communications crossed the Jezireh, connecting northern Mesopotamia with the Mediterranean via Aleppo. Until recently, this area had not been subjected to detailed archeological investigation, but it is now the scene of expeditions from Japan, Russia, and Great Britain (see Umm Dabaghiyah in Chapter 6).

Foothills and Intermontane Valleys

As we go farther north from the Assyrian Highlands and the Jezireh, we soon leave the dry grassland of the piedmont zone and the semiarid uplands and enter the undulating, hilly country of the Taurus and Zagros ranges (Figures 2-4, 2-5, and 2-11). This environmental zone has been characterized as having foothills and intermontane valleys, ranging in elevation from 350 to 1,500 meters (Braidwood and Howe 1960). The average annual rainfall is from 500 to 750 millimeters—adequate for dry farming. The region was once covered with an open woodland of oak and pistachio trees. These "hilly flanks of the Fertile Crescent" are watered by moist winds that come from the Mediterranean through the break in the Lebanon and Anti-Lebanon Mountains known as the Syrian Saddle. As in most areas of the Near East, precipitation is not reliable and figures for average rainfall give only an approximation of the amount of rainfall in any given year. The major physiographic features of this zone are the parallel ridges and valleys that make up the foothills of the Zagros and Taurus mountains. Because of overgrazing, poor agricultural techniques, and cutting timber for fuel and housing, this region today is almost totally devoid of its native trees. In protected areas, such as cemeteries, there are remnants of the oak and other trees that once covered the landscape.

River regimes

   The relationship between the early settlements of the Mesopotamian Plain and their ecological settings is primarily determined by the location and regimes of the two major rivers—the Tigris and Euphrates—originating in the Anatolian Highlands. The Euphrates is fed chiefly by melted winter snow, receiving two left-bank (as seen while facing downstream) tributaries: the Balikh and the Khabur (Figure 2-1). No significant tributaries are received from the Syrian or Arabian deserts, but a large number of wadis (occasionally flooding stream beds) suggest that at one time water may have entered from the right bank. The Tigris, lying close to the Zagros Mountains, is primarily rain-fed, and along its whole length it receives many tributaries, some of which are quite large, such as the Greater and Lesser Zabs, the Diyala, and the Karun (Figure 2-1). The entry of tributaries has important consequences on the regimes of the rivers. The Euphrates depends on the rainfall of a single and relatively restricted catchment area; consequently, the volume of the river does not fluctuate rapidly in its middle and lower courses. The Tigris, on the other hand, draws its water from a much wider catchment zone and local rain in a single district soon affects the height of the river, making sudden floods much more a feature of this river. A local rainstorm in the Zagros can produce marked changes in the height of the Tigris within a few hours, and it is not unusual for the river to rise from 2 to 3 meters in 24 hours.

   The Tigris River descends nearly 300 meters between the Turkish frontier and Baghdad (the gradient is 1:1,750). It carries a greater volume of water than does the Euphrates and is subject to greater seasonal fluctuations. Both rivers are at their lowest levels in September and October. Flooding of the Tigris is greatest in April and the high water for the Euphrates is in May. These floods are poorly timed with respect to the prevalent winter agricultural schedule: the high water comes at a time when crops are mature and ready to be harvested; therefore, rather than helping their growth, it is a major threat to their harvesting.

Some ridges that are not easily accessible to the ubiquitous wood-gatherers or grazing goats may still retain scattered clusters of scrub oaks. Deforestation has led to widespread erosion of the excellent terra rosa soils, which increases the difficulty of farming in a formerly productive environment. In this zone of foothills and intermontane valleys, evidence for the earliest experiments with agriculture is plentiful. The size and the inferred architecture of the prehistoric agricultural villages are not significantly different from many of the agricultural villages occupied today by peasant farmers. Many of the houses, especially those in the mountains, are made of pressed mud, or mud brick, whereas those closer to sources of stone have stone foundations and mud walls or stone walls plastered over with mud. Wheat and barley are the primary crops in this region, and herding of sheep, goats, and cattle is actively pursued. In addition to the upper courses of the Tigris, Euphrates, and their major tributaries, countless minor streams drain the intermontane valleys, successively cutting through each of the ridges on their way down to the Mesopotamian Plain (Figure 2-12, page 36). Some of these streams are perennial, but most are seasonal, carrying only winter rain water. Scattered parts of many of the seasonal streams retain water during the dry season.

Taurus Mountains

   Moving in a northwest direction through the successively higher valleys of the Taurus foothills, we enter a zone of high mountains (Figures 2-4, 2-5, and 2-13). Many of the peaks in eastern Anatolia retain snow throughout most of the year and are sparsely inhabited. The high mountains receive

Figure 2-11
Foothill valley of the southern slopes of the Taurus
Mountains. The ancient site of Çayönü is adjacent to
the stream in the foreground. (Photograph from the
Joint Prehistoric Project of the Universities of Istanbul
and Chicago.)

Figure 2-12
Upper Tigris River as it descends
from the Taurus Mountains near
Diyarbakir, Turkey. (Photograph
from the Joint Prehistoric Project
of the Universities of Istanbul
and Chicago.)

Figure 2-13
Obsidian flows in the Taurus Mountains of eastern
Anatolia. (Photograph from the Joint Prehistoric Project
of the Universities of Istanbul and Chicago, R. Watson.)

Figure 2-14
Valley within the Anatolian plateau, near modern city
of Elizag. (Photograph from the Joint Prehistoric Project
of the Universities of Istanbul and Chicago.)

1,000 or more millimeters of rain annually and below the timber line of approximately 2,000 meters there are dense forests. A few large valleys within the mountain range have sufficient rainfall and are not excessively cold; they have been centers of occupation for many millennia. In general, however, the terrain of the upper Taurus and Zagros mountain slopes is too rugged and the winter too cold for farming. The area is frequently used as summer pasture for the animals of pastoral nomads. Many nomadic groups, if not all of them, move from one location to another along a customary, relatively fixed route as the seasons change, to follow the usable pastureland. During the summer and autumn, the higher intermontane valleys are green and offer ample grazing for herds of animals. During the winter, the cold and snow in these higher locations makes them inhospitable, forcing the pastoral nomads to seek pastures at lower altitudes. They move their herds and communities down into lower valleys or even into the piedmont zone, where the winters are not harsh and the vegetation is richest during the winter and

spring. The nomadic pattern of subsistence is now vanishing because of fixed national borders and attempts by governments at sedentarization, but it was probably an important aspect of early agricultural life in this region and in adjacent ones. The mountainous zone is also utilized for its natural resources of timber and minerals. There are a few routes of communication through these mountains that have been used for thousands of years. The route through the Cilician Gates was probably the most traveled route from Mesopotamia or the Levant to Anatolia—a strategic location whose control was sought by early states (Figure 2-1).

Anatolian Plateau

Having crossed the Taurus Mountains, we enter the eastern edge of the central Anatolian plateau, which is another example of a semiarid upland environmental zone (Figures 2-4, 2-5, and 2-14). Anatolia is like a bowl with its center surrounded by mountains. The plateau itself is undulating upland broken by sunken basins and scattered

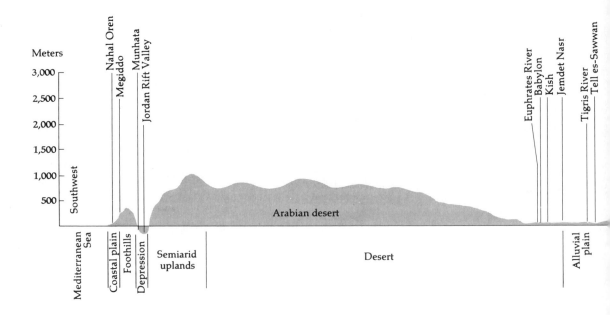

Figure 2-15
Altitudinal cross section of the Near East from southwest to northeast.

peaks. Because it is surrounded by mountains, the plateau is dry, supporting only grassland vegetation with isolated areas of woodland in the immediate rainshadow of the Taurus. Farther from the Taurus, rainfall increases and dry farming is possible. The plateau slopes slightly downward toward the west where today there are productive areas of dry farming and where in prehistoric times important early villages existed.

Pontic Mountains

Continuing our journey, we reach the northern border of the Anatolian plateau, the Pontic Mountains (Figures 2-4 and 2-5). These rugged mountains slope precipitously down to the narrow coastal strip along the Black Sea. Many rivers and streams cascade down the northern slopes into the sea. Rainfall is abundant even during the summer and the weather stays relatively warm. The combina-

tion of year-round precipitation and mild temperatures produces rich vegetation, including deciduous trees.

Having reached the Black Sea, our first journey is completed. We have traversed much of the area that was the setting for important stages of development in the rise of civilization.

Southwest to Northeast Journey

The orientation of our second journey is roughly perpendicular to the first one, taking us from the southwest to the northeast and crossing the route of our first journey at Babylon (Figure 2-15). We begin at the Mediterranean coast of Israel and travel through the Jordan Rift Valley, the Arabian desert, the Mesopotamian Plain, the Zagros Mountains, the Iranian plateau, and the Elburz Mountains, before descending to the Caspian Sea.

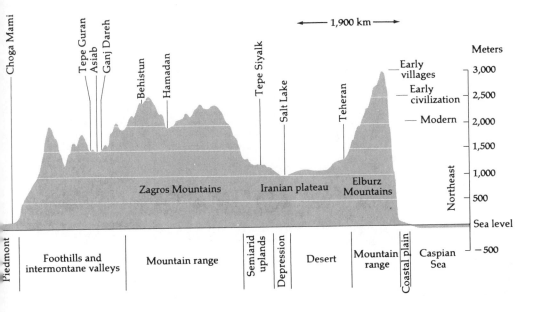

Coastal Plain

The Mediterranean coastal plain of the Levant (Figures 2-4, 2-15, and 2-16) is narrow and discontinuous in the north but widens toward the south. In Syria, it consists merely of a series of small valleys, or coves, separated by mountain spurs that reach the sea. This topography extends to Lebanon and northern Israel, except the proportion of plain increases. At Mount Carmel in Israel, for example, there is a 200-meter expanse between the mountains and the sea, but this opens up to the Plain of Sharon to the south, which is between 15 and 25 kilometers wide, and widens even more in the vicinity of Gaza. The Plain of Sharon is formed of alluvium brought down from the interior hills of Israel, and hence the soil is quite fertile. Water is the limiting variable for successful agriculture in this region, but there is also the problem of sand dunes encroaching on cultivated land. The amount of rainfall diminishes farther south, and at Gaza the coastal plain is arid. Farther to the north, where irrigation water can be obtained, the coastal plain supports citrus trees and other crops.

Foothills

Inland from the coastal plain are the mountains and foothills of the Levant (Figures 2-4 and 2-15). In the north, the mountains are quite high, creating a formidable barrier to the accessibility of the interior for both moist winds and people. However, there are breaks in the mountains that allow moisture-bearing winds from the Mediterranean to cross into the interior and bring rain to the foothills of the Taurus and Zagros mountains. Few well-developed rivers exist in the Levant, the largest being the Orontes, which runs northward through a depression in the mountain range and breaks through to the sea just beyond the Turkish border.

Figure 2-16
Mediterranean coastal plain in northern Israel.

Figure 2-17
Hilly region of Samaria in southern Levant.

The Lebanon Mountains are the largest range in the Levant, the highest peak being slightly more than 3,000 meters. Farther south, the mountains are low and look like foothills. In northern Israel, the extension of the uplands is known as the Galilee plateau, which has an average height of 500 meters with a few minor peaks of 1,000 meters (Figures 2-1 and 2-17). These uplands are rounded, grassy hills with open woodlands where the soils will support them. Cutting across the region of uplands is a lowland valley, the Plain of Esdraelon, which currently supports intensive agriculture and has throughout history been a major route of communication. As we continue southward in the upland belt, we pass through Samaria, a somewhat drier area, and enter Judea. Judea is a dissected upland region slightly lower in elevation and somewhat drier than Galilee or Samaria. Cultivation in Judea is limited to scattered patches of alluvium in the deeper valleys where water is obtainable.

Interior Depression

Moving east from the uplands of Israel, we descend into the Jordan Rift Valley (Figures 2-4, 2-15, 2-18, and 2-19). This geological trough is bounded on the west by the uplands of Galilee and Judea, and on the east by the Arabian platform. Because most of the Jordan Rift Valley is below sea level and the surrounding plateaus are 1,000 meters above sea level, the boundaries are often precipitous. In the north, basalt flows across the trough at two points caused the formation of lakes. The smaller and northernmost is Lake Huleh, a shallow body of freshwater overgrown by papyrus swamps, whose surface level is about 50 meters above sea level. Farther south is Lake Kinnereth (Sea of Galilee), which is 20 kilometers long and from 8 to 13 kilometers wide, its surface being 209 meters below sea level. The waters of the Jordan River emerge from Lake Kinnereth through a narrow channel and then meander extensively across the floor of the Jordan Rift Valley moving southward toward the Dead Sea. In this area of the valley, as well as in the Huleh basin, there are remains of important early villages. The river is deeply incised

Figure 2-18
Bank of the Jordan River south of
Lake Kinnereth.

Figure 2-19
Western shore of the Dead Sea at the lowest point in
the Jordan Rift Valley

into the valley bottom and a dense jungle of willow trees, tamarisk, and aquatic plants cover the banks. Lower in its course the river becomes strongly saline, and the Dead Sea, which has no outlet, is extremely saline. The southern half of the Jordan Rift Valley is relatively uninviting for human occupation, with the exception of a few scattered oases at springs (e.g., Jericho, 10 km northwest of the Dead Sea).

Semiarid Uplands and Desert

Climbing out of the Jordan Rift Valley to the east, we enter the uplands of the Arabian plateau

(Figures 2-4 and 2-15). The region east of the Levant mountain chain is in a very effective rainshadow in which there is only negligible precipitation. The land is rather barren with at the most only steppe vegetation. This great expanse of dry uplands slopes downward to the east where it becomes more desertic. The distance of 650 kilometers from the parts of the Levant that have adequate rainfall or groundwater to the valley of the Tigris-Euphrates (at Baghdad) is an effective barrier to human movement and communication. Because there are few oases in this desert, crossing it before the invention of motor vehicles was not easily

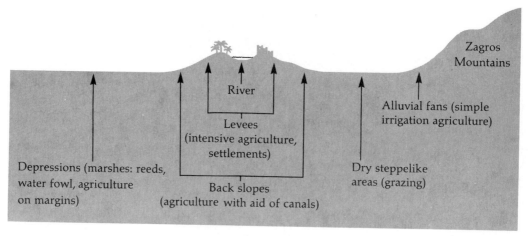

Figure 2-20
Cross section of topography near natural river courses in Mesopotamia.

done; communication between Mesopotamia and the Levant was by way of a northerly route—up the Euphrates across to Aleppo, and then down the Levant (or up through the Cilician Gates to Anatolia).

Alluvial Plain

After crossing the northern extension of the Arabian desert, we enter the Mesopotamian alluvial plain (Figures 2-4, 2-10, and 2-15). As far north as Babylon, where our journey takes us across the river, the Euphrates is not confined to a single permanent bed; rather, it meanders and bifurcates into more than one course. This means that we cross the two main river beds plus many smaller streams as we traverse the alluvial plain. There were probably even more minor streams in antiquity before the inhabitants of the region attempted to keep the river in its main bed and in artificial canals.

The general topographic sequence of the Mesopotamian Plain on either side of a river influenced the selection of settlement locations (Figure 2-20). Farthest from the river are lowland areas that are marshes during the flood season and dry the rest of the year. Some of these lowland areas are saline; others, on the other hand, support natural grass

cover, which makes them useful for grazing animals. Nearer the river are low-lying farmlands within reach of irrigation water; the closer to the river, the greater the productivity of these areas. Along the banks of the river are the levees, which are higher and better drained than the surrounding plain and are the best locations for cultivation and settlement. A levee has the natural advantage of being fertile, quickly drained, and least vulnerable to winter frosts. Equally important, it affords access to river water during years in which the river level is low (Adams 1965:9). On the other side of the river the topographic sequence is reversed, from levee, to farmland, and then to depressions. This topography is similar for each major stream bed until we reach the uphill side of the Tigris River Valley in the direction of the highlands.

Piedmont

From the west to east there is only a short distance from the Tigris River to the first foothills of the Zagros Mountains (Figures 2-4, 2-15, and 2-21). In this narrow piedmont zone, agriculture is possible in years of normal or better than normal rainfall, but cannot be relied upon every year, and so a strategy of farming mixed with herding is employed. Early sedentary farming would have

Figure 2-21
Piedmont zone of Zureh River
valley in southern Khuzistan.
In the background are the barren
slopes of the southern Zagros
Mountains.

Figure 2-22
Intermontane valley in central
Zagros Mountains near the
modern town of Khorramabad,
Iran.

been successful where surface water or semipermanent streams allowed for simple irrigation.

Intermontane Valleys

The Zagros Mountains ascend quickly from the
Tigris-Euphrates Valley in a series of successively
higher ridges (Figures 2-4, 2-15, 2-22, and 2-23).
These "steps" are long parallel folds that trend
southeast to northwest and form the "grain" of
the Zagros Mountains. Numerous well-developed
rivers have cut water gaps that form valleys between the folds and weave a tortuous route across
or around the ends of ridges, gradually descending
westward toward the Tigris River and Persian
Gulf. The mountains are rugged, but the valley
floors have a grass cover; those at higher elevations
have natural woodlands of oak and pistachio if
unaltered by people (Figure 2-24, page 44). A no-

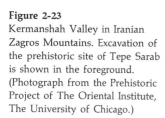

Figure 2-23
Kermanshah Valley in Iranian
Zagros Mountains. Excavation of
the prehistoric site of Tepe Sarab
is shown in the foreground.
(Photograph from the Prehistoric
Project of The Oriental Institute,
The University of Chicago.)

Figure 2-24
Highland area east of the modern town of Rawanduz
in northeastern Iraq, at about 1,500 meters elevation.
(Photograph from the Prehistoric Project of The
Oriental Institute, The University of Chicago.)

madic existence is common in this zone of intermontane valleys. The movement to higher, cooler
pastures in the summer and lower, warmer valleys
in the winter may have been practiced as long ago
as the time of the domestication of sheep and goats
(and the wild flocks may have done it on their own
before that).

Semiarid Uplands

After crossing the Zagros Mountain peaks, we
descend into broader and longer valleys that open
onto the interior plateau of Iran (Figures 2-4, 2-15,
and 2-25). Water for the villages in these valleys
comes from the nearby mountains by means of
underground irrigation tunnels, or qanats, to support cultivation. The interior slopes of the Zagros
range are spotted with trading centers that participated in a trading network skirting the central
desert to the east and west across the Zagros Mountains down onto the Mesopotamian Plain. Rainfall
is low on the interior plateau of Iran, and it diminishes to almost zero farther east where the elevation is lower, grading into the true desert areas
(see Figure 2-2). Half of the total area of Iran is
composed of a series of enclosed basins from
which there is no outward drainage. The plateau
itself is from 900 to 1,500 meters high and its depressions collect the surface runoff created by the

Figure 2-25
Edge of Iranian plateau looking west at Zagros Mountains in the general vicinity of the ancient site of Tepe Siyalk.

Figure 2-26
Atrek River Valley in the foothills of the Elburz Mountains of northern Iran.

sparse rain. This water then evaporates to create salt marshes and dry salt flats. Both the desert and the salty depressions, with their extremes of temperature, are inhospitable locations for human habitation.

Elburz Mountains

Our journey continues across the Dasht-e-Kavir desert toward the northeast where we reach the slopes of the Elburz Mountains (Figures 2-4, 2-15, and 2-26). This mountain range forms the north-west boundary of the Iranian plateau and contains the highest peak in the Near East, Mount Dama-

vand at 5,760 meters. The interior slope of the Elburz is very dry and is without any significant vegetation. However, the northern slopes of the Elburz are very well watered by winds coming off of the Caspian Sea. The transition line is a cloud line, and the change from semiarid to rain forest is spectacular. These slopes of the Elburz and the coastal plain of the Caspian Sea receive more than 2,500 millimeters of rain annually and support a rich vegetation. On the coastal plain, which supports a relatively dense population, the winters are not cold, precipitation occurs year-round, and tea and rice are grown with great success.

River regime

The regular annual flooding of the Nile is caused by spring and summer rainfall occurring over the highlands of eastern Africa. The single stream of the Nile that flows through Egypt is a combination of three principal streams: the White Nile, the Blue Nile, and the Atbara. The White Nile is the most regular of the three, being responsible for 80 percent of the total flow during the dry season, but only 10 percent during the flood period. Its source is Lake Victoria, and the river is relatively slow moving and does not carry much sediment in suspension by the time it is joined by the other tributaries. The Blue Nile originates in Lake Tana of the Ethiopian highlands; it contributes 17 percent of the low-water flow, but it rises rapidly and flows swiftly, contributing 68 percent of the high-water. The Atbara, which originates in the Sudan and Ethiopa, contributes very little water during the dry season, but it contributes 22 percent of the total high-water flow. Both the Atbara and the Blue Nile carry large quantities of sediment down into the Nile Valley during the flood season. About 110 million tons of sediment are carried annually past Wadi Halfa (Fisher 1963:490). This silt is rich in mineral substances. Before construction of the Aswan high dam, approximately half of this reached Cairo and, of that, 7.5 million tons are fully dissolved, consisting principally of calcium and magnesium carbonates and sodium chloride. Hence, the importance of the Nile is not merely for the water itself; it is also for the fertilizing mud laid down annually. The river can deposit sediment on a field at a rate of about 1 inch per 100 years of flooding.

The minimum water level in Egypt is reached during May and early June. The first flood waters arrive in the third or fourth week of June; they come from the White Nile and have a greenish tint caused by suspended algae. Later, the major flood waters come from the Blue Nile and the Atbara. The maximum flood level is usually reached in mid-September. At this time, the river water may turn reddish brown because of decaying algae from the earlier flood, and on occasion may thicken the Nile water and give it an offensive odor. If the maximum flood occurs early, such as in late August, the minimum water level will be reached in April instead of in May or June, thus producing crop failures. Despite the general regularity in the onset of the Nile floods, the actual height, periodicity, and, hence, value to agriculturists is distinctly variable.

Nile River Valley

A major region that played an important role in the rise of civilization not included in our two journeys is the Nile River Valley of Egypt (Figure 2-4). The long and narrow river valley of the Nile is distinctly different in many ways from the Tigris and Euphrates alluvial plain. Until it broadens into the delta north of Cairo, the Nile River Valley is about 10 kilometers wide, and the river itself about 1 kilometer wide (Figure 2-27). Because of this distinct linearity, the Nile Valley has been conceptualized as two regions both by archeologists and by the ancient Egyptians. To the south is Upper Egypt where the valley is narrow and the river deeply incised in its bed, and farther to the north is Lower Egypt, which includes the delta region (Figure 2-28, page 48). The delta region begins at Cairo, with two main distributaries: the Rosetta branch, which flows to the west, and the Damietta branch, which flows to the east. The delta is a triangular area, approximately 250 kilometers wide at its base and 150 kilometers long, that is crossed by a very large number of small streams branching off the two main distributaries. About half the delta area consists of lakes and swamps, most of them near the Mediterranean coast.

The environmental conditions created by the

Figure 2-27
A broad section of the Nile River Valley near the ancient site of Thebes.
(Photograph from The Oriental Institute, The University of Chicago.)

Nile are more favorable for agriculture than are those of Mesopotamia. The part of the Nile that flows through Egypt is a single stream with no tributaries, whereas both the Tigris and Euphrates have several channels at their southern ends. The Tigris is fed by tributaries that carry masses of sediment, which blocks the lower courses of both rivers, giving rise to swamps, lagoons, and shifting banks. In addition, the floods of Mesopotamia are more variable than those of the Nile because they are a result of rainfall that tends to be unpredictable. Because of their direct relationship to winter precipitation (runoff either from rain or melting snow), Mesopotamian floods occur in spring (not, as in Egypt, in the late summer) and are followed by a long dry period lasting more than half of the year. In Egypt, on the other hand, floods complement the sparse rainy season by splitting the year into four shorter seasons: one of slight rainfall, one of flood, and two of drought.

Although there are many loops and meanders in the Nile's course, it generally flows close to the eastern valley wall. Thus, the greater part of the potentially cultivatable area is west of the river. The natural vegetation of the valley consists of acacia and tamarisk, as well as sycamore and wil-

low, especially on the levees. The natural undergrowth is dense stands of aquatic grasses, papyrus, lotus, and reeds. The best-drained areas are the most favorable sites for human habitation, either directly on the levees of the river or in the low desert adjacent to the floodplain.

Because of its low relief and landlocked position, Egypt's climatic conditions are remarkably uniform throughout the country. Summers are hot, with daytime temperatures reaching 40°C in most places, but nights are distinctly cooler. July is the hottest month, with the highest temperatures being reached earlier in the south than in the north. The Mediterranean coastal temperatures are moderated by the proximity of the sea and are distinctly lower in the summer than they are in the rest of the country. Winters are mild, allowing continuous plant growth, and severe frosts are unknown in the Nile Valley. Occasionally, there are short cold spells, but more harmful is the occurrence of hot dry desert winds that may scorch the crops along the river banks. Rainfall is limited in Egypt to 200 millimeters or less, with 50 millimeters of annual precipitation being the average for the region south of Cairo (Figure 2-2).

The fertile narrow strip of the Nile Valley is

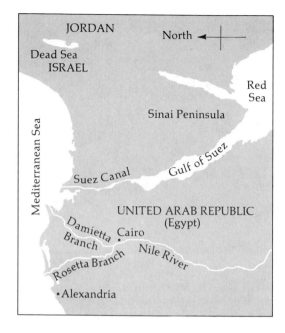

Figure 2-28
The Nile River delta and the adjacent parts of the
southern Levant: (above) Gemini photograph (NASA);
(right) diagram of the region shown in the photograph.

bounded on both sides by broad expanses of barren
deserts. To the east is a highland belt separating
the Nile Valley from the Red Sea that is heavily
dissected by wadis running toward the Nile or
toward the Red Sea. Because of this, the edge of
the Nile Valley on the east is less well defined than
on the west where there are virtually no wadis. The
western desert is a broad horizontal expanse, the
average elevation of which is about 200 meters.
The expanse is broken by a number of deep basins,
many of which contain oases. Aside from these
basins, the desert surface consists of bare rock outcrops, stone wastes, and loose sand.

There is evidence to suggest that the ecological
conditions outside the Nile floodplain were comparatively more favorable in Post-Pleistocene
times until the Sixth Dynasty (c. 2350 B.C.) (Butzer
1965:35). Because of somewhat greater amounts of

rainfall then, the low desert areas were covered
with a sparse growth of acacia and tamarisk together with grass tufts and desert shrubs, which
made up a savannah type of vegetation. Plants
were probably concentrated close to or within the
wadis where there was supplementary ground
moisture between rains. The desert belts may have
been shifted from 80 to 250 kilometers back from
the river valley by a rainfall in the desert of only
100 to 150 millimeters annually. Hence, the absolute change in the local climatic regime was minimal, but its ecological effects were significant. This
type of vegetation on the fringes of the river valley
could have supported a scattered population of
food gatherers and pastoralists. This population
in an area that today is totally uninhabitable could
have contributed a great deal to development of
early Egyptian civilization.

The Environmental Setting of the Near East

Knowledge of several characteristics of the Near Eastern environment is important for an understanding of the natural matrix within which cultural developments took place.

1 The Near East is a topographically diverse region, with high mountains, rolling hills, and a broad alluvial plain. Zones having their own distinctive natural resources are distributed roughly in bands across the region. The proximity of different environmental zones and the localized nature of certain resources encouraged the exchange of goods and the movement of people.

2 The Mediterranean climate of hot summers and cool winters combined with winter rainfall in the intermontane valley and foothill regions nurtured the growth of annual grasses, some of which became the earliest domesticated plants.

3 The existence of large, alluvial valleys adjacent to the Nile, Tigris, Euphrates, and Karun rivers allowed plants domesticated in the uplands to be cultivated intensively with the aid of irrigation water. The rivers also facilitated communication and exchange.

It is the diversity and combination of landforms, climate, and natural resources that made the Near East a fertile environment for cultural developments.

3

CULTURAL BACKGROUND
Prologue to the Drama

*Human groups have inhabited the Near East for more than a half
million years. The Pleistocene societies of the Near East formed the
cultural background from which early agriculturalists
emerged. Information about these early societies is limited largely to the
animal resources they used and the stone tools they made. Nevertheless,
many hypotheses have been made about Pleistocene cultures
and the nature of their settlements—particularly those of the
Late Pleistocene period—including patterns of settlement, subsistence resources,
technology, and human physical development.
The immediate predecessors of village agriculturalists are
considered to have been intensive food collectors. It is in their
cultures that we find abundant evidence for "preadaptations" to agriculture
and village life. Throughout the Pleistocene period and during
the Agricultural Transformation, the people of the Levant and the Zagros
Mountains maintained significant cultural differences while participating in
similar overall developments. By relying on reasonable empirical
evidence, it is possible to describe the nature of the communities and the
prehistoric lifeways of these terminal Pleistocene intensive food collectors.*

A study of the lifeways and adaptations of the inhabitants of the Near East before the advent of agriculture reveals why the descendants of these people made such fundamental changes in human existence. It yields evidence that indicates which elements of the Pleistocene societies were pre-adaptations to agriculture—in other words, those aspects of their technology, subsistence systems, and organization that were crucial in initiating the innovations that subsequently led to much higher levels of organization and to civilization itself.

The Pleistocene prehistory of the Near East is a story of slow biological and cultural evolution that resulted in anatomically modern human beings that were culturally prepared to achieve the Agricultural Transformation. The earliest stages of human occupation in the Near East have been documented at a few sites, particularly in the Levant (Figures 3-1 and 3-2, pages 52 and 53). The Middle Pleistocene was a long period in which the climate of the Near East alternated between wet and dry periods. The people were unspecialized hunters and scavengers who relied on crude tools and a low level of organization to satisfy their needs, and the rate of cultural change was very slow. The primary archeological artifacts indicative of a slowly developing technology during this period are stone tools. Their invention may have been necessitated by new tasks, or it may have been a result of discovering different raw materials, or perhaps of an improvement in the skill of the makers. Some archeologists argue that, in addition to changes that were basically utilitarian, variations in the stone tools that may be related to stylistic differences also can be identified.

During the Late Pleistocene, the rate of cultural change began to accelerate. There are many more archeological sites dating to this period, some of which are demonstrably larger than those from earlier times. They indicate that settlement patterns changed, the predominant locations shifting from open sites on the Mediterranean coast or in the Jordan Rift Valley to cave and terrace sites in the same general regions. The stone tool inventories supply evidence of both an expansion in the tasks undertaken and a greater specialization in the tools used. The greatest developments were in organization and communication, but how they occurred is difficult to speculate on the basis of archeological evidence. Larger social groups, purposeful burial of the dead, and planned hunting activities are all first manifest during this period.

Archeologists have identified the cultures of Western Europe at the end of the Pleistocene (terminal Würm) as *Mesolithic.* The tool inventory and the way of life of the people living then were strikingly different from those of their Upper Paleolithic ancestors. Some scholars have used the term Mesolithic in referring to cultures of the Near East at the end of the last Ice Age. However, these cultures and their tools are not so markedly different from those of their predecessors; hence, most Near Eastern archeologists refer to this period as *Epipaleolithic.* Important changes nevertheless did take place in the lifestyle of the Epipaleolithic people. Among the changes were a continued increase in the size of communities and more technological specialization, especially with the introduction of such facilities as storage pits and grinding stones. It is reasonable to assume that organization of subsistence pursuits and community interaction were significantly transformed, but as yet this is difficult to document archeologically. Although these changes have their roots in earlier periods, the first communities that manifest these preadaptations to agriculture are those of the final Upper Paleolithic and the Epipaleolithic.

The Paleolithic Transformation: An Hypothesis

The Paleolithic Transformation laid the foundation for the spectacular human accomplishments that were to follow. The causes and nature of this transformation are difficult to discern, because it occurred during the inadequately understood early stages of cultural development. It consisted of two transitions. The first was a change in adaptive strategies and organizational abilities at the beginning of the Upper Paleolithic. This transition signifies the rapidly increasing ability of human beings to recognize the environmental potentials that

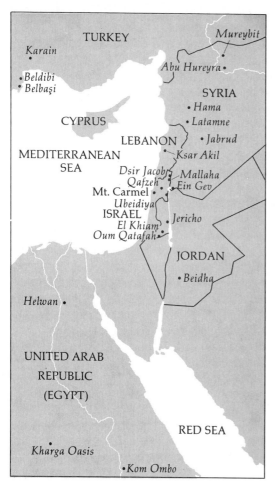

Figure 3-1
Archeological sites in the Levant and adjacent regions.

of foods consumed was broadened to include small mammals, snails, waterfowl, fish, mussels, and plants (Flannery 1969). Both ways of improving subsistence strategies enabled a community to remain in one location for a greater period of the year, and eventually to become a permanent year-round settlement.

Certain societies that existed at the end of the Paleolithic period incorporated the advances of the Paleolithic Transformation into features that can be considered preadaptations to agriculture. Those that relied on hunting and gathering for subsistence began to experiment with the plants and animals being used as resources. Many communities developed into permanent settlements with substantial architecture and a fair amount of immovable equipment designed to aid in the preparation and storage of plant material. Each of these developments can be regarded as distinct adaptations of the particular culture, but from a general perspective they form a continuum of changes that were initiated sometime during the Late Pleistocene and paved the way for agriculture.

Earliest Evidence of Human Occupation in the Near East

Research conducted in recent years increasingly documents that the earliest humanlike creatures lived in either East or South Africa. New discoveries have shown that, of our earliest predecessors, the first bipedal, erect-walking, tool-using hominids lived from at least three to five million years ago. The discoveries and interpretations of the biological and cultural evolution of early human beings in Africa are testimonies to the great strides that archeology has taken in solving one of its central problems, human origins (see Howell 1973). Sometime between one million and one-half million years ago, human beings moved out of Africa into other regions of the Old World, and the earliest evidence of human habitation of the Near East comes from this period, known in geological terms as the end of the Early Pleistocene. Although anatomically human, those who first lived there

existed, to communicate these potentials to others, and to take advantage of them. The second transition within the Paleolithic Transformation can be considered the culmination of the first transition, or the early stages of the Agricultural Transformation leading to the formation of permanent communities with immovable cultural equipment. For some societies, this meant that subsistence pursuits were modified to allow concentration on one or two animal species as the primary source of meat (Binford and Binford 1966a); for others, the variety

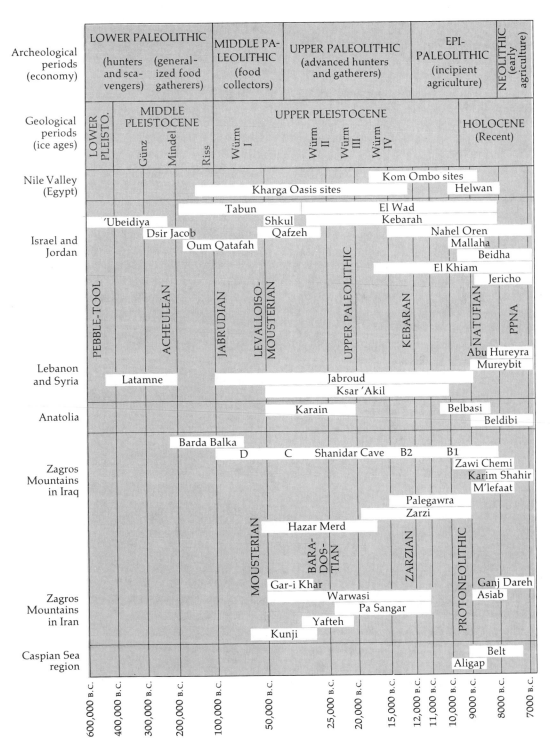

Figure 3-2
Chronology of Pleistocene archeological sites by subregion.

lacked certain physiological characteristics of modern human beings. They were hunters and scavengers who made and used very simple stone tools. They probably communicated with one another by means of sign language, and their lifestyle and social organization were very simple.

Changing lifestyles and adaptations, unfortunately, are not what is excavated at archeological sites; archeologists uncover chipped stone tools, animal bone fragments, and occasional evidence of a prehistoric feature such as a hearth. Hence, Paleolithic lifeways can only be interpreted from the objects that are found. However, careful investigation of changing technological patterns and of the varieties of animals consumed can yield information about what the changing lifeways of the people might have been. Unfortunately, the study of the organization and. lifeways of Paleolithic hunters is in its infancy (see Binford and Binford 1966b, Isaac 1972).

The oldest known site of hominid occupation in the Near East is 'Ubeidiya, located in the Jordan River Valley 3 kilometers south of Lake Kinnereth (Stekelis 1966; Stekelis, Bar-Yosef, and Schick 1969). This archeological site is composed of twelve superimposed levels of sediment, each one containing simple stone tools left by the people who visited this area more than one-half million years ago. 'Ubeidiya was at one time adjacent to a freshwater lake and marsh with grassland and open woodland on the nearby hillslopes. The shore of this lake was periodically visited by animals and by ancient people who hunted the large game that came to drink at the lake and who also subsisted on small animals and plants found along the shore of the lake and in the marsh. The human groups that visited 'Ubeidiya probably consisted of no more than a dozen people each.

The earliest remains at 'Ubeidiya (i.e., at the lowest stratigraphic level) include stone tools thought by the excavators to be indicative of a "pebble tool industry" that is comparable to what archeologists call Developed Oldawan in Africa. Among these crude tools are flaked cobbles of lava, limestone, or chert that could have been used for battering and chopping and simple tools made of

flakes that might have been used for cutting (Figure 3-3). These tools are similar to those found in Bed II of the archeological site of Olduvai Gorge in East Africa (Leakey 1971). On the basis of these similarities in tool types, geological evidence, and potassium-argon radioisotope dating, the earliest deposits at 'Ubeidiya are at least 600,000 years old.

The site of 'Ubeidiya was visited intermittently by prehistoric people over a long period. Close examination of the stone tools found in successive stratigraphic levels of the site demonstrates that the stone tool technology and probably other aspects of the culture of these people changed with the passage of time. Later tools were more carefully fashioned than earlier tools had been—an increase in proficiency that is probably due both to greater motor control of the hands and to attempts to use the raw material more efficiently. In addition to pebble tools, the lowest levels contain choppers, polyhedrons, spheroids, and picks. Archeological deposits of subsequent inhabitants of 'Ubeidiya include a chipped tool inventory similar to that found in earlier deposits, but with the important addition of a few stone hand axes, which are believed to have been used for a variety of chopping and cutting tasks. The presence of hand axes in the inventory of chipped stone tools is significant because the manufacture of such tools required skill and foresight to chip the rough piece in such a way that a hand ax was the result. Only a single blow was required to make a pebble tool (Figure 3-3). Hand axes similar to those found at 'Ubeidiya have been found at sites in different regions of the world and are considered to be indicative of an advanced level of biological and cultural development. The archeological evidence from 'Ubeidiya and other early sites in the Levant does not present a complete picture of the lifeways of the first settlers of the Near East, but it does indicate that the time at which they lived was twice as far back as had been thought and it gives a general idea of their capabilities.

Latamne, a site on the middle Orontes River in northcentral Syria, may be as old as one-half million years. Owing to the rapid burial of this site, it is believed that some of the material is still in the

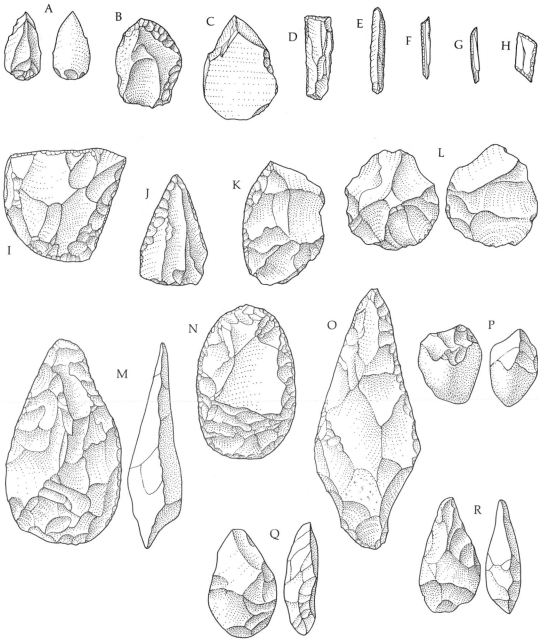

Figure 3-3
Characteristic tool types found at Paleolithic sites in the Levant: (A–C)
Upper Paleolithic point (A), scraper (B), and burn (C); (D–H) terminal Upper
Paleolithic truncated blades and geometrics; (I–L and O) Middle Paleolithic,
Mousterian scraper (I), point (J), scraper (K), core (L), and biface (O);
(M and N) Lower Paleolithic, Late Acheulean bifaces; (P–R) Lower Paleolithic
'Ubeidiya chopping tool (P) and Djisr Banat Jaqoub bifaces (Q and R).

Figure 3-4
Excavated living surface at the site of Latamne, Syria. The large boulders were
brought to the site by ancient inhabitants; the smaller debris is from tool
manufacture and use. (Courtesy of J. Desmond Clark.)

same position and context as it was originally
(Figure 3-4). The Acheulian stone tool inventory
found there, including hand axes, gets its name
from the site in Europe where tools of this type
were first excavated. Because of the nature of the
inventory at Latamne, archeologists have suggested
that it is similar to contemproary African assemblages—a similarity that may imply similar lifeways and a direct relationship with the makers of
the African tool kits. The site also contains large
limestone blocks, brought to it from elsewhere,
that might have been used to form the base of a
structure (Clark 1966; 1968). During excavation of
Latamne, attention was paid to the distribution
and orientation of stones within the archeological
deposit. Because of the presence of cores and
waste material from stone tool manufacturing,
the excavator, J. Desmond Clark, surmised that
the small tools had been made at the site. The hand
axes, however, had been made elsewhere and

carried to the site. Most of the stone tools had
fresh edges and no traces of abrasion, an indication
that they had not been abandoned elsewhere and
carried by a stream to the site. The animals available to the people of Latamne for hunting or
scavenging included elephants, rhinoceros, hippo-
potamuses, horses, bison, camels, giant deer,
gazelle, and other antelopes (Hooijer 1961). These
fauna suggest a primarily open environment with
gallery forest along the river and woodland steppe
at higher elevations. From the condition and distribution of the artifacts and stone debris at Latamne, the excavator inferred the existence of
what may have been the earliest structure in the
Near East. Depositional and artifactual information
imply that the occupants remained there for a
relatively long time. Hence, Latamne is the earliest
undisturbed site at which people are known to
have lived in the Near East.

The prehistoric population of the Near East of

Figure 3-5
View of the Mount Carmel caves in Israel: Tabun is the opening at the
right; El-Wad is the double opening in the center; and Es-Skhul is at the
left. (Courtesy of the Israel Department of Antiquities and Museums.)

approximately 100,000 years ago was large enough
to enable archeologists to discover several sites for
each succeeding period. The biological and cultural
evolution of the inhabitants of the Near East during the first one-half million years was slow and
gradual. Human groups were small, probably consisting of no more than from 10 to 25 members,
and technology changed slowly. Modest developments in stone tool manufacturing and the appearance of what seem to be "stylistically" distinct tool
kits at different sites are suggestive of changes for
which there is clear evidence in the remains of
subsequent societies. Middle Pleistocene settlements, as far as we know, seem to be predominantly on open sites, although some were in caves.
Favored locations included the Mediterranean
coastal plain and the Jordan Rift Valley. There
was a distinct lack of specialization in subsistence.
Wherever the evidence is available, it indicates that
hunters relied on a combination of large and small
animals. This lack of specialization in hunting
probably implies that Middle Pleistocene societies
did not hunt efficiently. It has been suggested that,
rather than by hunting, most meat was obtained

through scavenging dead or lame animals. It is
likely that the early inhabitants of the Near East
also collected plant material, but plant remains
have not been found, nor have tools for harvesting
plants been recognized among the artifacts. Although the developments during the first one-half
million years of human occupation in the Near
East were modest, they formed the technological
and cultural base from which a transformation
of greater magnitude could occur during the Upper
Pleistocene.

Hunters and Gatherers of the Levant

Sequence of Paleolithic Occupations

The first substantial Paleolithic discoveries in the
Near East were made at a series of caves in Mount
Carmel, Israel, by Dorothy Garrod in the 1920s
(Garrod and Bate 1937). One of them, Tabun Cave,
contains evidence of a long succession of human
occupations and stone industries (Figures 3-3 and
3-5). More recent excavations at Tabun promise to

refine the known sequence when analysis is complete (Jelinek et al. 1973).

The stone tools that have been found at Mount Carmel demonstrate an accelerating rate of technological innovations. Evidence of the earliest of the stone industries indicates that it was a crude flake industry, called Tayacian (or Tabunian), which was followed by a hand-ax culture of Acheulean type. The Acheulean was succeeded by the Jabrudian industries, which were characterized by thick scrapers on flakes with plain platforms. Bifaced tools have been found alongside some of the scrapers in considerable quantities. Closely following the Jabrudian was a stone tool industry called the Amudian, which includes tools in the form of blades, presaging the blade industries of the Upper Paleolithic.

At the Tabun Cave, the Jabrudian stone industry was succeeded by the Levalloiso-Mousterian, which has been dated at about 40,000 years. This industry includes points, Levallois cores, disc cores, many triangular flakes, and a few hand axes. It was during this Middle Paleolithic period that the nearby Mount Carmel cave of Es-Skhul was also occupied. Skeletal remains of eleven human beings have been recovered from the two caves. The excavators, Ted McGowan and Dorothy Garrod, suggested that all the skeletons were intentionally buried and come from the Lower or Middle Levalloiso-Mousterian deposits, as do the skeletons from Qafzeh cave near Nazareth, Israel (Garrod and Clark 1965:14). The Es-Skhul skeletons are the center of a controversy over the evolutionary history of early *Homo sapiens sapiens*, which is discussed in the next section.

The Transition to Upper Paleolithic Cultures

Although archeologists are only beginning to understand the sociocultural patterns that accompany the stone tool industries manifested at various archeological sites, it has been frequently suggested that the boundary between the Middle and Upper Paleolithic represents major changes in human lifeways. This transition is the one identified previously as the earlier component of the Paleolithic Transformation. There are several changes in the

stone tool inventory that signify this transition. A larger variety of tools that are generally smaller and more carefully worked distinguish the Upper Paleolithic. The Upper Paleolithic stone assemblages are characterized as blade tool industries because many of the retouched tools are made on elongated blade fragments. The production and use of blades and blade-related tools are a major technological advance, in terms of both manufacturing skill and the ability to produce more specialized implements.

Archeologists have identified what they consider to be a fundamental change in subsistence strategies of the Near Eastern hunters during this same transitional period. This change consists of a reduction in the variety of foods that were utilized. During the Lower and Middle Paleolithic periods, hunters exploited the full range of game resources in their environments, presumably because they ate whatever was available. However, this pattern is not characteristic of much of the Upper Paleolithic when human groups often concentrated their hunting efforts on a single species. The change is probably indicative of greater planning, communication, and organization in carrying out the hunt, and of a difference in attitudes toward food and the environment. The earliest evidence for this transition to systematic exploitation of a single species comes from the Mount Carmel cave of Es-Skhul (Binford and Binford 1966a). Unlike the earlier deposits of the neighboring cave of Tabun, which contain evidence that a variety of animals were slaughtered, the final Middle Paleolithic deposits of Es-Skhul contain an extremely large number of wild cattle bones (Garrod and Bate 1937). Because cattle are large and travel in herds, it would have been necessary to organize into hunting bands to slaughter them in large numbers.

It is interesting that, at this period of transition in stone tool technology and subsistence strategy, there is also evidence for a change in the morphology of the human skeleton. As is discussed later in this chapter (see Figure 3-10), skeletons unearthed at Es-Skhul reveal certain traits that are more characteristic of *Homo sapiens sapiens* than of the preceding Neanderthal remains.

The transition to the Upper Paleolithic is still poorly understood, but it may be that a fundamental change took place in the human career after a long period of slow development of protohuman and protocultural characteristics—development that crystallized during this transition into a society possessing many of the characteristics and capabilities of modern society. From the archeological evidence, it seems that this transition was more gradual and perhaps earlier in the Near East than it was in Europe where it has been better studied. The changes in stone tool technology and skeletal morphology were preceded by early innovations. In the Levant at sites such as Tabun, Israel, or Jabrud, Syria, there is evidence of a blade industry—the Amudian—mixed into a sequence of early Middle Paleolithic deposits. Although this precursor of later blade tool industries had a relatively short life, blades are often found in Levalloiso-Mousterian deposits at all stages of the Middle Paleolithic. It is not until the first stage of the Upper Paleolithic that deposits contain evidence of a definite blade industry. The Middle to Upper Paleolithic boundary has been reasonably well dated with the aid of carbon-14 samples from numerous caves in various regions of the Near East and northeast Africa. Although the information is not entirely uniform, the bulk of evidence implies that the Middle Paleolithic industries ended in the Near East from about 40,000 to 45,000 years ago (Farrand 1965:44). The earliest Upper Paleolithic date is about 35,000 B.P., but the difference in dates may be reduced after further determinations.

Upper Paleolithic Cultures of the Levant

Upper Paleolithic sites are widely distributed throughout the Levant, as well as the rest of the Near East. Most of the deposits are found in caves and rock shelters. The only site in the Levant in which the Upper Paleolithic sequence seems to be complete is the rock shelter of Ksar Akil, Lebanon. In general, the succession of stone tool industries in the Near East is comparable to that in Western Europe. In both regions, Mousterian industries are succeeded by blade cultures with Aurignacianlike

characteristics, which are themselves succeeded by Gravettianlike industries (Figures 3-2 and 3-3). On the other hand, it is precisely during this range of time that the stone tool industries of the Near East increasingly began to take on an aspect of their own, resembling those of Europe less and less. No counterpart has been discovered in the Near East for the rather spectacular stone tools made during the Solutrean period in France. There are two alternative explanations for this dissimilarity: either the Lower and Middle Paleolithic cultures of Europe and the Near East were tied together by movements of people or else advances in fashioning tools and localization of subsistence pursuits encouraged increased regional diversification in tool kits to the extent that they can be readily recognized by archeologists. In addition to the differences in the stone tools of the Upper Paleolithic, there are no known cave paintings or incised bone and stone in Near Eastern sites, whereas they have been found in Europe. Although the Near Eastern inventories seem to be less spectacular than those of their neighbors to the northwest, this should not be interpreted as an indication of a difference in intelligence or organization. Rather, the technology of the Near Eastern Upper Paleolithic should be viewed as a fully efficient and functional means of adaptation so far as their technology or lifestyle permitted to the prevailing ecological setting.

Many of the tools found in the Near Eastern Upper Paleolithic stone industries do not fit easily into already developed terminology for Western European stone tools. Consequently, archeologists have adopted a somewhat more general system of subdividing the period by separating it into six phases denoted by "Upper Paleolithic 1 through 6" (Neuville 1951; Howell 1959). In addition, individual excavators named each of the various industries after the site where it was first discovered. Different forms of scrapers, points, backed blades, burins, and other carefully fashioned tools characterize each succeeding stage (Figures 3-2 and 3-3).

The coastal areas of the Levant offered a rich and varied environment for the prehistoric hunter. Four major environmental zones were available to the inhabitants of the Mount Carmel caves (similar zones exist near Ksar Akil): on the craggy limestone cliffs of Mount Carmel, there were wild goats; the wooded wadi bottom contained fallow deer and wild cattle; herds of gazelle and onagers probably grazed on the coastal plain; and pigs and aquatic birds inhabited the swamps along the coast. The diversity of these resources simplified the hunter's task and enabled people to remain in the area for long periods.

Sites of the final Upper Paleolithic are referred to as Kebaran after a coastal cave site in Israel at which the type was first recognized. The Kebaran stone tool inventory is sophisticated in that it demonstrates increasing skill in manufacturing, greater specialization in tool kits, and the greater significance of plant-collecting implements. The diagnostic chipped stone tools of Kebaran sites include microlithic blades; long, narrow, double-pointed blades; long, narrow bladelets with obliquely truncated points; back-blunted blades; curved points; and asymmetric triangles (Figure 3-3). Blades with silica sheen—a deposit caused by contact with plant material—and stone mortars that may have been used in plant food preparations have been found in Kebaran deposits, although in small numbers. The frequency of bone implements such as fish hooks increases as does the presence of bone hafts (handles) for small flint pieces.

Most Kebaran deposits—dating at approximately 12,000 to 16,000 years—have been found in cave and rock shelters like those of Mount Carmel, but Kebaran remains are now being discovered at open sites such as El Khaim in the Judean desert, Nahal Oren on a terrace in Mount Carmel, and Ein Gev, on the eastern shore of Lake Kinnereth. At Ein Gev, a small, semisubterranean, circular hut has been excavated that contained two pestles, a basalt mortar, flint blades with silica sheen, scattered animal bones, and the skeleton of a woman buried beneath the floor (Bar-Yosef 1970). These findings are very suggestive of a village farming economy, but there is no primary evidence for any kind of agriculture. Clearly, the Kebarans had learned to collect plants and to hunt animals effectively. Wild barley was plentiful throughout the Ein Gev deposits, and the animal bones excavated suggest that the Kebaran hunters specialized in wild goats and gazelle.

The transition that occurred in the 10,000-year period starting 20,000 and ending 10,000 years ago in the Levant included attempts at village life, increasing use and preparation of plant material, and perhaps more effective social organization. The number of Kebaran archeological sites is larger than that for earlier periods. The Kebaran sites are also somewhat larger than their Upper Paleolithic predecessors, although they still average only 200 square meters (Bar-Yosef 1970). Despite the incompleteness of the evidence, it is possible to suggest that during the Kebaran period both the size of individual groups and the general density of population increased in the Levant. These changes taken together represent a major transition that further laid the foundation for the agricultural revolution that was to follow.

Upper Paleolithic Cultures in Areas Adjacent to the Levant

Areas adjacent to the Levant are well explored and are yielding important Paleolithic sites. Until recently, Paleolithic finds in Anatolia were restricted to scattered surface finds and some river gravels. Excavations carried out in the Karain cave, near Antalya, have produced a Middle to Upper Paleolithic sequence resembling that of the Levant (Kiliç Kökten 1955). On the coast in the Antalya region, there is evidence of an Epipaleolithic culture similar to the Kebaran in the Levant. This is best known from the cave site of Belbaşi, which contains a stone tool industry characterized by a microlithic repertoire of points, triangles, and obliquely truncated blades. It seems that the inhabitants were predominantly hunters of deer, ibex, and cattle, and did some fishing, as evidenced by the presence of bone harpoons in the excavated assemblage.

The intense archeological reconnaissance and excavation in the Nile Valley prompted by the construction of the Aswan high dam has led to the discovery of numerous Paleolithic sites both in Nubia and in Egypt (Wendorf 1968; Smith 1966). One of the densest areas of Upper Paleolithic occupation is the plain on the east bank of the Nile at

Kom Ombo. This plain is more than 500 square kilometers, and several early sites were discovered there in the 1920s (Vignard 1934; Smith 1966). An industry known as the Sebilian was defined as consisting of three stages. More recent work has shown that there were at least six other distinctive stone industries in the period between 20,000 and 10,000 B.C., a period of rapid development and dense population in Upper Egypt. Early microlithic tools including backed bladelets, geometrics, microburins, burins, and scrapers were used. Bone tools were also developed, and large numbers of grinding stones and flint tools exhibiting sheen—both presumed to have been used for wild grain—have been found that are earlier than 10,000 B.C. The excavators interpret these artifacts as strong evidence for the collection and grinding of grain as an important economic activity (Wendorf, Said, and Schild 1970:1170). Although the population density and the inventories of artifacts of these Upper Paleolithic people of the Nile Valley parallel the situation in the Levant at the time of the Kebaran, the transition to agriculture was not developed directly by the descendants of Nile Valley inhabitants. The Upper Paleolithic assemblages—made by people who successfully relied on collecting plants and on hunting and fishing—persist at sites in the Nile Valley well into the Holocene, and it is only from sites dating at 5000 or 6000 B.C. that primary evidence for agriculture has been found in Egypt.

Hunters and Gatherers of the Zagros Mountains

Sequence of Paleolithic Occupations

Available evidence of human occupation in the eastern half of the Near East indicates that it was not as early as it was in the Levant. The first Paleolithic research in the Zagros was that of Dorothy Garrod, who spent a season excavating in Northern Iraq before embarking on her pioneering excavations at the Mount Carmel caves in Israel. Garrod excavated for short periods at Hazar Merd, which contains Middle and Upper Paleolithic deposits, and at Zarzi, which contains Upper and Epipaleolithic remains

(Garrod 1930). Since Garrod's investigations in 1928, enormous amounts of information have been gathered on the Paleolithic occupations in the Zagros region, especially by archeologists working on three American projects. The Iraq-Jarmo project, directed by Robert J. Braidwood, was a survey of several regions of the Zagros foothills and included the excavation of a number of important sites. Ralph Solecki headed a Columbia University project, concentrating his work at Shanidar Cave in northern Iraq. The third project was an expedition directed by Frank Hole and Kent V. Flannery that focused on the various Paleolithic occupations in the Khorramabad Valley of Iran. As a result of the fine work carried out by members of these three expeditions, as well as the work of others, there is now sufficient information to construct a picture of the prehistoric lifeways of this area during the Paleolithic.

More has been published about the sequence of occupations at Shanidar Cave than about any other site in the Zagros. This cave is located in the south face of the Baradost Mountain at an elevation of about 822 meters (Figure 3-6, page 62). It overlooks Shanidar Valley and is a short distance from the Greater Zab River, a tributary of the Tigris. The cave is large, having about 1,000 square meters of floor space and prehistoric deposits as much as 13 meters deep. The deposits have been divided into four major archeological levels spanning the past 100,000 years (Figure 3-7, page 63). The level of earliest occupation is a thick deposit of Middle Paleolithic, Mousterian remains called Shanidar D. These remains are characterized by points, flakes, scrapers, and several human skeletons. From an examination of the fossilized pollen contained in the earth surrounding these skeletons, it seems that at least one of the bodies was purposefully buried with flowers strewn across it (Solecki 1971). This type of attention to burials at least 50,000 years ago is the earliest evidence anywhere for careful and probably ritualistic treatment of the dead.

The deposits in the next level, Shanidar C, are Baradostian, after the name of the mountain range, and are characterized by an Upper Paleolithic industry. Above the Baradostian are deposits similar to those found at Zarzi Cave by Garrod. This level

Figure 3-6
Archeological sites in the Zagros Mountains.

has been divided into two cultural strata by Solecki, the lower layer being Epipaleolithic, or Zarzian (Level B2), and the upper layer being Proto-Neolithic (Level B1). Shanidar B2 contains a large number of microliths and expertly chipped flint burins, backed blades with points, notched blades, and gravette-type points. Several pits were found in this level that protrude into lower deposits. These pits may have been for storing food, suggesting that the people at Shanidar were perhaps preserving plant food. Among the tools found in Shanidar B1 are some that are similar to those in Shanidar B2. In the Shanidar B deposits, there are an arc-shaped alignment of stones that may have been part of a structure and a cemetery area with twenty-six burials. The industry in general is similar to that found at the nearby open site of Zawi Chemi Shanidar,

which is discussed later in this chapter. The uppermost level of Shanidar Cave (Level A) contains materials that range from Neolithic times to the present. Today the cave is occupied during the winter months by local villagers and their livestock, mainly goats. They live in brush huts, each with its own fireplace, and they probably lead a life that is somewhat similar to that of the inhabitants of level B1.

Robert J. Braidwood sought evidence on the origin of agriculture in the lower valleys of the Zagros Mountains and attempted to discover and to excavate the Paleolithic predecessors to agricultural communities. The sites excavated produced information on specialization of activities and on food resources being used. The earliest site found in the Zagros is Barda Balka which probably predates and overlaps Shanidar D. At Barda Balka, archeologists

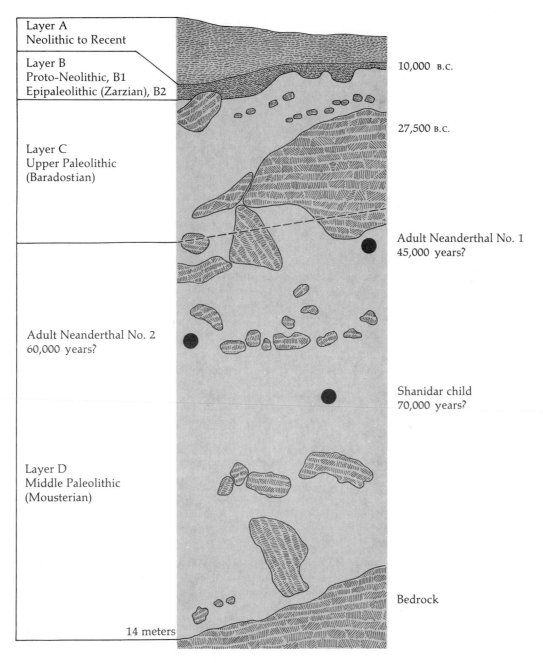

Layer A
Neolithic to Recent

Layer B
Proto-Neolithic, B1
Epipaleolithic (Zarzian), B2

Layer C
Upper Paleolithic
(Baradostian)

Adult Neanderthal No. 2
60,000 years?

Layer D
Middle Paleolithic
(Mousterian)

14 meters

10,000 B.C.

27,500 B.C.

Adult Neanderthal No. 1
45,000 years?

Shanidar child
70,000 years?

Bedrock

Figure 3-7
Stratigraphic layers in Shanidar Cave. The locations of the Neanderthal
skeletal finds are marked by solid circles. (After Shanidar Cave by Ralph S.
Solecki. Copyright © 1957 by Scientific American, Inc. All rights reserved.)

uncovered a series of simple stone tools (Braidwood and Howe 1960:150, 165). Pebble tools, tools made out of flakes, and core bifaces similar to hand axes characterized the tools used by the people of Barda Balka. The inhabitants were big-game hunters to judge from the animal bones recovered. Remains of wild cattle, Indian elephants, rhinoceros, wild horses, and sheep or goats were excavated together with the stone tools. Open sites from this general Middle Paleolithic time lack some of the finer retouched pieces found in contemporary cave deposits, which means that they may have been communities that specialized in food gathering, whereas a complete range of domestic activities may have been carried out in the cave sites.

Industries of the Zarzian type are from one of the last periods during which food collecting was the primary means of subsistence and, hence, may be a source of insight about the origin of a food-producing economy. At the shelter of Palegawra, the animal bones recovered in the Zarzian levels included gazelle, red deer, roe deer, wild cattle, wild goat, equid, and probably wild sheep, pig, fox, wolf, as well as those of a lynx-sized cat, and what has been identified as a domestic dog (Turnbull and Reed 1974). The diversity of animals demonstrates the intensive hunting that was being done by these Epipaleolithic hunters and gatherers. From a single camp, they exploited several of the adjacent environmental zones, bringing in a variety of animals. The hills in this region were covered with an open deciduous forest that harbored large wild cattle, red deer, and a diversity of smaller mammals; on the higher and rockier ridges there were wild sheep and goats; and in the open valley bottom below the site were equids, and in more distant and opener valleys, gazelle. The chipped stone tools from Palegawra are part of a diminutive blade industry containing various kinds of microliths, including such geometrics as triangles, lunates, trapezoids, and rectangles. A few obsidian tools were found at Palegawra, as well as in the deposits of Shanidar and Zarzi. The presence of obsidian, the closest source of which was more than 250 kilometers away near Lake Van in Turkey, suggests that during this Epipaleolithic period there was some form of long-distance communication.

Further to the south in the Zagros Mountains, information on Paleolithic lifeways comes from the Khorramabad Valley of Iran. This small valley, about 10 kilometers wide and 15 kilometers long, is nestled between high ridges of the Zagros Range at an elevation of 1,170 meters. Unlike many of the surrounding valleys, the Khorramabad Valley has many freshwater springs and large caves. Hole and Flannery located seventeen Paleolithic sites in this valley and have conducted excavations at five of them. Of the total number of sites, at least five contain Middle Paleolithic (Mousterian) occupations, six contain Upper Paleolithic (Baradostian) occupations, and at least two have terminal Upper Paleolithic (Zarzian) levels (Hole and Flannery 1967:151).

The Mousterian remains found at Khorramabad sites (Kunji Cave and Gar Arjeneh) are probably a late variety and seem to represent the first extensive habitation of the Zagros Mountain area. The stone tool industry is characterized by unifacial triangular points made on flakes and by sidescrapers. There are also some simple burins and borers. The core preparation technique of the Mousterian of Khorramabad and elsewhere in the Zagros is not Levallois and is thus distinctive from that of the Levant (Hole and Flannery 1967:155). By comparison with the Mousterian deposits, the subsequent Baradostian deposits at Yafteh Cave and Pa Sangar contain a greater variety of tool types and evidence that there was much greater emphasis on the technique of making blades. Characteristic of the Baradostian are small slender points, backed blades, retouched bladelets and scrapers, discoidal scrapers, simple burins, and polyhedric burins. Microlithic blades were introduced during the Baradostian, presaging the following Epipaleolithic industry. Several coarse stones used for grinding ochre—similar to pieces found in the Upper Paleolithic deposits of Ksar Akil, Lebanon—were found at Yafteh Cave; they are the first evidence of a ground stone technology that was a prerequisite for early agriculture.

Pa Sangar was the only Zarzian site excavated in the Khorramabad Valley. Many tools of the Baradostian were still used during this later period, some of them, such as round-ended scrapers, increasing and others, such as the Arjeneh points, decreasing in frequency. Appearing for the first time were notched blades and geometric microliths. Blades were becoming an increasingly important aspect of the chipped stone industry, which was developed even further in early agricultural communities. Also found in the Zarzian deposits of Pa Sangar are unshaped sandstone abraders and grooved rubbing stones similar to those found at Zarzi—additional early examples of a ground stone industry that took on central importance in succeeding stages of agricultural development.

To understand the total sequence of occupations in the Khorramabad Valley and the Zagros Mountains, it is necessary to determine whether there was cultural continuity between the Mousterian, Baradostian, and Zarzian occupations of this region. Increasingly, evidence seems to reveal that there was a generally uninterrupted continuum. The changing proportions of "characteristic" tool types from the Khorramabad sites portray clear differences, but no discontinuities, between levels. Occupation levels in the various sites exhibit this continuum with the exception of the Mousterian-Baradostian transition, which is poorly documented in the sites that Hole and Flannery excavated. The deposits excavated by Bruce Howe from the nearby rock shelter of Warwasi also supply evidence of the continuity of cultural and technological traditions, particularly covering the exception in the Khorramabad sequence.

Although single names can be given to each of the relatively contemporaneous industries, there is a definite trend toward regional technological specialization following the Mousterian occupations (c. 40,000 B.C.). This probably indicates that these Paleolithic hunters were moving about less than their predecessors had. The evidence suggests intensified occupation of single areas or adjacent ranges of valleys. Geographically, the known Mousterian and Upper Paleolithic occupations in the Zagros are very tightly restricted. As is shown in Figure 3-6, these sites form a narrow band oriented from northwest to southeast, parallel to the Zagros Mountain chain. They are located in areas receiving adequate rainfall at intermediate altitudes where there would have been maximum alternative possibilities for hunting game. This type of "vertical

economy" would have allowed the food gatherer to exploit different environmental zones and the changing seasons with a minimum amount of movement. Habitats at intermediate elevations with great ecological diversity also proved to be favorable for subsequent changes in subsistence strategies resulting in the introduction of primitive agriculture.

General Patterns of Paleolithic Society

Hypothetical Settlement Model

The diverse sets of data from the various archeological sites in the Near East can be classified according to settlement patterns and their relation to subsistence pursuits (Hole and Flannery 1967; Binford and Binford 1966a; Wright 1971). Three types of sites are hypothesized to account for the variations in the observable archeological remains: seasonal base camps, butchering stations, and transitory stations. Data for this model come from ethnographic examples of modern hunters and gatherers, evidence of the animals hunted by the prehistoric inhabitants of the Near East, and statistical analyses of chipped stone tool assemblages that have been found.

The largest of the three hypothetical types is a *seasonal base camp*. Most known base camps are located in large, chambered caves commanding a good view of passing game. The camps are large enough to accommodate from two to five families (10 to 30 persons) and are close to sources of water, fuel, and flint. A base camp would have been occupied by an economically self-sufficient and politically autonomous hunting band. Most tool manufacturing and food preparation took place at these base camps, resulting in a great density and diversity of refuse in the archeological deposits. Excavations at base camps produce concentrations of chipping debris, identifiable bone fragments, tools for making other tools, food-processing tools (e.g., grinding stones), ornaments, and, in general, a wide range of artifacts. Base camps have more hearths than other types of settlements, and they have clearly defined living floors. In the Zagros, the base camps in lower mountain valleys were probably occupied during the winter months, and open camps or shelters at higher elevations lived in during the summer.

The second type of site in the Paleolithic settlement model is a *butchering station.* Most butchering stations were small rock shelters, seldom more than 10 square meters in area. These camps were used by groups of hunters (from two to six in a group) who made a kill, butchered the animal, and later returned to the base camp. Assemblages at butchering stations include killing and butchering implements but lack other tools found at base camps. Each living surface of a butchering station contains the remains of one or two animals, whereas the bones on the living surface of a base camp may be from many different animals and species. At the Khorramabad sites, Hole and Flannery have found the remains of complete sets of bones for wild goats and sheep at the base camp, but not for wild cattle, red deer, and onager, which leads to the conclusion that the primary dismemberment of large animals took place at the butchering station, and only selected parts of the carcasses were carried back to base camps.

The third type of hypothetical site is a *transitory station.* Many such sites may have served as lookouts for hunters searching for game and passing the time by preparing new tools and weapons; they may also have been used for catching small animals and gathering plants during the appropriate seasons of the year. Scattered chipping debris characterizes such sites, a greater amount being present if they were hunting outposts and fewer traces if they were food-gathering stations.

Despite the rather incomplete picture archeologists have given of even the best-known areas, it is possible to hypothesize what type of settlements the Paleolithic sites of the Near East represent. In the Khorramabad Valley of Iran, the Kunji, Yafteh, and Gharmari caves probably functioned as base camps and Gar Arjeneh and Pa Sangar as butchering stations. Along the Levant coast in Lebanon, Ksar Akil probably functioned as a base camp, several small rock shelters in the area as butchering stations, and a number of very small sites up the wadi as transitory hunting stations. In the Mount Carmel area, the caves of El Wad, Tabun, and Kebara may have functioned as base camps, whereas Es-Skhul, further up the wadi, may have been a station for butchering wild cattle, and artifact scatters reported along the adjacent coastal plain may have been transitory stations (G. Wright 1971:466). Other groups of base camps and nearby butchering or hunting stations can be identified both along the Levant and in the Zagros Mountains.

Changing Subsistence Strategies

Flannery maintains that it is possible to discern a slow but very significant change in the subsistence pursuits of the Upper Paleolithic peoples of the Near East (1969). During the Mousterian and the early part of the Upper Paleolithic period, the major food source of the inhabitants of both the Zagros Mountains and the Levant was hoofed mammals, which account for 90 percent of the bones found in these archeological sites. Calculation of the weight of the meat represented by these bones indicates that ungulates contributed 99 percent of the meat eaten (Flannery 1969:77). Although the natural habitats of some of these animals were largely determined by local topography, other animals migrated with the seasons, seeking available grasses and moderate temperatures. To facilitate hunting, settlements were located in places in which animals would be close enough to be hunted for as much of the year as possible. In certain seasons, it was necessary to move the base camps to different locations to follow the game. Because of the greater topographic and climatic variation in the Zagros than in the Levant, the Paleolithic occupation sites are more obviously seasonal, being lived in for short periods of the year only. In the Levant, the moderating effects of the Mediterranean Sea and the close proximity of different environmental zones allowed the prehistoric hunters to spend more time in one location before they had to move because the local game had been exhausted or had moved into another area. There is evidence that the mobility and migration of the prehistoric inhabitants of the Zagros region and the relative sedentism of the Levant constitutes a duality that persisted in the adaptations in these two regions after agriculture had been introduced and to a certain extent is present today.

A gradual change in food resources after approximately 20,000 B.C. is apparent in archeological deposits. This change consisted of a significant broadening of the subsistence base to include progressively greater amounts of fish, crabs, water turtles, molluscs, land snails, birds, and possibly plant foods. The hunting of ungulates remained the main subsistence pursuit, but the addition of smaller animals, birds, aquatic creatures, and invertebrates was the precursor of a major change in lifestyle. These additional sources were more consistently available than the migratory game and provided food when the game was not available. People who used these consistently available sources could remain in one location longer than those who relied heavily on hunting large and migratory game. Thus, people began to settle and to develop local traditions of technology. Being in one place for a long period enabled them to spend time and effort in the development of nonportable equipment, such as heavy ground stone tools, elaborate dwellings, and a means of storing food. The change in subsistence base and the accompanying cultural changes were by no means sudden nor universally adopted. The increase in sources of food may have come about very simply: what might have been eaten by hunters waiting for the first kill, or by children exploring their surroundings, could have been occasionally eaten by other members of the community until it became an accepted source of food to be sought on its own.

At present the archeological evidence for this transition is meager, but that which has been found is probably a result of more complete recovery techniques utilized by archeologists in the past twenty years, or at certain sites. Examples of new foods are the thousands of snails recovered in the upper levels at Ksar Akil in the Levant (Ewing 1947:262) and the abundant remains of snails, mussels, and crabs found in the deposits at Palegawra in the Zagros (Braidwood and Howe 1960:169). However, certain other contemporary sites, such as the Mount Carmel caves and the Khorramabad caves, do not yield significant numbers of invertebrates such as these. Two different patterns of subsistence strategies developed during the Upper Paleolithic. Some societies were developing regionally specific procurement strategies that relied on a "broad spectrum" of local resources. Other societies became more species specific, "harvesting" only a few species but in quantity. The difference may have been due to the differential availability of ungulates or to cultural decisions about the desirability of theretofore unutilized food sources.

The transition to a broad base of subsistence resources was probably crucial to later developments. People who viewed almost all living organisms as potential sources of food and were willing to organize their activities to collect them would have been developing an awareness and organizational system potentially receptive to the collection and eventual domestication of wild cereal grasses and leguminous plants. Heavy ground stone tools first appear in late Upper Paleolithic levels at Ksar Akil, Yafteh Cave, and a number of other sites. These particular implements may have been used to grind ochre or other minerals, but their users became familiar with the characteristics and potential of ground stone implements which later could be adapted to grinding plant food. As already noted, several pits in the Zarzian levels of Shanidar Cave have been identified by the excavator as possibly being used to store food (Solecki 1959). The ability to store food is an essential prerequisite for plant cultivation and permanent communities.

Although the effect of this transition to a broader subsistence base is important, what caused it is difficult to detect. The disappearance of big wild game, such as elephants and rhinoceros, occurred much earlier during the Mousterian period and so cannot be an immediate cause. Climatic change may have been instrumental, but the relationship is not clear. Environmental change is discussed in detail in Chapter 4, but it should be noted here that the glacial maximum was reached about 18,000 B.C. after which the climate of the Near East became increasingly warmer and wetter until it attained conditions approximating those of today at about 8000 B.C. (Wright 1968; 1976). The ecological significance of this change is questioned by some scholars because during this entire period the range of animals available to Paleolithic hunters did not change. Nevertheless, the changing climate may have altered the migratory patterns of the animals or their relative abundance and, hence, affected the people who relied on them. The utilization of new sources of food may have been a result of an attempt to maintain a former lifestyle in the face of a changing environment: the same effort may have been directed toward hunting game, but other members of the community may have collected other types of food.

In modern day hunting and gathering groups, the young and middle-aged men do the hunting, whereas the women, children, and the elderly collect and prepare other sources of food. In light of this model, the broad-spectrum collecting pattern may be an indication of more participation by women in the subsistence activities of the community. Many ethnographic studies reveal that it is the women and so-called weaker members of a community who bring in most of its food, especially when game is unavailable. The elevated importance of women is accompanied by a more distinct division of labor according to sex and age. Because prehistoric women collected a wide variety of small animals, invertebrates, and plant foods, they may have been instrumental in effecting the recognition of these resources as edible substances. Such recognition was a change in the information content of the culture, which in turn altered the information flow among members of the society—changes typical of those that contributed to the introduction of agriculture several thousand years later. Thus it may have been the women and other "weaker" members of society who prompted the reorganization of activities necessary for a food-producing economy.

The Evolution of Technology

During the Paleolithic, there was a slow development of a stone tool technology from large, multipurpose tools to smaller specialized ones—a development that became more rapid toward the end of the period. The introduction of a ground stone technology and the possible use of storage pits are first manifest during the second half of the Upper Paleolithic period. These initial steps in specific processes of technological development, which became intensified in succeeding periods, were the foundation for early agriculture.

The general trend toward smaller chipped stone tools culminated at the end of the Upper Paleolithic in the introduction of carefully worked microliths. The use of microlithic stone tools in combination with bone or antler hafts was a major technological and intellectual innovation. Although tools were probably hafted (furnished with handles) as early as the Mousterian, the hafts were only an extension of the stone tool itself. However, the introduction of composite tools made of several microliths set into a handle or shaft is a qualitatively different invention: small pieces, each of a simple form, were combined to make a single complex, and hence specialized, tool. The practice of combining simple elements to form a complex tool was ancestral to many later technological and mechanical innovations. The use of microliths, along with hunting as the primary subsistence activity, diminished, but composite tools are still in use today. One chipped stone tool that is sometimes found hafted in a bone or an antler handle is a series of flint blades with a shiny patina coating, called sickle sheen. It has been suggested that these implements were used in reaping grain, and it is clear that they were used to cut some sort of vegetable matter. Their presence in late Upper Paleolithic deposits is evidence of increasing attention having been given to plant resources, furnishing another example of a preadaptation to the subsequent agricultural technology.

Human Evolution in the Near East

Changes in skeletal morphology are indicative of changes in physical and mental capabilities that influenced the course of history. The oldest evidence for the presence of human beings in the Near East is from the lowest deposits at 'Ubeidiya, which are more than 600,000 years old. Although no early skeletal remains have been uncovered, it is likely that the inhabitants of this site were of an archaic form of the human species, such as *Homo erectus*. By Middle Paleolithic times, from about 100,000 and 50,000 B.C., people had migrated to several parts of the Near East, and archeologists have found a significant number of human skeletons of this period. Middle Paleolithic people were ungulate hunters and used what have been called Mousterian stone tools. The skeletal morphology has prompted anthropologists to identify them as Neanderthals (*Homo sapiens neanderthalensis*). During the Upper Paleolithic, skeletons took on a modern form, classified as *Homo sapiens sapiens* and, by the end of the Pleistocene, their form had become completely modern, resembling that of the people of the Mediterranean race who occupy parts of the Near East today.

The evolutionary and cultural relationship of the Neanderthal types found in Mousterian deposits is a point of some uncertainty and controversy despite a relative abundance of information. The quandry has developed because of the discovery of what seem to be two distinct sets of skeletons from relatively contemporaneous deposits. The skeletons found in Tabun Cave and Shanidar are considered close to classic Neanderthal types, whereas those unearthed at Es-Skhul exhibit both Neanderthal and modern characteristics (Figure 3-8, page 70). Three sets of hypotheses have been put forth to explain the known evidence (Mayr 1963). The first, and classical, one is that the Neanderthal is an ancestral stage leading to *Homo sapiens sapiens*, which is unlikely in view of what is now known about physical evolution. The second hypothesis is that the Neanderthal is a species contemporary with *Homo sapiens* but reproductively isolated from it. This is a possible explanation, but it is more complicated than seems necessary. The third hypothesis is that the Neanderthal is a subspecies of early *Homo sapiens*. This seems most plausible, although not definite. According to the third hypothesis, Neanderthals of Tabun and Shanidar were probably representatives of a variety having

Neanderthal characteristics, which was genetically bred out of the population by social selection, whereas the Es-Skhul skeletons represent an early variety of *Homo sapiens sapiens* that manifest the characters being selected for. Although the tool assemblages found with the skeletons at Tabun and Es-Skhul are similar to one another, it is interesting to note that it is at about this time that blade tools appear in the Mount Carmel deposits, interbedded with more typical Levalloiso-Mousterian assemblages. The associational evidence does not support it, but it is tempting to hypothesize that it was this ancestor of *Homo sapiens sapiens* who made these early blade tools, ultimately gained demographic ascendancy over the Neanderthal population of the Near East, and later moved into Europe with these new tools.

At no time during the Paleolithic were there great numbers of people in any one place. Even in an area like the Khorramabad Valley, excavators suggest that there were never more than from fifteen to twenty people living in a valley of about 150 square kilometers (Hole and Flannery 1967:165). A general estimate of population density for the Late Pleistocene Near East might be close to one person per 100 square kilometers.

Perhaps by the Upper Paleolithic, and certainly by the end of the Pleistocene, the occupants of the Near East has the mental and physical capabilities of modern human beings. Language and other forms of symbolic communication were probably well developed, and standardized tool production was common. It is likely that the people who lived at the end of the Pleistocene and initiated the rise of civilization were as intelligent and capable as people are today. At that time, cultural evolution began to outstrip biological evolution as the most important factor determining the mode of human existence. The process described in this book is not a result of biological changes in an evolving human species; rather it is a result of a changing series of adaptations and organizations owing to fundamental alterations in conceptual, behavioral, and organizational patterns of anatomically modern human beings during approximately the past

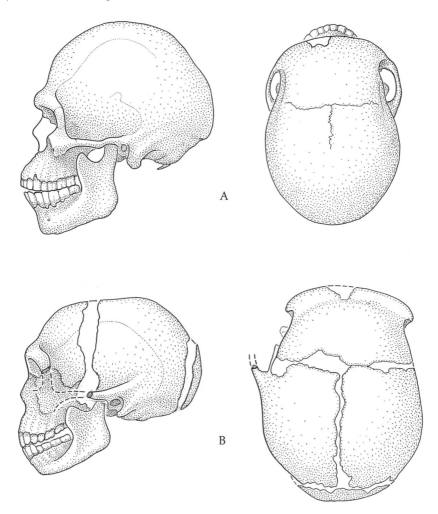

Figure 3-8
Two types of skulls from the Mount Carmel caves (A) Skhul V (transitional)
and (B) Tabun I (Neanderthal). (After McCown and Keith, 1939.)

15,000 years. During this time, the physiological changes in human beings due to biological evolution were insignificant, but the changes in their way of life due to cultural evolution were world shaking.

The biological and cultural evolutions represented by the Paleolithic occupations in the Near East are not particularly unusual or spectacular when compared with contemporary developments in other regions of the world. The earliest human-like creatures were in Africa, the densest known Paleolithic population was in southwestern France, the most substantial Paleolithic architecture was in Eastern Europe, and the most spectacular expression of art and symbolism was in France and Spain. However, the end of the Pleistocene is a definite turning point in the focus of cultural development. Although people in many regions of the world attained at least the sophistication of the Upper Paleolithic advanced hunters and gatherers of the Near East, they did not continue to develop into what is called civilization. The Mesolithic and Epipaleolithic groups of Europe, Asia, and Africa continued to hunt and collect food long after many of the peoples of the Near East had given up these pursuits in favor of agriculture. According to almost any measure of cultural development or change, the rate of innovation in the Near East accelerated to a pace theretofore not achieved. Even more important, there was an aspect of early Post-Pleistocene Near Eastern societies that not only stimulated innovation, but also incorporated each creation so that they become cumulative. In this manner, most innovations were institutionalized and passed on to form the basis of modern-day Near Eastern and Western civilization. At 12,000 B.C., the Kebaran and Zarzian communities of the Near East may not have seemed different from or more advanced than their contemporaries in Europe, Africa, or Asia, but in fact a seed had been sown and was soon to grow into full bloom.

Intensive Food Collectors of the Levant

Natufian Settlements

Many of the cultural advances made by the advanced hunters and gatherers at the end of the Pleistocene became more important and widespread with the succeeding cultures in both the Levant and Zagros regions. Large, seemingly permanent communities, substantial architecture, storage facilities, and food-processing equipment were no longer rare; they were integral parts of the cultural inventory. Although people still lived in caves, the proportion of open sites increased. After these developments, caves were no longer a major community form in the Near East. It is in the remains of Epipaleolithic intensive food collectors that archeologists find the evidence for the birth of village life with all of its technological and organizational implications. This transition was

not universal, nor was the change irreversible; however, those prehistoric people who successfully settled in permanent villages took a step that changed the course of history.

In the Levant, a widespread cultural assemblage has been found that followed the Kebaran occupations and is referred to as the Natufian, after its discovery at the Cave of Shukbah in the Wadi Natuf (Turville-Petre and Keith 1927). The Natufian culture flourished from at least 10,000 to 8000 B.C. and possibly earlier, but the scarcity of radiocarbon dates from Natufian sites makes precise dating difficult. The area in which Natufian materials have been found is limited to a band about 80 kilometers wide from the Mediterranean coast inland and extending from Beirut to Cairo. Natufianlike assemblages have been found outside this area, but they do not display all of the technological and representational characteristics that have been used to define an occupation as Natufian. Unlike the Upper Paleolithic deposits, the Natufian sites have yielded many skeletons, and so there is a relatively good picture of the morphology of the Natufians and of some of the diseases that afflicted them. Natufians were biologically modern human beings similar to modern Mediterraneans. Their stature was slightly smaller than that of their present-day counterparts, but in other respects they would be indistinguishable from them.

Soon after the first discovery of Natufian materials, Dorothy Garrod excavated the important Natufian deposits of the El Wad Cave and terrace at Mount Carmel, Israel (Garrod 1957). At first she claimed it was a Mesolithic culture of food producers, the first agriculturalists! Later evidence has shown that the Natufians were not true agriculturalists but carried on experimental activities with plants and animals. Robert J. Braidwood has given the name "incipient agriculturalists" to those living in such close relationship with wild plants and animals. In addition to the wide range of wild game hunted and aquatic resources gathered, the Natufians expended considerable effort—as reflected in their tools—in the gathering and preparation of cereal grains, such as the wild emmer wheat and wild barley that still grows in the Levant.

Figure 3-9
'Ain Mallaha ('Enyan) and Lake Huleh basin at the northern end of the Jordan Rift Valley. (Copyright Mission Archéologique Francaise en Israél.)

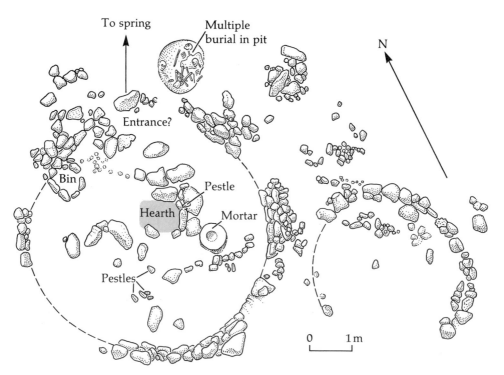

Figure 3-10
Plan of two structures from the lower level of Mallaha: a hearth is in the center of the larger structure, as are tools and a basin mortar. (After Jean Perrot, L'Anthropologie, vol. 7, nos. 5 and 6, 1966. Masson & Cie., Paris.)

Figure 3-11
Structure shown in Figure 3-10, Mallaha. (Copyright Mission Archéologique Française en Israel.)

The artifact assemblage that characterizes Natufian occupations consists of large numbers of microliths, lunates and sickle blades with retouch on both edges, decorated and slit bone tools, notched flakes and blades, microburins and geometrics (refer to Figure 3-12). Pestles, mortars, basins, slabs, rock-cut installations, and enclosure walls are characteristic of these sites. Although Garrod's work at El Wad supplied the information necessary to define the Natufian assemblage, it was later found that other sites contained tool inventories very similar to those at El Wad, but with widely varying proportions of tool types. These differences are probably due to the different activities required for adaptation in each area.

Excavations at the open "village" site in the upper Jordan Rift Valley of 'Ain Mallaha ('Enyan) have yielded the most complete picture of a Natufian settlement (Perrot 1966a). Mallaha is located adjacent to a spring on what were the prehistoric shores of Lake Huleh, which is now largely drained (Figure 3-9). Until the excavation of this site, Natufian remains had been found only at cave and terrace sites, but Mallaha is an open site covering at least one-quarter hectare. The inhabitants of this village lived in semisubterranean, stone-founded circular houses that were as much as 7 meters in diameter (Figures 3-10 and 3-11). Some of these structures were partly paved with flagstone, and some had well-built hearths and bins. This site was occupied for a significant length of time and contains three distinct strata in which building remains have been found. The excavator has correlated all three strata with the Lower Natufian as it is known from other sites. There are no radiocarbon dates from Mallaha but it probably was occupied for several hundred years sometime within the range of 11,000 to 9000 B.C.

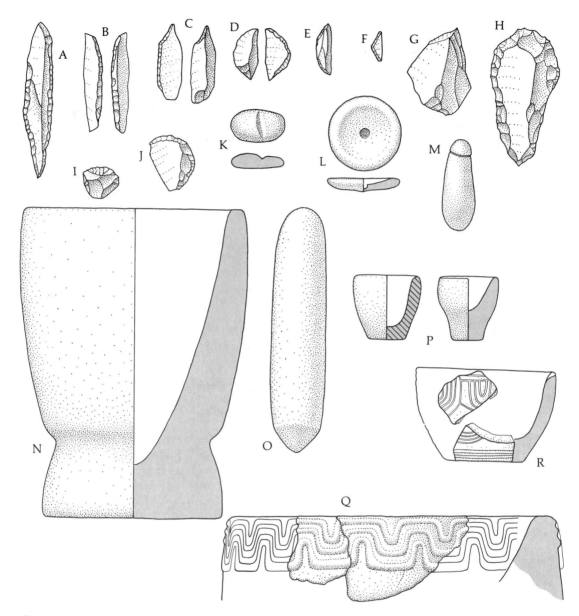

Figure 3-12
Chipped stone tools (A–J), ground stone vessels (N, P–R), and implements (K–M, O) from Mallaha.

The most outstanding feature of Mallaha is its architecture. Evidence shows the structures to have been large, well made, and numerous. They are the earliest known examples of "substantial" architecture, and they constitute the earliest known true village anywhere in the world. It has been estimated that there were fifty houses in this community of between 200 and 300 people. The houses in the lower stratum vary from 7 to 9 meters in diameter; those in the upper two strata are from 3 to 4 meters in diameter. The structures are close to one another and are in hollows dug about 1 meter deep. The

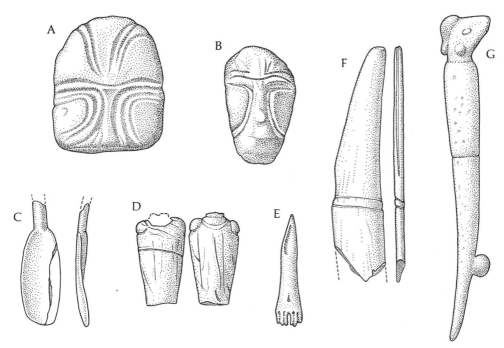

Figure 3-13
Bone implements (C, E–G) and artistic representations in bone (D and G)
and stone (A and B). Artifacts A–F were found at Mallaha; G was found at
Kebara.

hollows are lined with stones, and the superstructures were probably made of reeds and supported by wooden posts. The whole community is on a hillside, and the entrances of most structures are located on the downhill side in the direction of the spring. Most buildings have centrally located stone-lined hearths that are either square or oval in shape. In many, there is a pavement of stones or flat slabs near the hearth. Round storage pits as much as 1 meter deep are located outside the structures. One of the more complete examples of the Mallaha huts is shown in Figures 3-10 (at the left) and 3-11. This hut has an inner diameter of 6 meters with sections of the walls preserved to a height of 0.9 meter. Near the center of the hut is a square fireplace (0.7 meter on a side) that was full of grey ashes when unearthed. To the south of the hearth was a large mortar of heavy stone, and ground stone pestles were scattered across the floor. In the middle of the hut lay a beaker-shaped basalt vessel. Built against the north wall was a semicircular stone bin. Under

one of the flat slabs on the floor was a skeleton of a newborn infant. By close inspection of the walls, it was determined that the hut had been rebuilt twice, each time with a slightly smaller inside diameter and with different artifacts scattered on the floor.

Approximately 50,000 chipped stone tools have been excavated and recorded from Mallaha. In contrast to El Wad, where the majority of pieces were microliths, at Mallaha only 13 percent were microliths. The flint assemblage is largely a blade industry with backed blades, notched blades, burins, and scrapers being the most common categories. More than three hundred pieces of ground stone were recovered (Figure 3-12). Both basalt and limestone were used for grinders, grinding stones, polishing stones, pestles, mortars, and stone vessels. Flat pebbles with notches on the opposite sides may have been used as fishing net sinkers. Bone implements were common, including awls, skewers, needles, fish hooks, a bone haft for sickle blades, and a flat, spoonlike spatula (Figure 3-13C).

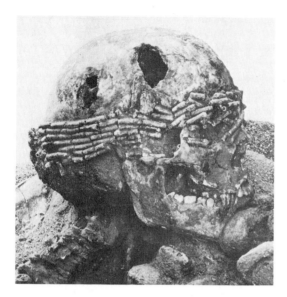

Figure 3-14
Burial from Natufian levels of El Wad, Israel, with
headdress of dentalium shells. (Courtesy of Israel
Department of Antiquities and Museums.)

Artifacts that can be interpreted to have been
ornamental or symbolic were also found at Mallaha.
Two incised pieces of stone, each probably representing a human head, are among the earliest
representational art in the Near East (Figure 3-13A
and B). Other pieces of bone and stone from Mallaha and other sites were carved into the forms of
animals (Figure 3-13G). Incised geometric designs
were used to decorate the outsides of some of the
stone vessels uncovered at Mallaha. Burials with
necklaces of bone or dentalium shell beads have
been found at several sites and attest to some trade
and to additional care given certain members of the
community (Figure 3-14).

Natufian burials are relatively common. More
than two hundred skeletons have been found in
archeological context at various sites, including
those of all three topographic locations—caves, terraces, and in the open. There are both primary and
secondary burials, with no uniform orientation or
treatment of the bones. Most burials are individual,
but some are multiple. Some skeletons are extended, others are tightly flexed, and the remainder are
loosely contracted. Many burials have grave goods

such as dentalium shell or bone necklaces. The
diversity of burial treatment probably indicates that
burial of the dead was a relatively new custom and
had not yet been culturally restricted to one form.
The presence of both primary and secondary burial
practices may be related to the seminomadic nature
of Natufian settlement patterns. Secondary burials
might have been those of people who died or were
killed while away from the base camp. The bodies
would have been allowed to decompose and then
buried when they were brought back "home."

It is difficult to reconstruct the subsistence pattern of Natufians in great detail because, at least so
far, few examples of vegetable food have been
recovered. Yet on the basis of finding flint blades
with silica sheen and the large quantities of grinding
stones, the inference can be made that plant foods
played a major role in the economy. Wild emmer
wheat and wild barley, which would have grown
abundantly in the Jordan Rift Valley and in the hills
beyond the coastal plain, were gathered, as were
acorns and other nuts and fruits. Fish was a significant source of food, as documented by the
abundance of fishbones and the presence of bone
fish hooks and harpoons. Still, the largest source of
food was the hunting of large game. Gazelle account
for almost one-half of the animal bones excavated
and various species of deer for one-third. Other
animals hunted included wild pigs, wild goats, and
large wild cattle. The large number of gazelle and
deer bones found at Mallaha (and other Natufian
sites) suggests that the herds may have been controlled to an extent. The lush environment created
by the marshes of Lake Huleh provided potential
sources of food for a large permanent community
such as Mallaha. Given this ecological potential, it
was up to the inhabitants to develop various techniques, such as intensive harvesting of cereal
grasses and incipient control of herd animals, that
insured year around supplies of food.

It is difficult to estimate population for Natufian
times, but it is clear that it was much larger than that
of Upper Paleolithic Levant. At least thirteen major
Natufian sites are known, which is dense considering the restricted geographic extent of Natufian
settlements. This is a larger number of sites than are

known to have existed during any preceding short period (Wright 1971:467). The Natufian sites are on the average larger than preceding settlements and some of them contain substantial architecture. The number of inhabitants of some of the sites may have been as many as 200, but groups ranging from 50 to 100 were more common. Two zones that had been inhabited during the Paleolithic were also the primary homeland for the Natufians. Densely occupied terrace sites were located in the valleys that opened onto the Mediterranean coastal plain, whereas seasonal hunting or gathering stations were situated in the semiarid hill country of the interior and the south. The increase in community size over the Upper Paleolithic camps, which seldom would have included more than twenty-five people, is probably related to a change in the organizational structure of the groups. To use the terminology of Elman Service (1962), some Natufian communities may have made the transition from band-level organization to tribal organization with all of the accompanying cultural changes. This is discussed in detailed in Chapter 6.

Later Cultures of the Natufian Tradition (Derived Natufian)

By the ninth millennium, many of the Natufian sites had been abandoned by their inhabitants. This is especially true of the cave sites, such as El Wad and Kebara. However, some of the sites first occupied by Natufians, such as Jericho, Beidha, Nahal Oren, El Khiam, and Tell Abu Hureyra, continued to be occupied for long periods (refer to Figures 3-1 and 3-2). The fortuitous natural settings that prompted the establishment of these open and terrace communities during Kebaran or Natufian times proved well suited for those economies in which the collection of certain categories of plants and animals was intensified. The inventories of the various sites inhabited in the Levant during the ninth and eighth millennia have been given the name "Proto-Neolithic" or "Pre-Pottery Neolithic A," but the similarities in their lifeways make it reasonable to refer to them as later cultures of the Natufian Tradition, or as Derived Natufian. The material inventory and the way of life during the eighth and ninth millennia were essentially the same as before except for a gradual change in economic dependence and settlement types. On the average, sites grew in size and permanence. Architecture becomes more widespread and substantial. Variations in building techniques begin to be exhibited. Although there is no definite evidence for either plant cultivation or animal domestication, there is evidence for intensified experimentation with wild progenitors of cereal grasses and herd animals.

The site of Nahal Oren was occupied during both the Upper Paleolithic and the Natufian periods, but it is best known for its Pre-Pottery Neolithic occupation (Stekelis and Yizraely 1963; Noy, Legge, and Higgs 1973). This community was located on a terrace in front of a cave in a valley leading out to the coastal plain from Mount Carmel (Figure 3-1). At one time, a small stream flowed through the valley. There are three springs within a kilometer of the site. The abundant local supply of water and the diverse ecological zones available to the food gatherers of Nahal Oren made this a favorable location for continued occupation. The excavated part of the Pre-Pottery Neolithic strata contains fourteen houses, each covering an area between 9 and 15 square meters (Figures 3-15 and 3-16, pages 78 and 79). The steep slope upon which the village was built had been terraced into four steps and on each step there were several of these houses, some of them joined by common walls. The structures were either round or oval, the floors were of pounded earth, and in most there was a centrally located, stone-lined hearth. The walls were built of large, undressed stones placed either side by side or one on top of the other. Some of these walls have been preserved as high as 1 meter and as thick as 0.8 meter.

The artifact assemblage at Nahal Oren is similar to those at Natufian sites. Microliths are rare and for the first time there are chipped stone pieces that have been identified as arrowheads. The presence of arrowheads, even in small numbers, is one of the characteristics that differentiates inventories in the Natufian Tradition from the earlier Natufian sites. There is also a greater number of thick imple-

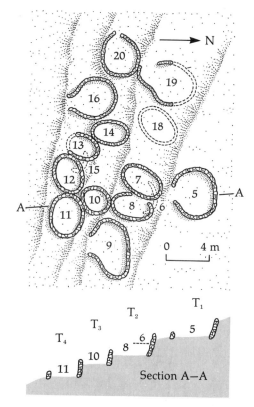

Figure 3-15
Plan and cross section of structures on the terraced mountain slope at Nahal Oren, stratum II. (After Excavations at Nahal Oren by M. Stekelis and T. N. Yizraeli. *Israel Exploration Journal* 13(1), 1963)

ments, such as axes, adzes, and picks. Sickle blades and knives continue to be present in large quantities, as do burins, scrapers, and retouched blades. Borers and awls of bone, ground stone pestles, grinding stones, and querns are also characteristic of Pre-Pottery Neolithic A inventories. Stone vessels continued to be used, and there are examples of artwork consisting of incised stone pebbles. The settlement at Nahal Oren housed from 50 to 100 inhabitants who were already carrying on activities significantly different from those of the Upper Paleolithic occupants of the same area, as indicated by the size of the settlement and by the details of the architecture and artifacts.

During the eighth millennium, there was another settlement atypical of early villages at Jericho in the arid lower Jordan Rift Valley (Figure 3-1). The site of Jericho had first been occupied during the Natufian period, but the remains are not of a substantial nature and the excavator, Kathleen Kenyon, considers the Natufians of Jericho to have been nomadic hunters. However, the next stratigraphic levels are Pre-Pottery Neolithic A and contain evidence of massive architectural construction. Because the area of the site is large for a settlement of that early period, Kenyon and others have even called this community a city. However, the simplicity of subsistence pursuits and its moderate size, compared with that of later urban centers, preclude the use of the term city to describe Jericho even though it was a spectacular settlement for its time. Unfortunately, the Pre-Pottery Neolithic A deposits known are from only three deep, narrow trenches dug in different parts of a large mound. Hence, the structures that have been exposed are incomplete, and so the relationships of the buildings and the contents of the intervening areas can only be hypothesized. If the presence of Pre-Pottery Neolithic A remains in the three widely separated trenches is interpreted as demonstrating that the total area of the mound was occupied at this time, then Jericho of the eighth millennium covered about 4 hectares. This size suggests a population of 500 or more. However, the organization required to integrate and feed this many people would have been so difficult that it is doubtful that all of the area between the trenches was densely occupied.

Jericho is located in a uniquely favorable environmental setting, which may help to explain how such a large community might have existed (Figure 3-17). It is in an arid region adjacent to a copious spring (Ain es-Sultan), which would have attracted animals from some distance and allowed plants to grow thickly. In addition to controlling this ample water supply, the people of Jericho may have controlled the burgeoning trade network in which they participated. Traded goods discovered at Jericho include salt, bitumen, and sulfur from the Dead Sea area, turquoise from the Sinai region, cowry shells from the Red Sea, and obsidian and greenstones from Anatolia. Widespread trading contacts may be a key to Jericho's prosperity. The inhabitants of

Figure 3-16
Stone foundation of circular structure from stratum II, Nahal Oren. (Courtesy of the Israel Department of Antiquities and Museums.)

Figure 3-17
Ancient mound of Jericho surrounded by the modern city; the Dead Sea is in the distant background (Jordan Rift Valley).

Jericho may have ventured to the sources of raw materials and brought them back (a form of long-distance procurement and not really trade) or they may have obtained raw materials, and perhaps other less easily identifiable goods, from other groups. It is likely that such groups consisted of mobile hunters and gatherers or at least the mobile members of otherwise sedentary villages. Exchange might have been directly with the groups that procured the raw materials or through intermediaries. We can assume that a general reciprocity existed, a balance in value being exchanged both ways.

The people of Jericho may have traded their salt, bitumen, sulfur, or fresh water for less easily obtainable materials such as turquoise, cowry shells, or obsidian. It is likely that the business of trading included ceremonial practices and the exchange of gifts, which established and maintained loose social ties between the participating groups.

Trade in many primitive societies tended to redistribute wealth within a community and maintain equality. It is not certain whether the exchange of goods at Jericho functioned in this way or whether it contributed to what must have already

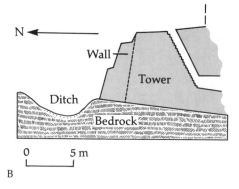

Figure 3-18
A. Pre-Pottery Neolithic A stone tower at Jericho: the square opening is to a stairway that descends through the center of tower. (Courtesy of Jericho Excavation Fund and K. Kenyon.)
B. Cross section of the tower, wall, and ditch. (After Kenyon, 1960b.)

been an emerging social differentiation. Single burials at other Natufian sites that included adornment consisting of imported dentalium shell headdresses imply that, as early as the ninth millennium, certain traded goods may have been reserved for people of high status.

Although the architectural remains of Jericho are those of an advanced community, there is no evidence indicating that the inhabitants of Pre-Pottery Neolithic A Jericho were familiar with farming techniques. Their subsistence was by means of hunting and gathering: gazelle, large wild cattle, and wild pigs, which were probably hunted while the animals were in the vicinity of the Jericho springs or in the not-too-distant hills, were the sources of meat; and cereal grains may have constituted most of the nonmeat diet (what have been interpreted as silos were uncovered in Pre-Pottery Neolithic A deposits).

Most of the structures found at Jericho are similar to structures uncovered at other contemporary sites.

Round semisubterranean houses with stone foundations and mud-brick superstructures were common. The average size is from 4 to 5 meters in diameter, but several single-roomed structures may have been connected to form multiroomed complexes. The architectural accomplishments that best attest to the industry of the Jericho inhabitants are the defensive wall and tower uncovered in the west trench (Figure 3-18). The stone wall is 1.6 meters thick and is still preserved to a height of 2 meters. It is surrounded by a ditch 8.5 meters wide and 2.1 meters deep cut into bedrock. On the interior side of the wall is a circular stone tower preserved to a height of more than 8 meters in which there is an enclosed staircase of twenty-two well-dressed stone steps leading down through the center of the tower to a passage at its base. This rather amazing set of stone constructions was the work of skilled laborers and an organized community, but there is no reason not to believe that a moderately well organized tribal community of several hundred people could not have constructed these works, given sufficient time. The valuable local resources, the water supply, stored food stuffs, and the concentration of trade goods were ample reason to build these defensive works. Ceremonies and the exchange of gifts may have helped to maintain friendly relations between groups, but a breakdown in alliances or the incursion of new groups into the region might have led to the abandonment of trading in favor of raiding, given the concentration of wealth at Jericho. Hence, the defensive constructions were reinforcement for the ceremonial and economic means of maintaining peace. The monumental scale of these stone works is one of many examples of the ingenuity and workmanship of prehistoric peoples.

Mureybit, a large village located on the east bank of the Euphrates River in Syria, was occupied during the eighth millennium (Van Loon, Skinner, and Van Zeist 1968). The maximum extent of Mureybit is 250 by 125 meters, but during most of its occupation it was considerably smaller. Seventeen occupation strata have been identified, each representing one of a series of successive communities at Mureybit. These strata can be grouped into three basic phases, the earliest being characterized by round houses, the middle by fire pits, and the latest by square houses. The architecture of the lower levels comprised rather crude constructions of rough stone and clay. These structures were roughly circular and varied in diameter from 2.7 to 4 meters. The houses of the upper levels are composed of several rectangular rooms but are of a later period than the material described in this chapter.

The artifact assemblage from Mureybit has not been completely published, but it seems similar to assemblages from contemporary Levant sites. The two basic components are small implements made of very thin and straight flint blades and rather large, heavy-duty tools made of rough chert. Tanged points and sickle blades have been found, especially in the upper levels. Querns and mortars of ground stone are common, but the mobile elements, pestles and hand stones, have not been found. It is possible that the inhabitants of Mureybit used another type of implement with their mortars and querns, such as a rounded flint nodule.

The economy of Mureybit is important because, unlike other early sites, it was located in the semiarid Syrian desert. There are no fish bones in the deposits and only a few mussel shells, which implies that the inhabitants were not relying heavily on the river resources. Hunting was a primary activity, with large wild cattle, Syrian onager, and gazelle each accounting for about one-third of the animal bones recovered. Analysis of the plant remains found in the deposits reveals that only wild forms of plants, especially einkorn wheat, were used; wild barley, lentils, and vetch were found carbonized in the deposits. This implies that a wide range of potentially domesticable plants was being collected. However, according to what is known about the environment of this region during the eighth millennium and about the natural habitat of wild einkorn, there should not have been any stands of wild einkorn closer than what is now the Turkish border, 150 miles away. Three interpretations are possible: (1) our paleoenvironmental inferences are wrong and the climate was cool enough for wild einkorn to grow near Mureybit; (2) the inhabitants of Mureybit went to what is now Turkey during the harvesting season to gather the grain or to trade for it; and (3) although the grain found was morphologically wild, it had in fact been planted and harvested. If this were an early example of cultivation, it would be revealed by morphological changes in the grain. However, Mureybit's agriculture might have been in the short transitional period from wild to domestic grain. These possibilities, among others, are being investigated by members of expeditions currently working at Mureybit and other Syrian sites.

Generally, the settlements in the Levant at the end of the eighth millennium were large and predominantly sedentary; architecture was substantial (buildings having stone foundations); and subsistence was by means of intensive hunting and gathering of a variety of resources. Although the wild progenitors of domesticable plants and animals were commonly exploited, there is no primary evidence for their domestication anywhere in the Levant during the eighth and ninth millennia. The people developed sophisticated facilities and tool inventories that enabled them to harvest and hunt to support the population, and the technological and organizational advances accompanying large sedentary settlements stimulated subsequent changes that led to agriculture.

Intensive Food Collectors of the Zagros Region

The Zagros region offers a markedly different environment from that of the Levant. The elevations are much higher, the distances between areas greater, and the bodies of water limited to a few rivers. These conditions affected the cultural adaptations in the region. The most direct environmental effect was on the distribution of wild flora and fauna. Although many of the species of plants and animals found in the Levant were available to the people of the Zagros, their densities and distributions were different. The hills of the Zagros were more suitable for animals whose natural habitat was rugged country, such as sheep and goats, than for those living in open country, such as cattle or gazelle. Wild progenitors of wheat and barley were also present in the Zagros, but not in stands as thick as those in the Levant. Despite these ecological differences, the people of the Zagros also developed adaptations that led toward agriculture and sedentary village life. Although the adaptations in the Levant and the Zagros were generally similar, they differed in several important details, which may explain why the early cultural developments in the Levant were more advanced than those in the Zagros. However, soon after the beginning of agriculture, cultural developments in the Zagros seem to have accelerated, and the Levant entered a long period without major advances.

Epipaleolithic Settlements

The best-known Epipaleolithic settlement of the ninth millennium in the Zagros region is the open site of Zawi Chemi Shanidar in northern Iraq (Solecki 1964). Zawi Chemi is located about 4 kilometers downstream from Shanidar Cave at an altitude of 425 meters above sea level (see Figure

3-6). It is on a terrace above the Greater Zab River in a valley surrounded by mountains that reach heights of more than 1,800 meters. Artifacts on the surface of the site cover an area of about 215 by 275 meters, of which 112 square meters has been excavated. The deposits are more than 2 meters deep and consist of two basic levels: the upper one is a mixture of recent material, but the lower one contains the remains of a "Proto-Neolithic village." Architecture is not well developed at the site, but there is a scatter of stones throughout the deposits, and in one part they are arranged in what seem to be rough walls outlining a circular area about 4 meters in diameter. These walls were constructed of stones, river boulders, and ground stone artifacts and the area that they encircle does not contain a hearth, but there is evidence that the building that may have been there had been rebuilt more than once. There are large storage pits elsewhere on the site, and domestic refuse in the form of a thick scatter of animal bones covers the entire area.

The tool inventory from Zawi Chemi exhibits a trend toward increasing reliance on plant foods similar to that which typifies the Natufian sites. There are pecked and ground stone artifacts in considerable variety and abundance. Mullers, or hand grinding stones, are extremely abundant, as are trough querns and combination quern-mortars. Pestles were used, but clearly defined mortars were not. Grooved steatite pieces that functioned as smoothers or bone tool sharpeners have also been uncovered. More than sixty-five whole or broken celts (ax- or adze-shaped implements) with polished or chipped bits were found in the excavations. The flint industry was basically one of notched blades and flakes, with a small proportion of microliths and a characteristic type of backed microblade. A small amount of obsidian was used (only one piece was found). Sickle sheen on flint blades is rare. As in the Natufian deposits, there is an abundance of bone tools: more than one hundred points and awls have been recovered, as have a large number of flat pieces that could have been used as chisels or hide burnishers. Several pieces are perforated or incised. A crescent-shaped piece of antler 22 centimeters long with a longitudinal groove probably held flint blades at one time, possibly serving as a sickle haft for harvesting grain.

Information on the economy and life style of the people of Zawi Chemi, although not definitive, suggests a major step toward food production. The presence of many ground stone plant-processing artifacts indicates that the people depended on gathered plants (probably wheat, legumes, acorns, and pistachio nuts) for a large part of their diets, but no carbonized remains of plant materials have been recovered. Hence, we can only guess at what plant foods were eaten and whether all were wild forms. The abundance of bones in the deposits at Zawi Chemi and in contemporary deposits at Shanidar Cave allow a precise knowledge of the animal resources used, including red deer, wild sheep, and wild goats. Wild pigs, cattle, fallow deer, wolves, and smaller mammals were also used but to a lesser extent. Concentrations of snail shells were found throughout the deposits.

In the upper part of the Proto-Neolithic strata at Zawi Chemi, there is evidence for what has been interpreted as the first domestication of an animal species other than dog. On the basis of a statistical study of the ages at which the Zawi Chemi sheep were killed, Dexter Perkins suggests that the high proportion of bones of young animals means that the animals were being herded and, hence, were under the immediate control of human beings (Perkins 1964). However, it is difficult to determine whether the high proportion of bones of young animals was a result of selectively hunting abundant herds or whether it is indeed an indication of control. Considering the close relationship that had existed between human beings and animals in this region, the assertion that man was controlling this docile species is not difficult to believe. Although the animals were selectively slaughtered, there is no evidence for a morphological change in the animals' bone structure, which develops after many generations of domestication (see Chapter 4).

Radiocarbon dates from Zawi Chemi and from contemporary levels at Shanidar Cave suggest that these sites were occupied between 9000 and 8550 B.C. It is very likely that these two sites, and others like them, were part of the same settlement system

and that inhabitants of the Shanidar sites were migrating from one area to another during different seasons of the year. The thick archeological deposits and the presence of architecture and storage pits at Zawi Chemi suggest a substantial occupation over a long period. However, it is likely that Zawi Chemi was a spring and summer station for people who lived in Shanidar Cave or at some lower elevation during the harsh winter months.

There are several other settlements of the eighth and ninth millennia that have been excavated in the Zagros region. Three of the sites—Karim Shahir, Tell M'lefaat, and Tepe Asiab—were found and investigated by Braidwood and Howe (see Figure 3-6). Karim Shahir is a hilltop site on a terrace above a small river at an elevation of about 800 meters in northern Iraq (Braidwood and Howe 1960). It has a single shallow occupation deposit made up of a scatter of fist-sized pieces of cracked limestone that had been carried there to form a rough stone pavement (Figure 3-19, page 84). This pavement has no apparent architectural features but is broken by numerous pits. About 30,000 chipped stone artifacts have been recovered. Most of the tools are notched blades or flint blades with silica sheen. There are abundant grinding stones and polished celts, but generally the emphasis at Karim Shahir—unlike that at Zawi Chemi—was on chipped stone implements rather than on ground stone (Figure 3-20, page 85). Ornamental objects such as beads, pendants, stone rings, and stone bracelets have been found, and two clay pieces modeled into animal forms are the earliest known examples of representational work in clay from the Near East. As at Zawi Chemi, no carbonized grains were recovered at Karim Shahir; so it is not possible to infer the vegetable diet of the inhabitants. The animals found in the Karim Shahir deposit include a high proportion of sheep or goats or both, cattle, onagers, and wolves. No claim has been made for the domestication of any of these animals.

The site of Tell M'lefaat is about as old as Karim Shahir, but it is located at a lower elevation, at about 300 meters. The distinguishing feature of this site is the evidence for round, semisubterranean houses with well-marked floors. These structures vary in

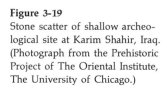

Figure 3-19
Stone scatter of shallow archeo-
logical site at Karim Shahir, Iraq.
(Photograph from the Prehistoric
Project of The Oriental Institute,
The University of Chicago.)

size, averaging less than 4 meters in diameter and
are set as much as 1 meter below the surrounding
surface. The chipped stone industry is similar to
that of Karim Shahir, but with more mortars and
pestles, and there is an abundant quantity of
polished celts. Several clay rods and balls have been
recovered, together with a schematic figurine.

At an elevation of about 1,400 meters in the Ker-
mansheh Valley of the Iranian Zagros is the site of
Tepe Asiab (Braidwood, Howe, and Reed 1961).
The deposits at this site produced plentiful yields
of animal bones and flint artifacts. Recent studies
suggest that the people of Asiab were keeping domestic goats in addition to hunting and gathering
(Bökönyi 1969). The chipped stone is generally
similar to that of Karim Shahir. A few lightly baked
clay objects have been found. The only architectural
remains found consist of a semisubterranean structure 10 meters in diameter, but whether this was a
roofed or open-air structure has not been determined. The general impression of the site is that it
did not support a permanent community and was
occupied only during certain seasons of the year. A
location so high in the mountains would have been a
good summer-pasture hunting ground, and the
people who occupied it might have spent the cooler
months at a lower elevation, such as at Karim Shahir
or Tell M'lefaat.

Another site whose basal layers probably date at
this period of intensive collecting and incipient
agriculture is Ganj Dareh (Smith 1968). Ganj Dareh

is also located near Kermanshah, Iran, at an elevation of about 1,350 meters. It is a small conical
mound about 60 meters in diameter and 8 meters
high. The earliest occupation excavated is composed of shallow pits and hollows that are roughly
circular in plan and contain ashes and burnt stones.
One area is partly enclosed by an arc of stone slabs
set on edge and may have been used for roasting or
heating. There is no evidence of substantial architecture in this level. The community was probably
of a seasonal type, like the other settlements of this
region and period. The deposits have been carbon-
dated at the mid-ninth millennium. The later
levels of Ganj Dareh apparently date at the late
eighth millennium and are similar to sites described
in Chapter 5.

**General Developments in the Near East:
12,000 to 8000 B.C.**

The end of the Pleistocene was a period of relatively rapid alterations in the life styles of Near
Eastern peoples. Although there is clear continuity
with Upper Paleolithic economies and settlement
types, fundamental changes occurred. The transitions were initiated during the final phases of the
Paleolithic in both the Levant and the Zagros re-
tions. Caves were no longer the predominant
locations for human occupation. By 8000 B.C., a
typical settlement was out in the open and had a

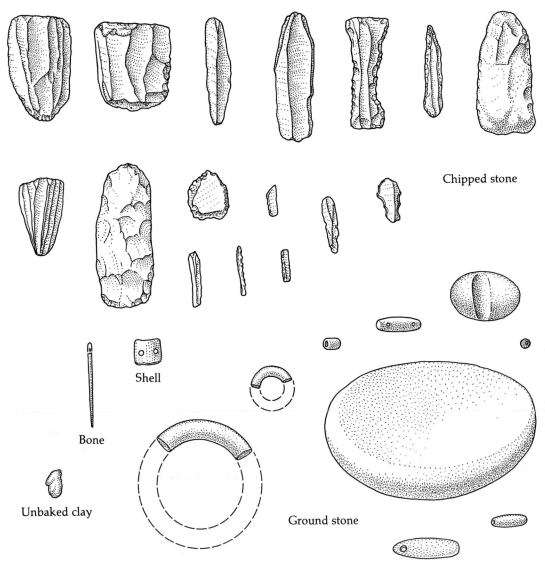

Chipped stone

Shell

Bone

Unbaked clay

Ground stone

Figure 3-20
Tools and other objects from Karim Shahir.

significantly larger population than those of earlier periods. The collecting and processing of plant material was intensified and it is possible that some plant species were controlled, although there is no specific evidence for this. Hunting certain ungulates continued to be the basic means of obtaining food, but very close relations existed between the hunters and the hunted. Settlers both in the Levant and in the Zagros were hunting a limited number of species—two or three at the most—for their major source of meat. In the Levant, it may have been possible to live at one campsite during the hunting season because the herd animals, such as goats or gazelle, would not have covered great distances. In the Zagros, where the elevational differences are great and the extremes of climate more varied, the animals would have normally moved a long distance in the course of a single year. Hence, their hunters either would have had to follow them and establish seasonal settlements at different elevations or would have had to restrict the movement of the animals. Both courses were probably followed.

The increasing importance of the ground stone and bone tool inventories of these peoples is a manifestation of their changing subsistence activities and the increasing permanence of their settlements. Specialization and division of labor must have increased during the Epipaleolithic period. Human groups engaged in a diversity of activities and started to build cultural inventories to aid in the efficient adaptation to the new life styles. The development of substantial architecture allowed people to live in open locations even during the winter and to move into such sparsely inhabited, but ecologically rich, areas as the upper Jordan Rift Valley. More successful techniques of gathering and processing food also allowed people to move into marginal areas that could not have supported large or permanent settlements earlier. One of them is the semiarid area on the edge of the Syrian desert in Jordan and Syria (e.g., Beidha, which is described in Chapter 5).

Another fundamental technological change is first documented in the Upper Paleolithic and plays an increasingly important role in the rise of civilization. This change consists of the use of two basic kinds of human artifacts: implements and facilities (Wagner 1960). Implements are the human artifacts—such as a hand-ax or knife—that transmit or move kinetic energy. Facilities such as storage pits, pottery, and ovens store potential energy, or impede its transfer (Flannery 1972b:26). A major long-term trend in human technology is an increasing reliance on facilities rather than implements. Prehistoric human groups were laboring to build facilities, supposedly during slack seasons, to increase their capabilities during active seasons. Because the fabrication of facilities is most effective if occupation is permanent, a reliance on newly invented facilities such as storage pits and on heavy artifacts such as grinding stones would have en-couraged the users to remain in one place. If the settlement was maintained on a permanent year-round basis, then it would have been increasingly worthwhile for its inhabitants to invest their labor in manufacturing more facilities. The long-range implications are great: facilities were a means for storing "labor" and increasing the group's future producitvity in a cumulative fashion. It is only through the investment in facilities—in a manner, capital goods—that prehistoric society could eventually develop the subsistence potential to support full-time specialists.

Composite tools became more widespread with the hafting of flint blades in bone and antler handles. Objects such as fish hooks and net sinkers attest to the increased consumption of fish and other aquatic resources. Just as the creation of composite tools was a technological innovation with far-reaching consequences, so were the early experiments with clay, as evidenced by the small figurines and other objects in lightly baked clay found at some of the Zagros settlements. The formation of objects by molding them out of a pliable material, which was then dried or baked, was a basic innovation in manufacturing technology. Ceramics, mortar, metallurgy, and glass are descendants of this initial discovery. These early innovations were probably accomplished accidentally and in themselves must not have seemed important, but their effect on a person's conception of the environment and the materials within it must have been enormous. The modeling of clay exemplifies human control of the earth itself. From our perspective several millennia later, it symbolizes our own efforts to control the environment and to shape our destiny. It is not accidental that the first experiments with clay took place at the same general time as did early experiments in food production.

Other conceptual changes revealed in the archeological data are increasing attention to the burial of the dead and to representational artwork. The Natufians and their contemporaries in the Zagros were purposefully burying many of their dead, both mature adults and infants. Although there was no uniform method of burial, attention was often paid to the positioning of the body and to the objects left with it. Concepts of an afterlife, the control of death, and ancestor worship may be implied in these patterns. Jewelry and other ornamental objects adorn burials and have also been found in other deposits at these settlements. Representational art in several different media appeared for the first time in the Near East at the end of the Pleistocene. Animals and other geometric forms were incised or carved in bone by the Natufians. The incised stone pieces from Mallaha may have been early representations of human heads. The clay figurines from the Zagros sites representing animals and other forms also indicate that prehistoric people used symbols to recreate the natural world. Such representations can be interpreted in a number of ways: some scholars suggest that these symbolic forms were elements in an early religion based on animal and fertility cults, whereas others view them as children's playthings or as the incidental creations of adults. Whatever their meaning, these objects are evidence of increasing attempts to understand, categorize, control, and reproduce the natural surroundings. Human groups during Late Pleistocene and early Post-Pleistocene times were increasing their understanding of their surroundings and were manipulating their environ-ments more efficiently than had been done in earlier eras.

By 8000 B.C., major differences were already apparent between the Epipaleolithic cultures of the Levant and those of the Zagros. Their predecessors, the Zarzian of the Zagros and the Kebaran of the Levant, had relatively similar technologies and subsistence bases. The Epipaleolithic cultures continued to have generally similar life styles, but in the Levant there was greater emphasis on substantial permanent settlements than elsewhere. 'Ain Mallaha and the later sites of Jericho, Nahal Oren, and Mureybit are clear examples of well-organized and architecturally sophisticated villages. In the Zagros, Zawi Chemi is the most substantial example of an open settlement, and it was probably occupied only seasonally. That nomadism continued in the Zagros was related to the fact that sites were located in areas that were not so rich environmentally and subject to wider variations in climate than those of the Levant. Although these environmental factors may have retarded the establishment of large and architecturally sophisticated villages at the end of the Pleistocene, they encouraged interregional movements of people and goods, which later stimulated the growth of early Mesopotamian civilization.

C   H   A   P   T   E   R

4

THE ORIGINS OF AGRICULTURE

A Giant Step for Humankind

*The introduction of food production and a settled village
existence are among the most important achievements of the human
career. A variety of hypotheses have been formulated to explain
these developments in the Near East. Climatic changes, conducive natural
habitats, population growth, and demographic disequilibrium are
alternately cited as primary causes. In this chapter, a synthetic approach to
investigating the origin of agriculture is taken as a means
of understanding current information and organizing future research.
Natural scientists are an integral part of an archeological
investigation into questions of early plant and animal domestication. Thus
it is necessary to know the methods they use and the results they
obtain to be able to evaluate the limitations of potential
data collection and the feasibility of testing hypotheses. Paleoenvironmental
reconstruction requires the participation of geologists, palynologists,
botanists, and zoologists. The work of paleoethnobotanists in recovering and
identifying ancient plant remains has added a new dimension to archeological
information. Zooarcheologists supply detailed information on the
kinds of animals consumed by early agriculturalists, as well as on the
nature of the animals themselves.*

In the full sweep of human history, no development has had a greater effect than the introduction of agriculture. Agriculture created the economic base and the social milieu from which state societies could emerge. For 99 percent of the time during which human beings have inhabited this planet, they lived by hunting and gathering. They were cunning and successful animals in nature's ecosystem. The ability to produce food enabled people to increase their control over nature, and the human population began to multiply at a rapid rate. In addition to increasing the food supply and the population, early agriculture accelerated the rate of technological innovation and was accompanied by rapid changes in social organization. The period in which farming was introduced has been referred to as the "Neolithic Revolution" (Childe 1936). The term revolution is appropriate both for the speed with which the transition occurred, only a few millennia, and for its fundamental effect on human life.

History of Investigation and Working Definition of Agriculture

The importance of the origin of agriculture has prompted several generations of scholars to hypothesize about its causes. This interest has been shared by people of diverse training encompassing a wide range of perspectives, including historians, anthropologists, geographers, botanists, and zoologists. Many of the hypotheses are related to more general ones about cultural development, agriculture being only one component. Only since 1950 has the origin of agriculture become a field of inquiry of its own. The hypotheses formulated before 1950 depended on inferences made from secondary evidence because there had been no direct archeological investigations of early farming communities. Historians claimed that the earliest agriculturalists must have lived in the same locations as the earliest literate civilizations. Geographers and botanists considered the present locations of wild strains of domesticated plants and the centers of maximum diversity for particular

plant species to be the places of origin of the first domesticates.

One of the earliest attempts to understand the origins of cultivated plants was by Alphonse de Candolle (de Candolle 1884; Wright 1971). He utilized information from a variety of scientific fields to determine the conditions under which the cultivation of plants might be initiated and the kinds of data necessary to test his hypothesis. De Candolle suggested that the following five conditions had to be met before a given location could be identified as the site of the original domestication of an individual plant species: (1) that the species had grown wild there; (2) that the climate was mild; (3) that the temperatures were high for part of the year, accompanied by drought; (4) that human beings are known to have settled there; and (5) that resources from hunting, fishing, or the gathering of wild plants were insufficient to support local human communities (de Candolle 1884:2). By combining the available evidence in botany, archeology, history, and philology, de Candolle was able to suggest where certain plants were first domesticated. Considering that he had no archeological evidence with which to test his ideas, de Candolle's conclusions were surprisingly close to those drawn from present knowledge. He maintained that some forms of wheat were first cultivated in Mesopotamia, particularly in the Euphrates Valley, whereas einkorn wheat was domesticated in Serbia, Greece, and Anatolia; and that barleys were first cultivated in western temperate Asia, in an area bounded by the Red Sea, the Caspian Sea, and the Caucasus. His formulation, as well as those of other scholars, identified the Near East as one of the earliest centers of domestication in the world.

Although the interests of the theorists attempting to explain the introduction of agriculture varied, several questions were of concern to all. Three general questions that guided early archeological investigations of farming were modified as researchers began to gather primary data.

1 When and where was agriculture first invented, and was it invented more than once?

2   Were plants or animals domesticated first?

3   Was agriculture the invention of an individual genius, or did it evolve over a long period?

Answers to the first and second questions remain matters of disagreement among archeologists. Although it is likely that agriculture was introduced more than once—in several different regions—some of the earliest evidence for agriculture comes from the Near East. There are conflicting opinions concerning the priority of plants or animals, but the weight of the evidence, as it now exists, suggests that animals were domesticated earlier, but not at every community nor in every region. The third question is more amenable to solution. Accumulated evidence documents the introduction of agriculture as a process that took thousands of years to be fully accomplished.

Because many archeologists have adopted an ecological approach to cultural developments and explanatory goals, they have reformulated the third question to ask why agriculture was introduced when it was? Recent observations made by ethnographers on the lifeways of contemporary hunters and gatherers raise the question whether agriculture was a welcome invention. The traditional view of the life of hunters and gatherers is that it was an incessant search for food with little time for leisure or contemplation. This characterization of the rough life of the hunter and gatherer was often contrasted with the view that peasant farmers had plenty to eat, considerable leisure, and time to develop crafts and art. Because of this belief, it was thought that prehistoric people would have considered farming a major advance and been quick to adopt it. A corollary assumption was than an agricultural life was conducive (because of allowing time for leisure) to the development of cultural innovations.

Ethnographic observations of hunting and gathering groups, especially the work of Richard Lee on the Kung bushmen of South Africa, have shown that at least for some hunting and gathering groups life was not a constant struggle (Lee 1968). The Kung live in a dry, seemingly desolate environment, yet are able to gather sufficient food without working long or regular hours. Most of the diet is made up of vegetable material gathered by the women of the group. In one 6-hour day, a woman can gather enough to feed her family for three days. The men hunt on a rather irregular basis, the amount of hunting done depending more on the desire and skill of the hunter than on the need for food. Both the men and the women of the Kung have time for leisure and rarely suffer from a lack of food. On the other hand, evidence suggests that being a primitive farmer was a rather difficult task. Crop yields were variable, depending on the amount of rainfall and the number and kinds of pests present. Stored grain was susceptible to damage by fire, water, insects, and rodents. Long-term sedentarization and crowding in villages encouraged human disease. A farmer may have found it necessary to resume hunting and gathering if his crops failed, but soon after farming has become widespread in a region the wild animals and plants diminish in number and are no longer alternative sources of food.

Another study undertaken at about the same time compared the productivity and efficiency of collecting wild grain with that of farming. Jack Harlan, an agronomist participating in an archeological project in southcentral Anatolia, was impressed by the density of the almost pure stands of einkorn, a variety of wild wheat, growing in certain locations (Harlan 1967). By conducting a practical experiment of harvesting grain himself, first using only his hands and then using a simple hafted sickle blade, Harlan demonstrated how much wild grain could have been collected. The quantity collected from this stand of wild grain was surprising: an average of a little more than 1 kilogram of edible grain per hour using hands alone and about 20 percent more using the primitive sickle. The food value of this wild grain proved to be superior to much of the grain cultivated today. In prehistoric times, wild grain growing on the slope of a mountain would have ripened at different times, the stands higher up the slopes maturing later than those below. Thus, a family or small group of gatherers could have collected grain from one of these dense locations for several weeks. Harlan estimated that a family, using stone-bladed sickles or their hands, could have harvested in three weeks more grain than they would have eaten in an entire year. Farming would not have been necessary for the people who had access to stands of wild grain such as these.

All of these observations raise yet another question: Why was agriculture developed at all? If sufficient food was obtained by hunting and gathering and if early farming had little apparent advantage, then why would anyone have made this important step in human history? Many early explanations took a vitalistic form: for example, agriculture was the logical outcome of a developmental process; or, the advantage of farming was so clear-cut that it would have been adopted as soon as any genius or intelligent group of people happened upon it. But in light of recent observations, the latter explanation is no longer tenable. The advantages of agriculture were not obvious at the outset and often were not apparent until hundreds or even thousands of years after its initial introduction. So the question "Why agriculture?" confronting archeologists has evolved from an inquiry into the first cultivated plant or herded animal to an examination of why early agricultural experiments were adopted on such a scale that farming soon became the dominant form of subsistence throughout the world.

The origin of agriculture has become a challenging problem of primary interest to many archeologists. Almost all evidence that would enable us to answer the question, Why was agriculture introduced? lies buried in the ground. Archeologists are well suited to organize an inquiry into the subject, but they require the expertise of specialists in allied natural sciences. Archeologists are not only data gatherers seeking evidence of early transformations, but also synthesizers bringing together the ideas of botanists, zoologists, geneticists, geographers, geologists, palynologists, and fellow archeologists.

To formulate and test hypotheses about the introduction of agriculture, it is necessary to develop a working definition of agriculture. It is important to recognize that agriculture is neither a concrete technological invention nor a single-valued discrete entity; rather, it is a series of new relationships formed between people, land, plants, and animals. It is a transition to an ecosystem fundamentally different from any that existed before, and it entails new structural relationships between the participants. Agriculture assumed many forms in various parts of the world and even exhibited diversity within the bounds of the ancient Near East. Throughout this volume, the terms *agriculture, domestication,* and *food production* refer to a reliance on domesticated plants or animals or both. In a fully developed agricultural community, there are four basic sets of activities that are necessary components of a food-producing subsistence system: (1) *propagation,* the selective sowing of seeds or breeding of animals; (2) *husbandry,* the care of plants or animals while they are growing; (3) *harvesting,* the collection of the food resources that have been fostered by the first two sets of activities; and (4) *storage* of seeds and maintenance of select animals, to insure an adequate reproductive source for the subsequent year. The terms agriculture, domestication, and food production imply all four sets of activities.

Hans Helbaek makes a further distinction between the use of the terms cultivation and domestication. Cultivation consists of activities that affect the natural ecology by furthering the growth and yield of one or more plant species (Helbaek 1970:194). Natural vegetation is suppressed or removed; the biology of the topsoil is changed by hoeing or plowing; and seeds of the desired species are dispersed at a suitable density, or seedlings are planted. In certain cases, water is drained off the terrain; in others, it is supplied artificially. Weeds are suppressed and predatory animals warded off. A cultivator's motive is the expectation that the yield will be increased. Any plant may be subjected to cultivation but, within a given ecological area, comparatively few pay back the expended labor. If cultivation is discontinued, most plant species will revert to their former status as members of the ecological complex from which they were drawn.

Some obviously profitable food plants were, at the start, subjected to cultivation by ancient people. In concentrating on pure populations of one of the wild grasses or large-seeded legumes, a cultivator might eventually have observed certain abnormal plants growing in his fields. These were plants in which gene mutation had taken place, a process that happens everywhere in nature but at a very low rate, one in several million plants (Helbaek 1970:194). In the wild, such mutants would usually be suppressed by their normal brethren. However, a mutant discovered in a cultivated field could be considered economically promising; thus, it might be cared for in a way that was most propitious for its survival. By this means, it would not be subjected to the pressure of natural competition and selection that prevails in any plant community, whether spontaneous or artificial. If the treatment of the mutants were continued, the survival of the plants would then be tied to human survival; they would become *domesticated.*

The most important single evolutionary characteristic of a domesticated plant is its loss of dispersal power, on which its continued propagation depends. Conversely, this loss is fundamentally advantageous to people because human control of a plant's dispersal means that its progeny can be exploited to human advantage.

Thus, it can be concluded that a cultivated plant need not necessarily be domesticated, whereas a fully domesticated plant can exist only as a cultivated plant. Cultivation is a matter of governing the ecology, whereas domestication depends on a physiological limitation in a plant of which the farmer takes advantage (Helbaek 1970:195).

Unlike agriculturists, gatherers harvest food resources by reaping or hunting and do not purposefully propagate or tend the growing organisms. *Intensive hunters and gatherers,* through an intimate knowledge of the potential resources of an area, utilize a wide variety of food resources. Evidence that this type of subsistence economy was widespread during terminal Pleistocene times has been uncovered in the Near East.

If, in addition to gathering the resources, prehistoric people also took care of the plants or animals they gathered, the form of subsistence pursued is called *husbandry.* It is likely that the Natufians and the inhabitants of Zawi Chemi Shanidar subsisted by this means. In some ways, the concept of husbandry parallels the idea of experimentation embodied in Braidwood's term, *incipient agriculture.*

Flannery suggests that the crucial element in the transition from food collecting to agriculture is not planting and herding, but the alteration of ecological relationships that resulted from the transfer of plants and animals, by human beings, to environmental zones to which they were not adapted (1965:1251). Their transfer removed certain pressures of natural selection, which allowed more deviants to survive and the eventual development of characteristics not beneficial under conditions of natural selection. These factors are important in the development and spread of agricultural communities, but it remains to be demonstrated whether they were crucial to the earliest experiments with agriculture. At which stage the adaptation to new environmental zones and the accompanying change in ecological relationships took place is crucial to the acceptance of either the nuclear zone or the marginal zone hypothesis for the introduction of agriculture.

Agriculture's introduction was rapid only in relation to the millions of years of hunting and gathering that preceded it. Although current data are not exhaustive, it seems that there were from several hundred to several thousand years between the first domestication of plants and animals in any given area and a heavy reliance by the people in that area on agriculture for food.

Available evidence supports the proposition that the introduction of agriculture was an incremental process. Domestication played a minor role at first, but in certain communities it assumed successively greater significance. Most theorists reject the idea that agriculture was invented by an individual genius, because there are many ethnographic examples of hunters and gatherers who have a great deal of knowledge about plants and animals. Therefore, it is illogical to assume that prehistoric hunters and gatherers were ignorant of their surroundings. However, before they could recognize the importance of cultivating a particular species of plant, or of maintaining a particular species of animal, they would have had to collect its wild progenitor for a long time.

Given the prehistoric collector's knowledge of the

ecology, the introduction of agriculture must have been related to its adaptive advantage. When agriculture produced greater yields than did other types of subsistence, it would have been economically more efficient to pursue that course.

Environmental Hypotheses for the Introduction of Agriculture

Environmental setting and climatic variation have frequently been cited in explanations of cultural change. The basic format of these explanations has been deterministic: in certain environments, a radical change in climate led to a radical change in cultural behavior. An example of this thinking is the belief that a climatic change at the end of the last Ice Age stimulated the introduction of agriculture. The widely held assumption (until recently) was that at the maximum of the last glaciation in Europe, temperature-rainfall patterns were deflected southward to the Near East and North Africa, producing a more temperate climate than exists today. As the ice sheet retreated northward, so did these temperate climatic belts, resulting in the desiccation of the Near East. It was assumed that this major change in the climatic regime of the Near East was the primary stimulus for people to change from a hunting and gathering existence to an agricultural life in an effort to adapt to the significantly deteriorated environment.

Oasis Hypothesis

Although several scholars utilized this environmental perspective, it was the insight and talent for synthesis of V. Gorden Childe that produced the most persuasive hypothesis. Childe began his studies in comparative philology and entered archeology to determine the birthplace of the Indo-Europeans and their ancient culture (Wright 1971). When Childe examined archeological materials, he recognized the inadequacy of using the system of the Stone, Bronze, and Iron Ages as evolutionary stages. The ancient use of these raw materials was

related to technological sophistication but did not always parallel what Childe interpreted as major changes in human lifeways. As a substitute, he organized information about prehistoric cultures and all of human history into a system oriented toward economics. Hence, he viewed the major evolutionary advances of history as economic revolutions and coined the terms Neolithic Revolution and Urban Revolution as earlier parallels to the recent Industrial Revolution. Childe redefined Neolithic to indicate not solely the presence of ground stone tools and pottery but also the existence of food-producing communities. Childe considered the deliberate cultivation of plants and the domestication of animals to be the greatest economic revolution after the mastery of fire: "It opened up a richer and more reliable supply of food, brought now within man's own unaided efforts" (Childe 1952:23).

Childe formulated a logical and convincing explanation for the invention of agriculture from earlier theories (see, e.g., Pumpelly, 1908) and from the understanding of paleoclimates at the time (Brooks 1926). Unfortunately, there was no archeological evidence about the location or nature of early farming villages with which Childe could test his ideas. Childe's "oasis" or "propinquity" hypothesis has been generally disproved by the archeological and natural scientific information gathered in the past two decades. Nevertheless, it greatly influenced archeological thinking and research.

Childe's oasis hypothesis for the invention of agriculture centers on his belief that a climatic crisis adversely affected those countries in which the earliest farming was done (Figure 4-1). He believed that much of the Near East had been fertile and well-watered before it began to dry up as the glaciers retreated about 10,000 B.C. Many rivers stopped flowing, and deserts of shifting sand replaced forests and grasslands. The hunters and gatherers who had sparsely inhabited these areas would have been forced to take refuge in the few remaining well-watered places such as the river valleys of the Nile, Tigris, and Euphrates, or near oases that had not dried up. In Childe's words, the desiccation supplied

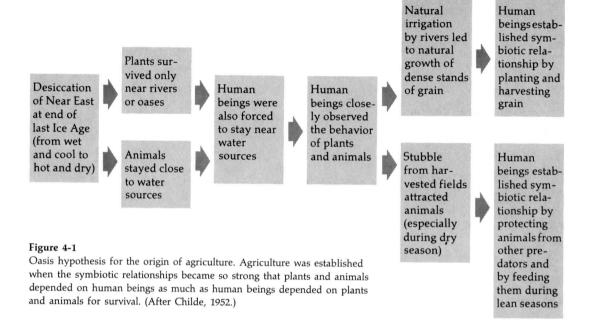

Figure 4-1
Oasis hypothesis for the origin of agriculture. Agriculture was established when the symbiotic relationships became so strong that plants and animals depended on human beings as much as human beings depended on plants and animals for survival. (After Childe, 1952.)

a stimulus towards the adoption of a food-producing economy. Enforced concentration by the banks of streams and shrinking springs would entail a more intensive search for means of nourishment. Animals and men would be herded together in oases that were becoming increasingly isolated by desert tracts. Such enforced juxtaposition might promote that sort of symbiosis between man and beast implied in the word "domestication." (1952:25)

Childe outlined the factors that caused the development of this symbiosis known as agriculture (see Figure 4-1). Because of the change from a cool and wet climate to a hot and dry one throughout the Near East, people and animals were forced to gravitate toward locations having permanent water. Plants continued to grow densely only near sources of water. Because of the proximity of the plants and animals, people had opportunities to observe the behavior and year-round life cycles of those that were subsequently domesticated. Childe asserted that plants were the first to be domesticated and that this was accomplished in the Nile River Valley. Rich soil deposited by the annual flood caused seeds dropped on the ground to germinate without human intervention. Given the presence of the appropriate wild progenitors of wheat and barley on the fringes of the Nile Valley, the Nile River would, by means of its "perfect irrigation cycle, be growing wheat and barley for the Egyptians." Eventually, according to Childe's explanation, some early agriculturalists dug channels to spread the flood water over greater areas and artificially sowed seeds to increase the density and distribution of the harvestable grain. He left open the possibility that these early farmers were still seminomadic: it would have been possible to plant the seeds, go away, and then come back to harvest the grain later in the year. The recognition that there was not an equivalence between agriculture and permanent communities presages archeological discoveries in the Near East and other parts of the world.

After the hunter had become a cultivator of grain, it became easier for him to domesticate some of the animals he had been hunting: the stubble of the cultivator's already harvested field offered the animals grazing, especially during the dry season. Predatory animals that encroached on the area of the oasis were probably chased off or killed, hence protecting the ungulates from attack. Occasionally, the hunters may have made pets of young animals and fed them from their supply of stored grain. By this means, these animals were tamed and they then attracted other herd animals to the settlement. Such a relationship between hunter-cultivator and the still-wild herd animals ultimately resulted in the animals no longer being able to survive on their own. The animals in turn fertilized the harvested field with their manure. They supplied secondary products such as milk and wool, and if selectively killed maintained their numbers while being a source of meat for the community. Keeping animals would also have been insurance for the primitive farmers against years in which their crop yields were inadequate, because keeping the animals was "banking food on the hoof" ready to be eaten whenever necessary.

Some scholars readily accepted elements of Childe's hypothesis and incorporated them into their own interpretations of world history. One of them was Arnold Toynbee, who utilized the oasis hypothesis in formulating his "challenge and response" hypothesis of cultural developments (Toynbee 1934). For Toynbee, the challenge was the Terminal Pleistocene desiccation. The responses were either to become extinct, to become nomadic herdsmen, or to change both habitat and way of life in the "dynamic act which created the Egyptian and Sumerian civilization out of the diminishing Afrasian grasslands." Other scholars did not accept the oasis hypothesis in its details, but were convinced that climatic change was the most important if not the sole variable in stimulating the invention of agriculture.

There was an alternative reaction to Childe's oasis hypothesis and other attempts to explain agriculture by climatic change. Childe's hypothesis was amenable to testing. Did the radical climatic change essential to Childe's theory actually occur? Did major cultural innovations take place simultaneously with the climatic change? Are the earliest examples of farming communities found in the areas suggested by Childe? The logical scientific response was to collect data that would confirm or discredit Childe's hypothesis.

Nuclear Zone Hypothesis

Robert Braidwood was a pioneer in gathering data relevant to the introduction of agriculture. Braidwood and others were influenced by the writings of Harold Peake and Herbert Fleure who attempted to locate the area in which food production began on the basis of a number of working assumptions about the climate, human settlement, and available plants. They concluded that wheat and barley cultivation began somewhere near the eastern highlands of Anatolia, and they were especially interested in the hilly regions adjacent to the area of the Near East that James H. Breasted had called the "Fertile Crescent" (Peake and Fleure 1927). Braidwood organized an archeological expedition to gather information with which to test the two competing hypotheses about the origin and introduction of agriculture; that is, that of Peake and Fleure versus that of Childe. He sought to find settlements that fit into the chronological and developmental interim existing between cave-dwelling hunters and gatherers and established village farmers (Braidwood 1969). Braidwood chose to investigate the lower foothills of the Zagros Mountains in northern Iraq. In these hilly flanks, the wild progenitors of potentially domesticable plants and animals were found in their natural state, and conditions would have been favorable for early experimentation with agricultural techniques. Braidwood briefly excavated at a prehistoric mound named Qalat Jarmo in 1948 and then conducted major excavations there in 1950 and 1951. For the 1954–55 Jarmo season, besides the archeologists who conducted the excavations and additional site survey, a botanist and a zoologist were recruited to help identify the food resources the inhabitants of Jarmo had been eating and the range of wild species that was available; a geologist was included to examine the evidence of past climatic conditions in the region. The plentiful and significant results of that expedition led Braidwood to formulate his thoughts about the origins of

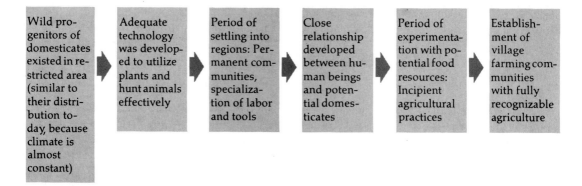

Figure 4-2
The nuclear zone hypothesis (natural habitat) for the origin of agriculture.
(After Braidwood, 1967.)

agriculture—an hypothesis that has come to be known as the "natural habitat zone," or "nuclear zone," hypothesis.

Braidwood has since altered his ideas in response to new information, but the basic premise of the natural habitat zone hypothesis is that there existed an area within the Near East where a constellation of wild progenitors of potentially domesticable plants and animals coexisted at the end of the last Ice Age. On the basis of his own work and that of his colleagues, Braidwood suggested that there has not been a significant climatic change in the Near East in the past 12,000 years and that the natural habitat zone could be looked for in places where the appropriate plants and animals exist in the wild state today. Synthesizing the various natural scientific and archeological evidence available, Braidwood hypothesized that the piedmont hills and lower intermontane valleys of the Zagros-Taurus arc of mountains was an ideal location (refer to Figure 2-4 on page 26). The zone suggested was that which lay above the hot and almost rainless floodplains yet below the cold and damp mountain peaks. Ranging in elevation from 300 to 1,500 meters, with rainfall between 250 and 500 millimeters per year, this region was ideal for naturally irrigated agriculture. Areas with more than 500 millimeters of rain would not have been optimum, for that much rain would have produced dense forests that would have had to

be cleared in order to cultivate crops. Braidwood called the optimum area the hilly flanks of the Fertile Crescent, and he has spent the past 30 years investigating various sections of it for evidence of early agricultural communities. The exact boundaries of the nuclear zone are a matter of debate and have been redefined several times. They coincide roughly with environmental zone 5 of Figure 2-4.

Besides relying on the proper environment, Braidwood's hypothesis depends on the presence of innovative cultural mechanisms for the introduction of agriculture (Figure 4-2). During the final part of the Upper Paleolithic period, people in the Near East were developing a more effective technology for gathering foods than had been theretofore known. Grinding stones for the preparation of plant material enabled them to utilize the abundant wild cereal grains. More effective weapons and organization aided in the hunting of what might have been a diminishing supply of large game. Cultural norms were relaxed, allowing the utilization of food sources not formerly relied upon, such as small mammals, snails, and various aquatic species. The improving technology and wider variety of food sources enabled hunting and gathering groups to move about less and less and to spend more time in each location than previously. This process of settling into a limited number of locations allowed the people to observe the plants and animals more closely than before. A close and regular relationship developed between these collectors and certain species of wild plants and animals. Stands of wild grain were harvested year after year on a regular basis. The hunting of ungulate herds was carried out so as not to reduce the number of females who could reproduce. This relationship might have been extended by experimentation to the sowing and cultivating of grain, or to the capturing and keeping of animals. This period of experimentation with plants and animals is referred to by Braidwood as a time of *incipient agriculture*, which in some instances led to successful and well-established agricultural communities. Hence, Braidwood's hypothesis relies on a favorable environment, the proper plants and animals, and a sufficient level of cultural development. The basic shortcoming of the nuclear zone hypothesis is that it relies on a so-far-unexplained human inventive faculty for the introduction of agriculture. Why was agriculture invented at *this* time? Given what *did* happen, we must assume that, in the proper circumstances, cultural development would have progressed toward agriculture, and that there were traits inherent in human society at that time that stimulated the experimentation leading ultimately to agriculture. Although these characteristics were generally present, and the thesis is correct so far as it goes, the explanation is not complete. More data must be gathered about the process that brought the circumstances into coexistence and about the factors that stimulated technological improvements and early experiments.

The discoveries by Braidwood and others of the remains of early farming villages in the foothill regions of Iraq, Iran, and the Levant give considerable support for the nuclear zone hypothesis. The finding that there is no evidence for significant climatic change in recent times dealt a heavy blow to the oasis hypothesis of V. Gordon Childe. However, Childe's hypothesis did not go down easily. The excavation of the early levels of the site of Jericho in the lower Jordan Rift Valley is an example of a community that supports Childe's position. In its basal levels there is evidence for a very large and probably fortified community (see pages 78–81). Radiocarbon dates taken from these deposits are

6700 B.C. and earlier. The first series of radiocarbon dates from Braidwood's site of Jarmo (4750 B.C.) implied that Jarmo is more recent than Jericho, but later carbon-14 dates pushed the date of Jarmo's lower levels back to 6750 B.C. A rather acrimonious debate concerning the relative priority of these two sites ensued with claims and counterclaims. Braidwood asserted that the dates from Jericho were unreliable and that its antiquity was not so great (1957). Kathleen Kenyon replied that, on the basis of depositional information, the 6700 B.C. date made sense and that Jarmo must have existed in some sort of "cultural backwater" (1959b). The importance of this debate was that Jericho and Jarmo were the only known communities relevant to the theories on the origin of agriculture, and they seemed to supply contradictory information.

Further excavations at Jarmo revised its dating to be roughly contemporaneous with that of Jericho. Other sites of early farming communities were found in both the Zagros foothills and in the low hills of the Levant. These areas fit into what Braidwood had defined as the natural habitat zone, whereas no other early villages were uncovered in dry river valleys or near oases. The balance of archeological evidence tipped in the direction of Braidwood's hypothesis. The combination of contradictory climatic interpretations and only one archeological site left Childe's hypothesis with few adherents, and it is virtually discounted today. An interesting footnote to this controversy, bearing on intellectual history in general, is that, as the debate was originally stated by the two antagonists, Braidwood's position on the relative dating proved to be wrong, whereas Kenyon's date for Jericho was correct. Nevertheless, Braidwood's hypothesis was generally confirmed and, although he might have lost the "battle" over that particular set of data, he clearly was the victor in the "war" of ideas, and the effect of his formulation on subsequent research has been enormous.

Neoclimatic Change Hypothesis

Although Braidwood's nuclear zone hypothesis has many adherents today, it is not all-inclusive, and

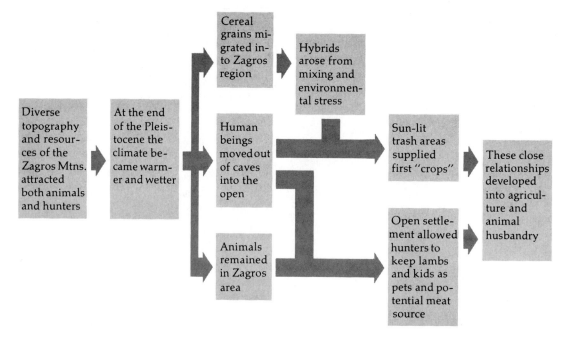

Figure 4-3
The neoclimatic change hypothesis for the introduction of agriculture.
(After Wright, 1968; 1976.)

it has been substantially revised in accord with recent research. Several archeological sites with evidence of early farming or incipient agriculture have been found at elevations both too low and too high to be included in the natural habitat zone of the potential domesticates as it is currently understood. Information produced by Braidwood's own expeditions has reintroduced the proposition that there was significant climatic change in the Near East at the end of the last Ice Age. The evidence came first from pollen cores taken by Herbert Wright and Willem van Ziest in western Iran (Wright 1968; van Ziest and Wright 1963). The details of this procedure and their results are discussed in the section of this chapter on paleoclimatic information. Briefly, their results and those of other researchers imply that before 9000 B.C. the climate of the Near East, or at least large parts of it, was colder and drier than it is today. Areas of the nuclear zone that today support an open forest of oak and pistachio trees

were an *Artemisia* steppe during the Late Pleistocene. This type of change is very different from that suggested by Childe and further diminished the likelihood of the oasis hypothesis. Wright claims that the change to a warmer climate that occurred at about 9000 B.C. is the most significant in the Near East during the past 100,000 years. The amelioration of the climate stimulated the migrations into the present natural habitat zones of certain species of plants and trees essential to the introduction of agriculture.

Wright has formulated an hypothesis related to the nuclear zone hypothesis that relies on climatic change as a major motivating factor (Figure 4-3). He suggests that the Zagros Mountain region of diversified habitat was an attractive area for certain wild animals and for the men who hunted them (1968; 1976; 1977). The abundance of limestone caves and rock shelters made the Zagros hospitable to the hunters of the last Ice Age. As the climate of the

Zagros region became warmer and wetter at the end of the Pleistocene, a different vegetative community developed in the area—the oak and pistachio open woodlands, which included the wild progenitors of potentially domesticable wheat and barley. These plants existed in temperate refuges during the Ice Age (possibly nearby in isolated valleys or as far away as Morocco) and spread rapidly at its conclusion. The warmer climate did not affect the habitats of the animals as strongly as it did the distributions of certain plants. Sheep and goats are more directly tied to the nature of the topography than to the temperature and rainfall of a region. Hence, Wright's proposition is that the appropriate constellation of plants and animals did not exist in Braidwood's nuclear zone until 9000 B.C.

The warmer and wetter climate also stimulated other changes. Migration of the plants at the end of the Pleistocene and the accompanying environmental stresses would have encouraged hybridization of the wild species, some of which might have been beneficial to agriculture. The less-harsh winters allowed people to move their settlements out of the protection of caves into open areas more convenient for collecting plants. The open settlements afforded sun-lit trash areas that were ideal locations for discarded seeds to sprout. The space that an open settlement afforded made it easier for hunters to keep animals as pets; lambs or kids captured and kept as pets were potential sources of food for the community when game animals were scarce. It is under these favorable conditions that agriculture developed. The key difference between Wright's neoclimatic change hypothesis and the nuclear zone hypothesis derives from the palynological research that implies that the appropriate plants and animals were not in close geographic proximity until after the climatic change accompanying the end of the last Ice Age.

This hypothesis supplies an ecological reason for agriculture's having been introduced at the end of the Pleistocene, but it does not attempt to give cultural reasons for its having developed as it did. There is considerable controversy over the nature of the climatic change, how widespread it was, and how it affected the distribution of wild plants and

animals. A good deal more paleoenvironmental information will have to be collected before it is possible to describe in detail the environmental setting of 10,000 years ago throughout the Near East.

Demographic Hypotheses for the Introduction of Agriculture

Population Pressure Hypothesis

Recently, many scholars have begun to consider demography and population growth as an independent variable affecting other cultural and environmental factors, as well as being affected by them. Whereas Malthus argued that a society's food supply is limited and that it governs population growth, Ester Boserup has suggested the reverse (Boserup 1965). Boserup asserts that population growth is in itself the autonomous, or independent, variable and was a major factor in changing agricultural technology and productivity. In other words, population pressure was responsible for certain economic and social innovations. Boserup relates the basic changes in agricultural technology and the intensification of land use to historical patterns of population growth. Her proposition is that changes in food-gathering techniques and agricultural systems of individual farmers were not voluntary decisions to produce more food than was necessary to meet the needs of domestic consumption but resulted from the pressure of a growing population on the food supply.

Elements of this treatise are adopted by Philip E. L. Smith and T. Cuyler Young, Jr. (1972) in their formulation of an hypothesis for the origin of agriculture and its early development (Figure 4-4, page 100). Developments described in the population pressure hypothesis took place in Braidwood's nuclear zone, which afforded the greatest supply of food for the initial population growth and subsequent innovations. Smith and Young relate the fragmentary archeological evidence for prehistoric population estimates and knowledge of agricultural tools to developing subsistence systems. Their basic premise is that, owing to a series of environmental

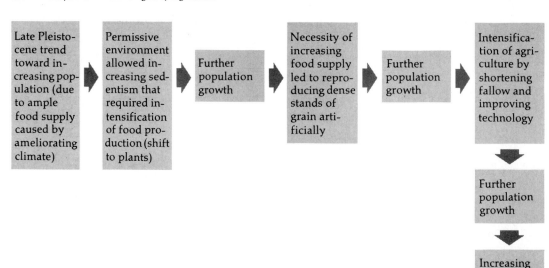

Figure 4-4
The population pressure hypothesis for the origin of agriculture and the rise of early civilizations. (After Boserup, 1965; Smith and Young, 1972).

and cultural factors, Near Eastern population has grown during the past 20,000 years. Periodically, the size of the population increased to a point at which methods of food procurement then in use were no longer sufficient. To counteract this, additional food supplies had to be secured. The first period of population growth was during the Late Pleistocene. According to Herbert Wright (1968), the climate in the Zagros region became more hospitable and plant resources more plentiful than they had been. The population increased until further intensification of the food supply was necessary. This shortage stimulated an increased reliance on plant sources. The increase in available food enabled the population to continue to grow. In the Late Pleistocene, there was also an increasing tendency toward sedentism. The less often a group moved about, the easier it was for women at childbirth, and for children and the elderly to remain with the group. Hence, population grew rapidly with the advent of sedentism. A result of this further population growth was an attempt to increase the food supply once again. One method available to the people was

to plant cereal grasses in order to artificially increase the distribution and density of the grain that they already depended on for most of their diet. Thus, early experimentation with agriculture was done in or near areas where the plants grew naturally. Successful experimentation increased the supply of food, allowing further population growth. Continuing population pressure stimulated a further series of technological innovations, increasing the productivity of agriculture. Shortening the length of the fallow period and using hoes, plows, and irrigation canals were some of the improvements in agricultural technology, which in turn stimulated population growth.

Smith and Young, as well as others, present an interesting argument for the demographic pressures that probably led to the rapid adoption and spread of agriculture (Pfeiffer 1977; Cohen 1977). However, it is debatable whether people confronted with a burgeoning population and a scarcity of food resources would have taken the crucial step of saving a major part of the harvest of a given year to use as seeds for the next year's crops.

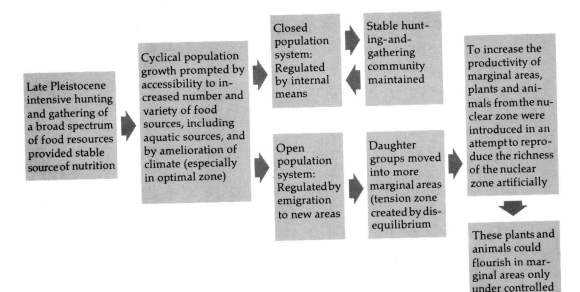

Figure 4-5
The marginal zone hypothesis for the origin of agriculture. (After Binford, 1968; Flannery, 1969.)

Marginal Zone Hypothesis (Demographic Shift)

Another hypothesis has been formulated by combining demographic factors with the presence of early villages outside the boundaries of the nuclear zone. This hypothesis, suggested by Lewis Binford (1968) and refined by Kent Flannery (1969), attempts to explain the origin of agriculture in the Near East as a response to cyclical demographic pressure on the margins of the optimal environmental zone for wild progenitors of domestic plants and animals (Figure 4-5).

Binford rejects the earlier concept that human beings normally look for methods of increasing their food supply. Recent ethnographic evidence suggests that the food-gathering activities of most of today's hunting and gathering groups are not overly strenuous. Hence, under normal conditions, adaptive pressures to increase a group's food supply are not strong. Binford regards Late Pleistocene hunting and gathering groups as having participated in an equilibrium system. By shifting from the pursuit of predominantly large game to that of a mixture of large and small game, invertebrates, and plant food, people were able to maintain relatively stable and nutritious food sources while decreasing their seasonal movements. This "broad spectrum" economy enabled communities to increase their populations and become semisedentary or even sedentary. On the basis of studies by scholars in various fields, Binford asserts that populations in equilibrium systems homeostatically regulate their numbers, keeping them below the carrying capacity of the local food supply. If this is true, then the major question to be answered by archeologists is: Under what conditions is there pressure to change one's adaptation? Or more specifically: When would the introduction of agriculture be advantageous?

Binford suggests that there are two possible conditions under which a change in adaptations is advantageous: (1) *a change in the physical environment*, especially one that reduces the biotic mass; or (2) *a change in the demographic structure* of a region that brings about the impingement by one group on the territory of another. He eliminated the first alternative because, at the time he formulated this theory, the recent information on climatic change in the Near East was not widely known. The new information (Wright 1968) implies an increase in the biotic mass, not a decrease; so the first alternative remains unlikely. Binford concentrated on the second alternative—that cultural change can be brought about by disequilibrium in local ecosystems.

An investigation of the possible effects of a change in demographic structure requires an understanding of two types of population systems. In a *closed population system*, a steady state is maintained by internal mechanisms. The number of births is balanced by the number of people dying. Abortion, contraception, and abstinence serve to lower the birth rate and infanticide increases the morality rate so that the size of a given population is homeostatically regulated (Binford 1968:329). An *open population system* is one in which size is maintained by the budding off of new groups or by the emigration of individual members: a community *from* which members migrate is a donor; communities *to* which they migrate are recipients. Open and closed systems can be continental in scope or restricted to, say, a section of a country, an environmental zone, or an individual valley. The areas of the Near East in which there were early villages are topographically diverse, exhibiting a mosaic of favorable and less favorable areas. There were a number of short-distance moves by settlements, which were made in regular patterns that were part of a single closed system. However, when part of a group deviated from its pattern and entered a new area, a donor-recipient relationship was created.

Two working assumptions of the marginal zone hypothesis are: (1) by 10,000 B.C., people had migrated to almost every part of the world; and (2) with respect to subsistence strategies and available resources, most regions were in general equilibrium. This implies that at the level of technology of that time, the world was filled up! In the Near East the population was probably the highest it had ever been, although not denser than some other regions of the world. A marginal zone exists where there is a marked difference in degree of sedentism between two sociocultural units within a relatively restricted

geographical region, creating a tension zone in which colonies from the more sedentary unit periodically disrupt the density equilibrium balances of the less sedentary one. Under these conditions, there is strong selective pressure favoring the development of more effective means of food production for both units.

Binford suggests that an important stimulus for cultural change was the cyclical demographic pressure exerted on these marginal habitats by their neighbors in optimal habitats. It is the optimal habitats that are regional growth centers (the donors in an open system). They were located within Braidwood's nuclear zone where wild plants and animals were most abundant, frequently near bodies of water supplying aquatic sources of food. The use of a broad spectrum of food, including aquatic resources, small game, and plants, led to cyclical population growth, resulting in emigration to the margins of the optimal habitat. The pressure for the exploitation of new food sources would have been felt most strongly at the margins of population growth centers, not in the centers themselves. Hence, a tension zone existed between the successful sedentary intensive hunters and collectors and the more nomadic hunters and gatherers. According to Binford and Flannery, the introduction of agriculture was an attempt to meet the food crisis created when human groups were forced into this tension zone and artificially produced the dense stands of grain that characterized tracts of the optimal zone. Moving cereal grains out of their natural habitat would also increase selective pressures, favoring new strains of plants. Control of these processes rapidly led to more productive and tolerant species of plants.

Binford does not rely on a single area in which population growth was cyclical as a basis for his statements; rather, he bases most of them on events in the coastal areas of Europe and the Levant. The major factor responsible for the increasing population density at that time was the settling-in of groups into coastal environments during the Mesolithic and the subsequent rise of sea levels at the end of the last Ice Age, diminishing the area of optimal land available.

Flannery's primary example in support of the marginal zone hypothesis is in the Zagros Mountains—Ali Kosh, a site that he excavated in the Khuzistan piedmont of southwestern Iran. Because of its low elevation, Ali Kosh is hotter and drier than is believed to be optimal for the wild progenitors of domestic plants and animals. Hence, these organisms were probably first experimented with elsewhere and then brought down to Khuzistan and to Ali Kosh. Flannery suggests that population growth in the intermediate elevations of the Zagros Mountains had begun 20,000 years ago owing to what he calls the broad spectrum revolution (see Chapter 3, pages 66–68). Reliance on a broad range of food sources allowed sedentism to increase, which in turn supported widespread population growth. This caused the optimal zone to become populated to capacity, initiating the movement of groups into more marginal environments, such as that of Ali Kosh, taking their sheep, goats, wheat, and barley with them.

The marginal zone hypothesis is important because it focuses attention on the changes in demographic structure, in the equilibrium of local subsistence systems, and in local environmental factors. Potentially, this hypothesis could be tested with data from the archeological record in the Near East. If the marginal zone hypothesis is correct, then the following conditions should be true: (1) the population increased in the optimal zones earlier than the oldest evidence that we have of domesticates; (2) the earliest evidence for domesticates is not from the optimal zones, but from the margins of these zones; (3) the material inventories of the earliest domesticators are stylistically similar to those of their neighbors within the optimal zone; and (4) rather than in a single center of domestication, evidence of early domesticates appeared in a number of places (Wright 1971:461). Given the nature of archeological data available, whether these conditions did exist cannot be conclusively evaluated, but directions for future research are outlined.

The marginal zone hypothesis minimizes the importance of the "invention" of agriculture and concentrates on the behavior of population systems and

defining adaptive behavior. Binford and Flannery, like the other demographic theorists, are not searching for the first person to have planted wheat or barley, because it is assumed that most hunters and gatherers knew the life cycles and methods of propagation of wild cereals. Rather, at the heart of their inquiries are two questions: What made cereal agriculture advantageous? What helped stimulate changes in the early domesticates? Groups accustomed to the plentiful fields of the optimal zones that moved into less favorable environments were motivated to improve food gathering techniques, and such moves created the environmental stress that favored genetic hybridization of the plants. Although the marginal zone hypothesis is informative and helpful in focusing research, it has not yet been substantiated by available evidence, it does not treat animal domestication adequately, nor does it explain in detail the process that took place.

Toward a Multifactor Explanation of the Origins of Agriculture

The Primary Force as an Element in Formulating Hypotheses

A first step in understanding any important change in the human career, such as food production, is to determine whether the observed changes were due largely to stimuli from the biophysical environment, the cultural milieu, or social institutions. Stimuli from each of these spheres were often interrelated and seldom functioned in isolation. Nevertheless, it is possible as a first approximation to delineate which sphere was the primary mover, and which were secondary or static. Although each of the hypotheses discussed in this chapter contains the assertion that an interrelated set of factors caused the introduction of agriculture, it is possible to abstract a "primary force" from each theory. Cultural systems and the transformations of these systems are extremely complex processes. However, for a general perspective on cultural development, the investigation of primary forces can be enlightening and educational.

It has frequently been suggested that the *environment* was a crucial element in many fundamental developments in the human career. Climatic change is suggested as the primary force in the introduction of agriculture in both Childe's and Wright's hypotheses. Braidwood and Wright emphasize the importance of the proper environmental circumstances, especially the presence of the appropriate wild plants and animals. Despite the variety of information used to reconstruct paleoenvironments, the question of the importance of the environment has not been conclusively answered. The first priority in such an inquiry is to determine what constitutes a relevant climatic change or environmental circumstance in relation to the subsistence patterns and lifeways of prehistoric people. The assumptions should not be made that people utilized only those resources adjacent to their own communities or that changes in the vegetation surrounding a lake in one part of the Near East were paralleled by those taking place in all localities. Ethnographic and archeological evidence suggests that groups often traveled hundreds of kilometers to gather certain resources. In geographic areas with vertical relief, several climatic and biotic zones would have been available within as few as 20 kilometers or less. This makes an archeologist's task more difficult. To ascertain the effects of a climatic change or particular environmental circumstance in a given region, the archeologist must gather climatic information from surrounding regions to compare the plants and animals used by the ancient communities with those available in each of these regions. This is a monumental task that has only begun to be accomplished.

If climatic change or other environmental variables are basic causal factors in the origin of agriculture, are they determinant? (cf. Wagner 1977). This question pervades all inquiries into human adaptations and cultural developments. The critical test is a detailed examination of areas that seem to share the same crucial environmental factors, but in which agriculture did not develop. Explanations for the different courses of development should also be sought because, if they were convincingly related to certain environmental variables, then the case for the environment playing a deterministic role would be considerably strengthened.

Culture also could have been responsible for the introduction of agriculture. For the present purpose, culture comprises all things learned and transmitted by people, including technological equipment and techniques, as well as knowledge. It has been suggested that a sufficient level of technology and an intimate knowledge of the potential plant and animal domesticates are key elements in the origin of agriculture (Braidwood 1975). Although this is a difficult concept to define objectively, it is clear that certain implements for harvesting and preparing food would have been necessary for agriculture to succeed. Inventions such as storage facilities make the cultivation of storable grains a worthwhile undertaking.

There are two types of technological inventions that enhance both the production and the establishment of agriculture: (1) innovations that help to increase production, which might include such devices for facilitating the procurement of food as efficient harvesting equipment; and (2) those that increase the usefulness of the yield, which include the selection and breeding of more productive plants and animals and implements that facilitated their preparation. The major question is whether the inventions came first and allowed agriculture to be introduced or whether the inventions were in response to the needs of a developing agriculture.

Population growth and density has been cited as a factor in the rate of cultural innovation (Figure 4-4; Smith and Young 1972). As a population increases, existing resources are strained, which might stimulate innovation. This idea has been countered by some scholars who suggest that, under conditions of stress, new technologies are not developed, but old ones are intensified. Some geographers maintain that in the early history of America the most important inventions were made along the sparsely inhabited agricultural frontier; given a potentially rich environment and insufficient labor to exploit it, people will attempt to create efficient mechanisms for collecting the resources. Whether the rate of cultural innovation was accelerated by population pressure or sparse population is a question that can be answered archeologically only after sufficient data have been collected.

Social organization as a primary force is often discussed but infrequently documented archeologically. In many ways, it could have been organizational changes that were crucial to the introduction of agriculture. Integrating larger communities, organizing the scheduling of activities, and developing a radically new ethic were among the most revolutionary aspects of early agricultural society. The social institutions being developed can be classified as those related to subsistence pursuits and those related to prolonged sedentism.

Subsistence-related institutions may have either caused the introduction of agriculture or resulted from it. They include the specialization and division of labor required for efficient farming pursuits, the greater concentration of people in one place permitted by an increasing food supply, and the participation of the young and old in subsistence activities. Such developments removed some of the population restraints but, even so, population growth did not continue unrestrained. Other resource limitations, diseases, and limits on social interrelationships inhibited growth at a certain level. Agricultural subsistence also made necessary the development of new forms of redistribution by a community: the permanent herds and fields of the agriculturist demanded different redistributive mechanisms from those used by hunters dividing their occasional kills of big game. Trade and exchange between communities developed during this period and may have made early farming more profitable than hunting and gathering. The trend toward specialization and exchange accelerated in the era of early agriculture and has been a fundamental characteristic of human society ever since.

A major sedentism-related change was an increase in community size. A mobile group was ordinarily limited to 25 to 50 people during lean seasons of the year, but the populations of early sedentary villages ranged between 100 and 200 year-round. Organizing the interrelationships and scheduling the activities of a community of this size necessitated major changes in its social structure. It is probable that ranked society became more prevalent and tribal organization was common (Chapter 6; Service 1962). Long periods spent in one location probably led to the manufacture of nonportable items: people who stayed in one place for many years were probably motivated to create querns, mortars, pottery, elaborate architecture, and so forth, because they could use them for a long time. As the nonportable cultural inventory grew and houses became more substantial, there might have been a tendency toward the acquisition of personal property.

The success of early farming depended on the willingness and ability of people to store enough of their crop yields to use as seed in the subsequent year, as well as for insurance against lean seasons. It is unlikely that initial attmpts at farming or the yields of early domesticates were very impressive. Only with the ability to store large quantities of food was a sedentary farmer able to survive under circumstances that a mobile hunter and gatherer would have found difficult. In addition, the social organization of a community was changed to allow the production and storage of surplus food to be used by the community as a whole. The institutions and value systems required to persuade people to work harder and to produce more than they themselves can consume were fundamental innovations of the early village era that continue to be exemplified in today's society (see Chapter 7).

Model for a Subsistence-Settlement System

The model to be described in this section grew out of an attempt to integrate the hypothesized effects of various factors on the efficiency of different subsistence activities with the possible transitions in settlement forms. It is not intended to be a conclusive presentation of a simplified theory explaining why agriculture was introduced when and where it was; rather, it affords an investigatory framework with which to evaluate current hypotheses and archeological evidence.

In using this model, it is not necessary to assume that the introduction of agriculture was by means of

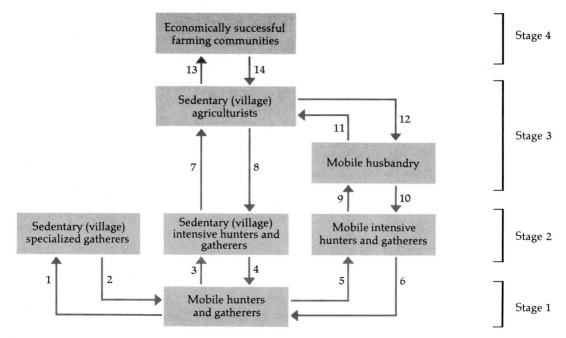

Figure 4-6
Model of the alternative subsistence-settlement forms that prehistoric communities might have taken in the transition from mobile hunting and gathering to sedentary agriculture in the Near East. The numbered arrows indicate possible transitions from one form to another.

a single pathway taken by every prehistoric group, even within the same region. Such a conclusion is to be confirmed or discounted by the archeological evidence. Although every cultural event was unique and similar events occurring at different sites had distinguishing characteristics, there are regularities to be found in events that were taking place in different regions. The most important goals of an inquiry into the origins of agriculture are to discover these regularities in development and to explain the differences observed.

The model shown in Figure 4-6 and the information in Figure 4-7 (pages 108–109) are a first step in an analytical approach to the origins of agriculture. The alternative subsistence-settlement forms diagrammed in Figure 4-6 have been constructed on the basis of archeological evidence from the Near East. As the model shows, the transition from

a hunting and gathering community to an agricultural one was not necessarily permanent: under certain conditions agriculturists resumed a hunting-and-gathering strategy. Thus, the factors that favorably influenced transitions leading to agricultural communities and inhibited transitions back to hunting and gathering were critical.

The model shows two pathways that mobile hunters and gatherers could have taken to become sedentary agriculturists: one was to first become sedentary intensive hunters and gatherers (transition 3) and then sedentary agriculturists (transition 7), as was done in some areas of the Levant; the other was to first become mobile intensive hunters and gatherers (transition 5), then to engage in mobile husbandry (transition 9), and then to become sedentary agriculturists (transition 11). It can be argued that the second pathway is characteristic of the Zagros-Khuzistan area. The model also includes a transition from mobile hunters and gatherers to sedentary specialized gatherers and back (transitions 1 and 2). Specialized gatherers depended almost entirely on a single resource that was easily gathered. Although such extreme specialization occurred in other parts of the world—for example, on the northwest coast of North America where fish were the main resource—it does not seem that it was common in the Near East (with the possible exception of the Upper Nile Valley) or that it would ultimately have led to agriculture. Therefore, the transition from sedentary specialized gatherers to sedentary agriculturists has been omitted from the model, though it could be included without substantially changing the remainder of the model.

There are two ways in which the various factors can be shown to have affected the introduction of agriculture: one way is in terms of how they affected the *general* transition toward a food-producing way of life; the other is in terms of the effect of each one on the possible *specific* transitions included in the systems model in Figure 4-6. As is done in Figure 4-7, the effect of each factor is classified according to the primary force to which it is related (i.e., barrier, environmental, cultural, subsistence, or organizational). Some of the factors will be discussed in the text; others are self-explanatory. The effect of each factor on each of the transitions shown in Figure 4-6 is indicated by one of three symbols: pr, for *prerequisite* to a transition; a plus sign for a *positive effect;* and a minus sign for a *negative effect.* Another relationship to consider (of which only a few examples are shown in Figure 4-7) is the positive effect that one factor has on another. Some factors seem to be present together and to facilitate one another. The complete delineation of these linkages is of fundamental importance and should be a high priority for future research.

An enumeration of the factors that affected early agriculture must be derived from close examination of the characteristics of early farming and prefarming communities. The factors must be so defined as to be recognizable in the archeological record, so that their effects on other variables, and on the

general transition, can be assessed. The ultimate goal is to cull those factors whose effects were both necessary for the transition to food production and sufficient to have stimulated this transition.

The factors in Figure 4-7 were not independent of each other, nor were their effects of equal magnitude in every case. Some were mutually reinforcing, whereas others impeded specific changes or the effects of other factors. Some positively influenced certain kinds of subsistence-settlement transitions, whereas others exerted a negative, or impeding, influence on other kinds of transitions.

There were many thresholds of change in the evolving subsistence-settlement systems of the late prehistoric Near East. Sedentism can be thought of as a threshold that was difficult to reach; yet its attainment facilitated other developments that would have been less likely to occur without it, such as population growth and the invention of heavy, nonportable food-processing equipment. Many more thresholds had to be crossed before prehistoric groups achieved the social organization required for managing a large community.

Barriers to Successful Agriculture

The effects of many factors made early agriculture difficult, and prehistoric farmers had to make adjustments to counter them before farming could be an economically successful way of life (Flannery 1973). The transitions that were strongly inhibited by these barriers are noted in Figure 4-7A.

Annual fluctuations in the climate of the Near East made early farming unreliable (B1 in Figure 4-7A). Because of the wide fluctuations in rainfall characteristic of many regions, prehistoric farmers probably harvested bountiful supplies of cereal grain in some years, but very little in others.

The localization of dense cereal stands limited the areas in which harvesting was practical (B2). The stands growing on certain limestone massifs and basalt plateaus were extremely dense (Harlan and Zohary 1966), but many areas such as these do not lend themselves to farming and, in the areas lying between them, little or no grain grew wild.

Harvesting wild wheat and barley was difficult because of the brittle rachis that is characteristic of

		1	2	3	4	5	6	7	8	9	10	11	12	13	14
A.	**Barriers to the Introduction of Agriculture**														
B 1.	Annual fluctuations in climate (increase in lean periods)	+		−	+			−		−	+	−	+	−	
B 2.	Extreme localization of dense cereal stands			−				−				−		−	
B 3.	Brittle rachis of wild wheat and barley			−		−		−				−			
B 4.	Tough glumes of wild grain					−		−							
B 5.	Necessity for harvesting tools, containers, and transport			−				−				−			
B 6.	Necessity for waterproof storage facilities			−				−				−			
B 7.	Either migratory or mountain-adapted habitats of hunted animals			−		+		−		+		−			
B 8.	Ability to induce animals to change seasonal routine			−				−				−			
B 9.	Interpersonal stress of larger agricultural communities			−				−				−		−	
B.	**Effects of Environmental Factors**														
E 1.	Availability of potentially domestic plants and animals	+		+		+	+	+		+		+			
E 2.	Ecological uniformity in vicinity			+		+	+	+		+		+			
E 3.	Ecological diversity in vicinity (including wild grain, sheep, and goats)			+				+			+	+			
E 4.	Climatic change that improved conditions for domesticable plants			+				+			+	+			
E 5.	Climatic change that worsened conditions for domesticable plants				+				+		+		+		+
E 6.	Climatic change that produced temperate conditions allowing open settlements	+		+				+				+			
	Positive-feedback relationship established with agriculture														
E 7.	Culturally altered environment: Increasing land clearance ⟶ diminishing resources for for agriculture ⟵ hunting and gathering							+			−			+	−
C.	**Effects of Subsistence Strategies**														
S 1.	Dependence on migratory herd animals	+		+				+		+					
S 2.	Dependence on nonmigratory animals	+		+			+	+							
S 3.	Dependence on tree nuts (autumn harvest)	+		+			+	+							
S 4.	Dependence on cereal grasses (spring harvest)			+			+	+							
S 5.	Dependence on combination of plants and animals			+			+	+							
	Positive-feedback relationship established with agriculture														
S 6.	Selective killing of young male animals ⇄ Maintain herd size	+		+		+		+		+		+		+	
S 7.	Field stubble eaten by animals ⇄ Fields manured by animals						+	+			+	+		+	
S 8.	Increasing productivity of grain ⇄ Denser stands of grain			+						+		+		+	
S 9.	Transfer of plants into new ⟶ Selection for hardier strains environmental zones ⟵ and increased hybridization							+		+		+		+	
S 10.	Abandonment of other activities ⇄ Increased during planting and harvesting ⟵ agricultural yield							+	−	+	−	+		+	
S 11.	Transfer of settlement to location near ⟶ Diminishing importance of agricultural activities ⟵ hunting and gathering				−			+				+		+	
S 12.	Increased production of food ⇄ Increased population growth			+				+				+		+	

D. Effects of Cultural Innovations

Item							
C 1. Microlithic composite tools	+	+ +	pr	pr	pr	pr	pr
C 2. Understanding environmental potential							

Positive-feedback relationship established with agriculture

Item							
C 3. Investment in inventory of specialized harvesting tools or techniques ⇌ Greater yield per hour of harvesting	+	+	+	pr	pr	pr	pr
C 4. Investment in inventory of food, processing equipment, ⇌ Greater nourishment per kilogram and techniques harvested	+	+	−	+	+	+	+
C 5. Use of heavy plant-processing ⇌ Increase in sedentism of equipment communities	+	+	−	+	+	+	+
C 6. Fabrication and use of ⇌ Increase in sedentism of storage facilities communities	+	+	−	+	+	+	+
C 7. Construction of substantial ⇌ Increase in sedentism of architecture communities	+	+	−	+	+	+	+

E. Effects of Organizational Variables and Social Relations

Item							
O 1. Ability to organize scheduling of activities for group	pr	pr	pr	pr	pr	pr	pr

Positive-feedback relationships established with agriculture

Item							
O 2. Establishment of sedentary ⇌ Young and elderly allowed communities to live and work	+	−	+		+	+	+
Population growth ⇌ Agricultural activity supplying greater proportion of food supply							
Population growth ⇌ Population growth							
O 3. Increased concern for human life ⇌ Population growth	+		+		+		
O 4. Long-distance trade ⇌ Exchange of ideas and species of plants		+	+	+ +	+	+	+ +
O 5. Increasing scope and frequency ⇌ Increased likelihood of of human contacts innovation			+ +	+ +	+	+	+ +
O 6. Local exchange or redistribution ⇌ Production of surplus	+	+ +	+ +				
O 7. Tribal or ranked organization ⇌ Control of surplus	+		+	+	+	+	+ +
O 8. Spatial impingement by other ⇌ Clearer delineation of a groups group's territory		+			+	+	

pr: factor is a prerequisite for transition
+: factor favorable, affects transition
−: factor impedes transition

Figure 4-7
Factors affecting the introduction of agriculture.

these grains; when the grain is ripe the slightest movement will disperse the seeds (B3). Thus, the development of the grain would have had to be carefully observed by the farmers, for the time at which it is harvested is critical: too early would have meant inedible grain, and a little too late would have meant that the rachis would have broken and dispersed the seeds. In addition to the difficulty of harvesting wild grain, the tough glumes (husks) that encase the edible kernels had to be removed before the grain could be eaten (B4).

Harvesting tools, containers, and a means of transport were necessary for an efficient large-scale harvest (B5), and storage facilities were necessary for keeping a large harvest to be used throughout the year (B6). Such facilities would have had to have been waterproofed to prevent the seeds from sprouting during the rainy winter months.

The animals hunted by prehistoric people were either migratory or adapted to rough topography (B7). Moving their communities to open locations brought early villagers nearer to the harvestable wild grain but took them away from the habitats of wild goats.

The organizational problems and interpersonal tensions created by large groups (B9), which are more efficient agricultural communities than are small groups, discouraged prehistoric people from forming them.

Preconditions for Agriculture

Certain factors were necessary preconditions for the introduction of agriculture. Other factors favorably influenced the transformation to a food-producing economy, but their effects were not as widespread or as essential as were the prerequisites. The transitions in settlement form directly dependent on each precondition discussed are noted in Figure 4-7B–D.

The availability of potentially domesticable plants and animals is generally agreed on as a prerequisite for early farming (E1). People living in a region for a long time developed an understanding of the environmental potential of that region (C2).

Dependence on a combination of different plants and animals led to a more balanced and stable diet

because periods spent collecting or maintaining them were distributed throughout the year (S5). This mixed strategy stimulated the rapid growth and spread of the agricultural way of life, as well as the development of large sedentary communities.

The selective killing of young male herd animals was a first step in their domestication and demonstrated a knowledge of the requirements of animal husbandry (S6).

The development of specialized harvesting tools and techniques enabled greater amounts of grain to be gathered by each worker during the short harvesting periods (C3). The development of food-processing equipment and techniques produced a greater amount of nourishment per kilogram of plant material gathered than before (C4). Grinding stones and roasting ovens were innovations that simplified the process of freeing the cereal kernel from its tough glume. The fabrication and use of storage facilities increased the amount of foodstuffs that could be kept in reserve for those periods of the year in which plants were not harvestable (C6). This made possible larger, year-round settlements.

Other important prerequisites for the introduction of farming are included among the other factors listed in Figure 4-7B–E.

Factors That Stimulated the Introduction of Agriculture

The stimuli, both from external and internal sources, that precipitated the introduction of agriculture were manifold and complex. Some were related to the changes in climate that occurred at the end of the Pleistocene, whereas others were the thresholds attained in long-term cultural development, such as the invention of tools and facilities. Other stimuli may have been related to the organization of groups and the local population densities in each region. A few of the more important stimuli are discussed herein; others are included in Figure 4-7B–E.

Prehistoric human groups inhabiting regions of great ecological diversity had available a wide variety of food sources (E3), because such regions are natural habitats for sheep, goats, and cereal grains. This diversity helped communities to become sedentary and led to careful scheduling of activities by the members of the community.

The climatic change toward a warmer and wetter climate in the Near East at the end of the Pleistocene led to the spread of open woodlands with their potentially domesticable grasses and harvestable nut trees (E4). The temperature climates during the winters allowed more groups to move their communities out of caves and zones of rugged topography into areas more convenient for collecting grain (E6).

The gathering of wild cereal grasses, such as wheat and barley, was a major stimulus because it initiated the creation of a whole range of items, such as sickle blades, grinding stones, and storage facilities, that were preadaptations to agriculture (S4). Early experiments of planting harvested wild grains led to a great proportion of these plants having a tough instead of brittle rachis (S8). Transporting these grains into new environmental zones hastened the processes of natural selection for hardier strains that resulted from mutation (S9).

Probably the single most important stimulus for the introduction of agriculture was the establishment of sedentary communities in the Near East (O2). Permanent communities allowed for and ultimately stimulated the use of heavy food-processing equipment and the expansion of storage facilities. They also obviated the need for infanticide and long intervals between pregnancies, because the effects of a rigorous nomadic life on a mother were minimized. It was no longer necessary for elderly members of a community to be subjected to the hardships of the long trips of a nomadic group. Thus, populations grew and communities became larger. The children and elderly participated in agricultural activities more than in the hunting and gathering of distant resources. Possibly related to the greater longevity of elderly people and the consequent increase in their number is the evidence for religion and careful burials uncovered in preagricultural sites. The higher regard for life may have been precipitated by sedentary life, which eliminated the need for certain mechanisms of limiting the number of members in a group. The general effect was population growth and, in some cases, a change in the age structure of the population.

The establishment of long-distance trading contacts, as exemplified by the presence of obsidian artifacts hundreds of kilometers from their sources, was probably a mechanism both for the exchange of ideas and for the transport of cereal grain species, if not of other domesticates (O4). As the scope and frequency of human contacts stimulated by trade increased, so did the number of innovations (O5): growing populations and growing networks of interrelations constantly increased the pool of innovators and improved the means of communication. These processes were responsible for the geometrically accelerating rate of cultural innovation that continues today.

Feedback Relationships Established by the Initial Practice of Agriculture

Given certain preconditions and stimuli, a series of mutually reinforcing, positive-feedback relationships were established, which encouraged the development of agriculture and made it economically feasible. Although many specific factors and events discouraged agricultural development, most feedback favored the establishment of sedentary agricultural communities. Reliance on domestic plants and animals began as a minor part of a general subsistence strategy, but the effect of the deviation was to amplify feedback relationships; thus, this reliance rapidly grew until agriculture was the almost universal means of subsistence. Some of these feedback relationships not only improved the efficiency of agriculture, but made reverting back to semisedentary hunting and gathering increasingly difficult (e.g., E7, S10, C5, C6, C7, O7, O8).

Use of the Multifactor Approach

This approach to understanding the origin of agriculture and village life is designed to allow a researcher to evaluate the effects of various natural and cultural factors on communities at different levels of organization and under diverse environmental conditions. Whether a particular behavioral response or technological innovation is adaptive in a positive sense depends on the specific conditions of the situation. The purpose of the model portrayed in Figures 4-6 and 4-7 is to incorporate available empirical evidence and to facilitate the evaluation of the relative importance of various factors under different situations. Several steps can be followed:

1 Specific occupations at each site can be classified according to the suggested community forms in Figure 4-6.
2 For each relevant site in a particular region, values for each factor should be recorded. Where absolute values are not discoverable, relative values might be obtainable from an examination of their occurrence at several sites.
3 The empirical values and changes derived from the archeological evidence should be compared with the hypothesized effects given in Figure 4-7, any discrepancies between the model and the empirical data are then examined to determine their cause or whether the model must be adjusted.

The overall value of this approach is that it focuses inquiry on anomalous categories, methods of obtaining values for the postulated effects, and objective definitions of the factors and their interrelationships.

The remaining sections of this chapter treat the methods used by natural scientists to collect data for the investigation of early farming. Knowledge of the techniques for reconstructing paleoenvironments and identifying the remains of plants and animals is necessary for evaluating the work that has been done and for assessing the kinds of data that are currently being obtained.

Reconstructing the Paleoenvironment

The effects of environmental variables and climatic changes are often manifested in specific cultural processes. For developing his theory, V. Gordon Childe relied on climatic change in the Late Pleistocene Near East as a stimulus for agriculture.

Robert Braidwood, in his concept of the nuclear zone, suggests that the introduction of agriculture could have occurred only in the appropriate environmental setting. The marginal zone hypothesis is based on the importance of the interface between two environmental zones. These theories and many others require a thorough understanding of past environmental conditions and climatic changes. With the widespread adoption of an ecological view of culture, the importance of the environment has been emphasized, and the changing relationship between human beings and their biophysical surroundings has become the central theme of prehistoric studies.

The paleoenvironment has been inferred from a variety of biological and geological evidence, but each source of information has relative merits and shortcomings. Different sources of data vary in chronology, and each method of obtaining evidence is limited by distribution, preservation, and ambiguity of interpretation. There are three major categories of information about the paleoenvironment of the Near East: (1) geological information on sedimentology, the extent of glaciers, sea levels, and local hydrological regimes; (2) the remains of animal bones recovered from archeological deposits or other dateable samples; and (3) the pollen and other plant material preserved in either archeological or natural deposits.

Geological Data

Although geological data on past climates can be collected from several sources, often they are difficult to date and do not record short periods. Raised terraces surrounding inland lakes, such as those around the Dead Sea, imply that at some time in the past there was either greater rainfall or less evaporation. Alluvial terraces along the coastal streams of Lebanon and Israel attest to periods of drier and wetter climatic regimes in the past. The dating of these climatic periods is difficult in the absence of material for radiocarbon determination. Because of the lack of such material, a correlation is made with related climatic stages in Europe. However, even though the climatic changes taking place in Europe during the Pleistocene probably affected the rest of the world, it is hazardous to assume that they can be extrapolated to the Near East. Childe relied on climatologists who assumed that the climatic belts of the Northern Hemisphere were uniformly shifted southward. This view can no longer be accepted because of evidence to the contrary: the pattern of climatic change was far more varied and regional than formerly thought. Even in Europe, during the last glacial maximum the temperature depression was 12°C near the ice sheets, 8°C elsewhere in central Europe, and only 4°C at lower latitudes (Wright 1960:83).

We know that glaciers occupied the high parts of the Zagros during the Pleistocene and that, during the coldest spells, they moved down to elevations 1,200 to 1,800 meters lower than those at which they are found today. This implies that the climate in the mountains and adjacent regions was much colder then than it is now.

An effective means of correlating geologically derived climatic sequences from different regions, in the absence of radiocarbon samples, is by changes in sea level. Presumably, sea level reveals the extent of glaciation and changing conditions on the major land masses. The problem that is particularly troublesome in the Levant, where correlation on the basis of sea levels is possible, is to find links between dated archeological deposits and the terraces that indicate changes in sea level. This can be done for only a few of the sites that are near the sea, primarily Ksar Akil. Even with reliable correlations, sea-level information and geological data are valuable only for understanding major long-term changes. The introduction of agriculture was a rapid process in a geological sense, and hence our reconstructions do not benefit greatly from this type of data.

Faunal Data

Information obtained from animal bones is suggestive, but lacks the necessary reliability for detailed climatic reconstruction. As early as the original Mount Carmel cave excavations, Dorothy Garrod inferred fluctuations in climate on the basis of the stratigraphic alternation of two common types of animals (Garrod and Bate 1937). She assumed that gazelle inhabited a grassland environment and deer a woodland one. The relative abundance of deer and gazelle varied throughout the stratigraphic succession of deposits and could be correlated with the known climatic sequence of European glaciations. Critics of this technique were quick to point out that the Mount Carmel caves are in a hilly environment in which both woodland and grassland exist nearby today. Even if this had not been the case, the changing hunting habits of the occupants of the caves might also account for this variation. Another problem with relying on animal remains for environmental information is that many wild species are not restricted to a single environmental zone. For example, wild pigs inhabit the Zagros Mountains at elevations ranging from sea level to the upper limits of the forest zone; consequently, evidence of pigs can be used in making only the most general inferences on the environment of the time. This problem is compounded by the fact that the distribution and habitat preferences of wild game in the Near East today may not be the same as they were even in the recent past. The introduction of firearms, the elimination of natural predators, and the clearance and erosion of large tracts of land have drastically altered the Early Holocene setting.

Despite these limitations, animal bones may be the only source of information available. Therefore, attempts should be made to minimize the shortcomings described. Certain species of small mammals are particularly sensitive to variations in environment. Species of rodents that are present in deposits and can be closely linked to known environmental conditions are useful climatic indicators, as are certain species of snails. Before a reliable assessment of past climatic conditions can be made from this type of zoological information, the habits and natural ranges of these animals must be known.

Pollen Data

Of the techniques available to the archeologist for reconstructing paleoenvironments, recent studies of

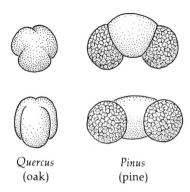

Quercus   Pinus
(oak)   (pine)

Figure 4-8
Pollen grains.

ancient pollen have produced the most promising results. Unfortunately, adequate deposits of pollen are few in number. When found, they usually present a detailed, reliable, and readily interpretable picture of the ancient vegetation of a region. A special merit of pollen analysis of stratified material is that it reveals relatively rapid and subtle changes in regional ground cover. Pollen analyses are successful because pollen is very durable and is shed by most wind-pollenated trees, shrubs, and herbs in great quantities. Pollen grains suspended in the air are widely dispersed by the wind, often as far away as 200 kilometers from the parent plant. The annual pollen "rain" in a vegetated area can amount to several thousand grains per square centimeter (Butzer 1971:244). Thus, the assemblage of pollen grains deposited at any given spot is an indicator not solely of the plants in the immediate area, but also of the regional vegetation.

Bogs and lake beds are favorable to pollen preservation. In such environments, pollen is deposited in stratified layers, each one containing a sample of the pollen in the air during the period represented by that layer. This produces a vegetational record that can be analyzed under chronological control.

The pollen grains from different plants are quite distinctive; the generic and, in some cases, the specific identification can be made of many of those present in deposits (Figure 4-8). The collection and preparation of samples for pollen analysis must be

done carefully and with the reason for analysis in mind. Pollen samples from floors of archeologically excavated rooms or from the general matrix of archeological sites yield interesting information on both the vegetation in the region and the plants that had been brought to the site. Samples collected from a stratigraphic column, such as the profile of an archeological trench, can yield a record of the pollen dispersed in the course of the deposition of those strata. Each sample must include at least 20 cubic centimeters of soil to contain an adequate number of pollen grains, and it must be collected in a manner that prevents contamination by modern pollen (Butzer 1971:244).

Pollen from a cultural context is not the most reliable material for reconstructing the paleoenvironment; it is preferable to collect samples from natural deposits unaffected by cultural factors. The pollen samples that have produced the most data about the past climate in the Near East come from cores, several centimeters in diameter, of lake sediments. Often, sufficient organic material is found at various layers within a core to permit radiocarbon dating.

After the samples have been collected, it is necessary to concentrate the microscopic pollen grains. Solvents are used to remove unwanted material, leaving the pollen intact (the solvent used depends on the nature of the matrix). A very small quantity of the pollen is examined under a microscope at a magnification ranging from 300 to 1,000. Generally, from 200 to 500 pollen grains are identified per sample. The percentages of the pollen types present in the sample are used to construct a diagram of the plants that were present. If stratigraphically related samples are analyzed, a diagram of the successive assemblages of pollen is constructed. The assemblage of pollen at a single level is known as a pollen spectrum. A comparison of several successive spectra from a core reveals the changing proportions of plants (Figure 4-9).

It is not possible to extrapolate the proportion of plants of a particular species from the number of pollen grains found. Some plants produce more pollen than others; some pollen is nonaboreal, and so it does not travel far; and plants that are insect-

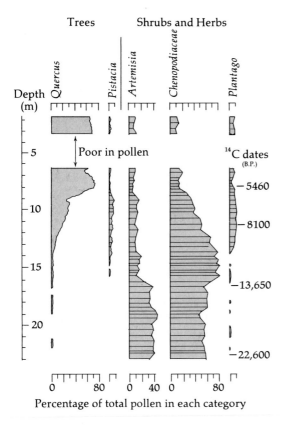

Trees   Shrubs and Herbs

Depth
(m)

Poor in pollen

^{14}C dates
(B.P.)

— 5460

— 8100

—13,650

—22,600

0   80   0   40 0   80

Percentage of total pollen in each category

Figure 4-9

Pollen spectra from core taken from Lake Zeribar, Iran. (After Natural environment of early food production north of Mesopotamia by J. Wright. *Science* 161(1968): 334–339. Copyright © 1968 by the American Association for the Advancement of Science.)

ronments. Macrobotanical and other categories of data often strongly support the vegetative information in the pollen record. Although the advantages of pollen analysis are great, there are problems both with finding usable samples and with their proper interpretation.

Near Eastern Paleoclimate

Fieldwork and analyses conducted by Wright, van Zeist, and others have begun to yield data for reliable interpretations of the climatic sequence and environmental setting at the end of the Pleistocene, when the initial steps toward agriculture were taken. The most important collection of evidence comes from a core taken from the bed of Lake Zeribar in western Iran. Lake Zeribar is at an elevation of 1,400 meters and in the middle of a vegetation zone of natural oak woodland, which has now been drastically altered by cutting and grazing. The elevation of this woodland belt ranges from 200 to 600 meters; it is from 50 to 100 kilometers wide. On the Iranian and Anatolian plateaus to the north, the climate is cool and the steppe vegetation is characterized by *Artemisia* (Wright 1968).

The sediments from the Lake Zeribar core date from 21,000 to 9000 B.C. and contain a pollen assemblage similar to that of modern surface samples collected from the steppe of the Iranian and Anatolian plateaus. There are relatively large proportions of *Chenopodliaceae* and *Artemisia,* whereas tree pollen is virtually absent. The absence of tree pollen is very significant, because it is known that samples will be 2 percent oak pollen, even if oak woodland belts are more than 75 kilometers away. It is unlikely that the oak woodland was located at lower altitudes because a core taken further south at Lake Mirabad at an elevation of 800 meters has an assemblage dating earlier than 9000 B.C. that is essentially the same as the one from Zeribar. Hence, the evidence implies that the Zagros Mountains were largely treeless, with perhaps a few isolated refuges of trees. It is likely that the main Pleistocene refuge for oak trees and associated plants, such as wheat and barley, may have been as far away as the Levant. It should be remembered

pollinated do not shed pollen into the air. It is difficult to differentiate between species that constituted only a small proportion of a local community and species that were more numerous but distant from the point of collection. The information derived from pollen cores is more important in a relative sense; that is, in showing changes in flora through time rather than in allowing precise reconstruction of the past vegetation of a region. Expected frequencies for certain kinds of environments can be established from samples collected from modern pollen-containing deposits from a variety of envi-

that not only low temperatures, but also dryness could account for the lack of trees. Hence, the climate of the Lake Zeribar region of the Zagros mountain range before 9000 B.C. was cooler and probably drier than it is today.

From 900 B.C. and later, the pollen core documents a change in climate, with annual precipitation and temperature both increasing (van Zeist 1969). There is evidence that soon after 9000 B.C. the first trees appeared in the Zeribar region and that they continued to increase in number as *Artemisia* diminished. For several thousand years after 9000 B.C., the Zeribar region was an oak-pistachio savanna like that found today on south-facing slopes near the lower tree line of the Zagros foothills. There was also an increase in plantain, which is a plant naturally found today in the lower steppe. All of this indicates that the climate was warmer and drier than it is today at Lake Zeribar. The core shows that after 6000 B.C. the percentage of oak had greatly increased, and by 3500 B.C. it comprised from 50 to 70 percent of the vegetation. This proportion of oak is similar to that which is present there today, which indicates that by 3500 B.C. a vegetation of the present constitution had been established.

The general paleoenvironment, based on the analyses of pollen cores from Zeribar, Mirabad, and the Ghab in Syria, was a cool dry climate with steppe vegetation for most of the Near East from about 33,000 to 9000 B.C. (Wright 1976). Forests and steppe forests were confined to a few areas of rainfall at lower elevations. After about 9000 B.C. precipitation steadily increased and refuges of trees started to enlarge. During the crucial period from 8000 to 6000 B.C., steppe forest prevailed where oak forests exist at present. The climate was somewhat drier than it is today and, in general, the vegetation was more open than would be supported naturally today, had it not been for 8,000 years of cutting, cultivation, and dense human occupation.

The foregoing description, although corroborated by evidence other than that from pollen-core analysis, is not complete nor universally accepted. Climatic patterns derived primarily from evidence

taken from mountainous regions cannot be easily extrapolated to other zones of the Near East. The environmental picture at 8000 B.C. was of a complex set of zones with varying rainfall and temperatures. This picture will improve with extensive collection and analyses of pollen cores from diverse regions. Wright and van Zeist have given us the most complete and reliable information so far possible about the environment in which agriculture was introduced. Time and future work will determine if their evidence is sufficient for inferences concerning other regions of the Near East.

Botanical Evidence for Early Agriculture

The presence of agriculture is implied by many categories of artifactual evidence, such as grinding stones and sickle blades, but there always remains the uncertainty of whether the plants were wild or domestic. The most straightforward method of answering these questions is to identify the plants themselves. During the past 20 years, the effort to recover and analyze plant remains from archeological sites has increased. Full-time specialists in plant identification accompany archeological expeditions to the field and establish laboratories at their home institutions. Such specialists are often referred to as paleoethnobotanists. Paleoethnobotany is the study of the remains of plants cultivated or utilized by human beings in ancient times (J. Renfrew 1969; 1973).

Preservation

Plant remains are relatively fragile and are not usually preserved in their natural state for long periods. Fortunately, there are several conditions under which botanical remains preserve their general character for thousands of years. A great quantity of the botanical material present at archeological sites has been preserved in carbonized form. Grains, seeds, and, in some cases, complete fruits have been reduced to carbon by fire or overheating and have retained their characteristic shapes. Such materials may have fallen into a hearth, been in a parching oven, or simply been inside a house or other structure that burned—events that are commonly recorded at archeological sites and have led to the preservation of enormous quantities of recognizable botanical remains. Occasionally, these carbonized remains retain some of the finer morphological details of the plant parts, but more often there is significant deformation and obliteration of details. Most carbonized grains recovered from archeological sites were not in direct contact with fire, because then they would have been reduced to dust or exploded. More likely, they were protected by a container or a layer of dirt and were heated slowly.

The normal deformation caused by burning can be observed by burning fresh grain samples of various species of plants. Prolonged indirect exposure to heat seems generally to expand the breadth of the grain and to contract the length. Because relative size and proportions are an important aspect of plant identification, the understanding of these changes in dimensions during carbonization is essential.

Another paleoethnobotanical source of information is the impressions of grains and seeds in clay, especially handmade pottery and mud-brick walls. Grains could have become imbedded in the clay either by accident or by having been put there deliberately as part of a vegetable temper. While in wet clay, the grains swell by absorbing water, and then shrink when the clay is heated. Because the clay often forms a detailed cast of plant remains, impressions can be a valuable source of information not preserved in carbonized samples. For example, grain impressions from the crude handmade pottery at Jarmo are the primary evidence for the use of domestic wheat and barley by the inhabitants of that site.

In certain temperate locations, immense amounts of botanical material can be preserved in a waterlogged condition. In the peat bogs of Denmark, for example, entire corpses have been found with the contents of their intestines (their last meals) easily recognizable. Settlements submerged close to the shores of Swiss lakes have been similarly preserved. Unfortunately, waterlogged remains have not been found in the Near East.

Extremely dry and constant climatic conditions can also lead to the fine preservation of plant material. Desiccation of remains allows them to endure close to their original state. Numerous examples of wood objects and stored food have been discovered in silos and ancient Egyptian tombs. Dry conditions also premit the preservation of human feces and even of bodies. Macrobotanical remains and pollen grains in desiccated fecal specimens can yield information both on the types of plants that were used by prehistoric people and on the proportions and nature of their diets. Although some fecal material has been located in Near Eastern sites, it has not yet yielded information about diet at the time that agriculture was introduced.

Collection

Of the various means of preserving botanical remains, carbonization is by far the most widespread and has yielded the most information to date. It is possible to collect carbonized grains and seeds by picking them out of the dirt individually in the course of excavating—a practical technique to use if a silo full of grain has burned or a storage jar is uncovered full of grain. Unfortunately, hand picking carbonized material from normal excavation deposits often damages it, in addition, it is likely that only the larger pieces will be selected by the excavator. A more efficient method of recovery is to separate the carbonized plant material from its dirt matrix by flotation (Struever 1968; Weaver 1971).

Flotation depends on the relationship of the specific gravity of the carbonized seeds to that of the flotation medium and on the amount of porosity within the seed. The true specific gravity of charcoal is from 1.4 to 1.7, but because of the high percentage of porosity the apparent specific gravity ranges between 0.3 and 0.5. Water's specific gravity, by definition, is 1.0. Most inorganic material has a higher specific gravity than that of water, about 2.5, and sinks to the bottom if water is used as the flotation medium (J. Renfrew 1973:14). The technique of flotation consists of pouring the dried carbonized material and soil into a liquid medium, such as water, at a slow, steady rate. The surface tension of the liquid and the lower specific gravity of the carbonized material combine to keep the carbonized seeds floating at the surface of the medium, or just below it, and the inorganic material sinks.

Water as a flotation medium has the advantage of being cheap and easy to handle, but not all seeds will float in it. Small seeds and fragments of seeds that are not sufficiently porous internally to bring their specific gravities below that of water will sink, instead of float. One solution to this problem is to use a flotation medium whose specific gravity is higher than that of water, such as carbon tetrachloride or carbon tetraiodide. These chemicals are expensive and somewhat difficult to handle at the sites; they require that the recovered botanical material be carefully washed to free it of traces of the chemical before storage or analysis. Several machines have been developed that float the deposit in a heavy chemical medium and then wash the botanical material. One such machine uses what is called froth flotation: it recycles the flotation medium and enables the investigator to process large quantities of dirt with uniform thoroughness (Jarman, Legge, and Charles 1972).

Whether flotation is done by machine or by hand, the floating botanical material is collected on a fine-mesh screen and then allowed to dry slowly before analysis (rapid drying can damage the seeds). After the seeds have dried, they are examined by means of a hand lens or low-power microscope and their characteristics are recorded.

Flotation is a means of obtaining fairly representative samples from ethnobotanical remains because it allows the collection of samples containing seeds from a large number of different cultural contexts. Thus inferences can be made about the variety of plants utilized. There is a danger that, if seeds are collected only from charcoal-rich midden deposits, the resulting plant identifications may contain not the species and plant parts eaten, but those discarded or that grew wild on the village dump. To make reliable quantitative statements about the proportions of plants used, it is necessary to collect as many samples as possible, each with

as many seeds as possible. Multiple samples should be collected from each archeological unit. It is best to adopt a systematic strategy for selecting soil for flotation during the excavation of an archeological site. A fixed percentage of the dirt excavated—such as 20 percent—should be floated. This can be accomplished simply by saving every fifth bucketfull for flotation. A larger percentage of soil can be floated from contexts believed to be particularly rich and, given sufficient resources and time, it would be best to examine all of the soil from a site.

Identification

Archeologically recovered botanical remains are identified by carefully comparing the minute details of morphology preserved in the ancient grains and seeds with the corresponding parts of fresh plants of the same species. Each species has its own characteristic ranges of size and shape.

Identifying the species of carbonized plant remains is only the first step in an analysis of botanical material. Information about the nature of the prehistoric plants and about the activities of their procurers can be gained from a careful study of ethnobotanical remains and their cultural context, including answers to questions such as: Why were certain plants chosen out of the wide range available for collection? Of these, why were only a few domesticated? What was the balance between domesticated and wild resources in the diet? Were the agricultural fields mixed or single-crop? Were the cereals ripe when harvested? Were they healthy? What were the proportions between cereals, pulses, and oilseed plants? Did the plants serve any purpose other than as a source of food?

Several factors should be considered in evaluating the interpretations offered by paleoethnobotanists and archeologists about prehistoric plant material (Harlan and de Wet 1973):

1   The authenticity of the find
2   The abundance of the plant in archeological contexts
3   The kind of evidence (impressions or carbonized seeds)

4 The identification and interpretation of the material

5 The integration of this information with other botanical and cultural evidence for the particular site and region

With this information, one can evaluate the reliability of the diverse statements that are often made at preliminary stages of analysis. Fortunately, the plant remains from early villages in the Near East have been examined by such outstanding and competent researchers as Helbaek, van Zeist, Harlan, Stewart, Hopf, Zohary, and Renfrew.

The Nature, Distribution, and Uses of Major Plant Species

As long ago as 10,000 years, the prehistoric people of the Near East used a wide variety of plants as sources of food. Wild varieties of cereals, pulses, and tree-nuts made up an increasing proportion of the diet. A good deal of effort has been made by paleoethnobotanists and archeologists to learn what plants were used, which species were domesticated, and how domestication was accomplished. The method of investigation currently being followed is to determine the genetic ancestors of early domestic plants and then to locate the modern distribution of these wild species. The distribution of ancestral species of major domesticated plants, adjusted for changes in climate, combined with the increasing amount of information obtained from the plant remains in early agricultural sites will yield data on where and under what circumstances each species was domesticated. Harlan and Zohary, professors of agronomy and botany, have pioneered this line of research by compiling already collected data on the distribution of plant species and by conducting extensive field surveys of their own (Harlan and Zohary 1966; Zohary 1969; Zohary and Hopf 1973; Zohary and Spiegel-Roy 1975).

Cereals

The most frequently reported early domesticated plants in the Near East are cereal grains. Other types

Figure 4-10
Early domestic wheat: (A) einkorn (*Triticum monococcum*); and (B) emmer (*Triticum dicoccum*).

of plants were also domesticated at an early date, but they were not as common and have not been given the same attention by researchers. The brief description that follows of the morphology and behavior of wheat and barley is intended to apply to cereals in general.

Cereals, which consist of annual grasses such as wheat and barley, are grown chiefly because their large grains are a concentrated source of carbohydrates that can be stored easily (J. Renfrew 1973:30). In many cereals, the grain is located at the top of a stem in a dense spike. Figures 4-10 and 4-11 show the general morphology of a cereal spike. The central column is the axis, or rachis, and is made up of the nodes and internodes. The nodes are the points at which wild brittle-spike cereal comes apart, each section consisting of the internode, node, and attached spikelet. These disintegration points may become solid by mutation; then the axis does not fall apart, but remains a single tough column. The toughness of the spike is the property of domes-

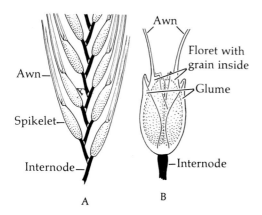

Figure 4-11
A. A cereal spike.
B. A spikelet.

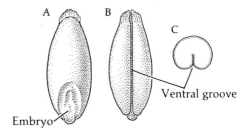

Figure 4-12
Wheat caryopsis (grain): (A) dorsal view; (B) ventral view; and (C) cross section.

ticated cereals that made them worthwhile crops for early farmers.

The spikelet consists of two glumes enclosing one or more florets. The floret consists of two inner bracts, the lemma and palea, which contain the stamens and pistil; the ovary, which is part of the pistil, eventually develops into a fruit (caryopsis, or grain). In wheat, each node bears a single spikelet, whereas, in barley, each node bears three spikelets, each consisting of a single floret and a pair of reduced glumes. In two-row barley, the ancestral form, only the middle spikelet bears a fertile floret and can therefore produce a grain; the two lateral ones are sexually imperfect and thus sterile. By genetic mutation, the lateral florets have become fertile; hence, each of the three florets of the spike can produce a grain, making the barley six-row.

Cereal grains are generally egg-shaped, being pointed at the lower end, or base, where the grain was attached to the floret and blunt at the upper end (Figure 4-12). The dorsal surface is round and the ventral side has a longitudinal groove, which is deeper in wheat than it is in barley (J. Renfrew 1973:31).

Barley

Barley was one of the economic cornerstones upon which Near Eastern civilization was built. On

the basis of careful study, Helbaek (1970) and others conclude that all early species of domestic barley were descendants of *Hordeum spontaneum*. This species of wild barley is the most widespread of the Near Eastern cereals, tolerating the greatest range of environmental conditions. Barley grows best where the ripening season is comparatively long and cool and the annual rainfall is moderate, not exceeding 90 centimeters. Well-drained, deep loam soils are well suited for barley. High nitrogen content is desirable, and barley is remarkably tolerant of saline and alkaline conditions (J. Renfrew 1973:81). Wild barley does not tolerate extreme cold and is infrequently found today at elevations greater than 1,500 meters. It is almost totally absent from the high continental plateaus of Anatolia and Iran. On the other hand, it penetrates warm steppe and desert areas in the Near East in the form of a slender, small-seeded desert variety and can be found in dry water courses and in steppe from the Negev to the Turkish border and eastward to Iran and Afghanistan (Zohary 1969). An exceptionally robust, large-seeded variety still thrives in the upper Jordan River catchment area.

Wild barley comprises a number of distinct races differing in natural habitat or morphology. Some races seem to be adapted to rather primary habitats, whereas others are very weedy and have spread as a result of the disturbances of agricultural settlement (Harlan and Zohary 1966). Although the weedy varieties of barley can be found in many locations, the best clues to the economically useful distribution of wild barley in the past are the locations of

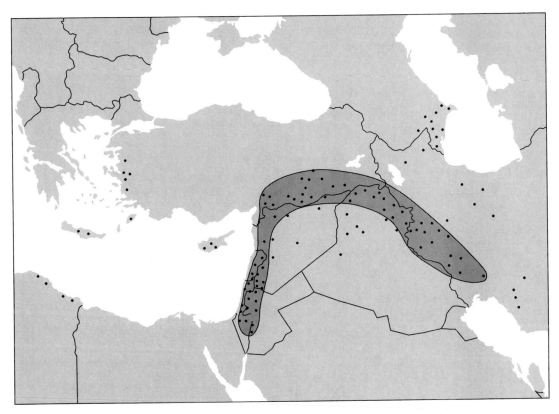

Figure 4-13
Distribution of a species of wild barley (*Hordeum spontaneum*) in the Near
East. Solid circles represent known sites, and shaded area is that of primary
habitats. (After Distribution of wild wheats and barley, by J. R. Harlan and
D. Zohary. *Science* 153(1966):1074–1080. Copyright © 1966 by the American
Association for the Advancement of Science.)

primary habitats today. There are massive stands of
wild barley in primary habitats along the lower part
of the deciduous-oak woodland belt circling the
Syrian plains and the Euphrates basin, including the
western Zagros, the southern Taurus, the mountains
of the Levant, and the Jordan River catchment area
(Figure 4-13). From this open forest belt, wild barley
spreads down the wadis to the more desertic sage-
brush belt (Harlan and Zohary 1966:1076). If the
climate from 10,000 to 12,000 years ago was cooler
than that of today, the distribution of wild barley
would be expected to have been somewhat more
restricted, perhaps to an elevation not exceeding

1,200 or 1,300 meters, rather than the 1,500 meters
of today.

The distribution of wild barley in disturbed
habitats is far wider than that in primary habitats.
The weedy race is found along roadsides, along the
edges of fields, in gardens, and even on rooftops and
mud walls. The geographic range of weedy barley
has been greatly broadened by agriculture, and it
now grows in mountain forests, on coastal plains, in
the shade of rock outcrops in semidesert areas, and
as a weed in the fields of every type of cultivated
crop from Libya to Turkestan. Wild barley seems
to flourish rather than retreat under conditions of

human exploitation of the natural environment (Helbaek 1960:112).

The spikes of wild barley break up at maturity by disengaging at their nodes. The sections, each consisting of one developed grain and two empty spikelets, are then transported (sometimes by animals) to distant places or they fall to the ground at the base of the plant. The seeds have a sophisticated mechanism that enables them to self-plant. However, in barley that has undergone mutation to produce grains in the lateral florets as well, the triplets are too heavy to be carried very far and the mechanism for self-planting is also lost. This mutation probably happened sporadically in the wild, but with no one to observe it and to plant the seeds, they did not develop into new plants.

The mutation causing toughness of the axis also occurs sporadically in populations of wild barley. This development, too, inhibits dispersal and propagation, unless there is human intervention.

It is possible to infer from the archeological evidence that people were improving the ecological conditions for wild barley plants and harvesting them long before 7000 B.C., and the evidence for the planting of barley and selection for a tough axis soon after 7000 B.C. is clear. The transition to a tough axis could have happened in at least two ways. The harvesting of wild barley must have taken place before the grains reached their full maturity; otherwise many of the grains would have been wasted because of the brittle axis.

Should a mutant have developed a tough axis that allowed its spikelet to remain in place after maturity, it would most probably have been noticed by the harvesters. Recognizing the economic importance of this difference, they could have retained these valuable spikelets and used their seeds for planting the subsequent year's crop. Several successive seasons of careful selection and propagation would have led to a predominantly tough-axis crop. The other way in which this transition could have been accomplished would not have required any explicit decisions on the part of the farmer, and may have happened often. If a cultivator used part of the seeds harvested each season for planting the succeeding year's crop, then there would have been slow na-

tural selection of any tough-axis mutants which developed. Statistically, grains from tough-axis plants would have been more likely to end up in the harvester's basket than the brittle-axis variety. Each season, the proportion of tough-axis spikelets harvested and subsequently sown would have increased. Starting as only a small percentage of the crop, the tough-axis variety probably did not predominate for hundreds of seasons. The archeological evidence seems to imply a long period of transition from brittle-axis to tough-axis barley. Although the earliest evidence for domesticated (tough-axis) barley is at about 7000 B.C. (Beidha; Bus Mordeh Phase, Ali Kosh), of the axes recovered from the Mohamad Jaffar Phase of Ali Kosh (at the end of the seventh millennium) only from 10 to 15 percent were tough.

Six-row hulled barley, which has not yet been documented for any of the earliest farming villages, appeared for the first time about 6000 B.C. at Tell es-Sawwan and in the Mohamad Jaffar Phase of Ali Kosh. It seems to have been well established by mid-sixth millennium at Tepe Sabz, where irrigation was probably practiced. The six-row hulled variety is absent in rainfall-agriculture regions and is found only in those places where irrigation was likely. It is interesting to note that six-row hulled barley is limited to later periods and depended on irrigation, whereas six-row naked barley—although difficult to recognize archeologically—appeared earlier and in areas of rainfall. The reason for this difference awaits solution by paleoethnobotanists.

Wheat

Einkorn wheat is another cereal found in most early village sites. Like those of barley, its wild and cultivated forms are very closely related. The main trait distinguishing wild einkorn (*Triticum boeoticum*) from domesticated einkorn (*Triticum monococcum*) is the mechanism of seed dispersal and depends on the morphology of the axis. Wild einkorn has a brittle axis and the individual spikelets disarticulate at maturity to disperse the seed. In domesticated einkorn, this essential adaptation to wild conditions no longer exists: the mature axis stays intact and breaks only upon threshing, and survival depends on reaping and sowing (Zohary 1969). As it did in barley, this development makes einkorn not only dependent on human beings for continued existence, but also attractive to them because it facilitates harvesting.

There are two distinct ecogeographic races of wild einkorn: a small, usually one-seeded one characteristic of the Balkans and western Anatolia, and a much larger, usually two-seeded one found in southern Turkey, Iraq, and Iran. The two-seeded race is adapted to arid regions because one of the pair of grains germinates early and the other much later.

The distribution of wild einkorn is relatively wide. Although it is found from the southern Balkans to Iran, its primary habitats are at the fringe of the Fertile Crescent in southern Turkey, northern Iraq, and adjacent territories of northern Syria (Zohary 1969:48). Wild einkorn is more mesophytic and tolerant of cold than is wild barley and grows in massive stands at elevations as high as 2,000 meters. Today, it is a weedy plant growing along roadsides, field margins, and paths, often invading fields of cultivated wheat in quantity. Like that of barley, its most intense and widespread habitat is the Taurus-Zagros arc but, unlike that of barley, its center is not the Levant (Figure 4-14, page 124). An example of a primary habitat for wild einkorn is in southeast Turkey on basaltic cobble. The slopes of the volcanic mountain Karacadag in the province of Diyarbakir are covered with basalt, weathered and broken sufficiently for wild stands of grasses to grow on it, but only in a few pockets on the lower slopes is the soil sufficiently deep for cultivation. Dozens of square kilometers of the rocky slopes are covered with almost pure stands of wild einkorn and *Triticum speltoides* (Harlan and Zohary 1966:1078). Over many thousands of hectares, it would be possible to harvest wild wheat today from natural stands almost as dense as a cultivated wheat field. If the present abundance is any indication of the situation 10,000 years ago, food gatherers and collectors would surely have been attracted to the stands of southeastern Turkey. As mentioned earlier, Harlan demonstrated by experiment that, even with the most primitive implements, a family could easily have gathered sufficient grain in a few weeks to meet its needs for the remainder of the year (Harlan 1967).

Emmer wheat (*Triticum dicoccum*) is another important cereal grain from early farming villages. The domesticated species of emmer is very similar to its wild progenitor, *Triticum dicoccoides*. The most conspicuous difference between them is the more fragile rachis of the wild species. Domestic emmer is a glume wheat that does not thresh cleanly; additional processing is required to free the naked seeds from the glumes. Some botanists hypothesize that, in the remote past, diploid einkorn (which has 2 × 7, or 14, chromosomes) and diploid (2 × 7) *Aegilops speltoides* (goat-face grass) hybridized to produce the tetraploid (4 × 7, or 28, chromosomes) wild emmer wheat (Flannery 1973:277). Although the identity of the parent species remains a subject of controversy, the distribution of goat-face grass overlaps that of einkorn, and the hybridization could have taken place in many locations.

Wild emmer is more restricted in its distribution and habitat than wild einkorn or barley; hence, of the three cereals, it is probably the most sensitive as an indicator of initial region of domestication. It is not a weedy plant, and it is rather demanding in its requirements. The best areas for emmer have a comparatively high mean winter temperature and an annual rainfall between 500 and 750 millimeters. The optimal soil is a stiff clay loam that is well drained. Wheat exhausts the land relatively quickly, therefore flourishing under conditions favorable for nitrate formation (J. Renfrew 1973:66).

The restricted distribution of wild emmer is due to the fact that it does not tolerate cold as well as einkorn, or heat and aridity as well as wild barley. Its range is split into two distinct parts, separated by the Syrian mountains, where no wild emmer grows (Figure 4-15, page 125). The race of emmer found in the Taurus-Zagros mountain ranges of Turkey, Iraq, and Iran is a small-seeded plant that was never very abundant. It grows sporadically in isolated patches and thin, scattered stands in the

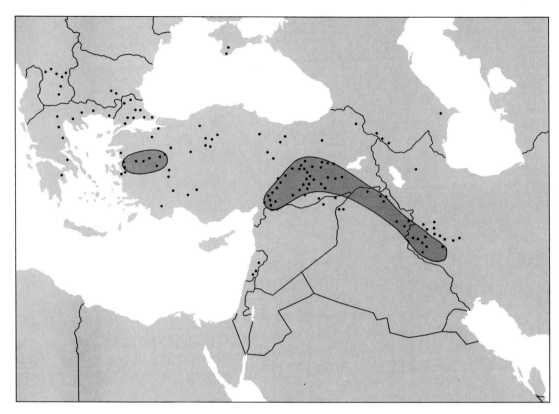

Figure 4-14
Distribution of wild einkorn (*Triticum boeoticum*) in the Near East. Solid
circles represent known sites, and shaded areas are those of primary
habitats. (After Distribution of wild wheats and barley, by J. R. Harlan and
D. Zohary. *Science* 153(1966):1074–1080. Copyright © 1966 by the American
Association for the Advancement of Science.)

lower oak-woodland belt. It is never the dominant
species of the grassland flora.

The other race is found in the upper Jordan Rift
Valley and is remarkably large and robust with large
seeds. It grows in massive stands on basaltic and
hard limestone slopes from eastern Galilee to
Mount Hermon and the Golan plateau. Where
grazing is currently controlled, nonarable sites support stands as dense as cultivated wheat fields.
These areas would have been rich harvesting
grounds for the prehistoric inhabitants of the
Galilee basin.

Harlan and Zohary suggest, on the basis of the

distribution of wild progenitors of the three important domesticable cereals, that emmer was probably
first domesticated in the upper Jordan watershed,
that einkorn was first domesticated in southeast
Turkey, and that barley could have been domesticated almost anywhere within the arc bordering
the Fertile Crescent. As a caution to those who
might accept these conclusions at face value, Harlan
and Zohary (1966:1079) pose the question: Why
should anyone have cultivated a cereal where natural stands were as dense as cultivated fields?
Primary habitats and ranges of wild progenitors are
essential sources of information but, until the

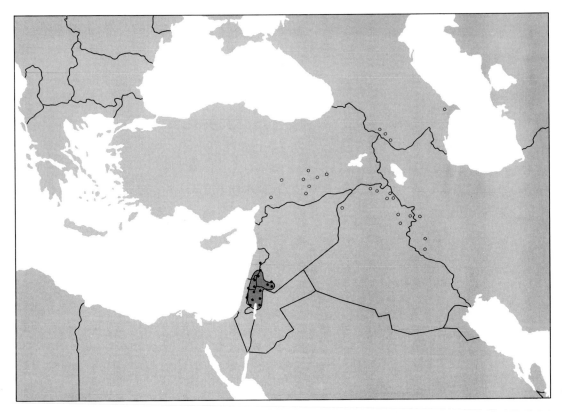

Figure 4-15
Distribution of wild emmer (*Triticum dicoccoides*) in the Near East. Solid circles
represent known sites, and shaded area is that in which wild emmer is
common. Open circles represent known sites of wild tetraploid wheats,
including *T. dicoccoides* material. (After Distribution of wild wheats and
barley, by J. R. Harlan and D. Zohary. *Science* 153(1966):1074–1080. Copyright © 1966 by the American Association for the Advancement of Science.)

process of the introduction of agriculture is more
fully understood, distributions do not offer easy
answers to the questions where and how it took
place.

Legumes

The cultivation of leguminous crops is probably
as old as that of cereals, and remains of legumes are
found in most early farming villages of the Near
East. Legumes constitute an essential element of
early food production and must have been an important ingredient in the early farmer's diet. They
are valued for their seeds, which contain a high
percentage of protein, and for their root nodules,
which are beneficial to the soil. The outgrowths on
the roots are caused by the presence of the bacteria
Rhizobium. These bacteria are capable of converting
free nitrogen in the air into a form that can be used
by the host plant; in turn, they rely on the plant for
carbohydrates. This enables the legume to grow
without drawing on the nitrogen compounds in the
soil. In time, the nodules decay, making more nitrogen available in the soil for use by other plants.
Thus, the cultivation of leguminous crops enriches

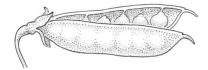

Figure 4-16
A typical pod of the family Leguminosae; the pod is
split along its midline, showing the row of seeds within.

the soil, whereas cereals tend to impoverish the
land on which they are grown.

The fruits of leguminous plants are known as
pulses. The pulse consists of a pod derived from a
single carpel, usually opening at maturity along
both edges into two halves, revealing a single row of
seeds attached to one edge (Figure 4-16). The seeds
of the different species vary in size and shape. The
pulses which have most frequently been found in
early village sites include the field pea, lentil, bitter
vetch, and chickpea (Zohary and Hopf 1973). Carbonized pea seeds have been found in seventh millennium deposits at several village sites. In contrast
to those of wheat and barley, archeological remains
of peas do not supply simple diagnostic traits for
easy and reliable recognition of domestication. Peas
that have been cultivated generally have larger
seeds, but such a change takes place gradually
through repeated cultivations; thus, size is not a
dependable archeological indicator. The most reliable evidence for domestication of peas is provided
by the surface of the seed coat: that of wild peas is
rough or granular, but cultivated varieties have
smooth seed coats (Zohary and Hopf 1973).

Two species of wild peas are genetically related to
the cultivated pea *Pisum sativum:* a tall wild pea with
purple-blue flowers (*Pisum elatius*), which is distributed throughout the more humid parts of the
Mediterranean Basin; and a smaller one (*Pisum
humile*), which is geographically restricted to the
Near East (Figure 4-17). *P. humile* grows in areas of
open vegetation, mainly in steppe. Its primary
habitat is the belt of oak parkland and forest that
supported the wild progenitors of cultivated wheats

and barley. It also invaded secondary habitats: it
grows like a weed at the edges of cultivation, and it
penetrates cereal fields (Zohary and Hopf 1973:889).

Cytogenetic studies of *P. humile* and its presence
in early archeological sites indicate that it is probably the wild ancestor of domesticated *P. sativum*. The
transition took place somewhere in the open oak
forest of the Near East.

Lentils are another important pulse crop found in
most early village sites in the Near East. Not only are
they found in the earliest farming villages, but there
are even specimens in the remains of the prefarming
community of Mureybit (van Loon, Skinner, and
van Zeist 1970). As with peas, it is very difficult to
differentiate between the wild *Lens orientalis* and the
subsequently domesticated *Lens culinaris* on the basis of carbonized remains. The only conspicuous
development under domestication is an increase in
seed size; wild lentils have a relatively small seed,
from 2 to 3 millimeters in diameter, whereas the
seeds of modern cultivated forms are from 5 to 8
millimeters. Obviously, this change took place very
slowly. Almost all lentil seeds found at early village
sites are relatively small. The morphological information is inconclusive, so ethnobotanists have
relied on ecological characteristics to determine
whether the plant remains from any given site are of
domestic or wild lentils. Two categories of evidence
are cited in support of its domestication by at least
the sixth millennium: (1) *L. orientalis* rarely grows in
large stands, and so collecting an adequate amount
of seeds from the small plants would have been
extremely difficult; and (2) wild lentils today do not
grow in the vicinities of many of the sites in which
their remains have been unearthed (Figure 4-18,
page 128). This is so at Jericho, where the surrounding lower Jordan Rift Valley is too dry for
wild lentils (Zohary and Hopf 1973:891).

Other pulses are found in remains of early farming villages, but information on their characteristics
and distributions is less complete than that on lentils. The bitter vetch (*Vicia ervilia*) is common in
some early village sites such as Çayönü in southeast
Turkey. The wild ancestor of the cultivated bitter
vetch has been determined, and its primary distribution is in Anatolia, with little conclusive

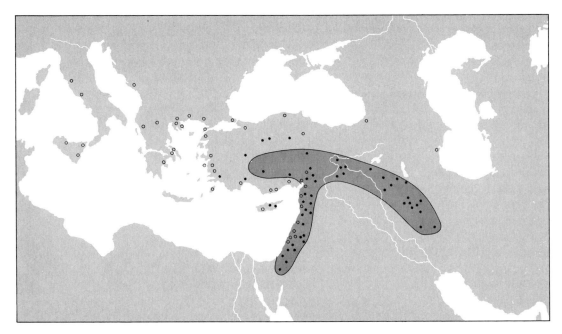

Figure 4-17
Distribution of wild peas (*Pisum humile* and *Pisum elatius*) in the Near East.
Solid circles represent known sites of *P. humile*, open circles those of *P. elatius*,
and shaded area is that of primary habitat. (After Domestication of pulses
in the Old World, by D. Zohary and M. Hopf. *Science* 182(1973):887–894.
Copyright © 1973 by the American Association for the Advancement of
Science.)

evidence for it elsewhere. As its name implies, bitter
vetch is a bitter seed and it was not frequently used
by prehistoric people for food. It was probably
grown to feed animals and may have been consumed by people during food shortages.

Chickpeas (*Cicer arietinum*) have been found in
early contexts, and probably contributed to the diet
of the early villagers of the Near East. The wild
ancestry of the cultivated chickpea is not yet definitely known, but two races, one in the Levant and
the other in southeast Turkey, are the best can-
didates, as are these regions for the place of its
earliest domestication (Zohary and Hopf 1973:893).

Nut Trees

According to the climatic reconstruction of the
Late Pleistocene, much of the open steppelike area
of the Near East was colonized by oak and pistachio trees beginning at about 9000 B.C., reaching a
maximum about 4000 B.C. These two types of
trees and others, such as the almond, provided the
local inhabitants with plentiful supplies of nutritious edible nuts (Figure 4-19, page 128). Because
oak and pistachio trees grew in the natural habitat
of wild wheat, barley, and pulses, the intensive
collectors and early farmers would have come in
close contact with them. Quantities of oak (*Quercus
robur*), pistachio (*Pistacia atlantica*), and almond
(*Prunus amygdalus*) nuts have been located in seventh millennium sites such as Çayönü, where they
were probably a substantial part of the vegetable
food during the early occupation (van Zeist 1972).
An important characteristic of these nut trees is
that their fruit ripens in the autumn, whereas cereal
crops ripen in the spring in the Near East. Also, the

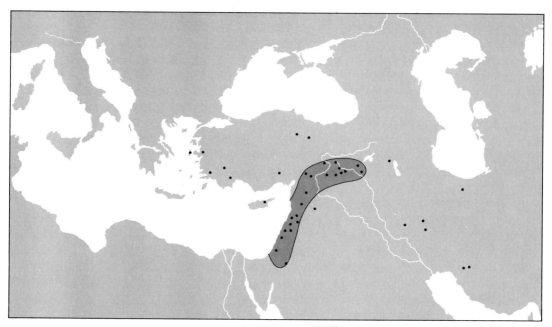

Figure 4-18
Distribution of wild lentils (*Lens orientalis*) in the Near East. Solid circles represent known sites, and shaded area is that of primary habitat. (After Domestication of pulses in the Old World, by D. Zohary and M. Hopf. *Science* 182(1973):887–894. Copyright © 1973 by the American Association for the Advancement of Science.)

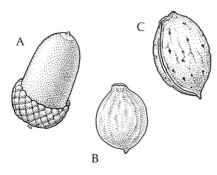

Figure 4-19
Tree nuts: (A) acorn (*Quercus robur*); (B) pistachio (*Pistacia atlantica*); and (C) almond (*Prunus amygdalus*).

harvesting season for nuts is longer than that for cereals. The widespread availability of pistachios and oaks 10,000 years ago in close proximity to potentially harvestable stands of wheat and barley provided an adequate food supply for preagriculturists. The availability of plentiful nuts aided in the establishment of permanent communities by providing food during the otherwise lean autumn season, and by allowing the inhabitants to concentrate on the harvesting and processing of grain and legume crops during the spring and early summer.

Fruit

Although the evidence is relatively scarce, it seems that olives, grapes, dates, and figs were important additions to the Near Eastern farming complex by the fourth or third millennia (Zohary and Spiegel-Roy 1975). Fruit-tree cultivation took place long after the successful establishment of grain agriculture, probably in different localities from those of the earliest villages. Olives, grapes, and figs were widespread throughout the Near East by the end of the third millennium and may have been first domesticated in coastal regions of the Levant or Anatolia. The earliest evidence for the domestication of dates is from the 'Ubaid levels of the site of Eridu in southern Mesopotamia; it is likely that they were first cultivated in that area. Dates soon became a crop of enormous importance for early Mesopotamian society.

The domestication of all four of these fruit trees took the form of altering the way in which they were reproduced: in the wild such trees reproduce sexually (i.e., by means of seeds); prehistoric people domesticated them by the vegetative propagation of clones, using simple techniques (cuttings, basal knobs, and suckers). Zohary and Spiegel-Roy (1975) view these plants as having been preadapted for domestication by their ability to be reproduced by the relatively simple methods of vegetative propagation.

Food Value and Dietary Strategies

Any discussion of the plants that made up the food supply of the earliest farmers would not be complete without taking into account their relative food values (J. Renfrew 1973). In the Near East, hunted, and later domestic, animals contributed significantly to the diets of these early farmers, yet the variety and balance of vegetable sources suggest the importance of plant resources (Table 4-1, page 130). Cereals were used for making either porridge or bread, having been threshed, winnowed, and ground to course groats on querns. They were the principal source of carbohydrates and vitamins B and E. Pulse crops were the main source of vegetable protein. The protein content of leguminous seeds is not as concentrated as that of meat, fish, eggs, and milk; consequently when vegetable proteins are relied on exclusively, a greater bulk of food needs to be eaten to obtain the same quantity of protein.

Oil seeds were recognized at an early stage of agriculture to have nutritional value, and the first crop of this type to be cultivated for food was flax. The first evidence for flax cultivation is from the late seventh-millennium levels of Tell Ramad (van Zeist 1976). Linseed is from 30 to 40 percent oil, varying with the variety and the environment in which the crop is grown; linseed is also from 20 to 25 percent protein. Tree nuts were another rich source of fats, proteins, and carbohydrates, as well as minerals, especially iron and lime. However, nuts become rancid after a few months, even if stored with great care (J. Renfrew 1973).

From a knowledge of the natural habitats, the regional distributions, and the estimated food values of the plants that grew wild in the Near East, it is possible to hypothesize the nature of early farming crops and their selection by intensive hunters and gatherers for propagation. There are several basic decisions that prehistoric people must have had to make, although they may never have recognized them as such. The first decision was whether to concentrate on perennial or annual plants. The wide seasonal fluctuations in climate in the Near East and the winter-rain-and-summer-drought regime favored the growth of annuals and limited the number of perennial plants. Perennials require less labor each year, but also produce less. The perennials which grew wild in the Near East 10,000 years ago were not particularly suitable for domestication.

The second decision was how many crops to concentrate on. Relying on many different species has the advantage of stabilizing the food supply and insuring against years in which crops fail. However, the cost of multiple species is a loss in efficiency and lower productivity of each plant species (Zubrow 1973). The decision made by most early farming communities in the Near East was to favor the production of several species. The mixture of cereals and legumes was favorable with respect to both regenerating the nitrogen content of the soil and to supplying proteins and carbohydrates for the diet. Oil seeds and tree nuts provided other necessary components of the diet. For the prehistoric villagers of Çayönü, tree nuts were a major source of protein

Table 4-1

Composition of foods per 100 grams of edible portion for various plants and animals consumed by early villagers.

Food	Food energy (kcal)	Protein	Fat/Oil	Carbo-hydrate	Fiber	Ash	Water
Cereals							
Bread wheat	331	14.8	1.7	67.1	2.6	1.6	12.2
Emmer wheat	333	12.5	2.4	68.3	2.7	1.8	12.3
Six-row barley	337	10.0	1.6	70.2	6.0	2.3	9.9
Legumes							
Peas (dried)	339	22.3	1.1	56.3	5.7	3.6	11.0
Lentils (dried)	345	24.9	1.2	57.2	3.9	2.9	9.9
Vetch	343	27.6	1.7	55.2	2.0	2.4	11.1
Tree nuts							
Almonds (dried)	605	16.8	54.9	21.5*		2.0	4.8
Pistachios (dried)	598	18.9	54.0	19.7*		3.2	4.2
Acorns	268	3.0	2.6	57.8*		1.1	35.5
Fruits							
Figs (dried)	303	4.0	1.2	62.6	5.8	2.4	24.0
Dates (dried)	318	2.2	0.6	73.0	2.4	1.8	20.0
Grapes (raisins)	289	2.5	0.2	76.5	0.9	1.9	18.0
Olives (ripe)	207	1.8	21.0	1.1	1.5	2.8	71.8
Domestic animals							
Cattle (medium fat)	240	18.7	18.2	0.0	0.0	1.0	62.1
Sheep	267	17.0	21.0	0.0	0.0	1.0	61.0
Goats	157	18.4	9.2	0.0	0.0	0.9	71.5
Pigs (medium fat)	377	13.0	36.0	0.0	0.0	1.0	50.0

Source: After FAO, 1968; Pellett and Shadarevian, 1970; Watt and Merrill, 1963.
*Amount of carbohydrate including fiber content.

and oil when plant domestication was beginning and animal domestication was not practiced. Later, when plant domestication had been firmly established and domestic sheep and goats were commonplace, the vegetable source of oil and protein was no longer necessary. Carbonized remains from the later phases do not contain large proportions of tree nuts, which could be a result of a change in dietary needs or of subsequent deforestation due to climatic or culturally induced factors, or both.

It is important to note that the genetically induced morphological changes that made wheat and barley such productive plants did not occur immediately upon the planting of seeds. Many generations of plants were required for these changes to take place and for the altered species to become the predominant members of the plant community being cultivated. When hunters and gatherers first settled in permanent communities, intensive collection of cereals was only a minor component of the total plant gathering activities. After people began to plant cereals, and cultivate them, they soon recognized the advantageous mutants and hybrids. As the advantages of certain cereals and legumes were recognized, extra effort was expanded for their care and processing, but alternate food sources were not abandoned. It was the increasing attention to the selected plant species that further stimulated important changes. However, it was a long time before these early agriculturists could rely completely on cereals. During the period of transition, a wide variety of plants were used, indicating an attempt to secure an adequate and stable food supply from the environment in the most effective manner. The mixed strategy of (1) diversity of plant crops, (2) variety of domestic animals, and (3) procurement of wild resources made the early farming complex of the Near East overwhelmingly successful and stimulated its rapid spread in all directions.

The Animals of Early Farming Communities

Animals were not only a source of protein for early farmers, but also a means for storing surpluses on the hoof. Herd animals, which fed off the stubble of harvested fields, could be slaughtered when other food sources were in short supply. These domestic animals were also a source of other important products, such as milk, wool, manure, and skins.

Preservation

Fortunately for archeologists, the bones of animals are the most tangible remains of human subsistence activities of the past. Bone is a relatively durable material and survives in various depositional environments in both fresh and fossilized form. Increasingly, the careful recovery and preservation of animal bones found during excavations are primary goals of archeologists. The bones of most animals, especially those used for food, are not

found in the form of articulated skeletons, nor are they even whole; thus, it is necessary to remove fragile specimens with care and to recover all of the bone fragments. Zoologists who analyze archeologically recovered bone have found it useful to accompany archeologists to the field. This enables them to participate in the excavation, supervise the extraction of fragile specimens, and regulate the recovery of small pieces through the systematic screening of earth from the excavations. Frequently, it is necessary to apply preservatives to the bones or to remove them with the aid of a plaster cast. While at the excavation sites, zooarcheologists can observe the local environment, examine collections of animals in local museums, and collect skeletons of wild and domestic species of the area. This enables them to make accurate identification of the archeological specimens and meaningful interpretations about the natural wild life that once surrounded the prehistoric community (Reed 1963).

Identification

A well-trained zooarcheologist can determine many things about the animals used at a prehistoric site from the morphology and composition of the bone fragments recovered. At most sites, the vast majority of pieces are small, smashed fragments of long bones, which makes the identification of species or body part difficult. These unidentifiable fragments can account for as much as 90 percent of the bones found. Although marks of butchering may be preserved on them, which can yield information on food-preparation techniques, such fragments offer little information about diet. Of the remaining bones, many are ribs or vertebrae, for which identification of body part is easy but of species is difficult or impossible. Others are fragments or complete bones of certain skeletal parts that do allow identification of species. Upper and lower jaws, teeth, horn cores, and articular surfaces of long bones are among the most useful remains for identifying species, which can be done by comparing the archeologically recovered bones with examples of bones from known specimens in museum collections or in the zooarcheologist's own collection. Some species of early domestic animals, such as sheep and goats, are particularly difficult for zooarcheologists to distinguish, because only a very small number of their skeletal parts reveal differences between them. On the other hand, the skeletal parts of other animals can yield information not only on the species, but also on the size, age, and sex of the animal, and even on how it was slaughtered and prepared.

The material from the Turkish site of Suberde is a good example of how successively smaller proportions of animal bone yield increasing amounts of information per piece. Approximately 300,000 pieces of bone were recovered during two seasons of excavation at Suberde, of which all but 25,000 were unidentifiable scraps (Perkins and Daly 1968). Of those that were not scraps, 11,000 were pieces, such as ribs, for which the species could not be identified. Hence, for only 14,000 of the original 300,000 bones (about 5 percent) could the species be identified. Most of them were from either sheep or goats (about 9,000 pieces), but only 700 of these 9,000 could definitely be attributed to one or the other. Hence, the proportion of sheep to goats, the major food animals of this early village, must be inferred from only 700 bones. A good deal of research in which metrical and microscopic methods of identification are employed has been undertaken to discover other skeletal parts that allow the identification of species. For this research, it is necessary to understand the range of variation in wild and domestic populations. Many past interpretations of archeological material have been made without taking into account the complexity and difficulty of making zoological identifications and will doubtless be revised as more information is obtained.

Wild versus Domestic

A primary purpose of the zooarcheologist's work is to ascertain whether the food animals of a community were hunted in the wild or kept in domestic herds, and to investigate the nature of the transition from hunting to domestication in subsistence activities. In trying to understand the early domestication of animals, one wonders why, out of so many possible orders of wild animals, so few species were developed into productive domestic animals? There is no simple answer, but an examination of exactly what is meant by animal domestication aids in the inquiry.

Animal domestication can be defined in terms of three general factors:

1 Tameness, implying that the animal neither flees from nor attacks human beings
2 Behavioral changes, including changes in seasonal migrations, in daily behavior, and in herd composition or size
3 Breeding control, including selective slaughter, castration, and selective mating, and thus creating new gene pools and new selective pressures (Bökönyi 1969)

There are two major stages in animal domestication as it was practiced in the ancient Near East. The first stage was animal husbandry, which required the capture and taming of predominantly young animals. The keepers did not practice purposeful breeding or even close control of feeding. It was more a matter of keeping a meat supply close at hand. In return, the herders protected the animals from other predators and supplied them with food during lean seasons. A herder might have purposefully selected the animals to be killed for food on the basis of age and sex in order to maintain or increase herd size. This type of animal husbandry led to few, and very gradual, morphological changes in the animals.

The second stage of animal domestication is animal breeding. At this stage, not only was breeding selective, but both the quantity and quality of feeding was controlled (Bökönyi 1969:220). The animals were no longer treated as a single herd, but as individuals. Particularly tame and early-maturing animals were encouraged to breed, whereas the more obstreperous males were castrated or killed for food. Mutations that enhanced the value of the animals to their herders occurred with increased frequency in captivity; such mutants might not have survived in their natural habitats. The herders accelerated the process of domestication by encouraging the mutants to reproduce, while limiting the reproductive activities of others. Even with these artificial selective pressures, morphological changes in the animals were not instantaneous and were probably not obvious until many generations had been bred. According to modern experiments, well-defined morphological changes do not occur before about thirty generations (Bökönyi 1976). Because the length of a generation is from 2 to 3 years for small species such as dogs, sheep, goats, and pigs and from 5 to 6 years for larger species such as cattle, one could expect to detect morphological changes in bones dating from 50 to 200 years after domestication began.

Animal husbandry and the first breeding experiments resulted in a decrease in the size of animals compared with their wild progenitors. After breeding and feeding were carefully controlled and their effects understood, the size of most domestic animals increased, with the exception of a few dwarf breeds. The two stages of animal domestication are not as clear-cut as might be assumed from their brief description: for a long period after domestication was first established, people replenished and increased their herds by capturing young wild animals. This practice was continued into historic times and had the effect of reintroducing wild traits into the gene pool of the domestic herd. Because of this practice, the range of variation in early herd animals was greater than would be expected from a study of modern herds.

There are several changes that occur in most species of animals after domestication. These changes do not necessarily result from new characteristics, but from existing ones that are selected for, either because of controlled breeding, or because of the conditions of herd life, or because of selective slaughtering (Zeuner 1963).

1 Growth rates are frequently affected; thus, many early domesticated animals were smaller than their wild relatives.
2 Coat color usually changes, with the wild varieties often having more color.
3 The morphology of the skull changes. The general tendency is for the facial part of the skull to be shortened relative to the cranial, which is little

affected. This may also cause a reduction in tooth size.
4 The morphology of the postcranial skeleton changes. Such changes are very difficult to recognize, but considerable research is being done to solve this problem. Post-cranial morphological changes are induced by the changes in habit and amount of movement allowed by the removal of predators, by restricted ranges, and by the crowding that results from animal herding.
5 The underlying shorter hair of certain species changes. Such changes in sheep can be very important to their herders, but very difficult to recognize archeologically.
6 Animals change physiologically: for example, they develop fat accumulations, their brains become smaller, and their musculatures are altered. These changes can be recognized archeologically only if they produce changes in an animal's skeletal structure.

There are a number of different means by which zooarcheologists can determine whether the inhabitants of a prehistoric community were animal keepers or animal breeders. Evidence leading to the conclusion that animal keeping was being practiced includes the presence of animals outside their natural geographic range, such as mountain goats in a lowland plain. If a large proportion of the bones found are those of a particular species or if the remains indicate that the number of animals of a given age or sex was different from that expected in a hunted wild population, chances are the animals had been kept. These two types of evidence were found at Zawi Chemi Shanidar, implying that sheep were being herded by the inhabitants as early as 8900 B.C. Wild goats had been the predominant animal hunted at the nearby cave of Shanidar. Coinciding with the shift in settlement from the cave to the open site, the remains of sheep outnumber those of goats by 16 to 1, and the percentage of animals one year old or less increased from approximately 25 to 60. This pattern is strong evidence for animal keeping or even early breeding, but it could also be interpreted as solely a change in hunting strategies. Further research on the initial morphological changes in herded animals or in the artifactual changes associated with early animal herding might supply an answer to this important question. Artistic representations of domestic forms of animals, such as clay figurines, are also evidence of domestication. The presence of objects associated with animal husbandry would also be strong evidence, but they have not been recognized in early village contexts in the Near East.

A recently developed scientific technique for determining whether a bone is from a wild or a domestic animal relies on variations in the microstructure of the animal's long bones (Drew, Perkins, and Daly 1971). Examination of bones of prehistoric animals by a standard petrographic thin-section technique indicates that there are well-defined characteristics distinguishing specimens of wild animal bones from those of domestic animals. The crystalline substances in the bones of wild animals are more randomly arranged than they are in those of their domestic counterparts. This technique is still in a developmental stage, but it is promising.

Having identified the bones from a site, and having determined whether they are wild or domestic, the zooarcheologist tries to determine the relative proportions of different kinds of animals used for human consumption. This information is crucial to an understanding of the underlying causes for domestication. One of the simplest methods of determining proportions of animals is to calculate the number of bones recovered from each species and then to calculate percentages. The figure obtained is very crude, because some animals have many more identifiable skeletal parts than others, whereas other animals offer much more edible meat than others. To compensate for these facts, the minimum number of animals represented by the bone inventory is calculated. This is done by counting the most common single skeletal element in the collection in order to know how many individual animals were required to yield that many pieces. This method gives a reasonably reliable figure, but unfortunately it utilizes only a part of the already small number of identifiable fragments to calculate the proportions.

Other somewhat more sophisticated methods have been developed to take into account all identifiable pieces of bone by working out an index of the number of identifiable parts per animal species and relating that to the findings (Perkins and Daly 1968). This method also yields the number of individual animals per species. This figure, or the minimum number of individuals, is multiplied by the average quantity of edible meat for an animal of that species. Adult sheep and goats each yield about 35 kilograms of meat (50 percent of their live weight), red deer yield about 100 kilograms of meat (50 percent of their live weight), large cattle about 500 kilograms (50 percent of their live weight), and pigs about 100 kilograms (70 percent of their live weight). In this way, it is possible to get an accurate idea of the relative importance of each species in the diet of the prehistoric people.

Process of Domestication

Although they do not generally agree about what the process of domestication was, there are certain factors zooarcheologists consider important. All of the animals that were first domesticated have a "natural sociability" and "herd instinct." They moved in groups, often following leaders. Assuming that people and potentially domestic animals shared ecological ranges before domestication, there would have been sufficient opportunity for animals and people to build up symbiotic relationships under natural conditions. The protection of herds from attack by other carnivores may have encouraged herds to stay closer to villages. The protection of herds may also have been a stimulus for people to domesticate the dog. Keeping young animals as pets led to their taming and eventually to keeping and breeding adult members of the species. With the increased sedentism of early village life, there were more favorable circumstances for keeping animals and greater motivation to have food available on the hoof for an unexpected lean season than before.

An important factor in the selection of certain animals for domestication is their ability to digest cellulose. Animals such as sheep, goats, and cattle are able to eat dry grasses, leaves, straw, twigs, and other food not digestible by human beings (Reed 1969). These ruminants have multichambered stomachs and a fermentation vat anterior to the intestine that contains bacteria to help break down cellulose. Because of their physiological characteristics and their ability to recycle nitrogen from their own urea, these animals are able to survive on a diet high in cellulose and low in protein. Hence, they are not in direct competition with people for available food. It is highly inefficient for people to consume animals that consume the kinds of food that people can consume themselves, because the amount of meat obtained from them is only a fraction of the amount of plant food required to produce it. Therefore, by relying on animals that eat food that they themselves cannot digest, people are not diminishing the food available to them, but are extending their resource base to include plants that would otherwise go largely unused. The bovids were of high priority for domestication because they can convert cellulose-rich materials, otherwise unavailable to humans, into carbohydrates, fats, and proteins, in the form of flesh and milk, and into secondary products such as hides, hair, and dung.

Dogs do not have the ability to digest cellulose-rich material; pigs do, but are inefficient at it. Because of this physiological limitation, the pattern of exploitation of dogs and pigs was significantly different from that of sheep, goats, and cattle (Reed 1969). It seems that dogs were not kept in large numbers, nor did they serve as a significant food source in the Near East. Pigs, on the other hand, were hunted by most early villagers and their bones are present in small numbers in the remains of almost all early agricultural communities. They were never the primary food animal, but were probably kept for variety and were maintained in sufficient numbers to consume garbage and human waste but not in such abundance that primary food would have had to be given to them. It is also obvious that these animals would have been the first to suffer during lean periods, which may have limited their numbers.

Dogs

There is significant evidence that dogs were among the earliest, if not the first, animals to be domesticated (Figure 4-20, page 136). There has been considerable controversy over the wild ancestor of the domestic dog (*Canis familiaris*), but it is now generally agreed that it was the small wild wolf (*Canis lupus*). The distribution of various varieties of wolf spans almost the entire Northern Hemisphere, and it is likely that dogs were domesticated independently in several different regions, including the Near East (Figure 4-21, page 136). Early examples of domesticated dogs are claimed for Jaguar Cave, Idaho, and Star Carr, England, The earliest domestic dog known in the Near East was found in Palegawra Cave and has been dated at 11,000 B.C. (Turnbull and Reed 1974). The evidence reveals that, by 7000 B.C., domestic dogs were present in several early villages in the Near East, such as Cayönü, although in small numbers. It is interesting to speculate whether dogs played a part in hunting activities or in the early domestication of herd animals. At this time, there is no clear evidence indicating how they were used.

Sheep

According to current information, the first animal to be domesticated, or at least husbanded primarily for food, was the sheep (*Ovis aires*). According to ratios of sheep of different ages, the people of Zawi Chemi Shanidar in northern Iraq were keeping sheep 11,000 years ago. The wild ancestor of domestic sheep was *Ovis ammon*, which is distributed throughout the Zagros-Taurus mountains and foothills across Iran (Figures 4-22 on page 137 and 4-23 on page 138). Wild sheep prefer rolling, hilly topography, which is less precipitous than the natural habitat of goats. Wild sheep graze on short grasses and gravitate to open pastureland. Sheep with definite morphological changes indicative of domestication, such as the hornless female sheep in the Bus Mordeh Phase deposits of Ali Kosh, appeared about 7000 B.C. in the Near East.

The main morphological change in sheep is in the animal's coat. This change is not easy to recog-

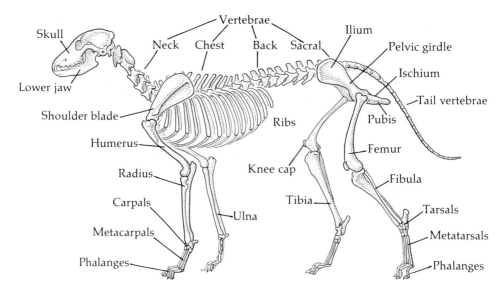

Figure 4-20
Skeleton of a dog.

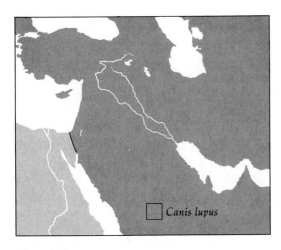

Canis lupus

Figure 4-21
Distribution of the wild ancestor of domestic dogs
(*Canis lupus*).

nize archeologically, but it had an important effect on the uses of domestic sheep. Wild sheep, like wild goats, have coats of long hair and much shorter undercoats of wooly fur (Figure 4-24, page 138). The wool of wild sheep is not obvious and could not have been the main reason for their early domestication. After sheep had been domesticated, however, several changes occurred that affected the coat (Ryder 1969). The coats of wild sheep and of several primitive domestic breeds are colored, whereas most domestic varieties have no pigment. Domestic sheep do not moult their coats as do their wild progenitors, and their hairiness is also diminished. The most important change in early domestic sheep is that, although the hair of the coat decreased in length, the wooly undercoat grew until it was the predominant element. It is difficult to determine how quickly this transition took place and how early wool became an important by-product of sheep domestication. It is likely that it took several thousand years and that the wool industry did not develop until at least protohistoric times (c. 4000 B.C.).

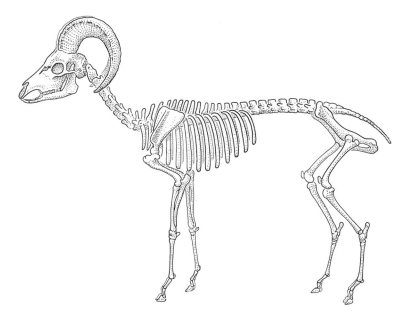

Figure 4-22
Skeleton of a wild sheep (*Ovis ammon*).

Goats

The domestic goat (*Capra hircus*) of the Near East is descended from the wild bezoar, or pasang (*Capra aegagrus*), which is indigenous to the uplands of southwest Asia (Figure 4-25, page 138). It is at home in rugged and craggy topography at a wide range of elevations. It feeds mainly on leaves and hence can survive in bushy environments in which grass is not abundant. The wild goat and sheep had overlapping natural ranges, but were adapted to slightly different environments. There must have been a period when early domestic goats, like other early domesticates, were morphologically identical with their wild relatives, but there are no conclusive archeological examples of this. Soon after domestication was initiated, the shape of goat horns began to change. The bony cores of these horns are preserved archeologically and their cross sections reveal different stages of animal exploitation (Figure 4-26, page 138): the horn cores of wild goats are normally irregular quadrangles in cross section; those of early domestic goats were almond-shaped; later there was a flattening of the medial

surface (Reed 1960:130). After many generations of domestication the horns acquired a twisted shape. Why the horns become flattened and twisted is not fully understood. The shape of the horn cores is determined by a series of independent genetic characters, each of which is probably controlled by several genes. It seems unlikely that these characters would have been consciously selected by the animals' keepers; rather, it is possible that these characters are genetically linked to other attributes that were purposefully selected (Hole, Flannery, and Neely 1969:277).

Early evidence for domesticated goats comes from a number of early villages, such as Asiab, where the bones of morphologically wild goats were almost all male, Ali Kosh, where during the Bus Mordeh phase domestic goats accounted for 72 percent of the animals utilized, and Ganj Dareh, where the hoof print of a goat was found on the remains of a mud-brick roof fragment. Although both sheep and goats contributed to the diets of most early villagers, usually one or the other was predominant. It would be very interesting to know

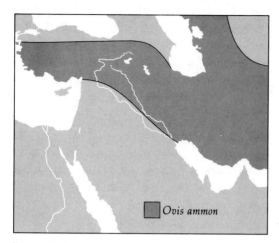

Figure 4-23
Distribution of wild sheep (*Ovis ammon*).

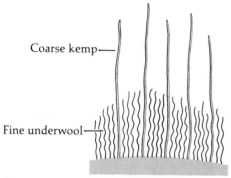

Figure 4-24
The structure of the hair and wool coat of wild sheep.

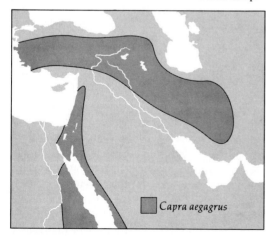

Figure 4-25
Distribution of wild goats (*Capra aegagrus*).

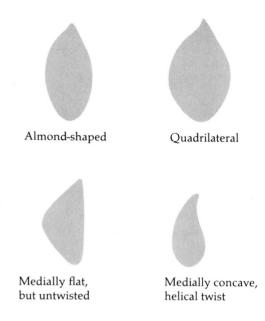

Almond-shaped   Quadrilateral

Medially flat,   Medially concave,
but untwisted   helical twist

Figure 4-26
Cross sections of goat horn cores showing the
progression from wild (quadrilateral) to domestic
(concave and twisted). (After Hole, Flannery, and
Neely, 1969.)

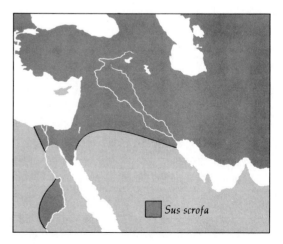

Figure 4-27
Distribution of wild pig (*Sus scrofa*).

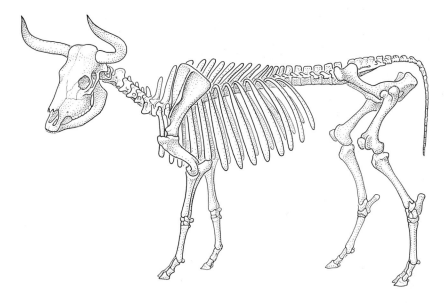

Figure 4-28
Skeleton of wild cattle
(*Bos primigenius*).

more about the relative proportions of these two species and their distribution at individual sites, but it is still very difficult to tell them apart from fragments of most bones. With the solution to this problem it might be possible to determine whether goats and sheep were herded together by prehistoric groups or whether certain households specialized in one species or the other.

Pigs

The wild ancestor *(Sus scrofa)* of the domestic pig is widely distributed throughout Europe, Asia, and parts of Africa (Figure 4-27). Wild pigs are omnivorous and live mainly in forests, although their ecological range is very wide. Pigs are found in diverse habitats, such as marshes, forests, or open plains, but individual pigs do not range widely, nor are they ever found far from a source of water (Reed 1960:139). Despite the wild nature of the mature wild pig, young animals are quite easy to tame. This characteristic may have facilitated their widespread domestication. They could have lived

off garbage and human waste products and furnished a high proportion of edible meat per pound of live weight. There is a good deal of controversy over whether the evidence for pigs in early villages is from domesticated or wild animals. The location of the earliest pig is unknown, but it is clear that by the second half of the seventh millennium pigs, like sheep and goats, had become basic staples in the diets of Near Eastern villagers.

Cattle

The ancestor of domestic cattle was the large wild aurochs *(Bos primigenius,* Figure 4-28). The natural range of this species included a diversity of habitats spreading across Europe, southwestern Asia, and northern Africa (Figure 4-29, page 140). Aurochs were probably large, long-horned, fierce animals, standing as high as 2 meters at the shoulders. They did not live in the high mountains or in the subtropical plains but preferred open, parklike areas. Cattle were probably domesticated in several locations. It seems that the earliest examples (7000

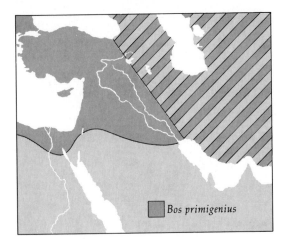

Figure 4-29
Distribution of wild cattle (*Bos primigenius* inferred).

B.C.) are from southeastern Europe. Domestic cattle have been identified as the predominant animal used for food at Çatal Hüyük in central Anatolia at about 6000 B.C. (Perkins 1969). This is a relatively late date for the first domestication, but cattle soon became the most important domestic animal for many Near Eastern societies. As a source of meat, milk, and hides, and as beasts of burden, they were indispensable to early Mesopotamian civilization.

Other animals were domesticated and became important to the economies of early civilizations in the Near East. The horse, camel, donkey, and other species were crucial to various adaptations. Even after the domestication of sheep, goats, pigs, cattle, and other animals, hunting still played a major role in the economy of early villagers, and to a lesser extent in the economies of the early urban societies. Fishing, which had been of some significance during hunting and gathering and early farming periods, became an industry in the early state. The identification of the wide variety of animal, fish, and bird remains is basic to an understanding of the diverse economies of later societies.

5

FIRST VILLAGE FARMERS

The Silent Revolution

*When originally conceived, the Agricultural Transformation
was believed to have been a uniform phenomenon. Thirty years of field
investigations in the Near East and elsewhere have documented the diversity
of paths by which a food-producing economy was achieved. In
this chapter, a village site from each of three major regions
of the Near East—the Levant, Anatolia, and the Zagros Mountains—is
examined in detail and is compared briefly with other sites in its region.
Despite the differences between the early village communities, it is
possible to suggest some generalities about the nature of cultural change
during the introduction of agriculture. Similarities in house
form, technology, local ecological diversity, range of food sources utilized, and
attempts at symbolic representation can be seen at numerous
archeological sites. As more sites are excavated, it is becoming apparent
that variation in the developmental patterns of early villages also existed but,
at the same time, some general developmental notions seem to
hold up. To evaluate the validity of the hypotheses presented in
Chapter 4 explaining the introduction of agriculture, it is useful to
identify both the central tendencies within the expanding body of evidence
and the range of variability.*

When V. Gordon Childe (1936) introduced the term Neolithic Revolution, he believed it represented a uniform transformation that was characterized by the same basic traits everywhere. The Neolithic signified the relatively synchronous introduction of sedentary village life, a food-producing economy, ground stone tools, and the widespread use of pottery. The Neolithic was thought of as a complete transformation affecting every aspect of life. As archeologists began to excavate remains of early villages, this simple picture became more complex. Each new site excavated revealed its own unique characteristics, confirming that the Neolithic Revolution was neither instantaneous nor uniform, even within the bounds of the Near East.

Archeologists soon discovered that well-fired pottery was not present in the earliest villages nor as part of the inventory of the earliest farmers. Excavations of sites such as Mallaha, Suberde, and Mureybit demonstrated that agriculture was not a necessary prerequisite of sedentary village life, and that sedentary villagers were not always agriculturalists. As more sites were investigated, it was learned that two communities within moderate distance of each other could have subsisted with different economies. The hunting community of Suberde is only 200 kilometers from the roughly contemporary early farming village of Hacilar. Several early villages—as they are known from recent archeological excavation—are examined in this chapter to demonstrate both the similarities and the differences between the various peoples who first employed agriculture. Because no early village has been either completely excavated or exhaustively published, our knowledge is not complete or uniform from region to region and site to site. Nevertheless, the intensity of research in the past twenty years into the origins of agriculture has produced an abundance of data that begins to make generalizations possible.

General Characteristics of Early Village Life

Despite the diverse cultural manifestations from the early villages (c. 7500–6000 B.C.), the uniqueness of each village should not be overemphasized. Many general characteristics can be discerned in the combined processes of sedentarization and early food production. One of them concerns the transition from hunting and gathering to farming, which spans a long period and a broad geographic area. The Agricultural Transformations's temporal span is shown to be broader with each new discovery of either Pleistocene communities with incipient forms of agriculture or established villages that continued to subsist by hunting and gathering. A second characteristic is that the geographic distribution of preagricultural villages is great but is usually limited to areas of ecological diversity. Such a location permitted a vertical economy that had as its basis many different sources of food available at different times of the year. A third characteristic is related to both biological and archeological information. Early farming was not a great economic advantage for its first practitioners. At almost every site, evidence shows early domestication to be only a modest addition to normal activities, whereas a major proportion of food continued to be obtained by hunting and gathering. Two activities involving wild resources that were to form the basis of early farming subsistence were grass collection and ungulate hunting. The exploitation of both plants and animals by early agriculturalists was an effective strategy for maximizing potential sources of food. Because of biological alterations resulting from early experiments with these plants and animals and the cultural alteration of the landscape, dependence on domesticated resources became increasingly advantageous and soon supplanted hunting and gathering as the major subsistence activity. Because of increasing dependence on domesticated plants and animals, mixed farming became firmly established as the primary economic form in the Near East. The adoption of agricultural techniques, and greater dependence on them, was an incremental process that produced a few major changes in short periods. Decisions made from year to year of the participants in this transformation about how to obtain enough food were imperceptibly, but irreversibly, changing the course of human history.

Sedentary communities often preceded agriculture, especially in the Levant. In the Zagros area, permanent communities and agriculture developed at roughly the same time, but a few scholars suggest that agriculture may have preceded sedentism. Most early farming villages had populations ranging from 50 to 200, but some communities in the Levant, such as Jericho or Beisamoun, may have been much larger. The general arrangement of early communities was nucleated, the farmers commuting to their fields from a village. In preagricultural communities, most houses were circular, semisubterranean, single-chambered buildings. The foundations were of uncut stone and the superstructures were probably of wood and skins. Early agricultural villages were characterized by rectilinear architecture. Many of the buildings were multi-roomed structures with specialization of rooms and differentiation between some of the structures. Like those of the preagricultural villages, the buildings had stone foundations, but their superstructures were of tauf or mud brick, some of which was made by being pressed into a mold. Although there is evidence for the alignment of buildings, there probably was no standard organization of town plans. Buildings might have abutted against one another for support, but shared walls were not the rule. Each building housed a family having from five to eight members. An entire agricultural community might have consisted of several extended families organized as a tribal society.

The artifactual inventory of early villagers included a diversity of tools made from many different raw materials. Although many were modifications of implements already in use, there was a clear trend toward specialization. Composite tools made of several materials were commonly used for manufacturing and for subsistence. Projectile points first made their appearance in the Levant during the early farming period. Figurines of human beings and domesticated animals were present at most sites, as were such ornamental pieces as beads, pendants, and bone and stone engravings.

From the excavation of early villages, there is considerable evidence of a trading network in the Near East that extends from Anatolia to locations a long distance away (G. Wright 1969). Obsidian from two major source areas in central and eastern Anatolia has been found at sites as much as 800 kilometers away; for example, small quantities of this volcanic glass have been found at many sites in the Levant as far south as Beidha and at sites across the Taurus and Zagros all the way to Ali Kosh (Figure 5-1, page 144). Other materials of specific origin, such as marine shells from the Red Sea and the Persian Gulf, have been found far from their native sources. These items are probably a small segment of the range of materials traded. It is difficult to archeologically determine whether there was long-distance trading in bulk commodities. However, the trading of special goods was an important economic step because they became items of widely recognized and standardized value and, because of their limited availability, their possession was an indication of status—an important aspect of later society. The movement of goods also implies the movement of people, although perhaps of only a few traders and small nomadic groups. Such movement was a ready conduit for the exchange of ideas, as well as a mechanism for the genetic mixing of the cereal plants of different regions (the seeds of which were carried for food). It has been suggested that the transport of cultivated emmer out of the Levant and domestic sheep into the Levant was facilitated by the trading of obsidian (G. Wright 1969).

During the early farming period, there was also an increase in the attention paid to the dead, especially in the Levant. Standard burial practices characterize many of the sites of the seventh millennium in the Levant. Skulls were removed from the bodies, plastered over in a naturalistic manner, and sometimes painted red. A similar technology was applied in decorating the floors of some of the buildings, which were plastered and decorated with red painted designs. The uniformity of burial and building practices from the southern Levant north and west across Anatolia to Hacilar suggests a widespread system of belief that has not been recognized as existing in earlier human history. These practices might be related to what could be called a religion. The attention to burials is also

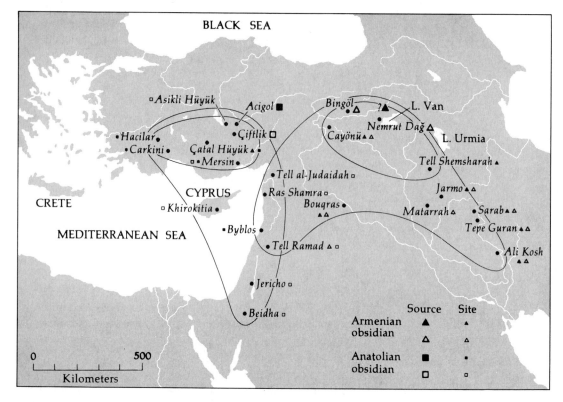

Figure 5-1
Distribution in Near Eastern villages of obsidian for which the source is
known. (From Obsidian and the origins of trade by J. E. Dixon, J. R. Cann,
and Colin Renfrew. Copyright © 1966 by Scientific American, Inc. All
rights reserved.)

indicative of the regard for older people in early
agricultural society.

Early Villages of the Levant

The region that today includes Israel, Jordan,
Lebanon, and western Syria played a primary role in
the origin of sedentary communities. The diverse
topography and the accessibility of marine and
freshwater sources of food have made it suitable for
human habitation since people first lived in the Near
East. Large hunting-and-gathering communities
developed where a wide variety of food resources
were locally available. With improved techniques

for processing food, some of these communities
grew into larger sedentary settlements. Mallaha, in
the upper Jordan Valley, is an example of a sedentary community comprising from 100 to 200 people
who did not practice agriculture. Preagricultural
sedentism is also evident at other Natufian and
Post-Natufian settlements, such as Jericho, Mureybit, and Nahal Oren.

The period following these preagricultural settlements has come to be known as Pre-Pottery
Neolithic B (PPNB) from its levels at Jericho, which
are dated at roughly the seventh millennium (Figure
5-2). Remains from this period contain the earliest
evidence of simple forms of agriculture at sites such

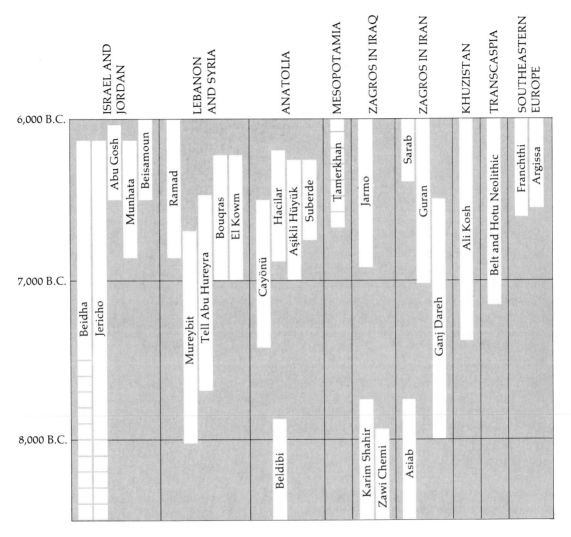

Figure 5-2
Chronological chart of the excavated early villages in the Near East.

as Beidha, Jericho, and perhaps Ramad. Hunting and gathering was the main subsistence strategy for these communities and the only one for others, such as Munhata. Nevertheless, the number of large sedentary communities with architectural sophistication increased. Uniformity of certain aspects of these sites has been discerned, implying at least a minimum amount of interaction between them. It has been documented that, during the Pre-Pottery Neolithic B, significant trading of Anatolian obsidian and other items took place. During the eighth and seventh millennia, the Levant was a crucial center of development, attested to by the abundance of advanced communities. The Levant did not return to this position of primacy in economic development for several thousand years.

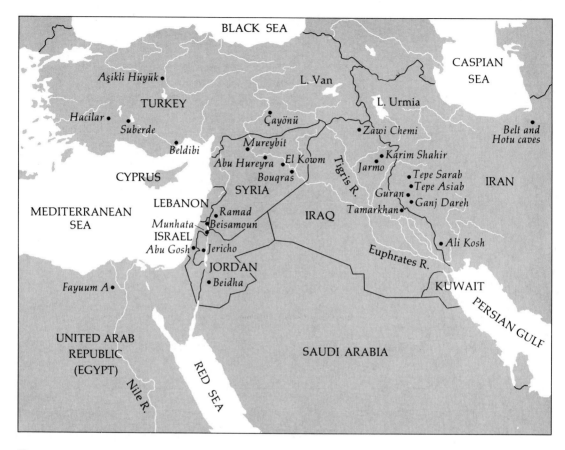

Figure 5-3
Locations of early village sites.

Beidha

Although it is not the largest nor the first discovered, the site of Beidha in southern Jordan is the best-known early village in the Levant (Kirkbride 1966a; 1966b; 1967). Seven seasons of excavations by Diana Kirkbride have unearthed the largest area of any early village in the Near East (more than 2,000 square meters). Beidha is located on a terrace above a wadi in a region of rough terrain in southern Jordan, a few kilometers north of the classical site of Petra (Figures 5-3 and 5-4). Its elevation is 1,000 meters and it probably received from 300 to 500 millimeters of rain annually. Although the region today has the appearance of aridity, the diverse topography included wide wadi bottoms and areas with sufficient moisture for the collection and eventually the cultivation of wild grain. In surveying the region, Kirkbride located several other sites that seem to be roughly contemporaneous with Beidha, which suggests that this area was a favorable environmental setting for early villages. Nine thousand years ago, Beidha's valley was surrounded by forests of oak, pistachio, and juniper covering the sandstone cliffs. Bones of aurochs, wild boars, ibex, wild goats, gazelle, hares, jackals, hyrax, and wild horses show that such animals lived in the vicinity of the site. The nearest perennial water supply today is a spring 4 kilometers northeast of Beidha on the slope of Jebel Shara (Mortensen 1971:3).

Figure 5-4
View of architecture uncovered at Beidha after five seasons of excavations.
(Photograph by Diana Kirkbride.)

The most important information obtained from the excavation at Beidha is from its well-preserved architectural structures. There were several successive occupations (levels) of the site, each with its own characteristic form of buildings. The major occupation of Beidha was within the first half of the seventh millennium (Figure 5-2). There are four major building levels above the considerably earlier Natufian remains. The earliest examples of buildings above the Natufian levels are found in level 6. There are two types of structures: a roughly polygonal house that Kirkbride considers an attempt to build a round house; and clusters of large circular "post houses." The post houses were substantial semisubterranean structures as much as 4 meters in diameter; the wall of such a house was built of stone and it surrounded an inner skeleton of wooden posts, which together with a central post supported a heavy roof made of reeds and clay. These roughly round houses were arranged in clusters, like cells in a honeycomb, and were connected to one another by rectangular passageways. Storage units were built into the spaces between dwellings (Figure 5-5, page 148). There were separate clusters of structures at Beidha, each surrounded by a wall outside of which lay a courtyard plastered with sandy clay. The village itself was protected by a terrace wall to retain the sand on which it was built. Subsequently, in level 5, there were free-standing circular buildings, several examples of which have been excavated. Each building had wide stone walls and a sandy clay plaster on its floor and lower walls.

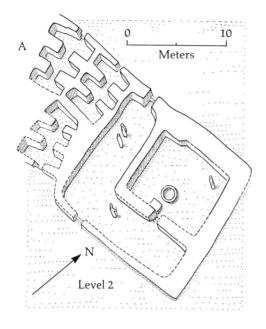

A

0   10

Meters

N

Level 2

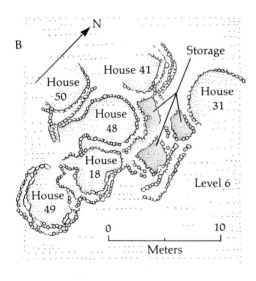

B

N

Storage

House 41

House 50

House 31

House 48

House 18

Level 6

House 49

0   10

Meters

Figure 5-5

Architectural structures uncovered at Beidha: (A) corridor and large-roomed buildings in upper level (2); and (B) circular cluster housing in lower level (6). (After Kirkbride, 1966a; 1968.)

In level 4, the structures were more rectilinear, but retained round corners and curving walls. These buildings can be thought of as subrectangular, and are examples of the finest workmanship at the site. Most structures were single-roomed and semisubterranean, and were entered by three descending steps. Several of the larger houses were about 5 by 6 meters in area and might have supported a second story.

The buildings built in levels 2 and 3 are rectilinear in plan and exhibit a high degree of complexity and specialization. The continuity of architectural development recorded in the lower levels is interrupted at levels 2 and 3. They contain a large rectangular house 9 by 7 meters with evidence of a collapsed, burned roof and a plastered floor (Figure 5-5A). The plaster was creamy yellow with red bands painted around such features as hearths. The plaster used was a compound of white lime that had a finer texture than that used on houses in the earlier levels. The house is semisubterranean and is made of roughly square boulders, with small stones used as chinking. An enclosed area around the large structure may have been a pen for animals. Besides the large single-roomed structure, several "corridor buildings" have been excavated (Figure 5-5A). Each consisted of a narrow central corridor, 1 by 6 meters, that opened into six small rooms, three on each side of the corridor. Each room was approximately 1.5 by 1 meter in area. The rooms were separated from each other by wide baulks, which implies that the rooms supported a lightly built upper story. Kirkbride's hypothesis is that the corridor rooms were workshops for the manufacture of bone tools, beads, horn objects, and so forth, and the second story was the living quarters. Clusters of tools and raw materials in many of the corridor building chambers, and the absence of hearths, tends to support this idea. The way in which artifacts are distributed among the buildings is interpreted as evidence for specialization of manuracturing tasks. Kirkbride interprets the large rectangular structure to have been a communal building used, among other things, for food preparation; it contains the only hearth discovered in this level.

Another group of structures was uncovered at

Beidha, approximately 50 meters from the main settlement. The three building levels containing this group closely parallel the early circular building levels of the main site. These buildings have floors of either sandstone slabs or gravel. Several large slabs might be interpreted as having served some purpose connected with rituals; thus, it is possible that this group of buildings functioned as a center for special activities.

The importance of the architectural sequence at Beidha is that it exemplifies the development of structures from small round huts to larger circular houses, then to subrectangular buildings, and eventually to substantial, rectilinear multiroomed structures. At each successive stage, the arrangement of buildings was different from that of the preceding stage, and the technology required to build them had changed. However, the general architectural features of stone walls and plastered floors, as well as a Pre-Pottery Neolithic B tool inventory, are found at each level.

The remains of six adults and twenty children were found buried within the confines of the excavated area of the village. They had been placed in individual graves; four of the bodies were interred after they had been allowed to decay for a period. Two of the adults were headless, the decapitation of corpses having been a frequent practice during this period in the Levant.

Although there is no pottery at Beidha, there are several objects made of clay. In level 6, a small clay figurine in the form of an ibex was found, as was a tiny, crudely made bowl preserved by an accidental fire. A small (2.8 centimeters in height) clay figurine interpreted to have been a "mother goddess" was found in a level 2 workshop in one of the corridor buildings. It is made of unbaked clay, modeled to be armless, and the head is missing.

Ornamental objects were common; beads were made of shell, bone, and stone. The shell came from either the Mediterranean or the Red Sea, the most abundant type being cowrie shell. The long bones of gazelle were the usual raw material for bone beads.

Bone tools are found in a variety of forms, but were predominantly utilitarian, with no representational carving, such as is found on early Natufian

bone tools. Awls or points, made from the long bones of goats or ibex are the most numerous type. Pieces that Kirkbride interpreted to have been bodkins were made from the ribs of wild aurochs and imply the practice of weaving.

The ground stone industry is abundant, the tools having been made mainly of limestone or, in a few cases, of sandstone. Most of the tools found are querns and grinders, probably used in the preparation of wild and cultivated cereals. Mortars and pestles have also been found and might have been used in the preparation of wild nuts, such as pistachio. Polished stone axes and adzes were made of basalt; most of the ones found are coarse, only their tips being polished, although there are few miniature examples carefully polished in their entirety.

The chipped stone industry from Beidha has been carefully studied by Peder Mortensen (1970). Three pieces of obsidian and 44,000 of flint were examined. The two major sources of the flint were nodules collected in the nearby wadis and tabular flint from the limestone strata of Jebel Shara. The obsidian pieces come from the Çiftlik source in Anatolia (which also supplied Jericho and Ras Shamra) and from a Lake Van source in eastern Anatolia (almost 900 kilometers from Beidha).

In most of the excavated levels at Beidha, less than 10 percent of the flint pieces are distinct tools. Of these tools, 80 percent are made on blades and the remaining 20 percent from flakes. Most of the chipped stone tools are arrowheads. They are made on blades, with converging edges. Some of the blades have been retouched along the edges, and the points trimmed on the reverse. Mortensen has worked out a detailed classification system for the arrowheads according to the shape and treatment of the base, tang, and shoulders. In general, these arrowheads are similar to those found at other Pre-Pottery Neolithic B sites in the Levant (Figure 5-6, page 150). Arrowheads are not found in significant numbers in the roughly contemporaneous sites of the Zagros Mountains—an important difference between the respective inventories.

Borers and knives make up the next most abundant categories of chipped stone tools. Scrapers, burins, denticulated pieces, and sickle blades are

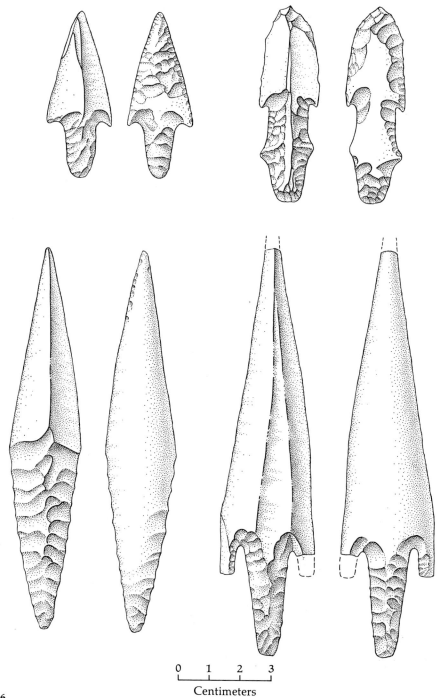

0   1   2   3

Centimeters

Figure 5-6
Projectile points from the preceramic levels of the early village of Munhata.
(Mission Archéologique Française en Israél.)

also present in large numbers. Another distinctive artifact of the Beidha chipped stone industry is the firestone, which is characterized by having sharp, irregular breaks and scars at one or two places along the edges. It is believed that these flints were used for striking fire. Similar artifacts are known from sites in Lebanon, Anatolia, and Europe. So far, firestones have not been discovered at sites in the Zagros Mountains nor on the Mesopotamian Plain. Firestones are another distinctive element of the eastern Mediterranean assemblage.

An analysis of the animal bones recovered during the Beidha excavations leads to the conclusion that goats were domesticated at Beidha, although the inhabitants hunted wild animals, such as ibex, gazelle, and aurochs (Perkins 1966). There are two reasons for believing that goats were domesticated: (1) many young animals were slaughtered; and (2) the difference in the number of young *Capra* (possible domesticated goats) and *Gazella* (clearly wild) killed. Neither kind of evidence is unequivocal, nor is stock breeding necessarily implied. However, considering the evidence from other similar sites in the Near East, the suggestion that the goats at Beidha were domesticated is not unreasonable.

The soil at Beidha does not lend itself to the preservation of individual carbonized grains, but a good deal of information has been obtained from plant impressions in the clay walls of the many burned houses, and from a few caches of carbonized plant material that did survive (Helbaek 1966). Thousands of imprints of barley have been examined. Morphologically, the recovered grains are members of *Hordeum spontaneum*, the wild barley species, but Helbaek suggests on the basis of their size and the cultural milieu that they were "cultivated" wild barley. They are examples of a cereal that is under cultivation but has not had sufficient generations for the morphological changes to become widely established. Impressions of a transitional form of emmer wheat were also observed. In addition to the two cultivated crops, large numbers of pistachio nuts, acorns, and various leguminous plants were collected by the inhabitants of Beidha.

Other Villages in the Levant

The evidence yielded by the excavations at Beidha of the architectural development, artifactural assemblage, and subsistence economy is similar to that found at other early villages in the Near East, especially those of the Levant. The Pre-Pottery Neolithic B occupation at Jericho, like its earlier community of Pre-Pottery Neolithic A, was larger than that of most villages (Kenyon 1960a). Jericho was probably a settlement of almost 4 hectares and, if all of it was densely occupied at one time, it would have had more than 500 people. The architecture at Pre-Pottery Neolithic B Jericho is rectilinear and arranged around courtyards. A feature of the architecture is polished plaster floors, the plaster being carried up the face of the walls, which are made of elongate, cigar-shaped mud bricks with herringbone patterns of thumb imprints. Unlike those at Beidha and other early villages of the Levant, few of the Jericho buildings had stone foundations.

Further north in the Jordan Rift Valley of Israel, 15 kilometers south of Lake Kinnereth, is the site of Munhata. The lower levels of Munhata are roughly contemporaneous with Pre-Pottery Neolithic B Beidha. Munhata is located on a high terrace of the Jordan River Valley at an elevation of 215 meters below sea level. Large exposures have been made by the excavator, Jean Perrot (1966a; 1967). The bottom levels are preceramic and have an artifact assemblage similar to that of other early villages in the Levant, with an especially impressive arrowhead industry (Figure 5-6). The architecture is characterized by plastered areas and raised platforms of stone. Structures are both circular and rectilinear and many are quite large. One building type has a rectangular outline foundation with several cross foundations that probably supported a raised floor. A similar type of grill foundation is common at the site of Çayönü in southeastern Anatolia.

North of Munhata and 15 kilometers southwest of Damascus, is the site of Ramad (de Contenson 1971). It is situated on a basalt plateau on the edge of the Wadi Kattana at an elevation of 850 meters above sea level (Figure 5-3) in an area that had more rainfall than did the other early villages described herein. Ramad is generally similar in size, architecture, and artifacts to Beidha and Munhata. A distinctive artifact found at Ramad, as well as at Munhata, which characterizes the later part of the Pre-Pottery Neolithic B period in the Levant, is a vessel made of mortar. This white ware, or *vaisselle blanche,* is a composite of lime and salty grass ashes. It is soft enough at first for the fabrication of vessels by coil techniques, then hardens into a cement (Balfet et al. 1969). By this process, large bowls with thick walls could be produced. The surfaces of the vessels were then made smooth and sometimes painted. This unbaked ware, used before the discovery of baking clay, was relatively widespread for a short period (c. 6250 B.C.).

Several other early village communities in the Levant and adjacent to it are similar to those just described. The basal levels of Ras Shamra in Syria, the enormous site of Beisamoun in the Jordan Rift Valley of Israel, the upper levels of Mureybit and Abu Hureyra on the Euphrates in Syria, the upper levels of El Khiam in the Jordanian desert of the west bank, and a variety of other sites have yielded early village material (Figure 5-3).

Continuing excavation will reveal both the similarities and the differences between early villages in the Levant. The seventh-millennium human settlements of the Levant were denser, as a result of an increase in the population, than those of earlier periods, but after 6000 B.C. there was a general hiatus of occupation, especially at sites in Israel and Jordan. Perrot suggests this was due to a slight drying in the climate, which had theretofore yielded the barest minimum of rainfall. This lack of adequate rainfall prompted the abandonment of almost all sedentary sites. As a result, the Levant fell from the forefront of the developmental process. What followed in this region was the reintroduction and consolidation of village life over a period of several thousand years.

Several important generalizations can be made—from the data in this section—about how early villages in the Levant were distinguished from villages in other regions of the Near East.

1 Most villages in the Levant were large, architecturally substantial settlements. The stone foundations and sophisticated building techniques attest to the year-round occupancy of these communities.

2 There was widespread and reasonably uniform use of certain distinctive elements of technology and decoration. These included *vaisselle blanche,* plastered floors that had been painted red, and plastered skulls.

3 Although the excavated remains have been interpreted to be documentation of animal herding and plant domestication, these assertions are not accepted by all experts. There remains the possibility that continued studies and better techniques of recognition will change current interpretations about the economy of these sites. Evidence does indicate that, even if early forms of agriculture were practiced at some villages, others such as Munhata may have been subsisting without the aid of food production.

Early Villages of Anatolia

Until recently, early villages were largely unknown in Anatolia, and it was assumed to be an area of little importance. Excavations and surveys during the past 15 years have completely changed this picture. Instead of proving to be a peripheral backwater, Anatolia was a center of development and an important conduit of information from the Aegean, Levant, and lowland Mesopotamia. The links between western Anatolian sites and southeastern Europe are being documented, as are those between the sites of eastern Anatolia and northern Mesopotamia. In addition to connections fostered by geographic characteristics, the various obsidian trading networks that reached out across both the Levant and the Zagros Mountains originated in Anatolia (see Figure 5-1). The villagers of seventh-millennium settlements near these obsidian sources, or on the trade routes, must have participated in this system and may have controlled it. Hence, Anatolia was at the center of a system that prompted the establishment of impressive early villages.

Figure 5-7
Airview of excavations at the early village site of Çayönü after four seasons
of excavations: distance between two white squares in foreground is
50 meters. (Photograph from the Joint Prehistoric Project of the Universities
of Istanbul and Chicago.)

Çayönü

The largest archeological exposure of an early village in Anatolia is the site of Çayönü Tepesi (Braidwood et al. 1971; 1974). Çayönü is a low oval mound about 250 by 150 meters adjacent to a tributary of the upper Tigris in the Diyarbakir province of Turkey (Figure 5-3). On the basis of radiocarbon determinations, the prehistoric occupation of Çayönü can be reasonably dated at between 7300 and 6500 b.c. During four seasons of excavation, more than 5 percent of the 2.5-hectare mound was exposed (Figure 5-7), and from the abundance of material uncovered it is possible to learn about many aspects of the life of these early villagers. Çayönü was selected for excavation because of its location in the foothills of the Taurus Mountains, a region intermediate between the archeologically better known Levant and the Zagros Mountains. The surface yield from the site suggested artificial

abundance and sophistication, which was borne out by the results of excavation. In addition, impressive architectural remains have been found in all levels of Çayönü but the earliest one. The technology and organization necessary to design and construct the large stone-founded buildings attest to the ingenuity of the people.

Çayönü is at an elevation of 830 meters in an open valley in the lower reaches of the Taurus Mountains. The local vegetation during the period of occupation was a steppe forest composed of pistachio and oak trees. Potentially domesticable plants, such as wild wheats and barley, were available in the vicinity. Jack Harlan's experiment demonstrating the productivity of harvesting wild einkorn took place on the slopes of a mountain near Cayönü (Chapter 4, pages 90–91). Wild aurochs, pigs, sheep and goats inhabited the surrounding countryside. Analysis of the faunal and floral remains has shown that the people of Çayönü

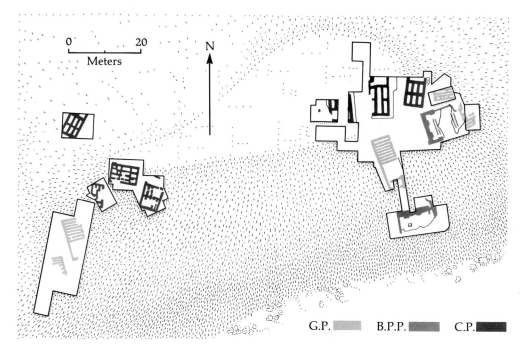

0   20
Meters

N

G.P.   B.P.P.   C.P.

Figure 5-8
Contour map of the mound of Çayönü showing substantial building remains
uncovered during four seasons of excavations. Buildings are from three
subphases: grill plan (G.P.), broad-pavement plan (B.P.P.), and cell plan (C.P.).
(Recorded by T. Rhode, the Joint Prehistoric Project of the Universities of
Istanbul and Chicago.)

relied on wild animal resources and a combination
of wild and domesticated plants. At the end of the
early village occupation, from about 6800 to 6500
B.C., the people at Çayönü utilized large numbers
of domestic sheep and goats.

The size of the occupation mound of Çayönü
suggests that from 100 to 200 people lived there at
any given time. Excavations have shown that the
mound was occupied for a long period by several
successive communities. Each community contained from twenty-five to fifty buildings that were
predominantly, if not entirely, domestic structures
(Figure 5-8). To study the form of each community
and to ascertain whether it was part of a continuous
development or a discrete settlement, the stratigraphic sequence of deposits was divided into a

series of subphases (Figure 5-9). The divisions were
made on the basis of general stratigraphic and
architectural correlations observed during the excavations. The length of time represented by each
subphase is a subject of investigation. Major differences in the form and orientation of the architectural complexes are the primary criteria for division
into the stratigraphic subphases. An examination
of the nature of the occupation in each subphase
and how it changed from one subphase to the next
reveals the complexity of life in an early village.

In the earliest known subphase, basal pits (B. P.),
the remains that were uncovered do not include
buildings; rather, they consist mostly of small circular cooking pits filled with stones, burnt bark, and
wood, giving an impression of a limited type of

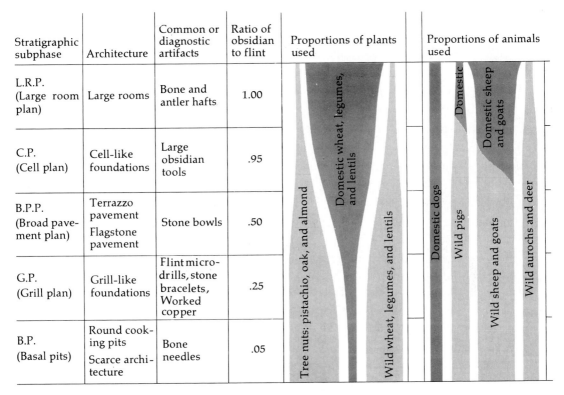

Stratigraphic subphase	Architecture	Common or diagnostic artifacts	Ratio of obsidian to flint	Proportions of plants used	Proportions of animals used
L.R.P. (Large room plan)	Large rooms	Bone and antler hafts	1.00		
C.P. (Cell plan)	Cell-like foundations	Large obsidian tools	.95		
B.P.P. (Broad pavement plan)	Terrazzo pavement / Flagstone pavement	Stone bowls	.50		
G.P. (Grill plan)	Grill-like foundations	Flint micro-drills, stone bracelets, Worked copper	.25		
B.P. (Basal pits)	Round cooking pits / Scarce architecture	Bone needles	.05		

Figure 5-9
Summary of some of the diagnostic attributes of Çayönü assemblage and how they changed during the occupation of the site as exemplified in the five subphases (B. P. is earliest and L.R.P., latest).

encampment. This may simply be an accident of sampling resulting from the small exposure of this lowest level, or it may be that the community at that time was not yet a well-established village.

The subsequent subphase, grill plan (G.P.), produced an abundance of architectural and artifactual information. The remains of five separate buildings have been uncovered, each with at least one superimposed rebuilding (Figure 5-8). This subphase gets its name from the unusual stone foundations that characterize its buildings. The five structures are uniform in design, size, and orientation, and the best-preserved among them is about 5 by 10 meters in area and retains much of the plasterlike floor that covers its foundation (Figure 5-10, page 156). The parallel foundation walls

probably supported wood beams on which the plaster floor was laid. In this way, the floor of the building was off the ground and would have remained dry throughout the damp winter. The spaces between the foundation walls permitted subfloor air circulation, which also would have helped to keep the building dry. The bases of the interior partitions have been preserved, which allows a fairly accurate determination of the interior parts of this building: there were two long and narrow chambers and three small rectangular areas between them (Figure 5-10). The three small units, each little more than 1 meter square, may have been storage bins rather than rooms. A large rectangular area on the southern end of the building was also enclosed by walls, but was without foundations or

Figure 5-10
Çayönü grill-plan foundation with plaster floor and bases of partitions still
in place. The undulation seen in the plaster floor is probably due to the
decay of supporting material. (Photograph from the Joint Prehistoric Project
of the Universities of Istanbul and Chicago.)

Figure 5-11
Foundation walls of another grill-plan building at Çayönü, in which the
floor has not been preserved, but the tightly packed pebble pavement at the
left has been. (Photograph from the Joint Prehistoric Project of the
Universities of Istanbul and Chicago.)

Figure 5-12
Large structure with carefully executed terrazzo floor uncovered at
Çayönü. Note the two sets of parallel white lines set into the pavement and
the features at the upper left, center, and right, just inside the wall of the
structure (center of floor was apparently destroyed in ancient times).
(Photograph from the Joint Prehistoric Project of the Universities of Istanbul
and Chicago.)

preserved flooring. In each of two other buildings at
Çayönü having grill foundations, there is an area in
which the flooring is a tightly packed pebble pavement (Figure 5-11). Such areas may have been used
for preparing or cooking food.

The three dominant features found in the next
subphase, broad-pavement plan (B.P.P.), are too
extraordinary to be interpreted simply as domestic
architecture. One feature is an open area having
four or more large free-standing stones. Another is a
building whose partial remains include a neat arrangement of large limestone slabs for flooring and
free-standing stones. A third feature is a 9 by 10
meter structure with a brilliantly executed terrazzo
floor (Figure 5-12). This floor is constructed basically of white limestone cobbles and crushed rock
set in a concretelike bonding. A surface layer of
primarily salmon-pink calcareous pebbles was set
into the concrete while still wet, as were two sets of

parallel strips of white pebbles, making white bands
5 centimeters wide and more than 4 meters long.
After the concrete had bonded, the entire surface of
the floor was ground smooth and polished. The
walls of this structure had buttresses on the inside.
Unfortunately, the artifactual contents of these impressive structures were either lacking or poorly
preserved, few pieces being found in situ either
within the structures themselves or close by.

Many buildings of the next subphase, cell plan
(C.P.), are well preserved owing to the burning of
their mud-brick superstructures. These structures
are referred to as cell plans because their stone
foundations form six or eight small cell-like units.
The units vary in size, and the foundation walls that
have been preserved range from one stone to as
many as ten stones high (more than 70 centimeters),
some of which still have the remnants of the mud-
brick superstructure. It is not certain whether these

Figure 5-13
Çayönü cell-plan building preserved by burning. Note the openings (arrows) in the stone foundations for passageways and the clusters of artifacts that either were left in the cells or fell from the floor above. (Photograph from the Joint Prehistoric Project of the Universities of Istanbul and Chicago.)

cells functioned as rooms, as storage spaces, or simply as air spaces. In the three best-preserved structures, openings in the interior stone foundation walls suggest passageways between the cell-like rooms (Figure 5-13). In the other three relatively complete foundations, the cells are too small to have been used as rooms but could have been used for circulation of air. In two of the three buildings whose foundations have room-size cells, large quantities of ground stone and antler tools indicative of manufacturing activities have been preserved. In each of these buildings, different cells contained different types of artifacts, implying that specific parts of a building were used for specific tasks.

It has been hypothesized that the building shown in Figure 5-13 had two stories, with the living area on the upper story and work rooms below. None of the six cells contains a hearth; nor do they contain any of the querns, mortars, and pestles used in food preparation that are common in the rest of Çayönü. There is a walled area to the north of this cell building that contains a hearth, quern, and handstone. It is possible that food was prepared in this partly enclosed area.

A description of some of the objects found in the cell building in Figure 5-13 indicates not only the diversity of implements used in a single building, but also the specificity of the use of each cell. The cell in the southeast corner contained the greatest abundance and variety of artifacts, the most numerous of which were small limestone spheres, which may have been used as sling stones. Adzes, two palettes, and a perforated doughnut-shaped object

Figure 5-14
Clay model house found in the cell-plan building shown in Figure 5-12 (upper middle cell). The modelled door jamb on the right, the roof supported by twigs, and the parapet running around the roof (with openings) may be indications of building techniques utilized at Çayönü. (Photograph from the Joint Prehistoric Project of the Universities of Istanbul and Chicago.)

were made of polished stone. Several long flint and obsidian blades were found in the cell, as were numerous bone objects including a blade haft and a cylindrical haft of antler. Also found in this cell was a shallow, sun-dried clay bowl, which had been molded in the bottom of a basket—an example of the use of clay for vessels before the introduction of fired pottery. The middle cell on the south is distinguished by the remains of two small clay model houses (Figure 5-14). In addition to several limestone spheres, there was a scatter of large

chunks of obsidian, which had not yet been worked into tools but seemed to be smashed from one or more large cores. The southwest cell was characterized by a large number of small, highly polished adzes and chisels. Several architectural elements of the building, such as roof fragments and a door lintel, were preserved by a fire in the chamber. The northwest chamber contained more than twenty marine shells, neatly piled next to a complete antler blade haft. The most unusual object of the middle room on the north was a complete scapula of a large *Bos primegenius*, which may have been used as an anvil for manufacturing activities. The northeast chamber was almost devoid of artifacts.

In each of two of the cell buildings, three human skeletons were found in the northwest cell. Also found in the deposits of one cell building were caches of large-sized obsidian implements, including blades, points, and specialized tools that measured as much as 20 centimeters in length, and a single obsidian flake weighing more than 400 grams. Both the burials and special artifacts may be evidence of rituals having been performed in these buildings.

The final preceramic subphase, large-room plan (L.R.P.), contains several complete structures, the best-preserved of which is a single-roomed structure, 5 by 9 meters in area, with half of its floor area preserved in situ. Evidence from the part of this open room that was preserved indicates that it was used for vegetable food preparation. Large basalt handstones, pestles, and quern fragments were common and were found close to a clay-lined bin (Figure 5-15, page 160).

The artifacts found at Çayönü are similar in some respects to the assemblages of early villages in both the Levant and Zagros regions. Less than 10 percent of the pieces had been shaped into distinctive tool types, whereas more than 33 percent of the pieces had no evidence of use. Flint is the more common raw material, especially in the earlier subphases (Figure 5-9). In the first subphase (B. P.), there is from six to ten times as much flint as obsidian, whereas, in the cell-plan subphase, there are as many obsidian as flint pieces. The chipped stone inventory is basically a blade industry of retouched

Figure 5-15
Foundation of a building from the large-room-plan
subphase at Çayönü, with food preparation implements
near the foreground. (Photograph from the Joint
Prehistoric Project of the Universities of Istanbul and
Chicago.)

tools (Figure 5-16). As shown in Figure 5-17 (page
162), proportions of the major categories of chipped
stone pieces are constant through all the subphases
of occupation of the site, with small differences
between obsidian and flint artifacts. The most
abundant category of pieces consists of blades and
flakes modified by use. Borers, drills, scrapers, and
sickle blades are the most common types of obsidian tools. Almost all tool types are present throughout the Çayönü occupation, but their proportions
vary significantly from one subphase to another.
This variation is related to the variety of activities
at Çayönü and the changing location of these
activities.

The ground stone industry was predominantly of
basalt, which was brought from basaltic flows about
20 miles away. Large numbers of pestles and hand-

stones have been recovered, and smaller numbers of
querns and mortars (Figure 5-16). Because of the
effort required to bring large pieces of basalt from
the source area, the inhabitants of Çayönü used
their querns until they wore out. In addition, local
limestone outcrops were used as bedrock mortars.

Bone and antler tools were a major component of
the Çayönü inventory (Figure 5-16). Awls and other
types of points were the most numerous. Finely
worked, slender bone needles with carefully engraved eye-holes were abundant in the lowest
levels. A variety of bone pieces with drill marks and
incisions may have been forms of artwork, attempts
at recording, or haphazard results of use and manufacture. In the later subphases, antler pieces were
used as hafts or handles for stone tools. There are
two basic forms of hafts: one on a curved antler with
a long groove for a blade, and the other on a stubbier
antler with an oval hole in one end for hafting a
cylindrical stone object, such as an adze or a scraper.

A wide variety of ornamental objects were produced by the people of Çayönü (Figure 5-18, page
163). They used many raw materials, some of which
had to be procured through trade. Hard stone,
bone, and shell were used to make rectangular,
tubular, and uniquely shaped beads and pendants.
Objects that look like chess pawns, which might
be figurines, were also made out of stone. Carefully
worked and sometimes decorated stone bowls were
found in small numbers only in the deposits of the
broad-pavement-plan subphase (B.P.P.).

Although fired pottery was not yet in use at
Çayönü, the people used sun-dried clay for a
number of purposes. The superstructures of their
houses and features within them were made of clay;
there is evidence of experiments at modeling clay
vessels in the bottoms of baskets; and small objects
made of clay in a variety of shapes are plentiful
(Figure 5-18). Small geometric objects, such as
spheres, disks, cones, and hourglasses, were
modeled, as were abstract shapes that might be
stylized representations. Small figurines of animals
and humans have been found in all subphases:
sheep, goats, pigs, cattle, and dogs were all represented in clay, in addition to a tiny, pregnant, seated
human female (see Figure 5-25A).

Figure 5-16
Stone, bone, and antler implements found at Çayönü: (A) flint blade core; (B) obsidian scraper; (C) flint scraper; (d) flint microdrill; (E) flint pointed piece; (F) bone awl (G) bone haft; (H) bone "wristlet"; (I) bone "hide rubber"; (J) sharpening stone; (K) stone chisel; (L) stone adze; (M) stone adze; (N) basalt pestle. (Photographs from the Joint Prehistoric Project of the Universities of Istanbul and Chicago.)

Like the inhabitants of Çayönü, those of other early farming villages in the Near East used clay for functional and representational objects. However, the clay models of small houses (one of which is shown in Figure 5-14) are unique for this period. Each house is single-roomed, with a thick clay base. In one wall there is a large doorway with a rounded door jamb. The walls are solid and had been surmounted by small twigs upon which was laid the clay roof. The parapet along the edge of the roof has openings, perhaps for drainage. It is difficult to determine how precisely these models reflect the appearance of houses of that day, but the use of timber to support the roof (documented by impression in a fallen section of roofing) and the discovery of a rounded piece of clay that may have been a doorjamb or lintel imply that they do incorporate some of the building techniques that were being used.

In the earlier subphases of Çayönü, a number of cold-hammered copper pieces have been found. They had been beaten into pins, a reamer, and

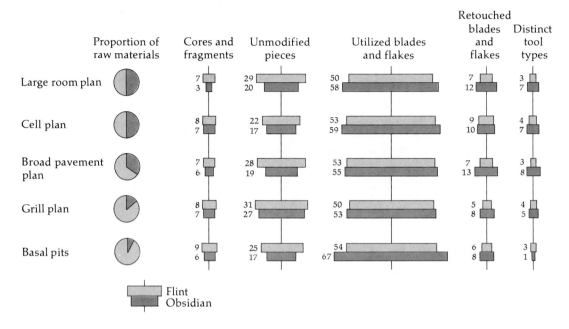

	Proportion of raw materials	Cores and fragments	Unmodified pieces	Utilized blades and flakes	Retouched blades and flakes	Distinct tool types
Large room plan		7 / 3	29 / 20	50 / 58	7 / 12	3 / 7
Cell plan		8 / 7	22 / 17	53 / 59	9 / 10	4 / 7
Broad pavement plan		7 / 6	28 / 19	53 / 55	7 / 13	3 / 8
Grill plan		8 / 7	31 / 27	50 / 53	5 / 8	4 / 5
Basal pits		9 / 6	25 / 17	54 / 67	6 / 8	3 / 1

Flint
Obsidian

Figure 5-17
Changing proportions of raw material and major categories of chipped stone tools in five subphases of occupation at Çayönü. Although the amount of obsidian used for tools increased markedly during the occupation, the relative proportion of cores and waste, utilized, and retouched pieces changed only slightly.

flat-rolled tubular beads. A major source of copper lies approximately 20 kilometers to the north at the Ergani Maden, Turkey. The surprising aspects of this example of metal working are both its early occurrence and the fact that, after the grill plan subphase, copper was apparently no longer used at Çayönü. From today's perspective, the discovery of metal-working techniques was one of the most important technological breakthroughs in human history. However, to the people who inhabited the grill buildings of Çayönü, metal working was probably not particularly significant and evidently was discontinued when other reasons for traveling to the source area no longer existed.

Of central importance to the excavations at Çayönü was the gathering of data on the subsistence resources of the inhabitants, especially data that bear on the development of effective food pro-

duction. With regard to meat sources, the general pattern was a shift from dependence on the big wild game animals of the area—aurochs and red deer—to the use of domestic sheep and goats. In the early subphases, aurochs bones were slightly more abundant than those of deer, and those of aurochs and deer together were approximately twice as numerous as those of sheep and goats. In the later subphases, the evidence was reversed: sheep and goat bones together were about thirteen times as numerous as those of aurochs and red deer. Such a shift in the principal food animals is by itself a strong indication of animal domestication by the latest subphase—an indication that is reinforced by the slightly smaller size of the sheep and goats and by certain changes in their body proportions. For both sheep and goats, the percentage of bones of young animals is higher in the later subphases;

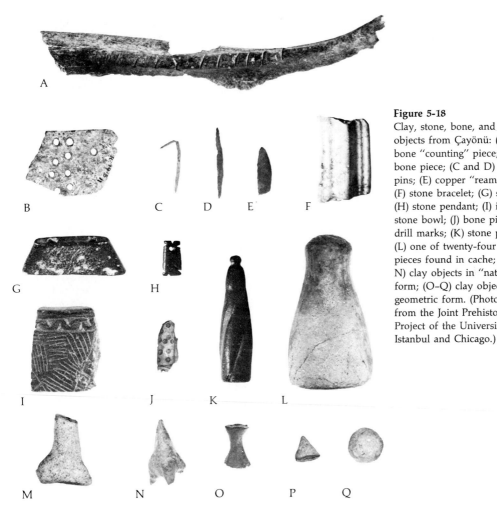

Figure 5-18
Clay, stone, bone, and metal objects from Çayönü: (A) incised bone "counting" piece; (B) drilled bone piece; (C and D) copper pins; (E) copper "reamer"; (F) stone bracelet; (G) stone bead; (H) stone pendant; (I) incised stone bowl; (J) bone piece with drill marks; (K) stone pestle; (L) one of twenty-four stone pieces found in cache; (M and N) clay objects in "naturalistic" form; (O–Q) clay objects in geometric form. (Photographs from the Joint Prehistoric Project of the Universities of Istanbul and Chicago.)

cranial fragments of sheep include three that are hornless. What occurred in the earlier subphases is more difficult to interpret: the change seems to have been abrupt and perhaps did not take place simultaneously throughout the entire community. Hunting was continued throughout, and it may have been only a small group of families who began to keep sheep and goats.

Pigs were abundant in all subphases and there is some evidence, although not conclusive, that they had been domesticated by the last subphase (L.R.P.). An interesting faunal discovery is the lower jaws of four large pigs buried together in the southeastern cell of a cell-plan foundation. Their placement there may have been a primitive form of the later Mesopotamian custom of including offerings in the foundations of new buildings.

The floral remains recovered through flotation imply a subsistence strategy that combined a variety of wild and domesticated sources of food. The people at Çayönü engaged in agriculture, if only to a limited extent, even in its earliest occupation; through time, its importance increased. Evidence of the cereals at Çayönü includes domesticated einkorn and emmer wheat. Large numbers of leguminous seeds of domesticated plants, such as pea, lentil, and bitter vetch, as well as wild vetch have been recovered. Pistachios and almonds constituted a plentiful and valuable source of carbohydrates, proteins, and oil, and the remains of these nuts are especially abundant in the early occupations. It is interesting to note that, although wild barley was available in the vicinity, the inhabitants of Çayönü seem deliberately to have excluded it from their diets and collected wild einkorn and emmer wheat only in small quantities. The pattern seems to have been one of rapid adoption of certain domesticated plants, such as emmer and einkorn, with continued dependence on selected wild resources such as tree nuts. This contrasts sharply with what was found in the early levels at the site of Ali Kosh (see pages 167–169) where there was a heavy reliance on the seeds of wild plants well after domestic cereals had been used (van Zeist 1976). The difference may have been due to different environmental conditions, Ali Kosh having been located in a dry area relatively marginal to farming and Çayönü in a region well suited for agriculture with a mean annual precipitation of about 700 millimeters.

The work at Çayönü continues. With each new field season and period of analysis new information is obtained and further questions are raised. In general, Çayönü seems to have been an active community in contact with other early villages and participating in local and long-distance trading networks. Although there was a basic continuity in technology and subsistence pursuits, the people of Çayönü were attempting to improve their exploitation of the environment by organizing their activities to take advantage of what was available to them. The grill-plan subphase is especially noteworthy for its great diversity of activities and experimentation, using many different raw materials and techniques for working them. In addition, the scale of the construction of the large buildings and their uniform orientation and spacing suggests rather advanced community organization and cooperation.

Other Anatolian Villages

Many other early village sites have been discovered in Anatolia, several of which have been excavated. The first of these is Hacilar, near Burdur in southwestern Anatolia. A small village of the early seventh millennium, it was uncovered by James Mellaart (1970). At its lowest levels, Hacilar was a small community whose inhabitants cultivated barley and emmer wheat and probably had domestic animals, although the faunal remains have not been studied in detail. Some of the characteristics of early Hacilar resemble those of the Pre-Pottery Neolithic B of the Levant, such as plastered floors with red painted designs, attention to skulls in burial practices, and the absence of pottery. Hacilar is better known for its late sixth-millennium village which contains fine examples of painted pottery and naturalistic clay figurines.

In central Anatolia, the relatively large village site of Aşikli Hüyük has been carefully examined and surface collected, but not yet excavated (Todd 1966). The site lies in a well-watered valley about 25 kilometers southeast of Aksaray. It consists of a large mound partly eroded by the Melendiz River. The valley is narrow but fertile and is surrounded by areas suitable for dry farming. The sections eroded by the river are sources of information normally obtainable only through excavation. The architecture seems to consist entirely of mud-brick buildings with no evidence for the use of stone. In some parts, walls are preserved to heights ranging from 1 to 1.5 meters. Fragments of red burnished plaster indicate the existence of plastered floors, which probably also covered the lower parts of the walls. Most of the artifacts found consist of chipped stone implements and waste material. Of the 6,200 pieces of chipped stone collected, all were made of obsidian except for one piece of chert. The chipped stone industry is characterized by circular and leaf-shaped scrapers, borers, and retouched blades. Complete unifacial retouching is rare, bifacial retouching is absent, and the percentage of projectile points is very low. The polished stone industry is represented by a small number of objects, including two heavy axes, one small celt, and fragments of pounding and rubbing stones. Several bone awls have been found with what seems to be a fragment of a pierced belt hook. Little is known of the economy, but it is likely that the trade in obsidian was influential in the growth and maintenance of the community. On the basis of radiocarbon dates and typological similarities, Aşikli Hüyük can be dated at approximately 7000 B.C.

Suberde is another seventh-millennium village in southcentral Anatolia (Bordaz 1969b). It is a small site, covering half an acre, on a rocky knoll beside Lake Sugla south of the modern city of Konya. The lower deposits contain floors with ashes but no permanent structures, whereas the upper levels have plaster floors and mud-brick walls. Pottery is not present in the Suberde deposits. From a careful analysis of the 300,000 fragments of animal bones recovered during the excavations, it has been suggested that the only domestic animal kept by the people of Suberde was the dog, and that the inhabitants' meat was supplied entirely by hunting (Perkins and Daly 1968). Most of the animals hunted were red deer, wild sheep, wild cattle, and pigs. From a detailed faunal analysis, it has been inferred that the larger animals were butchered where they had been killed, the meat being dragged back to the village inside the hides, whereas smaller animals, such as sheep, were usually carried back whole. Because Suberde is dated at the second half of the seventh millennium, its economy is enigmatic. By that time, several other villages in Anatolia were already relying on domestic plants and animals as a major source of food, whereas Suberde remained basically a hunter's camp. This is a good example of how developmental processes are not completely uniform nor unilinear. The people of Suberde did not find it necessary or even advantageous to keep domestic animals and their success with a continued hunting strategy is amply attested to by the enormous quantity of animal bones found at the site.

Early Villages of the Zagros Mountain Region

The first major archeological research into early agriculture and sedentary life was undertaken in the foothills of the Zagros Mountains of northern Iraq when Robert Braidwood brought to the field a group

Figure 5-19
Aerial view of Jarmo during the third season of excavations, northeast of Iraq. (Photograph from the Prehistoric Project, The Oriental Institute, The University of Chicago.)

of archeologists, botanists, zoologists, and geologists. Fieldwork in the Near East and the discipline of archeology has not been the same since. The problem-oriented and interdisciplinary field team has become the model for all subsequent research projects. Fieldwork in the Near East on the origins of agriculture has intensified, many of the researchers having had their first exposure to this problem in working on Braidwood's Prehistoric Project.

Jarmo

Qalat Jarmo was the center of Braidwood's earliest investigations into farming. Because it was the first early village to have been found and described, Jarmo became the prototypical early Near Eastern village.

Jarmo is located on the top of a bluff at an elevation of 800 meters. It lies in the hill country east of the modern town of Kirkuk (Figure 5-19). The remains of the prehistoric community cover about 1.5 hectares and are preserved to a depth of about 7 meters. As many as twelve layers of architecture have been identified, representing a community of between 150 and 200 people over a period of several

Figure 5-20
Tauf and stone foundations in lower levels at Jarmo. Note the traces of reed matting on several of the floors, the circular domed feature in the lower left (possibly an oven), and the parallel foundations walls in the upper right (which may be the subfloor support for a grill-plan building. (Photograph from the Prehistoric Project, The Oriental Institute, The University of Chicago.)

Figure 5-21
Stone foundation walls of a building in the upper level at Jarmo. Note the variation in room size, the possible hearth (burned area to right), and the possible stone mortar at the top of the photograph. (Photograph from the Prehistoric Project, The Oriental Institute, The University of Chicago.)

hundred years. Because of the substantial architecture, constructed largely of pressed mud, or tauf, Jarmo has been identified as a permanent settlement. The buildings, which were rectilinear, consisted of several rooms and many of them had small courtyards (Figures 5-20 and 5-21). The site has been dated at approximately 6750 B.C., and those parts of it that contain crude pottery in their upper levels probably continued for 500 more years (Figure 5-22A).

The economy of Jarmo had as its basis settled agriculture, although food collecting was of considerable importance. Goats, and to a lesser extent sheep, had been domesticated and they supplied large quantities of meat. Barley, einkorn, and emmer wheat were domesticated, but the emmer seems to have been a transitional form midway between the wild and fully domestic types. In addition to these sources of food, the people of Jarmo relied on potentially domesticable animals such as pigs, cat-

A   B

Figure 5-22
Containers from Jarmo:
(A) example of crudely made
pottery found in some of the
excavation unit's upper levels;
(B) one of the finely worked
stone bowls found throughout
the Jarmo deposits. (Photographs
from the Prehistoric Project, The
Oriental Institute, The University
of Chicago.)

tle, and horses, as well as on such ubiquitous creatures as land snails.

Tools used in the collection and processing of both wild and domestic plant foods are common at Jarmo. Flint blades with sickle sheen, mortars, querns, and handstones are abundant, and there are several ovens that might have been used for parching the grain. The chipped stone industry consists of unretouched blades, with a significant number of obsidian tools, especially microliths. One of the most characteristic features of the Jarmo assemblage is the quantity and variety of the clay objects. Pieces are molded into abstract or geometric shapes, as well as into figurines representing animals or human beings. More than 5,000 clay objects were recovered during three seasons of excavation. Bone implements are an important element in the tool inventory, the awl being the most common item. Objects of polished stone, such as axes and adzes, were found, but the most remarkable objects are a large number of finely worked stone bowls (Figure 5-22B). Considering the technology available to the inhabitants of Jarmo, we know that the work required to produce these aesthetically pleasing stone bowls was tremendous.

Ali Kosh

As more early villages were discovered and excavated, the original definition of the nuclear zone in which early farming began had to be revised continually. The site of Ali Kosh, in the Deh Luran Plain of Khuzistan, Iran, was one of the first sites excavated outside Braidwood's original conception of the nuclear zone. Whereas an elevation of 300 meters might be considered a lower limit for the distribution of potential domesticates in this region and hence of early dry farming, the elevation at Ali Kosh, which contains evidence of early plant and animal domestication, is 145 meters (Hole, Flannery, and Neely 1969). Ali Kosh is an example of an early farming village established at the margin of a natural-habitat zone, where early domesticates could survive but not grow in abundance without human help.

Ali Kosh is a roughly circular mound 135 meters in diameter and 7 meters in depth. Its remains have been subdivided by the excavators into three general phases: Bus Mordeh, Ali Kosh, and Mohammad Jaffar (Figure 5-23, page 168). Bus Mordeh is the earliest phase of occupation at Ali Kosh and dates from 7500 to 6750 B.C. Crude rectilinear structures of mud brick were uncovered. The people of the Bus Mordeh phase relied on a combination of wild and domestic resources for their subsistence. Most of the carbonized seeds recovered during the excavations were those of wild annual legumes and grasses native to the local steppe environment. A small percentage of the seeds found were of cultivated varieties of two-row hulled barley and emmer wheat, neither of which is native to the region. Apart from their seed-gathering and cereal-harvesting in the late winter and spring, the people of the Bus Mordeh phase were herdsmen, mainly of goats—animals not normally inhabiting the Deh

1963 Excavations   1961 Test excavation

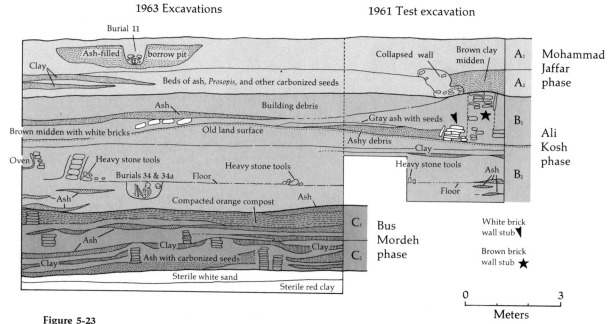

Figure 5-23
Stratigraphic section of the Ali Kosh excavations showing different strata,
wall stubs, and burials. (After Hole, Flannery, and Neeley, 1969.)

Luran Plain but found in the wild state in the rugged cliff areas not far away. Northern Khuzistan is an excellent area for winter grazing, a fact that may have had a great deal to do with the beginnings of food production there. Sheep were also herded, but in much smaller numbers than goats. Hunting and fishing constituted another major component of the subsistence activities of these early villagers.

The artifact inventory of the Bus Mordeh phase is similar to that found in other early village sites. A flint blade industry consisting of chipped stone tools was supplemented by a small number of obsidian pieces. Ground stone pounders, chipped stone picks, bone awls, and ornaments of stone and shell were also discovered. The Bus Mordeh phase community is thought to have been a small, relatively insubstantial settlement of people who brought the knowledge of agriculture with them and had close relations with the nearby highland regions of the Zagros Mountains. It is possible that this community was not occupied year-round, but rather served

as a winter-spring station with most of the inhabitants moving to higher pastures for the summer months.

For the subsequent phase of occupation (the Ali Kosh phase from about 6750 to 6000 B.C.) there is evidence of a substantial community, perhaps more settled and larger than earlier ones. The architecture developed into larger buildings with better construction (Figure 5-24, pages 170–171). The effectiveness of the dependence on domesticated resources improved during the Ali Kosh phase. Collection of wild legumes diminished, and wheat and barley became more prevalent. Domestic goats continued to be the animals most commonly eaten. The abundance of sheep was greater and the hunting of large ungulates continued. Development of the artifact inventory continued from the Bus Mordeh phase, with blade tools, especially sickle blades, being very common. The use of containers is documented in the Ali Kosh phase, stone bowls and impressions of basketry being recovered with greater frequency than in the earlier phase. Clay figurines increased in number and in variety of forms, a goatlike representation being especially common. The inhabitants of Ali Kosh participated in a far-reaching trading network that brought sea shells from the Persian Gulf, copper from central Iran, turquoise from northeastern Iran, and obsidian from eastern Turkey. Several of the burials found in the Ali Kosh levels suggest careful treatment of corpses. Often the body would be coated with red ochre, tightly flexed, and wrapped in a reed mat. The bundle was then buried, along with items of personal adornment, in a shallow pit under the floor of a house. Occasionally the burial was delayed to allow the body to decompose.

During the latest phase of occupation (the Mohammad Jaffer phase from about 6000 to 5600 B.C.), there were many innovations, including the introduction of pottery. Building techniques improved and the agricultural tools used became task specific. The effectiveness of the domesticated resources continued to increase, but the productivity of the land after 1,000 years of occupation was quickly diminishing. This probably led to changes in farming activities and ultimately to the site's abandonment.

Ganj Dareh

The discovery of the site of Ganj Dareh pushed the upper limit of the elevation of early villages higher, just as Ali Kosh had extended the lower limit. It is near the modern town of Kermanshah, Iran, at an elevation of 1,400 meters. Ganj Dareh is a small oval mound about 1 hectare in area with 8 meters of early Neolithic deposits (Smith 1972b; 1975). The upper levels of the site contain the remains of an early village with solid mud-brick architecture dated at about 7000 B.C. The remains of what the excavator named Level D were partially destroyed by fire, which has led to fine preservation. The architecture of that level is mainly of rectilinear structures with small chambers constructed of long plano-convex bricks. Some of the buildings may have had a second story consisting of a lightly built living floor supported by wooden beams overlying the small chambers that made up

the basement. The lower chambers may have been storerooms and are generally similar to the corridor rooms of Beidha and the cell-plan structures of Çayönü. The roofs were made of beams and reeds overlain with clay.

A discovery of interest at Ganj Dareh was that of the earliest pottery known in the Near East. It is a lightly fired, chaff-tempered coarse ware that includes large vessels as much as 0.8 meter high and small pots only 5 centimeters in height. Some of the pots were found in the small chambers, which supports the hypothesis that the chambers were storage rooms. Other clay objects, both containers and figurines, were discovered. Small geometric clay pieces, and human and animal figurines are similar to those found in other early villages of the Near East.

Flint artifacts are abundant, having undergone little change from the earliest to the latest levels of the site. No obsidian has been recovered from Ganj Dareh. Backed bladelets, truncated blades, heavy flake scrapers, end scrapers, use-retouched pieces, and fine bladelet cores are characteristic. Blades with sickle sheen are common, as are ground stone mortars, pestles, and handstones. There are no ground stone axes or celts and only a few fragments of polished stone vessels, which is surprising. Among the bone tools were awls, fragments of grooved sickle hafts, and large, corner perforated flat pieces that are interpreted to have been wrist-guards.

The economy of Ganj Dareh is not yet completely known but, from preliminary analysis, it seems that goats were domesticated and domesticated plants may have been utilized (Smith 1972b).

An unusual feature preserved in a burned building in Level D is a cubicle containing two skulls (without their lower jaws) of what were probably wild sheep attached one above the other to the plaster interior of a small niche build against the wall. It is likely that this room had a ritualistic function. This feature is another example of the growing number of buildings or parts of buildings used for rituals, a development that became more prevalent in subsequent cultures throughout the Near East.

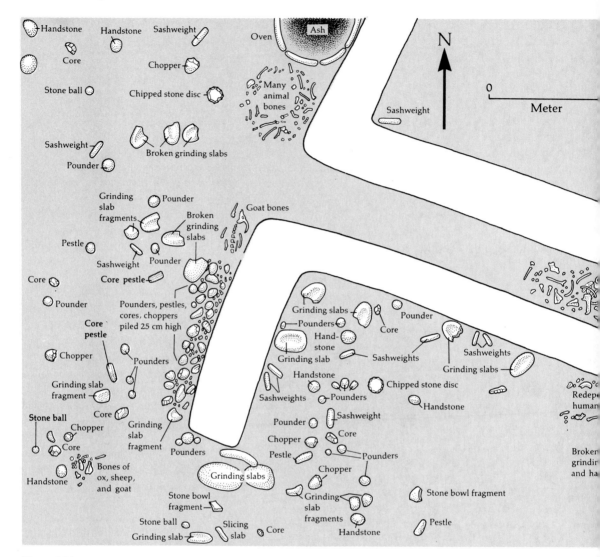

Figure 5-24
Plan of parts of two structures from the Ali Kosh phase of the site of Ali Kosh, with all tools larger than a flint blade plotted in situ. (After Hole, Flannery, and Neeley, 1969.)

Other Sites in the Zagros Mountain Region

Several other early village sites have been excavated in the Zagros mountain region and even more sites are known from surveys. The remains of Tepe Guran in Luristan, Iran, at an elevation of 950 meters, have been carefully investigated by a Danish archeological team (Mortensen, Melgaard, Thrane 1964). This site has yielded a long sequence of early village material: twenty-one levels have been identified, which make up from 6 to 7 meters of occupation debris dated roughly at 6500 to 5500 B.C. At Guran, the earliest settlers lived in wooden huts in

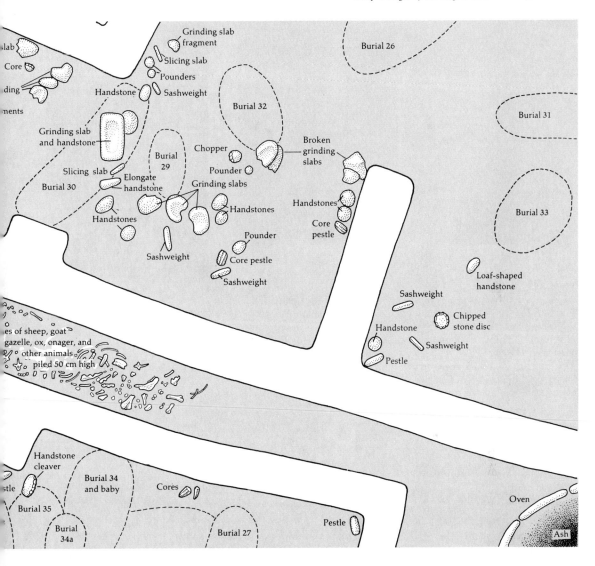

which there are traces of what may have been matting on the floors. It is likely that the early levels constituted a semipermanent winter camp for a group of nomadic herdsmen who also hunted gazelle and some of the seasonally available water fowl. In the later levels, mud-walled houses predominate and there is abundant evidence for both farming and gathering. Two-rowed hulled barley, pistachios, gazelle, and domestic goats are the major subsistence resources.

The three lowest levels at Guran do not contain ceramic remains, but subsequent levels yield evidence of the development of the potter's craft and increasing use of such wares. Soon after coarse

A   B

Figure 5-25
Clay figurines of human figures from early villages in three regions of the
Near East: (A) female figurine found at Çayönü in southeastern Anatolia
(photograph from the Joint Prehistoric Project of the Universities of Istanbul
and Chicago); (B) female figure found at Tepe Sarab in the Iranian Zagros—
the figurine is composed of several separate parts that fit together (photograph from the Prehistoric Project of The Oriental Institute, The University of
Chicago); (C) human figurine from the preceramic levels of Munhata, Israel
(photograph from the Israel Department of Antiquities and Museums).

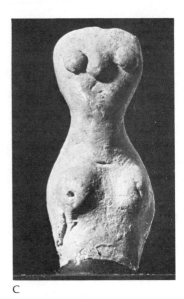

C

plain pottery was introduced, it was also painted.
This standard painted ware is decorated with red
strokes that resemble small tadpoles—a style of
painting also found on the pottery in the upper
levels of Jarmo and in other early villages in the
Zagros (see Figure 6-4 on page 190). The flint and
obsidian tools were made on flakes and blades,
some of which are characterized as microlithic. A
large percentage of the chipped stone pieces are
unretouched.

Changes can be observed in the architecture, the
faunal resources, and the artifacts, indicative of a
transition from a semisedentary to a year-round
occupation. During the summer months, some
members of the community took the goat herds to
higher mountain valleys to take advantage of late-
ripening pastures (Mortensen 1972).

Tepe Sarab is an early village located 7 kilometers east of Kermanshah and at a higher elevation
(1,300 meters) than Jarmo or Guran (Braidwood,
Howe, and Reed 1961). The excavations did not reveal substantial mud-walled architecture, but the
evidence from the animal bones suggests a year-
round occupation by at least some of the village's
occupants. Sarab may also have been temporary
quarters for people living in communities at lower
elevations, such as Jarmo or Guran. Some of the
people from those communities may have moved
from one site to the other in pursuit of pastures,
while the remainder stayed home to continue activities that could be carried out during the summer.
The artifactual assemblage from Sarab is similar to
that of Jarmo and the other early villages of the
Zagros, but seems to be slightly later and less varied
than that of Jarmo, although Sarab did produce an
abundance of realistically modeled clay figurines.

There are well-made human female figures with stalklike heads (Figure 5-25B), as well as realistic representations of animals.

Settlement in the Zagros Mountains consisted of a large number of villages that were modest in size, relied on a mixed strategy of farming and gathering, and developed into reasonably substantial communities. There continues to be uncertainty about whether the villages were totally sedentary or whether many of their inhabitants led nomadic lives. The sharp differences in elevation between adjacent valleys, the extremes of climate, and the dependence on domestic herd animals for food would have encouraged a nomadic mode of existence (Mortensen 1972).

Early Villages in Adjacent Regions

There are three ways in which the patterns of life in regions adjacent to the Near East might have affected developments there:

1 Agriculture might have been introduced in other regions earlier, and the idea might have been borrowed or early domesticates imported by the Near Eastern villagers.
2 People living in settlements in peripheral regions might have interacted with those living in settlements in the Near East.
3 The ideas, domesticates, and organizational skills originating in the Near East might have been exported to settlements in the adjacent regions.

Southeastern Europe

From what can be inferred from current evidence, the only region that might have acted as a stimulus through its interactions with the Near East seems to be southeastern Europe. Early village assemblages and sites in several locations in Greece are dated at the seventh millennium. The materials from Franchthi Cave, in the eastern Peloponnese, are as early but not as substantial as those from the neighboring sites of Anatolia (Jacobson 1969). The site of Argissa in Thessaly, Greece, is another im-

portant example (Milojcic, Boessnick and Hopf 1962; Prosht and Berger 1973). The remains at Argissa imply that certain animal species were domesticated there at least as early as they were in the Zagros-Taurus mountain arc, probably indicating an independent center of early animal domestication in Greece. There is strong support for the view that the orginal domestication of cattle took place in southeastern Europe and was later adopted in Anatolia and eventually in the rest of the Near East. A well-known example of an early village in Greece is the site of Nea Nikomedeia in Macedonia (Rodden 1965). The site dates from the end of the seventh millennium to the middle of the sixth millennium and yields a developed village inventory, including pottery.

Transcaspia

Although the area of northeastern Iran and Turkmanistan in the USSR is only now becoming adequately known, there is substantial evidence for early villages. Along the piedmont of the northern slopes of the Kopet Dagh Mountains in the USSR, streams water a narrow strip of land between the mountains and the sands of the Karakum Desert. The villages discovered in this area generally resemble those of the Zagros-Taurus arc of the Near East. The excavator, V. Masson, has named this group of villages the Jeitun culture after the best-known site, Jeitun (Masson 1971). Jeitun is a moderate-sized village with evidence for early domesticates, two-row barley, sheep, and goats. The area is marginal in terms of natural rainfall, and a very primitive form of irrigation, perhaps the damming of small streams running out of the mountains, supplied the necessary water during the drier years. Although radiocarbon dates are rare, the early levels of the Jeitun culture are dated at the sixth millennium. Considering the presence of pottery and the carbon dates, one would expect early Jeitun to be contemporary with or somewhat more recent than the upper levels of Jarmo and Guran. Although there is no clear evidence for antecedents to the Jeitun culture in Transcaspia, it is possible that it developed from the culture of the cave sites of the southern Caspian area or was influenced by the contemporary cultures of the highlands of northwestern Iran. Generally, Transcaspia is thought to have developed somewhat later than did the neighboring areas of the Near East.

Egypt

As described in Chapter 3, the Nile Valley was the scene of early settlements of intensive hunters and gatherers with some agricultural equipment. Despite the early appearance of sickle blades and grinding stones, there is no primary evidence for agriculture or substantial permanent communities before the end of the sixth millennium (see Chapter 9). Until new evidence is discovered, the Nile Valley must be considered to have been influenced by its neighbors, and not to have been equal to them, in the development of early villages.

Developmental Patterns of Early Villages in the Near East

Several general patterns emerge from the complexity of information available about early villages. To identify regularities, various shortcomings of the data must be accounted for, because the information produced is directly related to the researcher's perspective, what is considered important, what is deemed possible to accomplish, and the fortuitous circumstances that some researchers find themselves in. The temporal and distributional patterns of early villages are becoming increasingly clear. The picture has been somewhat complicated by the assumption that a substantial village must have had an agricultural base—a notion that has been revised in light of communities such as Mallaha and Suberde, although inferences based on the necessity of a food-producing base for certain sites remain in the literature. Other problems arise because of sites being treated as single-period occupations. Many of the early villages may have been reoccupied several times and thus span a considerable length of time. Because of the assumption of uniformity, inferences based on domesticates found in an upper level

may be made about the earlier levels; similarly, the absence of domesticates in lower levels may be construed as evidence of a hunting and gathering community throughout.

Geographic Focuses

In general, the presence of at least some primary evidence for domesticated species of plants and animals is attested to at early seventh millennium sites throughout the Near East, from Beidha in the southwest, to Çayönü, on the north, to Ali Kosh in the southeast. Agricultural practices had spread to these villages by at least 7000 B.C. However, agriculture was not yet the predominant subsistence base for any of them, nor was it universally adopted by all communities. Hunting villages continued to exist for considerable lengths of time alongside communities that were largely agricultural.

The geographic distribution of early examples of both agriculture and sedentism is continually being revised in light of continuing research. Of prime importance is the fact that the distributions of sedentism and agriculture are not the same. There are substantial permanent villages without domestic resources both in the lowlands and in higher locations (e.g., Mureybit, Mallaha, perhaps Bouqras, and Suberde). Villages that remained somewhat transient, yet accomplished a food-producing economy are more difficult to identify; examples may be Sarab and the Bus Mordeh phase of Ali Kosh. In the Levant, there are sites for which the inference can be made that the early emergence of sedentism and substantial architecture occurred in the Natufian. However, predominant reliance on a food-producing economy in the Levant is not documented until the sixth millennium. On the other hand, the evidence in the Zagros Mountains suggests that domestication was practiced as early as 8900 B.C. at Zawi Chemi Shanidar. However, the architectural sophistication and magnitude of the Levantine villages is not yet known to have been paralleled in the Zagros. Hence, the emphasis in the Zagros seems to have been on food production, especially animal herding, rather than on substantial, architecturally sophisticated settlements. It is interesting that the site of Çayönü, situated between the Levant and Zagros, contains evidence for both early domestication of plants and substantial architecture.

Nuclear versus Marginal Zones

Another important aspect of the distribution of early villages is where they were located in relation to the nuclear zone as first proposed by Braidwood. Investigators have searched in regions within the natural habitat zone more intensively than they have in areas outside the suggested range of potential domesticates. Nevertheless, sites are being found in environments other than those that have been interpreted to be suitable for the wild progenitors of domestic plants and animals. For example, Mureybit lies in the Syrian desert in an area too hot and dry for the appropriate plants and animals. The sites of Bouqras and El Kowm in Syria and Tamarkahn in Iraq also are too low for the nuclear zone. Other sites with evidence for domesticated plants and animals have been found in areas located on the dry margins of the nuclear zone. Ali Kosh is the best known example. Although wild progenitors of domestic plants and animals may have been present in these areas, or close to them, they would not have thrived in sufficient numbers to be the basis for an "incipient" form of agriculture. The suggestion has been made that occupants of Ali Kosh brought plants and animals from adjacent regions to the site in an attempt to reproduce the abundance of the nuclear zone in a marginal setting (Flannery 1969). If in fact, evidence of domesticates at Ali Kosh predates that at sites within the nuclear zone, the Flannery-Binford marginal zone hypothesis for the origins of agriculture gains strong support.

However, the primacy of Ali Kosh is not only unproved but, at this time, seems unlikely. Evidence from sites such as Zawi Chemi Shanidar, Çayönü, and Ganj Dareh lend support to the hypothesis that the earliest evidence for domesticated plants and animals comes from within the bounds of the natural habitat zone (although Ganj Dareh is at the upper extreme of the nuclear zone). If farming originated in the nuclear zone and was "transported" to a marginal environment, the domesticated resources would probably have contributed substan-

tially to the diet from the outset, and morphological changes would have been relatively rapid at the marginal site. In contrast, domesticated resources would have constituted only a small fraction of the diet at sites in the nuclear zone at which domestication was being introduced. The proportion of domesticates consumed would have then become larger as yields improved. Acceptance of the marginal zone hypothesis implies that farming was introduced largely as an exigency to solve the problem of a shortage of resources in an environmentally marginal area. Acceptance of the hypothesis that farming first developed in a nuclear zone implies that agricultural techniques were initiated and adopted as part of the interdependency between beginning sedentism and the exploitation of local resources (refer to Figure 4-7 on pages 108–109). The evidence is not yet at hand to differentiate clearly between these two alternatives, and it is not altogether certain that agriculture did not originate in both ways. A solution might be forthcoming with closer relative chronological controls, more standardized criteria of domestication, and better demographic information.

What influenced the precise location of a settlement within a general zone? Most early villages were close to areas with differences in elevation: for example, Çayönü, Ali Kosh, and the Kermanshah sites are on valley floors within walking distance of mountains; Beidha and Jarmo are on bluffs or terraces high above wadis; and Suberde, Jericho, and Munhata are in depressed valleys near sources of fresh water. The primary considerations in choosing a location for an early settlement must have been to maximize the range of habitats available and to be close to a source of water. Defensive considerations and control of important passes or trade routes were probably not primary determinants of early settlement location.

Adaptive Trends

There is a wealth of architectural information about early villages, but it is difficult to generalize from site to site. The almost universal appearance of rectilinear and multiroomed structures with agriculture is striking, and is probably related to a change in househould activities and community organization. Rectilinear houses are more easily added to than are round structures and can be efficiently subdivided into separate chambers, each for a different set of activities. The transition to rectilinear architecture can be viewed as one of a large number of changes that early villagers went through in the process of coping more effectively with the environment and with each other.

The changing subsistence activities and the rapid changes in architecture are manifestations of tendencies toward specialization and flexibility. If more were known about the prehistoric uses of the artifactual inventories, they, too, might be indicators of these tendencies. Flexibility and specialization are somewhat contradictory and can only be achieved at different levels of organization. Flexibility could have been instituted at a general level, in basic building technology, in the manufacture of artifacts, and in subsistence strategies. Obtaining raw materials and manufacturing and distributing the products made from them must have been so organized as to accommodate changes in needs and potentials. Specialization would have been achieved in the products themselves, both in the compartmentalization of buildings and in the artifacts (or kits of implements). Other manifestations of the trends toward flexibility and specialization are the increasing number of artistic pieces and enigmatic objects, the increasing amount of ornamentation and decoration, the use of new raw materials, experimentation with containers, and the manufacture of other specialized items.

In addition to the universality of rectilinear architecture in early farming villages, there is a widespread distribution of multichambered foundations that probably supported second stories. The upper deposits of Mureybit, the corridor building of Beidha, the cell-plan structures of Çayönü, and the cubicles of Ganj Dareh conform to this pattern. Except for Mureybit, these sites have also yielded definite evidence for very early domestication (the Bus Mordeh phase at Ali Kosh may contain evidence for similar buildings and equally early domestication). It is unlikely that the chambers were used primarily for storage because the winter rainfall at most of these sites was heavy and the dampness would have impaired the preservation of the grain stored in them. Also there is no clear evidence for carbonized remains of seeds in these chambers, even in those that were burned. A great deal of evidence supports Kirkbride's suggestion that the Beidha chambers were crawlways and workrooms. The artifactual yield of many of the chambers at Beidha and Çayönü is abundant and diverse, which supports the suggestion that the chambers were workrooms. The upper stories could have been used for living areas. At Cayönü, food preparation probably took place in a sheltered area next to the building.

The significance of this interpretation is the importance it gives to manufacturing activities in the village. Such activities might have been carried out by farmers when they were not engaged in agricultural activities. At both Beidha and Çayönü, the chambered buildings are in the upper levels, by which time agriculture had been sufficiently established to have been the major source of food for the community. It is interesting that their location on the site is not limited to one part of it, which would indicate that there had been a class of craftsmen in the community. At Çayönü, all buildings from the cell-plan levels are generally similar, implying that every family did its own manufacturing and that specialization was occurring within the family (or other minimal economic unit) and not between families. At later sites in the Near East, this pattern changed and the minimum economic unit in which specialization occurred was much larger.

The settlements containing cell buildings probably represent the optimal adaptation to early agricultural life within the framework of single-family organization. Subsequent developments required increasingly larger organizational units. The early villages of the Near East resulted from the most fundamental transition in human history. Although they seem primitive from the perspective of later millennia, many of the innovations in subsistence and technology necessary for urban society were developed within them. From then on, primary developments were those of organization and the means of handling increased complexity.

6

DEVELOPMENT OF THE VILLAGE ECONOMY

The Process Becomes Irreversible

The advanced farming village, an end product of the Agricultural Transformation, was a very successful community form that was adopted in many different regions and endured almost unchanged for millennia. The success of these villages was related to three accomplishments: sources of food were improved by domestication, becoming more productive and, hence, more attractive; the technology of food production was developed to the extent that it facilitated agriculture and discouraged people from returning to their former lifeways; and adaptations in community size and organization were made to facilitate a food-producing economy and subsequently became self-perpetuating. Thus, farming became much more advantageous than hunting and gathering, making it almost impossible for people to revert to their earlier subsistence pursuits.

In this chapter, information on the archeological sites of the three major regions of the Near East is presented region by region. However, in this period the Levant was no longer the pivotal region that it had been during the development of early villages. Although some of the most spectacular discoveries have been made in Anatolia—the town of Çatal Hüyük was larger and in many ways more complex than any of its contemporaries—it was the Zagros foothills and the adjacent fringes of the Mesopotamian Plain that predominated in the development of advanced villages and the foundations of urban civilization.

The nature of archeological excavation and the materials analyzed are somewhat different from those in the investigation of earlier periods. The most abundant artifacts are ceramic, and their design and form are used to classify the societies that developed and used them. The important cultural developments that took place in this period were the changing forms of community organization. It is possible to identify complex forms of organization, though embryonic, in the advanced villages and to trace the emergence of various regulatory institutions.

Although agriculturists of the Near East drastically altered their subsistence pursuits and organizational forms, their lifestyles remained relatively primitive. They relied on wild plants and animals for much of their food, and so their achievements do not seem to be superior to those of sedentary hunters and gatherers.

Developments during the sixth and fifth millennia completely changed this situation. By 4000 B.C., and earlier in many places, the agricultural village had established itself as the most effective economic strategy, allowing some communities to grow into large towns. Hunting had become a subsidiary subsistence pursuit. Nonagricultural communities were no longer the cultural equivalent of the ubiquitous farming communities. The distribution of farming villages and emerging towns had been extended far beyond the limits of the nuclear zone of the Near East to include highland Iran, Transcaspia, Afghanistan, lowland Mesopotamia, the Nile Valley, and southeastern Europe. Farming was becoming a way of life for an increasing proportion of the world's population. The effectiveness with which a farming village dealt with adverse climates in order to produce a consistent supply of food steadily improved until it became the dominant community form. Established villages were the culmination of the Agricultural Transformation and are the fourth phase of development in the systems model shown in Figure 4-6 on page 106.

What Caused the Success of Village Farming Communities?

Among the environmental, cultural, and organizational factors that favored the growth of villages (refer to the positive effects on transition 13 in Figure 4-7 on pages 108–109), the most important are those that create a positive-feedback situation. Positive feedback magnifies change because a small increase in one factor causes a second to increase, which in turn causes the first factor to increase again. Hence, the change becomes greater and greater, until some force diminishes the effect of the feedback.

Three important positive-feedback relationships had been set in motion during the period of early villages. These feedback relationships improved the workability of the village farming economy, making it the primary means of subsistence throughout the Near East. And the village farming economy facilitated rapid population growth. The first feedback relationship concerned the physiological improvement of the domesticates used by the early farmers (S-9 in Figure 4-7C). Herders might have deliberately selected more productive animals for reproduction; cultivators might have saved the largest seeds for planting the next year. Equally important were the events that were not deliberate: transporting early domesticated plants and animals outside of their natural habitats increased the likelihood that certain mutations would succeed under the pressure of natural selection.

When farmers moved domestic species to the lower elevations of Khuzistan and lowland Mesopotamia, only heat-tolerant animals and aridity-tolerant plants could survive and reproduce. In time, the proportion of species that had adapted to lowland conditions increased. As plants and animals became more effective food sources than they had been in the wild, people relied more heavily on them. The increasing number of domesticates enlarged the gene pool in the herds and fields, which increased the likelihood of favorable hybridizations. Hence, by having been moved into new areas and relied on more and more as a source of food for human consumption, the early domesticated plants and animals became more productive sources of food for their keepers. This is not to say that all such experiments were successful. However, in terms of the statistical success of a process, the expansion of early agriculture into new geographical regions was instrumental in making food production more effective and, the more effective it became as a way of life, the greater the tendency was to adopt it in new regions.

The second positive-feedback relationship that contributed to the success of farming villages was technological. As farming became the predominant subsistence activity of many communities, efforts were intensified to improve the tools and techniques for procuring, processing, and storing domestic plants and animals (C-3, C-4, C-5, and C-6 in Figure 4-7D). Improvements in plant-processing equipment included grinding tools, parching ovens for separating the grain from its husk, and domed ovens for the preparation of bread. One of the more significant technological innovations was in making containers. Those used by early villagers for carrying, trading, preparing, and storing their food had largely been made of organic material or stone. The introduction of well-fired pottery vessels in the seventh millennium made possible relatively light, water-tight, and inexpensive containers. Pottery was soon produced throughout the Near East. It made the transport and storage of agricultural products easier and more efficient than ever before, which, in turn, made farming even more attractive.

The third positive-feedback relationship concerned the organization of human communities (Figure 4-7E, O-1, O-6). Remaining in the same location year-round was an advantage to cultivators, for it enabled them to construct substantial buildings, storage facilities, and nonportable implements, and it allowed the material inventory of the villagers to proliferate. As farming became a more effective means of subsistence, community size increased, as did regional population densities. These changes in turn necessitated alterations in community organization and intercommunity relations. Strong bonds developed within the growing communities, and intergroup alliances became necessary. Some results of these changes, as they are preserved in the archeological record, are examined in this chapter. House form, community layout, and special goods are indicators of prehistoric organizational changes. Because new forms of organization improved the cooperation and productivity of farming communities, they stimulated further growth of farming villages.

These three general feedback relationships helped to make farming an increasingly attractive, effective, and stable form of existence. Another important process was at work that insured that most of the population would never revert to a hunting-and-gathering subsistence: this was the cumulative effect of village farming communities on the landscape. Domestication and cultivation disrupted the natural ecological balance, resulting in an inexorably and irreversibly altered landscape. Killing predators, capturing domesticable wild animals, eliminating competitors, cutting down forests to clear land and to build houses, and encroaching on unused land are all inevitable elements of a developing agricultural way of life. As the population increased, farming villages increased in number and penetrated new areas, and farmers consciously and unconsciously destroyed the basic subsistence resources of hunters and gatherers. The newly domesticated plants and animals could no longer exist without human care and attention, just as human beings became increasingly dependent on agricultural resources. The increasing effectiveness of the agricultural way of life derived from a combination of explicit decisions and inventions that led to changes that made any reversal of the process practically impossible. People were on the way to becoming food producers and eventually urban dwellers.

Established Farming Villages of the Southern Levant

The pre-eminence of early village developments in the southern Levant diminished at the beginning of the sixth millennium. The Natufians and early villagers of the Levant had been at the forefront of the movement toward substantial sedentary villages and a farming economy. However, the inhabitants of the southern Levant during the succeeding millennia were no longer in the vanguard. Rather, the conditions that had encouraged the development of the earliest substantial villages in the Near East also restricted further development, allowing them to continue at only a basic level of organization.

At approximately 6000 B.C., many of the communities in the southern Levant were abandoned, and large areas were not reoccupied for at least a thousand years (Figure 6-1). Their abandonment does not seem to be a result of invasion because there is no evidence of burned buildings in the

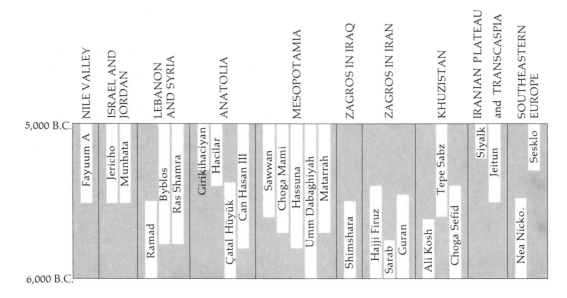

Figure 6-1
Chronological chart of Near Eastern advanced villages.

archeological remains. It was probably caused by a drying of the climate that reached a maximum at about 6000 B.C. As a result, areas in which dry farming had been marginal would than have become too dry for any farming, and areas that had supported a dense agricultural population could then have supported only small groups. Some archeological sites continued to be occupied after 6000 B.C., especially those in the upper Jordan Rift Valley and Damascus area. In general, movement was to the north and to coastal areas where the effects of drought were minimized. Tell Ramad is one of the early villages that continued to be occupied.

It has been suggested that the villages established after the hiatus indicate that a new population moved into the area, rather than that the people already there moved to different locations. Whether the former interpretation or the latter is correct cannot be proved by the archeological evidence, but it is likely that there was a combination of both.

The best known sixth-millennium site is the settlement of Byblos in Lebanon (Figure 6-2). Byblos was a large community located on sand dunes

on both sides of a deep wadi that ran into the Mediterranean. The buildings at Byblos had stone foundations and plastered floors. They were free standing and some of them contained two rooms, one being smaller than the other. Little is known of the economy of the people at Byblos, but they were probably agriculturists who supplemented that resource with marine foods. Pottery was abundant at Byblos and at other sixth-millennium sites in the Levant. The pottery was relatively well made. Although it was not painted, many pieces were decorated with incisions and with relief techniques. The ware is monochrome, burnished, and usually grit tempered. The shapes are plain, many of the jars being round or globular. Similar pottery has been found in sites having an Amouq A inventory to the north in the Plain of Antioch in southcentral Turkey (Braidwood and Braidwood 1960).

Somewhat later, during the fifth millennium, a related but significantly different cultural inventory from that found at Byblos was utilized in southern Levant. Archeologists have given the name "Yarmukian" to this assemblage. The pottery shapes are somewhat sophisticated, jars with collar necks and

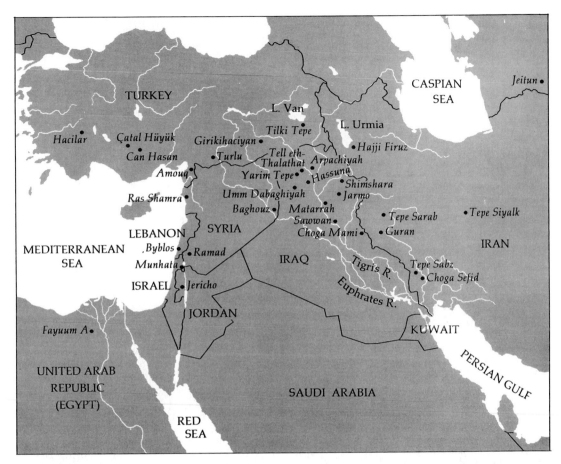

Figure 6-2
Prehistoric advanced villages in the Near East.

handles being common. The pottery is coated with a red slip and is decorated with incised or combed patterns. Clay figurines with emphasized features are distinctive elements in the Yarmukian assemblage (examples from Munhata are shown in Figure 6-3, page 182). These were found in addition to the incised pebble figurines already known from the preceding Byblos occupations.

Little is known about the community layout or economy of the sixth- and fifth-millennium sites in the southern Levant because Byblos and Munhata are the only broadly excavated ones. The architecture, built of stone and mud brick, varies from rectangular structures to round huts. Most of the

communities of this period relied on domesticated plants and animals for most of their subsistence. Domestic emmer, barley, sheep, goats, and possibly cattle are all documented in the archeological record. The settlements of the Levant show no significant improvements over those of the early villagers except for the introduction of pottery. The population does not seem to have increased significantly nor did the size of individual settlements. Architecture was neither more substantial nor widespread than in early villages. The pottery is generally similar to that found at contemporary sites in Anatolia and northern Syria. Inhabitants of the region were coping effectively with the

Figure 6-3
Clay figurines from the upper levels of Munhata (the two at the right are front and side views of the same piece). (Courtesy of the Israel Department of Antiquities and Museums.)

environment, but it seems that a village-level economy and organization was sufficient for the potential of the environment. Because of this, the Levant ceased to be a primary center of economic and organizational developments for this period and for the succeeding millennia.

**Emerging Towns of Anatolia:
A Flash of Brilliance**

Anatolia had been a major locale for the development of early sedentary villages. The people of the Anatolian plateau and the slopes of the Taurus Mountains knew the techniques of domestication and utilized stone and mud architecture. Unlike those in the Levant, however, the developments in

Anatolia that followed the simple farming villages were characteristic of the growth of complex societies in the Near East. Because there are no early historic records of Anatolia and because it does not contain examples of large urban centers contemporary with those of Mesopotamia, it was assumed that developments in Anatolia were peripheral to the main ones taking place in the Greater Mesopotamian Basin. The work of James Mellaart and others in the past twenty years has done a great deal to correct this misconception.

Çatal Hüyük

More than those of any other site, the excavated remains of Çatal Hüyük have demonstrated the sophistication of the ancient inhabitants of Anatolia and the complexity of their communities (Mellaart 1967). Çatal Hüyük is the largest known archeological site in the Near East dated at the seventh millennium. Although only part of it has been excavated, the mound itself covers about 13 hectares and rises 17.5 meters above the surrounding plain. It is located in a dry, open valley southeast of the modern city of Konya at an elevation of 900 meters. During three seasons of excavation at the site, Mellaart uncovered about 0.5 hectare of the deposits, and in a limited exposure plumbed the bottom of the mound through fourteen building levels. More is known about the lifeways of some of the prehistoric people who lived at Çatal Hüyük than about those at any other site contemporary with it because of two factors: (1) buildings and objects were beautifully preserved by a catastrophic fire that consumed a great deal of level 6; and (2) Mellaart's strategy of broad horizontal exposures took maximum advantage of the fine preservation. The levels investigated date from about 6250 to 5400 B.C., and all the levels contained pottery. If the entire area of the mound had been occupied simultaneously, and at the same density as were the excavated parts, then the population of Çatal Hüyük would have been several thousand. Although current knowledge does not allow a precise determination of the population, it is the largest known aggregate of this era. Whether, in fact, Çatal Hüyük should be considered a city, as the excavator and others have called it, is more a matter of definition of the word than of the number of people who lived there.

The economy of Çatal Hüyük was largely an agricultural one, though its inhabitants also engaged in trade and craft production. The major source of meat was cattle, most of which were domesticated (Perkins 1969). Possibly, domestic sheep and hunted animals constituted the balance of faunal resources. Domestic emmer, einkorn, bitter vetch, and peas were grown by the people of Çatal Hüyük (Helback 1964b; 1970). In addition, two hybrid varieties were grown—bread-wheat and six-row naked barley—which produced much higher yields than did their predecessors, but which probably required irrigation to survive in a region such

as the Konya Plain. The other vegetable food sources utilized, such as acorns, pistachios, and almonds, were native to the surrounding mountains some distance from the site. The reliance on cattle herding and the possible introduction of a simple system of irrigation were economic innovations that may have enabled Çatal Hüyük to achieve the size that it did. Although the people of Çatal Hüyük participated in several major advances of subsistence technology, their accomplishments in other realms were even more noteworthy.

The architecture at Çatal Hüyük reveals the sophistication and organization that distinguishes this site from earlier villages of the seventh millennium. The buildings, which were constructed of mud brick and wood, conformed to a standard rectilinear plan. Each room was roughly square and had an area of about 25 square meters. It seems that all the buildings were single-storied and that access to their interiors was by climbing down ladders through openings in the roofs. Because they were built one against the other with no lanes or alleyways between them, most pedestrian traffic between structures in the community must have been on the roofs. Many of the rooms, which the excavator has interpreted to have been separate units or houses, are arranged around courtyards, some of which consisted of an area in which an earlier house had fallen into decay. Each house contained built-in mud furniture, including platforms for sleeping and an area for food preparation in which there was an oven and in most cases a hearth. New houses were built on the foundations of old houses that had collapsed. In this way, the mound developed rapidly. At any given time, the houses were at slightly different levels, permitting light-admitting windows in the upper walls of some of them. Timber frames in the walls supported large roof beams, which in turn supported smaller timbers, reeds, and mud roofing. The overall appearance of the community was very much like that of an Indian pueblo in the southwestern United States.

Mellaart interpreted at least 40 of the 139 structures that he unearthed in three seasons of excavation to be shrines. They are distinguished from domestic houses by their decoration, associated finds, and burials. They do not differ structurally from the houses and are interspersed among them. As yet, no structures that could be interpreted to be manufacturing centers have been uncovered. Mellaart suggests that the craft and trading quarters are located in the unexcavated part of the site.

Trade and industry were probably important aspects of Çatal Hüyük's economy. A great many raw materials used for the manufacture of the artifacts found at the site were probably imported from distant sources. It is likely that the inhabitants of this large town traded manufactured goods in return. Perhaps this trade also filled some of their subsistence needs. It is possible that the people of Çatal Hüyük controlled the trade in obsidian from the central Anatolian sources. Obsidian from these sources has been discovered at sites as far away as Jericho, a distance of almost 1,000 kilometers. Among the raw materials or manufactured objects from distant places that have been found at Çatal Hüyük are fine tabular flint from the southern slopes of the Taurus Mountains, about 200 kilometers away, that was used for making some of the chipped stone tools; cowrie and other marine shells from the Mediterranean, 100 kilometers away, or even the more distant Red Sea; and copper and turquoise from eastern Anatolia, 500 kilometers away, or the Sinai peninsula, 1,000 kilometers away. Some materials had to be brought to the settlement in large quantities from distances that required special organization: timber for houses came from the surrounding hills and mountains more than a day away by foot; the obsidian that made up 90 percent of the chipped stone artifacts, plus that which was used in trade, was brought from volcanic flows perhaps as much as 250 kilometers away. All these materials may have been brought to Çatal Hüyük by its inhabitants, perhaps with the aid of their domestic cattle as beasts of burden, or it could have been obtained by trading for it through a network that included many intermediaries.

In addition to procuring and distributing raw materials, some members of the Çatal Hüyük community probably spent part of their time converting the obsidian and other raw materials into finely crafted products. The quantity of magnificently made but unused obsidian points, the abundance of personal ornaments, the evidence for basketry, wooden containers, and woven goods suggests a craft industry that may have comprised the work of individual households.

The chipped stone industry of Çatal Hüyük is characterized by bifacial, flat retouched tools for which the workmanship is of high quality. Large spearheads, knives, and arrowheads are the most distinctive pieces. Awls, needles, beads, spatulas, and polishers dominate the bone industry, which is similar to that of other settlements of the period. Items of rare distribution include a dagger haft, carved animal heads, forked hairpins, a cosmetic stick, and a fish hook.

The pottery found in Çatal Hüyük's earliest level is cream colored and burnished with a straw temper. In level 7, a better-fired, dark-burnished ware with grit temper predominates. This ware appears in higher levels with modifications in the slip color, but there are few attempts at decoration. These pieces were clearly meant to be used for the preparation of food and its storage. The craftsmen of Çatal Hüyük found expression for aesthetic creativity in other media, like wall paintings and decorative objects.

A variety of clay objects have been recovered, and animal and human clay figurines, like those carved in stone, are common. Two unusual representations are of a plump woman seated on a bench flanked by leopards, done in clay, and a stone carving of two couples lying next to each other. A number of large clay seals with geometric designs have also been recovered. Whether these seals were used for decoration or for symbolic communication, the technique was an important advance in the development of communication.

In addition to the rich and well-preserved material inventory uncovered at Çatal Hüyük, there are diverse wall paintings and molded clay objects, which can shed light on certain aspects of an extinct society often guessed about but rarely observed. Paintings on the plastered walls of many of Çatal Hüyük's buildings are the earliest known examples of this craft. Each room was replastered often, perhaps annually. In one room, forty layers of plaster were peeled off the wall, exposing many different designs. Other decorative techniques included plastering over molded clay relief and intaligo (incised carving). The wall paintings were in monochrome or polychrome, and some were combined with molded relief. Some of their designs were linear or geometric, resembling designs commonly used by weavers. Mellaart suggests that, because of the similarity of these designs to those of traditional Turkish kilims (flat-woven rugs), the people of Çatal Hüyük may have woven kilims. A painted design of great interest is a series of squares below a twin-peaked erupting volcano: this panel is interpreted by the excavator to be a representation of the town of Çatal Hüyük with the then active volcanic mountain peaks of Hasan Dag, about 100 kilometers away, in the background. There is also a room that contains several panels depicting a hunting scene or ritual in which numerous hunters surround large animals in a way that suggests to Mellaart an animal rite rather than a hunt.

One wall painting that may elucidate the treatment of the dead contains large birds, which seem to be vultures, and human bodies, some of which are decapitated. The interpretation that Mellaart gives is that, when people died, they were put on platforms to be defleshed by vultures, leaving the bones to be buried. There is a good deal of evidence for this type of secondary interment at Çatal Hüyük; in some cases, the skulls were treated separately. Most of the burials found have been under the floors of houses; in some of them, the bones are tightly wrapped in basketry containers.

The use of clay and plaster relief, sometimes in combination with paintings or with faunal remains, was common in many of the rooms identified as shrines and may symbolize a combination of life and death. In one room, vulture beaks are encased in clay and plastered on a wall in forms that resemble a woman's breasts. In another room, pig jaws are treated in a similar manner. Other reliefs are of such animals as leopards and of human females, often in a spread-eagled position that suggests the

act of giving birth. The interpretation of these spectacular works of art and symbolism is a difficult task, but in any case it seems likely that the rooms identified as shrines had a primarily ritualistic function. The wall paintings were probably made during ceremonies: such a painting might have been exposed for a year or less, and then the wall would have been replastered and repainted the subsequent year during a particular ceremony. The features in relief were probably repainted frequently, but their basic forms remained the same during the entire use of the room. Hence, the features displayed in a particular room were probably associated with a particular ritual. The seemingly disproportionate number of rooms used for ritualistic activities has been the subject of conjecture about the role of religion in the community organization of Çatal Hüyük. It has been suggested that Çatal Hüyük was a religious city, serving as a center for a large region. Part of the subsistence of the community could have been derived from the payment for conducting ceremonies that it received from people in the surrounding region.

The interpretation that Çatal Hüyük was a regional religious center is not necessary to explain the abundance of ritualistic rooms and decorations. Another, ecologically oriented interpretation is that it was a community that developed along certain lines more rapidly than its neighbors in response to a favorable economic situation. Because abundant economic returns resulted from a few technological advances, a community of great complexity and size grew. Economic breakthroughs enabled movement into a relatively unoccupied ecological niche. Previously, there had been few agriculturists on the potentially productive Konya Plain, and little organized control of the trade in obsidian. To become agriculturalists in the hot and dry Konya Plain, additional water, heat-tolerant animals and salt-resistant plants were necessary. Simple irrigation, better strains of plants, and cattle breeding were the probable solutions developed by the early settlers of Çatal Hüyük. Equipped with these subsistence resources, they produced agricultural returns from the Konya Plain far exceeding those produced by dry farming in the hill country. Perhaps the agricultural activities were so successful that a segment of the community was freed from subsistence activities for a substantial part of the year and could pursue the obsidian trade and time-consuming craft production. With an effective subsistence base and additional economic activities, the population grew. Relaxation of culturally imposed limits on fertility and increasing longevity might have accompanied the economic surpluses. In addition, Çatal Hüyük would have been a great attraction to people from small rural communities who came in contact with its relative opulence. The reasons for twentieth-century rural populations flocking to big cities probably had parallels in the time of Çatal Hüyük. The difference between Çatal Hüyük and its contemporaries was great—in terms of size, sophistication of material inventory, opportunities for employment, and general excitement.

Given that Çatal Hüyük was a community with an efficient subsistence base, a lively series of other economic activities, and a rapidly growing population, basic organizational changes were necessary to maintain the stability of the community. Throughout the period of the rise of civilization, human groups created diverse methods for regulating community activities. The need for these regulating mechanisms and their complexity increased as communities expanded. Not only were they necessary for the organization of economic activities, but also for the use that people made of the environment. So long as the basic economic unit was a single family and the size of the community was small enough so that all interaction was on a personal level, the organizational mechanisms could also have been on a personal level. In small-scale communities, regulation was incorporated as part of the kinship system and the relatively simple religion. However, organizational mechanisms that regulate villages of one or two hundred people are not adequate for maintaining order in a community of several thousand. When a system, such as a prehistoric settlement, increases in size, the natural tendency is for its regulating mechanisms to retain their basic structure while becoming elaborated to accommodate the additional flow of information and the larger constituency. Çatal Hüyük

is an extreme example of this tendency. The primitive rituals that had guided the activities of people living together in a village and had helped to create bonds between individual families were increased and elaborated at Çatal Hüyük to accommodate the tenfold increase in its size. To organize a system that had increased tenfold, the mechanisms for regulating organization and flow of information would have had to increase more than tenfold. Hence, it is not surprising that extraordinary attention was given to ritualism and that rooms whose functions were ritualistic were abundant.

There are two possible outcomes of such growth as that undergone by Çatal Hüyük: either the organizing institutions and regulating mechanisms continue to be elaborated, becoming more complex as the system increases in size until a point is reached at which further elaboration is impossible and the system can no longer accommodate the population and subsequently breaks down; or new forms of organization and regulation develop, which at first supplement the older forms of organization and later replace them. At Çatal Hüyük, the outcome was the first alternative. The site was ultimately abandoned and its successors, both in the Konya Plain and in other parts of Anatolia, lived in smaller communities without some of the economic complexities of Çatal Hüyük. Cultural systems for which the outcome was the second alternative could sustain major growth and internal change, producing a stable system at a new scale of complexity. This is what happened in lowland Mesopotamia, and it eventually led to state society.

If the people of Çatal Hüyük had initiated new organizational institutions to regulate their larger community by introducing mechanisms leading to simplification rather than continual elaboration, the earliest urban civilization in the Near East might have been centered in highland Anatolia rather than in lowland Mesopotamia. However, their potential for further growth and stability may have been restricted by other circumstances: the Konya Plain was a clearly circumscribed area of smaller extent and less agricultural potential than the Mesopotamian Plain. Furthermore, for trade and industry to succeed on a large scale, an economic center must have large markets for its goods: Çatal Hüyük was almost alone in its massive size, and the economies of surrounding villages were self-sufficient and did not rely on externally produced goods. Hence, although the vacant ecological niche of the Konya Plain and the subsistence innovations the people of Çatal Hüyük used to occupy the area were sufficient to initiate a period of rapid growth, the physical environment, cultural setting, and organizational innovations of Çatal Hüyük were not adequate to sustain and eventually stabilize this growth at the level of urban complexity. It is interesting to postulate how many developments similar to that of Çatal Hüyük remain undiscovered or unrecognized. A popular notion is that the rise of civilization was a cumulative and uninterrupted process of growth in community size and complexity. Contrary to this notion, Çatal Hüyük exemplifies those communities that may have made many of the crucial advances leading to civilization, but for one reason or another did not become urban societies. In some ways, the town of Çatal Hüyük and its inhabitants should be considered a premature flash of brilliance and complexity that was a thousand years before its time.

Other Anatolian Sites

The period of time represented by the upper levels of Çatal Hüyük and immediately following is known from a number of smaller Anatolian sites. A sister mound, Çatal Hüyük West, has not been excavated, but surface finds suggest that it might be the immediate successor to the main site. Other Anatolian sites that follow closely in time are Çan Hasan near the town of Karaman, Erbaba near Beysehir, and Hacilar near Burdur. The occupations of all three of these sites are dated at the second half of the sixth millennium; they were villages of modest size whose architecture was of stone and mud; and food production was the basis of their economics. Of the three, Hacilar is the best known, having produced a material inventory that is aesthetically attractive, if not revolutionary.

The sixth-millennium deposits on the mound of Hacilar cover an area of about 100 meters in diameter and include about thirteen building levels (Mellaart 1970), the most important of which are level 6, dated at about 5400 B.C., and levels 1 and 2, dated at about 5200 B.C. The mud-brick buildings of level 6 were large rectangular units built on stone foundations. The community was small, having a central courtyard and a wall encircling the entire compound. The preservation of materials from this level is excellent owing to a fire that swept the community. It seems that the entire settlement was composed of a dozen large buildings as much as 10 by 6 meters in size, with walls 1 meter thick. Because of the fire, certain architectural details were preserved, such as evidence of room dividers made of plastered matting and a flight of steps presumably leading to a second story. The level 6 occupation was characterized by well-baked, burnished monochrome pottery with a small proportion of painted vessels. Chipped stone tools were made of a local flint, and a small proportion of them were of obsidian from central Anatolia. Bone tools and several antler hafts for flint blades also have been recovered.

The most remarkable finds in this level are naturalistically modeled, baked-clay figurines. Most of them are representations of voluptuous women. The only representations of human males are as consorts or children of the women. The female figurines are large, as much as 25 centimeters tall, and are modeled in a variety of positions. The sensitivity in modeling and the diversity of forms reveal a degree of creativity not theretofore seen in the plastic arts.

The upper levels of Hacilar are dated from about 5200 to 5000 B.C. and only a part of the community is preserved. It was composed of large mud and stone buildings, and the two upper building levels were surrounded by what seems to be a fortification wall. The painted pottery from these levels is notable for its quality of execution and aesthetic appeal. Most of it is painted red on a cream background, and the designs are for the most part geometric. The proportion of bowls to jars is roughly equal, and decorated molded relief is common. In the latest levels, there are a few jars that are anthropomorphous in shape, and animal shapes appear throughout all the ceramic levels. The figurines from the later levels are of burnished clay; most are painted, but they are not as impressive as those of the previous period (level 6).

The economy of sixth-millennium Hacilar is not completely known, but it probably was a fully agricultural community. Carbonized remains of domestic emmer, einkorn, bread wheat, naked barley, peas, bitter vetch, and collected acorns have been recovered (Helbaek 1970). Insufficient animal bones have been analyzed to determine whether the cattle, sheep, goat, and pig bones found were from domesticated species. Nevertheless, it is most probable that the people at Hacilar were herding these animals.

The remains of the community at Hacilar record what was in some ways typical of what was happening throughout the Near East. The modal settlement size did not increase significantly beyond that in early villages. The economy became more dependent on food production. The diversity and yield of the domestic resources were improving. The number of settlements in all regions probably increased. Ritual practices and means of symbolic communication were becoming more complex and more important. The figurines and finely painted pottery were probably elements in this process. The increased means of symbolic communication was largely a result of the increasing quantity of information that had to be transmitted even in these relatively small communities. The economic innovations and incipient forms of organization did not lead to obvious changes in society. Rather, they laid the foundation for the rapid growth in community size, which subsequently led to urban society.

The Growth of Villages in the Zagros Foothills and the Peopling of Mesopotamia

The general pattern that can be discerned from the evidence found in the Zagros Mountains and their foothills is one of continued occupation by increasing numbers of people. With the improvement in the effectiveness of domesticates and certain technological inventions, such as pottery, the communities in this region developed a more effective economic base than that of the earliest farmers. There was growth in population, but the average size of communities was not significantly larger than that of the ancestral early villages; that is, from 100 to 200 people. Architecture became more substantial and the artifactual inventory more complex than those of earlier villages; however, for the most part the changing lifeways of the mountain folk are not central to our study of civilization because the focus of development moved to lower elevations and out onto the Mesopotamian Plain.

During the sixth millennium, the area of settlement in the Zagros foothills was enlarged to include the land at lower elevations, close to the alluvial plain. The first steps toward the colonization of lowland Mesopotamia, taken at the beginning of that millenium, were not rapid, for it took many generations to develop crops and animals that could endure the heat and aridity of the lowlands. Thus, the initial expansion was limited to areas of possible, although unreliable, rainfall. Subsequently, with the aid of primitive irrigation systems, settlers moved into areas that had theretofore been uninhabitable by agriculturists.

Advanced Village Communities

At the beginning of the sixth millennium, most communities were manufacturing pottery decorated with incision or painting. Pottery is the most common artifact recovered by archeologists from sites of this period, and the characterization and chronological ordering of archeological sites is often directly related to the pottery produced by its inhabitants. Similarities in technology and in painting styles are interpreted by archeologists to be proof of contemporaneity and even of contact between the makers. It is commonly assumed that, if groups shared a distinctive style of pottery, they shared other things as well, and hence they are referred to as a distinct "culture." Absolute means of dating are important, but the primary basis for the relative chronology of Near Eastern sites is pottery, supplemented by other aspects of the material inventory. The assumed cultural groups are named after the site at which the pottery was first adequately defined. The assumption that pottery style is an indicator of cultural groups is an oversimplification, but it serves as a useful classificatory tool in the absence of more appropriate measures.

The remainder of the preliterate settlements discussed in this book, then, are classified according to the cultural groupings assumed from similarities in manufacturing and decorative techniques. The unit of interpretation and comparison is no longer the individual archeological site, but the groups of sites or levels within a site that share a particular pottery style. However, there are definite limitations to relying entirely on pottery for classification, because many factors affect the design and manufacture of ceramic vessels. Choices of raw materials, functions to be performed, manufacturing techniques, and learning behavior of the potters affect the final product. Former assumptions that people who used one type of pottery were of the same racial or linguistic group have been discredited. Different pottery styles have been found to have been in use at the same time in the same region, such as the Hassunan, Halafian, and Samarran pottery styles that will be discussed in this section. Despite the theoretical shortcomings of the pottery-culture interpretive framework characteristic of past work in Near Eastern archeology, the introduction of pottery and the systems that have been created to classify it have given the archeologist a powerful tool. The relative chronologies of various regions have been refined on the basis of ceramic studies, and so dating is more accurate than that which can be accomplished for preceramic sites using carbon-14 alone. Hence, it is possible to undertake complex analyses, using pottery as a sensitive indicator of interaction between communities.

The widespread use of well-fired pottery was early in the communities of the Zagros range. Pottery has been found in level 3 of Tepe Guran, level D of Ganj Dareh, the beginning of Tepe Sarab, the

upper levels of Jarmo, and the beginning of Tell Shimshara. This means that by about 6500 B.C. at Tepe Guran and Ganj Dareh, and by 6000 B.C. at the other sites, pottery was a common artifact. Coarse monochrome vessels were the earliest known, but they were soon followed by simply painted vessels of improved workmanship.

Among the earliest pottery, a painted ware has been found at several different sites in relatively similar form. Designs resembling tadpoles painted in red on buff-colored background are common on sherds from Jarmo, Guran, Sarab, and other early ceramic communities (Figure 6-4, page 190). So there is evidence for communication and standardized decorative techniques even by 6000 B.C. The mechanisms for communication may have been of many forms, such as the obsidian trading network. The distribution of similar pottery styles in addition to other items of the cultural inventory is strong evidence in support of a common pool of ideas. The exchange of information, as well as the exchange of goods, increased with the growth of civilization.

Hassunan Communities

One of the first regions to be colonized by agriculturalists using hardy domestic plants and animals was the northern section of the Mesopotamian Plain, especially the area later called Assyria (refer to Figure 2-1 on page 20). Most of this region is within the Piedmont environmental zone and is composed of undulating hills cut by rivers and seasonal wadis. The 200-millimeter rainfall isohyet cuts across this territory; hence, part of Assyria was suitable for agriculture that depended on natural precipitation and part of it was too dry.

The first sixth-millennium site to be excavated in northern Mesopotamia was Hassuna, located 14 kilometers south of the modern city of Mosul, Iraq (Lloyd and Safar 1945). The mound is approximately 200 by 150 meters and contains occupational residues of several distinct communities. The material inventory includes pottery representing the three major cultural-chronological groupings discussed in this section: Hassunan, Samarran,

Figure 6-4
"Tadpole style" potsherds from
Jarmo (A) and Tepe Sarab (B).
(Photographs from the Prehistoric
Project of The Oriental Institute,
The University of Chicago.)

A   B

and Halafian. Although the site of Hassuna yielded all three types of pottery and is the site after which Hassunan ware was named, subsequent excavations at other sites have produced more detailed and complete evidence of each type.

The lowest level of the Hassuna deposits yielded traces of three distinct superimposed campsites, with no evidence of substantial structural remains (level 1a). The pottery from the three encampments consisted almost exclusively of large, coarse, straw-tempered storage vessels. The next occupation levels offered evidence of a different type of community: they contain substantial houses composed of rectangular rooms with walls of pressed mud (tauf) grouped around a courtyard. Domestic activities seemed to be carried out both inside the buildings and in the courtyard where ovens and grain bins were found (Figure 6-5). The buildings were arranged contiguously, with common walls between them. The well-developed architecture and complex plans contrast sharply with the lack of buildings in the earliest deposits.

Good examples of settled agricultural communities are recorded in the later levels at Hassuna, although the excavations were conducted before the recovery and identification of plant and animal remains had become a regular excavation procedure. Because of the dissected nature of the local terrain and low level of the river in relation to the land, irrigation was probably not used near Hassuna nor in most parts of Assyria. What the economy of the earliest communities at Hassuna was remains an unanswered question. Whether the

first occupation was by a semisedentary group or was simply a small settlement that required time to develop into the fully successful later communities is difficult to determine from the available evidence.

Along with the evidence for architecture, the levels above the first occupation contained large amounts of pottery. Three different pottery types characterized the Hassunan settlements: archaic painted, standard painted, and standard incised ware. The proportions of the three types found in the levels at Hassuna varied (Figure 6-6, page 192), as they did at several other, more recently excavated sites. The sites of Matarrah (Braidwood et al., 1952, and Figure 6-7, page 192), Yarim Tepe (Merpert and Munchajev 1969), Telul eth-Thalathat (Fukai, Horiuchi, and Matsutani 1970), and Umm Dabaghiyah (Kirkbride 1972) contain pottery resembling the Hassunan wares. Indications are that at each of these sites there are levels containing material contemporary with that of Hassuna level 1a and earlier, and, hence, each overlaps and predates the occupation at Hassuna.

Umm Dabaghiyah is the best known of these sites, having been excavated almost in its entirety (Kirkbride 1972; 1973a; 1973b; 1974; 1975). It is the southernmost of a group of early prehistoric sites located in the northcentral part of the Jezireh, between the Tigris and Euphrates rivers. Although the other sites have not yet been excavated, their surface yields and the excavated material from Umm Dabaghiyah demonstrate that this area was settled by agriculturists as early as 6000 B.C. and

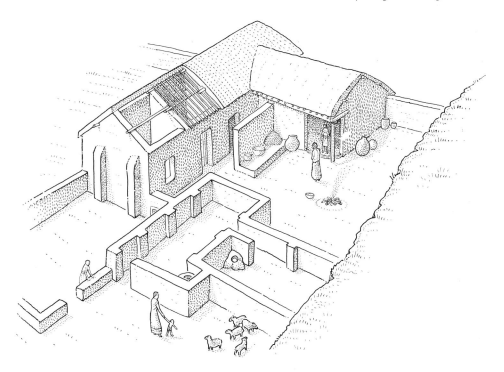

Figure 6-5
Isometric reconstruction of what a house at Hassuna (level 4) might have looked like. (The Oriental Institute, The University of Chicago.)

supported scattered small farming villages then much as it does today. The amount of land on which reliable rainfall agriculture can be practiced seems to be approximately the same now as it was during Hassunan times because the distribution of contemporary and sixth-millennium communities extends about the same distance south.

The excavator, Diana Kirkbride, suggests that the first inhabitants of Umm Dabaghiyah came from the region to the north and northwest, perhaps from the general vicinity south of Çayönü. Umm Dabaghiyah was a settlement on the margin of a more settled region in the better-watered uplands. The general growth of population in the earlier settled regions and the suggested movements of peoples during the sixth millennium encouraged the colonization of areas that had not yet been occupied. It is difficult to assess whether it was pressure from a growing population, an attempt to procure valuable local resources, or simply a desire to move into an unoccupied land that drew the people of the uplands down onto the hot and dry plain. Perhaps some of them realized the possible productivity in these areas, or maybe it was only a refuge for them. Whatever the case, the moves were made and important processes had begun.

Umm Dabaghiyah is a small mound about 100 by 85 meters, with a depth of cultural debris of 4 meters. Twelve building levels have been identified by Kirkbride, with pottery being an important part of the inventory from the beginning. The occupation was contemporary with the earliest levels at Hassuna and probably began earlier (first half of the sixth millennium). The architecture throughout the site is of packed mud, or tauf, without stone foundations. Most of the structures had plastered

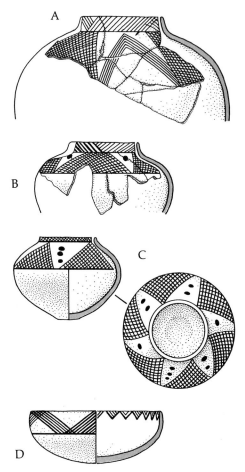

Figure 6-6
Standard painted Hassunan pottery from the site of Hassuna. (The Oriental Institute, The University of Chicago.)

Figure 6-7
Tauf foundations of a rectilinear building at Matarrah. (Photograph from the Prehistoric Project of The Oriental Institute, The University of Chicago.)

floors and walls. The earliest settlers at Umm Dabaghiyah built small, roughly curved structures that would seem to have been too small for habitation; they may have been storage bins or parching ovens. The next level contained substantial buildings made of tauf that were organized around large courtyards. Although the arrangement and details of buildings changed during the major occupation of Umm Dabaghiyah (levels 4 and 3), two primary building types can be described.

The structures that are thought to have been residential are located in the western and southern

sections of the site (Figure 6-8). A common house-plan was of two or three rooms arranged in a straight line: a living room, a kitchen, and another room of unspecified use. Often the southernmost room contained an oven; a chimney was built outside, against an exterior wall with an opening through the wall. The floors were of thick gypsum plaster and had depressions in them that may have been used for food preparation. The walls had niches that may have served as bins for food or tinder. The rooms were small, averaging only 1.5 by 2.0 meters, and the doorways were tiny, only 0.50 meters wide and 0.75 meters high. There are traces of steps and toe-holds in a few walls, which suggests that the primary means of entering buildings was through their roofs. The excavators found paint on the floors, as well as fragments of wall frescoes that seem to be part of an onager hunting scene.

The organization and uniformity of the large buildings located in the middle and in the northeastern part of Umm Dabaghiyah give the impression of having been built as single units and probably for nonresidential activities (Figure 6-8). These buildings comprise more than seventy small chambers (1.5 by 1.7 meters) arranged in two or three long rows. There are few doorways between these cells, their floors are of only hardened earth, their thick walls are not plastered, and they are

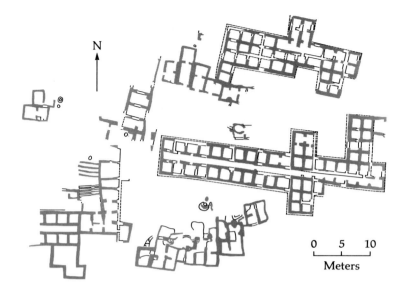

N

Figure 6-8
Plan of architecture uncovered in levels 3 and 4 at Umm Dabaghiyah. (After Kirkbride, 1975.)

0   5   10

Meters

thought to have been storerooms, for most of them lack hearths and significant contents. One chamber contained 2,400 baked clay sling missiles and about 100 large baked clay balls, apparently an ´arsenal used for large-game hunting.

The buildings in the uppermost levels were not as well built, although a large mud-brick courtyard was constructed. The artifacts in these levels were less varied than those in the earlier levels, creating an overall impression that the community underwent a period of decline toward its end.

Although the analysis of subsistence resources is not complete, the preliminary results have shown that Umm Dabaghiyah was to an extent an agricultural community relying on cultivated emmer, einkorn wheat, and barley, as well as on domesticated sheep, goats, cattle, and pigs (Helbaek 1972; Bökönyi 1973). However, hunting was apparently a more important activity, onager having been the most popular source of meat. The reliance on onagers (68 percent of the bones found) and to a lesser extent gazelle (16 percent) for food and on their hides for trading may have been the primary reason that these early villagers settled on the relatively dry piedmont. Kirkbride suggests that the small number of inhabitants of Umm Dabaghiyah,

perhaps only six families, were engaged in trading animal hides to a larger community elsewhere, receiving in return the agricultural products found in the excavations. If this community was a permanent trading outpost organized for the benefit of a powerful central community, then the current concepts of the self-sufficiency and interaction of communities of this period must be reevaluated.

The chipped stone industry of Umm Dabaghiyah exhibits similarities to the sites of both the Zagros and the Levant. Raw materials for flint and obsidian artifacts had to have been imported and, hence, the inhabitants seem to have used every piece, even the small flakes. Few pieces were finely worked or are identifiable as distinct tool types. Arrowheads similar to those found in the Levant were recovered, as were small quantities of blades, scrapers, and borers. In general, the chipped stone tools found are well made, but not exceptional, and probably most closely resemble those found at sites to the west and northwest.

Bone tools were common and were characterized by well-made awls, points, and spatulas. Polished stone axes and adzes of basalt and a fine green stone are part of the inventory, as are shell and stone beads. Spindle whorls, both flat and conical,

made of gypsum have been found. Clay figurines
of women have been recovered, but all are incomplete. All the figurines were found in the lower
levels and inside houses. The shapes are rounded
and one elegant example has a concave base, as
though it had been made to fit on some sort of seat.

Pottery was the most abundant artifact at Umm
Dabaghiyah. Thick and medium coarse wares predominated, although finer wares were present. The
clay was heavily chaff and straw tempered, with a
mixture of grits in some cases. All vessels were
handmade and most show the coils from which
they were constructed. A slip, usually cream or
white, was used for the medium and finer wares.
These wares are examples of an early stage in the
pottery-making craft and exhibit experimentation,
especially in the application of design. There are
four distinct types of decoration: burnishing, painting, applique, and incision. Most of the vessels are
undecorated and simple in shape, many having
rounded carination. The basic color for the painted
wares was red ochre but, after firing, the color assumed a variety of shades. Among design motifs,
dots, circles, snakelike squiggles, commas, and
ticks are most prevalent, plus a variety of linear
effects with straight lines. Applied decoration was
common on the pottery of all levels. In addition to
functional items, such as lugs and knobs, there
were decorative forms of human eyes and ears,
ram's heads, snakes, crescents, and one fine-horned
head.

Sites with Hassunan pottery are distributed
throughout the upper Tigris River Valley and on
the plains north and south of Jebel Sinjar to the
west of the modern city of Mosul. These regions
are part of the Assyrian Plain, which was composed
of piedmont and semiarid uplands where agriculture could have been successful without having
to resort to irrigation in most years. Sites with
Hassunan pottery are rare in the highland regions,
where the earliest village agriculture had been
undertaken 1,000 years earlier. There are also no
Hassunan sites at lower elevations on the Mesopotamian alluvium itself. The economy was based
on well-developed agricultural practices, but there
is no evidence for substantial irrigation or for

varieties of plants and animals able to withstand
the rigors of the lower altitudes. Many of the
Hassunan sites may not have been completely
sedentary communities. The frequency of years
during which rainfall was inadequate forced communities to leave their fields and move upland, or
to rely heavily on their herds and to graze them in
better summer pasturelands. This nomadic element
may have been restricted to only a part of the community, and it may have been necessary only every
few years. Until irrigation allowed a more dependable supply of food, the necessity of returning to
a more nomadic existence threatened the inhabitants of the Mesopotamian basin.

Samarran Communities

In the middle and later levels of Hassuna, a finely
painted, well-made pottery was found. This type
of pottery had already been named Samarran after
the site at which it was originally discovered.
Several years ago, there was controversy among
archeologists about whether Samarran ware represented the pottery of a separate group of people or
was the luxury ware of people who also used the
somewhat plainer Hassunan pottery. Since the discovery and excavation of other sites yielding
Samarran pottery, it is believed that this pottery
type characterizes a separate group of people
whose lifeways were distinct from those of the
people who made Hassunan pottery. Sites with
Samarran pottery were found throughout a large
area on the northern fringes of the Mesopotamian
alluvium, largely in regions theretofore uninhabited by agriculturists. The distribution of their
settlements extended from the Zagros piedmont
northeast of Baghdad to the middle Euphrates of
Syria, and reached as far north as Mosul on the
Tigris. The communities varied in size and character, but in general were substantial villages or small
towns with well-made mud-brick architecture. The
most distinctive aspect of their material assemblage
was the handsome and intricately painted pottery,
including shapes not formerly used, such as plates
(Figure 6-9).

The society originally responsible for Samarran
pottery has become better known through the re-

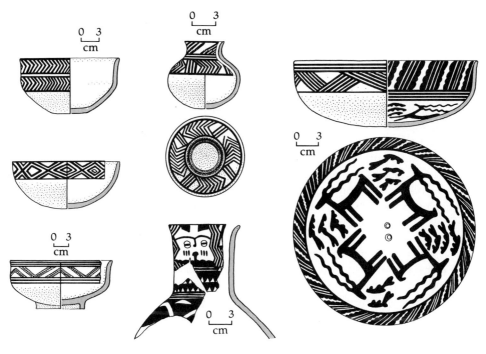

Figure 6-9
Painted Samarran ware from the site of Hassuna. (The Oriental Institute,
The University of Chicago.)

cent excavation of two Samarran settlements: Tell es-Sawwan (Abu al-Soof 1968b), situated on a bluff on the east bank of the Tigris River, and Choga Mami (Oates 1968), near Mandali at the foot of the Zagros Mountains (refer to Figure 6-2). One of the most interesting discoveries made at these two sites concerns their economy. Whereas Hassunan sites were located within an area where dry farming was regularly successful, the Samarran sites were located to the south, on the margin and outside of the dependable dry-farming zone. Tell es-Sawwan, Samarra on the Tigris, and especially Baghouz in Syria were situated in areas where dry farming was possible but was not adequate as a regular basis of support. Other Samarran sites, such as Choga Mami, were in regions where dry farming was possible in most years.

The botanical evidence recovered from the excavation of both Tell es-Sawwan and Choga Mami attests to the practice of irrigation by at least the middle of the sixth millennium (Helbaek 1964a; 1972). In the Mandali area, where Choga Mami is located, the Samarran sites are along low contours parallel to the nearby hills and at right angles to the natural flow of water into the plain. It is known that by the fifth millennium there was a canal along this line, and smaller channels, probably for irrigation, were found at Choga Mami. At both Tell es-Sawwan and Choga Mami, emmer, bread wheat, naked six-row barley, and hulled two-row barley have been identified by Hans Helbaek, in addition to considerable quantities of linseed. Linseed is a crop that probably could not have been grown in such a climate without artificial watering. This is also true of bread wheat and naked six-row barley, but the poor size of these grains makes it improbable that regular canalization had been instituted at that time. Because of this, Helbaek suggests that irrigation was by means of the seasonal flooding of the fields. If this technique were used, then irrigation would have been feasible on the river floodplain below Tell es-Sawwan.

At Choga Mami, the physical configuration was ideal for an early canal system because the site lies on a triangle of land between two rivers. The higher river provided a head of water and the lower river a natural drainage outlet. This was similar to the layout of the lower Tigris-Euphrates basin, but in miniature. The problems of drainage and salinization were partly eliminated by the sharp difference in land levels—and consequent rapid flow of water—that resulted from Choga Mami's position on an alluvial fan at the base of the Zagros foothills. Because the topography facilitated irrigation in the Choga Mami region, it was used there at a very early date. Subsequent improvements in irrigation technology allowed farming communities to move even further into regions that had until that time been ecologically hostile to farmers.

The faunal evidence from Choga Mami suggests fully developed domestication of cattle, sheep, goats, pigs, and dogs. At Tell es-Sawwan, fish and freshwater mussels were an important source of food. At both sites, the hunting of onagers, gazelle, aurochs, and fallow deer continued. The subsistence activities practiced by the inhabitants of these sites included a reliance on hunted and collected resources, but in general the Samarrans were highly advanced farmers.

Other aspects of the Samarran communities reveal that their inhabitants had acquired technological and organizational skills (Oates 1973). Tell es-Sawwan and Choga Mami were relatively large sites compared with those of earlier villagers. Choga Mami covered about 6 hectares and may have been inhabited by more than a thousand people. At Tell es-Sawwan (Figure 6-10), a ditch and wall surrounded part of the site, whereas, at Choga Mami, a tower guarded the only excavated entrance to the settlement. At both sites, the entrances required a bent-axis approach to the interior. This arrangement forced an attacker to traverse a longer entrance while being exposed to missiles hurled from the tops of adjacent walls. That they designed the gates in this manner is further evidence of the Samarran's concern with defense.

The buildings in each of these Samarran sites exhibit a regularity of plan, T-shaped at Tell es-Sawwan and rectangular at Choga Mami. Each building consists of many small rooms. The larger buildings had external buttressing at the corners and at wall junctions, perhaps to support roof beams (Figure 6-10). The use of buttresses became widespread in Mesopotamia during the fifth and fourth millennia. Buttressing was initially used in Mesopotamia as a structural element, but it later became a nonfunctional convention in religious structures.

Sun-dried bricks were used in construction for the first time in Mesopotamia at Choga Mami and Tell es-Sawwan (they were employed earlier in the uplands at Ganj Dareh and Çayönü). This technique contrasts with the exclusive use of tauf at such contemporary villages as Matarrah, Hassuna, and Yarim Tepe. Sun-dried bricks have the advantage of greater durability and strength than tauf, allowing larger buildings to be constructed than can be built of tauf. At Choga Mami, these bricks were long, cigar-shaped, and laid alternately along and across the axis of a wall.

Several kinds of data can be interpreted to be indicative of further development of the concept of property rights during Samarran times. Buildings were built directly on the ruined foundations of earlier buildings, a practice that developed during the early-village time range. The appearance of seals for stamping impressions at both Hassunan and Samarran sites, as well as at other advanced villages, might be interpreted as a concern for ownership, especially in the exchange or communal storage of goods. The new but widespread use of potters' marks is an indication of the increasing importance of craft activities and the sense of professionalism that might have accompanied the transfer of manufacturing activities from individual households to specialized manufacturing groups.

The presence of necessary surplus wealth to carry on nonsubsistence activities was further demonstrated at Samarran sites, especially at Tell es-Sawwan. At Tell es-Sawwan, beneath several unusually large buildings in the earliest community

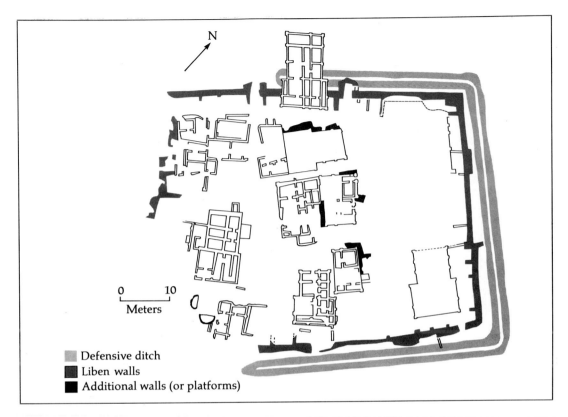

N

0   10
Meters

Defensive ditch
Liben walls
Additional walls (or platforms)

Figure 6-10
Plan of excavated remains of substantial walled community at Tell
es-Sawwan. (Courtesy of the Director General of Antiquities, Baghdad, Iraq.)

level, were found a large number of graves—many
of them burials of small infants—that contained an
extraordinary collection of objects. The buildings
may have had a religious significance that was
directly related to the richly adorned burials found
beneath them. Ground stone alabaster statuettes of
women (Figure 6-11, page 198) and handsome
alabaster bowls accompanied the burials. The alabaster figurines foreshadowed those made by the
early Sumerians during the third millennium.
There were numerous reasons for including valuable goods with burials (Ucko 1969; Brown 1971),
but in general it indicated a person's wealth or
status: a possible explanation for their presence in
the graves of infants is that the society was organized according to ascribed rank. In other words,
some families controlled more wealth than did

others, and age was only secondary in acquiring
high rank. The general implication is that Tell
es-Sawwan's social system was characterized by a
growing emphasis on social stratification.

In addition to the alabaster figurines, Samarran
sites have yielded a variety of baked-clay figurines,
which vary from site to site. Certain traits were
common to most of these figurines, such as the use
of "coffee bean" eyes, elongated headdresses, and
appliquéd necklaces. The figurines from Choga
Mami and some of the early examples found at
Tell es-Sawwan are quite naturalistic, resembling
later pieces from Mesopotamia of the 'Ubaid period, whereas pieces from the Samarran levels of
Yarim Tepe include figurines of women wearing
"flounced" skirts and having unusual "stalky
heads" (Oates 1973).

Figure 6-11
Stone statuette with inlay from Tell es-Sawwan.
(Courtesy of the Director General of Antiquities,
Baghdad, Iraq.)

A few pieces of hammered copper at Samarran
sites are the earliest metal objects found in Mesopotamia, but they are much later than the earliest
examples of hammered copper found at Çayönü.
Their presence is further evidence of the trading
network in which these communities participated,
because Tell es-Sawwan is far from sources of
copper in either Iran or Turkey.

Samarran sites are distributed across Mesopotamia roughly in a band north of Baghdad and
south of the rain-fed lands generally occupied by
the people who made Hassunan pottery. Samarran
pottery is also found further to the north on sites

that are otherwise Hassunan. There are several
ways of interpreting its presence at these northern
sites: it could represent a temporary intrusion or
an active trading network, or it could be that the
southern pottery was imitated by northern craftsmen. At any rate, there was a relationship between
the people who made Hassunan pottery and those
who made Samarran pottery. They were basically
contemporaneous groups who were organized into
established farming communities. They spread
into the lower foothills and plains, both because of
population growth in the uplands and because land
and resources were available at the lower elevations. It is likely that the people who occupied the
Samarran sites were pushed out of the higher land
where Hassunan sites were already reaching a high
density. The Samarrans colonized the lower areas,
first along the major rivers and their tributaries
and then branching out as their ability to deal with
the environment improved. The main innovation
that allowed these people to inhabit hot and dry
regions was their use of irrigation and of heat-
resistant varieties of plants. It was because of this
use of irrigation and their movement to lower
elevations that the Samarrans played a crucial role
in subsequent developments. The three positive-
feedback relationships discussed at the beginning
of this chapter were fully activated by the Samarrans. This led to the major advances of the people
of lowland Mesopotamia, of which the Samarrans
were among the early colonizers.

Halafian Communities

Following the Hassunan occupations in northern
Mesopotamia and overlapping in time with late
Samarran sites was the widespread cultural inventory known as Halafian (c. 5500–4800 B.C.). This
assemblage was distinguished by its handsome
painted pottery, circular buildings, and variety of
characteristic beads and amulets.

There were several important developments
associated with the period during which Halafian
pottery was used. The Samarrans and Halafians
maintained separate cultural traditions, but there
is ample evidence of contact. The Halafians were

heirs to the region where most Hassunan sites existed, including areas further to the west and north. The important innovation of the Halafians was not technological, economic, or demographic: they lived by basically the same economy as that of their predecessors, their technology had not measurably improved, and their communities were no larger. The major difference was in terms of social interaction and organization. For the first time in the Near East, there was a widespread cultural horizon. This horizon was defined by an amazing similarity of painted pottery motifs (80–90 percent of the sherds from any given Halafian site would not be out of place at any other Halafian site), the distinctive architectural styles common to all Halafian sites, and the similarities in small objects (LeBlanc and Watson 1973). The similarities are greater than any that have been demonstrated for earlier times and yet the distances are great, as much as 550 kilometers between the extreme locations of sites recognized as fully Halafian.

A number of factors may have been responsible for the spread of the Halafian traits and the presumed interaction between Halafian communities. Watson and LeBlanc (1973) suggest that their social organization changed from a tribal organization to a chiefdom. This required greater communication between elite groups of different communities and encouraged the sharing and imitation of status goods, such as the painted pottery. Their interpretation is that the various Halafian sites represented internally different cultures that had incorporated a set of common attributes.

Although the Halafian painted pottery style was first identified at Tell Halaf, in northern Syria, the assemblage is best known from the subsequent excavations at Arpachiyah, northeast of the modern city of Mosul in northern Iraq (Mallowan and Rose 1935a; 1935b). The mound of Arpachiyah is about 125 meters in diameter and contains 8 meters of Halafian occupational deposits. Although there is a striking similarity in the painted motifs found on Halafian sherds from many sites, as well as in other distinguishing characteristics, the finest examples of Halafian painted pottery and the largest structures attributable to Halafian settlements were found at Arpachiyah. A peculiarity of Halafian developments is that some of the highest-quality material and most substantial buildings have been found at a site that was no larger than a simple village that probably never had more than two hundred inhabitants.

Circular architecture predominates on Halafian sites, although some rectangular structures have been uncovered. The size of the circular buildings varies from the more numerous small buildings that were from 3 to 4 meters in diameter to the very large examples found at Arpachiyah that were from 7 to 9 meters across. The thickness of the walls also varied with the size of the buildings. None of the walls at the more impoverished Halafian site of Girikihaciyan in southeastern Anatolia exceeded 0.5 meter, whereas some of the larger buildings at Arpachiyah had walls more than 1 meter thick. In addition to stone foundations, the building materials included mud brick (at Tepe Gawra in northern Iraq) and tauf (at Arpachiyah), both being topped by reed or wood superstructures. Many of the round buildings had rectangular antechambers attached to them and are referred to as tholoi because their characteristic "keyhole" design is similar to that employed much later in the construction of burial tombs in the Aegean (c. 1200 B.C.), a fact that has led to some highly speculative discussions of cultural contact.

The well-made, thin-walled Halafian painted pottery included new and distinctive shapes (Figure 6-12, page 200). The handmade, wet-smoothed, and lightly burnished vessels were in the form of bowls having flared rims, concave sides, or round sides, vessels having small, round mouths, and jars of various profiles (LeBlanc and Watson 1973). Halafian designs were predominantly geometric, but there are some examples of naturalistic ones that incorporated birds, animals, plants, and the famous bucranium, or bull's head with horns. The exterior surface of most Halafian vessels was completely covered by decorations, and many of the bowls were decorated on their interior surfaces as well. The central motif on the interior of a bowl might have been a rosette, a Maltese cross, or a cross composed of bucrania. Although only the

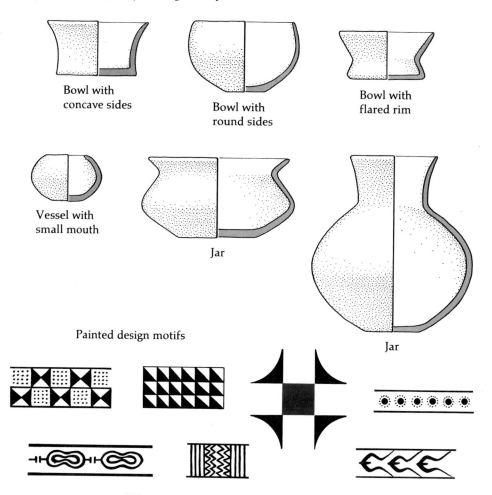

Bowl with
concave sides

Bowl with
round sides

Bowl with
flared rim

Vessel with
small mouth

Jar

Jar

Painted design motifs

Figure 6-12
Painted motifs and standard forms of Halafian pottery. (The Oriental
Institute, The University of Chicago.)

exteriors of jars were decorated, many had painted bands on the inside of the rim. Other common design elements were bands, cross-hatching, zig-zags, triangles, checkerboards, and dots. It is important to realize that not all the vessels used at any Halafian site were painted pottery: at some sites, such as Banahilk, in northern Iraq, and Arpachiyah, the painted ware was in the majority, whereas, at a peripheral site such as Girikihaciyan, it was only a small percentage of the total ceramic industry.

The remainder of the Halafian assemblage included items commonly found at non-Halafian sites, as well as some distinctive objects. The chipped stone tools of flint and obsidian were not particularly different from those in the village assemblages of northern Mesopotamia, with sickle blades, knives, scrapers, and borers predominating. Ground stone mortars, pestles, handstones, querns, and spheres were common, as were polished stone adzes and axes. Small objects of polished stone were more distinctive, such as seals with geometric designs and beads in the form of a double ax.

The economy of the Halafians, especially during their later stages, was clearly that of settled village agriculturalists. Domestic emmer, einkorn wheat, and barley were cultivated and sheep, goats, and cattle were herded. It is possible that the Halafians engaged in the domestication of cattle because cattle are rendered in the artistic artifacts found at Halafian sites. All Halafian sites are within the range of possible dry farming and it is unlikely that irrigation was used.

Models of Community Organization

The established villages of the sixth millennium represent the culmination of the Agricultural Transformation (Stage 4 of Figures 1-6, on page 9, and 4-6, on page 106). Interrelated developments in technology, economy, and settlement had created a successful community form. Although these material developments were crucial to the subsequent rise of civilization, equally significant organizational changes occurred during the sixth millennium. Inferences concerning prehistoric organization must be based on a thorough examination of the archeological record and on assumptions about the organizational achievements revealed in material remains. The patterns observed in the archeological material can be related to concepts developed from ethnographic studies by means of two different but parallel models of organization (Figure 6-13, page 202). The first model was formulated by Morton Fried and centers on mechanisms that societies use to differentiate their members (Fried 1960; 1967). The second model was devised by Elman Service and relates to overall community organization (Service 1962).

Fried's Model for the Evolution of Social Stratification

Fried recognizes four different types of societies in terms of criteria used for differential status: egalitarian, rank, stratified, and state society. Every human society differentiates among its members

and assigns greater or lesser prestige to them according to selected attributes. It is the nature of these attributes and the manner in which the structure is preserved and conveyed that separates one form of society from another. In an *egalitarian* society, the simplest criteria are used: age, sex, and a measure of ability. These criteria have probably been the major axes for the division of labor since earliest times and continue to function to a certain extent in all societies. An important aspect of a criterion such as age is that, whether increasing age means higher or lower status, the opportunity to attain that status is the same for everyone. In other words, the primary means of ascription in an egalitarian society is universal and open to all on an equal basis. Anyone who is of the appropriate sex and manages to live long enough automatically achieves the various statuses. Given the variations in individual skill and the advancement of age, the ascription to any particular status is rather ephemeral. The transient nature of status affects the attitudes of those who have achieved it because strong attachments and personal identification are not likely to develop in a system in which members move automatically from one status to another.

An egalitarian society can be defined as one in which there are as many positions of prestige in any given age-sex classification as there are persons capable of filling them. There is no predetermined number of openings in any particular status position: for example, if there are four young male hunters, then there are four positions; if there are only three such people, then there are only three positions. In other words, there are no limits on the number of people who can hold any particular status nor any limits on their attainment of any status.

A survey of the ethnographic literature on egalitarian societies reveals that they are almost exclusively hunting and gathering bands. The production of goods and procurement of subsistence resources is largely a household matter. Family groups are not specialized, and so each family replicates the same general activities carried out by every other family. Exchange in an egalitarian society is informal and takes place between individuals who be-

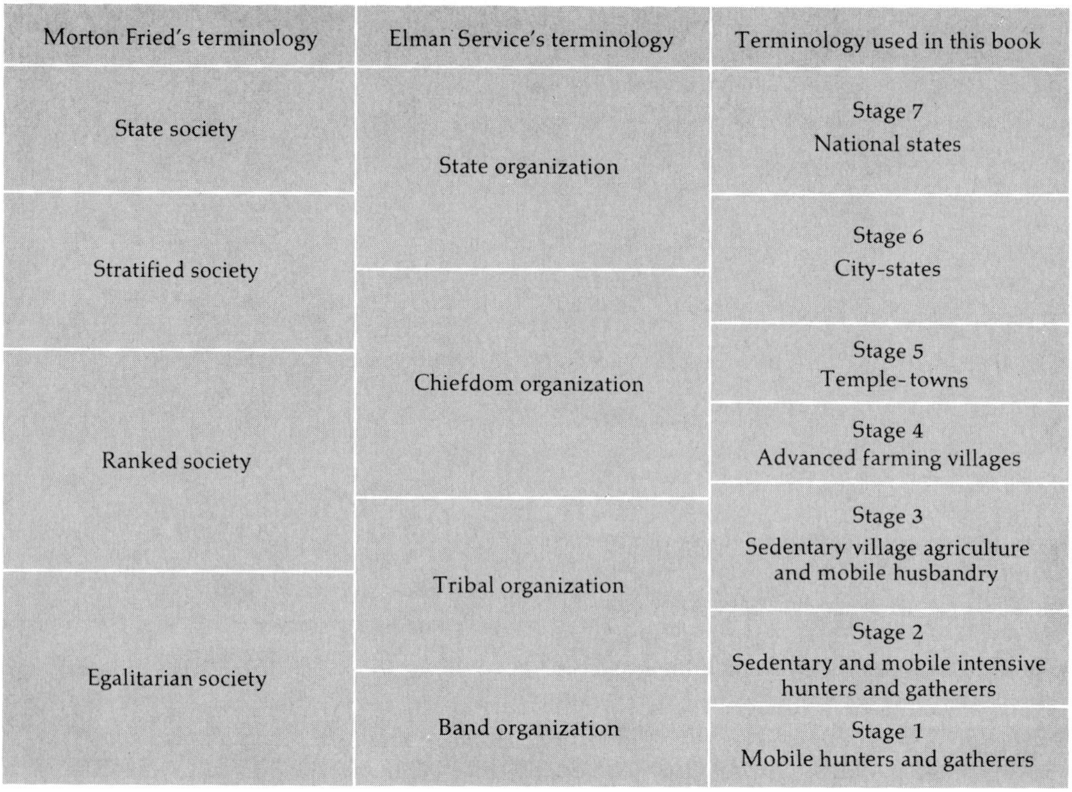

Morton Fried's terminology	Elman Service's terminology	Terminology used in this book
State society	State organization	Stage 7 National states
Stratified society		Stage 6 City-states
	Chiefdom organization	Stage 5 Temple-towns
Ranked society		Stage 4 Advanced farming villages
	Tribal organization	Stage 3 Sedentary village agriculture and mobile husbandry
		Stage 2 Sedentary and mobile intensive hunters and gatherers
Egalitarian society	Band organization	Stage 1 Mobile hunters and gatherers

Figure 6-13
Terminology used by Service and Fried and that used in this book.

long to different, small-scale kin groups. Within the society, the economy is reciprocal, although a balance in exchange of goods may not be attained. Good, or lucky, hunters may always be supplying their less-skilled relatives with more meat than they get in return, but the transient nature of these skills keeps this difference from becoming institutionalized.

The second form of differentiation in Fried's model is a *ranked* society. Because no totally egalitarian human society actually exists, the term rank is used as a relative measure. A ranked society differs from an egalitarian society in the way in which differential prestige is handled. The ranked society places limitations on access to valued status, and these limitations are only indirectly related to sex, age, or personal attributes. Because of these

limitations, ranked societies have fewer positions of valued status than the number of people capable of achieving them. Various techniques are employed for limiting status to certain persons or families, the simplest being dependent on birth order; that is, the firstborn is given the highest status. This can be repeated in succeeding generations, or, alternatively, all descendents of a particular person may hold high status. This can create general status differences between different lineages within the same community.

Whether accomplished by a rule of succession or by some other limiting device, the ranked society as a framework of statuses can be represented by a triangle, the vertex of which represents the leading status. The hierarchy of status positions usually has a very definite economic significance.

Fried suggests that the notion of rank is not inherent in human beings but is caused by economic and other external factors. The transition to a ranked society is often simultaneous with the emergence of a network of redistribution that does not have the family unit as its basis. An essential difference between egalitarian and ranked societies is that egalitarian economics is dominated by reciprocity, whereas a ranked society has redistribution as a major element in its economy. The key status is that held by the central collector of supplies, who also redistributes them. In most ranked societies, there is neither exploitative economic power nor genuine political power; rather, the two kinds of authority that people of high status have are familial and sacred. They do not have access to a privileged use of force; hence, the two methods by which they operate are by setting personal examples of industriousness and by utilizing the principles of reciprocity. A redistributive system may arise for any number of reasons, but its survival and growth are due to its superiority to reciprocal systems in a number of ways: an increase in productivity through specialization, a greater diversity of food resources and material goods, and the stability of redistribution.

A *stratified* society has institutionalized differential relationships among its members with respect to means of subsistence. A ranked society operates on the principle of differential status for members with similar abilities, but these statuses are without privileged economic or political power. In a stratified society, some members have unimpeded access to its strategic resources, whereas access to the same fundamental resources is denied or restricted for others (Fried 1960:721). The emergence of stratification also requires a more formal means of communication and regulation. Whereas, in a ranked society, social control rests on enculturation and internalized sanctions, a stratified society requires a formal statement of legal principles and mechanisms to adjudicate and enforce the rules. The prime authority in society is no longer based on kinships; rather, it is based on territorial groups. Stratification facilitates the increasingly complex divisions of labor that are required in urban so-

cieties. The causes of the emergence of stratification, its effects, and Fried's fourth type of society, state society, are discussed in the next chapter, which treats of the origin of cities.

Service's Model of Levels of Community Organization

Elman Service has given us an alternative model for analyzing changes in the organization of cultures. Four levels of sociocultural integration are defined on the basis of ethnographic information: band, tribe, chiefdom, and state. Each level is an ideal type exhibiting characteristics that result from the differing ways in which interactional problems are solved by a group organized at that level (Service 1962; Sanders and Price 1968). Some scholars have criticized both the general implications and specific details of each level of Service's model—criticisms that are valid if the four levels are conceptualized as being distinct forms that can neatly accommodate all cultures. However, Service's and Fried's models are not used in this book as ideal cultural types: rather, they are simply heuristic tools that facilitate communication and enable us to refine our understanding of organizational changes during the rise of civilization. It is not suggested that levels of organization of archeologically known groups exhibit all the details found in selected ethnographically recorded societies. Nevertheless, a rigorous cross-cultural study of the relations between organizational frameworks and potentially observable archeological remains is crucial for adequate explanations of changing community forms. The models designed by Service and Fried are useful frameworks for studies of organizational changes and social evolution in primitive societies. Certain low-level generalizations can be made that seem to be documented by both ethnographic and archeological investigations. These generalizations imply that the general evolution of social structure has been toward greater size and density of the social body, an increase in the number of groups, greater specialization in the function of groups, and new means of integrating groups (Service 1962:111).

This should not be taken to mean that all cultures pass through Service's four stages or that all groups in a particular region share a similar level of organization. The evidence seems to indicate that organizational evolution in the Near East was neither uniform nor strictly unilineal. Nevertheless, there are overall similarities, and the study of these two models of social organization helps to clarify them.

The simplest level of organization in Service's model is that of *bands*. Bands are small territorial hunting-and-gathering groups that range from 30 to 100 members. They tend to be kin groups of related men or women together with their spouses and unmarried children. Spouses are selected from outside groups and residence is with either the husband's or the wife's relatives, more often with the former. Sex and age are the primary forms of status differentiation. Political organization and economic specialization are normally absent, except as they relate to sex, age, and family. Rarely are there any social techniques for integrating local groups into larger aggregations. The diverse types of hunting-and-gathering economies that support bands necessitate various patterns of nomadism and frequent changes in group size. The band level of organization exhibits Fried's egalitarian form of differentiation.

Service's second level of organization is that of *tribes*. The major development that distinguishes tribes from bands is the creation of techniques to integrate local groups into a larger society. These mechanisms take the form of various sodalities that cross-cut local groups such as clans, associations of people of the same age, secret societies, and warrior and religious societies. Most tribal organizations remain egalitarian in Fried's model and so are horizontally integrated. Tribes usually have agricultural economies, although hunters and gatherers who are sedentary for much of the year may have developed the necessary integrative institutions to be considered tribes. There are no well-developed specialized craft groups nor is there highly organized trade between tribal groups. Warfare consists of ambushes and skirmishes and, if a tribe occupies several settlements, there is no hierarchy in importance of the settlements or

great differences in their sizes—a tribal settlement normally comprises from one hundred to several hundred people. The nature and distribution of tribal societies has been the center of significant controversy: many scholars believe that tribal organization is not an indigenous development but rather a response to neighboring militaristic states. According to this view, tribes exist only on the periphery of civilizations and may never have existed before the advent of civilization.

Service's third level of organization is that of *chiefdoms*. A chiefdom comprises several groups organized into hierarchical social systems. Variation in rank, with the associated privileges and obligations, is the primary technique of social integration. This hierarchical system centers on a single status position, that of the chief, and descent is frequently the primary determinant of the relative positions of different individuals and kin groups. A chiefdom is a well-developed form of Fried's ranked society. It does not have social classes in the modern sense, but some of its members attain social positions that carry with them enhanced power and privilege. There is usually craft specialization, as well as specialization in the production of subsistence resources. Because of this specialization, there is usually a mechanism for the redistribution of goods in which the chief plays an important role. Despite the importance of this role, the chief lacks, for the most part, the true differential access to and control of strategic resources that would constitute social stratification. In addition, the chief lacks formal delineation of power and coercive techniques of political control. His authority is based on the existence of sumptuary rules providing for elaborate ritualistic isolation by regulations of dress, ornamentation, food, and mobility. Warfare can consist of real campaigns and actual conquest on a limited scale. Compared with tribes, chiefdoms have considerably greater capacities for the incorporation of new groups. This is often facilitated by the chief's authority to coordinate economic, social, and religious activities. Populations of individual settlements in a chiefdom vary widely: there can be as few as one hundred people in one community or as many as several thousand. Thus, population density is higher in a chiefdom than in either bands or tribes. There is variation among chiefdoms in the degree to which systems of ranking are developed, as well as in the amount of power and reverence accorded a chief.

The fourth level of organization in Service's model is the *state*. The state, like the chiefdom, is hierarchically organized. The key difference is that state societies are larger and more complex than chiefdoms. The state makes explicit the manner and circumstances of its use of force and forbids other uses of force. States have a well-developed political organization, sharply defined social classes, intensive patterns of economic and social differentiation, and craft specialization. The definitions of the state, urbanism, and civilization are covered in greater depth in the next chapter.

Archeological Evidence for Changes in Community Organization

The two models of alternative forms of community organization make it possible to classify archeological data that are indicative of the organizational mechanisms of Near Eastern settlements. It should be borne in mind that, unlike a stone tool or an animal bone, a community's organization cannot be "dug up." Although there is no question that the organization of a prehistoric community definitely affects the nature and disposition of the archeological record, archeologists are not in agreement about exactly how this organization manifests itself. Hence, it is necessary to develop methods for recognizing types of organization in the material remains of a society similar to Fried's and Service's ideal types. Although there is considerable interest in this problem, attempts to solve it are few and of a very simple nature. The discussion that follows is another such attempt, offering promising, but not rigorously documented, categories of evidence.

Archeological Examples of Fried's and Service's Organization Types

It is possible to relate the early settlements in the Near East to the models of community organi-

zation formulated by Fried and Service. The categories of the two systems are generally parallel, but do not overlap entirely (see Figure 6-13). Service's bands and tribes are usually egalitarian in Fried's terminology. Ranked society is characteristic of chiefdoms and stratified society characterizes states.

The identification of organizational levels of archeologically known communities is dependent on inferences relating these institutional forms to potentially discoverable material remains. The difference between bands and tribes was both demographic and economic. Pleistocene hunting-and-gathering communities were organized as egalitarian bands. The transition to tribes may have accompanied the growth of villages composed of rectangular architecture (Stage 3). However, some of the larger Natufian sites, such as Mallaha (Stage 2), must already have had tribal organization. Village farming sites such as Jarmo, Beidha, Munhata, Ali Kosh, and Hassuna were probably all egalitarian tribal communities. There is no strong evidence for craft specialization, or for significant status or economic differentiation within these villages or between different settlements.

The identification of early chiefdoms in the archeological record has recently attracted the attention of numerous archeologists (Sanders and Price 1968; Renfrew 1974; Watson and LeBlanc 1973). According to Service, the distinguishing characteristics are as follows:

Chiefdoms are particularly distinguished from tribes by the presence of centers which coordinate economic, social and religious activities. . . . The great change at the chiefdom level is that specialization and redistribution are no longer merely adjunctive to a few particular endeavors, but continuously characterize a large part of the activity of the society. (1962:143)

There are several categories of data that can be used to distinguish tribes from chiefdoms (Watson and LeBlanc 1973). Tribes should exhibit more local differentiation in pottery types than do chiefdoms. The personal possession of pottery in a chiefdom was a means of demonstrating status and, hence, uniform decorative styles should be distributed throughout greater areas than they are for tribes. It can be expected that rare and exotic goods were of greater importance in chiefdoms than in tribes. In tribes, only people who had attained status were buried with material goods, whereas, in chiefdoms, the children of chiefs might also have received such treatment. Population size and density should be greater in chiefdoms than in tribes. One of three types of settlement pattern should be exhibited by chiefdoms:

1 A ceremonial center in which only a few people reside, with neighboring communities housing the other members of the chiefdom
2 A large center housing the entire chiefdom
3 A large center housing most of the population, with the rest of it in smaller nearby settlements

Çatal Hüyük might be an example of the second type of settlement pattern, in which all the members of a chiefdom resided in a single large community. The Halafian might represent the first or third types, with most of the excavated sites being the outlying villages. Except for the possibility of Arpachiyah, their ceremonial centers have not yet been discovered.

Evidence that can be interpreted to be indicative of chiefdom type organization has been uncovered at numerous sixth-millennium sites. The Halafian and Samarran sites with their intricately painted pottery distributed throughout large areas were probably chiefdoms. Çatal Hüyük with its well-developed craft specialization and ritualistic activities might have been a chiefdom, or it might have had a tribal organization with an elaborate religious regulatory system. There were different levels of chiefdoms, indicative of the importance of status positions and the degree of specialization within and between communities. There may have been short-lived, low-level chiefdoms earlier in the Near East, such as seventh-millennium Jericho or Çayönü, but this is difficult to demonstrate. Chiefdoms also developed into more highly ranked and differentiated communities as evidenced during the fifth-millennium in Mesopotamia at the 'Ubaidian site of Eridu.

The transition from chiefdoms to stratified and state societies took place in lower Mesopotamia during the fourth and third millennia. Details of this organizational transformation are discussed in Chapter 7.

Settlement Patterns

Probably the most direct form of archeological evidence for community organization is the nature of ancient settlements. Five general aspects of settlements can be examined for information: the size of houses, their shapes, their numbers, community layout, and the distribution of settlements. It is assumed that each of these aspects was related to the organization and economics of the society.

Circular Huts to Rectangular Houses

Kent Flannery has put forward an interesting hypothesis on the relationship between organizational and architectural forms of early villages (1972b). He cites four empirical generalizations as the basis of his analysis:

1 There is an average of one person per 10 square meters of floor area in village communities.
2 Circular dwellings tend to correlate with nomadic or seminomadic societies; rectangular dwellings tend to correlate with fully sedentary societies.
3 Rectangular structures replace circular ones through time in many archeological areas.
4 Although circular structures may be easier to construct, it is much easier to add units to rectangular structures.

Flannery uses the ethnographic record to suggest two alternative types of communities with which to compare the archeological examples. The first is the "circular hut compound" (Stages 1 and 2 of Figures 1-6 and 4-6, on pages 9 and 106, respectively). Formulated on the basis of information on African settlements of today, this type of community would have been composed of small circular huts, many of which had stone foundations and each of which housed one or, at the most, two persons. In Flannery's model, the family is not the basic organizational unit, and life is communal. Each hut houses either a man or a woman and her children.

The huts are arranged in a circle or oval around a large clear space or they are clustered so that the huts of a man and his wives are grouped together. The food supply and storage facilities are generally shared by the whole community, and the hunting and gathering activities are carried out by groups of men and smaller groups of women. The average size of a circular-hut compound is twenty people, but it could be as small as ten persons or as large as one hundred.

The second community type is a village of rectangular houses (Stage 3 of Figures 1-6 and 4-6). Such settlements range in size from one hundred to one thousand people and generally have predominantly agricultural economies. The houses are larger than most circular structures of earlier communities, accommodating families of at least three or four members rather than only one person. The rectangular plans of these houses make it easy to add or subtract rooms, which is useful in terms of both family growth and the need for rooms for diverse economic activities. Although there may be central storerooms, each house is equipped with storage facilities of its own. The general organization of such a community is egalitarian, but communal aspects of life are diminished and the notion of private property is introduced. Flannery interprets the change in community form to be indicative of a fundamental shift in social and economic organization from that having as its basis a polygynous extended household to one structured on a primarily monogamous nuclear family.

The changes suggested by Flannery were not universal or irreversible, as is exemplified by various Near Eastern communities. Circular and rectangular buildings exist together at some sites (e.g., Munhata); some communities have buildings that are subrectangular (e.g., Beidha); and some later agriculturalists have circular houses (e.g., Halafian). However, rectangular architecture and nucleated village communities eventually did triumph over the circular-hut compound as the predominant community form, the reason being at least twofold. First, the potential for expansion was greater with rectangular architecture: the ability to add rooms accommodated increasing family size in agricultural communities. In turn, the unifying social organization of nucleated rectangular villages and their natural advantage in wartime made them suitable for large populations. Second, the social organization of these nucleated villages favored the intensification of production. The communal living of the circular-hut compound would not have stimulated additional labor. Private storage facilities, increasing private ownership of houses and land, and growing trends toward specialization contributed to the increasing effectiveness of agricultural village economy. Hence, the village of rectangular units was superior to circular hut compounds in three crucial ways: defense, population growth, and production.

Additional Variability in Early Villages

It is useful to consider additional categories of evidence and alternative explanations in order to expand Flannery's model of settlement types. Although the average size of circular buildings at most sites was relatively small and each was perhaps adequate for only one person, there are examples of larger structures at several archeological sites that suggest a different kind of organization. At Mallaha in Israel, there were many small huts that may have housed only one person, but there were also several large circular huts more than 25 square meters in area and well suited to family occupation. However, Mallaha may be exceptional in that advances in organization may have been made even though the technological changes that normally accompanied such advances had not been fully achieved.

Communities with circular structures are organized in several ways. At Mallaha and Nahal Oren, the huts are predominantly free-standing, their doorways generally facing the same direction—in both cases toward the water source (generally downhill). At Beidha, the excavated circular structures are clustered into one group with shared walls (refer to Figure 5-5B on page 148). This complex structure served the same functions as a multiroomed rectangular building. Many of the architectural changes exhibited by the successive communities at Beidha had been foreshadowed in earlier levels: for example, the cluster buildings of level 6 may have been precursors of the multiroomed rectangular structures of levels 2 and 3. At other sites at which circular structures have been uncovered, such as Mureybit, Zawi Chemi Shanidar, and Jericho, the exposures or examples are too few to allow generalizations about the layout of structures or even about their typical form.

Excavated vaillages of rectangular houses also yield diverse settlement patterns, but their interpretation is severely limited by minimal archeological exposures. At Çayönü, where most rectangular buildings are surprisingly uniform in size (25–30 square meters) and form (either cell plan in the upper level or grill plan in the lower level), there is also a uniformity in layout and orientation. The buildings of a given level are generally oriented in the same cardinal direction. Where the exposure has been large enough to judge the relationship of neighboring buildings, they are aligned with approximately 5 meters between them (perhaps forming a pathway). All the buildings are free standing, and there is a possibility that some of them are arranged around a large open space. At Jarmo, the pattern is not so uniform, with both free-standing large buildings with stone foundations (see Figure 5-20 on page 166) and seemingly contiguous buildings made of pressed mud (Figure 5-19). At Beidha, in level 2, the rectangular buildings exhibit many forms, all stone founded. It may be possible to abstract a minimal free-standing unit as one or more large rooms connected to one or more series of small corridor buildings (Figure 5-5A on page 148).

The general picture of both the rectangular settlements of Stage 3 and the curvilinear ones of Stages 1 and 2 is one of great diversity. It might be useful to analyze these communities in terms of the ways in which they differ. Average house size would be one dimension of variability, but equally important would be the range of sizes in any given community. Related to variability in size would be the presumed functions of structures within a community. Other variables would be their shape and whether they were free-standing. The floor plans of individual structures are also central to any analysis. Owing to the limited extent of most archeological exposures of early villages and the even more limited amount of published information, it is currently impossible to carry out a complete analysis.

Patterns of Established Villages (Stage 4)

Another method of expanding Flannery's model of settlement type is to examine the archeological record at later sites in the rise of civilization. Generalities about community types become more difficult to make as one examines material from later and later periods, a situation indicative of the adaptation and specialization that took place. Following early villages with free-standing rectangular houses were established villages (Stage 4) with rectangular buildings and contiguous walls. The *community plans* of Çatal Hüyük, Hacilar, Umm Dabaghiyah (Figure 6-8), and Hassuna (Figure 6-5) typify this pattern. The rooms were of a size similar to or somewhat larger than those of the rectangular Stage-3 villages, but the buildings were attached to one another in large groups, many of them enclosing courtyards. The minimal unit was of a size similar to those of Stage 3, housing a family and having one large living room and one or more small storage rooms. These minimal units were combined in large groups that probably were occupied by large extended families or other solidarity groups. According to the rather scant available data, each minimal unit and each group of units was of uniform size and all were functionally equivalent. Although forms of social differentiation, including ranking, were more developed in these communities than in the earlier villages, they were not economically stratified in the sense that there were large differentials in wealth.

A settlement of this form is also indicative of further changes in the economic structure of the community. Whereas in earlier villages (Stage 3) each family had a house like those of other families and supplied most of its own needs, this was not the case in the established contiguous villages of Stage 4. Although the nuclear family remained the basic economic unit for most activities, the solidarity group living around each courtyard constituted an economic unit of perhaps fifteen to twenty-five people. In more highly developed communities, such as Çatal Hüyük, there may have been specialization not only within each group, but also between groups.

Although it is difficult to identify archeologically, the community organization of Stage 4 advanced to accommodate closer integration of its members. Increasing settlement size and density, as well as closer cooperation in building new houses, necessitated some sort of leadership. As they grew in size and wealth, Stage-4 communities probably had one person who served as chief.

An advanced form of Stage-4 communities was the large village or small town with separate buildings of different sizes. Samarran sites such as Tell es-Sawwan (Figure 6-10) and Choga Mami and Halafian sites such as Arpachiyah exemplify this change. This pattern was an important organizational stage in the rise of civilization and has only recently begun to be adequately documented archeologically. From inferences made from architectural and artifactual information, these communities had distinctly more complex organizational frameworks than those of their predecessors. There is clear evidence for the first known examples of Fried's ranked society and Service's level of chiefdoms (see pages 201–205). For example, at Halafian sites, most buildings were round and varied in size. They were free standing, and the only examples of multichambers were those to which rectangular anterooms were added at one end. At some Halafian sites, such as Girikihaciyan, the size of buildings was quite uniform (the average being 3.5 meters in diameter, with the range being from 4.5 to 2.25 meters), whereas at Arpachiyah the diameter of round structures was as much as 10 meters, but there were also smaller examples. This difference in size could indicate either that buildings served different functions or that there was differentiation in the status of their inhabitants. There were similar situations at Tell es-Sawwan and Choga Mami, where many of the rectangular structures were of modest size (5 by 10 meters), but several were larger (8 by 12 meters). Some of the larger structures have been interpreted to have been religious structures. The very presence of separate and

larger religious buildings implies that there were persons holding positions of high status even though they may not have lived in the buildings. Hence, at these late sixth-millennium sites there is definite evidence for architectural differences that had more than functional significance.

The settlement patterns of early cities and states were the next identifiable stages (5, 6, and 7) in this developmental process. These urban forms are discussed in detail in subsequent chapters and are only summarized here. The primary developments were distinct quarters of the city that were related to activities, social classes, and increasing differentiation in the relative size of dwellings. Although the minimal economic unit for a certain range of activities continued to be the nuclear family, economic specialization stimulated the growth of that unit to encompass the entire city and, for some activities, the whole state.

Only the most general statements can be made about the spatial *distribution* of settlements during Stages 1 through 4. With increasing amounts of survey work and more complete publication, it may soon be possible to supplement these observations with detailed descriptions. There has been a general tendency for population to increase during the last 10,000 years (Smith and Young 1972). Population density varied from region to region, but the overall pattern is one of increasing density. This growth was made possible by an increasingly efficient economic base and effective organizational mechanisms. Although total population increased several times between the tenth and fifth millennia, the size of individual communities remained relatively constant. There was an increase in settlement size between Stage-2 and Stage-3 communities. Intensive-hunting-and-gathering communities such as the Natufians usually numbered less than 100 people, but the early villages that succeeded them ranged between 100 and 200 inhabitants. After this early increase, only a few significantly larger communities developed: for example, early Jericho, Çatal Hüyük, and Tell es-Sawwan. Most other prehistoric settlements contained less than 200 people—a modal village size that is a very effective agricultural unit and has remained the most common village size up to the present. However, a process that is becoming increasingly apparent is the growing differentiation in the size of contemporary communities. These differences were related to economic success, and they engendered unequal distributions of power. The differentiation in community size and function presupposes a developed system of specialization and redistribution that are hallmarks of civilized society. Sixth- and fifth-millennia evidence for these developments is more plentiful; unquestionably, the civilizational process was underway.

The precise *location* of settlements must have been related to a complex combination of factors as perceived by the original inhabitants: among them are proximity to subsistence resources and raw materials; access to a year-round supply of water; and proximity to other communities or trading routes. It would be possible to determine the relative importance of these factors if all of the information were available and the location and chronology of more sites were published.

The relative importance of different factors can be discovered by assuming that people located their settlements according to what they discerned to be the best solution to the problem of minimizing work and danger. During Late Pleistocene times, the craft of building shelters was not highly developed, and so caves were frequently utilized. Access to diverse topographic zones and their related resources was important to Pleistocene hunters and gatherers. Many sites along the Mediterranean coast and in the Jordan Rift Valley satisfied this criterion. With the advent of early farming villages, the primary consideration was proximity to ample agricultural fields and to supplemental sources of food. Because architecture had improved, caves were no longer advantageous for shelter. Hence, most early villages were not only close to large open areas suitable for dry farming, but also close to zones of topographic diversity so that supplemental food resources could be collected.

With an increase in the effectiveness of agriculture, access to farmable land became the overriding factor. Regions that could be farmed had been

extended by improvements in crops, animals, and techniques. Population grew rapidly and new areas were colonized. Because of the increasing trade of raw materials, two factors grew in importance for the location of sites: one was proximity to sources of raw materials, such as obsidian and metal, and the other was proximity to the ensuing trading networks. The importance of these factors varied considerably from period to period, but became crucial during historic times.

With the introduction of irrigation agriculture and the increased yields it provided, proximity to usable sources of water became important. Locations along a river, at the base of an alluvial fan, or in the vicinity of a strong spring were favored. Just as the development of more effective crops and animals allowed agriculture to spread, the introduction of irrigation opened a few new areas to colonization, but it also severely limited the areas in which the most productive form of agriculture could be conducted. Hence, although irrigation allowed for a growth in the total amount of farmable land, eventually the amount of land producing the greatest yields was very limited. These sharp differentiations in land value were not characteristic of dry farming, which depended on broad rainfall patterns. Because of the increasing importance of both irrigation agriculture and control of trading routes, locations along rivers (e.g., Tell es-Sawwan), especially at the junction of a tributary, were particularly favored (e.g., Arpachiyah and Nineveh). Another prized location was the base of a mountain range where the damming and canalization of run-off was adequate for agriculture, especially if it was close to a potential trading route (e.g., Choga Mami).

Shared Ideas, Traditions, or Influence

The mechanisms for interaction between different groups, and the extent to which they interacted, can be indirectly inferred from a variety of sources. In several instances the actual volume, as well as the sources and distribution, of traded goods, especially of obsidian, has been carefully documented (G. Wright 1969). The presence of traded items that came from different regions documents the fact that the people of those regions were in contact, at least through intermediaries. Trade can be an effective conduit of information and ideas. If there are many intermediaries, the exchange of ideas between distant groups is only fragmentary.

A second source of evidence for contact are material objects and practices common to regions separated by great distances that are unlikely to have been introduced independently of one another. A most striking example of a shared tradition has been found at Pre-Pottery Neolithic B sites in the Levant and at their distant neighbors in western Anatolia. The presence of plastered floors frequently painted red and of naturalistically plastered skulls implies a commonality of ritual and technology. This distribution overlaps with the distribution of central Anatolian obsidian traded into the Levant.

The introduction of painted pottery makes it easier for the archeologist to recognize similarities of design occurring over long distances. An early example of such a similarity is the painted "tadpole style" on pottery from several early villages in the Zagros. The distance between sites yielding this type of pottery is as much as 300 kilometers.

The Samarran and Halafian pottery styles of the sixth and fifth millennia in northern and central Mesopotamia are highly developed and widely distributed. There are sites with distinctively painted Samarran ware across the northern fringe of the Mesopotamian alluvium for more than 400 kilometers. To the north, the Halafian painted style is found at sites that stretch from Tilki Tepe in the northeast to Turlu in the west, covering a distance of more than 500 kilometers. The extremely complicated design motifs of these two handsome painting styles leaves little doubt that the communities producing one or the other of them were in contact with other communities yielding that particular pottery style. Detailed studies have been undertaken on the distribution of design motifs at different Halafian sites (Perkins 1949, LeBlanc and Watson 1973). The conclusions vary, but the general finding is that the Halafian style is remarkably uniform. There are definite regional differences, which may be due to the varying distances between sites. Halafian sites also contained poorly made pottery, and at some of them it comprised most of the ceramics (e.g., Girikihaciyan). Hence, the handsomely painted wares may have been vessels for special purposes, perhaps made by craftsmen whose skills were specifically developed, and traded within and between communities. Their distribution probably indicates that they were valued as status objects by widely separated groups. It may also signify the existence of organizational bonds between spatially separated groups. The growing body of archeological evidence implies that the inhabitants of the Near East during prehistoric times included numerous distinct ethnic groups. These groups shared traditions that may be recognizable in their artifact distributions.

The Growth of Regulatory Institutions

The rise of civilization was characterized by the increasing size and complexity of communities and the development of mechanisms to regulate this complexity. Such development was due to various stimuli that initiated positive-feedback relationships between the mechanisms and other aspects of society. Many of these regulatory mechanisms, such as religion, probably originated as general practices in egalitarian communities. As the importance of these mechanisms grew and as a society became more ranked, the practice of religion became the responsibility of people of special status. During this period, regulatory mechanisms acquired special trappings making it difficult for the uninitiated to understand. Although status positions in their earliest forms did not entitle their holders to personal economic gains, this situation changed as the authority of the status positions increased. Eventually, regulatory mechanisms became more formalized, developing into institutions with limited access and definite ascribed power. With development of such a formalized structure, societies became stratified in Fried's terminology.

It is not possible to discern that formalized institutions or stratified societies existed in the Near East at the end of the sixth millennium. However, there is evidence that several regulatory mechanisms that eventually became central aspects of civilization were beginning to emerge in early villages (Stage 3), established villages (Stage 4), and small towns (Stage 4). Among them were warfare, concept of property, and formalized religious and ritualistic practices. In the following discussion, the earliest evidence for the appearance of these regulatory mechanisms is briefly described. The ultimate forms, roles, and reasons for the emergence of these mechanisms and others are discussed in Chapter 7.

Organized warfare was a crucial element in the early formation and maintenance of cities and states. Warfare had two important effects: (1) people who were being attacked were forced to consider defensive strategies; and (2) the attackers had to organize offensive operations. Large, densely nucleated population aggregates were advantageous for defense, but their concentrations of material wealth made them rich sources to plunder. In the absence of written records, it is difficult to determine whether prehistoric hostilities took the form of raids, skirmishes, or organized campaigns; however, some forms of combat and raiding were a part of human society at least as far back as the beginning of village life.

Community defense is evidenced in the massive stone wall and rock-cut ditch constructed at the end of the eighth millennium at the site of Jericho (refer to Figure 3-18 on page 80). The concentrated wealth of this precocious settlement and fear of being raided were strong enough stimuli to prompt the largest cooperative architectural effort of that period. It is more difficult to identify weapons used in war with certainty. However, the prevalence of arrowheads and slingstones at the same time that a reliance on domesticated animals was increasing supports the interpretation that these weapons were not intended solely for animals.

Because there are many methods of defending a community that would be difficult to detect archeologically, the absence of defensive walls does not mean that there was no warfare. After Jericho, the next archeological evidence for defense comes from several sixth-millennium sites. The agglomerative

arrangement with access only through the roofs of the dwellings at Çatal Hüyük has been interpreted by its excavator to have been an attempt to fortify the settlement. The wall and ditch surrounding early Tell es-Sawwan and the tower at Choga Mami imply that people at Samarran sites had reason to undertake defensive works. Enclosure walls have been unearthed at other late sixth-millennium sites, such as those in the upper levels of Hacilar. Each community with defensive works was a settlement with a concentration of portable material wealth. It was unlikely that attacks on these settlements were well-organized campaigns, and there is little archeological reason to believe that any of the aforementioned communities were destroyed by attackers. The first unambiguous archeological evidence for organized warfare is dated at the beginning of the fourth millennium, on the basis of a combination of written and excavated evidence.

The development of the concept of *property ownership* was an essential element of early civilizations. Pleistocene hunting-and-gathering bands had basic notions of territoriality and of private property in terms of their own weapons. With the advent of settled agricultural communities, the investment in material objects increased. The time-consuming construction of houses and the necessity for storing large quantities of food engendered the notion of private property. In the egalitarian villages, most land and implements were held in common with only the property and the boundaries of the total community being well defined. The growth of private ownership was probably a slow process paralleling the growth of ranked and stratified society. It is only in subsequent communities with irrigation, craft specialization, and social stratification that property ownership became an essential regulatory mechanism and was formalized as an institution. The private ownership of productive resources and differential access to them formed the basis of stratified society. Although ownership (i.e., impeded access to goods) attained formal status with the first cities, simple forms of ownership may have been already present during the sixth millennium. The stamp seals of Çatal Hüyük and of Halafian sites, and the potters' marks on Samarran pottery document the growing importance of symbolic communication involving either administrative regulation or the ownership of material goods. Ownership or restricted access to agricultural land may have also developed at this time. The authority over land ownership shifted considerably during subsequent stages of the rise of civilization. Until the sixth millennium, land was probably held by an entire community. During the sixth millennium, private holdings by groups within the community may have started to become distinct.

The institution that has received the most attention from scholars, but remains poorly understood, is that encompassing *religious* and *ritualistic practices*. Such practices were important regulatory mechanisms in hunting-and-gathering groups, but significant material evidence of them has been found only in the remains of the first villages.

At Natufian settlements and even more so at early farming villages, there are several types of data that may be interpreted as evidence for ritual. The careful burials at Natufian sites and the standardized burial practices of the Pre-Pottery Neolitic B Levant are clear indications of a concern for the dead and for rituals of interment. The increasing quantity and diversity of personal ornaments also is suggestive of ritualistic behavior and status positions. A third form of early evidence for religion, which has been the subject of controversy, is representational figurines. Made from incised stone in Natufian times and from clay at early villages, these objects are characteristically small, crudely made, and in the form of human females or animals. The early figurines may simply have been children's toys, but the spectacular statuettes of Hacilar and Tell es-Sawwan probably had special significance for their makers.

At several early villages, it is possible to identify rooms that were probably used for a religious or ritualistic purpose: a rectangular room at Jericho has a niche in one of its walls and contains a large volcanic stone; a room at Çayönü has a terrazzo floor; and a room at Ganj Dareh contains plastered animal heads. At each of these sites, only one such room has been excavated. At the later site of Çatal Hüyük, about one-third of the rooms in the best-preserved level have been identified by the excavator as shrines. The proliferation of evidence for religious or ritualistic activity at Çatal Hüyük is extreme for the village level of organization. The rooms used for such purposes were not larger than their domestic counterparts nor were they architecturally distinct from them. Instead of being the domain of a few priests of high status, the religious-ritualistic regulatory mechanism was employed by members of almost every family in the community.

An alternate mode of development for religious or ritualistic practices was for them to be controlled by a small number of people who conducted these practices for the benefit of the entire community. This was probably the case at Tell es-Sawwan, where a large excavated building may have been used exclusively for religious activities. Below it were numerous burials with finely carved statuettes and stone bowls. These burials have been interpreted to be those of members of a special status group, or perhaps even of a stratified class. The similarity of the statuettes, the buildings, the location, and the economy of Tell es-Sawwan to later Sumerian materials suggests that this site might be directly ancestral to elements of early Sumerian civilization. Whether archeologists have uncovered an early form of Sumerian religion in the special building at Tell es-Sawwan remains questionable, but that Tell es-Sawwan people and others in the Near East had come to rely on a religious hierarchy is becoming increasingly evident.

Near Eastern urbanism, religious institutions, and government strongly influenced the course of subsequent civilizations. Although the formation of cities and states has produced spectacular material and written evidence, the earlier organizational innovations of prehistoric villagers created the structure that enabled later civilizational developments. The literate civilizations discussed in the following chapters were the culmination of a long, gradual process that had begun at prehistoric villages across the uplands of the Near East.

7

THE ORIGINS OF URBAN SOCIETY

In Search of Utopia

The physical focus for the rise of civilization in the Near East is the city. But the urban phenomenon is so complex that its treatment by researchers varies greatly, either because their perspectives differ or because their reports have been written in response to the general intellectual atmosphere of a given period.

Several alternate hypotheses for the formation of cities and states have recently been put forward. Among the organizational variables that have been suggested as primary causes for their formation are such factors as managerial control of a hydraulic society, population pressure or conflict, and exchange systems. These ideas are evaluated in this chapter and aspects of each are integrated into a multifaceted approach to determining how cities could have developed.

The archeological investigation of urban societies requires a different approach from that used to study small villages. In such large-scale investigations, the complexity of material demands that emphasis be on sampling and locational analysis. In addition, urban societies often leave written records that add new dimensions to the information available for interpretation.

Of the three major transformations described in this book, the Urban Transformation is the most immediate in terms of contemporary society. The continuing importance of the organizational changes that accompanied urbanization in the fourth and third millennia is evident in many aspects of our lives. Thus, understanding the nature of urbanism and how it came into being are matters of widespread interest.

A result of the change in scale that accompanied the Urban Transformation was the complexity of societal organization that it prompted. Quantitative growth in community size led to more than quantitative changes in organizational mechanisms. Entirely new forms of integrating institutions emerged, establishing the Urban Transformation as a major development in human history.

Cities, Civilization, and the State

Toward a Definition of Cities

Not only was the city the central entity in the rise of early Near Eastern civilization, but in one form or another it has become the primary community type throughout the world. Thus, a knowledge of its earliest appearance is an aid to understanding the growth and functioning of contemporary society. An examination of cities in their pristine state and a knowledge of the processes that led to their formation should be sources of insight into both the achievements and the failures of our own cities.

A good deal of anthropological and sociological literature addresses the question of what a city is, and whether one archeological site or another should be considered a city. I do not want to dwell unnecessarily on the distinguishing characteristics of cities nor on whether Jericho and Çatal Hüyük should be considered cities or towns. Rather, my approach is to examine characteristics that distinguish cities from earlier settlement forms, to emphasize the diverse forms that early cities assumed, and to outline the relevance of these forms for the rise of civilization.

Early cities have assumed many different forms, depending on the processes by which they were formed and their roles within the total civilizational structure. Most Mesopotamian cities could be described as large sprawling population centers that grew by acretion, without careful planning. They were densely populated and divided into districts. In other regions of the world (e.g., Indus Valley and North China), early cities were regular in plan, a result of greater planning and more rapid growth. In some early civilizations, such as in Egypt, not all cities were centers of large populations; there were also communities in which there was a good deal of monumental architecture but only a small number of inhabitants. These ceremonial centers were seats of power in the Nile Valley, performing many of the same integrating functions as the Mesopotamian city. Similarly, most of the "palaces" of the Cretan and Mycenean civilizations in the Aegean were not major population centers but functioned as secular centers that helped to integrate and organize those societies.

Although the terms city and urbanism are used somewhat interchangeably throughout this book, it should be borne in mind that there is a distinction between the two. Urbanism implies the characteristics that distinguish cities from simpler community forms; it also refers to the organization of an entire urban society, which includes not only cities, but also towns and villages. A city, on the other hand, is the physical center manifesting many important characteristics of the urban condition.

A primary characteristic in any definition of a city is its population, in terms of both size and density. Cities are generally larger and denser than other types of settlements. It might be possible to set a lower limit to the size of a city, but this would deny the special character of an urban complex. A lower limit of 5,000 people is a useful rule of thumb for differentiating cities from towns, but it must be kept in mind that population aggregates of even larger size do exist without the integration characteristic of a city, whereas communities with fewer people might have all the other requisite urban criteria. Hence, large size is diagnostic of cities, but not a sufficient definition.

The most important quality defining a city is its complexity and form of integration. Cities are made up not simply of large populations but of large *diverse* populations that account for the economic and organizational diversity and interdependence that distinguishes a city from simpler settlement forms. Archeologists and social historians measure these factors in several ways. The presence of monumental architecture is easily discoverable evidence for organizational mechanisms that control large groups of people. It is also an indication of the probable participation of craftsmen. Manufactured goods suggest craft specialization, and an uneven distribution of such goods implies a wealthy elite. To support the craftsmen and the elite—both of whom probably do not grow their own food—the agricultural base must be efficient so that farmers can produce more than they need, and there must be mechanisms for collecting and redistributing these surpluses.

Most cities have the following characteristics:

1   A large and dense population
2   Complexity and interdependence
3   Formal and impersonal organization
4   Many nonagricultural activities
5   A diversity of central services both for its inhabitants and for the smaller communities in the surrounding area

Each of these characteristics can be measured in a variety of ways, although absolute values have little meaning except in a general sense. More appropriate to an investigation of emerging urbanism are relative measures that reveal changes in these values through time and among different contemporary settlements. Although it is possible to measure most of these characteristics in terms of the city alone, the very essence of an urban society dictates that measurements take into account the relation of the city to the surrounding region. Thus, the fifth characteristic defines a city as a functioning node in a broader civilizational network. The importance of this criterion is that it can be evaluated only in terms of the system as a whole. A node is defined as a junction in a network. In a complex society, there can be different kinds and levels of interaction that create networks at different levels of organization. Each of these net-

works has functioning nodes. The differentiating characteristic is that a city is a node within a civilizational network serving as a center for the very institutions and mechanisms that characterize that society as a civilization.

Cities exist only within the context of a civilization. Hence, to be able to understand and distinguish a city, one must have an understanding of civilization. Definitions of the two terms are closely interrelated, as are the phenomena themselves. The terms *city* and *civilization* are often loaded with connotations of good and evil, deriving from our firsthand experience of cities and civilization and from our knowledge of them through popular literature. The definitions given in the discussion that follows allow one to distinguish between cities and noncities and between civilizations and noncivilizations—distinctions that are prone to bias and the subject of much controversy. For the present purpose, whether a specific settlement was a city is only of peripheral interest; more important is the functioning and systemic context in which it existed.

Historical Treatment of Civilization

To construct a working definition of civilization, it is useful to review the previous treatment of the concept of civilization. The work of late-nineteenth-century evolutionists, such as Edward B. Tyler and Lewis Henry Morgan, casts the development of cultural forms into a series of stages that all societies pass through. The first, or primordial, stage was *savagery*, with little organization and a hunting-and-gathering subsistence base. The next stage was *barbarism*, roughly equivalent to tribal organization and primitive agricultural subsistence. The third and highest "ethical period" conceived by Morgan was *civilization*, with writing its distinguishing characteristic.

This three-part classificatory scheme was an attempt to categorize all of the ethnographically known cultures and to explain the rise of civilization in evolutionary terms. Like many other "world systems" that attempted to explain human development in a simplified manner, this scheme fails in a number of ways. Besides problems with data and its interpretations, there are two basic shortcomings in the Tyler-Morgan system. First, any classificatory scheme in which diachronic (through time) relationships are assumed on the basis of synchronic (at one point in time) examples is on weak ground. The study of different contemporary organizational forms of society does not support the projection of one or more of these forms into the past as ancestral to other current societies. It is true that the ethnographic record affords models to be tested by actual archeological data, but it cannot function simultaneously as both model and test case. The second shortcoming is the use of pejorative terms to classify societal forms. Implicit in the terms savagery, barbarism, and civilization is a value judgment; barbarism is better than savagery and civilization is better than barbarism. One may also get the false idea from any unilinear evolutionary scheme that there are inherent forces guiding the development of cultures that necessarily lead from one stage to another. Although peoples of many regions exhibit this general course of development, it is not the only route, and in certain circumstances savagery can be more efficient for survival than barbarism or even civilization.

Twentieth-century historians such as Oswald Spengler and Arnold Toynbee also attempted complete world histories. As universal syntheses based on very scanty data, except those drawn from the western civilization model, these attempts were inadequate. Nevertheless, both Spengler and Toynbee developed important concepts that were to affect subsequent investigations of the rise of civilization. Spengler attempted to counteract the western centrists of his time, and his ideas were a reflection of his general pessimism (1926–28). He suggested that progress and history are not equivalent. In an attempt to reduce the humanist aspect of his interpretations, he employed a biological model of development. In addition to suggesting similarities between the structure and form of plants and animals on the one hand and civilizations on the other, Spengler asserted that civilizations pass through a life cycle. Each civilization goes through the same developmental phases: youth, maturity, and senescence. Spengler was an environmental determinist to the extent that he believed that the characteristics of a civilization are closely related to its region. After a civilization has realized its potentialities in terms of people, arts, and sciences, it soon passes into a phase of senescence and then dies. Spengler's belief in the close connection between a civilization and its surroundings and his concentration on the changing stages in the growth of societies were important influences on later theorists.

Arnold Toynbee's work, *A Study of History,* is another massive attempt at explaining the course of world history (1934). The concept of progress and a belief in the "upward movement" in history permeates his work. Toynbee saw the direct relationship between the form of the civilization and its physical surroundings. The primary mechanism of societal growth and "progress" consisted of society's meeting the challenge of the physical environment with a response that not only answered the particular challenge, but also exposed the society to a fresh challenge. Toynbee came to this conclusion by a somewhat superficial comparison of pairs of societies that developed in different environments. In each pair, the stimulus toward civilization was stronger in proportion to the difficulty of the environment. Toynbee cited the eventual superiority of the New England settlers over those of other more physically hospitable regions as an example of his "Challenge and Response" hypothesis. He championed the idea that a combination of physical factors influenced the growth of civilization in particular regions. The mechanisms initiating growth were largely psychological, but he did not carefully delineate them. Although the details of his hypothesis are given little currency today, a major one that grew out of Toynbee's form of environmental determinism is Wittfogel's hydraulic hypothesis, which is discussed later in this chapter.

Several anthropologists have tried to define civilization from the perspective of both delineation and explanation. Alfred L. Kroeber used the concept of a civilization to divide all of human history into analytical units (1953). These units were delimited primarily by their values and their qualities known as style. This ideational method of delineating civilizations is particularly useful in the investigation of material remains, such as artwork or dress, but does little to explain the differences and similarities between civilizations or their growth. Rather, it is a classificatory system based on a selected set of attributes.

Another method for defining civilizations is to distinguish them from their surroundings. Robert Redfield characterized societies in terms of opposing ideal constructs: folk and urban, great and little traditions (1953). Unlike Kroeber's approach, which was primarily meant to delineate different civilizations, Redfield's perspective helps to illuminate the nature of functioning civilizations. It encourages the researcher to look for patterns of interaction between different social constituencies that together formed the civilizational whole. Redfield's seminal contribution is the idea that great civilizational characteristics, as personified by the urban elite, cannot be fully understood without reference to little civilizational traditions, as practiced by the rural peasantry. These little civilizational traditions often have their roots in precivilizational folk societies. Although the Redfield ideal types are too general for use in detailed analysis, the emphasis on the relational aspects among constituents of a civilizational complex was of crucial importance for further study.

Trait-Complex Definition of Civilization

Another approach to defining civilization is to combine certain aspects of delineation with information on the nature of these societies by compiling lists of characteristics of different levels of societal organization. Gordon Childe (1950) compiled a list of ten characteristics of cities that were specifically chosen to be recognizable in the archeological record. Their concurrence at an ancient site signified an urban community that was part of a civilization. Childe used these characteristics to delineate and recognize early forms of urbanism, and he attempted to demonstrate how they functioned and how they were interrelated. However, it is not difficult to separate Childe's ten indices into primary and secondary characteristics of early

civilizations. The five primary characteristics refer to evidence of fundamental changes in the organization of society, whereas the five secondary characteristics refer to various forms of evidence documenting the presence of the five primary characteristics.

Primary Characteristics

1   Size and density of cities: the great enlargement of an organized population meant a much wider level of social integration.
2   Full-time specialization of labor: specialization of production among workers was institutionalized, as were systems of distribution and exchange.
3   Concentration of surplus: there were social means for the collection and management of the surplus production of farmers and artisans.
4   Class structured society: a privileged ruling class of religious, political, and military functionaries organized and directed the society.
5   State organization: there was a well structured political organization with membership based on residence. This replaced political identification based on kinship.

Secondary Characteristics

6   Monumental public works: there were collective enterprises in the form of temples, palaces, storehouses, and irrigation systems.
7   Long-distance trade: specialization and exchange were expanded beyond the city in the development of trade.
8   Standardized, monumental artwork: highly developed art forms gave expression to symbolic identification and aesthetic enjoyment.
9   Writing: the art of writing facilitated the processes of organization and management.
10   Arithmetic, geometry, and astronomy: exact, predictive science and engineering were initiated.

By separating and reordering these ten indices, one can appreciate the depth of understanding and insight that characterizes much of Childe's writing. The primary characteristics relate to demographic, economic, and organizational changes that were essential aspects of early civilization. Secondary characteristics document that certain primary characteristics existed. For example, a community that was able to build monumental public works probably had not only the craft specialists to work on them, but also sufficient surplus to support the work. Long-distance trade on a large scale also was indicative of the existence of primary characteristics. Craft specialization to create goods, the ability to concentrate surpluses, and sufficient political organization to conduct trade are all implied by the presence of a large-scale trading network. Two of Childe's characteristics have been the subject of considerable criticism: writing and standardized artwork. At first glance, such indices appear to be of very indirect importance, but they are in fact indications of fundamental changes in societal organization. Writing, especially in early Mesopotamian civilizations, was used primarily for the keeping of accounts. Writing or some substitute for the recording of complex transactions was necessary for the type of large-scale economic system that Near Eastern civilization required. The utility of standardized artwork is not so apparent as that of writing, but the themes of early standardized art seem to be of a nature that reaffirmed the social structure and codes of the early civilization. This is discussed in detail in Chapter 9. Writing, standardized artwork, and early civilizations that appeared coincidentally were clearly related and were elements in a functioning process.

Another trait-system for delineating civilizations and states from other organizational forms has been proposed by Elman Service. On the basis of worldwide ethnographic information, Service has formulated a series of theoretical levels of organization (1962). The simpler forms—band tribes, and chiefdoms—have been described in Chapter 6. Service uses the term *state* to avoid many of the connotations of the word *civilization*. He considered the state to be the highest form of sociopolitical organization, characterized by a very strong, centralized government with a professional ruling class largely divorced from the bonds of kinship. The state was highly stratified and extremely diversified internally with residential patterns often based on occupational specialization rather than on blood or affinal relationships. The state attempted to maintain a monopoly of force and is characterized by

the emergence of true law. The economic structure of states utilized both reciprocal and redistributive exchange and was largely controlled by an elite who had preferential access to strategic goods and services.

Ecological-Systemic Consideration of Civilizations

Whereas most of the approaches to a concept of civilization heretofore presented have had as their main purpose the delineation of civilizations both from each other and from simpler forms of organization, use of the ecological-systemic approach encourages study of the growth and functioning of civilizations. Investigators who follow this approach seek to discover the regularities that were shared by different civilizations, instead of merely the details that set them apart. Interrelational aspects that stimulated, regulated, and maintained civilizations are the primary goals of study. From this perspective, questions of a society's adaptive strategies and relationships to its environment are crucial. A civilization is viewed as a functionally interrelated system of basic components including the environment, the technology, and the human participants and their social organization. Social organization, value systems, and other cultural subsystems are analyzed in terms of their adaptative utility. One of the goals of these studies, and my goal in this chapter, is to suggest how external stimuli and internal interrelations functioned to change the form and relationships of each of these subsystems to culminate in the early civilizations.

Julian Steward was a pioneer in ecological studies of civilizations who formulated a useful conceptual framework (1949, 1955). He used an evolutionary perspective that related environmental variables to cultural developments in the rise of civilization (1949). His proposals are not based on simple unilinear evolution nor environmental determinism. Rather he suggested that at the "core" of the Urban Transformation there was a changing, functionally interrelated group of social institutions. This core was characterized by the structural relationships of interdependent institutions. Each society derives its distinctive set of social systems from its institutional core. Steward's framework for following the rise of civilization was to investigate each society in terms of its "level of socio-cultural complexity." The contributions of his studies were fundamental. The rise of civilization was viewed as a series of successive, major organizational levels. Steward conceived of cultural evolution as a succession of adaptive patterns, thereby emphasizing the ecological and economic arrangements as the primary sources of change.

Robert McC. Adams broadened Steward's viewpoint by considering the causation and structure of civilization from a multifaceted perspective. Although he acknowledged the importance of environmental and technological factors in the emergence of early civilizations, Adams stated that the evidence supports the position that "the transformation at the core of the Urban Revolution lay in the realm of social organization. . . . For the most part, changes in social institutions precipitated changes in technology, subsistence, and other aspects of the wider cultural realm, rather than vice versa." (Adams 1966a:12) To Adams, the Urban Revolution implies a focus on ordered, systematic processes of change that can be described in terms of a functionally related core of institutions that interacted and evolved. In defining the end-product of the Urban Revolution, Adams attempts to avoid the term civilization, which he suggests refers to the totality of the culture and, hence, reduces the possibility of making models for analytical comparison. Adams does this in an attempt to understand the evolution that led to Near Eastern civilization by investigating the complex core of social institutions that interacted to form early state society.

The approach to civilization used in this book is an adaptation of the Steward-Adams perspective. Civilizations are best recognized and defined with reference to the complexity of their interacting sets of social and political institutions. Emphasis should be on the regularities found in civilizations and the processes by which they emerged rather than on the features that differentiate civilizations, except as sources of information about the variability in the civilizational process. I do not accept a priori that social institutions were the prime movers in the rise of civilization. Rather, my perspective is that stimuli and initial feedback cycles involved diverse elements in the prehistoric Near Eastern cultures. Environmental factors, technological innovations, and social institutions were crucial in the first strides toward state society (see Figure 7-7 on page 230). After the process was underway, changes in social institutions played an increasing role in initiating changes in other realms of behavior, yet always with feedback.

Although in a general sense cities, states, and civilization appeared at approximately the same time in the Near East, it is useful to regard them as three distinct entities and to examine the processes by which they interacted. Cities are defined in terms of their size, complexity, and position within a societal matrix; states in terms of their political organization, which are treated in Chapter 9; and civilization in terms of its great complexity, interaction, and accomplishment. Hence, civilization is a level of societal complexity, cities are elements within a complex society, and states are institutions based on a form of administration in complex societies.

The city is the dominant element in the settlement system of a civilization. It is larger, denser, and more internally diverse than other settlements in the civilizational system. Because of its large size and diverse inhabitants, a city is able to provide specialized services to those living both in it and in areas nearby. In return, the city receives raw materials, foodstuffs, and periodic manpower. This symbiotic relationship between a city and its surrounding area is not limited to subsistence matters but is apparent in all aspects of society.

Alternate Hypotheses of the Origin of Urban Society

In this section several hypotheses about the rise of civilization are outlined and discussed. Each one offers a slightly different perspective on the prob-

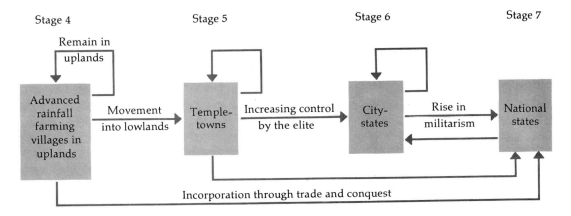

Figure 7-1
Development of dominant community forms during the emergence of urbanism in lowland Mesopotamia.

lem and concentrates on one or more factors as being most important. It is not a matter of whether one hypothesis is correct and the others false. Rather, each one is a source of insight into what influenced the rise of civilization, and each helps to explain the course of events in the Near East. A careful appraisal of the descriptions of early civilizations in Chapters 8 and 9 will enable the reader to judge which hypothesis most completely (or adequately) explains the data.

To make a meaningful examination of each hypothesis of the origin of urbanism and state society, it is useful to outline briefly the course of developments in the Near East (Figure 7-1). There were three general stages in the Urban Transformation in lowland Mesopotamia that were characterized by the emergence of temple-towns (5), city-states (6), and national states (7). The path of development in each region of the Near East was somewhat different from those of other regions. For example, in the upland regions of the northern Near East, large urban centers did not develop early, but town and townships did (Jawad 1965). In Egypt, the developments did not lead to cities as large population centers, but rather to moderate population centers, each with far-reaching administrative and religious responsibilities. The rate of development in Egypt was more rapid than that in Mesopotamia,

after the process had begun. As the archeological record is now understood, the Nile Valley did not pass through stage 6, but went almost directly from temple-towns to a unified national state (see Chapter 9). With these stages of development and alternative pathways in mind, we can turn to the hypotheses for an explanation of these changes.

Hydraulic Hypothesis

Karl Wittfogel (1957) and Julian Steward (1949) have pointed out the simultaneous occurrence of early civilizations in regions where large-scale irrigation agriculture was practiced. Wittfogel presented this idea in a lengthy theoretical exposition in which he attempted to explain the major political systems of the world (1957). The relevant aspects of Wittfogel's hypothesis are his discussion of the importance of water as a natural resource and the suggestion that large-scale irrigation required centralized coordination and direction (Figure 7-2). Water was no more essential to agriculture than several other basic factors, such as temperature, fertility of the soil, and topography of the land. However, it was a crucial variable because it could be manipulated and agglomerated in bulk. Water management was especially important in places where rainfall was insufficient, but water existed

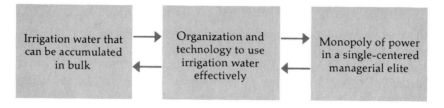

Figure 7-2
Interrelationships of variables in the hydraulic-managerial hypothesis of the formation of a state. (After Wittfogel, 1957.)

nearby—for example, in semiarid river valleys. To make large water-deficient areas fertile, people had to create large-scale enterprises that were usually operated by a central government.

Wittfogel describes the range of activities necessary in a society that relies on large-scale irrigation works (his term "hydraulic society"): the planning and construction of the irrigation works, the scheduling of water use, the maintenance of canals, and the defense of canals from hostile neighbors. Although these activities can be carried on by small groups on an informal basis, it is more efficient and leads to greater growth if there is central management. In return, the person who manages the water resources has tremendous power over the farmers. If one source of power is so much more important than all others, a monopoly develops within a society. Thus, a single-centered government arises in the form Wittfogel has called "oriental despotism." He contrasts this kind of development with what happens in more temperate climates in which rainfall agriculture prevails and alternate bases of power, such as the church, guilds, and propertied classes, arise to give a more balanced, or multi-centered, government. In Mesopotamia, where control of the water resources was very important, the managers of water also became the primary managers of trade, industry, and property rights. This power was originally vested in the temple elite, but slowly the secular state organization wrested it from the temple. There is a strong environmental element to Wittfogel's hypothesis, but it is far from deterministic. Wittfogel asserts that, although the environment supplied the setting,

hydraulic society was developed by its members, and this development was organizational and not technological.

Two major criticisms have been made of Wittfogel's hypothesis. First, available archeological and historical data imply that large-scale irrigation works were not prevalent in Mesopotamia until long after the rise of the state. If this is true, hydraulic society should be viewed as a result of state formation rather than as a cause. However, it is possible that centralized administration and large-scale irrigation works were present at an early date, but because their growth was incremental they only became obvious in the archeological and textual records after they had reached major proprotions. The second criticism is based on studies of several modern communities in Mesopotamia where small-scale cooperative irrigation works without centralized external control are sufficient for an adequate agricultural livelihood. Although the possibility for this being accomplished weakens Wittfogel's hypothesis, it does not deny that managed irrigation and overall agricultural planning were effective, leading to greater success than in communities without them.

Wittfogel's hydraulic hypothesis is a more workable construct if the emphases are somewhat altered (Mitchell 1973). It is unlikely that Wittfogel intended to imply that large-scale irrigation works preceded centralized government. Clearly, the institutions of central government and large-scale irrigation would have grown incrementally, side by side. Small-scale irrigation would have required a certain amount of administration, which would

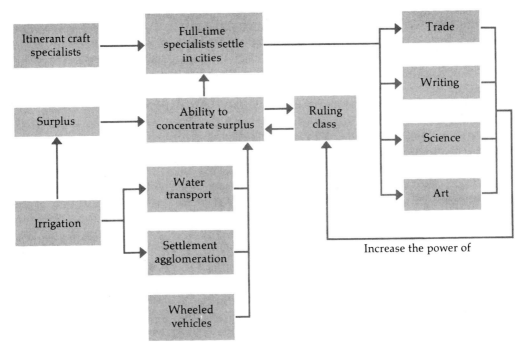

Figure 7-3
Interrelationships of variables in the craft-specialization-and-irrigation
hypothesis for the growth of urbanism. (After Childe, 1950.)

have expanded the irrigation system, which in turn
would then have required greater administration,
and so on. In this manner, a feedback relationship
between increasing irrigation and growing authority of the government would have been established,
eventually leading to large-scale irrigation works
and to a state political organization with a monopoly of power. Another factor that should be emphasized in addition to the necessity of centralized
control for the minimal functioning of irrigation
works is the adaptive advantage of a centralized
system. Perhaps in many situations the farmers did
not allow centralized control to develop, but in
those in which it did develop the economy expanded, and then the managers could not be dis-
placed. Hence, a useful restatement of Wittfogel's
hypothesis is that it was not irrigation itself, but the
centralized coordination of irrigation activities that
had important social consequences. Centralized

coordination resulted in greater political integration, and this organization was then expanded because of its economic advantages (Mitchell 1973).

Childe's Craft-Specialization-and-Irrigation Hypothesis

Childe (1950) suggested a series of factors that
enabled the growth of cities (Figure 7-3). Full-time
craftsmen existed before the advent of cities but
in order to earn their keep as metal workers, for
example, they would have had to travel from village to village. Childe suggested that the specialization of labor began with itinerant experts.
However, in the fourth millennium the development of effective irrigation agriculture combined
with fishing and raising animals in the alluvial
valleys of Mesopotamia and Egypt afforded the
surplus necessary to support a growing number of

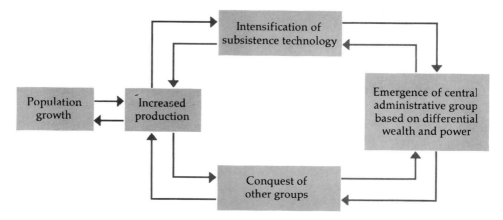

Figure 7-4
Interrelationships of variables in the population-pressure-and-conflict
hypotheses of the formation of a state. (After Carneiro, 1970; Diakonoff,
1969; Smith and Young, 1972; Gibson, 1973.)

resident specialists. Two other aspects of irrigation agriculture also facilitated the growth of cities. First, water transportation along with pack animals and newly invented wheeled vehicles made it possible to gather large quantities of foodstuffs at a few centers. Second, the use of irrigation restricted the areas that could be cultivated effectively; that is, those near water courses and canals. Hence, Childe's approach was to outline some of the technological factors that enabled urbanism to develop, rather than suggesting factors that strongly stimulated or forced the development of cities.

Population-Pressure-and-Conflict Hypotheses

Several hypotheses for the formation of a state include the view that the mechanisms of conflict or warfare stimulate the growth of powerful administrative organizations (Figure 7-4), and population pressure and economic factors are the most pervasive conditions for causing conflicts. Robert Carneiro formulated a broad hypothesis using South American examples, but he applied it to the Near East as well (1961; 1970). Carneiro's hypothesis is based on what he observes to be a general regularity about the environmental settings of early civilizations throughout the world—that is, they

are areas of circumscribed agricultural land. Each area is bounded by mountains, seas, or deserts—environmental features that sharply delimited the area that simple farming people could have occupied. In circumscribed areas, an expanding population cannot accommodate itself by colonizing new lands; rather, it must intensify its production on lands already being used. A result of such intensified land use is that military conflicts between groups become more frequent, with the losers not being able to flee to new farmlands. Thus, communities tend to enlarge as a defensive measure, and the losers of a conflict may be assimilated into the winner's society as a lower class. Successful militarists are rewarded by economic wealth, increasing amounts of land, and a conquered class of workers. The adaptive advantages of organizing and controlling a successful military operation quickly lead to its institutionalization in the form of an early state. The state grows in size as a result of external conquests. Their internal structures continue to be elaborated by increasing differences in wealth and status. Carneiro makes clear that population growth in itself is insufficient to engender warfare, but population pressure does encourage warfare if the expanding population is constrained either by environmental barriers or by competing social groups whose populations are so dense as to preclude expansion.

Another hypothesis for the formation of the state in southern Mesopotamia that relies on conflict is that of Igor A. Diakonoff (1969). He posits that increases in agriculture, in supplemental food production, and in craft goods led to specialization that created differentials in wealth, constituting the basis of socioeconomic class differentiation. Differences in economic status led to class conflict and ultimately to the formation of the state as the agent for the maintenance of ruling-class dominance. Diakonoff's approach is similar to that of Carneiro's because in both conflict is seen to arise from differentiations in wealth in a situation of increasing population.

Philip Smith and Cuyler Young also have formulated a hypothesis that rests directly on population pressure as a major causal variable (1972). Increasing population necessitated improvements in the subsistence activities of the Mesopotamian settlers. Agriculture was intensified, labor became more specialized, and mechanisms for controlling economic institutions were developed. Further population growth encouraged these tendencies and gave rise to increased competition, which led to conflict, agglomeration into larger settlements, and, eventually, state organization.

Another population-pressure hypothesis closely related to those just described is that of McGuire Gibson (1973). He suggests that the environment of Mesopotamia created chronic problems of population movements and relative overpopulation. The major rivers—the Tigris and Euphrates—meandered across southern Mesopotamia, periodically changing their courses. Most of the population was settled along the banks of these rivers and relied on them for irrigation water. Gibson suggests that, whenever the Euphrates River changed its course, those living along its banks were subjected to population pressure that necessitated organizational changes.

The common shortcoming of the various population-pressure hypotheses is that they do not explain why groups of people who had theretofore kept their population within limits allowed it to

grow so large as to become a crisis. Socially approved methods of regulating group size had been used for millennia and could have been tightened in face of subsistence stress (Birdsell 1958). However, these groups did allow their populations to continue to increase, and the manner in which this growth stimulated organizational changes is at the crux of the rise of civilization.

Interregional- and Intraregional-Exchange Hypotheses

Several theorists have suggested that the development of complex, large-scale trading networks stimulated the growth of urban society (Figure 7-5, page 226). This hypothesis has been most carefully worked out for Mesoamerican civilizations (Sanders 1968; Flannery 1968; Rathje 1971), but it has also been examined with reference to the Near East (Wright 1972; Wright and Johnson 1975). Southern Mesopotamia does not contain very many raw materials, such as metal ores, large timber, building stone, or stone for tools. Thus, in some cases, the inhabitants of Mesopotamia substituted available resources, such as clay, for unavailable materials. In addition, they traded for other materials on a large scale. The advent of large-scale trade necessitated an administrative organization to control the procurement, production, and distribution of goods. Such an organization would have had access to a major source of wealth in the community and, hence, its power might have been extended to other aspects of society. To increase production further, and perhaps to supply a growing population, continued specialization and intensification would have been necessary. Larger settlements would have resulted from the competition, produced by a growing population, for agricultural land. This enlargement of settlements was adaptive because of the greater efficiency of production of large population aggregates and the relative ease of controlling people in nucleated settlements.

It is certain that trade was important in early Mesopotamian civilizations, but once again it is unclear whether it was a cause of the rise of civilization or an effect of an administrative elite that

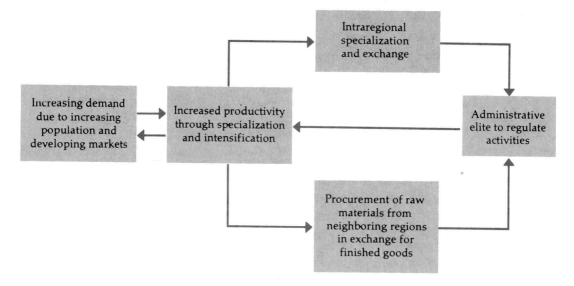

Figure 7-5
Interrelationships of variables in the interregional- and intraregional-exchange
hypotheses of urban development. (After Sanders, 1968; Rathje, 1971;
Flannery, 1968.)

already existed. Hence, although trade is a key variable in the formation of urban society, it is not a
sufficient explanation in itself for this development.

Hypotheses on the Multiplicity of
Factors Affecting Urbanization

In each of the foregoing hypotheses, the complexity of the process of urbanization has been
recognized, but each of the theorists has attempted
to single out one or two major factors that contributed the most toward its initiation. In contrast,
the work of Robert McC. Adams (1966a) and others
has led to hypotheses that emphasize not only the
complexity of the process but also the multiplicity
of factors that triggered it (Figure 7-6). In addition,
Adams has taken the position that "primarily
changes in social institutions . . . precipitated
changes in technology, subsistence, and other aspects of the wider cultural realm, rather than vice
versa" (1966a:12). In *The Evolution of Urban Society*
(1966a), he describes three major transformations:

the first two led to urban centers that were controlled by a religious elite, and the third resulted in
the growth of secular state authority.

The first transformation consisted of changes in
subsistence strategies that had far-reaching ramifi-
cations, according to Adams. Mesopotamian civilization relied on a well-developed system of food
production and procurement: while some people
cultivated crops, others herded animals or fished
for food. The combination of these somewhat independent sources of food yielded a stable food base
that allowed the population to increase in size and
density. The exchange and redistribution of the
food produced were managed by the members of
the temple community. The growth of this centralized means of redistribution gave a group of people, the temple elite, the power to coerce farmers
or herders into producing surpluses, something that
could not be done by simple exchange.

The most important organizational changes resulted from the intensification of subsistence pursuits. With a growing population and a means for

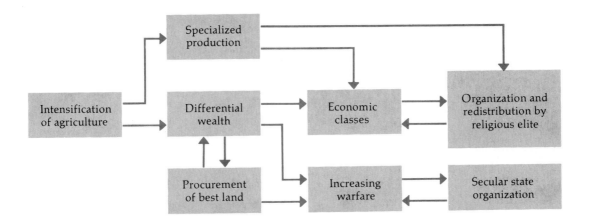

Figure 7-6
Interrelationships of variables in the multiple-factor-and-organizational
hypothesis of the formation of a state. (After Adams, 1966a.)

redistribution, the trend in early Mesopotamian agriculture was to produce more food. Adams suggests that what limited food production was not land but the availability of water. Natural water courses and small-scale irrigation works allowed only a part of the available land to be adequately irrigated. Even areas that were irrigated were not equally productive and, in years in which the water level of rivers was low, only the land closest to them would have had enough water for successful crops. Hence, with the increasing amount of land put under cultivation and the intensification of agriculture on already farmed land, there emerged an important differential in the productivity of different tracts of farmland. Those who controlled the land close to the natural courses of a river were able to produce more crops and to produce them even in years of low precipitation. This led to a major differentiation of wealth among farmers, which was compounded by their ability to buy additional irrigable land. Adams identifies differential access to the primary productive commodity,

water, as the first step in the emergence of class society.

The increasing craft specialization and differential wealth based on land holdings helped to stimulate the second major transformation Adams has identified—a shift from kin-based to class-structured society. Kinship was the basis for organizational structure in early Mesopotamian society and such ties were influential in early administrative efforts. The economic division of subsistence activities and craft production led to specialization by family in one or more economic pursuits. The wealth accumulated by controlling good land and by managing the distribution of its products resulted in the acquisition by a few families of great wealth and power. It is likely that these families attempted to retain their wealth and power by advocating an organizational structure that institutionalized the differences that were emerging—a structure largely based on economic activities connected with a person's lineage. The religious elite, who controlled production and redistribution, and the propertied elite who controlled the best agricultural land, formed the upper strata of society.

The third transformation identified by Adams is the transfer of administrative power from the temple to the state largely because of increasing militarism. This is treated in detail in Chapter 9.

Adams's hypothesis has had several important effects on the study of the rise of civilization. Most significantly, he has shown that the evidence from Mesopotamia does not strongly support any of the simpler, single-factor explanations of urbanism. He presents a convincing argument in favor of the complexity and interrelatedness of the process by discussing several important transformations and the mutually amplifying relationship of certain variables. By emphasizing these feedback relationships and how on a general level they can also be identified in Mesoamerica, Adams has encouraged the investigation of early civilizations within a systems-comparative framework.

Building largely on the work of Adams and on his own research in Mesoamerica, Kent Flannery has modified Adams's hypothesis and put it into a more explicitly systems-oriented perspective (Flannery 1972a). Flannery conceptualizes the rise of the state as a process of increased segregation and centralization within a society. *Segregation* is the internal differentiation and specialization of subsystems of the society, and *centralization* is the linkage between the subsystems and the highest-order controlling apparatus in the society (Flannery 1972a:409). Flannery points out that an adequate explanation of the rise of the state would carefully distinguish between:

1 The processes of segregation and centralization
2 The mechanisms by which they take place
3 The socioenvironmental stresses that select for those mechanisms

Even if one accepts the assumption that the processes in the rise of civilization are the same in different regions of the world, the mechanisms may or may not be the same, and almost certainly the socioenvironmental stresses vary.

The importance of this approach is that it emphasizes the various levels of control appartus that maintain the ongoing system. A control apparatus

keeps the system working within bounds that are acceptable. If the apparatus fails, then another mechanism must take over or the system will "devolve" to a lower level of organization. In most complex systems, such as a civilization, there is a hierarchy of controlling mechanisms, with higher-order apparatus controlling lower-order apparatus, which in turn control the functioning subsystems. There is relative stability in systems in which the subsystems are relatively insulated from each other so that a problem in one does not immediately affect the others. However, the hallmark in the evolution of such complex systems as the state is the increasing centralization and interdependence of the various subsystems. In such cases, there is a tendency for aberrations in one subsystem to affect all other subsystems and to create instability. To offset this instability, powerful centralized management often evolves at the top of the hierarchy.

Control apparatus usually assumes the form of institutions of varying kinds. Such an institution may have been created for a certain range of purposes and, concomitant with the evolution of the general system, the institution may assume other purposes and increasingly direct its own destiny. Among the most important institutions are those that regulate the flow of information to constituent groups within a society (Flannery 1977a:411). As discussed in Chapter 6, a central development in the rise of civilization was the increasing necessity for mechanisms with which to communicate information. Societies for which the basis of organization was kinship or religion could handle a considerable amount of detailed information, but the highly formalized institutions of early civilizations carried information regulation and dissemination much further than had theretofore been done and enabled the scale of organization that developed into the state.

Flannery adopts two evolutionary mechanisms from systems theorists to explain many of the changes that took place during the rise of the state. The first is *promotion*, by which a low-level special-purpose institution becomes a higher level institution serving a more general purpose during a time of stress. A military coup in which the leader takes control of the state government is an example of promotion. The second mechanism is *linearization*, by which low-level controls are permanently bypassed by higher-level controls. The take-over of local irrigation management by the state government is an example of linearization. Various forms of promotion and linearization led to increasing centralization of control during the formation of the state in Mesopotamia, but centralization can progress too far in terms of the maximum stability of the total system. If a system of control becomes too centralized, then once again small stresses in any component of the system will have reverberations throughout the entire system. Examples of how this overcentralization led to the recurrent demise of early Mesopotamian states during early historic times are described in the second half of Chapter 9.

A Systems-Ecological Model

Using many of the ideas of Adams and other theorists, one can design an investigatory framework for the rise of civilization that takes into account many of the factors and their systemic relationships that stimulated the growth of the state. Urbanism, or civilization, is viewed as a complex social system with great internal differentiation organized along class-stratified lines and an administrative elite controlling the major organizational institutions.

Urbanization was not a linear arrangement in which one factor caused a change in a second factor, which then caused a change in a third, and so on. Rather, the rise of civilization should be conceptualized as a series of interacting incremental processes that were triggered by favorable ecological and cultural conditions and that continued to develop through mutually reinforcing interactions. The developmental process comprised five positive-feedback interrelationships, three of which (A, B, and C in Figure 7-7, page 230) were prompted by the ecology and gave rise to institutions that characterized early Mesopotanian cities. The fourth and fifth positive-feedback relationships (D and E in Figure 7-7) were stimulated by early urban developments and helped transform the independent cities into members of a centralized na-

tional state. None of these feedback relationships functioned for a long period in an administrative vacuum, with an administrative elite suddenly appearing "full blown" to control the already developed institutions. Rather, each institution started at a simple level and increased by small increments. These processes deepened the growing divisions within society, which became institutionalized as economic strata within a hierarchical society. These feedback relationships also stimulated the growth of a class of administrators who increasingly controlled the productive resources of society and who reinforced the emerging divisions in the class structure.

The successive phases of urban development diagrammed in Figure 7-1 were not followed by all the communities in Mesopotamia. Many towns and villages continued to exist and function within the emerging civilizational network. However, the structure of Mesopotamian society was greatly affected by the larger communities, which were the centers of civilizational developments. Hence, although it is necessary to study both large and small settlements to understand an urban society, the systems model focuses on changes that led to the differentiation of community types.

The most important single variable by which to measure the development of urbanism is the relative increase in formalized internal complexity as evidenced by the emergence of stratified society. The aspect of class-stratified society that is directly relevant to our study is the increasing control in the hands of an administrative elite. Figure 7-7 shows the feedback relationships between elements of early Mesopotamian society that effected the growth of an administrative elite. The elements in the diagram are not arranged chronologically from left to right; rather, the diagram is intended to show the interrelationships of the factors at work at all times throughout the process.

A favorable ecological situation was instrumental in the formation of Mesopotamian civilization. At about 5500 B.C., an enormous and potentially productive area of Mesopotamia was unoccupied. The southern Mesopotanian Plain may have been sparsely inhabited by seminomadic people, but it was apparently void of farming communities. With

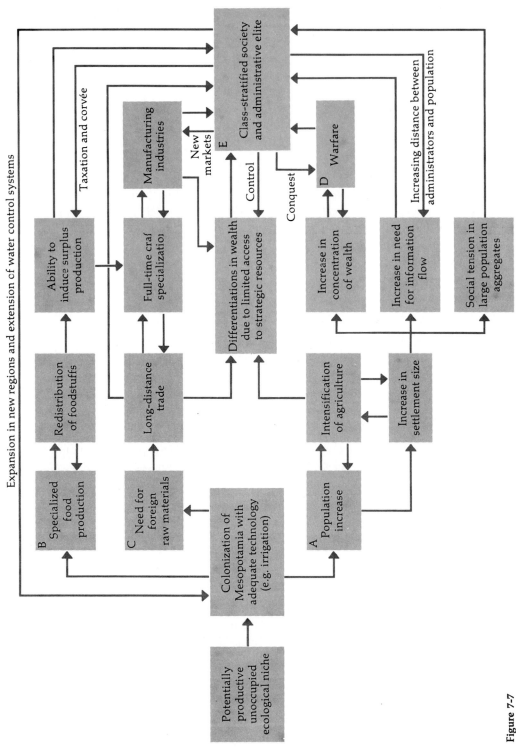

Figure 7-7
Interrelationships between cultural and environmental variables leading to the increasing stratification of class structure in Mesopotamian society.

the appropriate technology, the agricultural potential of land adjacent to the natural water courses was immense. The limitations were insufficient rainfall for dry farming and the inability of the upland plants and animals to tolerate the environmental conditions of the lowland river valley.

However, by 5000 B.C., important strides toward forming the basis for Mesopotamian urbanism had already been taken. Village farming communities had spread beyond the areas in which plants and animals had first been domesticated. Some of the new areas imposed environmental stresses on the plants and livestock, stresses that encouraged selection for more tolerant strains. At the same time, it seems that some of the people who had moved to the margins of the southern Mesopotamian lowlands, such as those of Tell es-Sawwan or Choga Mami, were beginning to rely on simple forms of irrigation to supplement the meager rainfall. In addition, there is evidence that the members of these communities developed more complex forms of organization than had their early village predecessors. Ranked society in Morton Fried's terms and a chiefdom level of organization in Elman Service's model had emerged. Hence, four advances—heat-tolerant animals, salinity-resistant plants, simple irrigation systems, and ranked, chiefdom organization—laid the groundwork for the rapid emergence of urbanism in lowland Mesopotamia.

The habitation by advanced farming communities of the Mesopotamian lowlands led to several major changes, creating three deviation-amplifying relationships that eventually resulted in class-stratified society (A, B, and C in Figure 7-7). Although the movement to lower elevations by the villagers of the sixth millennium and the later movement onto the Mesopotamian Plain by advanced villagers set in motion the growth of urbanism, I am not suggesting that the participants necessarily recognized the entire importance of the changes that were taking place. Rather, this whole process of movements of peoples, colonization of new regions, and stimulation of important feedback mechanisms can be understood in terms of natural, incremental processes that required people only to react to what they perceived as their most advantageous short-range choices. Hence, it was the environmental, technological, and social systems that primarily directed the evolution of these societies. Although individual people and unique circumstances may have caused minor deviations in the process of civilization, its general course was charted in a seemingly irreversible manner, given the aforementioned initial steps.

Emmigration to adjacent valleys was probably a common solution to the problem of a growing population in early Mesopotamia. In the course of seasonal migrations of the herding segment of semisedentary villages, the early farmers of the uplands came to know parts of the lowland areas. Whether people moved to new areas because of population growth or soil depletion or both, it is logical to suppose that in a two-thousand-year period (possibly eighty generations) people would have attempted to live at lower elevations among other alternatives. Not every village established in the lower, piedmont areas succeeded, but those that used irrigation water and relied on hardy strains of plants and animals were most successful. The process did not require foresight, nor the desire of people to move into Mesopotamia, nor any conception of the complex society that would develop there. Instead, it relied on the natural small-scale movements of human groups and on the existence of requisite conditions for the survival of a community in the Mesopotamian lowlands.

The establishment of agricultural communities along the natural river courses of lower Mesopotamia initiated three processes that set up crucial positive-feedback relationships (Figure 7-7A–C):

1 Slow, but steady population growth within a circumscribed productive region
2 Specialization in food production by different units within a society
3 Acquisition of foreign raw materials needed for utilitarian purposes

The increasing population of the Mesopotamian Plain, resulting from internal growth and immigration, initiated several crucial transitions. Unlike areas that have rainfall, where the prime determinant of productive locations is the fertility of the soil, the alluvial plain was agriculturally productive only if water was available. This meant that the best land was close to the natural courses of the major rivers, where small-scale irrigation could be employed. As the number of inhabitants increased, so did the amount of farmland utilized; it soon became necessary to cultivate land without direct access to a river by obtaining water from canals that ran through the land of other farmers. This situation might have been workable so long as the farmers remained amicable and there was sufficient water for everyone. However, in dry years, a farmer with direct access to a river might have used all the available water on his own fields. The problem would have been compounded as the population grew, because all the desirable land would have been in use; thus, less-desirable land would have had to be cultivated. The effects of the problem were twofold (Adams 1966a): (1) some land produced more crops per work hour than did other land; and (2) some farmers found that they had power over their neighbors. Consequently, irrigation works were built that would water greater areas.

The larger the population and the greater the amount of land under cultivation, the more advantageous it became to control the land with direct access to irrigation water. The wealth accumulated by the farmers who had better land allowed them to acquire additional land. By controlling the source of irrigation water, an already wealthy farmer would also have been the first to benefit from any further construction of canals that passed through his land. Differential land values would have encouraged those who owned the most valuable land to be in favor of the concept of private property rather than communal ownership. The inheritance of property and wealth would have been a logical next step, prompting the recognition of ascribed status, which was a basic regulating mechanism in early civilizations. Hence, the social division between rich and poor began 6,000 years ago. As Adams has stated (1966a), the successive intensification of agriculture and the ensuing differential access to strategic resources was a major cause for the emergence of class-stratified society.

There are several elements in this situation that reinforce each other and lead to a complex positive-feedback relationship:

1 The more people there are, the more land must be cultivated, or the more intensive must be the cultivation of each field, or both. The more intensive the agriculture, the more food there is to support a growing population.
2 Another method for increasing agricultural production for a growing population is through the centralized planning and administration of agricultural activities. Among other things, this would include the construction, maintenance, and management of irrigation works.
3 A growing population in a circumscribed productive area is also forced to live close together. Settlements would increase in size, which would in turn necessitate increasingly intensive agriculture, especially in the vicinity of large settlements.
4 The outcome of this intensification of agriculture in Mesopotamia was differential access to strategic resources—that is, irrigable farmland—and the basis for a growing administrative elite.

The growth of demographic centers stimulated the formation of several regulating institutions. The concentration of large numbers of people in nucleated settlements, with their stored food supplies and tools, created concentrations of wealth in amounts formerly unknown. The fact that only a few families in these large settlements benefited from such wealth accentuated its concentration. The concentration of wealth stimulated a concern for defense, and professional armies for regulating and maintaining the growing divisions within society became an institution. Another need created by the growth of large settlements was for improved information flow, requiring formalized rules and structure for conveying technical information concerning the productive economy. Tasks such as these seem to have been taken over by the temple community in early Mesopotamian cities, with writing and standardized art work being the two major mechanisms used. A third effect of large settlements was the social tensions created by the dense masses of people. New integrating mechanisms, closer regulation, and adjudication would have been necessary. In early cities, these institutions were administered by the temple elite and were enforced through social sanctions or the newly created military establishment.

The agricultural potential of the Mesopotamian Plain and the intensification of food production through the widespread use of irrigation made it advantageous for production to become specialized. It is possible to achieve greater production in a number of ways: (1) by utilizing more land; (2) by producing more food per unit of land; or (3) by increasing specialization and exchange. All three avenues were pursued in Mesopotamia. The specialization of productive tasks meant that workers became strictly fishermen, herders, or farmers. Each worker could have been more effective in doing one of the jobs on a full-time basis than was possible if all three tasks had to be accomplished by a single family (cf. Lees and Bates 1974). Specialization created a need for a means of exchanging goods, and a system of collection and distribution was organized by the temple elite. Thus, the temple directly employed a large part of the settlement's population in productive tasks (Gelb 1965).

The redistributive economy increased the efficiency of food production, but more important than that for the emergence of urbanism it placed additional power in the hands of the administrative elite, especially those in the temple community (Polanyi, Arensberg, and Pearson 1957). A major requirement of a complex society is that a surplus of food must be accumulated from the productive segment of society to support craftsmen, traders, and the elite. A redistributive system allows the administrator to set the amount of food a farmer must contribute to get a certain quantity of fish or meat in return. In this manner, the temple elite could have encouraged the production of a surplus by setting high requirements. It also gave the administrators another weapon against deviants. Specialization in food production, therefore, both created the need for a managerial elite and vested in their hands the means for supporting themselves and other specialists not engaged in the production of food.

The third major process that was initiated by the movement into Mesopotamia was the acquisition of raw materials from other regions (C in Figure 7-7). Southern Mesopotamia did not have adequate building stone, timber, bitumen, metal, nor stone for tools, grinding slates, or vessels. Substitute materials were used in some circumstances, such as baked clay instead of stone for tools and mud brick instead of stone masonry for buildings; nevertheless, significant amounts of material had to be imported.

Trade can assume a number of forms, depending on a society's organization and its need for goods. For example, raw materials can be either procured directly from the people who manufacture or mine them or obtained through intermediaries. Transactions can consist of the exchange of goods of equal value, but frequently one side may give more than it receives, in an effort to maintain the trading relation or establish an alliance. Ceremonies can accompany the exchanges in which "gifts" are given and solidarity reaffirmed.

To understand how trading networks affected societal organization, it is necessary to identify the persons or groups conducting the trade, how the goods were distributed, and the local goods received for payment. Although archeological evidence is inconclusive for the fifth and fourth millennia, it is likely that long-distance trade was conducted through the temple community. Trading parties may have been sent to regions in which the sought-after goods were available. By the fourth millennium, villages concentrating on the extraction and production of raw materials, such as copper and obsidian, probably existed in Iran and Turkey. The Mesopotamian traders may have exchanged textiles, pottery, foodstuffs, or craft goods for the raw material. As early as Jemdet Nasr times, there may have been communities of Mesopotamian traders living in distant centers to carry on trade—for example, Godin Tepe in Iran and Tell Brak in northern Syria. The goods that were brought back to Mesopotamia would have become part of the temple community inventory for manufacturing goods that was subsequently either distributed to the population or retained in the temple. The first trade may have been in utilitarian commodities, but after a short time rare metals, semiprecious stones, and other exotica also were traded, because the emergence of a wealthy class vested with authority stimulated the need for status goods that could be obtained only by trade. The increasing scale of trade had several important effects on Mesopotamian society: it required central administration to carry out long-distance trade efficiently and agricultural surplus to support the full-time traders.

The earliest traders are thought to have been functionaries of the temple. Later, however, during the second half of the early dynastic period, traders acted for the temple, but they also worked on behalf of the king and wealthy citizens, according to written evidence from that time. In addition, traders may have done business for their own benefit, leading to a semi-independent class of traders who conducted both official and private transactions (Adams 1974a).

Mesopotamian administrators collected surplus food from the agrarian population to support full-time craftsmen who fabricated the pottery, agricultural tools, textiles, sculpture, and metal goods that were used to pay for raw materials. The craftsmen became well organized, and there is good evidence that certain goods were mass produced at a very early date (e.g., pottery by 3000 B.C. and textiles by 2700 B.C.). The manufacturing industries required administration, and their control had to be coordinated with the control of the trading networks because craft specialization and industrialization placed new demands on trade. Thus, trade and industry further increased the complexity that characterized urban society.

A fourth feedback relationship (D in Figure 7-7) is partly due to the transformations caused by the first three feedback mechanisms. The increasing size of individual settlements and differential wealth created major concentrations of such material as agricultural produce, portable equipment, and status goods. Such valuable goods were a temptation to raiders from outside the community and to the poorer classes within it. In either case, the wealthier classes and, to a certain extent, all members of the society required some sort of military force to protect themselves. At the same time there was reason to use military forces in offensive campaigns. These armies might have been used to settle

disputes about land, protect trading routes, or loot goods from other communities. The greater the threat by the armies of others, the greater the necessity for building an army of one's own. However, once a militia is formed, even for defensive purposes, it is not economical to allow this potential armed force to remain idle. Hence, it might have been sent out to earn its keep. The vicious cycle of plunderable wealth leading to militarism leading to greater wealth is one that has continued to the present day.

The growth of militarism had important effects on the growth of urbanism. First, the army had to be supported by surpluses accumulated by the administrative elite. In return, the army helped to enforce the directives of the elite. Second, in times of instability, militarism encouraged the occupants of the countryside to move into defendable cities, which brought these peasants under more direct control of the urban elite than before. Third, militarism soon became an independent force of its own within the emerging civilizational hierarchy of administrative groups. Whereas the elite of the temple community might have been able to exercise power by informational, ritualistic, and economical means, the army could exact its authority directly through the use of force. This authority became extremely important after cities had been established and was instrumental in the formation of secular state governments.

Besides the positive-feedback relationships that increased the complexity of Mesopotamian society, there were numerous negative-feedback relationships that had a regulating or inhibiting effect on the growth of the system. It is the articulation and relative importance of the positive versus negative relationships that determine which systems grow, which remain static, and which diminish. No society steadily continues to grow in size and complexity without interruption. Mesopotamian civilization developed in stages, each one attaining a level of stability and then retrogressing in terms of size and complexity. Negative-feedback relationships were crucial in determining the level of stability achieved and the kinds of institutions that emerged to regulate the changing society.

Many of the factors in Figure 7-7 have potential

negative interrelationships; however, two of them are critical: production of agricultural surplus and increasing militarism. The production of agricultural surplus was central to the development of Mesopotamian civilization. It enabled a redistributive economy, crafts, trade, and industries. Agricultural surplus was also used to support the growing administrative elite and other specialists that were at the core of early urbanism. However, various processes in the growth of urbanism had a negative effect on the production or utilization of agricultural surpluses:

1 Short-term efforts at increasing production led to overintensification that frequently resulted in long-term economic disaster. Decisions not to allow sufficient fallow periods between crops or to continuously irrigate without taking proper precautions increased the probability of the water table rising and the farmland becoming salinized and unusable (Gibson 1974). Hence, administered efforts to increase production might in time have diminished production, in some cases even leading to abandonment of a region.

2 As is known from ethnographic studies, redistribution can function as a mechanism to equalize wealth. It is doubtful that it served as a leveling mechanism in Mesopotamia because of ethical considerations created by the productive situation. Much of this is embodied in the shift from ranked to stratified society in Fried's terminology. In ranked society, status is maintained through accomplishments and redistribution of wealth, whereas, in a stratified society, status is formalized, not requiring continual affirmation through distribution of wealth. What caused this change in ethics in early Mesopotamia is difficult to determine, but the unequal land values and need for imported utilitarian goods were probably important.

3 The concentration of population in cities reduces the amount of potentially cultivable land. Probably the ideal agricultural situation would be an even distribution of people over the entire agriculturally productive landscape. Concentrations of people can be supported by intensifying agriculture in the vicinity of the city, but there are limits. Improved transportation due to canal construction allows for the importation of foodstuffs with which to feed the inhabitants of large urban centers. However, the trends toward urban growth and potential agricultural production are inversely related.

4 The increasing size and wealth of the administrative elite drained capital from the productive segments of society. Excessively large classes of administrators and bureaucrats consumed an increasing proportion of the available agricultural surplus. This trend was intensified by the desire of the elite for status goods and the periodic immobilization of these goods in burials. Because of this trend, less surplus would have been available for investment in improving agriculture, for supporting craft production, or for industry. Thus, the difference between rich and poor would have become greater, and this could have caused both internal strife and invasion by outsiders.

The establishment of a standing army would have been a means to obtain wealth for the city through conquest and tribute. It also would have helped to increase the city's population because military activity in rural areas would have encouraged their inhabitants to migrate to the city. However, militarism also had several negative effects:

1 Agricultural production decreased when farmers moved to the cities.

2 Long-distance trade became hazardous and more costly to protect in areas of military activity.

3 The support of a standing army and an active state of militarism funneled off large amounts of potentially productive resources. The manpower and subsistence needs of the army itself reduced production capabilities that could have been channeled elsewhere. The defensive constructions around the city and the army equipment required large quantities of labor and raw materials. Warfare itself destroyed capital resources and already accumulated wealth.

Thus, the growth of urbanism stimulated by militarism was inhibited by negative-feedback relationships that acted to keep societies from developing into totally militaristic enterprises.

The increasing complexity, social stratification, and emergence of managerial institutions were initially caused by a series of interrelated systemic ecological factors stimulated by the colonization of the Mesopotamian Plain by agriculturalists. However, the elite they created were participants in the fifth positive-feedback relationship; that is, purposeful strategies of the elite to stimulate further growth of the institutions that gave them their power and wealth (E in Figure 7-7). This elite may have been either a single group or several groups, each attempting to extend the scope of its authority. It is logical that the administrative elite would have encouraged continued growth of managerial institutions to regulate the positive- and negative-feedback relationships. By doing so, they would have increased the scope of their control, making society more dependent on them. Each of the regulating institutions was a source of economic and administrative power for its manager, and various social codes and ethics were established to maintain and extend that power. Private or institutional property, ascribed status, differential access to productive resources, military force, elements of religion, myth, and artistic works—all contributed to societal division.

Although the course of cultural change is determined by diverse factors, an important element is the cumulative decisions made by the participating population. These decisions are made using the information at hand, and those who participate in making them do not always realize their true significance. In an urban society, decisions made by a small elite group influence the course of events for a large population. Even decisions made by the entire population are affected by the elite, who formulate courses of action for the populace to choose from and then influence those choices. This power of the elite might be especially evident in time of crisis: strong individuals or groups may gain power and be unwilling to relinquish it after the crisis has passed. The growing influence of the elite does not mean that other members of a complex society no longer react to environmental or economic exigencies; nevertheless, the elite are intermediaries who both interpret the situation and offer alternatives. They often have enough control

to be able to direct a society in courses initially at odds with the necessities of the environment and its own societal system. Eventually, however, these nonadaptive decisions must fail. By examining length of occupation and patterns of population growth, it is possible to determine from archeological evidence which societies were successful in coping with complexity and which remained at a lower level or disappeared altogether.

Future Research and Evaluation
of Hypotheses on Urbanism

General models of formation processes are difficult to test with data from the archeological record. The systems model depicted in Figures 7-1 and 7-7 is an attempt at further specifying the interrelationships between variables that prompted the emergence of Mesopotamian civilization. It does not pretend to offer simple answers nor to be a total departure from earlier attempts (Figures 7-2, 7-3, 7-4, 7-5, and 7-6). Rather, it affords an intellectual framwork within which research can proceed and current results can be evaluated.

Three directions that further investigations might take are:

1   Terms and categories must be operationally defined as they relate to the development of urbanism in Mesopotamia. These include the nature of class divisions, composition of an administrative elite, activities of ethnic groups, mechanisms of trade and industry, and power bases of early city rulers. It is necessary to develop relevant archeological yardsticks to measure civilizational variables in the archeological record. Methods of recognizing economic classes, conical clans, ethnic groups, mechanisms of trade, and patterns of control are poorly developed in archeology. A rigorous methodology based on a quantitative approach and historical inferences is essential to future investigations.
2   Comparative studies should be made of the variables present in regions where urbanism developed with those present in regions where it did not. Such studies could suggest the crucial variables that were necessary for urbanism. An examination of why Çatal Hüyük apparently did not evolve a centralized administrative elite is an ex-

ample of this type of study. Çatal Hüyük's early growth was the result of villagers moving into an unoccupied ecological niche and possibly becoming irrigation agriculturalists on the Konya Plain. Although Çatal Hüyük became the largest known demographic center in its time, it lacked several key variables that were present in Mesopotamian civilization: instead of importing major raw materials, Çatal Hüyük exported them to less-developed trading partners; the size of the Konya Plain was small compared with southern Mesopotamia, and this did not encourage specialization of subsistence pursuits; and there were no competing centers of population to threaten hostilities. Although major developments took place, the centralized administrative structure necessary for urbanism did not emerge. Consequently, Çatal Hüyük was unable to increase or even maintain its size and complexity.

3 One of the most direct tests of a hypothesis such as the one incorporating the systems ecological model presented herein would be to investigate the societies directly preceding the formation of states and cities to see whether the institutions discussed were already at work before the total crystallization of the administrative elite. Support for the interpretation summarized in Figure 7-7 would include good evidence for increasingly intensive agriculture, a redistributive economy, differential wealth, small-scale warfare, and increasing trade and manufacturing during the fifth and fourth millennia in Mesopotamia. If these institutions took on importance after the formation of the state, then they were not essential elements in the formation of a stratified society with an administrative elite. Chapters 8 and 9 contain information on Mesopotamian communities leading up to the earliest national state in the mid-third-millennium. This information is to be examined in light of the diverse hypotheses that have been formulated to explain the rise of civilization.

Investigating Complex Societies

Difficulties

The problem of determining the origins of cities, states, and complex societies is one of the funda-

mentally important areas of inquiry confronting the archeologist. However, an understanding of the processes that led to these phenomena is difficult to obtain from archeological materials. The remainder of this chapter is an introduction to some of the methodological considerations inherent in a study of complex societies. One problem is that the hypotheses presented to explain the origin of urbanism rely on many cultural variables, some of which are difficult to recognize in the archeological record. The evidence about certain cultural variables requires competence in specific subjects and must be examined by scholars in allied disciplines. Philologists to read early economic texts, chemists to determine the source areas of exotic raw materials, and statisticians to help with analytical techniques are just a few of the specialists needed. Another problem confronting the archeologist of complex societies is the scale of a civilization. Cities are by definition large in area, and to understand their relationships with their own surroundings and with other cities, an investigator must examine a huge area. In addition to large physical size, the hallmark of many civilizations has been the ability to produce great quantities of material objects, which means that there are enormous numbers of artifacts to identify from even a single site. A related problem is that, because the scale of interaction of a civilization makes large areas part of a single example, there are few independent examples of urbanism against which to test regularities. Because of the small number of examples of pristine urbanism, the normal statistical methods for identifying covariants cannot be applied. Consequently, systems models and simulation analyses seem to be the most appropriate means of testing hypotheses about the origin of urbanism.

Approach

The cultural units and processes of the origin of village life are very different from those of the origin of urbanism; hence it is necessary to adapt the scale of investigation, the techniques employed, and the range of data collected to the nature of the remains. The kinds of data to be collected are those that provide measures of the variables shown in Figures 7-2 through 7-7. Among these variables are demographic patterns, means of transmitting information, trade, industry, differential access to strategic resources, social organization, warfare, stratification, and the nature of the administrative elite. Not only must these variables be identified, but their interrelationships must be delineated in successive periods of urban development. To identify relevant variables in the archeological record, one must rely on information from ethnographic examples and the historical record. The difficulties of identifying sociocultural variables and the enormous scale of urban society should not be cause for abandoning rigorous archeological investigation; rather, they constitute a challenge to the resourcefulness of the archeologist.

The greatest difference between investigating complex societies and investigating village societies lies in the size of the unit under investigation. Although it might be possible to understand the origin of village life by studying the processes at individual sites or in small regions, this procedure is insufficient for the study of urban society. The very definition of a city emphasizes its interdependence with surrounding communities. The central functions and services of a city develop in response to the needs of its own inhabitants and those of the region it serves. Hence, the unit of investigation for complex societies must be a region containing major centers, and not just the city itself. This increase in the scope of investigations emphasizes the interrelatedness of the elements of the civilizational system. The assumption that entities within an ongoing system are interrelated means that it is not possible to understand an entity only in terms of its own characteristics. Rather, the study must include not only the characteristics of the entity itself, but also the characteristics that it derives from its position within the functioning system. As Robert Redfield suggested (page 220 herein; and Redfield, 1953), it is not possible to understand the great civilizational traits of any society without understanding the small civilizational traits of the entire region. The unique character of most urban societies, although manifested largely within the bounds of the central cities, develops from a city's interaction with the surrounding areas. Thus rural

traditions are strong influences on urban concepts and practices.

In conducting field research into complex societies, the initial work should be on the central city or the urban complex. The difficulties of archeological investigations of large cities are many. The deep cultural deposition on most Mesopotamian mounds covers stratigraphic levels of immediate interest to the origin of cities. Thus, it is difficult to unearth sufficient horizontal exposures and to control them properly. Compounding this difficulty is the fact that, because they are so complex, cities must be extensively sampled. In the investigation of a village it is possible to assume that, because the society was egalitarian and the basic economic unit was the household, remains of houses in different parts of the village will be relatively uniform. This assumption cannot be made at an urban center, which by definition is an integrated series of differentiated groups performing specialized activities. Hence, with complex societies the sites are bigger, the need for a representative sample more acute, and the information sought more subtle than for villages. Because of these limitations, archeological excavations in Mesopotamia have thus far contributed only certain kinds of information for the study of early urbanism. Most of the excavations undertaken have been of temple buildings, with the purpose of elucidating chronological sequences. More recently, archeologists have attempted to gather data on the variables necessary to the formulation and testing of systems models, but much more must be gathered than has been so far.

After the initial investigation of the city itself, its relation to the surrounding area must be researched. The relationship is measured in terms of demographic patterns and central services supplied by the city, services of a religious, economic, political, or military nature. These services may have been extended to the entire region, their organization being centralized in the city. Investigations should include a search for evidence of the central services supplied by the city, a quantitative measure of the area served by the city, and the degree to which the city depended on the smaller communities around it. Regional data can then be integrated with the data derived from the study of the center itself.

Sampling

Confronted with the difficulties imposed by increasing scale and new variables to be recorded, archeologists have begun to adopt new methods of investigation. Because of the immensity of the investigations that would have to be carried out to study an entire civilization, sampling techniques must be employed. Parts of regions to be surveyed intensively or sections of sites to be excavated can be selected on the basis of probability so that human biases are minimized. From the evidence obtained, patterns for the entire region or urban site can be inferred, within limits of probability. There are diverse sampling strategies available to archeologists, each designed to solve somewhat different problems (Redman 1974a). The selection of appropriate sampling strategies depends on the nature of the remains, the substantive questions being pursued, and the resources available. Combined strategies of excavations or surveys of small, scattered areas and large, contiguous ones yield a diversity of information on questions concerning complex society (Binford 1964; Redman 1973b).

Locational Analyses

The problem of measuring the increasing number of variables in an analysis of complex societies has been partly answered by careful study of the location and spatial arrangement of archeological remains. In addition to the formal properties of artifacts and settlements, their distribution and context are extremely useful sources of information, especially concerning questions of systemic relations. Spatial data give important clues to the way in which people lived. The placement of artifacts, features, structures, and the archeological sites themselves is indicative of the kinds of decisions made by ancient people, the environmental forces present, and the organizational structure of a community. Thus, archeologists are paying more attention than they formerly did to the horizontal placement of artifacts within excavated sites

(Whallon 1973; Dacey 1973). This type of study has helped in the functional identification of excavated areas. Studies of the distribution of specific designs painted on pottery have allowed inferences about social organization to be made (Hill 1970; Longacre 1970). Locational analysis of artifacts promises to open new areas of archeological inquiry, and to support inferences made about activities, residence patterns, and ancient social organization.

Another form of locational analysis that has contributed directly to an understanding of the rise of civilization is the study of changing settlement patterns (Braidwood 1937; Adams 1965; Adams and Nissen 1972; Johnson 1973b; 1977). Settlement-pattern studies are a valuable source of data for testing a wide range of hypotheses. From successive configurations of communities, inferences can be made about population, subsistence, sociopolitical systems, trade, and warfare. The investigation of settlement patterns takes place on three levels: the first concerns the shape of individual buildings; the second, the layout of communities; and the third, the spatial relationships of one community to another. The use of house plans and village layouts for determining changing village organizational mechanisms was discussed in Chapter 6.

Information on the spatial arrangement of communities can be collected by surveying a region on foot, by jeep, or by air. Archeological sites can be detected by, among other things, topographic differences and artifacts exposed by erosion. After a site has been discovered, its location, size, chronology, and other details are recorded. Questions are answered on settlement size, distribution of settlements according to size, the number of communities in each period, and the spatial arrangement of sites for each period. It can be expected that changes in administrative structure, the amount of warfare, or the routing of trading networks directly affected the nature of the settlement pattern at any given time.

The work of geographers is a valuable source of analytical techniques for understanding distributional data about ancient settlement patterns. Like

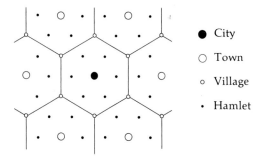

- ● City
- ○ Town
- ○ Village
- • Hamlet

Figure 7-8
Central place model of hexagonal settlement distribution.

archeologists, geographers are concerned with description, comparison, and process, but their data are primarily from the present and historical periods. Archeologists examine settlement data concerning the density, agglomeration, scatter, extent, orientation, shape, and topography of prehistoric communities.

Many settlement-pattern models used by geographers have been applied productively to archeological data and may soon be brought to bear on the problem concerning the rise of civilization. One of these models—which has as its basis the principle of least cost—has been used to investigate settlement patterns in the southwestern United States (Fritz and Plog 1970; Plog 1974a; Gumerman 1971). The basic assumption is that settlements were located so as to minimize the effort expended in dealing with the environment. Thus, such necessities as water, fuel, agricultural land, or collecting territory could have been prime determinants of site location, depending on their relative value to the ancient inhabitants. The distances of these resources from each site in a given region during successive occupations, the environmental zone, and the topography yield information concerning their relative importance in determining settlement location in the respective periods.

There are a variety of statistical methods that allow a researcher to determine whether the distribution of settlements is nonrandomly patterned and, if so, what the pattern is (Haggett 1965; King

1969; Smith 1976; Hodder and Orton 1976). Statistically determined site distributions become more relevant to the origin of cities if combined with data on settlement size. The variation in site size and the proportion of large sites to small ones are useful in developing models of community organization and change. In many developmental processes, there were absolute changes in numbers of people, whereas, in others, people simply moved from one type of community to another. By calculating community sizes, an archeologist can determine whether there is more than one mode to the distribution of size. If there is, then there may have been a hierarchical system, such as village, town, and city. The hierarchy of settlement sizes may be the result of economic or political variables. Different approaches can be taken to explain these settlement hierarchies and the distribution of communities within a region. One hypothesis states that most state-organized societies are characterized by a three-tiered hierarchy of settlement size, indicating different types of administrative and productive units.

An important geographic model formulated by Walter Christaller and adapted by August Lösch is known as central place theory (Haggett 1965; Berry 1967; King 1969). Its basic assumption is that only a small number of cultural variables affect the location of settlements. The primary postulate is that larger communities provide services for the surrounding smaller communities and should have more extensive hinterlands than do smaller settlements. The second postulate is that, in locating new settlements or in expanding older settlements, the inhabitants attempt to maximize the available resources. The most efficient use of an agriculturally homogeneous plain is made if the farming settlements on it are arranged in a hexagonal lattice distribution. This distribution places each settlement as far from all others as possible. If a larger settlement is to supply central services, then its most efficient location is in the center of hexagons of small villages (Figure 7-8). If mountains limit the expanse of productive agricultural land or if river courses and trading routes give a linearity to productive locations, then a modified distribution would be expected. By discovering the critical variables for settlement location and by knowing the environmental limitations and potentials, one can construct a hypothetically optimum distribution of villages, towns, and cities in a region. In reality, this distribution is modified by other factors, such as means of transportation, topography, local natural resources, external influences, and the extent to which the prehistoric inhabitants recognized the potential of their surroundings. Actual settlement patterns discovered during a survey can be compared with the derived ideal model and important ancient organizing factors can be inferred from the comparison. The deviations of the observed patterns from the ideal also yield valuable data on settlement interaction. By examining the changing patterns of site distribution and related causal factors, one can identify some of the major organizational changes that occurred during the rise of civilization.

Combining data on relative site size within a hierarchy with that on the location of the sites allows the identification of some settlements as central places. A medium-sized community can serve as a central place that supplies a narrow range of services to a relatively small surrounding area. Several of these medium-sized central places can exist in one region, with specific services being supplied by each one or with each of them supplying all services. Large central places, on the other hand, supply a wide range of services for large areas. The services themselves can be identified archeologically by the types of activities for which there is evidence at a given site but no evidence for surrounding smaller sites. The smaller sites being served might be inferred from geographical proximity and stylistic similarity of artifacts. The investigation of protourban and urban development depends directly on the discovery of these patterns.

An experimental study that includes detailed investigations of site functions, interrelations, and central place services has been conducted by Gregory Johnson (1972) on the distribution of Early Dynastic I settlements in the Diyala Plain, a region surveyed by Robert Adams (1965). Johnson attempted to use some of the postulates of central place theory to explain the location of sites in this early urban situation. He found that the general mode of distribution was in rhomboids rather than hexagons, possibly because of the parallel watercourses. Johnson examined the importance of least-cost considerations in determining site location. Maximization of usable land (even spacing of settlements) was found to be less important in determining settlement location than were considerations of transport networks. Settlements of successively smaller size were located (nested) around larger settlements along routes of communication between the larger settlements (Figure 7-9, page 242). The relative importance of towns as centers of distribution and the various routes of communication could be tentatively assessed on the basis of their distribution. Although no definite conclusions can be drawn from Johnson's preliminary analysis, it does demonstrate how locational analysis and central place principles can be useful tools in the formulation of hypotheses on the organization of early urban centers.

Additional Sources of Data for Civilization Studies

The student of complex societies benefits not only from the development of new methods of investigation and analysis, but from new categories of data that are not available to those who study simpler societies. The most important new source of data for early civilizations in the Near East is decipherable written records. The art of writing began at approximately 3400 B.C. in southern Mesopotamia. Most of the documents recovered from deposits of the following thousand years are records of goods stored, taxes paid, land rented, and offerings to the temple. It is possible to reconstruct the general outlines of economic systems, property rights, and some administrative and religious organizations from a careful study of the documents.

At approximately 2500 B.C., the written records became more diverse, and historical texts, mythologies, and literature became common. The tales of adventure, parables of morals, and stories of everyday experiences included in these writings are

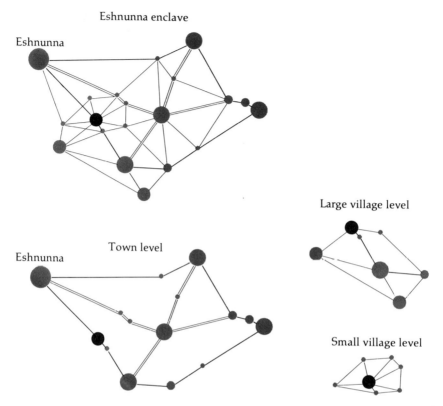

Figure 7-9
Distribution of Early Dynastic settlements in the vicinity of Tell Asmar (Eshnunna). Their subsystem nesting is exhibited by each large settlement being surrounded by evenly spaced smaller communities with even smaller villages located along the routes of communication between them (black circle is the same site in all four diagrams). (After Johnson, 1972.)

sources of insight into early Mesopotamian society, especially that of the Early Dynastic period, which was considered to be a Golden Age by later peoples (see Chapter 9). Some scholars have interpreted the myths transcribed in 2000 B.C. to have as their bases events that took place a thousand years earlier but, until we have evidence to support such interpretation, it remains speculative. Despite the uncertainities, later writings do afford interesting and testable models of organization and change.

Representational art often can be of assistance in understanding the lifeways of a period. Buildings are sometimes represented, as are productive and ritualistic activities. Art also served as a mechanism for conveying information, which archeologists can use to enhance their understanding of the organizational structures of the period.

To a greater extent than in earlier periods, the people of early cities buried their dead in cemeteries and included grave goods with the bodies. Careful study of the skeletons gives information on diet, disease, age profile, sex ratio, and sometimes ethnic groups. An investigation of the nature and quantity of grave goods can help in studies of rank society and social stratification.

These are some of the major new sources of information available to archeologists studying early civilizations in Mesopotamia. Some of these sources hold more promise than accomplishment. Examples of information derived from each is discussed in the remaining two chapters.

Having examined hypotheses on the formation of cities and methods of investigating them, one should consider briefly the effect of these early cities on their inhabitants. The density and regimentation necessitated by an urban community effected a life style for these urban dwellers that must have contrasted sharply with that of their village ancestors. The difference between an urban lifestyle and a rural one in early Mesopotamia must in many ways have been as great or greater than is found in the Near East today. Despite certain negative aspects, the early urban centers must have exerted a strong attractive force. The excitement of living with large conglomerations of people, the awesome monumental architecture, and the attitudes toward the newly formed elite are difficult for archeologists to excavate. The question whether the early cities grew through force of arms or through voluntary immigration is yet to be determined. Irrespective of the cause for urban growth and whether people who lived in the fourth-millennium Mesopotamian cities recognized what was happening, they were participants in one of the most fundamental and far-reaching transformations in human history.

C H A P T E R

8

FIRST STRIDES TOWARD URBANISM

The Emergent City

*During the fifth and fourth millennia, the people of southern
Mesopotamia achieved most of the landmarks of an urban civilization. In
this chapter, the archeological information from this period is discussed
according to the sequence of occupations, which are differentiated
largely on the basis of changing pottery styles and stratigraphic superimposition
of temple buildings. Descriptions of characteristic items of the
archeological inventory and building forms are included for each
occupation, as are data on settlement patterns and the
accompanying demographic changes.*

*Of great archeological interest are the subsistence resources used during
this period, the growth of organized industries, and the invention of writing.
These cultural achievements, as well as the early development
of social institutions and the appearance of civilizational attributes,
are the subjects discussed in the last half of this chapter.*

The formation of cities and of a civilizational network on the Mesopotamian Plain was relatively rapid: only two thousand years after its earliest-known occupation in the mid-sixth millennium cities emerged and writing and the other traits of urbanism appeared. The innovations and changes in organizational structure that produced complex societies were constantly occurring in what was an almost unbroken sequence of development. Some elements of urban society appeared earlier than others, perhaps stimulating further growth. Writing, industry, religious elite, monumental public works, and representational art were all in the archeological record before the crystallization of state society.

During the fifth and fourth millennia, many of the technological inventions and organizational innovations essential to later civilizations appeared. The first communities of sufficient size and complexity to be considered true cities also emerged. By 2900 B.C., when the events described in Chapter 9 began, the people of southern Mesopotamia had already taken giant strides toward the realization of civilization. From then on, the process was self-sustaining. The advances made during the fifth and fourth millennia were crucial to the development of cities.

Early Mesopotamian Chronology and Settlement

Chronological Sequence of Occupations

The primary means for subdividing the fifth and fourth millennia into shorter periods is by the changes in pottery. The manufacturing techniques, the clay used, the shapes of vessels, and the painted designs changed with relative rapidity. By carefully studying the characteristics and the stratigraphic relationships of the ceramic pieces found in excavated deposits, archeologists have been able to subdivide the two thousand years covered in this chapter. Other aspects of the cultures were also incorporated into these subdivisions, including artwork other than pottery, clay tools, architec-

tural information, and recent radiocarbon age determinations. The details of this chronological system are presented in Figure 8-1 (page 246). Although this sequence is commonly accepted, it is by no means the only system of subdivision in use. It should be understood that each system has advantages and disadvantages. However, the details of chronological ordering are less pertinent for the present purpose than the use of this chronological system as a tool for analysis and communication. Poorly understood artifact inventories recovered from partial exposures of selected sites cannot be expected to yield sufficient information for subdividing protohistoric Mesopotamia. However, if we were to wait for a system based on reliable dating, it would not be possible to interpret the information about the rise of civilization that is already available, nor would it be possible to plan effective future investigations.

The seven chronological periods used in this chapter are subdivisions of three major periods of time (Porada 1965; Adams and Nissen 1972): the earliest is the 'Ubaid period (c. 5300–3600 B.C.), subdivided into 'Ubaid 1 through 4; the next is the Uruk period (c. 3600–3100 B.C.), subdivided into Early Uruk and Late Uruk; and the last is the Jemdet Nasr period (c. 3100–2900 B.C.). Like those of earlier periods, cultures were usually named after the archeological sites at which their distinguishing characteristics were first discovered. 'Ubaid and Jemdet Nasr are not the most important sites for their respective periods, but Uruk (Warka) is the primary source of information for the period of that name.

During the 'Ubaid period, especially 'Ubaid 3 and 4, the culture of the entire Mesopotamian Plain and of the lands extending in all directions from it was generally uniform. The 'Ubaid culture probably began in southern Mesopotamia, where it had the greatest effect on subsequent developments. To put these developments in perspective, it is useful to look briefly at the cultural inventory uncovered at Tepe Gawra in the north as well.

There is little question that the cultures of the south were in the forefront of development by the end of the 'Ubaid 4 period, and most of the infor-

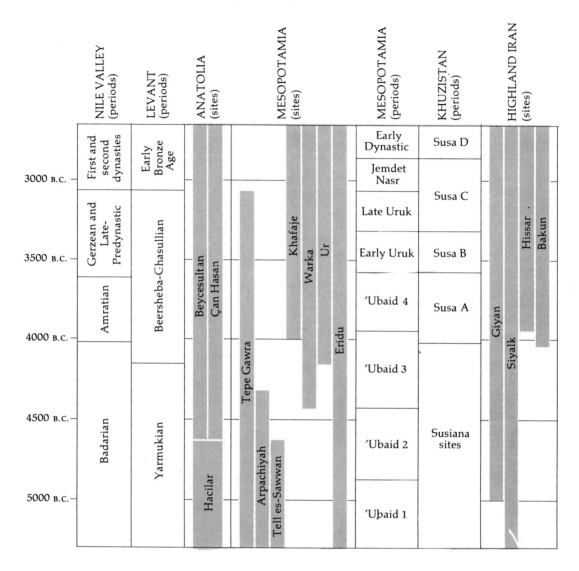

Figure 8-1
Archeological periods for each region of the Near East, including the dating of early towns and cities in Mesopotamia.

mation on the next period, the Uruk period, has come from the extensive excavations in the temple precincts of Warka (whose ancient name was Uruk, referred to in the Old Testament as Erech). Consequently, the data on this period consist predominantly of architectural information concerning large-scale religious structures and the artifacts that have been found in them and at smaller sites.

The Jemdet Nasr period is not well known archeologically. The painted temple at Tell 'Uqair and the temple complexes at Warka are perhaps its best examples of achievement.

'Ubaid Occupations of the South

Although the 'Ubaid period received its name from a small site, Tell Al 'Ubaid, in the vicinity of Ur, it is best known from the larger site of Eridu (see Figure 8-2). Eridu and other 'Ubaid-period sites of southern Mesopotamia were founded on virgin soil. Hence, 'Ubaid 1 (also referred to as the Eridu culture) seems to be the time of initial colonization of southern Mesopotamia by sedentary agriculturists. Whether there were earlier nomadic groups or settlements that have not yet been discovered remains to be seen. The evidence that would establish the details of the 'Ubaid 1 subsistence systems is not yet available, but it is clear that the agriculture of this period relied on irrigation. Eridu was in the extreme south of Mesopotamia on the edge of the Arabian desert and had insufficient rainfall for dry farming. It is likely that the first inhabitants of this region were able to farm on the banks of the Euphrates River and on the margins of the swamps, where access to water would have been relatively easy.

Although the earliest deposits at Eridu of the 'Ubaid 1 period did not cover so large an area as did later deposits, it is likely that some of the 'Ubaid-period sites were larger than most early villages in the upland regions. From the 'Ubaid 2 period (also known as the Hajji Muhammad phase), sites as large as 4 hectares are known (Adams and Nissen 1972). By 'Ubaid 4, the site of Eridu may have been as large as 10 hectares. Sites of this size cannot be considered villages. Eridu probably housed from 2,000 to 4,000 people at its maximum. The size of this community has organizational implications, which are considered later in this chapter.

The artifacts that have been used to distinguish 'Ubaid-period occupations and to subdivide the general period are diverse (Porada 1965). The characteristic pottery of 'Ubaid 1 was a fine monochrome ware, with small rectilinear patterns painted in a chocolate color. These patterns are similar to those on Samarran vessels and include grids, triangles, and zig-zags. 'Ubaid 2 pottery had dark purplish-black paint, often thickly applied, pro-

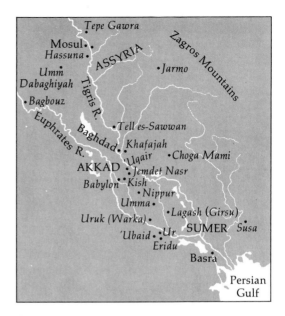

Figure 8-2
Fifth- and fourth-millennia sites in Mesopotamia and Khuzistan.

ducing a metallic luster. The patterns were close together, creating dark zones on the light buff clay background. Common shapes for these two periods include shallow, wide bowls, jars with narrow mouths, and tall beakers Figure 8-3, page 248).

The 'Ubaid 3 assemblage found in large areas of Greater Mesopotamia has several distinctive elements. Tools made from hard-fired clay were used. Sickles, hammers, axes, and bent nails were common (Figure 8-4, page 249). Clay was used for objects normally made of stone, evidence both of the absence of stone in southern Mesopotamia and of the inventiveness of the people. The painted designs on the pottery of 'Ubaid 3 were simpler than those of 'Ubaid 2, with less painting but bolder designs. This trend toward simplification continued into the 'Ubaid 4 period. Most 'Ubaid pottery was made on a slowly turning wheel (turnette) and was a major means of artistic expression. However, after the 'Ubaid period, the fast wheel was introduced, as were other means of artistic expression, and painted pottery declined in importance and eventually disappeared completely.

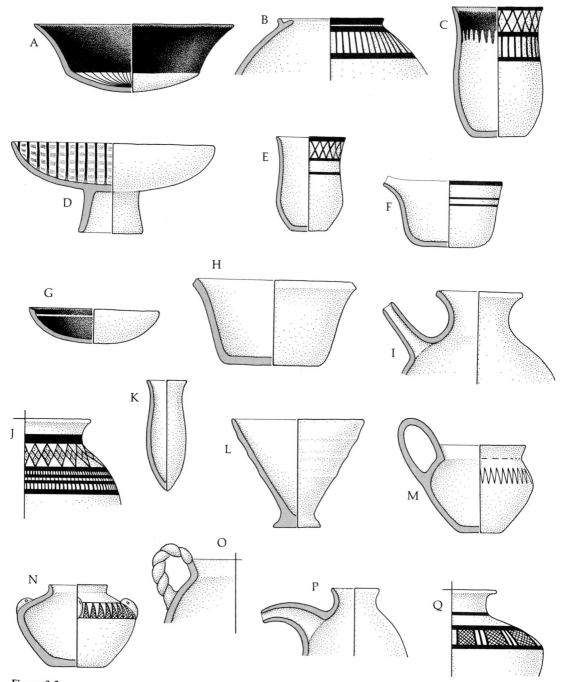

Figure 8-3
Pottery profiles for diagnostic Mesopotamian types from the 'Ubaid (A–G),
Uruk (H–O), and Jemdet Nasr (P and Q) periods. (After Adams and Nissen,
1972.)

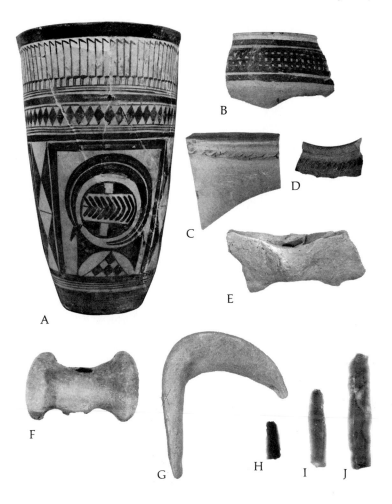

Figure 8-4
Clay objects characteristic of 'Ubaid-period sites: (A) beaker from Susa (Musée du Louvre); (B–D) ceramics from a small site near Nippur; (E and F) clay tools; (G) clay sickle; (H) obsidian blade; (I and J) flint blades.

Distinctive clay figurines have been discovered in deposits of both the 'Ubaid and the Uruk periods (Figure 8-5, page 250). They are made from the same type of clay as the pottery, but have a greenish color. The figurines are fairly large (from 14 to 17 centimeters high). The heads are almost reptilian in character with long oblique gashes to represent eyes. They were all in standing positions and both sexes are represented.

Despite the fact that painting declined in importance during the 'Ubaid period, there was a greater variety of pottery shapes than ever before. Spouts and handles became common appendages to aid in the utilization of the vessels. It seems that pot-

tery was relegated to a largely utilitarian status. As with other nonsymbolic artifacts in the cultural inventory, tendencies toward specialization were strong. The variety of shapes and the modifications of vessels indicate that tasks were becoming more specialized.

The evidence for changing forms of architecture is of as much interest as the artifactual inventory of the people of southern Mesopotamia during the 'Ubaid period. Little is known about the construction of houses, but it is commonly assumed that most domestic buildings were made of a combination of reeds and mud brick. The best information about the architecture and the religion of this pe-

Figure 8-5
Clay figurines typical of 'Ubaid
and Uruk periods. (Courtesy of
the Director General of
Antiquities, Baghdad, Iraq.)

1   8
Centimeters.

riod comes from several temples at Eridu. Thirteen
superimposed foundations of increasingly larger
structures were uncovered by Seton Lloyd and
Fuad Safar at Eridu (Safar 1950). What is remarkable about these buildings is that they contained all
of the elements of later Sumerian temples. The
earliest complete temple in the Eridu sequence
(level 16) was a thin-walled square building with
a deep recess in which a small pedestal probably
served as an altar (Figure 8-6A). On a second, similar pedestal in the center of the building there are

signs of burning, which probably means that it
was an offering table. The building was constructed
of long, prismatic mud bricks.

Subsequent buildings in this sequence were a
good deal larger; their floor plans were more complex, and they had regular buttresses. The temples
were built on raised platforms. The dominant element of each building was a large rectangular room,
later known as a cella, with an altar at one end.
Behind the cella were two small rooms, which
served as a passageway and a side chamber, respec-

tively. The last temple in this sequence had a definite tripartite plan, which was characteristic of subsequent Sumerian construction. The area of the high platform on which it sat was 20 by 10 meters. The building contained a large central room (cella) with smaller rooms on either side (Figure 8-6B). A stairway led from the ground level to the platform and then to the temple entrance.

Each building in this sequence is separated from the others by deposits of debris containing bones of small animals and fish that might have been part of the offerings made inside the temple. It has been suggested on the basis of the fishbones that the deity worshipped in these temples was Enki, the god of water, who is known to have been the city-god of Eridu in historic times. The identification of the patron deity of these protohistoric people and the similarity in architectural design with subsequent temples is strong evidence for the continuity of tradition and population in southern Mesopotamia from the first settlers to early historic times.

'Ubaid Occupations Adjacent to Southern Mesopotamia

To understand the origin of the 'Ubaid culture in the south and the growing civilizational network during this period, one should be familiar with available evidence from other 'Ubaid settlements. Assemblages resembling the 'Ubaid materials of the south have been found in numerous sites of the north. The best-known sequence of 'Ubaid occupations in the north is at Tepe Gawra (Figure 8-2). The earliest 'Ubaid deposits at Gawra, and most other northern sites, overlie a series of earlier occupations. Halafian material precedes the 'Ubaid deposits at Gawra. Although some evidence points to a continuity between the Halafian and 'Ubaid in the north, it is likely that many aspects of the 'Ubaid culture were influenced by the south. The 'Ubaid economy was of predominantly rainfall agriculture and the villages were from small to moderate in size. Cultivation did not require irrigation in most locations and goats, sheep, and cattle were herded. Because there were sources of stone in the north, there was little need for the baked

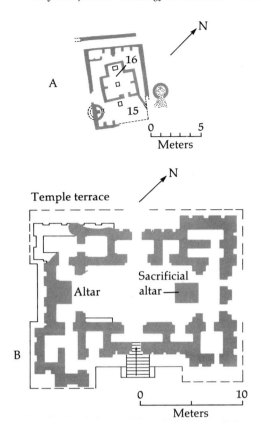

Figure 8-6
Plans of temples at Eridu: (A) levels 16 and 15; (B) level 8.

clay tools that were common in the south. Some "bent nails" of clay have been found at Gawra, reinforcing the similarity observed in the pottery of the north and south. Stamp seals were more common and more developed in the north than in the south. Nearly six hundred stamp seals and impressions were found at Gawra, most of which were made of stone although some were made of other materials. Most designs were engraved and not drilled, among which geometric designs predominated, with only a few animal representations.

The remains of what have been interpreted to have been a series of temples were uncovered at Gawra. There was greater diversity in the design of the Gawra temples, but many of the elements are similar to those in the temples of Eridu. In the

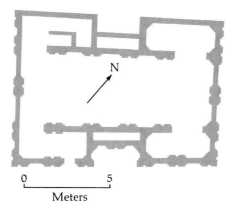

Figure 8-7
Plan of temple of level 13 at Tepe Gawra ('Ubaid 4 period).

main sequence of superimposed temples at Gawra, there was a circular building referred to as a tholos, the same term used for earlier, Halafian buildings. Its presence in the temple sequence term used for earlier, Halafian buildings. Its presence in the temple sequence has been interpreted as confirmation that the larger Halafian tholoi were religious structures rather than domestic ones (Perkins 1949:65). The foundations of several large buildings arranged around an open plaza have been found in the last 'Ubaid levels at Gawra. These buildings exhibited many of the characteristics of southern Mesopotamian temples and their superimposition over earlier temples is reminiscent of a "temple precinct." The northern temple was the best preserved and most closely parallels the temples of Eridu (Figure 8-7).

These remains of the 'Ubaid 4 period are the most monumental of Gawra; they are indication of a turning point in the history of northern Mesopotamia. During the development of agriculture and the establishment of village life, northern Mesopotamia was in the forefront. However, starting with the 'Ubaid period, the situation reversed. The settlers in the south were subjected to new forces not present in the north. Although the people in the north continued to subsist in a fashion similar to that of previous millennia, the communities of the

south were forced to reorganize their activities. Neither irrigation nor great quantities of traded raw materials were needed in the north. Agriculture and economic pursuits could be successfully carried out in small groups, and so the stimulation for growth in settlement size and reorganization of structure was largely absent.

Another region of important settlement during the 'Ubaid period was in Khuzistan, Iran, east of the Tigris and Euphrates rivers (Figure 8-2). Khuzistan, like the north, had been occupied long before the 'Ubaid period. The economic necessities of Khuzistan lay somewhere between those of northern and southern Mesopotamia. Areas of Khuzistan could support agriculture without irrigation, but the heartland of Susiana (refer to Figure 2-1 on page 20) could be effectively farmed only with the aid of irrigation. Tepe Sabz was a late-sixth-millennium and early-fifth-millennium village in the Deh Luran Valley of Khuzistan (Hole, Flannery, and Neely 1969). It was a small village of agriculturalists who used irrigation and herded cattle, sheep, and goats. Although these people were simple farmers, they had the plants, animals, and skills to live on the alluvial plain. About forty sites of this general time range are known in Khuzistan, which means that the area was densely populated by agriculturalists who successfully adapted to the piedmont zone and the edges of the alluvial plain.

During the fifth and the first half of the fourth millennia Khuzistan continued to be densely populated. Larger settlements developed, with the primary community being Susa (Figure 8-8).

The period in Khuzistan referred to as Susa A was roughly contemporary with 'Ubaid 3 and 4 in southern Mesopotamia (LeBreton 1975). The settlements of the Susa A period in Khuzistan indicate that the population density and perhaps other aspects of their culture peaked. There were large numbers of villages in the Susiana Plain and neighboring areas of Khuzistan. In addition, there were several intermediate-sized communities as much as 10 hectares in area in the adjacent valleys (Nissen and Redman 1971). The largest Susa A community was at Susa itself, covering from 25 to 30 hectares

Figure 8-8
Aerial view of the site of Susa
and the surrounding Susiana
Plain in Khuzistan. (Photograph
from Aerofilms Ltd. Copyright
reserved.)

with a "high terrace." The complex system of set-tlements of varying sizes in Khuzistan is currently being studied by archeologists on several expeditions and promises to yield information about an early, large-scale development leading to urbanization (Wright, Neely, Johnson, and Speth 1975).

The people of Khuzistan were certainly in contact with those of southern Mesopotamia, but to a large extent the developments in the two areas seem to have followed separate paths. The increase in population and settlement size in Khuzistan was earlier than it was in Mesopotamia, but it did not continue after the end of the fourth millennium. Rather, the city of Susa continued to grow in population and power, seemingly at the cost of developments in the remainder of Khuzistan. As more becomes known about developments in this region, there will be an example of early civilization that will complement and contrast with that of southern Mesopotamia.

Uruk Occupations in Southern Mesopotamia

By 3600 B.C., when the period identified as Uruk began, the primacy of southern Mesopotamia in the development of urban centers was assured. The chronological sequence and material inventory of this period are best known from the excavations at Warka (see Figure 8-2). However, the artifactual assemblage identified as Uruk, and the cultural system it represents, was widespread, appearing throughout the Mesopotamian Plain and beyond. The distinguishing feature of the Uruk artifact assemblage was that painted pottery was being replaced by unpainted or light-colored pottery. Much of this pottery was made on a wheel and decorated with incised patterns. Handles and spouts were common, and there was greater variation in shape and rim treatment than there had been in earlier ceramics. Because of the absence of painted designs, archeologists must rely on other changing characteristics to differentiate within the Uruk period. This is a difficult task and is only now producing the detailed chronological picture required for analysis. Changes in the shape and other features of the pottery, as well as the absence of decorative motifs, are evidence of different periods. Major technological innovations and institutional developments also are being used more and more

Figure 8-9
Uruk or Jemdet Nasr cylinder seal: modern impression of cattle of a sacred
herd emerging from a reed structure. (Photograph from The Oriental
Institute, The University of Chicago.)

to define the chronological periods starting with
the Uruk period. The introduction of wheel-made
pottery is the hallmark of the Uruk period; the appearance of certain mass-produced types of pottery indicates the beginning of the Late Uruk
and the end of the Uruk period is signaled by the
first evidence of writing. The major chronological
dividers for periods subsequent to the Uruk are
architectural changes, glyptics, and historically
known dynasties.

The Early Uruk period is characterized by the
introduction of plain gray and red slipped pottery
and the sharp decrease in painted wares. This period is roughly equivalent to the stratigraphic levels
14 to 7 of the Eanna precinct at Warka. Overfiring
or possibly different clay resulted in a greenish
color during the 'Ubaid period, but this was less
frequent during the Early Uruk period. The architecture of the Early Uruk period is not so well
known as that of the Late Uruk period, but the
'Ubaid-period temple series at Eridu continued into
the Early Uruk period, with new structures being
built on top of the earlier temple platform. Although there were changes, the general picture is
one of continuity between 'Ubaid 4 and Early Uruk
periods.

The Late Uruk period (c. 3400-3100 B.C.) is characterized by technological innovations, design

changes, and major architectural achievements. The
most striking addition to the material inventory
during the Late Uruk period is the abundance of
bevel-rimmed bowls (see Figure 8-3H). These
crudely made, chaff-tempered vessels are distinguished by their obliquely cut rims. They were
manufactured in large numbers with little attention
paid to finishing. It has been suggested that they
were mass produced by pressing sheets of clay
into a mold, and that their abundance and widespread appearance might be related to a role they
played as a standard measuring vessel for the increasingly centralized redistributive economy
(Johnson 1973b). If this were the case, bevel-
rimmed bowls are the earliest strong evidence for
a managed economy. Other recognizable changes
in the ceramic inventory during the Late Uruk include applique, finger impressions, incision (Figure
8-3M), and twisted "rope" handles (Figure 8-3O).
Seals have been found in large numbers, both
stamp and cylinder types. In addition to geometric
designs, naturalistic motifs of animals and people
became more prevalent (Figure 8-9).

Among the most impressive material achievements of the Uruk period are the monumental
buildings uncovered at Warka, a community established during the 'Ubaid period on the banks of the
Euphrates River about 65 kilometers northeast of

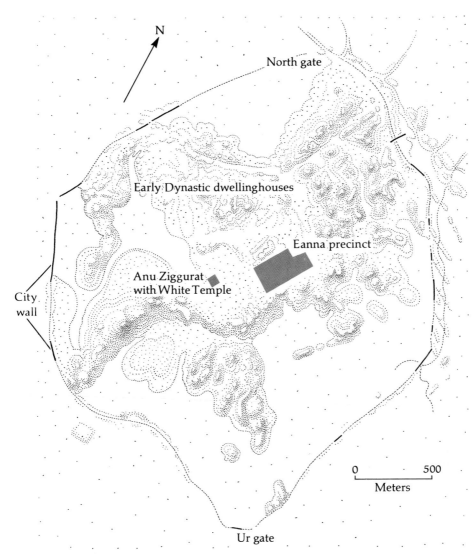

N

North gate

Early Dynastic dwellinghouses

Eanna precinct

Anu Ziggurat
with White Temple

City
wall

0　　　500

Meters

Ur gate

Figure 8-10
Plan of the site of Warka (ancient Uruk) showing the excavated areas of the
Anu ziggurat, the Eanna precinct, and the city walls.

Ur (see Figure 8-2). The fluctuating size and density of occupation is not well documented for the settlement at Warka, but it is clear that during the Uruk period this community attained urban status. It is possible that the city covered as much as 80 hectares and had a population of 10,000. The two areas within the city of Uruk that have been intensively investigated by archeologists underlie the Anu ziggurat and the Eanna precinct of the historical period (Figure 8-10). These areas of the city were the sites of temples during the early historic periods, and they are assumed to have been temple precincts during the Uruk period. Other parts of the city have not been thoroughly explored, and

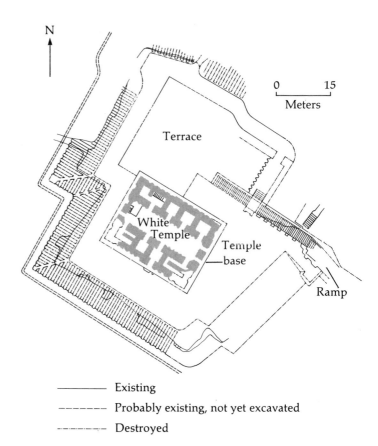

Figure 8-11
Plan of the Anu ziggurat with the White Temple at Warka.

N

0   15
Meters

Terrace

White Temple

Temple base

Ramp

——————— Existing

— — — — — Probably existing, not yet excavated

—·——·——·— Destroyed

large areas of domestic architecture, craft quarters, and nonreligious civic buildings have yet to be discovered and excavated. Hence, what is known of the early history of Warka, as well as of Eridu and other Mesopotamian cities, is from temples. This has given archeologists a wealth of information about ceremony and religion but almost none about the mundane aspects of early society. The degree to which this situation changes depends on whether archeologists expand the scope of future excavations to include the utilitarian along with the exotic, the domestic along with the religious.

The earliest-known monumental architecture at Warka is the series of building levels collectively referred to as the Anu ziggurat. The structures there reached their maximum size and best-preserved form immediately after the end of the Uruk period, but below this level were similar structures dated

at all phases of the Uruk period and at 'Ubaid times. The best-preserved building, known as the White Temple because of its color, was built on a high platform, creating a visual effect of monumentality. The ascent to the platform was a combination of ramps and steps. The construction of the platform was of complex brickwork, and included foundation deposits in the east corner. A hollow space was left in the lowest course of bricks and in it were laid the skeletons of two carnivores: a leopard and probably a young lion (Perkins 1949:111).

The White Temple itself measured 17.5 by 22.3 meters and had a tripartite plan (Figure 8-11). It contained a long, central room with two rows of smaller rooms, a plan similar to that of the final 'Ubaid temples at Eridu. In the central room, or cella, were two features that were probably used in the rituals taking place in this building: one was

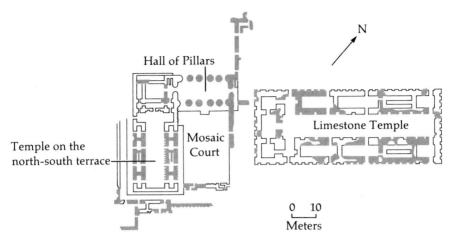

Figure 8-12
Plan of the Limestone Temple, the Mosaic Court, and the Hall of Pillars at Warka.

a free-standing rectangular pedestal with a semi-circular step that shows evidence of burning, perhaps of offerings; the other was a high platform at one end of the cella with steps leading up to it, perhaps the base for a monumental sculpture. The temple interior contained many niches, and the exterior was regularly buttressed. The size, layout, and features of this temple were vey much in keeping with later historic Sumerian temples and can be assumed to be ancestral to them. The inference that this temple and platform complex was for the worship of Anu is based on the temple's proximity to later historical temples dedicated to the sky-god Anu, who was a primary god in the Sumerian pantheon.

The presence of the Anu platform and White Temple are of major significance in terms of the changes in society that they manifest. Whereas the earlier Eridu temples were indicative of a religious elite with well-defined canons of architecture and a modest control over the populace, the Anu complex gives evidence of an elite with tremendous control over a highly organized labor force. It is estimated that it required 7,500 man-years of physical labor to construct this monumental edifice (Mallowan 1965). The size of the labor force, the

skill in planning and execution, and the repeated rebuildings imply an institutionalized hierarchy with access to large economic resources, pools of laborers, and skilled craftsmen.

A fact that supports the inferences about centralized control made on the basis of the Anu complex is that it was one of several other contemporary temple complexes at Warka. The most monumental of all the excavated ruins at Warka is the series of superimposed and contemporary temples uncovered in the Eanna precinct. This area, in the center of Warka, was dedicated to the worship of Inanna during early historic times. Inanna was Warka's most prominent patron deity. Inanna in the semetic form, Ishtar, was considered to be the goddess of love and war represented by the planet Venus (Saggs 1962). The earliest reconstructable temple in the Eanna precinct is known as the Limestone Temple because it was erected on a base of limestone blocks brought from the escarpment of the Arabian plateau about 60 kilometers away to protect it from rain and moisture (Figure 8-12). The temple itself was enormous, measuring at least 76 by 30 meters. Its plan was tripartite, but the central room was T-shaped and there were several entrances to the building. The symmetry of the

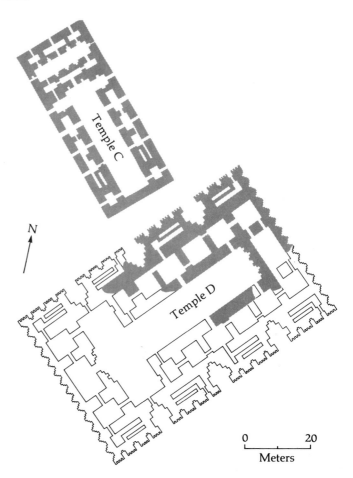

Figure 8-13
Plans of temples C and D
at Warka.

architectural design and the intricately niched interior and buttressed exterior are testimonies to the sophistication of the planners and craftsmen of fourth-millennium Warka.

Located near the Limestone Temple and probably overlapping it in time was a building referred to as the Pillar Temple (Figure 8-12). This structure was built on a complex of terraces that also were to serve as the foundation for later temple complexes. The distinguishing features of the Pillar Temple were its free-standing columns, clay cone mosaic decoration, and unusual design—instead of being a single building, it consisted of several. A moderate-sized, tripartite temple adjoined a large court whose entrance was through an area in which there were two rows of decorated pillars. The pil-

lars were 2.6 meters in diameter and are the earliest free-standing columns known in Mesopotamia. To form the columns, the mud bricks were laid radially and thickly plastered with clay. Thousands of clay cones were stuck into this plaster while it was still wet (Perkins 1949:122). The visible ends of the cones were colored red, white, and black; all three colors appear in most of the mosaic fields. The geometric designs made by these cones were composed of zigzags, lozenges, triangles, and diagonal bands. It has been suggested that the model for these mosaic designs came from the reed matting used as wall coverings.

Eventually the Pillar Temple was covered over and served as the foundation for two larger temples of the traditional tripartite plan. The central chamber of each of these temples was T-shaped, and the side chambers were further elaborated (Figure 8-13). The larger temple (Temple D) was about 80 by 60 meters, with extremely elaborate buttressing around its exterior.

In general, the religious architecture during the Uruk period at Warka is strong evidence for a powerful elite. Temples in different sectors of the site were uniform in design, which remained conservative for a long time. Whatever physical differences there were between temples were probably due to a difference in beliefs and the rituals performed for specific deities or to the members of the elite responsible for their construction. In the temples of the Anu ziggurat, there is clear evidence for altars and burnt-offering pedestals. In those of the Eanna precinct, there is a complex design of interior niches that may have served both decorative and ritualistic functions, although this is not the case in other temples nearby. The scale of both the buildings themselves and the precincts at Warka was enormous; the Eanna precinct alone covered about 9 hectares.

Chronologically, little is known of Warka before the Uruk period, but it is assumed that by the 'Ubaid period the settlement was growing and temples were being built. By the end of the Uruk period there were several elaborate and monumental temples at Warka, demonstrating both the strength and the diversity of the religious elite. Many of these temple areas continued to be used during subsequent periods. From what archeologists have discovered so far of the Uruk period, Warka was the largest and most impressive site in Mesopotamia. Although there is no archeological evidence that suggests that the inhabitants of Warka controlled more than their immediate vicinity, it seems that for the 400 or 500 years following the construction of these large temples (c. 3200–2800 B.C.) Warka was the supreme example of Sumerian accomplishment.

In addition to the pottery that identifies the Uruk period and the architecture that is its monumental feature, there are other important aspects of the material inventory. Stone vessels of a variety of shapes and raw materials were found in Uruk-

Figure 8-14
Stone vase from Warka with registers depicting different activities. (Courtesy of the Director of Antiquities, Baghdad, Iraq.)

period deposits. The most impressive stone vessel is a pedestaled vase about 1 meter high from Warka (Figure 8-14). The exterior of the vase is decorated with three registers of scenes from domestic and religious life: the lowest register portrays rows of plants and animals; the middle one is a procession of nude males with shaven heads carrying offerings of food and wine; and the upper one is a complex scene, probably depicting a ritual in which a goddess (Inanna?) is presented with offerings of food

Figure 8-15
Marble head from Warka; the eyes and eyebrows
were of inlaid material. (Courtesy of the Director of
Antiquities, Baghdad, Iraq.)

(Mallowan 1965:58). The Warka vase is a fine example of the artistic skill of craftsmen of the period,
and may represent the artist's rendition of both the
social order at Warka and one of its important
rituals.

A superb example of sculpture, an art form that
also emerged at the final stage of the Uruk period,
is a white marble head from Warka (Figure 8-15).
The head was probably part of a composite statue
with a wooden body and inlaid eyes and eyebrows.
It is almost life-size and the sensitive, naturalistic
treatment of its facial features was unequalled for
some time. This head, which may be of a woman,
is the earliest-known monumental sculpture in the

round and is a precursor of a major artistic tradition developed by the Sumerians.

Jemdet Nasr Occupations

The time span following the Uruk period is
known as the Jemdet Nasr period (c. 3100–2900
B.C.). Many important innovations that may have
first been developed during the Uruk period were
discovered in deposits of the Jemdet Nasr period.
These innovations were consolidated and improved
to the point at which they coalesced to form a new
society. The mass-produced pottery that first appeared with the crude bevel-rimmed bowls of the
Uruk period were expanded to include a variety of
conical cups made on a potter's fast wheel. Artwork
exemplified by the Warka vase and the sculptured
head was found in levels of the Jemdet Nasr period.
The large temples of the Late Uruk period at
Warka were rebuilt during the Jemdet Nasr period.
Most important of all, the few early attempts at
writing in Uruk-period levels were multiplied and
improved during the Jemdet Nasr period. It was
during this period that the early Mesopotamian
city stabilized its organizational foundations. The
temple was its center both architecturally and organizationally, and the temple elite probably ran both
the economics and the politics of the city. Because
of the absence of fortification, it does not seem
likely that warfare was a significant force during
the Jemdet Nasr period. The number of important
centers in southern Mesopotamia was under a
dozen, and some of these may have been only large
towns.

The Jemdet Nasr period is best known from the
excavations at Warka, but it is also well documented at several other major Mesopotamian sites.
Levels of the Jemdet Nasr period have been found
in sites in central Mesopotamia, such as Khafaje
and Tell 'Uqair, and in the extreme north at Tell
Brak in Syria. The similarity of the temple architecture, including cone mosaics at Brak, with buildings in the south is strong evidence of the close
contact between the two areas during this period.
The connection between Brak and the cities of the
south may be an indication of the growing impor-

tance of trade. An increase in the number of copper and silver vessels found at southern Mesopotamian sites also gives evidence of increasing trade. Brak may have served as a trading post where raw copper and silver were brought from Anatolia down into the Mesopotamian lowlands. Another traded item that was prevalent during the Jemdet Nasr period is the flint blade: denticulated flint sickle blades are common at many sites; they replaced the clay sickles that were no longer used.

Although ceramics remained relatively unimportant artistically, there was a revival of painted ware in the form of polychrome jars. The distribution of these vessels was limited, with the site of Jemdet Nasr itself being one of the primary sources.

Stone vases remained common with the important innovation of inlaid decoration on a few examples. Most of the inlays found are of colored stone or mother of pearl and are set in bitumen. The designs were either geometric or floral representations.

Glyptography, an art form that existed during the Uruk period increased in importance in the Jemdet Nasr period, and later became a fundamental part of early Sumerian society (Porada and Buchanan 1948). Whereas stamp seals had been more common than cylinder seals, during the Jemdet Nasr period this trend was reversed. Cylinder seals were in the majority throughout the remainder of early Mesopotamian history. Four different classes of cylinder seals can be identified from the Jemdet Nasr period (Falkenstein 1967:34). The first class consisted mostly of larger seals on which extensive naturalistic scenes were carved in intaglio. The effect is similar to that of such early sculpture as the Warka vase. Commonly found were scenes of worship, religious processions, battles, hunting, and animals. Often an important figure, such as a ruler or a deity, was distinguished by costume and by being larger than other figures. The second class of seals was decorated with "heraldic" compositions, often featuring paired animals facing one another. These first two classes were the beginning of major traditions in artistic expression that were to continue during the subsequent millenia in Mesopotamia. The third class is known

mainly from central Mesopotamia and consists of seals that are small. The designs are of schematized animals and the workmanship is crude. The fourth class is also most common outside of southern Mesopotamia; it is made up of seals having deeply incised abstract designs.

The cylinder seal of later periods was a sign of individual ownership. It is difficult to assign a function to the early seals, but it is likely that those with naturalistic designs had certain standard meanings, whether or not of ownership. A small number of subjects and arrangements were used on Mesopotamian seals, each having its own variations. In this way the seal not only stood for a particular owner, but also the owner could choose a specific glyph to portray his name. It is logical that at the time that glyptic art was maturing and becoming more complex, early attempts at writing were also being made.

The Jemdet Nasr period's continuity with both the preceding and following periods is well documented artifactually and architecturally. Whereas the organizational forms of the Jemdet Nasr period were similar to, but more efficient than, those of the Late Uruk period, these forms changed significantly during the subsequent Early Dynastic period. The developments that characterized this transition are described in Chapter 9.

Demographic Patterns in Early Mesopotamia

Rapid growth in the population of certain settlements is a major criterion of the Urban Transformation. In addition to being a method of marking the progress of urbanization, the study of demographic patterns is now considered an important key to understanding the causes for the urbanization process. Shifts in population, arrangement of settlements, and general increases in population density reveal the nature of growth of early civilization.

Origin of 'Ubaid-Period Settlements

The first substantial communities on the Mesopotamian Plain were established during the

'Ubaid period. At first there were sparsely scattered villages of modest size. Eventually a few of the settlements grew into large population aggregates. By the end of the 'Ubaid period, and even earlier in certain places, the artificial hallmarks of a 'Ubaidlike culture had spread throughout Mesopotamia and into Iran, Saudi Arabia, and the northern Levant. The people of that time took the initial steps toward urbanism and may in fact have been direct ancestors of the Sumerians, who completed the journey toward urban life. Two questions of great archeological interest are: What was the origin of the culture known as 'Ubaid and where was the homeland of the people who developed it in southern Mesopotamia? The earliest 'Ubaid occupations ('Ubaid 1) were established directly on virgin soil at several sites in southern Mesopotamia, and are dated at approximately 5000 B.C. or somewhat earlier.

In northern Mesopotamia, 'Ubaid-period levels are directly on top of occupation horizons of Halafian-period material, which suggests that the 'Ubaid developed out of Halafian culture. The problem with this explanation is that the earliest evidence of the 'Ubaid period in the north is 'Ubaid 3, which is dated later than its initial appearance in the south. In Iran, both in lowland Khuzistan and in the highland regions, cultures similar to 'Ubaid existed (e.g., Susa A) that came directly after earlier sequences of occupation. The development of the Iranian cultures of the 'Ubaid period seems to be indigenous, which supports the possibility that the Mesopotamian expression of the 'Ubaid came from Iran. Despite their physical proximity, however, early civilizations in Khuzistan followed distinctly different paths from those in southern Mesopotamia, although their developments were similar in many ways. Also, the earliest 'Ubaid-period cultures of Mesopotamia were near the Euphrates River in the extreme southwest of the Mesopotamian Plain. If the people from Khuzistan moved westward to influence early 'Ubaid-period settlement, then it would be logical to expect to find a string of settlements from the Susiana Plain to the Tigris River and then over to the Euphrates (see Figure 8-2). Few such settlements have been found.

Further, recent dating shows that the earliest painted pottery cultures of Khuzistan are no earlier than 'Ubaid 1 in Mesopotamia, if they are even as early (Hole, Flannery, and Neely 1969). This fact, combined with the judgment based on stylistic grounds that the two traditions were distinct and developed indigenously (Oates 1973), leads to the conclusion that Khuzistan culture was not the source of 'Ubaid culture, although it was contemporaneously related to it.

Another region that has recently been suggested as the homeland of the 'Ubaid culture is the Arabian shore of the Persian Gulf. Preliminary research has revealed major 'Ubaidlike occupations there (Bibby 1969; al-Masry 1973). The local environment was probably more suitable for settlement then than it is today. Trade may have been an important factor in the settlement of this region, as it was in early historic times. So far, it is not possible to determine whether the Persian Gulf settlements were ancestors, contemporaries, or descendants of the 'Ubaid-period settlements of southern Mesopotamia. The likelihood is that this area developed contemporaneously with southern Mesopotamia as one large interacting region.

The Samarran culture of the Mesopotamian fringes had the strongest ties to 'Ubaid 1. The painted pottery known as post-Samarran transition ware from Choga Mami is closely parallel to the 'Ubaid 1 material (Oates 1973:172). This relationship is also demonstrated in the clay figurines from the two regions. The architecture known from Choga Mami and Sawwan also seems to have been ancestral to later building techniques and design at Eridu. The situation is not completely convincing, because the earliest 'Ubaid material from southern Mesopotamia may predate the similar assemblages from Choga Mami. The alternative that may be the answer, but is extremely difficult to investigate, is the possibility of earlier settlements in southern Mesopotamia. Such pre-'Ubaid sites might be covered by deep layers of silt and can be discovered only accidentally through trenching that might be done for a construction project, although close surface examination might reveal a scatter of artifacts (e.g., Ras al' Amiya: Stronach 1961).

Flood deposits at Ur

At several different trenches in the excavations of Ur in southern Mesopotamia, Sir Leonard Woolley uncovered thick deposits of clean, water-laid sand. Close examination suggested that these deposits were a result of violent flooding of the Euphrates River (Mallowan 1967:29). The stratum of sand was more than 3 meters thick and overlay 'Ubaid-period remains. The sand layer is dated at about 3500 B.C. at the transition between the 'Ubaid and Uruk periods. The importance of these deposits is their correlation, by Woolley and others, with the catastrophic flood described in later Sumerian tablets. This account probably supplied the model for the later flood episode of the Old Testament. Ur was the city of Abraham's birth, and it seems logical for the flood to be documented there if it occurred. The suggestion that these deposits were caused by the flood of the Sumerian legend led to immediate criticism, mainly on two grounds. First, historians pointed out that the legend recorded on Sumerian tablets referred to a flood during the reign of King Ziusudra of Shuruppak, who supposedly reigned at about 2900 B.C., not at 3500 B.C., the time of the Ur deposits. Second, if this had been a pan-Mesopotamian flood, one would expect to find evidence at nearby Eridu. This is absent, but does not disprove the hypothesis. Floods leave a thick deposit only under certain conditions—for example, where flood waters are impeded by an obstacle. The weight of evidence, however, is against Woolley's tantalizing interpretation. Although other archeologists have made arguments that specific sand or clay strata are evidence of the biblical flood, it is not likely that, in a land in which floods are frequent and the major rivers often change course, a particular flood could be definitely identified. Rather, the Sumerian flood myth was probably more a generic story than a recounting of a specific event, and hence searching for its remains is futile.

Given the current state of archeological knowledge, a reasonable explanation for the origin of the 'Ubaid 1 culture is that the strongest influence came from the Samarran cultures to the north. The evidence for this link is that the two have similar pottery and figurines, parallel architectural forms, and early development of irrigation agriculture. The use of irrigation would have been a prerequisite to the agricultural settlement of southern Mesopotamia, and its indigenous development at locations such as Choga Mami was crucial. After initial settlements had become established in southern Mesopotamia, a period of interaction with Khuzistan, and with early settlers on the Persian Gulf and the communities of northern Mesopotamia followed. Hence, the flourishing of the 'Ubaid period by 4000 B.C. was influenced from many directions, but the initial impetus seems to have come from the Samarrans.

Urbanization in the Warka Region

Owing to the fine work done by Robert McC. Adams and Hans J. Nissen in the vicinity of Warka, detailed information is available on the changing settlement patterns there during the period of initial urban growth (1972). The demographic patterns near Warka are especially important because of the primacy of this site. Current archeological evidence indicates that Warka was the largest early city in southern Mesopotamia, and it achieved true urban status before other Sumerian centers. The textual evidence does not contradict this inference. Hence, if one is seeking to describe the earliest city in the earliest civilization, then Warka is the logical choice.

The general outline of population growth within the center of Warka is limited by a lack of excavations or intensive surface investigation over much

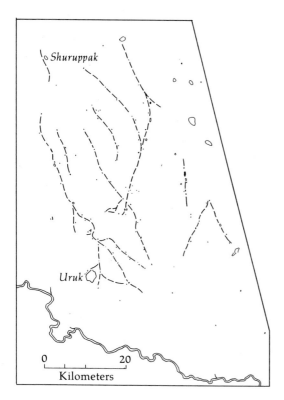

Figure 8-16
Jemdet Nasr settlements and watercourses discovered
by surveying the surface and by examining aerial
photographs taken in the vicinity of Warka. (After
Adams and Nissen, 1972.)

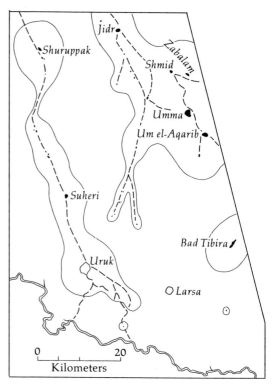

Figure 8-17
Late Early Dynastic settlements, watercourses, and
probable zones of cultivation suggested on the basis of
surveying the surface and examining aerial photographs. (After Adams and Nissen, 1972.)

of the site. Warka seems to have been established
during the 'Ubaid period and to have attained a
modest size by the end of this period. The Late
Uruk and the Jemdet Nasr periods were times of
rapid growth for the city of Warka. Its population
had probably reached 10,000 by the Jemdet Nasr
period. Warka grew to its maximum by the middle
of the Early Dynastic period (c. 2700 B.C.). At that
time, the great defensive walls were built, enclosing 400 hectares and a population that may have
numbered 50,000. Following this peak in relative
power and population, Warka's supremacy was
challenged by other early cities, and it diminished
in relative and absolute importance during the
succeeding periods.

Complementing the growth of the urban center
of Warka were the settlement patterns of the population that lived in the Warka vicinity (Adams and
Nissen 1972). The initial occupation of the Warka
vicinity was during the early part of the 'Ubaid
period. Settlement was in moderate-sized villages
evenly scattered throughout the countryside. The
average area of the 'Ubaid villages is estimated to
have been 4 hectares, which is larger than the average area of communities of subsequent periods.
Individual 'Ubaid 2 and 'Ubaid 4 sites of 4 and 10
hectares, respectively, were not simple farming
villages, but complex communities. An explanation
for this phenomenon may be that a larger economic
unit, possibly with a complex organization, was

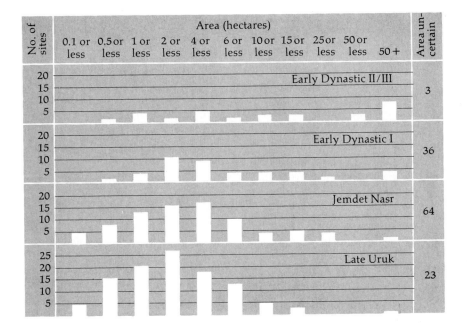

Figure 8-18
Classification of early sites in the vicinity of Warka by period and area.
(After Adams and Nissen, 1972.)

required for the initial colonization of southern Mesopotamia. After agricultural techniques were established, it was more efficient for small communities to break off, forming settlements along the natural river courses. The initial colonization of an area by a few large communities that subdivide into many smaller communities that later develop into larger ones is a pattern that is strikingly similar to the model of plant-community development offered by plant ecologists (Greig-Smith 1964).

During the Uruk period, the tendency was for the growing population to live in small clusters of communities instead of the scattered settlements of the preceding period. In the area that has been surveyed, there are only 21 known Early Uruk sites, whereas 123 sites have been identified as Late Uruk. Such population growth can be accounted for partly by fertility, but it probably also resulted from an influx of people who had not theretofore lived in settled communities in the area. The incoming people could have been either immigrants

from other territories or nomads who had been living in the Warka vicinity.

Urbanization in the Warka region from the Jemdet Nasr through the Early Dynastic periods is shown in Figures 8-16 and 8-17. A measure of the development can be obtained by comparing average settlement sizes: in the Late Uruk period, it was from 1 to 2 hectares; in the late Early Dynastic period, it was from 6 to 10 hectares. Whereas the distribution of settlement size in the Late Uruk period seems to be largely unimodal, that in the Early Dynastic period is bi- or even trimodal (Figure 8-18). This documents the increased complexity and integration of the settlement system in large areas (Berry 1967).

Between approximately 3100 and 2700 B.C., there were two major trends that were crucial to the development of urbanism (Adams and Nissen 1972: 11–12). The first trend was the redistribution of population in the Warka region: the number of rural communities reached a peak in the Late Uruk and Jemdet Nasr periods, and then declined sharply as the urban centers at Warka and elsewhere grew. It can be inferred that the growth of these centers was due less to an internal increase than to migration from scattered rural communities. The motivation to migrate was probably warfare, for large-scale warfare is documented by the construction of defensive walls around the major urban · centers during the Early Dynastic period. Unable to defend themselves, rural villagers undoubtedly sought refuge in the cities, where they were probably welcomed as an additional source of economic and military power.

The second trend was a reduction in the number of water courses utilized for settlement. The natural regime of the area was a network of small streams that were useful for short-range irrigation of small areas. To cultivate larger areas and maintain large permanent settlements and fields, the inhabitants had to turn the major stream courses into canals and drain much of the adjacent land. This comprehensive plan was necessary for the vicinity of Warka perhaps as early as the Jemdet Nasr period and certainly by the second half of the Early Dynastic period. The evidence gathered by Adams and Nissen shows a clear linearity of settlements by the middle of the Early Dynastic period (c. 2700 B.C.); sites, most of which were relatively large, were located along major streams, which had probably been kept in straight courses by levee construction.

A discovery relevant to new forms of water-control technology is the arrangement of communities in an area about 35 kilometers northeast of Warka (Adams and Nissen 1972:12). The area was not occupied until the Jemdet Nasr period, when several relatively large communities were founded. These settlements were arranged in a linear fashion along what must have been a canalized stream course. Subsequently, by the end of the Early Dynastic period, these settlements had been absorbed by nearby growing urban centers. This may be the earliest known evidence of a major water-control system that would have required the cooperation of several communities, perhaps in some federated form. The length of the canal was at least

15 kilometers; its construction would not have been a tremendous undertaking, but it was significant nevertheless. The discovery of this cooperative system raises the question of the importance of water control in initiating early urban growth and state formation. Although a single example that is moderate in scale does not prove or disprove any position, it should prompt a reexamination of the evidence. Irrigation was definitely a factor in the rise of civilization and probably affected the course of events in several crucial ways: namely, in determining which crops could be grown and which techniques could be used, in creating differential access to strategic resources, and in stimulating cooperative planning, construction, and control of water works.

The trend toward urbanism in the Warka region reached its first peak by the middle of the Early Dynastic period. The city itself contained about 50,000 inhabitants, and one other major city (Umma) and a half-dozen secondary urban centers had developed in the general vicinity (Figure 8-17). Almost no small communities remained, indicating a general depopulation of the countryside (Figure 8-18).

Depopulation of the countryside by urban centers would have been greatest in periods of warfare and general unrest, and would have been reversed in periods in which a strong centralized power was able to keep the peace throughout an entire region. This is exemplified by the settlement pattern of the Old Babylonian Empire period in the Warka vicinity (Adams and Nissen 1972:36), when there were large cities, towns, and rural communities. Order was maintained by the centralized authority, and agriculture was most effectively carried out by scattered settlements.

Urbanization in Other Areas of Mesopotamia

Archeological surveys made in various parts of the Mesopotamian Plain, although varied in intensity, make it possible to draw certain general conclusions about the similarities and differences between them (Adams 1969; 1972; Adams and Nissen 1972). To the southwest of Uruk, the vicinity of the early cities of Eridu and Ur was surveyed by Henry Wright (1969). Like Warka, Eridu and Ur had moderate-sized villages scattered throughout the surrounding area during the 'Ubaid period. Some of these settlements were more than villages, with temples and large populations. Eridu grew to the status of a large town during the late 'Ubaid and Early Uruk periods. Ur had become a major city-state by the middle of the Early Dynastic period. Accompanying the growth of Ur was a slight reduction in the number of rural settlements, but no dramatic depopulation like that of the Warka region.

The drainage of the Diyala River near the northern limits of the Mesopotamian Plain was surveyed by Robert McC. Adams (1965). The initial 'Ubaid-period occupation of this region also was in the form of scattered villages. The population grew rapidly during the Jemdet Nasr period, producing clusters of small settlements and the emergence of several large towns with temples. Contrary to the pattern near Warka, population growth in the Diyala region continued, with an increasing number of settlements of all sizes along with an increase in the size of the centers. There is no evidence for rural depopulation. The population centers of the Diyala region did not assume the full size of southern Mesopotamian cities, and so are better considered townships (Jawad 1965).

Other areas of central Mesopotamia that have been surveyed, with varying results, are Kish (Gibson forthcoming), Akkad (Adams 1969), and Nippur (Adams 1972). In each case, evidence showed a rapid growth of the number of settlements during the Uruk or Jemdet Nasr periods followed by a relative decrease in rural population, accompanied by a growth of urban centers. The exact timing of the growth, consolidation, and degree of depopulation varies in each instance.

The evidence of demographic patterns in early Khuzistan offers another example of early growth in number of settlements followed by decline in rural communities (Johnson 1973b; Wright 1970; Wright and Johnson 1975). The striking aspect of the Khuzistan example is its temporal priority over similar developments in southern Mesopotamia. There is no evidence so far that the depopulation of rural Khuzistan led to major organizational changes in the growing center of Susa. Adams suggests that the Khuzistan evidence should be considered a relatively independent example of urbanization under environmental and demographic conditions different from those of southern Mesopotamia (Adams 1972).

Adams summarizes the evidence from these diverse areas and suggests that, although there is no single pattern of development, three general stages can be identified (Adams and Nissen 1972: 90–91): (1) in all of the areas studied, the initial population was in scattered agricultural villages of moderate size; (2) the population increased rapidly during subsequent periods, shifting from the scattered distribution to a more clustered pattern of, on the average, smaller settlements; (3) then large populations concentrated in major centers either as part of a general population growth or by drawing in the surrounding rural communities.

The important effect of the second stage is that increasing population would have led to a scarcity of land accessible to irrigation water. This type of population pressure would engender differences in wealth between the initial inhabitants and any newcomers. These differences evidently widened in the growth of stratified society and eventually initiated widespread conflict. Identifying the causes of stage three, urban concentration, is not simple. It is likely that both force and persuasion played roles. The security and economic potential of urban life must have convinced many rural inhabitants to move into the growing cities. The rulers of these newly founded cities must also have used all of the power at their command to stimulate the immigration that added to the number of their dependents, and, hence, to their power.

Although these three stages are painted in rather broad strokes, they are important generalizations of the known archeological evidence. Until the beginning of the Early Dynastic period, urbanization produced only a small number of temple-centered cities varying in population from 5,000 to 50,000. Their populations must have been stratified, specialized, and led by an administrative elite. Although the temple-centered city was the earliest urban form and many of its achievements were not quickly surpassed, it was not to remain the dominant element of the sociopolitical scene.

Cultural Accomplishments in Early Mesopotamia

Subsistence Pursuits

Although the earliest communities in southern Mesopotamia may have relied on hunting, gathering, and fishing, agriculture soon became the dominant source of food. Several major technological innovations helped to make cultivation possible in the arid lowlands. Small-scale irrigation techniques had been pioneered on the edge of the alluvium by the sixth-millennium Samarran settlements. According to interpretations of Late Uruk tablets, it is believed that the plow was first introduced during the fourth millennium. This tool aided in the preparation of the hard alluvial clays of lowland Mesopotamia. Also, the first documentation of the invention of the wheel comes from remains of fourth-millennium culture. The wheel was used in pottery manufacture during the Uruk period, and is depicted later in artistic works. The invention of wheeled carts would have significantly improved transportation networks, which would have enhanced the redistributive economy.

These inventions were important factors in early Mesopotamian subsistence, but the effects of the environmental setting on early agriculture had other influences on the rise of civilization. In a general sense, three environments can be identified in southern Mesopotamia (refer to Figure 2-20 on page 42): the cultivable land, on or near the natural water courses; the depressions that were periodically covered by swamps or marshes; and the vast areas that were not well watered, similar to dry steppe. The important factor was that, during early Mesopotamian times, land in general was not in short supply. Only land for which there was access to irrigation water was especially valuable. Other farmlands were extensive, which made it possible to let the fields lie fallow in alternate years. This allowed the land to recover some of its nutrients, and it slowed the salinization of the fields. Salinization was rapidly becoming a crucial problem for

the early civilizations of the south. Paradoxically, the prevention of salinization of a field during a specific season was aided by overirrigating, which washed the salt out. However, practices such as this hastened the long-term process of salinization. Hence, annual decisions by independent farmers probably were in favor of short-term productivity at the cost of the long-term fertility of the land. It was only through comprehensive land planning by a centralized authority that major efforts at stemming salinization could be carried out.

The zone of swamps and marshes offered possibilities for farming along their edges, the hunting of water fowl, and the gathering of reeds to be used in Mesopotamian buildings. The steppe zone and the swamps that dried up in the summer offered ample land for seminomadic herders. It is important to note that the land necessary for herding did not diminish the land for agriculture (Lees and Bates 1974). These two pursuits were complementary and often pursued by the same economic group. Herding offered a hedge against the vagaries of the agricultural cycle with its frequent lean years. Farmers who were not favored with land on major stream courses probably kept herds in addition to farming. Consequently, in years when they did not receive adequate irrigation water, they could move with their herds and survive the drought. This produced an unstable population in that people might have been living in settled communities one year and moving about the next.

A second means of hedging against lean years would have been to band together in communal efforts. Often, when the water in one channel was insufficient, it was adequate in another. Thus, some farmers harvested plentiful yields, while others were without crops. Contributions made to a central storehouse were insurance against those lean years. Because of the insecurity of the harvest, the need for a redistributive economy was strengthened.

Dietary Changes

The Mesopotamian environment and technology affected the range of plants and animals consumed. The major crops were emmer wheat, breadwheat, barley, and flax. Barley was more salt-tolerant than wheat, and so as salinization became a problem there was a gradual shift toward the cultivation of more barley. About 3500 B.C., before salinization had become a problem, the amounts of wheat and barley grown were about equal. Records show that one thousand years later, during the Early Dynastic period, only one-sixth as much wheat as barley was grown (Jacobsen and Adams 1958). In later historic times, wheat almost disappeared, and the overall fertility of southern Mesopotamia diminished.

A new form of cultivation introduced some time before 3000 B.C. was the planting of orchards: dates in Mesopotamia, figs in the uplands, and olives in the Levant. The date palm is an efficient plant for southern Mesopotamia but requires a long period before bearing fruit, and the cultivator must expend a reasonable amount of labor per unit of production. However, date palms are rich sources of carbohydrates, require very little land, and are relatively salt tolerant. Once again, the spread of date palm groves would have been stimulated by comprehensive long-range planning and a stability in the water regime that canalization would have aided. Hence, the increasing use of dates may indicate the growing power of the city during the Jemdet Nasr period, for which dates are first documented.

Adequate levels of the three basic food categories—proteins, fats, and carbohydrates—as well as specific vitamins and minerals are necessary to maintain the nutritional status of a human population. A group may rely more heavily on one or another of these categories as prescribed by cultural norms to conduct its daily activities. Near Eastern villagers derived diverse nutritive elements from their plant foods: cereal grains, such as wheat and barley, were rich sources of carbohydrates; tree nuts, such as pistachios and almonds, supplied fats and protein; and a mixture of legumes growing in the fields not only was a source of protein for the diet, but also enriched the soil by increasing its nitrogen content. However, the inhabitants of southern Mesopotamia relied less on legumes and tree nuts than on other plants such as flax (linseed) for fats, on domestic animals for protein and fats, and on river fish for protein.

Effective use of domestic animals was essential to the success of early Mesopotamian civilization.

Although evidence for fifth- and fourth-millennia animal husbandry in Mesopotamia is scant, there is enough to suggest the general pattern of animal exploitation (Flannery and Wright 1966). Sheep and goats were the primary animals of the upland villages, as they were in the communities on the edge of the alluvium, such as Choga Mami (Oates 1973). However, through time the proportion of sheep to goats increased significantly. On the Mesopotamian Plain itself, cattle far outnumbered sheep and goats in the 'Ubaid-period samples from Eridu and Ras al' Amiya (Flannery and Wright 1966). Cattle continued to be the dominant animal herded in Mesopotamia, with sheep playing a secondary role. Cattle were very efficient to raise, largely because of their secondary products. Not only did they produce milk, but they were suitable as beasts of burden. Moreover, they rapidly became acclimated to the hot plains. Sheep also remained important, partly for their secondary products. Sheep's wool was one of the major raw materials needed by early Mesopotamian cities for their textile industries. Wool and flax for weaving were two of the few raw materials that did not have to be imported into Mesopotamia.

The increasing effectiveness of Near Eastern food production had direct effects on social developments. The ability to produce and collect surplus food is the cornerstone of a complex society, of which a large segment of the population is not engaged in food production. Improved plants and animals, new technologies, and the efficiency and control of the redistributive economy all contributed to the available surplus. A more significant figure than the absolute amount of food produced is the balance between the calories produced and the calories expended on producing the food. Improved technology, specialization, exchange, and a more sedentary lifestyle enabled the Mesopotamian settlers to expend less energy than the amount produced, thus leaving a surplus.

Of far-reaching—but hard to assess—significance is the effect of a more abundant and reliable diet on birth rates, a key element in population growth. Sedentism facilitated shorter periods between births, and improved nutrition may have increased the number of years during which a woman could reproduce. It is hypothesized (Frisch 1975) that the onset and maintenance of menstruation is related to attaining a critical body weight and a sufficiently high proportion of body fat (about 20 percent). Effective food production and the stability of a redistributive economy may have sufficiently improved nutrition so that fertility in women was achieved earlier and maintained more consistently. Furthermore, cereal grains may have been used to make pabulum for infants, supplementing mother's milk at an earlier age than previously possible and hence allowing the period between births to be shortened.

Industrial and Economic Developments

Craft specialization, industry, and trade are all characteristics of civilization. In addition, they stimulate civilization's further growth. There is ample evidence for their increase during the early occupation of Mesopotamia. The diversity of vessels and implements, as well as their standardization, implies their production by specialists. The skillful planning, construction, and decoration of the monumental buildings of the early cities is even more direct evidence for a growing number of specialists. Stone vessels, metal pieces, clay cones, and lapidary works imply full-time specialists.

Concomitant with the increase in specialists was the growth of industries that organized and employed them. Although there is no direct archeological evidence for it, industries producing textiles may have already developed. The production of bevel-rimmed bowls during the Uruk period and conical cups during the Jemdet Nasr period attests to the specialized industry that was emerging for the mass-production of pottery.

The trading network grew in importance as it supplied raw materials for industry and other aspects of daily life. Utilitarian materials such as bitumen from the middle Euphrates, flint from Arabia or the Zagros, limestone from Arabia, and timbers and basalt from the highlands were imported in quantity (Figure 8-19). In addition, Mesopotamia imported a variety of goods for the production of status objects. Gold, silver, copper,

and tin ores were sought by the growing metallurgical industry. Lapidaries were already making beads and pendants of carnelian, turquoise, amethyst, lapis lazuli, agate, quartz, jadeite, beryl, diorite, hematite, steatite, serpentine, ivory, and shell. These materials would have had to have been sought from many different localities. Their procurement, transport, and distribution was increasingly controlled by the central institutions that were developing in the early cities.

In return for raw materials imported, the people of southern Mesopotamia may have traded manufactured goods or foodstuffs. As mentioned at the beginning of this chapter, it was during the second half of the 'Ubaid that characteristics of a single pottery style were found across the Near East. It is likely that the expanding trading network for the procurement of raw materials also functioned to spread these "'Ubaidian" characteristics. People of high status in the peripheral towns and villages may have adopted the stylistic motifs and symbols of highly ranked members of the more organizationally advanced 'Ubaidian groups. In this way, the Mesopotamian people were trading status for the goods of their less-developed, but raw-material-rich, neighbors. A similar relationship has been suggested for areas of Mesoamerica (Flannery 1968; Rathje 1971).

Invention of Writing

Probably the single greatest Mesopotamian invention is writing. The concepts and techniques of writing were developed over a long period, some of them as major innovations, others as minor alterations. Systems of recording may have been used as long ago as the Pleistocene (Marshack 1972). Marks on bone or stone may have been used for calendars and other records but only locally and probably not with the intention of the record being used by other people. Geometrically shaped clay and stone pieces may have served as weights and notations at least as early as the beginning of the 'Ubaid period. However, there is abundant and easily recognizable evidence that, toward the end of the Uruk period, writing appeared for

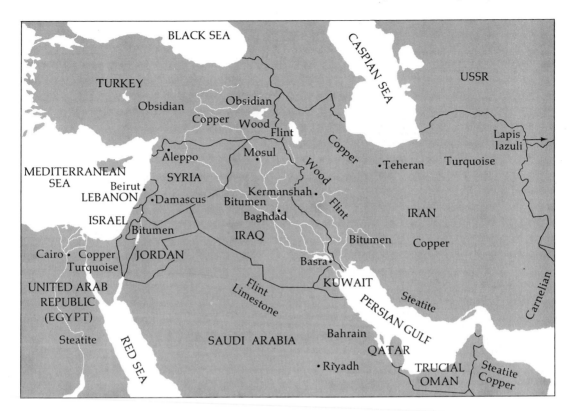

Figure 8-19
General location of well-known sources of important raw materials.

the first time anywhere in the world. Small clay tablets with incised markings were used as early as 3500 B.C. and were widely distributed through southern Mesopotamia by 3000 B.C. (Jemdet Nasr period). The earliest written signs were simple pictures of objects that were common in everyday life (Figures 8-20 and 8-21, pages 272 and 273). Symbols for cattle, sheep, grain, tools, fish, and other entities looked very much like the objects they represented. A common action might have been represented by an element in that action—for example, a human foot meaning the act of walking or a human head meaning the act of eating. The symbols were inscribed with a cut reed in wet clay, which was then dried to form a relatively permanent record of the message.

A crucial aspect of Mesopotamian writing was the effort expended to simplify its use and to make it efficient. Obviously, those who were using the writing system were striving for a means of communication that could be put into daily use. This was unlike the situation in Egypt, where the development of hieroglyphic writing led to increasingly difficult-to-execute symbols. Writing in Egypt served a small number of purposes and its use was not extended to most strata of society, as it eventually was in Mesopotamia. To simplify Mesopotamian writing, the Sumerian scribes substituted wedge-shaped marks for pictorial symbols, giving rise to the name *cuneiform* for subsequent Mesopotamian scripts (Figure 8-22, page 274).

Structurally, early Mesopotamian writing is logographic; that is, it is a word script in which each sign or group of signs corresponds to a single word (Falkenstein 1967). Initially, the number of signs was about 2,000, but for the sake of efficiency

Figure 8-20
Early pictographic script on obverse and reverse sides of Bau monuments
that deal with various professions. (Photographs © The Trustees of the
British Museum.)

this number was soon reduced. By eliminating re-
dundancies and by using the same sign for similar
sounds, the number of signs in use at the end of
the Early Dynastic period (c. 2400 B.C.) was reduced
to about 600.

A major innovation that was incorporated early
in Mesopotamian writing was the so-called rebus
principle. Instead of drawing the idea to be conveyed, a scribe drew pictures of other things that
when read aloud suggested the word to express
that idea. For example, this principle can be applied to expressing the concept "belief" in English
by drawing a bee and a leaf. The implications of
this improvement were enormous: the range of
concepts that could be expressed was vastly enlarged, the act of writing was simplified, and the
ambiguity of the symbols was reduced. With increasing use of the rebus principle, the emphasis
in writing shifted from representing the idea itself
to representing the phonetics of the spoken word
for the idea (Figure 8-21). Writing slowly developed
in the direction of a system of phonemes; it was
only after this development progressed to a stage at

which writing was more syllabic than logographic
that it could be used to express anything that could
be expressed in language. This "phoneticization"
had been accomplished by the end of the Early
Dynastic period, and after that time writing was
used for a wide range of functions (Jacobsen 1945).

During the Uruk, Jemdet Nasr, and first half of
the Early Dynastic periods, almost all tablets were
used for accounting purposes. Writing was used to
tally and record transactions that were negotiated
by the temple elite. Lists of rations, donors, productivity, and sales were the basic subject matter.
Eventually, writing was used for other administrative and legal tasks. Of all the clay tablets recovered from Sumer, more than 90 percent are
records of governmental affairs (Kramer 1957). It
was only in the last part of the Early Dynastic
period and in subsequent periods that writing was
used as a medium for recording historic events and
lists of rulers, for written communication, and for
the transcription of a large body of oral literature.
With these important additions to the repertory of
the scribes, writing assumed its full role.

Earliest pictographs (3000 B.C.)	Denotation of pictographs	Pictographs in rotated position	Cuneiform signs ca. 1900 B.C.	Basic logographic values	
				Reading	Meaning
	Head and body of a man			lú	Man
	Head with mouth indicated			ka	Mouth
	Bowl of food			ninda	Food, bread
	Mouth + food			kú	To eat
	Stream of water			a	Water
	Mouth + water			nag	To drink
	Fish			kua	Fish
	Bird			mušen	Bird
	Head of an ass			anše	Ass
	Ear of barley	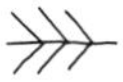		še	Barley

Figure 8-21
The development of Sumerian writing from a pictographic script to a cuneiform script to a phonetic system. The diacritical marks and subscripts on the transliteration of cuneiform signs are used to distinguish between signs having the same pronunciation but different meanings. (After *The Sumerians* by S. N. Kramer. Copyright © 1957 by Scientific American, Inc. All rights reserved.)

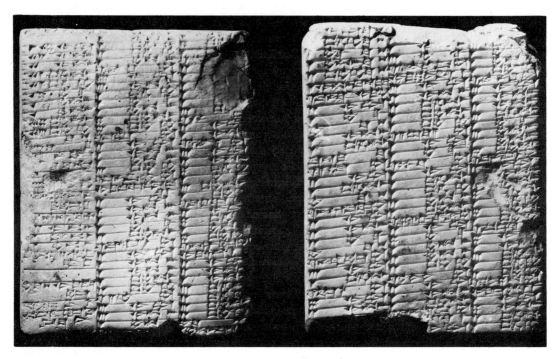

Figure 8-22
Well-developed cuneiform tablet (obverse and reverse sides) that is a ledger
dated at the 38th year of the king, Shulgi of Ur. It is an official account
treating the disposal of dead cattle turned in by the shepherds. (Photographs from The Oriental Institute. The University of Chicago.)

The invention of writing has had countless ram-
ifications throughout human history, but its immediate effects on early civilization were related to
problems of space, time, and complexity (Jacobsen
1946). Writing facilitated interaction between
groups separated by great distances. The standardization of early Mesopotamian writing is attested
to by the discovery of tablets containing word lists
used in the training of scribes, and identical word
lists have been uncovered from widely separated
settlements, suggesting efforts to effect uniformity
in the written word to facilitate interaction.

The use of writing also precludes the inaccura-
cies of recollection. Inscriptions on clay tablets
or stone monuments were durable records that retained their message for as long as they could be
read. This led to formalization of economic transactions, legal administration, and other aspects of
society. The written word facilitated the continuity
and tradition that became characteristic of Mesopotamian civilization.

The most significant contribution of writing, and
probably the major stimulus for its invention, is its
ability to facilitate the flow of information in an
increasingly complex society. Although the first
use of writing was for the keeping of records, a redistributive economy in which hundreds or thousands of people participated was too massive for
any simple form of recordkeeping. By facilitating
administrative activities, writing enabled the further
growth and centralization of Mesopotamian cities.
Writing contributed to the maintenance of large
economic and political units that could not have
persisted if the only form of communication had
been face-to-face.

Writing was also an effective means for accumulating information: agricultural techniques, mathematics, and predictive sciences were improved with writing as the means of transmission, both over long distances and through time.

Organizational Developments in Early Mesopotamia

Temple-Cities (Stage 5)

Rituals and sacred beliefs were a means of maintaining order as early as the first permanent settlements in the Near East. With the growth in size and complexity of communities during the 'Ubaid period, there was a concomitant need for greater mechanisms of integration. A religious order centered in temple structures assumed much of the burden of structuring the growing societies. Early Mesopotamian religion, like that of later societies, supplied its adherents with a simplified model of the acceptable social structure and rituals designed to mitigate the effects of natural forces (Frankfort et al. 1949). A moral framework and modes of interrelationships were set forth in the theological teachings of the religious elite. According to third-millennium texts, Sumerian religion was based on a fatalistic theology. The gods established laws that were unchanging. People did not have free will but were governed by the decisions both of the major gods and of their own personal intermediary gods. The gods were lords of the temple estates and the cities. Human beings had been created specifically to relieve the gods of the tedium of doing work. The gods appointed human representatives to direct day-to-day activities. They were the priests of the deity's temple, usually headed by a person holding the title of *En* (Saggs 1962).

Because of the instability and central importance of Mesopotamian agriculture, it is logical to suppose that the earliest deities would have been involved with fertility and natural forces. The Sumerian gods were related to life-giving powers in nature, such as water, earth, and air. The role and relative importance of each deity varied through time and between cities. The head of the pantheon was the god *Anu*, King of Heaven. His main characteristic was royalty, and it was from him that most individual human rulers received

their status. Anu was worshipped in many Sumerian cities, but his principal shrine was in Uruk (see Figure 8-10). Anu's consort, *Inanna*, Lady of Heaven, was also revered in Uruk, her cult centering in the major temple complex of Eanna (Figure 8-10). It is difficult to determine whether gods or зoddesses were more important in the early stages of Sumerian religion, but it seems that at the end of the third millennium the worship of Inanna in Uruk was of greater importance than that of Anu. Many of the early artistic representations of the Sumerian gods and goddesses during the Uruk and Jemdet Nasr periods were symbolic in form. For example, Anu was portrayed by a horned cap and Inanna by a bundle of reeds (Figure 8-23, page 276). Beginning in the Early Dynastic period, portrayal of the deities became increasingly anthropomorphic, often with distinguishing headdresses.

Enlil and *Enki* with Anu made up the triad of prominent Sumerian gods (Saggs 1962). Enlil was King of the Earth, just as Anu was King of Heaven. Enlil was considered the national god of Sumer, with his cult centered in Nippur. Enlil's association with Nippur gave that city a special pan-Sumerian religious significance. Enki was considered to be king of water and the subterranean and was believed to be sympathetic toward the plight of humankind. The city of Eridu, considered in Sumerian myths to be the oldest city, was the home of the cult of Enki.

A group of deities second in importance to Anu, Enlil, and Enki consisted of *Utu*, god of the sun (Shamash in Semitic), *Nanna*, god of the moon (Sin in Semitic), and *Inanna*, goddess of the planet Venus (Ishtar in Semitic). Of the three, the moon god was most prominent and his cult was centered at the city of Ur. Being controller of the night and the lunar calendar, Nanna was deemed responsible for creating many omens. Utu, god of the sun, was considered to be god of justice. Inanna's significance increased rapidly with the ascendency of Semites in Mesopotamia. Under the name Ishtar, she was virtually the only female deity, assimilating the personality and functions of other goddesses (Saggs 1962). She became goddess both of war and of sexual love, revealed to mankind as Venus, the morning and evening star.

Figure 8-23
Uruk-period cylinder seal (modern impression) showing a boat being poled and a bundle of reeds (symbol for Inanna) being carried by animal. (Photograph from The Oriental Institute. The University of Chicago.)

Daily libations and sacrifices of animals, fish, or plant material were offered to the city's patron deity at the temple. The priest of the temple was the deity's steward on earth, seeing to the god's needs and interpreting his omens. Periodic feasts or celebrations, many of which were attended by the general public, were carried out by the temple functionaries. We know from later periods that the most important religious ceremony was to ask for the annual regeneration of vegetation. The origin of this ceremony may be as early as the fouth millennium. The New Year festival was a series of rituals in honor of the "sacred marriage" between the city ruler and the goddess Inanna (or her representative). After the connubial activities, the goddess fixed the destiny of the king and his city for the next year.

Many elements of the structure and content of Sumerian religion became a part of subsequent religions. The construction of temples manned by full-time religious functionaries is a pattern that has continued in most major religions. The Sumerian creation myth, flood epic, and assorted parables are preserved in slightly modified form in Judeo-Christian scriptures. Of equal importance, the Sumerian religion created a creed of behavior and ideals of humaneness that strongly influenced all subsequent religious thinking.

The meteoric rise in importance of the temple community during the fourth millennium cannot be explained fully by the ability of religion to help order society or to allay fears about regeneration. The growth of the temple and of the early Mesopotamian cities around them was closely linked to the economic activities in which they engaged, the temple becoming the center for the redistributive economy. By banding together in this type of communal production and storage system, individual farmers were hedging against lean agricultural years. The temple was a logical place to center a redistributive economy, with all of its ritual concerning regeneration and its credos for order and fairness. Temple administrators soon did more than collect and distribute. They advised farmers about agricultural schedules, arranged for water control, initiated corporate ventures of larger groups, and rewarded cooperative individuals. The temple elite soon became managers of large sectors of the productive economy of the early cities. Temples owned land and employed workers directly. Because the temple elite controlled large quantities of foodstuffs, they were able to support full-time craft specialists, such as scribes, potters, masons, and textile workers. The temple also controlled the long-distance trade required to bring in raw materials for these specialists and received in return the status goods that helped to reinforce its position. Because the temple administrators controlled the collection of large quantities of agricultural produce, they accumulated reserves for lean years. The same methods that were used to encourage production of these reserves were employed to accumulate surpluses for craft activities, temple buildings, and status goods.

Because of its having the central role in the redistributive economy, the temple became the dominant architectural feature in the city; its administrators were economically and politically powerful; and it was the center for organizational and technological innovation.

The 'Ubaid-period temples of Eridu were small compared with the Uruk period's Anu ziggurat at Warka, which in turn was dwarfed by the later Eanna precinct buildings at Warka. It is likely that the economic and political power of the temple elite grew with the size of its buildings. As it gained power, the temple community set itself apart from the remainder of the city. Platforms and ziggurats elevated the temples above other buildings during the Uruk and Jemdet Nasr periods. By the Early Dynastic period, temples and houses for the functionaries were enclosed by high walls that served to differentiate them from other classes of people and to protect the increasing concentration of wealth within the temple precinct.

The extent of political control exerted by the early temple elite is not known, but it unquestionably was the single greatest economic power in early Mesopotamian cities. This practical consideration combined with the moral authority of the religion probably put the reins of command of the city in the hands of the En. Whether this control extended beyond the boundaries of the city is difficult to assess. A city as large as Warka of the Jemdet Nasr period must have exercised a strong influence over towns within a certain radius. How strong the control of the temple leaders was over the city or the surrounding countryside remains a matter for further investigation, but their primacy in early Mesopotamian cities was unchallenged.

Social Stratification and Emerging Class Society

Although social stratification is probably the single most important characteristic of civilization, it is difficult to document its development during the fifth and fourth millennia. In the absence of comprehensive written documents or archeological excavations that uncover broad areas of the early cities, one is limited to certain inferences about class society.

One form of archeological evidence does exist, but its interpretation as a measure of differential wealth remains open to question. Grave goods were buried with a body for a variety of reasons, but in some general way their quantity should be a rough indicator of the wealth of the person buried. Of the more than 200 graves of the late 'Ubaid period excavated at Eridu, there is little evidence for great differentiation in goods (Adams 1966:95). Normal grave goods include one or more vessels of pottery or, infrequently, of stone, occasionally supplemented by a clay figurine or a few strands of beads. By the Jemdet Nasr period, there was greater variation in the grave goods. About one-third of the 25 graves beneath the floors of private houses of the Jemdet Nasr period at the northern site of Khafaje contained stone bowls, and two contained somewhat larger accumulations, including a few well-made vessels of copper, lead, and stone (Adams 1966:96). Sixty-one of 340 graves from about the same period at Ur contained one or two metal cups, and two graves had substantial concentrations of material wealth. The general pattern, especially when compared with subsequent developments of the Early Dynastic period (Chapter 9), implies a society with only modest stratification and no sharp differentiations in wealth.

Unfortunately, the limited scope of written documents from the Uruk and Jemdet Nasr periods restricts to a few sources the possibility of discovering strong evidence for social stratification before the Early Dynastic period when the written record covers a wider range of topics.

Very few excavations of domestic architecture, which might yield information on differentiations in wealth, have been made. The work that has been done on sites earlier than the Early Dynastic period has been limited to temple buildings. However, excavators have uncovered tracts of buildings of the Early Dynastic period that did not serve a religious purpose that do indicate the existence of stratification. Before accepting the assumption that social stratification did not exist during the fourth millennium, one must evaluate the evidence for the emergence of social stratification during the Early Dynastic period: Is it indicative of the patterns that existed, or does it derive merely from the nature of earlier investigations?

Insofar as the functionaries and administrators of the temple shared in the obvious wealth at the temple's disposal, sharp differentiations must have been present as early as the Uruk period. The large quantities of status goods produced from exotic raw materials and characterized by fine artistic workmanship imply a class of people who were of high status. If these goods had been distributed solely within the temple, they would not imply a high status class so much as a powerful institution. However, because high status goods were not restricted to the temple precincts, although they are concentrated there, their distribution implies a stratification in society somewhat independent of the temple.

If elite classes did exist independently of the temple, then it is necessary to identify their source of wealth and power. Although the evidence is slight, it is likely that individual families or groups of families rose to positions of wealth and power on the basis of success in agriculture. If land was owned or leased by individual farmers, as well as by the temple, then some landowners might have been in better positions than others to control irrigation according to the model for urban growth posited in Figure 7-7 (on page 230). This would have led to differentiation in wealth and power among the landowners that would have increased if properly managed. It is likely that during the fourth millennium, along with the growing wealth and power of the temple community, there were in-dependent families or groups who had substantial wealth derived from agricultural and industrial enterprises. The degree to which these wealthy families worked in concert with the temple administrators is still a matter for investigation. In some cities there may have been an active conflict between private power groups and the temple, but during the fourth millennium the temple administrators seem to have been in the ascendancy.

Few inferences can be accepted with certainty about the social stratification during the crucial early phase of urbanization. Scanty archeological evidence combined with inferences based on later organizational structures do not supply enough information for one to determine what was happening during the fourth millennium. The unfortunate aspect of this situation is that it was during this first phase of urbanization, emergence of temple-cities, that the die was cast for so much of subsequent society. The lack of definitive information cannot be taken as a reason for delaying further interpretations. Rather, the inadequacy requires that the scholar examine the available information intensively to determine what additional categories of data are required. Although scholars have pondered about the beginnings of civilization as long as there has been a concern for history, in terms of empirical information and results, this study is still in its infancy.

9

THE RISE OF POLITICS
AND STATE SOCIETY

King of the Four Quarters

*The Sumerians and Akkadians brought new heights of creativity
and complexity to Mesopotamian civilization during the third millennium.
Political organization advanced with the formation of city-states, of
confederacies of cities, and for a time, of nation states under powerful military
rulers. While these developments were taking place, a state society
was being formed in the Nile Valley that was to interact
closely with Mesopotamian civilization, but maintain a form and
content very much its own.*

*The bulk of archeological information about the Sumerian
occupation of southern Mesopotamia is drawn from architectural changes
and items of material culture. Recently, extensive field surveys
have yielded data on successive settlement patterns. Objects of art and written
records take on greater weight in the interpretation of
Sumerian society and, consequently, the emphasis in this chapter
changes from matters of technology and subsistence to those of politics, kings,
religious pantheons, and economic administration.*

*During the second half of the third millennium, Mesopotamia
was dominated by two powerful state governments. The Akkadians, a group
of Semites under a leader named Sargon, formed what is considered
to have been the first empire in Near Eastern history. This
amalgamation was short lived and replaced by a resurgence of Sumerian
authority in the form of the Ur III state. Under both types of rule, there were
advances in administration, law, trade, and military organization.*

The culmination of the rise of civilization in the ancient Near East was the emergence of an urban society with city and state administrative organizations. Although many important innovations were to be introduced in later periods, the social institutions that characterize complex society had already evolved. While the Sumerian and Akkadian civilizations flourished during the third millennium in Mesopotamia, temple cities were transformed into politically autonomous city-states. Secular power emerged as the dominant force in early cities, which were eventually united to form loose confederacies that periodically were welded into national states. Many aspects of complex society matured during the first half of the third millennium through the genius of the Sumerians, including foreign trade, mass-production, metallurgy, animal-drawn carts, irrigation works, decorative arts, jewelry, law, and warfare. The urban development that had begun during earlier millennia in the highland areas reached maturity in southern Mesopotamia. In many respects the early civilization of the Sumerians was not to be surpassed by later generations. Only one major development eluded the Sumerians, political unification: the final stage of the rise of civilization, the formation of national states, was accomplished by another group, the Semites.

The emergence of the national state with its characteristic form of government is an achievement of long-range significance. The political history of the Near East from the third millennium until the spread of Islam in the seventh century A.D. has alternated between segmentation into small warring city-states and unification under a strong dynastic authority. The omnipresent tendency toward separatism and competition in Mesopotamia was overcome only periodically by integrative mechanisms that temporarily welded the feuding constituencies into a unified state.

Many scholars have attempted to define the state (Service 1962; Adams 1966a; Fried 1967; Wright 1970; Flannery 1972a). Generally the emphasis is on the following factors:

1 Concentration of economic and political power
2 Organization along political and territorial lines
3 Hierarchical and differential access to basic resources
4 Monopoly of force

Gregory Johnson suggests a definition of the state that builds on earlier ideas: a state is defined as a society that is "primarily regulated through a differentiated and internally specialized decision-making organization which is structured in minimally three hierarchical levels, with institutionalized provision for the operation and maintenance of this organization and implementation of its decisions" (Johnson 1973b:2).

Decisions are usually made and communicated to the populace through a complex set of administrators and bureaucrats. These decisions are often formalized into codes of laws that are supported by religious, cultural, and personal attitudes. Their enforcement is accomplished through the state's monopoly on the use of force. However, the strongest states do not find it necessary to utilize their ultimate persuasive techniques. Periods of strong state governments in Mesopotamia were often those of relative stability, which enabled trade, industry, literature, and the arts to flourish.

The use of the term state in this book to describe the nature of some third-millennium Mesopotamian societies has as its basis the similarities of those societies with current national states. However, it is not implied that Mesopotamian states share all characteristics with modern states. Mechanisms of organization of human societies have experienced a long and complex sequence of development, but the evolution of urbanism, stratified class society, and law codes are the basis of ancient civilizations as they are of our own. The "empires" of the Akkadian and Ur III Dynasties seem loosely structured in terms of subsequent administrations, but compared with their predecessors they were major innovations that contained many elements of future administrative developments.

Several overall trends are apparent in the rise of state administrations: (1) an increase in organized military power; (2) the emergence of rulers whose primary base of support is in the secular realm, although frequently reaffirmed by the religious sector; (3) a rapid growth in the size and complexity of government functionaries, the bureaucracy; and (4) the growing economic networks put a premium on centralized control of distant and local economic systems. These interrelated developments were a continued response to the same factors that led to urbanism in the fourth millennium (see Chapter 7); in addition, they were affected by the broader scope of interactions and greater productive capabilities that had been realized with the advent of urbanism.

The heads of early Mesopotamian states were often secular rulers who directly controlled the military establishment, but they were not the only powerful elements in society. The religious elite, although often appointed by the king, maintained considerable power and sometimes challenged the supremecy of the secular authorities. Wealthy families whose source of wealth may have been agricultural land or commerce may also have wielded power independently of the king. It is clear that these alternative power bases—the military, religion, and wealth—sometimes came together in creating a powerful dynasty, but at other times they led to separate, competing power groups within a particular society. Each group may have had its own means of influencing the course of events and selecting future rulers, but it was, the control of force, especially through the promulgation of laws and the support of the standing army, that gave the secular ruler primary authority. Different groups were alternately weak and strong, as was the overall power of central government, but the general trend that is discernible was of greater control in the hands of the central government. This trend was disrupted by interludes of segmentation or weak central governments, but each time another state emerged to take control.

Although this book is an attempt to explain the rise of civilization in greater Mesopotamia, emphasis on developments there is not meant to deny the importance of events in other regions of the Near East. Each major region—Mesopotamia, the Nile Valley, Anatolia, highland Iran, and the Levant—developed in partial isolation, but there were important interactions between them. The nature of the relationships and the priority of develop-

ments are subjects of considerable controversy and investigation. In Mesopotamia, there was a long and seemingly continuous development of social institutions and technology. Most scholars agree that the earliest examples of most civilizational traits are found there and that Mesopotamia strongly influenced the development of its neighbors.

In contrast to the development of Mesopotamia, where it took 4,000 years to get from early agriculture to early cities (with identifiable antecedents for most developments), the rise of civilization in Egypt was achieved more rapidly. From the introduction of agriculture to the establishment of the state in Egypt took about 2,500 years. The Pharaonic state was then maintained with relative stability for 2,500 years. The reasons for this aberrant development, though often sought in foreign influences, can be fully understood only in relation to the ecological setting and the social milieu that developed in Egypt.

Early Chronology of the Egyptian Civilization

Neolithic

Early farming villages in Egypt are known only in scattered locations and are dated relatively late in comparison with others in Southwest Asia. The sites in the Fayuum Depression that have been categorized as Fayuum A and B cultures manifest an established village economy (Figure 9-1). The Fayuum Depression was the site of a lake fed by the Nile River that enabled the villagers to take advantage of aquatic resources as well as to use the water for agriculture. Herding was practiced, and hunting supplemented the diet. The houses were small, some of them semisubterranean oval huts with mud walls. Although investigations of the Neolithic period of the Nile Valley are far from exhaustive, current evidence reveals that agriculture was introduced in about 5500 B.C. or later. This is far later than equivalent developments in the uplands of greater Mesopotamia and has led scholars to infer that the concept and technology of agriculture came to Egypt from Southwest Asia.

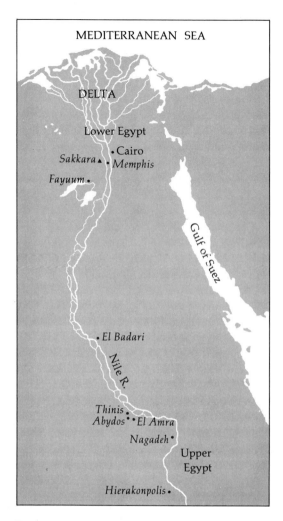

Figure 9-1
Early sites in the Nile Valley.

The early villages of the Nile Valley soon developed into large settlements with a substantial cultural inventory. Even during the Neolithic period, there was a pronounced difference between materials in the north and those in the south. (As described in Chapter 2, the Nile Valley is composed of two distinct regions: the Upper Nile (south) is a narrow valley with rock escarpments close to the river leaving a narrow cultivable plain; the lower Nile (north) widens out into a broad plain and eventually into the triangular Nile Delta.) Through-

out Egyptian prehistory and history, the cultures of the two regions were different from one another to a degree. Yet the success of the political administration of the Egyptian state can be measured by the degree of cohesion between the people of the two regions.

Badarian

The progression of predynastic cultures is best known from Upper Egypt because of less siltation and more intensive archeological investigation there. The first of three stages of the predynastic period in Upper Egypt is referred to as the Badarian culture from its early identification at the site of El Badari (Figure 9-1). The people of this culture did not live significantly differently from their Neolithic predecessors. They were simple farmers and gatherers, living in small mud huts. Their pottery was often burnished red with polished smudged black interior and exterior rims. Increasing attention was being paid to the burial of the dead, a custom that continued throughout Egyptian history. Many Badarian burials were in small wooden tombs, in which food and utensils were placed. Metalwork was being done in Egypt at this time but in small quantities and consisting of only the hammering of copper. Beads covered with a colored glaze are the earliest evidence for the production of a vitrified enamel ancestral to glass. Cosmetic palettes were carved out of schist, a practice that continued, with elaboration, for the next thousand years. Badarian remains include other artwork as well, such as combs, handles, and figurines carved from ivory, and molded clay statuettes. These objects have been discovered largely as part of burial offerings in the tombs of this period.

Amratian

The second stage of development in predynastic Egypt is referred to as Amratian, after the site of El Amra, near Abydos (Figure 9-1). Amratian remains have been found directly superimposed on Badarian deposits, which suggests continuity between the two periods. The people of the Amratian period continued to use the black-smudged, red-burnished ware first employed during Badarian times, but they developed other pottery types as well, including plain monchrome vessels and two-colored ones. The first decorated pottery in Egypt was evidently produced during the Amratian period. Geometric designs or naturalistic figures were painted on pots in dull white on a red-brown background; a few pieces had elaborate decorations in white on a black background incised on them (Vercoutter 1965). There is evidence that the Egyptians used green or gray eye make-up during this period. The make-up had a mineral base (malachite or galena), and its ingredients were ground together on stone palettes. Flint and other stones were used in the manufacture of tools more than was copper. A macehead in the form of a truncated cone was a common form of weapon. Although there are many sites with Amratian materials, the Amratian culture is known to have covered only a small part of the Nile Valley, the middle section of Upper Egypt.

Gerzean

After the relatively short lived Amratian period came a long period referred to as the Gerzean. Gerzean remains are widespread, being found in both Upper and Lower Egypt, and signify the crystallization of predynastic Egypt. Among these remains, evidence can be found for the first steps toward the national state that was to develop. The artifacts, burials, and settlements were given new forms. Gerzean pottery derived its distinctive color from the use of specific clay sources. On the characteristic light gray to buff background color, naturalistic designs were painted in dark red. The representations were stylized but were meant to be ibexes, flamingoes, mountains, and boats. These designs, as well as examples of human figures, were in many respects ancestral to common artistic and ritualistic works of later historic periods. Gerzean craftsmen were accomplished at the fabrication of stone bowls. The vessels were made from extremely hard stone, such as basalt, diorite, or breccia, specifically chosen so that the natural venation would decorate the vessel. Stone maceheads were also found in Gerzean deposits. Pear-shaped jewelry, metallurgy, and the importation of exotic raw materials increased in importance. More precious stones and gold were put in burials of the Gerzean period than had ever been before. Their presence there indicates that not only were trading networks within the Near East increasing in size, but Egypt's participation in them was becoming greater. Although it is difficult to determine from current evidence, the exotic materials and the increasing richness of some tombs probably indicate that craft specialization was increasing and society was becoming stratified. By late Gerzean times, the agricultural economy was highly developed and had probably produced a wealthy class of people. The agricultural elite may have been the core of the growing religious elite in Egypt, or the two groups may have been independent of one another.

Unification of Egypt

From what later, written sources say about this early period, it is possible to infer a hypothetical course of events. In early Gerzean times, there may have been several competing towns, each with its own patron deity. It is recorded that at some time during this predynastic period the towns of the north gained ascendancy over those of the south. This may account for the archeologically recognizable distribution of Gerzean cultural items from the north to the south. Subsequently, the south adopted many of the innovations of the north to become the leader in developments. At this time, each area may have become united in a loose confederation under the ruler of the most powerful town or cult. Inscriptions on later monuments describe these confederations as "kingdoms" and their leaders as "kings," but this may be a projection of later institutions backward in time. It was during this period of rivalry and confederations that much of the groundwork and trappings of the later Pharaonic state must have developed.

The final political developments that led to the formation of the First Thinite Dynasty can be hypothesized on the basis of several pieces of repre-

sentational artwork. All the palettes and maceheads
that portray this event in protohistoric times have
been found in the earliest temple at Hieraconpolis,
which was probably the last capital of the south
before unification of the country (Vercoutter 1965).
On one of the maceheads is the representation of
the king who had just vanquished an army in the
north, wearing the crown of Upper Egypt. Because
his name is written with an unreadable hieroglyphic symbol that includes a scorpion, he has
been called the "Scorpion King." Another important item is a huge and magnificent schist palette
with reliefs carved on both surfaces. On the one
side of the palette the king, who is identified as
Narmer by a readable hieroglyphic, is shown wearing the crown of Lower Egypt, striking Northern
enemies dead, and inspecting their decapitated
corpses.

On the basis of these sources of information and
others, it is thought that the towns of the north and
south were in conflict for a long period, perhaps
for several generations. It is likely that each side
banded together to form temporary confederations
headed by military leaders, who probably assumed
more responsibility than before. When the ultimate
victory was won by the army of the south, its leader
made the confederation permanent and put it directly under his own control. Hence, the unification
of Egypt and the early Pharaonic state seems to
have been born out of military unrest. The increasing power of the military ruler would have been a
natural result of the long period of warfare. It
would have been to the religious elite's advantage
to side with this new power base by giving religious
sanction to the position of the Pharoah.

First and Second Dynasties

With the establishment of the centralized government of the First Dynasty, Egypt entered the
historic period (c. 3100 B.C.). Inscriptions and monuments of the rulers of the early dynasties have
been discovered and identified. Later Pharoahs had
their scribes compile lists of all their predecessors,
leaving a record of the succession to the throne
starting with the first Pharoah. Unfortunately, sub-

sequent lists of kings are not completely preserved,
and even those compilations made during Greek
and Roman times are not available in their original
form. The most complete record is an inscription
on the Palermo Stone, which was made in about
2500 B.C. and which includes the name of each
Pharoah and the exact length of his reign. Using
this record and the recopied work of a third-century
B.C. Egyptian priest called Manetho, who compiled a master king list, it is possible to reconstruct
with some precision the names of the early rulers
of the Egyptian state and the lengths of their reigns.
The First Dynasty is dated at about the same time
as the beginning of the Early Dynastic period in
Mesopotamia. The identity of the first king of the
First Dynasty remains uncertain: the Narmer palette implies that the first king was Narmer, whereas
Manetho's list gives King Menes as the first ruler.
It is possible that the two names were among several used by a single king.

There is also some question of the location of
the capital of the First Dynasty. Manetho referred
to the First and Second Dynasties as Thinite, after
a city near Abydos in Upper Egypt. Although major
royal tombs of the First Dynasty have been discovered in the cemetery at Abydos, much larger
tombs have been uncovered at Sakkara, near
Memphis (Figure 9-2). The ruling family of the
First Dynasty came from the south, and Thinis was
probably its home. By the beginning of the Second
Dynasty, the capital of Egypt was definitely at
Memphis, near the angle in the Nile Delta. It would
have been a strategic move in terms of uniting the
feuding factions of the country to relocate the capital on the boundary between Upper and Lower
Egypt. It is likely that soon after unification, during
the First Dynasty, Memphis was made the main
capital. However, because the ruling family came
from the south, and the south was victorious in the
war with the north, it is reasonable to assume that
royal residences, or at least major monuments,
would have been built in the homeland of the
Pharoahs.

The unification of Egypt probably took many
generations to stabilize and make permanent.
Three techniques were used to foster national

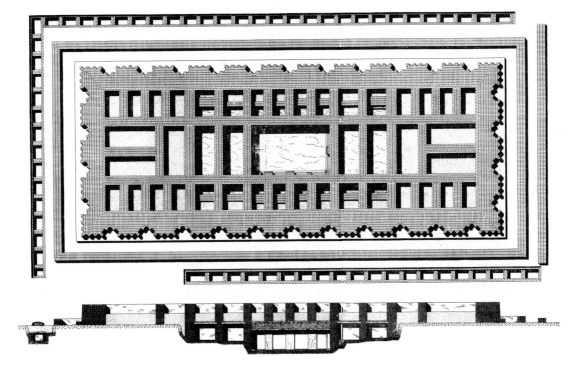

Figure 9-2
First Dynasty tomb at Sakkara. (After Walter B. Emery.)

unity: the transfer of the capital to an intermediary city, armed forces, and intermarriage. The use of force is attested to by several artifacts that portray warfare, such as the Narmer palette. The practice of intermarriage is inferred from the names of the queens of the First Dynasty, revealing that the kings from the south often took brides from the north. The success of these efforts at unification is unquestioned. The unity and relative internal peace is even more significant when compared with simultaneous events in the fragmented Mesopotamian Plain. The relative lack of internal dissention allowed the early kings of Egypt to concentrate on external menaces. There were campaigns to the south into Nubia and northwest against the Libyan desert dwellers.

International trade also was fostered by the Early Dynastic rulers. Wood and rare stones were brought in from the Levant, metal ore from Nubia, and ivory from farther south in Africa. The administration of long-distance trade and the increasing use of substantial irrigation works was controlled by the centralized authority at Memphis. During the first two dynasties, the offices and bureaucracy that were to characterize Egyptian government for 3,000 years first emerged: provincial rulers, census officials, and the grand vizier—all had early counterparts during this period. The king—later called the Pharoah—was the center of the administration, a position he maintained in the religion, artwork, and writing of Egypt. The monarchy itself established its special ideology of kingship; enthronement ceremonies became fixed. A festival closely linked to the ideology of royal power took place regularly, and a cult came into being centered on the person of the king. The Pharoah himself, representative and descendant of the god Horus, frequently was spoken of as a god (Vercoutter 1965).

With the establishment of the united monarchy in Egypt, writing and science flourished. Hieroglyphic writing was already known during late Gerzean times, but with the First Dynasty it became more common. Unlike the Mesopotamian pictographic script that soon developed into an abstracted and simplified symbol system, Egyptian writing maintained its precise ideograms. For the most part, ideograms were used to represent their facsimiles or related concepts. The rebus principle was adopted slowly, allowing for the communication of subtle concepts by means of similar sounding symbols. The major disadvantages of the Egyptian system of writing were the enormous number of symbols, the difficulty of executing these symbols, and the lack of any indication of whether a symbol was to be read as a word-sign (ideogram) or a sound-sign (phoneme).

Mathematics was already highly developed during the early dynasties, but largely in a nontheoretical, pragmatic manner. As was to be the case later, scientific developments were in the direction of precision of measurement. Astronomy was well established at this time. Originally, a lunar calendar was employed, but it was supplemented by a more accurate 12-month solar calendar. The locations of buildings and their orientation were determined by the astronomers.

Although there is little direct evidence for it, it is likely that during the first two dynasties the religion of Egypt with its characteristic pantheon was already established. Only one religious sanctuary of this period has been found, at Abydos. However, inscriptions on the Palermo Stone mention the building and rebuilding of many temples by the kings of the first two dynasties.

By the end of the Second Dynasty, at about 2600 B.C., the mold of what was to become Egyptian civilization had been formed. The legacy of the first rulers included an administration with the Pharoah at its center; a religion, with each city having a patron deity and a temple complex; and a system of writing and art that were to remain largely unchanged. Egypt had developed along

rather different lines from those followed by the Mesopotamian civilization. The late-beginning agricultural villages gave way quickly to towns and a successful agricultural base. Trade and irrigation played important roles from the beginning. Unlike what happened in Mesopotamia, the period of rival cities did not continue for long, nor did active rivalry continue after the establishment of the first national state government. Cities developed in Egypt, but not on the enormous scale of Warka or Nippur. Power was vested in the ruler and not in his city. The Pharoahs soon established shrines and temples throughout the country, which enhanced the maintenance of internal stability and unification; however, at certain times when central authority was weak, the provinces exhibited significant autonomy.

Urban development in Egypt had some of the characteristics of that in Mesopotamia, but they were different in duration and scale (refer to Figure 7-1 on page 221). In the Egyptian sequence of development, the phases of temple-cities (Stage 5 of Mesopotamian development) and warring city-states (Mesopotamian Stage 6) were combined into one short phase. Hence, although early advances in technology and organization of a farming economy probably did not originate in the Nile Valley, after they had been effectively adopted a national state developed with great speed.

Chronological Sequences of Major Mesopotamian City-States

The sixth general stage of community growth was introduced by the emergence of numerous city-states in southern Mesopotamia (refer to Figure 7-1 on page 221). This developmental stage is thought by archeologists to have occurred at roughly the period referred to as Early Dynastic I, II, and III. Written records from this period are more comprehensive than earlier ones and are the most important source of information. Cities became larger and the number of Sumerian centers grew to about one dozen. Sources of evidence of organized warfare are both the written records and the massive defensive walls built around the important cities. Social stratification is amply attested to, especially in the royal burials at Ur. The temple remained the center of economic, religious, and administrative affairs. However, during the Early Dynastic period, a secular authority developed that eventually separated itself from the temple, as evidenced by the palace buildings at several Mesopotamian cities.

The city-states of the Early Dynastic period were the culmination of the urbanization of the preceding 'Ubaid, 'Uruk, and Jemdet Nasr periods. Although each city often attempted to extend its dominion over neighboring cities, the basic unit of integration remained the city and its surroundings. Growth of the socioeconomic unit beyond the bounds of individual cities did not occur until the seventh phase of urbanization, the nation-state. Besides being a period of rapid political evolution, the Early Dynastic period was a time of great artistic achievement. Quantities of exotic raw materials were employed in diverse forms of artistic expression, from the minute glyptic designs on cylinder seals to monumental buildings and stonework.

Artifacts

The Early Dynastic period was not as distinctly set apart from its predecessors artifactually as archeologists would like. Technology developed and improved but did not change radically. Much of the pottery of the Early Dynastic period is indistinguishable from that of the Jemdet Nasr period. There are some additions to the ceramic inventory, such as the solid-footed goblet, fruit stands, heavy cylindrical beaker, and small cups with everted rims (Figure 9-3, page 288).

Whereas rapid changes in technology and style are not evidenced by Early Dynastic pottery, other parts of the material inventory indicate that creative changes were taking place. Representations on cylinder seals changed from solid figures to flat, overall patterns (Figure 9-4, page 289). Henri Frankfort has identified a "brocade style" among the seals from the Diyala region (1939; 1954). The subject matter of these seals was not substantively

changed; rather its arrangement was modified. The major figures of the design, such as goats or cattle, were carved in a row, and the remainder of the surface was ornamented with fishes, stars, crosses, lozenges, or other small motifs. These cylinder seals could be used to produce an unbroken frieze of any length.

Many of the cylinder seals found at southern Mesopotamian cities carry designs in which the cuneiform script is a major element (Porada 1965). Combinations of cuneiform signs and representational forms are common. The cuneiform signs served both as decorative motifs and as signs having meaning, such as a name or an incantation.

Architecture

The beginning of the Early Dynastic period is characterized at many sites by the introduction of the plano-convex brick. These cushion-shaped bricks were flat on one side and curved on the other. On the curved side finger marks have often been preserved from when the mud had been pressed into the mold by hand. Almost all major architecture in southern Mesopotamia and much of that in the rest of Mesopotamia was constructed of plano-convex brick during the Early Dynastic period.

Foundations of the larger buildings were constructed of rough, untrimmed blocks of stone at sites where stone was locally available, such as Mari and Al 'Ubaid. At Ur, stone blocks were used to erect corbelled vaults over tomb chambers built underground. The use of the vault in above-ground buildings of this period has not yet been discovered. However, arches made of plano-convex mud-bricks have been found over the doorways of the houses (Frankfort 1954).

The architectural design of major buildings shows a continuity with that of preceding periods. The layouts of temples constructed during earlier periods were maintained with minor modifications in rebuilding during the Early Dynastic period. Nevertheless, there were important innovations in architecture other than the use of plano-convex bricks. As evidenced from the remains of several

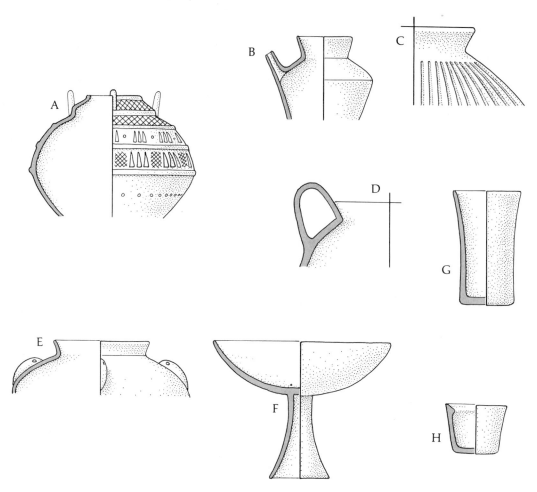

Figure 9-3
Profiles of Early Dynastic pottery types: (A-E) Early Dynastic I; (F-H) Early
Dynastic II and III. (After Adams and Nissen, 1972.)

buildings, increased attention was paid to the monumentality of major entrances. Towers or pillars embellished entrances of certain buildings at Kish, Mari, and Khafaje (Frankfort 1954). The construction of large oval compounds around major temples at Khafaje and Al 'Ubaid were unique to this period. Large architectural complexes from the second half of the Early Dynastic period at Mari, Kish, and Eridu were identified as palaces, manifesting the growth of a new element in the administration of the early cities.

One of the great monumental building com-

plexes preserved from the Early Dynastic period is the Temple Oval at Khafaje in the Diyala Valley (Figures 9-5 and 9-6). The Temple Oval was a walled-in sacred precinct that was self-sufficient in many respects. The massive perimeter wall enclosed an area of more than 3 hectares, including a huge courtyard, workshops, magazines, a priest's house, a second enclosure wall, and a temple-sanctuary on top of a platform (Mallowan 1968). The three rebuildings of the Temple Oval belong to Early Dynastic II and III; they are indications of the power in the hands of the temple elite and

Figure 9-4
Early Dynastic cylinder seals in the brocade style. (Photograph from The Oriental Institute. The University of Chicago.)

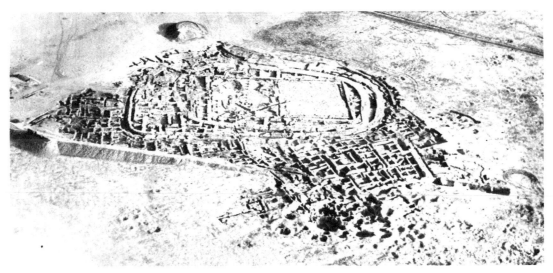

Figure 9-5
Aerial view of the excavations at the site of Khafaje, centering on the Early Dynastic Temple Oval and adjacent domestic buildings. (Photograph from The Oriental Institute. The University of Chicago.)

the scope of the activities in their control during these periods. Within the Temple Oval compound was a sculptor's workshop, and numerous pieces of human sculpture were found in various locations within the compound, including copper figures of nude males. These are among the earliest known objects fabricated by the lost-wax casting technique.

Another Temple Oval similar to the one at Khafaje was uncovered in the Early Dynastic levels of Al 'Ubaid. Large temples in the midst of oval-shaped, walled compounds are an architectural

manifestation of the growing power of the temple elite. Evidence that both economic and religious activities took place within the same compound, separate from the remainder of the community, is physical documentation of the developing social order. The Temple Oval was the center of many important economic and cult activities at Khafaje. Access was probably limited to certain persons or to specific times of the year.

The sequence of Sin Temples at Khafaje documents the continuity of architectural design from the Jemdet Nasr period through the end of the

Figure 9-6
Isometric reconstruction of the probable appearance of the Temple Oval of Khafaje and surrounding buildings and walls. (Photograph from The Oriental Institute. The University of Chicago.)

Early Dynastic period, while evidencing important changes. The first five rebuildings of the Sin Temple were undertaken during the Jemdet Nasr period, and the sixth through the tenth were done during the Early Dynastic period. The Sin Temple series was composed of relatively large buildings, but of importance to archeologists are its continuity of development and certain features of construction and design.

The first of the Early Dynastic Sin Temples (VI) was built directly on its predecessor, but the walls were for the first time built of plano-convex bricks. The main sanctuary of this structure was similar to earlier ones: an oblong room, approximately 12 by 4 meters with a large mud-brick box-podium at one end. It is assumed that, because of the single entrance to the sanctuary from the courtyard, access to the sanctuary was limited to priests and rulers, whereas the public could enter only the spacious courtyard to deposit offerings for the cult (Mallowan 1968:12).

Sin Temple VIII (Early Dynastic II) was larger than earlier temples but included several changes in layout (Figures 9-7 and 9-8). For the first time an open-air altar, or podium, was built in the courtyard, which may mean that larger numbers of people participated in the ceremonies than there was room for in the sanctuary. Other additions in-

cluded the use of a large mud column in the middle of an entrance from the courtyard to one of the large chambers, niches in the facade, and a stepped entrance to the building flanked by towers.

These three architectural features of Sin Temple VIII at Khafaje bear a striking resemblance to features of a larger architectural complex unearthed at the city of Kish to the south. According to later written records, Kish was acknowledged as one of the most important cities of Sumer during the Early Dynastic period, and at one time may have dominated the entire region. The best-preserved Early Dynastic architectural complex at Kish is the great Palace A (Figure 9-9; Mackay 1929). This complex shares various characteristics with Sin Temple VIII at Khafaje. This massive building with many rooms was divided into two parts. The entrance was flanked by fortified towers, and the perimeter wall of one of the parts was especially thick, perhaps for defensive purposes. Although this building shares features with the religious architecture at Khafaje, it is thought to have been the palace of a secular ruler. During Early Dynastic II and III, architectural complexes were built that for the first time rivaled the temple compounds in size and sophistication.

The presence of palaces in addition to temple compounds is an indication that authority and

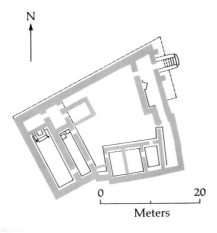

N

0   20
Meters

Figure 9-7
Plan of Sin Temple VI at Khafaje, showing open
courtyard, bent-axis approach, and monumental
entrance. (After Delougaz and Lloyd, 1942.)

Figure 9-8
The Sin Temple at Khafaje during
excavation. (Photograph from
The Oriental Institute. The
University of Chicago.)

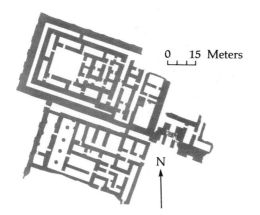

0   15 Meters

N

Figure 9-9
Plan of what has been interpreted to have been a
palace complex at the ancient site of Kish. Note the
thick (defensive?) wall enclosing the upper half of
the complex.

power was not solely in the hands of the temple elite within third-millennium society. Eridu, in southern Mesopotamia, and Mari, on the middle Euphrates River, also had large architectural complexes similar to the Kish palace and roughly contemporaneous with it. These buildings are as impressive in scale as the temple buildings excavated at those sites. It can be inferred from the architectural evidence that a separate and probably greater power base had developed in most Early Dynastic Sumerian cities to rival the authority of the temple.

Another building form that was developed in Early Dynastic times was related to the rise in secular power and accompanying warfare. The first massive defensive walls surrounding some of the Sumerian cities seem to have been constructed during the second half of the Early Dynastic period. The best-known example of these early fortifications is the wall surrounding the city of Warka. This massive construction is made of plano-convex bricks and is 9 kilometers long, enclosing an area of 400 hectares. The erection of this wall was credited to Warka's early king, Gilgamesh, in an epic poem about him. Gilgamesh seemed to personify many of the accomplishments and changes in the Early Dynastic period (see pages 305–306).

Settlement Patterns in Early Dynastic Mesopotamia

The second half of the Early Dynastic period marked the onset of the historical age and, in many respects, the crystallization of urban society. In southern Mesopotamia, especially in the environs of Warka, there was a distinctive shift from a pattern of rural occupation with small cities and towns to an abandonment of rural settlements and the growth of a few large urban centers. Archeological survey data can be supplemented by the use of the early cuneiform documents. By 2700 B.C., there were approximately a dozen major Sumerian cities, and several times that number of secondary centers. The locations of the major and minor centers

depended on numerous factors. Access to irrigation water was the primary determinant of site location and long-term economic success. Several of the Early Dynastic-period cities were located along the major courses of the Euphrates. The Euphrates River offered a more constant and manageable supply of water for simple, small-scale irrigation systems did the Tigris. Although location along a major river bed was crucial, the arrangement of large sites was not particularly linear. Each of the major rivers split into several large streams, and so the locations of cities formed a geometric pattern.

The basic pattern of settlement was of enclaves of communities spread out across the irrigable parts of the Mesopotamian Plain (see Figure 8-17 on page 264). Each enclave was dominated by one or more large centers. Smaller sites were located at short distances from the major centers and often in linear patterns, following the major stream course that the city controlled. Some of the enclaves were far enough apart that there would have been unfarmed land between them; others were side-by-side, in which case disputes over land and water were almost certain to have occurred. The proportion of the population that lived in rural communities, rather than urban centers, varied from region to region. In the Diyala region, the rural population grew along with the urban population during the Early Dynastic period, but the centers never attained the large size of those in the south. In the south near Warka, the countryside was largely depopulated when Warka grew to its maximum size during the second half of the Early Dynastic period. This pattern is indicative of a strong, centralized authority and of significant military strife. A large part of the population of Warka engaged in agricultural activities, probably farming the area immediately surrounding the city.

There were certain similarities in the layouts of Early Dynastic cities. Central temple complexes, large-scale palace buildings, and massive defensive walls are documented at several of the excavated sites. The infrequent archeological exposure of third-millennium domestic quarters suggests a density of buildings not unlike the older sections of modern Near Eastern cities such as Damascus,

Syria, or Erbil, Iraq (refer to Figure 1-4 on page 6). Two-story architecture was probably the rule, with houses arranged around small interior courtyards. The excavations of the Diyala sites revealed domestic quarters arranged in large "blocks" set off by roadways (see Figure 9-18 on page 302). Small alleyways twisted among the crowded houses. A large house of a rich family covered more than 200 square meters, whereas the house of a "middle class" family covered only 50 square meters and may have lacked an interior courtyard. Various estimates have been made for the average density of population in early cities: from what is known about the average house size, the average number of people in a family, and populations of analogous modern cities, it can be inferred that from 100 to 400 persons occupied 1 hectare (Frankfort 1950; Adams 1965; Adams and Nissen 1972). Although population density seems to have been generally constant over long periods, it did vary from community to community and from region to region. Even within a walled city, the entire enclosed area was not covered with buildings. It is believed that the largest cities, such as Uruk and Ur, did not consist totally of built-up areas but included open areas, orchards, and gardens. In addition, the temple precincts would have housed only a few people in large areas.

From general population estimates and calculations of available agricultural land, it is thought that the maximum Early Dynastic population of Warka was 50,000 (Adams and Nissen 1972). Warka was one of the two or three largest Sumerian cities. Most Sumerian cities had populations ranging between about 20,000 and 25,000. Allowing for the rural population, the total population estimated for the Mesopotamian Plain during the third millennium is between one-half million and one million (Adams 1966a:71). Although this population far exceeded those of earlier periods, it was small in comparison with fifteenth-century A.D. Mesoamerican civilization, which may have been ten times as large.

The evidence from early written sources implies that Early Dynastic cities were for the most part independent political entities. Although there were interregional trading networks that brought in raw materials, agricultural and manufacturing activities were centered in single cities. Each city grew out of its surrounding rural area, and control of that area was maintained. Small villages and moderate-sized towns were a part of each city-state. Thus, the city and its immediate surroundings constituted the basic political unit of the Early Dynastic period. The relationship between the central city and its dependencies was symbiotic. The smaller communities supplied the city with agricultural products and manual labor and received manufactured goods, protection in times of warfare, and religious and agricultural information in return. Although confederations of city-states have been ascribed to the Early Dynastic period, all were rather transitory.

Community development in Early Dynastic Mesopotamia can be classified as Stage 6 (refer to Figure 7-1 on page 221). In the lowland areas, independent city-states had developed and they fought with one another for supremacy. In northern Mesopotamia, and in certain areas outside Mesopotamia, large towns developed in ways analogous to the development of city-states (Jawad, 1965), but they cannot be considered city-states because of their small size and a lack of emphasis on central institutions and specialized activities. Throughout the Levant, Anatolia, and highland Iran were scattered large sites of from 5 to 50 hectares whose form was characteristic of the urban sites in the upland rainfall regions. During the third millenium, large cities developed only in extensive lowland areas where irrigation agriculture was necessary. Writing was unknown in most upland regions, and massive architectural structures characteristic of centralized control were not common.

Although the political pattern in lowland Mesopotamia, as well as in upland regions, seems to be that of independent entities, there is evidence of cooperation and specialization. Each city had its own patron deity or deities. Insofar as the Sumerian pantheon was a reflection of the structure of society as seen by its participants, each city must have been distinguished by certain traits or activities. Nippur was the city of Enlil, the god of the earth.

Being located midway between the cities of northern and southern Sumer, Nippur served as a religious center for all Sumerian cities. Its function as a religious center, however, did not make Nippur a political center, which implies a nonmilitary, nonpolitical form of cooperation between cities. Other cooperative aspects of the diverse Sumerian city-states are manifested in the wide distribution of identical tablets for teaching scribes the Sumerian language, as well as standardized measurement and numerical systems. The struggle between cities may not have been as constant nor as pervasive as the ubiquitous references in early historical documents imply. The confederation did not constitute a politically unified nation, but they may have cooperated culturally and economically in ways that led to the dispersal and standardization of Sumerian culture.

Material Culture of Early Dynastic Mesopotamia

The size and importance of the larger Sumerian cities attests to widespread prosperity during the Early Dynastic period. Material culture flourished and the artwork exhibited an excellence theretofore unattained. Behind this splendor was an effective economic system that produced the agricultural surplus to support full-time craftsmen and long-distance trade. Irrigation works must have grown in size and distribution. The emerging centralized power of the temples and then of the kings led to better organization and planning for regional water control, allocation, and land use than before. The salinization of the irrigated farmland was only beginning to be felt, and the population was not large enough to have occupied all potentially farmable land. Hence, with fertile land, high-yielding grain, cattle, and sheep, the Sumerian farmer was extremely successful. Also by this time the secondary products of sheep and cattle—wool and milk—were fully utilized. A fishing industry had grown to take advantage of the river resources, and orchards of date palms were probably producing an important dietary supplement.

Crafts and industry were also growing in scale. Mass-produced pottery continued to be used for food preparation and storage. The weaving of textiles out of wool and flax grew into an enormous industry. It is during the Early Dynastic period that slaves are first documented. They were workers in the burgeoning weaving industry. Metallurgy was being improved and became an increasing source of implements, containers, and artwork. Although hot hammering of copper and open stone molds remained important, the new process of lost-wax casting is documented by several Early Dynastic pieces. The lost-wax technique consists of molding in wax the object to be cast, building a clay mold around it, and melting the wax out, leaving the cavity to be filled with molten metal. The advantages of this process are that it allows for variation in the shapes being cast and that the molds are relatively simple to manufacture. Many of the important pieces of artwork from the Early Dynastic period and later times were made by lost-wax casting (Figure 9-10).

Accompanying the growth of crafts and industry were increases in the volume and extent of the trading network. Whereas the temple community was probably responsible for the procurement and distribution of imported goods during the fourth millennium, the palace assumed a share of this responsibility in the Early Dynastic period. Most of the intercity and interregional trade was conducted by a class of merchant agents (*dam-gar*) who acted on the king's behalf (G. Wright 1974). They received staples, such as cloth, garments, barley, oil, and flour, from the royal storehouse and exchanged them for foreign goods. The *dam-gars* acted as part of the administrative hierarchy of the early cities, but they probably supplemented those duties with private enterprise (Adams 1974a). Thus, although trade in early Mesopotamian cities was largely administered by those in authority, elements of private enterprise encroached on that territory, leading to the growth of private capital as a power base that competed with the established temple and newly founded kingship.

The increasing importance of trade to importers, exporters, and those who transferred the goods

Figure 9-10
Chariot cast in copper, from the site of Tell Agrab in the Diyala region. The chariot is drawn by four onagers. (Photograph from The Oriental Institute. The University of Chicago.)

stimulated the rise of communities that specialized in trade. A phenomena recognized in later history and probably present by Early Dynastic times is the "port of trade" (Polanyi, Arensberg, and Pearson 1957). Ports of trade allowed for neutral meeting places for traders from potentially hostile states that nevertheless carried on long-distance trade with each other. These towns might function as independent states, fixing prices and regulating the conduct of trade. They were often located on the coast, engaging in sea-going trade (e.g., Ugarit and Tyre), or near the boundary between two major empires. It has been suggested that Tepe Yahya, a town in southcentral Iran, and the Persian Gulf Island of Bahrein may have functioned as ports of trade for the Mesopotamian-Indus Valley. The excavator of Tepe Yahya interprets the evidence differently, viewing Yahya as a central place that procured and processed a raw material (green chlorite) and then traded it (Lamberg-Karlovsky 1971; 1972). An alternative to ports of trade was the establishment of foreign colonies of traders in regions that produced raw materials. This mechanism has been amply documented for the second millennium, during which there were trading colonies in Anatolia. Whereas the archeological evidence from Tell Brak supports the notion of southern Mesopotamian traders in northern Syria, there is little support for trading colonies in the Indus, nor of Indus traders in Mesopotamian cities, with the possible exception of Tell Asmar. The scant available evidence from Early Dynastic times implies that trade was conducted by functionaries of the major urban institutions and that this growing class of traders ventured to nearby regions for raw materials and dealt through intermediaries for more distant supplies.

Royal Cemetery at Ur

The most vivid testimony to the diversity and wealth of materials during the second half of the Early Dynastic period comes from the excavation of the Royal Cemetery at Ur. More than 2,500 graves, many of them of important personages, were excavated under the direction of Sir Leonard Woolley. The cemetery was in an open area of the city that had been a domestic sector during the Jemdet Nasr period and was subsequently covered with layers of debris. Most of the important burials in this cemetery are dated at Early Dynastic III. This cemetery was used for a long time, with many graves being dug through earlier ones or overlying them. This general disorder made the excavation and dating of the graves difficult, but it also allowed for the preservation of many of the tombs: a stratum of rich graves for which there is evidence for plunder probably protected the graves below.

The two best-known graves are vaulted chambers situated at the bottom of deep shafts. One tomb is presumed to have contained the remains of a king whose body was never identified because the grave had been entered through the roof and partly plundered. Adjacent to it was the vault of a queen, Shub-ad (also called Pu-abi), who was lying on her back upon a bed, accompanied by female attendants. Two wagons drawn by oxen and attended by male servants had been backed down the steep entry ramp, where fifty-nine bodies were on the ground near the tomb chambers. Most of the bodies were female. The few males seem to have

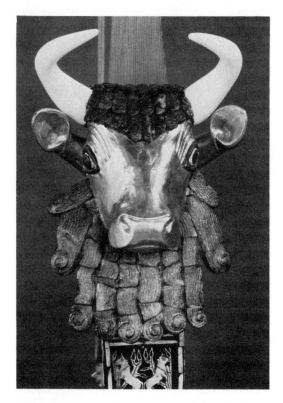

Figure 9-11
Bull-headed lyre of wood (reconstructed), gold, lapis lazuli, and other inlaid material from the Royal Cemetery at Ur. (Photograph © The Trustees of the British Museum.)

been soldiers. All of the attendants had lavish attire, including large quantities of gold, silver, carnelian, and lapis lazuli jewelry. There were many metal vessels and implements. Probably the most spectacular pieces from these graves were muscial instruments and decorative pieces made of gold, lapis lazuli, and delicately inlaid wood (Figures 9-11 and 9-12).

Woolley believed that all the people and animals buried at the time of Queen Shub-ad's funeral had descended into the pits alive. After a ceremony during which the queen's body and goods were placed in the vault, the animals were slaughtered by their attendants and the men and women probably took poison from little bowls that were ready for them in the shafts. From the arrangement and

composure of the bodies, a willing, nonviolent death can be assumed. After the tomb had been covered with dirt, another ceremony and a ritualistic meal took place.

In addition to preserving hundreds of magnificent pieces of Sumerian craftsmanship, the Royal Cemetery is a source of insight into the customs and beliefs of the protohistoric period. Inscriptions found with some of the burials document that the larger tombs held kings of the First Dynasty of Ur and members of their families. Although the entombment of servants and animals with the deceased is attested to in the archeological record at Ur, to a far lesser extent at an Early Dynastic cemetery at Kish, and at contemporary Egyptian cemeteries of Abydos and Saqqara, there is no explicit reference to this custom in the written records (Mallowan 1968:42–43). There is one possible reference in the *Epic of Gilgamesh* to a hero being accompanied to the grave by his retainers. There is little archeological evidence of the origin of this custom, except for the increasing practice of animal and material offerings in the temples of the Uruk and Jemdet Nasr periods, especially at Warka. Even more surprising than the unprecedented appearance of this cult of human sacrifice is its rapid disappearance. By the end of Early Dynastic III, the custom of human sacrifice had been discontinued, not to be revived again in Mesopotamia.·

Two competing hypotheses have been suggested to explain the occurrence of the royal burials. According to Sir Leonard Woolley, the main personages were the early rulers of the city of Ur. These rulers, having been considered part divine, were accompanied into the afterlife by their courtiers and material possessions. An alternative explanation was offered by the German scholar A. Moortgat. He suggested that the tombs were not the remains of the funeral rites of royal personages but of a primitive fertility cult (1949). The chief male and female participants were religious personnel who were put to death after representing the god and goddess in the sacred marriage ceremony upon which the fertility of the land was thought to depend. Literary and archeological arguments have been made in favor of both hypotheses, without either being conclusively accepted.

Even if it can be documented that religious ceremonies were related to the appearance and disappearance of large-scale human (and material) sacrifice during the second half of the Early Dynastic period, such documentation does not adequately explain why the phenomenon occurred. Rather, an explanation for these opulent graves may be related to organizational changes. During the first half of the Early Dynastic period, as well as during the preceding Jemdet Nasr period, the temple elite seem to have held most of the power in the early city. During the second half, massive palace structures were built that are attributed to an emerging secular elite. The architectural evidence combined with the written record implies that power changed hands; it went from the temple to the palace (Adams 1966a). When this change was taking place—that is, when the religious and secular elite were competing for power, the elaborate Ur burials occurred. The burial "goods" (human, animal, and artifactual) were forms of wealth. A significant proportion of a person's wealth was buried with the body, perhaps for use in an afterlife. There were few reasons that would compel the heirs to this wealth to bury it instead of retaining it for their own use. Customs of ritually destroying large quantities of goods are known ethnographically from several societies. In such cases, the destruction of wealth is often done so that the survivors maintain their status in society. Those who destroy the wealth implicitly receive recognition in return. Something similar may have been taking place at Ur. When a city ruler died, the position of authority had to be transferred: it may have been the custom that the new ruler (hereditary or not) could assume the reins of authority by renouncing (burying) the wealth of the former ruler. The underlying meaning of this custom may not have been explicitly understood by the practitioners, for early practices of exchanging goods for status may long have been a part of normal religious ritual.

The special significance of the royal burials is the possibility that these opulent burials may have

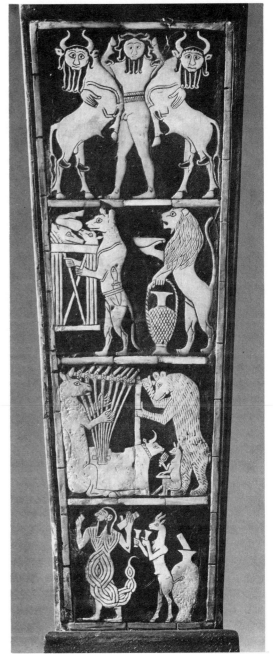

Figure 9-12
Detail from the front of the sound box of a bull-headed harp like the one in Figure 9-11. The depiction of animals engaged in human activities may be a portrayal of an important myth. (Photograph from the University Museum, Philadelphia.)

been one of the instruments in the emergence of secular power. The kings were powerful enough to accumulate great quantities of wealth during their reigns, but the institution was not so powerful and regularized that it could maintain itself. Rituals were still needed to maintain the authority of the king during periods of succession. As the position of the king became more firmly established during the second half of the Early Dynastic period, there was less necessity for this wasteful form of ritualistic reaffirmation. The last kings of the Early Dynastic period and those of the subsequent Akkadian Dynasty probably decided that there were better uses for the human and material wealth.

The short period of human sacrifice also demonstrates the power and wealth of the new ruling class and the lengths to which it would go to maintain power. What had started as a small-scale practice—the ritualistic offering of wealth in exchange for recognized status—was elaborated until it assumed major importance. The succession of kings seemed to be assured but at great cost in economic and human terms.

Ancient Art as a Medium of Communication

By the end of the Uruk period, about 3100 B.C., all of the traits of civilization (Childe's characteristics of cities discussed in Chapter 7) had been developed at least in embryonic form. However, it was during the Early Dynastic period that many of these characteristics developed to their fullest extent. Government, trade, crafts, and writing had all attained mature status by 2500 B.C. Probably the most spectacular achievement of the people of Sumer during the Early Dynastic period, at least from the point of view of archeologists, was their artwork. Early Dynastic art included sculpture in the round, relief, inlay, glyptics, and metal work, both cast and hammered. As is vividly documented in the grave goods at the Royal Cemetery of Ur, several arts had reached a level of creativity and sophistication not surpassed for millennia.

To understand the function of art in the context of the emerging organizational institutions of

Mesopotamian civilization, one must examine three interrelated ways of interpretating art (Conkey n. d.): as a means of classifying human experiences; as a regulating mechanism between human beings and their environment; and as an aspect of ritualistic behavior that transmits information about nature, society, and a world view. Art had been used by earlier societies as more than an outlet for creativity, and the Sumerians carried this trend further. Works of art were symbols of wealth and status, being manufactured for, possessed by, and buried with the rising administrative elite, who were able to marshall the resources and craftsmen necessary for the production of major artwork. Not only were the objects symbols of status, but many of them were representations of stratified roles among the members of Sumerian society. With the advent of cities, the balance between symbolic and representational art shifted toward a greater frequency of representational pieces. It is interesting to note that representational art and writing emerged and developed together in Mesopotamia. Writing could be considered the most explicit form of representational art. The earliest examples of both these phenomena, which flourished during the Early Dynastic period, are from the Uruk period. By 2000 B.C., both art and writing had been standardized in the forms of cuneiform script and the great art styles of the ruling dynasties. If writing and art are considered to be means of communication, then it is useful to examine the range of information conveyed by each and those segments of the population for which they were designed.

Throughout the Early Dynastic period, writing was the means of economic and administrative recording, with a good deal less attention given to historical and literary efforts. Literacy was restricted to only a few members of society, and of those many were scribes. It is difficult to determine which segments of the population were exposed to the finer pieces of Sumerian artwork, but large sculptures and wall reliefs must have been accessible to the general public during major festivals when rituals were performed in the temple complexes. Several different art forms would have

Figure 9-13
Hoard of Early Dynastic statues from Tell Asmar in the Diyala region.
(Photograph from The Oriental Institute. The University of Chicago.)

been displayed during such festivals. The architectural details of the temples themselves, such as raised platforms, niches, and wall coverings, would have been specifically designed to set them apart from other large structures. Gods, kings, and mythical characters were the subjects of large sculptural works (Figures 9-13 and 9-14). Smaller pieces of artwork carried specific information on such matters as proper behavior. For example, the Warka vase (refer to Figure 8-14 on page 259) explicitly communicates the appropriate categories of activities in a hierarchical society and the necessity of bringing offerings to the temple. The Ur Standard, found in one of the royal tombs, is a veritable en-

cyclopedia of information about the proper activities of residents of Sumerian cities (Figure 9-15, page 301). The standard portrays the activities of the king and his court during peace and war. It is in the form of a box of which one side relates domestic activities, food production, transport, and feasting. The reverse side contains chariots, foot soldiers, and fallen enemies. In a community where the vast majority of the population could not read, the Ur Standard would have been an effective means of communicating socially approved modes of behavior. Because the inhabitants of a Sumerian city were a large and diverse body of people who had not developed widely recognized

Figure 9-14
Profile of one of the statues of the Early Dynastic
hoard from Tell Asmar. (Photograph from The
Oriental Institute. The University of Chicago.)

forms of stylistic communication, the artwork was
less ambiguous than that of later periods. The Ur
Standard and the Warka vase, as well as many
other pieces of artwork, were means of communicating and reinforcing the social order prescribed
by the rulers (Figure 9-16). Perhaps only a small
segment of the population had frequent contact
with these works of art, but that segment administered the organization of the entire community.
Activities that served the elite and the structural
importance of the elite were recurrent themes of
early art.

Other examples of representational art are not
so readily understandable. The scenes portrayed in
glyptic art include geometrics and scenes of nature
that are not immediately recognizable. In many

such works, the primary purpose was to identify
the owner, and so the exact content was not important. In others, the representation may have
been of a mythical theme, a religious belief, or a
totem identification. One fine example of representational art that is not immediately interpretable
is the inlaid design on one of the harps from the
Royal Cemetery at Ur (Figure 9-12), in which animals are shown playing musical instruments and
feasting. Whether these are the episodes of a myth
or symbolic representations of human activities is
difficult to determine, but the sophistication of the
artist is unquestionable.

Other forms of craftsmanship and art, such as the
production of metal vessels and finely fashioned
implements, did not have direct representational
meanings, but were symbols of wealth. Some of
the more valuable vessels of gold were inscribed
with the names of the kings they belonged to and
were among their most prized possessions. This is
attested to in the burial of Mes-kalam-shar at Ur,
who was buried holding a gold bowl inscribed with
his name. Many of the vessels were hammered
from a single piece of metal, which was gently
fluted and required skilled workmanship. Possibly
the single most spectacular piece of metalwork
from the Royal Cemetery at Ur is a gold dagger
with a lapis lazuli hilt and a fantastically intricate
gold sheath (Figure 9-17, page 302). One side of the
sheath is decorated with rich filigree and exquis-
itely granulated gold work. The lapis lazuli hilt is
decorated with gold studs. Thus, the repertoire of
metalsmiths already included hot-hammering, lost-
wax casting, filigree, and granulated work. The
quality of this piece was not surpassed for many
generations.

Organizational Changes in
Early Dynastic Mesopotamia

Stratification

There is definitive evidence that the first sharply
defined social stratification within society occurred
during the Early Dynastic period. Stratification existed in earlier times within the context of the early
temple-cities, but it became the primary structuring

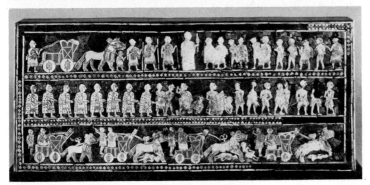

Figure 9-15
Scenes from an inlaid box found in the Royal Cemetery at Ur and known as the Ur Standard: (top) three registers depicting activities of a domestic and perhaps ceremonial nature; (bottom) three registers depicting the conduct of war. (Photographs © The Trustees of the British Museum.)

Figure 9-16
A stone plaque from Khafaje with a piece (lower left) from Ur showing both a feast in the upper register and a solid wheeled war chariot in the lower register. (Photograph from The Oriental Institute. The University of Chicago.)

of society during the Early Dynastic period. The most convincing evidence of increasing stratification is from the Early Dynastic cemeteries, especially from the Royal Cemetery at Ur: the royal graves, of which there are only a few, contain enormous quantities of goods; numerous graves contain modest amounts of material; and a great many graves at Ur contain little material wealth. Classifying the excavated graves according to the quantity of goods they contain is an oversimplification because it neglects quality, but the grave goods do reveal distinct stratification within the society.

The first adequate excavations of domestic architecture for indicating whether wealth differentials documented in the burials were paralleled by the sizes of houses were made in the Early Dynastic levels at Khafaje and Tell Asmar. The average house size was approximately 200 square meters, with many structures being only 50 square meters (Figure 9-18, page 302). Thus, the variation in house size probably related to whether the occupants were craftsmen, merchants, or peasants. The larger houses were arranged around central courtyards

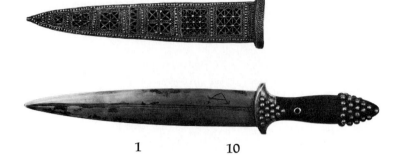

Figure 9-17
Gold daggar and sheath from the
Royal Cemetery at Ur. (Photo-
graph © The Trustees of the
British Museum.)

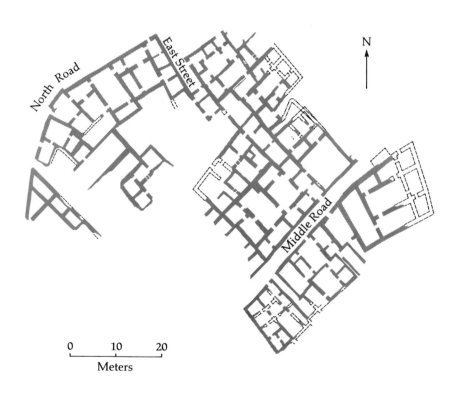

Figure 9-18
Plans of domestic architecture from the Early Dynastic levels at Tell Asmar.
(After Delougaz, Hill, and Lloyd, 1967.)

and had direct access to the major thoroughfares of the city. The smaller houses were without courtyards and were located on the narrow twisting alleyways that led off of the major streets (Frankfort 1950).

Several other categories of evidence imply the existence of a society stratified according to class at least as early as the Early Dynastic. Although slavery probably existed in Sumerian cities, the maintenance of an entire community never depended on slaves. Their numbers seem to have been small, consisting largely of prisoners of war. The written symbol for a female slave was basically "woman of the mountain," indicating that most slaves were procured through raids in the hill country. Historic records at the end of the third millennium describe situations in which free citizens became slaves either because of indebtedness or because they had been sold by their families. It seems that it was possible for such slaves to buy back their freedom. Most slaves seem to have been female. They were employed mainly in the workshops run by the temple for the spinning and weaving of textiles. Hence, slavery during the Early Dynastic was probably an additional incentive for offensive military campaigns because it was a source of supplementary labor for the growing mass-production industries of the Sumerian cities. However, it does not seem to have affected political developments of the period.

Political Evolution

Among the most significant developments of the Early Dynastic period in Mesopotamia was the emergence of a secular-based political authority. Archeologists have found information on this new elite by excavating palaces at Kish, Mari, and Eridu, as well as the royal cemeteries of Ur and Kish. However, their detailed interpretations and hypotheses have as their bases the decipherment of written documents of the period and the extrapolation of somewhat later ones. Many Early Dynastic writings chronicled past events. Thus, cultural development can be traced not only in terms of changing pottery styles, architecture, and artwork, but also in terms of the changing dynasties indicated in the lists of ancient kings (Table 9-1, page 304). There is sufficient information to indicate some of the kings of certain cities but not enough for a complete record. Consequently, the division of the Early Dynastic period into three phases is primarily according to its architecture and glyptics and only secondarily according to its rulers. However, with the end of the Early Dynastic period and the beginning of the succeeding Akkadian period, classification of all material is in terms of the dynastic rulers.

The nature of early city-state rule has been inferred from examining the titles of the rulers and the mythical accounts of their origin (Jacobsen 1943; 1945; 1957). Everyday public affairs are thought to have been handled by a council of elders in the sovereign communities constituting a city and its surrounding land. Crucial issues were decided by a general assembly of all the citizens. In times of crisis—for example, when there was threat of war—this assembly could confer supreme authority on one of its members, proclaiming him king. Such kingship presumably was held only for a limited period; the powers granted him were resumed by the assembly when the emergency had passed.

The titles used by city rulers of the Early Dynastic period and for some time later reveal that the origin of kingship was greatly diversified. There were cities in which the ruler was called *lugal*, or king, a title that suggests that the office was originally that of a warlord elected by the general assembly. Other cities had rulers known as *sangu*, or accountant. This was a term for the chief administrator of a temple, and it suggests that the office of ruler in that city-state originated as an extension of the powers of the chief administrator of the main temple. Another link to the temple elite is implied by the very common title *ensi*; the definition of *ensi* is unclear, but the word was related to an earlier term, *en*, which indicated the human spouse of the city goddess. Hence, the ensi seems to have originally been a member of the temple elite, perhaps the protagonist in festival rituals, who assumed broader authority, perhaps on the

Table 9-1

Partial list of kings of major Sumerian cities during the Early Dynastic period.

B.C.	Ur	Umma	Lagash	Uruk	Kish
2700				Gilgamesh	Mebaragesi
75					Aka
50					
25					
2600					
75			Enhengal (Mesalim)		
50					
25					
2500		*Ush**	Ur-Nanshe c. 2520†		
75	Mesanepada	*Enakale*	Akurgal c. 2490		
50	Meskiangnuna		Eanatum c. 2470		
25	Balulu	*Urlumma*	Entemena c. 2430	*Lugalkin-*	
2400			Enanatum II c. 2400	*geneshdudu*	
75			Lugalanda c. 2370		
50		*Lugalzagesi*	Urukagina c. 2355	*Lugalzagesi*	
25					Ur-zababa

Source: After Mallowan, 1968.

*Names in italics are those of rulers known from contemporary inscriptions.

†Names with dates preceded by "c." are only roughly dated, by synchronism with known rulers or by conjecture.

basis of his religious powers. A somewhat later example comes from the trading center of Assur in northern Mesopotamia where the ruler was occasionally called *ugula,* or foreman. The importance of manufacturing and trade in this city may have been responsible for the ascendancy of persons from the industrial sector of the community.

Whether the origin of secular authority was in the elected officials of an assembly of citizens, the economic administrator of a temple, the major actor in religious festivals, or the merchants of the city cannot be determined with certainty. It is likely that rulers emerged in different cities under varying circumstances, and that changes in early dynasties may have been due to changes in the power base. Although the earliest city rulers merely represented extensions of the power of one or another of the competing power bases in Sumerian society, each ruler soon established his own power base.

By the end of the Early Dynastic period, city-state rulers and the subsequent national-state rulers controlled the populace through a monopoly on the use of force, and soon thereafter the other sectors of the city were subservient to him. Religion was often used to sanctify the king, the king being the protagonist in the most important festivals.

A plausible hypothesis for the origin of secular city rulers has been made by Thorkild Jacobsen (1943; 1957). Jacobsen used written records, myths, and later historical documents to infer the events of the Early Dynastic period. He views the emergence of kingship within the context of an already existing form of local government, *primitive democracy.* Jacobsen refers to democracy in its classical sense, that is:

a form of government in which internal sovereignty resides in a large proportion of the governed, namely in all free, adult, male citizens without distinction of fortune or class. . . . Major decisions such as to undertake war are made with their consent, that these citizens constitute the supreme judicial authority in the state, and that rulers and magistrates obtain the positions with, and ultimately derive their power from, that same consent. (1943:159)

Early references to town assemblies and their appointed rulers come from a Sumerian epic poem about Gilgamesh. In this earliest record of intercity conflict in Mesopotamia, the ruler refrained from taking action until he obtained the consent of the town assembly. The story relates that King Aka of the city of Kish sent a messenger to Uruk demanding its surrender. Gilgamesh, ensi of Uruk, was determined to resist the seige, but he had to obtain approval for his plan. He first went to the council of elders and presented the reasons for his plan to take up arms against the soldiers of Kish. The council of elders considered the plan and approved it, but before it could be carried out the assembly of the entire male population had to be consulted. Gilgamesh did this and won their approval. Gilgamesh and his armed contingent were successful, the army of the King of Kish was defeated, and the siege was lifted. Gilgamesh's authority grew with time and became more independent of the councils.

It is difficult to determine whether this is a recounting of actual events, or an *a posteriori* story to help support an already existing kingship. Gilgamesh's reign was supposedly in the middle of the Early Dynastic period; however he is not mentioned on any monuments discovered from that time. Nevertheless, his feats were appropriate for the period, especially his construction of the city wall of Warka, which in fact is dated at this period.

The broad pattern that emerges from this and other hypotheses is that the office and power base of early kings originated from the need for efficient, full-time rulers to settle the problems of increasingly complex societies. The most plausible source of problems that demanded a strong leader was the increasing warfare. A war leader would have been called upon with greater frequency as intercity conflict became more common. The point would

soon have been reached when the position of war leader became a full-time job at the head of a standing army. After the position had been created and the power base of a standing army had been formed, it was not difficult for a war leader to usurp complete authority. When this had been accomplished, other segments of the society would soon have acknowledged his suzerainty.

Increasing warfare was not the only factor that demanded leadership. The growing system of irrigation and water control benefited from centralized government. Long-distance trade and participating industries were facilitated by integrated management and military protection. Hence, the origin of the king may not have been in all cases a war leader but may in certain cities have been a peace leader.

By 2500 B.C., the Mesopotamian Plain was composed of a scattered mosaic of small, relatively self-sufficient, politically autonomous city-states. In each state there was a principal ruler who united in his position the chief political powers: legislative, judiciary, and executive (Jacobsen 1943:160). Only he could promulgate and carry into effect new laws; he alone was personally responsible by contract with the city-god for upholding justice; as the supreme commander of all armed forces, he led the state in battle; and as administrator of the main temple complex, he controlled the most powerful single economic unit within the city-state.

Although Early Dynastic city-states were politically autonomous, intercity conflicts led to the temporary ascendency of certain city-states over others. For example, Lugalzagesi, ruler of the city of Umma, conquered several other cities, assuming the kingship of Uruk and the title of king of the land. He asserted that he ruled a confederation of fifty city-states, and he embarked on campaigns of foreign conquest. Whatever the truth of these claims, Lugalzagesi was the first of a series of leaders who created soldier-kingdoms loosely held together by military might.

Early Kings of Mesopotamia

The most important document for reconstructing the sequence of early rulers of Mesopotamian city-states is a king list that was formalized in about

1800 B.C. (Gadd 1964). The information supplied is uniform, but scanty in terms of what social historians would like to know. Lists of rulers and years of reign were compiled for the half-dozen greatest cities of early Mesopotamia. Occasionally a short note was added relating some incident or detail for which a king was celebrated, but this was done all too infrequently. Hence, what philologists are given to work with is a somewaht inflated chronological listing of competing and successive dynasties that must be intercorrelated with other inscriptions, archeological deposits, and accounts from later periods.

The earliest dynasties that began after the Sumerian flood were based in the three most important cities of the time—Kish, Warka, and Ur. Kish seems to have been the earliest power center, with the title "King of Kish" conveying special meaning for rulers of other cities. By assuming this title, a ruler of another city asserted that in fact he was ruling the entire land as a primary overlord with local city rulers under him. The early rulers of Kish were accorded the building of monuments in the holy city of Nippur, and one of them, Aka, came in conflict with the then ruler of Warka, Gilgamesh. In the struggle for supremacy among these three city-states, power was passed from Kish to Warka under Gilgamesh and his immediate successors. The rulers of Warka were also credited with temple construction in Nippur. By that time, the rulers of Ur also had become more powerful and were competing for supremacy. Supposedly, it was during this First Dynasty of Ur that the Royal Cemetery was used. However, the names of the kings of Ur given on the king list do not coincide with those of the royal personages in the tombs. This somewhat enigmatic situation could cast doubt on the precision of the king list or on the royal nature of the burials, but more likely it is evidence that early Mesopotamian kings had more than one name, like their counterparts in Egypt.

By 2500 B.C., Lagash emerged as one of the major competing city-states. Eanatum was one of the best-known early rulers of Lagash. Eanatum was ensi of Lagash, but assumed the title of king of Kish during his campaigns of conquest. According to written evidence, he fought Ur, Warka, Kish, Mari, and even with neighboring Elam. Many of these conflicts were rooted in controversies over water rights and boundaries. Supposedly Eanatum was successful in his encounters and became overlord to many of the Sumerian city-states (see Table 9-1). In this position, he was called upon to mediate disputes between neighboring cities who had common borders. On the basis of brief historical accounts, Eanatum seems to have split his time between military ventures, both offensive and defensive, and periods of construction, largely of canals and water works. These activities may be symbolic of the two realms of authority that concerned early kings and that brought them to power: war and water.

The last king of Lagash during the Early Dynastic period had a short but important reign. His name was Urukagina and he was better known for his social and ethical deeds than his military exploits. Early in his reign, Urukagina promulgated legal reforms that are preserved in inscriptions on buildings of his time. The reforms claimed to be attempts to "return to the good old days," when the temple was supreme and the rights of the people were protected. The motivation for these reforms may have been to strengthen Urukagina's position as king. Whatever the cause, these reforms mark a milestone in political history. These codes are the earliest-known formalized effort at promulgating a legal system that explicitly established rights, authority, and punishments. Urukagina claimed that he had a covenant with the city-god of Lagash, Ningirsu, so that "he would not deliver up the weak and the widowed to the powerful man." The intent was to lighten the burdens imposed on the general population by governors and priests. Working-class people were freed from certain taxes and from supervision by an overexpanded officialdom. Protection against usurpation of property and unfair business transactions also benefited the ordinary population. Social injustices involving marriage, divorce, and personal property were corrected. To placate the priests, who had been attacked in this code, Urukagina reestablished the authority of the temple over certain aspects of society.

The promulgation of Urukagina's code is an interesting commentary on the course of Early Dynastic developments. By this time, c. 2350 B.C., government bureaucracy had already grown out of proportion, the wealthy were cheating poorer people, the tax system had to be revised, and social customs had to be reviewed. The subject matter and intent of this early code was duplicated by many later legal documents and created an attitude that many subseqeunt rulers were to adopt toward the malpractices in society. Close examination shows that this reform acted to protect the working class and abolished many of their debts, but in such a way as to strengthen the central authority of the king and the temple that he directly controlled. The group of people who were the recipients of the most condemnation and restrictions were the independent wealthy families, who most likely were the king's major competition. It is important to note that within a short time after the emergence of the institution of kingship a legal code was promulgated. The legal code and the military power to enforce it were among the primary resources at the disposal of Mesopotamian kings.

The last great ruler during the Early Dynastic period in Mesopotamia was Lugalzagesi, from the city of Umma. During his twenty-year reign, Lugalzagesi spent much of his time on military campaigns. He soon subdued Urukagina, who ruled the city of Lagash. He then conquered Warka and assumed the titles King of Uruk (Warka) and King of the Land of Sumer. With these achievements, Lugalzagesi was supreme ruler of all of Sumer, and a new political era was beginning to emerge. He claimed to be the head of a confederation of city-states. The bounds of his political unit were no longer those of the individual city-state, but those of the entire region. It is unlikely that Lugalzagesi had the time or inclination to develop an administrative network that would have united his newly conquered territories into a national

state. Rather, his success was transitory. A prophetic description has been uncovered at Lagash, the site of Lugalzagesi's early triumph. It reads that Lugalzagesi by destroying Lagash had committed a sin against its patron god, Ningirsu. The hand that was laid upon Ningirsu should be cut off. Lugalzagesi's own patron goddess should make him carry his sin upon his neck. The prayer was soon answered. A new military king from the north, Sargon of Agade, defeated Lugalzagesi and brought him before the temple of Enlil in Nippur, his neck in a yoke.

The defeat of Lugalzagesi marked a major point of change in Mesopotamian history. Sargon of Agade and his successors molded the city-states of Mesopotamia into a national state and established the supremacy of the Semites over the Sumerians.

Chronology of Early Nation States in Mesopotamia

Our information about the second half of the third millennium is derived almost exclusively from the written records of southern Mesopotamia (Table 9-2, page 308). The excavation of sites in this area and other regions is expanding and soon archeological sources will supply much-needed information about material goods and developments in peripheral areas. Certain characteristics have been identified, such as cylinder seals, art styles, and pottery. Building sequences of distinctive architecture in regions such as the Diyala are known and recently the detailed plan of the town of Tell Taya in central Mesopotamia was reconstructed on the basis of visible surface remains and limited excavation (Reade 1973). The most important discovery of this decade concerning the second half of the third millennium has been the texts recovered in excavations of Tell Mardikh in northern Syria (Matthiae 1977). Nevertheless, the primary source of chronological information is the king lists. Even so, there are major uncertainties in the dating. Some kings are known from dated monuments, but others are known only

Table 9-2

Partial king list for major centers in southern Mesopotamia during the second half of the third millennium.

Agade	Gutium	Uruk	Lagash	Elam
*Sargon:** 2340–2284				*Luḫḫishan:* c. 2300
Rimush: 2284–2275			*Ki-KU-id:* c. 2280	
Manishtushu: 2275–2260			*Engilsa:* c. 2270	
Naram-Sin: 2260–2223			*Ur-a:* c. 2250	*Hita:* c. 2220
Shar-kali-sharri: 2223–2198			*Lugalushumgal:* c. 2215	*Kutik-Inshushinak:* c. 2200
	(Erridupizir)	(Urnigin)	(Puzur-Mama)	
	(Imta')	(Urgigir)	(Ur-Utu)	
	(Inkishush)	(Kudda)		
	Sarlagab: c. 2210	(Puzurili)		
	(Shulme')	(Lugalmelam?)	(Ur-Mama)	
Igigi Nanum 2198–2195 Imi				
Elulu	*Elulumesh*	(Ur-Utu)	(Lu-Baba)	
Dudu: 2195–2174	(Inimabakesh)		(Lu-Gula)	
			(Kaku)	
Shu-DURUL: 2174–2159	(Igeshaush)		*Ur-Baba:* c. 2164–2144	
	(Iarlagab)			
	(Ibate)			
	(Iarlangab)			
	(Kurum)		*Gudea:*	
	(Ḫabilkin?)		c. 2164–2144	
	(La'erabum)			**Ur**
	(Irarum)		*Ur-Ningirsu:*	*Ur-Nammu*
	(Ibranum)		c. 2124–2119	c. 2111–2094
	(Ḫablum)		*Pirigme:*	*Shulgi*
			c. 2119–2117	c. 2093–2046
	(Puzur-Sin)		*Ur-GAR:*	*Amar-su'ena*
	(Iarlaganda)	*Utuḫengal:*	c. 2117–2113	c. 2045–2037
		2116–2110		*Shu-Sin* c. 2036–2028
	(Si'um)			*Ibbi-Sin*
	Tiriqan: 2116		*Nammaḫani:* c. 2113–2109	c. 2027–2003

Sources: After Gadd, 1964, and Edzard, 1967.

*Names in italics are those of rulers known from contemporary inscriptions; names in parentheses, those of rulers who cannot be dated. Names with dates preceded by "c." are only roughly dated, by synchronism with known rulers or by conjecture.

from later sources or undateable contexts. Hence, certain entries in the king lists are reliable in cross dating and relative order, but others are less certain and correlation with absolute dates is weak for those reigning before the middle of the third millennium.

The history of Mesopotamia in the second half of the third millennium can be divided into three periods: Akkadian, Gutian, and Ur III (Neo-Sumerian). These divisions correspond to the dominant political forces in southern Mesopotamia, although competing centers existed and often information from provincial sites is clearer than that from the political centers.

The Akkadian empire was centered at the still unlocated city of Agade and ruled by a single dynasty of five kings from about 2340 B.C. to 2200 B.C. This was followed by a short period in which groups from the Zagros Mountains, known as Gutians, disrupted the empire of the Akkadians and took over political control of much of the lowlands. These groups were quickly assimilated and soon overthrown by groups that claimed to be Sumerian. Ur-Nammu was the founder of the second major Mesopotamian state, that of the Ur III dynasty. This dynasty lasted for approximately 100 years and centered in several of the southern Mesopotamian cities. The Ur III dynasty is frequently considered to have been Neo-Sumerian because there was a revival in the language, customs, and art forms that had been developed by the Sumerians during the Early Dynastic period.

The Akkadian State

Although the Akkadian empire seems to have been largely a conglomeration of different groups under a military power, important achievements in the political evolution of state administration are evident. A new language was used for official business and it eventually became the language of international affairs in the ancient Near East. A system of governors with military garrisons in the various provinces was created. Trade was conducted by means of a more integrated system than had existed before. There is evidence that this trade

extended as far as the Indus Valley, both overland (Lamberg-Karlovsky 1972) and by sea (Bibby 1969). The Akkadian period is not well known from archeological remains, partly because of its short duration and because its capital city, Agade, has not been identified. However, there is evidence from written records, cylinder seals, and excavations in provincial towns that gives a general picture of the lifeways and history of this era.

More than any dynasty that preceded it, the rise of the Akkadian state is attributed to a single man, Sargon. Because he came from humble beginnings, little is known of his early life. The name Sargon means "true king," and it represented the ideal military monarch to later people. In recounting Sargon's rise to power, the scribes had to create much of his biography. This "origin myth" may reveal some of the circumstances of Sargon's early life, but it probably incorporated themes common to the folklore of the period.

Sargon's father was one of the nonsedentary people of Sumer, living in the regions between the cities (Bottero 1967). His mother was a temple votary in one of the city sanctuaries. She cast the infant Sargon adrift on the river in a basket of rushes and a peasant found him and adopted him. The parallel between this story and accounts of the obscure early lives of other famous persons is striking. What seems to have happened is that Sargon was raised among the semisedentary peoples of southern Mesopotamia and then moved to Kish in the north where he was a cup-bearer of one of the last kings of Kish, Ur-Zababa. Sargon assembled a band of followers and led a revolt against Ur-Zababa after the king had lost a war. Sargon was successful and able to carve out a small domain in the north of Sumer, establishing a capital named Agade. From this base he soon extended his control over all of Mesopotamia.

Written documents report that Sargon was favored by good luck and attribute this to the fondness that the goddess Ishtar had for him. There, of course, were more fundamental events taking place. Probably throughout Sumerian history the population of Mesopotamia was a mixture of ethnic, and perhaps religious, groups. The language

Figure 9-19
Modern impression made with a greenstone Akkadian cylinder seal with
the inscription "Lugallam the scribe." (Photograph from The Oriental
Institute. The University of Chicago.)

Figure 9-20
Modern impression made with an Akkadian cylinder
seal. The inscription states the name and profession of
the owner. The various symbols may represent
deities. (Photograph from The Oriental Institute. The
University of Chicago.)

and names of towns suggest that there may have
been an indigenous population in Mesopotamia
before the entry of the Sumerian speakers (Jones
1969). Names of individual persons and rulers imply that people other than the Sumerians were
already in positions of power during the Early Dynastic. This tendency was especially true in the
northern sector of Lowland Mesopotamia in a region later known as Babylonia (a term that subsequently was used to refer to the entire south). On
the basis of linguistic similarities, many of these
people have been identified as Semites, the descendants of whom inhabit the Near East today. Sar-

gon's formation of the Akkadian state is considered
to be the first major accomplishment of the Semitic
peoples and was emulated throughout Mesopotamian history. The Akkadian language replaced
Sumerian as the official language and eventually
became the medium of international communication. In artwork, bearded faces and long hair replaced the shaven Sumerian heads on reliefs and
in sculpture (see Figures 9-19, 9-20, and 9-21).

For hundreds of years, large numbers of upland,
seminomadic peoples entered the alluvium, as they
had since its earliest occupation. Among these
were Semitic groups, some of whom maintained a
seminomadic lifestyle and others of whom adopted
urban lifeways in whole or part. After a period, this
element of society was powerful enough to have
members in the ruling class and eventually to take
complete authority. It is logical that this would
have occurred in the north first, where the greatest
proportion of Semites lived. The term Semite is
used rather loosely in this context and may have
included other linguistic groups who lived at the
edges of urban zones with the Semites.

Hence, Sargon's conquests were not all as an
invader; in some cases he may have been liberating
a city from Sumerian overlords. His first conquest
was the city of Kish, which was populated predom-
inently by Semites and therefore may have accepted him without substantial resistence. With
control of Kish, Sargon was master of all of north-

Figure 9-21
Modern impression made with an Akkadian cylinder seal made of shell and found at Tell Asmar. The scene is interpreted to be of the sun god in a boat, at the prow of which a long-haired, crowned figure holds a punting pole; at the stern is a snake's head. A human-headed lion in the boat is tied to the prow; above it are a plow, a vase, and two unrecognizable objects. Outside the boat the goddess of fertility, characterized by grain growing from her shoulders and her side, holds a flowering branch. (Photograph from The Oriental Institute. The University of Chicago.)

ern Babylonia and addressed his attentions to Sumer to the south. Sumer was controlled by a league of "fifty governors" headed by Lugalzagesi of Uruk. From the written evidence it seems that it took Sargon three campaigns and thirty-four battles to completely defeat Lugalzagesi.

After his successful conquest of Sumer, Sargon added to his titles those of "King of Agade," "King of Kish," "King of the Land." At this point he militarily controlled all of the Sumerian heartland, but urbanized society extended far beyond the southern Mesopotamian alluvium. Two great military campaigns to the northwest were conducted: the first was midway up the Euphrates River to the cities of Mari and Hit (a major source of bitumen), and the second was even more ambitious, bringing him all the way to the Mediterranean and the Taurus Mountains of Anatolia. With these conquests,

Sargon's empire stretched from the lower sea (Persian Gulf) to the upper sea (Mediterranean), a span of 1500 kilometers. Some records of a later date, and not totally reliable, report conquests in Anatolia, Cyprus, and Crete. Sargon also conducted campaigns against Elam to the southeast and against settlements in northern Mesopotamia.

The extent of Sargon's empire and the enormity of his military successes were without precedent. The scribes of his period and those of later times were to extol the Akkadian state and hold it up as a model for later generations. However, Sargon's empire was not an efficient administrative organization. The state was assembled by military power and was held together by local garrisons and long-distance campaigns to suppress revolts. Hence, the Akkadian state was able to exist by force of arms for about 150 years, but it eventually succumbed

Figure 9-22
Victory stele of Naram-Sin erected during one of his
campaigns into the Zagros Mountains. (Photograph
from the National Museums of France.)

to the forces of local independence and external
pressures.

Of the four subsequent rulers of the Akkadian
dynasty only Sargon's grandson, Naram-Sin, stands
out as a great militarist (Figure 9-22). Written
sources indicate that Naram-Sin's exploits were
largely military campaigns to put down revolts in
various parts of the kingdom, retracing Sargon's
original conquests. Naram-Sin's conquests ex-

tended beyond the old boundaries of the Akkadian
state. He therefore adopted a title additional to
those of his grandfather, "King of the Four Quarters." Despite these military conquests, there is
evidence that the Akkadian state was weakening
under Naram-Sin, heralding its collapse during the
reign of his successor. Naram-Sin was forced to
spend an enormous amount of time in maintaining
equilibrium by suppressing revolts and even found
it advantageous to make treaties. The most omi-
nous instability was in the northeast where groups
of people known as the Gutians who lived in the
Zagros were a serious threat.

Although many factors may have been motivation for assembling the first nation-state in the
Near East, probably the overriding consideration
was economic. The assembly of wealth acquired
both directly through looting and tribute and indirectly through a state monopoly on trade was a
crucial factor. Sargon and his descendants never
seemed to attempt to create a true political empire;
perhaps it was not necessary for their economic
goals. Rather, Sargon installed local rulers or agents
to oversee his interests. The appointed officials
were supported by a small army that lived in a
garrison within a conquered city (e.g., the Akkadian fortress at Tell Brak in northern Syria). In
addition to the booty collected through the initial
conquest, periodic tribute was collected. Related
to such tribute and of long-range significance was
the control that the Akkadians gained over the
sources of raw materials that they needed. Wood
was imported from Lebanon, the Taurus mountains, and the Zagros mountains. Metal (copper)
was secured in Anatolia or Iran. Bitumen was obtained from the middle Euphrates and stone from
surrounding upland areas.

The king and his court became the center of
economic activity under the Akkadians. A certain
amount of the administrative authority of the temple was preempted by Sargon and his successors.
Naram-Sin went so far as to take the title of "God
of Agade." Adoption of divine qualities by Akkadian rulers is an indication of their increasing control of the religious hierarchy and the assumption
by the palace of many temple-related activities,

such as legal jurisdiction, administrative authority, and trade. Although the religious elite periodically exerted independent authority, in subsequent Mesopotamian history the supremacy of secular authority under the king was firmly established. It is during the Akkadian period that private ownership of land is documented. Most property remained under the control of the palace or temple, but some tracts were sold or given in return for services rendered to the king.

To carry out the administration of tribute, trade, and militarism in the newly assembled empire, Sargon supported an enormous administrative personnel as part of the palace community. He boasted of feeding 5,400 men at his table every day. The scale of society and administration, even in the loose Akkadian fashion, required a large and growing bureaucracy. Functionaries of various kinds increased in number, which affected the course of development of Mesopotamian civilization.

Other important cities and states existed in the Near East in contact with Akkad but not directly under its control. One of these, Tell Mardikh, identified as ancient Ebla, for a long period was a major center on the trade route from the Euphrates to the Mediterranean (refer to Figure 8-1 on page 246). Although there remain some problems with dating, early indications from the excavated remains and preliminary examination of more than 16,000 tablets recovered suggest that Ebla was the center of a Semitic state that flourished at roughly the same time as Akkad (Matthiae 1977). Excavators have uncovered parts of a massive palace of this period that is believed to have been destroyed by Naram-Sin. This palace contained an enormous library of commercial, administrative, financial, economic, lexical, historical, and literary texts. The texts are written in a northwestern Semitic language (Eblaite), which has affinities to Ugaritic and Phoenician, but which was transcribed in Sumerian cuneiform. Of particular interest in the archives are copies of trading agreements and international treaties with neighboring cities in Syria, northern Mesopotamia, and Anatolia. Further study is necessary, but there is the suggestion in this material that many of the administrative and perhaps liter-

ary and artistic forms attributed to southern Mesopotamia may have originated at Ebla or elsewhere in Syria. These discoveries enhance our understanding of the internationalism of the third millennium and the diverse centers that participated in the development of early state society.

Without efficient mechanisms of integration to hold the diverse region together, the Akkadian empire began to disintegrate as soon as the military might of its rulers slackened. After Naram-Sin's reign, this process accelerated, with separate states being established or at least partial independence being gained by several cities. Under Shar-kali-sharri, the last effective ruler of the Akkadian dynasty, Uruk established itself as a power in the south and held sway over a considerable part of Sumer. The mountain group from Zagros, the Gutians, mentioned as a menace during Naram-Sin's reign, became the major disequilibrating factor in the empire. Although the exact sequence of events is not clear, there was a gradual dismemberment of the empire that culminated in the sack of Agade at about 2159 B.C. (Bottéro 1967).

What followed was a period in which separate city-states regained autonomy. Rulers with Gutian names controlled several city-states in the north, but their effect is difficult to discern. There is little that can be identified as Gutian-influenced art or architecture. Most certainly, the Gutians were profoundly changed by their subjects rather than the reverse. As it was for other seminomadic invaders of Mesopotamia, the momentum of civilization was too great to overcome or too desirable to interfere with. Assimilation into the ongoing system with minor modifications was the result. Centralized authority was already breaking down, owing largely to the Gutian disturbances. The Gutians did not introduce new mechanisms for integrating the pieces of the old Akkadian state.

While various Gutian rulers maintained supremacy over the north, local Sumerian rulers established themselves as ensis in southern cities. In addition to Uruk, the city of Lagash reasserted its independence and became very powerful. Under Ur-Baba's leadership, and thereafter, (c. 2164–2144 B.C.) the rulers of Lagash extended their power to

Figure 9-23
Stone sculpture of Gudea of Lagash. (Photograph ©
The Trustees of the British Museum.)

rule a large part of Sumer (Bottéro 1967). This was
not the reemergence of a powerful military state,
but the growth of an economic empire. The goals
of the rulers of Lagash paralleled those of the
Akkadian dynasty, but the means for achieving
them were different. The rulers of Lagash attempted
to monopolize trade in certain commodities, but
this time without a massive military commitment.
Commercial techniques were perfected and the
agents of the ensi traveled throughout the Near
East, securing supplies and raw materials. The
prosperity of these rulers is amply documented in
the number of buildings and works of art that were
made during this period (Figures 9-23 and 9-24).

The architectural and artistic creations of the
rulers of Lagash manifest Akkadian influence, but
they can be better understood as a revival of Sumerian ideas and authority. Long inscriptions in
Sumerian, sculpture resembling earlier Sumerian
works, and literary pieces like those of earlier
times document the revival. From what is preserved in the form of artwork and written materials, the Second Dynasty of Lagash seems to have
been a period of great prosperity in which the arts
flourished.

Third Dynasty of Ur

The expulsion of the Gutians from the cities of
the north is claimed by a ruler of Uruk named
Utuhengal. As part of his consolidation of power,
Utuhengal appointed a military governor for Ur,
Ur-Nammu, who soon proved to be an effective
military leader and ruler, overthrowing his former
master. Ur-Nammu founded a dynasty at Ur
(c. 2111–2094 B.C.) that was soon to control all
of Mesopotamia. Economics were a major motivation in the formation of this empire and attempts at improving the administration of the
Akkadian state were made. Ur-Nammu assumed
the title of King of Sumer and Akkad, expressing
the dual nature of southern Mesopotamia. Although Akkadians had for some time lived in both
regions, the south was still populated by predominantly Sumerian-speaking people. The organization of the affairs of state seem to have been
conducted in a more exact manner, with clear
definitions of authority and conduct, as evidenced
by the Code of Ur-Nammu, another state in the
development of legal codes. The avowed purpose
was to establish justice in the land, the code being
composed of a long preamble and a series of "if-
then" statements. The promulgation of such a code
could be considered a testimony to Ur-Nammu's
concern for the rule of law or, more likely, an effort
to establish the dominance of his governmental
apparatus and the support of the populace.

A second document that illuminates the administrative practices of the Ur III era is a text found

Figure 9-24
Head of Gudea of Lagash.
(Courtesy Museum of Fine Arts,
Boston.)

on a boundary marker. This text precisely outlines the jurisdictions of respective city rulers.

A measure of the resourcefulness and energy of Ur-Nammu and his successors is the impressive building program they carried out (Figures 9-25 and 9-26, page 316). The canal system was extended both to increase the amount of irrigable farmland and to improve intercity water transport. Temples were repaired and new ones erected. The greatest intensity of building was at Ur, Uruk, and Nippur. The ziggurat of the moon god Nanna at Ur was given its final form by Ur-Nammu (Edzard 1967b). What had originally been conceived as a platform for a temple in Uruk and Jemdet Nasr times was transformed into a monument consisting of sumperimposed platforms surmounted by a

shrine. Its design was perfected by Ur III architects and it remains *the* diagnostic building of ancient Mesopotamian civilization.

The rulers of the Ur III dynasty were absolute monarchs of what for Mesopotamia was a highly centralized state. The king was the supreme authority over every branch of government. Several of the rulers, including Shulgi, son of Ur-Nammu, assumed the title of a deity, albeit a minor guardian deity. Shrines were erected to the king and he was in full control of theocratic affairs. It is not certain, but probably by this time the king was playing the role of Dumuzi (Tammuz), the divine lover of Inanna (Ishtar) during the annual sacred marriage ceremony (Figure 9-27, page 317).

Other persons may have held considerable

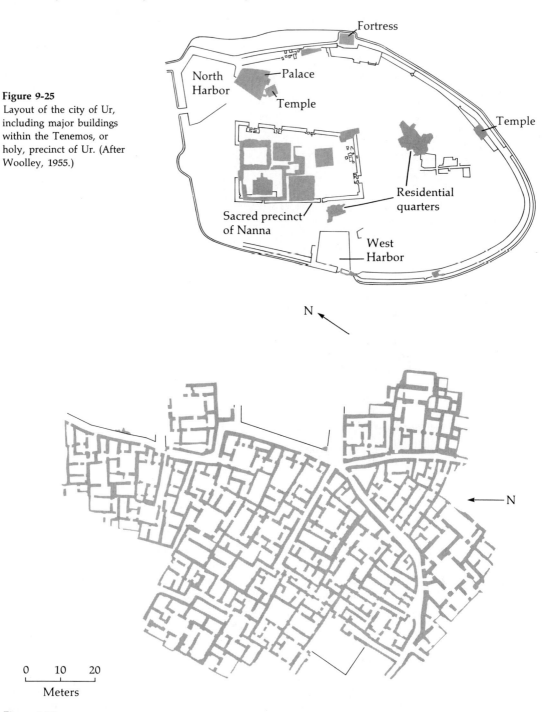

Figure 9-25
Layout of the city of Ur, including major buildings within the Tenemos, or holy, precinct of Ur. (After Woolley, 1955.)

Fortress

North Harbor

Palace

Temple

Temple

Residential quarters

Sacred precinct of Nanna

West Harbor

N

0   10   20

Meters

Figure 9-26
Plan of small, excavated section of the residential areas of the city of Ur during its third dynasty. (After Woolley, 1955.)

Figure 9-27
Modern impression made with an Akkadian cylinder seal found at Tell Asmar that depicts the annual fertility ceremony of the sacred marriage. (Photograph from The Oriental Institute. The University of Chicago.)

power but could be denied it by the king. The ensis of each city were given jurisdiction over their own affairs, but political decisions or major construction programs had to be initiated by the king. The king also employed many advisors in his court. Before making major decisions, the king usually consulted with the gods. Such consultation often required the services of priests skilled in reading omens in the livers of sacrificed sheep. These diviners were consulted about a wide variety of decisions, and a skillful practitioner might have had considerable power over the king. Another person who may have had considerable influence over the rulers of the Ur III dynasty was the grand vizier (sukkal-Mah) (Edzard 1967b).

Although numerous military campaigns are recorded against foreign adversaries and border provinces, it seems as if there was general stability within the empire. Unlike their Akkadian predecessors, the rulers of the Ur III dynasty were not preoccupied with holding their empire together. More efficient organization, stronger economic ties, and general material prosperity seem to have been strong unifying agents. This internal peace is especially well documented from the second half of the reign of Shulgi (total reign c. 2093–2046 B.C.). Historians refer to the Ur III period as a golden age of peace with a flourishing of arts, architecture, and literature. Nevertheless, the empire was periodically threatened by the neighboring groups, especially the Hurrians to the northwest and the mountain groups of the Zagros. Military campaigns were conducted against these insurgents to keep the trade routes to vital raw materials open. In addition to using arms, the Ur III rulers attempted to unite

their empire through royal marriages. It has been recorded that some of the daughters of Ur III kings married foreign princes. This mechanism for maintaining peace met with varied success, but became a common practice in later history.

The exact extent of the Ur III domain or that of any other early Mesopotamian state is difficult to delineate with certainty. It is likely that most, if not all, of the Mesopotamian Plain and some of the uplands to the north were controlled by the rulers of Ur.

For as long as the dynasty lasted, the royal residence was at Ur, but Uruk and Nippur were important cities, too. Nippur was the sacred city of the Sumerians and home of Enlil, chief deity of the Sumerian pantheon. The ensis of Nippur received preferential treatment and supreme religious prestige centered in the temple of Enlil.

The territories ruled by the Ur III dynasty were divided into approximately forty administrative districts. Each district was ruled by an ensi who conducted local business but was responsible to the king. Certain important or troublesome districts were run by military governors, or shagins. Ascendancy to the throne was hereditary, and the kings of Ur III took precautions to make certain that local ensis did not establish hereditary succession. Ensis were transferred to districts where they had not lived and even whole populations are known to have been relocated by the rulers of Ur III. These early attempts at reducing the potential power of local authorities and groups in order to maintain the strong centralized government were followed with greater frequency in subsequent dynasties.

The two major centers of administrative activity in each city were the palace and temples. These largely autonomous communities held land, carried on trade, and manufactured goods. The palace of the king was the primary administrative authority, but other productive communities existed, although they frequently took orders from the central authority. As far as can be inferred from available documents, land was not held privately, but only by temples and palaces, with tracts being temporarily rented or given to people for their own use. It was not until the following Old Babylonian period that the concept of private ownership of property became fully developed.

The administrative accounts kept by palace and temple functionaries were incredibly detailed. Daily records of goods brought in by individuals and balance sheet tallies of receipts and disbursements were kept by temple, palace, and city officials. Agricultural production was also recorded in detail. Although much of the exchange conducted at that time was for other materials, silver was used as a standard of exchange. One *mina* of silver equalled 60 *shekels*. Dry measures of volume were used, especially for allocating grain. One *gur* equalled 300 *sila*. The value of goods remained constant during most of Ur III period.

One mechanism for overcoming the great distances within the Ur III realm and to keep it closely tied together was a well-organized transportation system. Water transport by river and canal was highly developed and tightly controlled and recorded by administrators. Communications between officials in different cities were transmitted by messengers who traveled on foot or by donkey.

The legal system was another mechanism by which the disparate elements in Ur III society were held together. Legal codes such as the one promulgated by Ur-Nammu set standards of behavior and generally upheld the rights of the poorer classes. Courts were established to decide on disputed matters. Several judges would hear a single case and hand down a decision. Matters of family law, such as marriage, inheritance, and divorce were common. Ajudication of disputed land sales is not known, the absence of evidence being further indication that there was little or no private owner-

ship or exchange of land holdings. Even slaves had rights under the law and were able to sue in court. Native-born slaves who became indentured because of insolvency had most of the rights accorded to free people, but slaves who were foreign captives had few rights in the eyes of the law.

Several factors were responsible for the ultimate downfall of the Third Dynasty of Ur. Although the Sumerian and Akkadian elements of the population seem to have intermixed successfully, new semisedentary groups appeared within the empire. These groups were of different backgrounds but were often referred to as the Martu, coming from the north and northeast. Some settled near the cities and became part of the urban society, but many of them remained mobile, doing some kind of labor in some years and moving about in others. This type of group would present a periodic threat whenever subsistence was difficult or other unstabilizing events took place.

Internal problems also plagued the last Ur III ruler, Ibbi-Sin (c. 2027–2003 B.C.). Various city-states were declaring their autonomy and some local authorities seem to have gained significant independent power. This trend culminated in what seems, according to written evidence, to have been the betrayal of Ibbi-Sin by one of his military commanders, Ishbi-Erra (Edzard 1967b). Ishbi-Erra noted the incursions of the nomadic elements of the Martu peoples and demanded appointment as commandant of the city of Isin. He gained the upper hand by gathering surplus grain in the storehouses of Isin during a period of general famine in Sumer. The price of grain skyrocketed in Ur either because of crop failure or because incursions by the nomads disrupted agricultural work. The king in Ur no longer had the power to control his regional officials and was unable to challenge Ishbi-Erra, who eventually established what he considered to be a rival dynasty in the city of Isin and in fact soon gained control over much of southern Mesopotamia. Ibbi-Sin maintained his throne at Ur for a number of years until the region of Elam rose in revolt and invaded southern Mesopotamia. Ur was sacked. The greatest Sumerian empire, the model state for later ages, came to a tragic end. Hence, it was not the invasion of a nomadic group or the revolt of city-states alone that brought down the Ur III dynasty. Rather, it was the combination of the disequilibrating influences of semi-nomadic peoples, rebellious territories, and weak central control that eroded the administrative and military capabilities of the state.

General Processes in the Rise of Civilization

At the core of the rise of civilization in the Near East, from its earliest settlements to the first urbanized state societies, were two major transformations: the introduction of agriculture and the growth of cities. These developments have had an effect on all subsequent societies. The culmination of the process was the establishment of a food-producing, urban civilization that was periodically united under a state form of government. The Mesopotamian cities were the nuclei of the civilizational network, being centers of intellectual achievement, artistic creation, and organizational development.

In general terms, the Mesopotamian city can be described as a densely populated center serving many purposes. There is little evidence of overall planning in the early cities, yet certain areas, such as the holy precincts, were set apart for central functions. The city was the center of political administration, religious cults, and economic activities. The diversity of people and tasks performed within its boundaries was the key to its importance. It is this complexity that required new means of holding it together and keeping it functioning. Writing, laws, representational art, elaborate rituals, secular rulers, and bureaucracies are all responses to the need for regulation.

Early cities of Mesopotamia were not especially large compared with subsequent urbanism in other parts of the world. Populations of third-millennium centers ranged between 10,000 and 50,000. Although they were tightly nucleated and frequently surrounded by a defensive wall, the cities themselves were not the true economic and political units. The modal unit of the Mesopotamian countryside was the city-state, which comprised the urban center and the surrounding area directly under its control, much of it farmed by inhabitants of the city. The amount of surrounding area varied with the power of the city itself and the competition from neighbors. Early city-states probably directly controlled only the land within 5 or 10 kilometers of the city. When the number of city-states grew and their respective territorial ambitions increased, the boundaries of different city-states began to impinge upon one another. This may have set off the earliest round of organized militarism and urban population agglomeration, such as that during the Early Dynastic period in the vicinity of Uruk.

The ethnic group that peopled these first cities is known to us through its language, Sumerian. Although the contributions made by the Sumerians to the developments of later generations was pivotal, it seems from linguistic evidence that they had no direct successors. The wonderful confluence of productivity and creativity in the Sumerians of the fourth and third millennia can only be witnessed through discoveries in the archeological record. Although the artistic and linguistic evidence for a uniform Sumerian culture throughout lowland Mesopotamia is strong, it is not evidenced in their political history. City-states were the pervasive political units that were only temporarily unified into larger national states. The causes for these periods of unification and centralized authority are diverse, but economic factors seem to be a recurrent theme. Lowland Mesopotamia is devoid of some of the most basic raw materials that it needed for its economy. The importation of these goods may have been crucial in the emergence of urbanism in Mesopotamia, and control of this trade was a primary goal of subsequent city rulers. A monopoly over the trade of certain basic items, such as copper or wood, could have meant power and wealth. Two major forces were called upon to forge nation-states out of the heterogeneous Mesopotamian cities: militarism and complex administration. These two factors were the primary unifying elements, although in differing proportions, in all Mesopotamian state governments and in subsequent ones.

Demographic changes, especially population growth, were basic factors in the emerging civilizational patterns. Although it remains difficult to document archeologically, there was clearly a progressive general increase in population in Post-Pleistocene times. Some theorists have suggested that this population growth acted as an independent variable, promoting cultural innovation to keep abreast of growing subsistence needs. Whether this position can be accepted or not, large population units formed a necessary background for the hierarchical complex organization of early civilizations. The questions remain, Under what conditions does population pressure work as a stimulation to change? and What agents does it work through?

Food-producing technology is the basic resource upon which any civilization is built. The effective domestication of plants and animals allows for greater control over food resources. The early villagers of the Near East did not necessarily have an easier life than that of their hunting and gathering predecessors, but they were able to structure that life differently. Agriculture and storage allowed for (and necessitated) the establishment of year-round, permanent communities. The schedule of activities also changed from that of a constant, although not all-consuming, pursuit of food sources to that of periodic, intensive effort. Farmers had to work hard for short periods, but this was compensated during those periods in the agricultural cycle that do not require intensive labor. At first, farmers used the time to continue their collection of wild resources, but soon they spent it for craft and construction activities. The quantity of material goods increased dramatically with food production and this investment in capital goods led to greater productivity and even more goods.

The food-producing strategies themselves were also subject to change. New breeds of animals and new varieties of plants allowed for greater productivity and enabled farming in regions where it had not theretofore been possible. Productivity and the extent of arable land were also increased with the introduction of simple irrigation techniques. Early irrigation efforts allowed farming in regions where rainfall was insufficient in some years to support farming. When irrigation techniques had been improved, their effect was more fundamental. Irrigation and other means of intensifying agriculture

promoted differentiation in wealth and control of productive resources. This was one factor in the growth of stratified society. The potential gains of irrigation and other planned means of intensifying agriculture led to the adaptive strategy of centralized control of agricultural production. Communities could survive without centralized administration, but those communities that organized fared better. This was a second factor that favored class-stratified society and centralized administration.

Trade in raw materials, which is best known from the distribution of Anatolian obsidian, was practiced in the Near East from the time of the earliest farming villages and may have been important in the development and spread of early farming technology. Trade was of fundamental importance for the early Mesopotamian communities that were not self-sufficient in basic raw materials. It had to be organized so that large quantities of goods from diverse regions could be brought in continually. This favored the growth of an administrative class to orchestrate the procurement, payment, and distribution of goods, and of a class of functionaries to carry out the trading missions. The scale of trading activity also engendered the development of manufacturing industries to produce goods to pay for imports and probably a class of private venturers who sought to profit from trading across boundaries of differential accessibility.

Warfare of some sort has been practiced from the time of early villages to the present. It seems as if there was sufficient threat of warfare to stimulate the investment in massive defensive constructions as early as the Pre-Pottery Neolithic A community at Jericho. Warfare during early-village times was probably not highly organized. At that time, communities may have raided their neighbors if those neighbors possessed commodities, but it wasn't until the establishment of sedentary communities capable of producing enough food to support the manufacture of material goods that large-scale investment in defensive works became necessary. Eighth-millennium Jericho and sixth-millennium Tell es-Sawwan are examples of communities that had accumulated large amounts of material goods compared with their neighbors Such towns were worthwhile targets for raiding and, consequently, they had to protect themselves by building defensive walls and eventually maintaining armies. This process reached maturity during the second half of the Early Dynastic period for which there is widespread evidence for organized warfare and an elite whose primary purpose was to conduct armed campaigns. Archeological and written evidence indicates that militarism played a major role in the formation of early cities and states. The king lists show a preoccupation with war, many of the important monuments of the Early Dynastic period being portrayals of military campaigns.

The form and equipment of a city's army are best illustrated by the Royal Standard of Ur (Figure 9-15), and the Stele of the Vultures (Figure 9-28) erected by Eanatum of Lagash. The weapons, equipment, and organization of Sumerian military forces depicted in these two works imply a highly developed war machine. The discipline and tactics used were not those of a tumultuous, disorganized band. The Sumerian war machine had evolved a sophistication that was indicative of its role in precipitating major cultural developments.

The effect of organized militarism cannot be overestimated: it produced demographic changes that resulted in nucleated, defendable units, which were themselves very attractive to a potential aggressor. The creation of a standing army with its own administrators shifted the primary base of power in early cities from the religious leaders to the commander of the army. This transition in political history has never been completely reversed.

The *status of women* seems to have changed substantially with the emergence of complex society. Although archeological evidence has only recently contributed to our understanding, inferences can be drawn from a variety of ethnographic studies. It has been hypothesized that the advent of agriculture and sedentary village life initiated a series of changes that led to an increased inequality of status between men and women. Three interrelated factors are cited as the basic causes for this change in status (Conkey 1977; Quinn 1977): (1) the establishment of sedentary villages facilitated the partitioning of living and working areas; (2) the development of agriculture led to an expansion of the

Figure 9-28
Detail of the Vulture Stele, showing military equipment and organization during Early Dynastic times. (Photograph from the National Museums of France.)

food-processing responsibilities of women, activities that were largely restricted to the immediate environs of the home; and (3) men played the major role in the growing systems of exchanging goods and communicating knowledge (including rituals and symbolic communication). Hence, both the change in economic activities and the physical layout of houses promoted a growing discrepancy in the roles that men and women had in the productive and administrative aspects of society. With the intensification of agriculture and the growth of urbanism, these divisions were institutionalized through a variety of beliefs, customs, and even laws.

Specialization of activities and distribution of wealth are difficult processes to understand completely but are at the core of civilizational developments. It can be assumed that most preagricultural societies were largely egalitarian with little specialization except for that determined by age and sex. Urban societies, on the other hand, are developed through intense specialization of tasks and great inequalities in the distribution of wealth. Fundamental for these two processes was the availability of surplus wealth that could be invested in specialized activities and that supported wealthier classes. To accumulate such surpluses, agriculturalists had to be induced to produce sizeable surpluses; a central authority had to oversee their accumulation; and community norms had to be altered so that the redistribution of surpluses did not result in egalitarianism. From what can be inferred from the archeological and written records, the temple hierarchy was largely responsible for accomplishing these changes through the formulation of belief systems, control of information, and a redistributive economy.

For a complex society to continue, specialization of activities and differentiation in wealth must become institutionalized. Civilizations thrive on stability and order. Thus, class differences and specialized economies have to be formalized. The religious administrators in the Near East contributed toward this through mythical justification and ritualistic reaffirmation of the civilizational order as it was developing. The final stage in formalizing the new order was achieved by the early secular rulers in two ways: (1) to secure their authority, especially at times of succession of power, they appealed to religious deities for affirmation; and (2) they instituted legal codes. These codes not only protected the rights of the weak and poor, which enabled the secular rulers to gain popular support, but also limited the rights of competing power groups, which enabled those rulers to retain control over most aspects of society.

None of these processes took place in isolation, nor were their effects identical in every situation. The overall trend in the ancient Near East was that of a fluctuating but growing level of complexity of organization and an increasing network of interaction. Although there were temporary setbacks, the discernable trend has been toward more intense interaction and interdependence in prehistory, early history, and today.

Bibliography of the Prehistoric and Protohistoric Near East

BIBLIOGRAPHY OF THE PREHISTORIC AND PROTOHISTORIC NEAR EAST

Abu Al-Soof, Behnam

1967   The relevance of the Diyala sequence to southern Mesopotamian sites. *Iraq* 29:133–142.

1968a   Distribution of Uruk, Jamdat Nasr, and Ninevite V pottery as revealed by field survey work in Iraq. *Iraq* 30:74–86.

1968b   Tell es-Sawwan: Excavation of the fourth season (spring, 1967). *Sumer* 24:3–15.

1969   Two prehistoric sites in Iraq. *Archaeology* 22:70–71.

Adams, Robert McC.

1955   Developmental stages in ancient Mesopotamia. In *Irrigation civilization*, edited by Julian Steward. Pan American Union, Washington, D.C.

1958   Survey of ancient water courses and settlements in central Iraq. *Sumer* 14:101–103.

1960a   Early civilizations: Subsistence and environment. In *City invincible: An Oriental Institute symposium*, edited by Carl H. Kraeling and Robert McC. Adams. University of Chicago Press, Chicago.

1960b   The evolutionary process in early civilizations. In *Evolution after Darwin*, vol. 2, edited by Sol Tax. University of Chicago Press, Chicago.

1960c   Factors influencing the rise of civilization in the alluvium, illustrated by Mesopotamia. In *City invincible: An Oriental Institute symposium*, edited by Carl H. Kraeling and Robert McC. Adams. University of Chicago Press, Chicago.

1960d   The origin of cities. *Scientific American* 203(3):153–172.

1962   Agriculture and urban life in early southwestern Iran. *Science* 136(3511):109–122.

1965   *Land behind Baghdad: A history of settlement on the Diyala Plain.* University of Chicago Press, Chicago.

1966a   *The evolution of urban society.* Aldine, Chicago.

1966b   Trend and tradition in Near Eastern archaeology. *Proceedings of the American Philosophical Society* 110(2):105–110.

1968   Archaeological research strategies: Past and present. *Science* 160(3833):1187–1192.

1969   The study of ancient Mesopotamian settlement patterns and the problem of urban origins. *Sumer* 25:111–124.

1970   Review of *The domestication and exploitation of plants and animals* edited by Peter J. Ucko and G. W. Dimbleby. *Economic History Review* 23:380–382.

1972   Patterns of urbanization in early southern Mesopotamia. In *Man, settlement, and urbanism*, edited by Peter J. Ucko, Ruth Tringham, and G. W. Dimbleby. Duckworth, London.

1974a   Anthropological perspectives on ancient trade. *Current Anthropology* 15(3):239–258.

1974b   Historic patterns of Mesopotamian irrigation agriculture. In *Irrigation's impact on society*, edited by Theodore E. Downing and McGuire Gibson. Anthropological Papers of the University of Arizona, no. 25. Tuscon.

Adams, Robert McC. (*continued*)

1974c   The Mesopotamian social landscape: A view from the frontier. In *Reconstructing complex societies,* edited by Charlotte Moore. Bulletin of the American Schools of Oriental Research, No. 20. Baltimore.

n.d.   Notes on Nippur survey.

Adams, Robert McC., and Hans J. Nissen

1972   *The Uruk countryside: The natural setting of urban society.* University of Chicago Press, Chicago.

Al-A'dami, Kalid Ahmad

1968   Excavations at Tell es-Sawwan. *Sumer* 24:57–94.

Albright, William Foxwell

1957   *From the Stone Age to Christianity: Monotheism and the historical process.* Doubleday, New York.

1960   *The archaeology of Palestine.* Penguin, Baltimore.

Amiran, Ruth B. K.

1952   Connections between Anatolia and Palestine in the Early Bronze Age. *Israel Exploration Journal* 2:89–103.

Anati, Emmanuel

1962a   *Palestine before the Hebrews: A history, from the earliest arrival of man to the conquest of Canaan.* Knopf, New York.

1962b   Prehistoric trade and the puzzle of Jericho. *Bulletin of the American Schools of Oriental Research* 1967:25–31.

Arkell, A. J., and Peter J. Ucko

1965   Review of predynastic development in the Nile Valley. *Current Anthropology* 6:145–166.

Arkin, Herbert, and Raymond R. Colton

1962   *Tables for statisticians.* Barnes & Noble, New York.

Balfet, H., H. Lafuma, P. Longuet, and P. Terrier

1969   Une invention néolithique sans lendemain. *Bulletin de la Société Préhistorique Francaise* 66:158–192.

Bar-Yosef, O.

1970   The Epi-Palaeolithic cultures of Palestine. Ph.D. dissertation, Hebrew University, Jerusalem.

Barth, Fredrik

1956   Ecologic relationships of ethnic groups in Swat, North Pakistan. *American Anthropologist* 58: 1079–1089.

1961   *Nomads of South Persia: The Basseri tribe of the Khamesh Confederacy.* Oslo University Press, Oslo.

Bates, Marston

1953   Human ecology. In *Anthropology today,* edited by A. L. Kroeber. University of Chicago Press, Chicago.

Beek, Martin A.

1962   *Atlas of Mesopotamia.* Thomas Nelson, London.

Bennett, John W.

1969   Anthropological research bearing upon the use and development of water resources. Paper for the University of Kentucky Water Resources Institute Seminar on Water Resources and the Social Sciences.

Berry, Brian J. L.

1967   *Geography of market centers and retail distribution.* Prentice-Hall, Englewood Cliffs, New Jersey.

Berry, Brian J. L., and Duane F. Marble, eds.

1968   *Spatial analysis: A reader in statistical geography.* Prentice-Hall, Englewood Cliffs, New Jersey.

Berry, R. J.

1969   The genetical implications of domestication in animals. In *The domestication and exploitation of plants and animals,* edited by Peter J. Ucko and G. W. Dimbleby. Aldine, Chicago.

Bialor, Perry A.

1962   The chipped stone industry of Çatal Hüyük. *Anatolian Studies* 12:67–110.

Bibby, Geoffrey

1969   *Looking for Dilmun.* Knopf, New York.

Biernoff, D. C.

1969   The earliest painted pottery in western Anatolia and Greece: A study of development and diffusion. Manuscript.

Binford, Lewis R.

1962   Archaeology as anthropology. *American Antiquity* 28:217–225.

1964   A consideration of archaeological research design. *American Antiquity* 29:425–441.

1965   Archaeological systematics and the study of culture process. *American Antiquity* 31:203–210.

1968   Post-Pleistocene adaptations. In *New perspectives in archaeology,* edited by Sally R. Binford and Lewis R. Binford. Aldine, Chicago.

Binford, Lewis R., and Sally Binford

1966a   The predatory revolution: A consideration of the evidence for a new subsistence level. *American Anthropologist* 68:508–512.

1966b   A preliminary analysis of functional variability in the Mousterian of Levallois facies. In *Recent studies in paleoanthropology: American Anthropologist,* edited by J. D. Clark and F. C. Howell. 68(2, part 2):238–295.

Birdsell, Joseph B.

1958   On population structure in generalized hunting and collecting populations. *Evolution* 12(2): 189–205.

Bökönyi, Shandor

1969   Archaeological problems and methods of recognizing animal domestication. In *The domestication and exploitation of plants and animals,* edited by Peter J. Ucko and G. W. Dimbleby. Aldine, Chicago.

1973   The fauna of Umm Dabaghiyah: A preliminary report. *Iraq* 35:9–12.

1976   Development of early stock rearing in the Near East. *Nature* 264:19–23.

Bordaz, Jacques

1966   Suberde. *Anatolian Studies* 16:32–33.

1969a   Flint flaking in Turkey. *Natural History,* February, pp. 73–77.

1969b   The Suberde excavations, southwestern Turkey: An interim report. *Turk Arkeoloji Dergisi* 17: 43–71.

1973   Current research in the Neolithic of southcentral Turkey: Suberde, Erbaba, and their chronological implications. *American Journal of Archaeology* 77:282–288.

Bordes, Francois

1968   *The old Stone Age.* McGraw-Hill, New York.

Boserup, Ester

1965   *The conditions of agricultural growth.* Aldine, Chicago.

Bottéro, Jean

1967   The first semitic empire. In *The Near East: The early civilizations,* edited by Jean Bottéro, Elena Cassin, and Jean Vercoutter. Delacorte, New York.

Bottéro, Jean, Elena Cassin, and Jean Vercoutter, eds.

1967   *The Near East: The early civilizations.* Delacorte, New York.

Braidwood, Linda S., and Robert J. Braidwood

1969   Current thoughts on the beginnings of food-production in southwestern Asia. *Mélanges de l'Université Saint-Joseph* 45(8):149–155.

Braidwood, Robert J.

1937   *Mounds in the Plain of Antioch: An archeological survey.* Oriental Institute Publications, no. 48. University of Chicago Press, Chicago.

1952   *The Near East and the foundations of civilization.* Oregon State System of Higher Education, Eugene.

1957   Jericho and its setting in Near Eastern history. *Antiquity* 31:74–78.

1958   Near Eastern prehistory. *Science* 127(3312):1419–1430.

1959   Archaeology and the evolutionary theory. In *Evolution and anthropology,* edited by Betty J. Meggars. Anthropological Society, Washington.

1960a   The agricultural revolution. *Scientific American* 203(3):130–152.

1960b   Levels in prehistory: A model for the consideration of the evidence. In *Evolution after Darwin,* vol. 2, edited by Sol Tax. University of Chicago Press, Chicago.

1960c   Prelude to civilization. In *City invincible: An Oriental Institute symposium,* edited by Carl H. Kraeling and Robert McC. Adams. University of Chicago Press, Chicago.

1960d   Seeking the world's first farmers in Persian Kurdistan. *Illustrated London News* 237:695–697.

1961   The Iranian prehistoric project, 1959–1960. *Iranica Antiqua* 1:3–7.

1962   The earliest village communities of southwestern Asia reconsidered. *Atti del Sesto Congresso Internazionale delle Scienze Preistoriche e Protoistoriche* 1:115–126. Sansoni, Florence.

1965   The biography of a research project. *Chicago Today* 2:14–26.

1966   Review of *Earliest civilizations of the Near East* by James Mellaart. *Antiquity* 40:238–240.

1969   Cultures based on plant and animal domestication. Manuscript on file at The Oriental Institute, The University of Chicago, Chicago.

1970   Prehistory into history in the Near East. In *Radiocarbon variations and absolute chronology,* edited by Ingrid U. Olsson. Wiley, New York.

1972   Prehistoric investigations in southwestern Asia. *Proceedings of the American Philosophical Society* 116(4):310–320.

1973   The early village in southwestern Asia. *Journal of Near Eastern Studies* 32(1-2):34–39.

1974   The Iraq Jarmo project. In *Archaeological researches in retrospect,* edited by Gordon A. Willey. Winthrop, Cambridge, England.

1975   *Prehistoric men,* 8th ed. Scott, Foresman, Glenview, Illinois.

Braidwood, Robert J., and Linda S. Braidwood

1950   Jarmo: A village of early farmers in Iraq. *Antiquity* 24:189–195.

1953   The earliest village communities of southwestern Asia. *Journal of World History* 1(2):278–310.

1960   *Excavations in the Plain of Antioch.* Oriental Institute Publications, no. 61. University of Chicago Press, Chicago.

Braidwood, Robert J., Linda S. Braidwood, James G. Smith, and Charles Leslie

1952   Matarrah: A southern variant of the Hassunan assemblage, excavated in 1948. *Journal of Near Eastern Studies* 11:1–75.

Braidwood, Robert J., Halet Çambel, Barbara Lawrence, Charles L. Redman, and Robert Stewart

1974   Beginnings of village-farming communities in southwestern Turkey: 1972. *Proceedings of the National Academy of Sciences* 71(2):568–572.

Braidwood, Robert J., Halet Çambel, Charles L. Redman, and Patty Jo Watson

1971   Beginnings of village-farming communities in southwestern Turkey. *Proceedings of the National Academy of Sciences* 68(6):1236–1240.

Braidwood, Robert J., Halet Çambel, and Patty Jo Watson

1969   Prehistoric investigations in southwestern Turkey. *Science* 164(3885):1275–1276.

Braidwood, Robert J., and Bruce Howe

1960   *Prehistoric investigations in Iraqi Kurdistan.* Studies in Ancient Oriental Civilization, no. 31. University of Chicago Press, Chicago.

1962   Southwestern Asia beyond the lands of the Mediterranean Littoral. In *Courses toward urban life,* edited by Robert J. Braidwood and Gordon Willey. Aldine, Chicago.

Braidwood, Robert J., Bruce Howe, and Ezat O. Negahban

1960   Near Eastern prehistory. *Science* 131(3412):1536–1541.

Braidwood, Robert J., Bruce Howe, and Charles A. Reed

1961   The Iranian prehistoric project. *Science* 133(3469):2008–2010.

Braidwood, Robert J. and Charles A. Reed

1957   The achievement and early consequences of food-production: A consideration of the archeological and natural-historical evidence. *Cold Spring Harbor Symposia on Quantitative Biology* 22:19–31.

Braidwood, Robert J., and Gordon Willey, eds.

1962   *Courses toward urban life.* Aldine, Chicago.

Breasted, James Henry

    1916   *Ancient times.* Boston.

    1938   *The conquest of civilization.* New York.

Bright, John

    1959   *A history of Israel.* Westminster Press, Philadelphia.

Bronson, Bennet

    1977   The earliest farming: Demography as cause and consequence. In *Origins of Agriculture,* edited by Charles Reed. Mouton, The Hague.

Brooks, C. E. P.

    1926   *The evolution of climate,* 2d ed. Benn, London.

Brothwell, Don, and Eric Higgs

    1963   *Science in archaeology: A comprehensive survey of progress and research.* Basic Books, New York.

Brown, James A.

    1971   Approaches to the social dimensions of mortuary practices. *Memoirs of the Society for American Archaeology* 25(3, part 2):36.

Bunting, Brian T.

    1967   *The geography of soil.* Aldine, Chicago.

Butzer, Karl W.

    1965   Physical conditions in eastern Europe, western Asia, and Egypt before the period of agricultural and urban settlement. In *The Cambridge ancient history,* vol. 1, edited by I. E. S. Edwards, C. J. Gadd, and N. G. L. Hammond. Cambridge University Press, Cambridge.

    1971   *Environment and archeology: An ecological approach to prehistory,* 2d ed. Aldine, Chicago.

Caldwell, Joseph R.

    1977   Cultural evolution in the Old World and the New, leading to the beginning and spread of agriculture. In *Origins of agriculture,* edited by Charles Reed. Mouton, The Hague.

Caldwell, Joseph R., and S. M. Shahmirzadi

    1966   *Tal-i-Iblis: The Kerman Range and the beginnings of smelting.* Illinois State Museum Preliminary Report, no. 7. Springfield, Illinois.

Çambel, Halet, and Robert J. Braidwood

    1970   An early farming village in Turkey. *Scientific American* 222(3):50–56.

Campbell, Edward F., Jr., and David Noel Freedman, eds.

    1970   *The biblical archaeologist reader,* vol. 3. Doubleday, New York.

de Candolle, Alphonse

    1884   *Origin of cultivated plants.* Kegan Paul, London.

Cann, J. R., and Colin Renfrew

    1964   The characterization of obsidian and its application to the Mediterranean region. *Proceedings of the Prehistoric Society* (London) 30:111–133.

Carneiro, Robert L.

1961   The evolution of horticultural systems in native South America: Causes and consequences. In a symposium edited by J. Wilbert. *Antropologica,* suppl. 2, pp. 47–67. Venezuela.

1967   On the relationship between size of population and complexity of social organization. *Southwestern Journal of Anthropology* 23:234–243.

1970   A theory of the origin of the state. *Science* 169(3947):733–738.

1972   From autonomous villages to the state: A numerical estimation. In *Population, resources, and technology,* edited by B. Spooner. University of Pennsylvania Press, Philadelphia.

Caskey, J. L.

1965   Greece, Crete, and the Aegean Islands in the Early Bronze Age. In *The Cambridge ancient history,* vol. 1, edited by I. E. S. Edwards, C. J. Gadd, and N. G. L. Hammond. Cambridge University Press, Cambridge.

Caton-Thompson, G.

1952   *Kharga oasis in prehistory.* Athlone, London.

Caton-Thompson, G., and E. W. Gardner

1934   *The desert fayum.* Royal Anthropological Institute, London.

Cauvin, Jacques

1968   Les outillages néolithiques de Bylos et du Littoral libanais. In *Fouilles de Bybos,* edited by M. Donand, J. A. Maisonneuve, Paris.

Cauvin, Marie-Claire

1966   L'Industrie Natoufienne de Mallaha ('Eynan): Note préliminaire. *L'Anthropologie* 70(5–6):485–494.

Childe, V. Gordon

1936   *Man makes himself,* 1st ed. Watts, London.

1950   The urban revolution. *The Town Planning Review* 21:3–17.

1951a   *Man makes himself,* 3d ed. Watts, London.

1951b   *Social evolution.* World, Cleveland.

1952   *New light on the most ancient East.* Praeger, New York.

1957   Civilizations, cities, and towns. *Antiquity* 31:36–7.

Chisholm, Michael

1968   *Rural settlement and land use: An essay in location.* Hutchinson University Library, London.

Chorley, Richard J., and Peter Haggett, eds.

1967   *Socio-economic models in geography.* Methuen, London.

Clark, J. Desmond

1964   The prehistoric origins of African culture. *Journal of African History* 5:161–183.

1965   Changing trends and developing values in African prehistory. *African Affairs* (special number). Royal African Society, London.

1966   Acheulian occupation sites in the Middle East and Africa: A study in cultural variability. In *Recent studies in paleoanthropology, American Anthropologist,* edited by J. Desmond Clark and F. Clark Howell. 68(2, part 2):202–229.

1967   The Middle Acheulian occupation site at Latamne, northern Syria. *Quaternaria* 9:1–68.

1968   The Middle Acheulian occupation site at Latamne, northern Syria. *Quaternaria* 10:1–72.

Clark, J. Grahame D.

1961   *World prehistory: An outline.* Cambridge University Press, Cambridge.

1965   Radiocarbon dating and the expansion of farming culture from the Near East over Europe. *Proceedings of the Prehistoric Society* (London) 31:58–73.

Clarke, David

1968   *Analytical archaeology.* Methuen, London.

Cockburn, T. Aidan

1973   Death and disease in ancient Egypt. *Science* 181(4098):470–471.

Cohen, Mark N.

1977   *The food crisis in prehistory: Overpopulation and the origins of agriculture.* Yale University Press, New Haven.

Cole, John P., and Cuchlaine A. M. King

1968   *Quantitative geography: Techniques and theories in geography.* Wiley, New York.

Coles, J. M., and E. S. Higgs

1969   *The archaeology of early man.* Praeger, New York.

Conkey, Margaret W.

1977   By chance: The role of archeology in contributing to a reinterpretation of culture. *Abstracts of 76th Annual Meeting.* American Anthropological Association, Washington, D.C.

n.d.   Style and evolution of symbolic behavior. Unpublished manuscript.

de Contenson, Henri

1962   Pursuits des recherches dans le sondage. In *Ugaritica,* vol. 4, edited by C. F. A. Schaeffer. Gauthier, Paris.

1963   New correlations between Ras Shamra and al 'Amuq. *Bulletin of the American Schools of Oriental Research* 172:35–40.

1966a   Notes on the chronology of Near Eastern Neolithic. *Bulletin of the American Schools of Oriental Research* 184:2–5.

1966b   Ramad. *Syria* 43:153–154.

1966c   Les trois premières campagnes de fouilles à Tell Ramad. *Académie des Inscriptions et Belles-Lettres,* C.R. 1966:531–536.

1967   Troisième campagne à Tell Ramad: Rapport préliminaire. *Les Annales archéologiques arabes syriennes* 17:17–24.

1971   Tell Ramad, a village of Syria of the 7th and 6th millennia B.C. *Archaeology* 24:278–283.

de Contenson, Henri, and Willem J. Van Liere

1964a   Holocene environment and early settlement in the Levant. *Les Annales archéologiques de Syrie* 14:125–128.

1964b   Sondages à Tell Ramad en 1963: Rapport préliminaire. *Les Annales archéologiques de Syrie* 14: 109–124.

1966a   Premier sondage à Bouqras. *Les Annales archéologiques arabes syriennes* 16(2):181–192.

1966b   Premiers pas vers une chronologie absolue à Tell Ramad. *Les Annales archéologiques arabes syriennes* 16(2):175–176.

1966c   Seconde campagne à Tell Ramad, 1966: Rapport préliminaire. *Les Annales archéologiques arabes syriennes* 16(2):167–174.

Cook, Sherburne F.

1972   *Prehistoric demography.* McCaleb Module in Anthropology, no. 16. Addison-Wesley, Reading, Mass.

Coon, Carleton S.

1956   *The seven caves.* Knopf, New York.

1966   *Caravan: The story of the Middle East.* Holt, Rinehart & Winston, New York.

Cottrell, Leonard

1957   *The anvil of civilization.* New American Library, New York.

1963   *Land of the two rivers.* Brockhampton Press, Leicester, England.

1965   *The land of Shinar.* Souvenir Press, London.

Cressey, George B.

1960   *Crossroads: Land and life in southwest Asia.* Lippincott, Chicago.

Crown, Alan D.

1971   Toward a reconstruction of the climate of Palestine 8000 B.C.–0 B.C. Paper presented at the International Congress of Orientalists, Canberra, Australia.

Dabbagh, Taley

1966   Halaf pottery. *Sumer* 22:23–43.

Dacey, Michael F.

1973   Statistical tests of spatial association in the locations of tool types. *American Antiquity* 38(3): 320–327.

Dales, George

1971   Early human contacts from the Persian Gulf through Baluchistan and southern Afganistan. In *Food, fiber, and the arid lands,* edited by William G. McGinnies, Brian J. Goldman, and Patricia Paylore. University of Arizona Press, Tucson.

Daniel, Glyn

1968   *The first civilizations: The archaeology of their origins.* Crowell, New York.

Davis, Kingsley, ed.

1973   *Cities: Their origin, growth, and human impact.* Readings from *Scientific American.* W. H. Freeman and Company, San Francisco.

Delouqaz, Pinhas, Harold D. Hill, and Seton Lloyd

1967   *Private houses and graves in the Diyala region.* Oriental Institute Publications, no. 88. University of Chicago Press, Chicago.

de Morgan, J.

1905   *Mission scientifique en Perse.* Paris.

Diakonoff, Igor M.

1969   The rise of the despotic state in ancient Mesopotamia. In *Ancient Mesopotamia: A socio-economic history,* edited by I. M. Diakonoff. Mauka Publishing House, Moscow.

Dikaios, P.

1953   *Khirokitia.* Oxford University Press, London.

Dimbleby, G. W.

1970   Pollen analysis. In *Science in archaeology,* edited by Don Brothwell and Eric Higgs. Basic Books, New York.

Dixon, J. E., J. R. Cann, and Colin Renfrew

1968   Obsidian and the origins of trade. *Scientific American* 218(3):38–46.

Dornemann, R. H.

1960   An early village. *Archaeology* 22:68–70.

Dorrell, Peter

1972   A note on the geomorphology of the country near Umm Dabaghiyah. *Iraq* 24:69–72.

Downing, Theodore E., and McGuire Gibson, eds.

1974   *Irrigation's impact on society.* Anthropological Papers of the University of Arizona, no. 25. Tucson.

Drew, Isabella Milling, Dexter Perkins, Jr., and Patricia Daly

1971   Prehistoric domestication of animals: Effects on bone structure. *Science* 171(3968):280–282.

Ducos, P.

1969   Methodology and results of the study of the earliest domesticated animals in the Near East (Palestine). In *The domestication and exploitation of plants and animals,* edited by Peter J. Ucko and G. W. Dimbleby. Aldine, Chicago.

Dumond, D. E.

1965   Population growth and cultural change. *Southwestern Journal of Anthropology* 21:302–324.

Economist Intelligence Unit Limited

1960   The Middle East and North Africa. In *Oxford regional economic atlas.* Oxford University Press, London.

Edzard, Dietz Otto

1967a   The Early Dynastic period. In *The Near East: The early civilization,* edited by Jean Bottéro, Elena Cassin, and Jean Vercoutter. Delacorte, New York.

1967b   The third dynasty of Ur: Its empire and its successor states. In *The Near East: The early civilizations,* edited by Jean Bottéro, Elena Cassin, and Jean Vercoutter. Delacorte, New York.

Egami, Namio

1957   The excavations of Telul eth-Thalathat. *Sumer* 13:5–22.

Egami, Namio, Toehihiko Sono, and Kiyoharu Horiuchi

1966   Brief report of the third season's excavations at Tell II of Telul eth-Thalathat and some observations. *Sumer* 22:1–16.

Ehrich, Robert W., ed.

1965   *Chronologies in Old World archeology.* University of Chicago Press, Chicago.

El-Wailly, Faisal

1963   Foreword. *Sumer* 19(1-2):1-7.

El-Wailly, Faisal, and Behnam Abu al-Soof

1965   The excavations at Tell es-Sawwan: First preliminary report (1964). *Sumer* 21:17-32.

Emery, Walter B.

1961   *Archaic Egypt.* Penguin, Baltimore.

English, P. W.

1966   *City and village in Iran: Settlement and economy in the Kirman Basin.* University of Wisconsin Press, Madison.

Erman, Adolf

1966   *The ancient Egyptians.* Harper & Row, New York.

Evans, J. D.

1964   Excavations in the Neolithic settlement of Knossos, 1957-1960, part 1. *Annual of the British School of Archaeology* (Athens) 59:132-240.

Ewing, J. F.

1947   Preliminary note on the excavations at the Paleolithic site of Ksar Akil. *Antiquity* 21:186-197.

Fairservis, Walter A., Jr.

1961   Archeological studies in the Seistan basin of southwestern Afganistan and eastern Iran. *Anthropology Papers of the American Museum of Natural History* 48 (part 1).

Falkenstein, Adam

1967   The prehistory and protohistory of western Asia. In *The Near East: The early civilizations,* edited by Jean Bottéro, Elena Cassin, and Jean Vercoutter. Delacorte, New York.

Farrand, W. R.

1965   Geology, climate, and chronology of Yabrud rockshelter, 1. *Les Annales archéologiques de Syrie* 15:36-50.

Fisher, W. B.

1963   *The Middle East.* Methuen, London.

Fisher, W. B., ed.

1968   *The land of Iran.* The Cambridge History of Iran, vol. 1. Cambridge University Press, Cambridge.

Flannery, Kent V.

1965   The ecology of early food production in Mesopotamia. *Science* 147(3663):1247-1256.

1968   The Olmec and the Valley of Oaxaca. *Dumbarton Oaks Conference on the Olmec,* pp. 79-110. Washington, D.C.

Flannery, Kent V. (*continued*)

1969   Origins and ecological effects of early domestication in Iran and the Near East. In *The domestication and exploitation of plants and animals,* edited by Peter J. Ucko and G. W. Dimbleby. Aldine, Chicago.

1972a   The cultural evolution of civilizations. *Annual Review of Ecology and Systematics* 3:399–426.

1972b   The origins of the village as a settlement type in Mesoamerica and the Near East: A comparative study. In *Man, settlement, and urbanism,* edited by Peter J. Ucko, Ruth Tringham, and G. W. Dimbleby. Duckworth, London.

1973   The origins of agriculture. *Annual Review of Anthropology* 2:271–310.

1976   *The Mesoamerican village.* Academic Press, New York

Flannery, Kent V., and Henry T. Wright

1966   Faunal remains from "hut sounding" at Eridu, Iraq. *Sumer* 22:61–63.

Food and Agriculture Organization (FAO)

1968   Food composition table for use in Africa. U.S. Government Printing Office, Washington, D.C.

Frankfort, Henri

1939   *Cylinder seals: A documentary essay on the art and religion of the Near East.* Gregg, London.

1950   Town planning in ancient Mesopotamia. *The Town Planning Review* 21(2):99–115.

1951   *The birth of civilization in the Near East.* Doubleday, New York.

1954   *The art and architecture of the ancient Orient.* Penguin, Baltimore.

Frankfort, Henri, Mrs. H. A. Frankfort, John A. Wilson, and Thorkild Jacobsen

1949   *Before philosophy: The intellectual adventure of ancient man.* Penguin, Baltimore.

French, David H.

1966   Excavations at Çan Hasan: Fifth preliminary report. *Anatolian Studies* 16:113–124.

1971   An experiment in water-sieving. *Anatolian Studies* 21:59–64.

Fried, Morton, H.

1960   On the evolution of social stratification and the state. In *Culture in history,* edited by S. Diamond. Columbia University Press, New York.

1967   *The evolution of political society: An essay in political anthropology.* Random House, New York.

Fritz, John M., and Fredrick Plog

1970   The nature of archaeological explanation. *American Antiquity* 35:405–412.

Fukai, S., K. Horiuchi, and T. Matsutani

1970   *Telul eth-Thalathat: The excavation of Tell II.* Tokyo University Iraq-Iran Archaeological Expedition, report no. 2.

Gadd, C. J.

1964   The cities of Babylonia. *The Cambridge ancient history,* vol. 1, edited by I. E. S. Edwards, C. J. Gadd, and N. G. L. Hammond. Cambridge University Press, Cambridge.

Gardiner, Sir Alan

1961   *Egypt of the Pharaohs.* Oxford University Press, New York.

Garner, B. J.

1968 Models of urban geography and settlement location. In *Socioeconomic models in geography*, edited by Richard J. Chorley and Peter Haggett. Methuen, London.

Garrod, Dorothy A. E.

1930 The Palaeolithic of southern Kurdistan: Excavations in the caves of Zarzi and Hazar Merd. *American School of Prehistoric Research Bulletin*, no. 6, pp. 8–43.

1953 The relations between south-west Asia and Europe in the late Paleolithic Age. *Journal of World History* 1:13.

1957 The Natufian culture: The life and economy of a Mesolithic people in the Near East. *Proceedings of the British Academy* 43:55.

Garrod, Dorothy A. E., and D. M. A. Bate

1937 *The Stone Age of Mount Carmel*, vol. 1. Clarendon Press, Oxford.

Garrod, Dorothy A. E., and J. G. D. Clark

1965 Primitive man in Egypt, western Asia, and Europe. *The Cambridge ancient history*, vol. 1, edited by I. E. S. Edwards, G. J. Gadd, and N. G. L. Hammond. Cambridge University Press, Cambridge.

Garstang, John

1953 *Prehistoric Mersin*. Clarendon Press, Oxford.

Gelb, I. J.

1965 The ancient Mesopotamian ration system. *Journal of Near Eastern Studies* 24:230–243.

Ghirshman, R.

1938 At Sialk: Prehistoric Iran. *Asia* 38(11):645–650.

1954 *Iran.* Penguin, Baltimore.

Gibson, McGuire

1973 Population shift and the rise of Mesopotamian civilization. In *The explanation of culture change: Models in prehistory*, edited by Colin Renfrew. Duckworth, London.

1974 Violation in fallow and engineered disaster in Mesopotamian civilization. In *Irrigation's impact on society*, edited by Theodore E. Downing and McGuire Gibson. Anthropological Papers of the University of Arizona, no. 25. Tucson.

in press *The city and area of Kish.* Field Research Enterprises, Miami.

Gregory, S.

1968 *Statistical methods and the geographer.* Longmans, Green, London.

Greig-Smith, P.

1964 *Quantitative plant ecology.* Plenum, New York

Gummerman, George, ed.

1971 *The distribution of prehistoric population aggregates.* Proceedings of the Southwestern Anthropological Research Group, no. 1. Prescott College Press, Prescott, Arizona.

Gurney, O. R.

1964 *The Hittities.* Penguin, Baltimore.

Haggett, Peter

   1965   *Locational analysis in human geography.* Edward Arnold, London.

Hamblin, DoraJane, and the Editors of Time-Life Books

   1973   *The first cities.* Time-Life Books, New York.

Harlan, Jack R.

   1967   A wild wheat harvest in Turkey. *Archaeology* 20(3):197–201.

   1971   Agricultural origins: Centers and non-centers. *Science* 174(4008):468–473.

   1976   The plants and animals that nourish man. *Scientific American* 235(3):88–97.

   1977   The origins of cereal agriculture in the Old World. In *Origins of agriculture,* edited by Charles
           Reed. Mouton, The Hague.

Harlan, Jack R., and J. M. J. de Wet

   1973   On the quality of evidence for origin and dispersal of cultivated plants. *Current Anthropology*
           14(1-2):51–64.

Harlan, Jack R., J. M. J. de Wet, and E. Glen Price

   1972   Comparative evolution of cereals. *Evolution* 27:311–325.

Harlan, Jack R., and Daniel Zohary

   1966   Distribution of wild wheats and barley. *Science* 153(3740):1074–1079.

Harris, David R.

   1969   Agricultural systems, ecosystems, and the origins of agriculture. In *The domestication and exploita-
           tion of plants and animals,* edited by Peter J. Ucko and O. W. Dimbleby. Aldine, Chicago.

   1977   Alternative pathways toward agriculture. In *Origins of agriculture,* edited by Charles Reed.
           Mouton, The Hague.

Hassan, Fekri A.

   1972   Note on Sebilian sites from Dishna Plain. *Chronique d'Égypte* 47(93-94):11–16.

   1973   On mechanisms of population growth during the Neolithic. *Current Anthropology* 14(5):535–542.

   1975   Determinants of the size, density, and growth rate of hunting-gathering populations. In *Popula-
           tion, ecology, and social evolution,* edited by Steven Polgar. Mouton, The Hague.

   1977   The dynamics of agricultural origins in Palestine: A theoretical model. In *Origins of agriculture,*
           edited by Charles Reed. Mouton, The Hague.

Hawkes, Jacquetta G.

   1965   *Prehistory.* Mentor, New York.

Hawkes, J. G.

   1969   The ecological background of plant domestication. In *The domestication and exploitation of plants
           and animals,* edited by Peter J. Ucko and G. W. Dimbleby. Aldine, Chicago.

Helbaek, Hans

   1960   The paleoenthnobotany of the Near East and Europe. In *Prehistoric investigations in Iraqi Kurdistan,*
           edited by Robert J. Braidwood and Bruce Howe. Studies in Ancient Oriental Civilization, no. 31.
           University of Chicago Press, Chicago.

   1964a   Early Hassunan vegetable food at es-Sawwan near Samarra. *Sumer* 20:45–48.

   1964b   First impressions of the Çatal Hüyük plant husbandry. *Anatolian Studies* 14:121–124.

1966   Pre-Pottery Neolithic farming at Beidha. *Palestine Exploration Quarterly*. 98(1):61–66.

1969   Plant collecting, dry-farming, and irrigation agriculture in prehistoric Del Luran. In *Prehistory and human ecology of the Del Luran Plain: An early village sequence from Khuzistan, Iran*, edited by Frank Hole, Kent V. Flannery, and James A. Neely. Memoirs of the Museum of Anthropology, University of Michigan, no. 1. University of Michigan Press, Ann Arbor.

1970   The plant husbandry of Hacilar. In *Excavations at Hacilar*, vol. 1, edited by James Mellaart. Edinburgh University Press, Edinburgh.

1972   Traces of plants in the early ceramic site of Umm Dabaghiyah. *Iraq* 24:17–19.

1972   Samarran irrigation agriculture at Choga Mami in Iraq. *Iraq* 24:35–48.

Herre, Wolf, and Manfred Rohrs

1977   The origins of agriculture: Zoological considerations on the origins of farming and domestication. In *Origins of agriculture*, edited by Charles Reed. Mouton, The Hague.

Hermann, Georgina

1968   Lapis lazuli: The early phases of its trade. *Iraq* 30:21–57.

Higgs, E. S., and M. R. Jarman

1969   The origins of agriculture: A reconsideration. *Antiquity* 43:31–41.

Higgs, E. S., and C. Vita-Finzi

1972   Prehistoric economies: A territorial approach. In *Papers in economic prehistory*, edited by E. S. Higgs. Cambridge University Press, Cambridge.

Hill, James N.

1970   *Broken K: A prehistoric society in eastern Arizona*. Anthropological Papers of the University of Arizona, no. 18. Tucson.

1971   Seminar on the explanation of prehistoric organizational change. *Current Anthropology* 12(3): 406–408.

Hodder, Ian, and Clive Orton

1976   *Spatial analysis in archeology*. Cambridge University Press, Cambridge.

Hole, Frank

1971   The early phases at Chagha Sefid, Del Luran, southwest Iran. Paper presented at the 1971 meeting of the International Congress of Prehistoric and Protohistoric Sciences, Belgrade.

in press The emergence of settled life. In *Dictionary of Prehistory*. Scribner's, New York

Hole, Frank, and Kent V. Flannery

1967   The prehistory of southwestern Iran: A preliminary report. *Proceedings of the Prehistoric Society for 1967* (London) 33:147–170.

Hole, Frank, Kent V. Flannery, and James A. Neely

1969   *Prehistory and human ecology of the Del Luran Plain: An early village sequence from Khuzistan, Iran*. Memoirs of the Museum of Anthropology, University of Michigan, no. 1. University of Michigan Press, Ann Arbor.

Hood, Sinclair

1967   *The home of the heroes: The Aegean before the Greeks*. McGraw-Hill, New York.

Hooijer, D. A.

   1961   Middle Pleistocene mammals from Latamne, Orotones Valley, Syria. *Les Annales archéologiques arabes syriennes* 11:117–132.

   1966   Preliminary notes on the animal remains found at Bouqras and Ramad in 1965. *Les Annales archéologiques arabes syriennes.* 16(2):193–195.

Hooke, S. H.

   1963   *Middle Eastern mythology.* Penguin, Baltimore.

Howell, F. Clark

   1959   Upper Pleistocene stratigraphy and early man in the Levant. *Proceedings of the American Philosophical Society* 103:1–65.

   1973   *Early man.* Time-Life Books, New York.

Huntington, Ellsworth

   1945   *Mainsprings of civilization.* New American Library, New York.

Hutchinson, R. W.

   1962   *Prehistoric Crete.* Penguin, Baltimore.

Isaac, Glyn L.

   1972   Early phases of human behaviour: Models in Lower Palaeolithic archaeology. In *Models in archaeology*, edited by David L. Clarke. Methuen, London.

Jacobsen, Thomas W.

   1969   The Franchthi cave: A Stone Age site in southern Greece. *Archaeology* 22:4–9.

Jacobsen, Thorkild

   1943   Primitive democracy in ancient Mesopotamia. *Journal of Near Eastern Studies* 2(3):159–172.

   1945   Appraisal of Breasted and Childe on Mesopotamia. Manuscript on file at The Oriental Institute, The University of Chicago, Chicago.

   1946   The relative role of technology and literacy in the development of Old World civilizations. Manuscript on file at The Oriental Institute, The University of Chicago, Chicago.

   1957   Early political developments in Mesopotamia. *Zeitschrift für Assyriologie* 52:91–140.

   1958   Summary of the report by the Diyala Basin Archaeological Project, June 1, 1957, to June 1, 1958. *Sumer* 16(1-2):79–89.

   1970   *Toward the image of Tammuz.* Harvard University Press, Cambridge, Massachusetts.

Jacobsen, Thorkild, and Robert McC. Adams

   1958   Salt and silt in ancient Mesopotamian agriculture. *Science* 128(3334):1251–1258.

Jarman, H. N., A. J. Legge, and J. A. Charles

   1972   Retrieval of plant remains from archaeological sites by froth flotation. In *Papers in economic prehistory*, edited by E. S. Higgs. Cambridge University Press, Cambridge.

Jawad, Abdul Jalil

   1965   The advent of the era of townships in northern Mesopotamia. E. J. Brill, Leiden, Holland.

Jelinek, Arthur

  n.d.   The Tabun excavation project: A brief report on the 1969 field season. Manuscript.

Jelinek, Arthur, W. R. Farrand, G. Haas, A. Horowitz, and P. Goldberg

  1973   New excavations at the Tabun Cave, Mount Carmel, Israel, 1967–1972: A preliminary report. *Paleorient* 1(2):151–183.

Johnson, Gregory A.

  1972   A test of the utility of central place theory in archaeology. In *Man, settlement, and urbanism,* edited by Peter J. Ucko, Ruth Tringham, and G. W. Dimbleby. Duckworth, London.

  1973a   Implications of differential similarity among Halaf ceramic motif assemblages. Paper presented at the 1973 meeting of the American Anthropological Association, New Orleans.

  1973b   *Local exchange and early state development in southwestern Iran.* The University of Michigan Museum of Anthropology, Anthropological Papers, no. 51. Ann Arbor.

  1975   Locational analysis and the investigation of Uruk local exchange systems. In *Ancient civilization and trade,* edited by J. A. Sabloff and C. C. Lamberg-Karlovsky. University of New Mexico Press, Albuquerque.

  1977   Aspects of regional analysis in archaeology. *Annual Review of Anthropology* 6:479–508.

Johnson, James H.

  1967   *Urban geography: An introductory analysis.* Pergamon, Oxford.

Jones, Thomas B., ed.

  1969   *The Sumerian problem.* Wiley, New York.

Kees, Hermann

  1961   *Ancient Egypt: A cultural topography.* University of Chicago Press, Chicago.

Kenyon, Kathleen M.

  1956   Jericho and its setting in Near Eastern history. *Antiquity* 30:184–194.

  1957   *Digging up Jericho.* Praeger, New York.

  1959a   Earliest Jericho. *Antiquity* 33:5–9.

  1959b   Some observations on the beginnings of settlement in the Near East. *Journal of the Royal Anthropological Institute* 89:35–44.

  1960a   *Archaeology in the holy land.* Praeger, New York.

  1960b   *Excavations at Jericho,* vol. 1. British School of Archaeology in Jerusalem.

  1964   *Excavations at Jericho,* vol. 2. British School of Archaeology in Jerusalem.

  1967   Jericho. *Archaeology* 20:268–275.

Kenyon, Kathleen M., and Diana Kirkbride

  1960   Excavations at Jericho. *Palestine Exploration Quarterly* 92(2):1–32.

King, Leslie J.

  1969   *Statistical analysis in geography.* Prentice-Hall, Englewood Cliffs, New Jersey.

Kirkbride, Diana

  1960   A brief report on the prepottery flint cultures of Jericho. *Palestine Exploration Quarterly* 92(2): 114–119.

Kirkbride, Diana (*continued*)

1966a   Beidha: 1965 campaign. *Archaeology* 19:268–272.

1966b   Five seasons at the prepottery Neolithic village of Beidha in Jordan. *Palestine Exploration Quarterly* 98(1):8–72.

1967   Beidha 1965: An interim report. *Palestine Exploration Quarterly* 99:5–13.

1968   Beidha: Early Neolithic village life south of the Dead Sea. *Antiquity* 42:263–274.

1972   Umm Dabaghiyah 1971: A preliminary report. An early ceramic site in marginal north central Jazira, Iraq. *Iraq* 34:3–15.

1973a   Umm Dabaghiyah 1972: A preliminary report. *Iraq* 35:1–7.

1973b   Umm Dabaghiyah 1973: A third preliminary report. *Iraq* 35:205–209.

1974   Umm Dabaghiyah: A trading outpost? *Iraq* 36:85–92.

1975   Umm Dabaghiyah 1974: a fourth preliminary report. *Iraq* 37:3–10.

Kohl, Philip L.

1975   The archeology of trade. *Dialectical Anthropology* 1:43–50.

Kökten, Kiliç I.

1955   Ein allgemeiner Uberblick uber die prähistorischen Forschungen in Karain-Hohle bei Antalya. *Belleten* 19:284.

Krader, Lawrence

1968   *Formation of the state.* Prentice-Hall, Englewood Cliffs, New Jersey.

Kraeling, C. and Robert McC. Adams, eds.

1960   *City invincible: An Oriental Institute symposium.* University of Chicago Press, Chicago.

Kramer, Samuel Noah

1957   The Sumerians. *Scientific American* 197(4):70–83.

1959   *History begins at Sumer.* Doubleday, New York.

1961   *Mythologies of the ancient world.* Doubleday, New York.

1963   *The Sumerians.* University of Chicago Press, Chicago.

1975   *Sumerian culture and society: The cuneiform documents and their cultural significance.* Cummings Module in Anthropology, no. 58. Cummings, Menlo Park, California.

Kraybill, Nancy

1977   Pre-agricultural tools for the preparation of foods in the Old World. In *Origins of agriculture,* edited by Charles Reed. Mouton, The Hague.

Kroeber, Alfred L.

1953   The delimitation of civilizations. *Journal of the History of Ideas* 14:264–275.

Lamberg-Karlovsky, C. C.

1971   *Excavations at Tepe Yahya, Iran, 1967–1969: Progress report 1.* American School of Prehistoric Research, bulletin no. 27. Peabody Museum, Harvard University, Cambridge, Massachusetts.

1972   Trade mechanisms in Indus-Mesopotamian interrelations. *Journal of the American Oriental Society* 92(2):220–230.

Lamberg-Karlovsky, C. C., ed.

1972   *Old World archaeology: Foundations of civilization.* Readings from *Scientific American.* W. H. Freeman and Company, San Francisco.

Lampl, Paul
    1968   *Cities and planning in the ancient Near East.* Braziller, New York.

Leakey, Mary D.
    1971   *Olduvai Gorge,* vol. 3. Cambridge University Press, Cambridge.

LeBlanc, Steven A., and Patty Jo Watson
    1973   A comparative statistical analysis of painted pottery from seven Halafian sites. *Paleorient* 1(1):117–133.

LeBreton, L.
    1957   The early periods at Susa: Mesopotamian relations. *Iraq* 19(2):79–124.

Lee, Richard B.
    1968   What hunters do for a living, or how to make out on scarce resources. In *Man the hunter,* edited by Richard B. Lee and Irven Devore. Aldine, Chicago.

Lee, Richard B., and Irven Devore, eds.
    1968   *Man the hunter.* Aldine, Chicago.

Leemans, W. F.
    1950   *The old-Babylonian merchant: His business and his social position.* E. J. Brill, Leiden, Holland.

Lees, G. M., and N. L. Falcon
    1952   The geographical history of the Mesopotamian plains. *The Geographical Journal* 118:24–39.

Lees, Susan H., and Daniel G. Bates
    1974   The origins of specialized nomadic pastoralism: A systemic model. *American Antiquity* 29: 187–193.

Leighly, John, ed.
    1963   *Land and life: A selection from the writings of Carl Ortwin Sauer.* University of California Press, Berkeley.

Lenzen, Heinrich J.
    1964   New discoveries of Warka in southern Iraq. *Archaeology* 17:122–131.

Leonard, Jonathan Norton, and the editors of Time-Life Books
    1973   *The first farmers.* Time-Life Books, New York.

Lloyd, Seton
    1967   *Early highland peoples of Anatolia.* Thames and Hudson, London.

Lloyd, Seton, and Fuad Safar
    1945   Tell Hassuna. *Journal of Near Eastern Studies* 4(4):255–289.

Longacre, William
    1970   Archaeology as anthropology: A case study. *Science* 144(3625):1454–1455.

MacArthur, Robert H.
    1972   *Geographical ecology: Patterns in the distribution of species.* Harper & Row, New York.

MacKay, Ernest

    1929   *A Sumerian palace and "A" cemetery at Kish.* Field Museum Anthropological Memoirs, vol. 1, no. 2.

Mallowan, M. E. L.

    1947   Excavations at Brak and Chagar Bazar. *Iraq* 8:111–159.

    1956   *Twenty-five years of Mesopotamian discovery.* The British School of Archaeology in Iraq, London.

    1965a   *Early Mesopotamia and Iran.* McGraw-Hill, New York.

    1965b   The mechanics of ancient trade in western Asia: Reflections on the location of Magan and Meluhha. *Iran* 3:1–7.

    1967   The development of cities: From Al 'Ubaid to the end of the Uruk, parts 1 and 2. *The Cambridge ancient history*, vol. 1, edited by I. E. S. Edwards, C. J. Gadd, and N. G. L. Hammond. Cambridge University Press, Cambridge.

    1968   The Early Dynastic period in Mesopotamia. *The Cambridge ancient history*, vol. 1, edited by I. E. S. Edwards, C. J. Gadd, and N. G. L. Hammond. Cambridge University Press, Cambridge.

Mallowan, M. E. L., and J. Cruikshank Rose

    1935a   Excavations at Tell Arpachiyah, 1933. *Iraq* 2(1): 1–179.

    1935b   *Prehistoric Assyria: The excavations at Tell Arpachiyah, 1933.* Oxford University Press, London.

Mallowan, M. E. L., and D. J. Wiseman, ed.

    1960   Ur in retrospect. *Iraq* 22.

Manners, Robert A.

    1967   Review of *The evolution of urban society* by Robert McC. Adams. *American Antiquity* 32(4):552–553.

Margalef, Ramon

    1963   On certain unifying principles in ecology. *The American Naturalist* 97(897):357–374.

    1968   *Perspectives in ecological theory.* University of Chicago Press, Chicago.

Marks, A.

    1971   Settlement patterns and intrasite variability in the central Negev, Israel. *American Anthropologist* 73:1237–1244.

Marshack, Alexander

    1972   *The roots of civilization: The cognitive beginnings of man's first art, symbol, and notation.* McGraw-Hill, New York.

al-Masry, Abdullah H.

    1973   Prehistory in northeastern Arabia: The problem of interregional interaction. Unpublished Ph.D. dissertation, Department of Anthropology, University of Chicago.

Masson, V. M.

    1968   The urban revolution in south Turkmenia. *Antiquity* 42:178–187.

    1965   The Neolithic farmers of central Asia. *Atti del Sesto Congresso Internazionale delle Scienze Preistoriche e Protoistoriche* 2:205–215.

    1971   *The settlement of Jeitun: The problems of the economy of production.* Academy of Sciences, USSR, Materialy: Issledovaniya po Arkheologii SSR, no. 180.

Mattiae, Paolo

    1977   Tell Mardikh: The archives and palace. *Archaeology* 30(4):244–253.

Mayr, Ernest

 1963   The taxonomic evaluation of fossil hominids. In *Classification and human evolution,* edited by Sherwood Washburn. Viking Fund Publications in Anthropology.

McCown, Donald E.

 1942   *The comparative stratigraphy of early Iran.* Studies in Ancient Oriental Civilization, no. 23. University of Chicago Press, Chicago.

McCown, T. D., and A. Keith

 1939   *The Stone Age of Mount Carmel,* vol. 2. Clarendon Press, Oxford.

McLuhan, Marshall

 1964   *Understanding media.* New American Library, New York.

Meldgaard, Jorgen, Peder Mortensen, and Henrik Thrane

 1964   Excavations at Tepe Guran, Luristan. *Acta Archeologica* 34:97–133.

Mellaart, James

 1961a   Early cultures of the south Anatolian plateau. *Anatolian Studies* 11:159–184.
 1961b   Excavations at Hacilar. *Anatolian Studies* 11:70–75
 1961c   Roots in the soil. In *Dawn of civilization,* edited by Stuart Piggot. Thames and Hudson, London.
 1965   *Earliest civilizations of the Near East.* McGraw Hill, New York.
 1966   *The Chalcolithic and Early Bronze Ages in the Near East and Anatolia.* Khayats, Beirut.
 1967   *Çatal Hüyük: a Neolithic town in Anatolia.* McGraw-Hill, New York.
 1970   *Excavations at Hacilar,* vols. 1 and 2. Edinburgh University Press, Edinburgh.
 1975   *The Neolithic of the Near East.* Scribner's, New York.

Mendelsohn, Isaac, ed.

 1955   *Religions of the ancient Near East.* Liberal Arts Press, New York.

Merpert, Nicolai, and Rauf Munchajev

 1969   The investigation of the Soviet archaeological expedition in Iraq in the spring 1969. *Sumer* 25:125–131.

Michael, Henry N., and Elizabeth K. Ralph, eds.

 1971   *Dating techniques for the archaeologist.* M.I.T. Press, Cambridge, Massachusetts.

Milojcic, V., J. Boessnick, and M. Hopf

 1962   *Die deutschen Ausgrabungen auf der Argissa Magula in Thessalien,* vol. 1. Habelt, Bonn.

Minshull, Roger

 1967   *Regional geography: Theory and practice.* Hutchinson University Library, London.

Mitchell, William P.

 1973   The hydraulic hypothesis: A reappraisal. *Current Anthropology* 14(5):532–534.

Monkhouse, F. J., and H. R. Wilkinson

 1963   *Maps and diagrams: Their compilation and construction.* Methuen, London.

Moore, Andrew

1973   The excavation at Tell Abu Hureyra in 1972. Manuscript.

Moore, Charlotte B., ed.

1974   *Reconstructing complex societies: An archaeological colloquium.* Bulletin of the American Schools of Oriental Research, no. 20. Baltimore.

Moortgat, A.

1949   *Tammuz.* Walter de Gruyter, Berlin.

Morgan, Lewis Henry

1967   *Ancient society.* World, Cleveland.

Mortensen, Peder

1964   Additional remarks on the chronology of early village-farming communities. *Sumer* 20(1-2): 28–36.

1970   Tell Shimshara: the Hassuna period. *Historisk-Filosofiske Skrifter* 5:2.

1971   A preliminary study of the chipped stone industry from Beidha. *Acta Archaeologica* 41:1–54.

1972   Seasonal camps and early villages in the Zagros. In *Man, settlement, and urbanism,* edited by Peter J. Ucko, Ruth Tringham, and G. W. Dimbleby. Duckworth, London.

Mortensen, Peder, J. Meldgaard, and H. Thrane

1964   Excavations at Tepe Guran, Luristan. *Acta Archaeologica* 39:110–121.

Moscati, Sabatino

1960   *The face of the ancient orient: A panorama of Near Estern civilization in pre-classical times.* Doubleday, New York.

Movius, H. L., N. C. David, H. M. Bricker, and R. B. Clay

1968   The analysis of certain major classes of Upper Paleolithic tools. *American School of Prehistoric Research Bulletin,* no. 26. Peabody Museum, Harvard University, Cambridge, Massachusetts.

Mumford, Lewis

1961   *The city in history.* Harcourt, Brace and World, New York.

Murray, Jacqueline

1970   *The first European agriculture: A study of the osteological and botanical evidence until two thousand* B.C. Edinburgh University Press, Edinburgh.

Naroll, Raoul

1956   A preliminary index of social development. *American Anthropologist* 58(4):687–715.

Nasrallah, Mgr. J.

1965   Notes de préhistoire syrienne Qatana. *Les Annales archéologiques de Syrie* 15:51–64.

Netting, Robert McC.

1971   *The ecological approach in cultural study.* Addison-Wesley Modular Publication, no. 6. Addison-Wesley, Reading, Massachusetts.

Neuville, René

1951   Le paléolithique et le mesolithique du désert de Judée. In *Memoir 24 de l'Institute de Paléolithique Humain.* Paris.

Nissen, Hans J.

1968   Survey of an abandoned modern village in southern Iraq. *Sumer* 24:107–114.

Nissen, Hans J., and Charles L. Redman

1971   Preliminary notes on archeological surface survey in the Plain of Behbehan and the lower Zuhreh Valley. *Revue d'archéologie et d'art iraniens* 6:48–50.

North, Robert

1957   Status of the Warka excavation. *Orientalia* 26:185–256.

Noy, Tamar, A. J. Legge, and E. S. Higgs

1973   Recent excavations at Nahal Oren, Israel. *Proceedings of the Prehistoric Society* 39:75–99.

Oates, Joan

1966   First preliminary report on a survey in the region of Mandali and Badra. *Sumer* 22:51–60.

1968   Prehistoric investigations near Mandali, Iraq. *Iraq* 30:1–20.

1972   A radiocarbon date from Choga Mami. *Iraq* 24:49–53.

1973   The background and development of early farming communities in Mesopotamia and the Zagros. *Proceedings of the Prehistoric Society* (London) 39:147–181.

Olsen, Stanley J.

1971   *Zoo-archaeology: Animal bones in archaeology and their interpretation.* Addison-Wesley Modular Publication, no. 2. Addison-Wesley, Reading, Massachusetts.

Olsson, Ingrid U.

1970   *Radiocarbon variations and absolute chronology.* Nobel Symposium, no. 12, Stockholm.

Oppenheim, A. Leo

1964   *Ancient Mesopotamia: Portrait of a dead civilization.* University of Chicago Press, Chicago.

Orni, E., and E. Efrat

1964   *Geography of Israel.* Israel Program for Scientific Translations, Jerusalem.

Parsons, Jeffrey R.

1973   Review of *Man, settlement, and urbanism* edited by Peter Ucko, Ruth Tringham, and G. W. Dimbleby. *Science* 181(4100):646–648.

Payne, Joan Crowfoot

1968   Lapis lazuli in early Egypt. *Iraq* 30:58–61.

Peake, Harold, and Herbert John Fleure

1927   *Peasants and potters.* Oxford University Press, London.

Pearson, Kenneth, and Patricia Connor

1968   *The Dorak affair.* Atheneum, New York.

Pellett, P. L. and Sossy Shadarevian

    1970   *Food composition: Tables for use in the Middle East,* 2d ed. American University of Beirut, Beirut.

Perkins, Ann L.

    1949   *The comparative archeology of early Mesopotamia.* Studies in Ancient Oriental Civilization, no. 25. University of Chicago Press, Chicago.

Perkins, Dexter, Jr.

    1964   Prehistoric fauna from Shanidar, Iraq. *Science* 144:1565–1566.

    1966   The fauna from Madamagh and Beidha: A preliminary report. *Palestine Exploration Quarterly,* 98(1):66–67.

    1969   Fauna of Çatal Hüyük: Evidence for early cattle domestication in Anatolia. *Science* 164(3876): 177–179.

    1973   The beginnings of animal domestication in the Near East. *American Journal of Archaeology* 77: 279–282.

Perkins, Dexter, Jr., and Patricia Daly

    1968   A hunter's village in Neolithic Turkey. *Scientific American* 219(5):97–106.

Perrot, Jean

    1955   The excavations at Tell Abu Matar, near Beersheba. *Israel Exploration Journal* 5:17–40, 73–84, and 167–189.

    1960   Excavations at 'Eynan: Preliminary report of the 1959 season. *Israel Exploration Journal* 10:14–22.

    1961   Excavations at 'Eynan, Israel. In *Year Book of American Philosophical Society for 1960.*

    1962a   Excavations at a Natufian settlement. In *Year Book of American Philosophical Society for 1961.*

    1962b   Palestine-Syria-Cilicia. In *Courses toward urban life,* edited by Robert J. Braidwood and Gordon Willey. Aldine, Chicago.

    1964   Les deux premières campagnes de fouilles à Munhata (1962–1963): Premiers resultats. *Syria* 41:323–345.

    1966a   Le gisement natoufien de Mallaha (Eynan), Israel. *L'Anthropologie* 7(5–6):437–484.

    1966b   La troisième campagne de fouilles à Munhata (1964). *Syria* 43:49–63.

    1967   Munhata: Un village préhistorique. *Bible et terre sainte* 93:4–16.

    1968   La préhistoire palestinienne. In *Supplément au dictionnaire de la Bible,* no. 8, pp. 286–446. Letouzey & Ane, Paris.

Pfeiffer, John E.

    1977   *The emergence of society: A prehistory of the establishment.* McGraw-Hill, New York.

Phillips, James L.

    1970   Old World domestications. *Ecology* 51(4):752–754.

    1970   Travail récent sur le paléolithique final de la Vallée du Nil: Rapport préliminaire. *L'Anthropologie* 74(7–8):573–581.

Plog, Frederick

    1968   Archaeological survey: A new perspective. Unpublished master's thesis. Department of Anthropology, University of Chicago.

    1974a   Settlement patterns and social history. In *Frontiers of anthropology: An introduction to anthropological thinking,* edited by Murray A. Leaf. van Nostrand, New York.

    1974b   *The study of prehistoric change.* Academic Press, New York.

1975   Systems theory in archeological research. In *Annual Review of Anthropology* 4:207–224.

Polayni, Karl, Conrad M. Arensberg, and Harry W. Pearson
1957   *Trade and market in the early empires: Economies in history and theory.* Free Press, New York.

Porada, Edith
1965   The relative chronology of Mesopotamia: Part 1, Seals and trade. In *Chronologies in Old World archaeology*, edited by Robert W. Ehrich. University of Chicago Press, Chicago.

Porada, Edith, and Briggs Buchanan
1948   *Corpus of ancient Near East eastern seals in North-American collections,* vol. 1. The collection of the Pierpont Morgan Library. Pantheon, New York.

Prausnitz, M. W.
1959   The first agricultural settlements in Galilee. *Israel Exploration Journal* 9:166–174.
1966   A study in terminology: The Kebaran, the Natufian, and the Tahunian. *Israel Exploration Journal* 16:220–230.

Prescott, J. R. V.
1965   *The geography of frontiers and boundaries.* Aldine, Chicago.

Pritchard, James B., ed.
1958   *The ancient Near East: An anthology of texts and pictures.* Princeton University Press, Princeton, New Jersey.

Protsch, Reiner, and Rainer Berger
1973   Earliest radiocarbon dates for domesticated animals from Europe and the Near East. *Science* 179(4070):235.

Pumpelly, R.
1908   *Explorations in Turkestan, expedition of 1904: Prehistoric civilizations of Anau,* vol. 1. Publications of the Carnegie Institution, no. 73. Washington, D.C.

Quinn, Naomi
1977   Anthropological studies on women's status. *Annual Review of Anthropology* 6:181–225.

Rathje, William L.
1971   The origin and development of lowland classic Maya civilization. *American Antiquity* 36(3): 275–285.

Reade, J. E.
1973   Tell Taya (1972–1973): Summary report. *Iraq* 35:155–187.

Redfield, Robert
1953   *The primitive world and its transformations.* Cornell University Press, Ithaca, New York.

Redman, Charles L.
1972   Review of *Excavations at Hacilar,* vols. 1 and 2, by James Mellart. *American Anthropologist* 74(4): 946–951.
1973a   Early village technology: A view through the microscope. *Paleorient* 1(2):249–261.

Redman, Charles L. (*continued*)

1973b   Multistage fieldwork and analytical techniques. *American Antiquity* 38(1):61–79.

1973c   Multivariate approach to understanding changes in an early farming community in southeast Anatolia. In *The explanation of culture change*, edited by Colin Renfrew. Duckworth, London.

1974a   Archeological sampling strategies. Addison-Wesley Module in Anthropology, no. 55. Addison-Wesley, Reading, Massachusetts.

1974b   A conjunctive ceramic analysis for complex cultural processes. Manuscript. State University of New York, Binghamton.

1974c   Toward an effective approach to urban societies. In *Reconstructing complex societies*, edited by Charlotte B. Moore. Supplement to the Bulletin of the American Schools of Oriental Research, no. 20. Baltimore.

1977   Man, domestication, and culture in southwestern Asia. In *Origins of agriculture*, edited by Charles Reed. Mouton, The Hague.

Redman, Charles L., and Patty J. Watson

1970   Systematic, intensive surface collection. *American Antiquity* 35:279–91.

Reed, Charles A.

1959   Animal domestication in the prehistoric Near East. *Science* 130(3389):1629–1639.

1960   A review of the archeological evidence on animal domestication in the prehistoric Near East. In *Prehistoric investigations in Iraqi Kurdistan*, edited by Robert J. Braidwood and Bruce Howe. Studies in Ancient Oriental Civilization, no. 31. University of Chicago Press, Chicago.

1963   Osteo-archaeology. In *Science in archaeology*, edited by Don Brothwell and Eric Higgs. Basic Books, New York.

1969   The pattern of animal domestication in the prehistoric Near East. In *The domestication and exploitation of plants and animals*, edited by Peter J. Ucko and G. W. Dimbleby, pp. 361–380. Aldine, Chicago.

1977   A model for the origin of agriculture in the Near East. In *Origins of agriculture*, edited by Charles Reed. Mouton, The Hague.

Reed, Charles A., ed.

1977   *Origins of agriculture.* Mouton, The Hague.

Reed, Charles A., and Robert J. Braidwood

1960   Toward the reconstruction of the environmental sequence of northeastern Iraq. In *Prehistoric investigations in Iraqi Kurdistan*, edited by Robert J. Braidwood and Bruce Howe. Studies in Oriental Civilization, no. 31. University of Chicago Press, Chicago.

Renfrew, Colin

1973   Review of *Population growth* edited by Brian Spooner. *Science* 182(4107):46.

1974   Beyond a subsistence economy: The evolution of social organization in prehistoric Europe. In *Reconstructing complex societies*, edited by Charlotte B. Moore. Bulletin of the American Schools of Oriental Research, no. 20. Baltimore.

Renfrew, Colin, J. E. Dixon, and J. R. Cann

1966   Obsidian and early cultural contact in the Near East. *Proceedings of the Prehistoric Society* (London) 32:30–72.

1968   Further analysis of Near Eastern obsidians. *Proceedings of the Prehistoric Society* (London) 34: 319–331.

Renfrew, Jane M.

1969   The archaeological evidence for the domestication of plants: Methods and problems. In *The domestication and exploitation of plants and animals,* edited by Peter J. Ucko and B. W. Dimbleby. Aldine, Chicago.

1973   *Paleoethnobotany: The prehistoric food plants of the Near East and Europe.* Columbia University Press, New York.

Riley, Carroll L.

1969   *The origins of civilization.* Southern Illinois University Press, Carbondale.

Rodden, Robert

1965   An Early Neolithic village in Greece. *Scientific American* 212(4):82–92.

Rouse, Irving

1973   Review of *The Uruk countryside* by Robert McC. Adams and Hans J. Nissen. *Science* 181(4095):150.

Ryder, Michael L.

1969   *Animal bones in archaeology.* Blackwell, Oxford.

1969   Changes in the fleece of sheep following domestication. In *The domestication and exploitation of plants and animals,* edited by Peter J. Ucko and G. W. Dimbleby. Aldine, Chicago.

Sabloff, Jeremy A., and C. C. Lamberg-Karlovsky, eds.

1974   *The rise and fall of civilizations: Modern archaeological approaches to ancient cultures.* Cummings, Menlo Park, California.

1975   *Ancient civilization and trade.* University of New Mexico Press, Albuquerque.

Safar, Fuad

1950   Eridu: A preliminary report on the third season's excavations, 1948–1949. *Sumer* 6(1):27–35.

Saggs, H. W. F.

1962   *The greatness that was Babylon: A sketch of the ancient civilization of the Tigris-Euphrates Valley,* Hawthorn, New York.

Sahlins, Marshall, and Elman Service

1960   *Evolution and culture.* University of Michigan Press, Ann Arbor.

Sanders, William T.

1968   Hydraulic agriculture, economic symbiosis, and the evolution of states in central Mexico. In *Anthropological archeology in the Americas.* The Anthropological Society of Washington, Washington, D.C.

Sanders, Willaim T., and Barbara J. Price

1968   *Mesoamerica: The evolution of a civilization.* Random House, New York.

Schiffer, Michael B.

1976   *Behavioral archaeology.* Academic Press, New York.

Semenov, S. A.

1964   *Prehistoric technology.* Adams and Dart, Bath, England.

Service, Elman

1962   *Primitive social organization: An evolutionary perspective.* Random House, New York.

1975   *Origins of the state and civilization: The process of cultural evolution.* Norton, New York.

Singh, Purushottam

1974   *Neolithic cultures of western Asia.* Seminar Press, New York.

Sjoberg, Gideon

1960   *The preindustrial city: Past and present.* Free Press, New York.

1965   The origin and evolution of cities. *Scientific American* 213(3):54–63.

Smailes, Arthur E.

1966   *The geography of towns.* Hutchinson University Library, London.

Smith, Carol A., ed.

1976   *Regional analysis: Economic systems* (vol. 1); *Social systems* (vol. 2). Academic Press, New York.

Smith, Philip E. L.

1966   The Late Paleolithic of northeast Africa in light of recent research. In *Recent studies in paleoanthropology, American Anthropologist* 68(2, part 2):326–355.

1968   Ganj Dareh Tepe. *Iran* 6:158–160.

1970   Review of *Prehistory and human ecology of the Del Luran Plain* by Frank Hole, Kent Flannery, and James A. Neely. *Science* 168(3932):707–709.

1971   Iran, 9000–4000 B.C.: The Neolithic. *Expedition* 13(3–4):6–13.

1972a   *The consequences of food production.* Addison-Wesley Module in Anthropology, no. 31. Addison-Wesley, Reading, Massachusetts.

1972b   Survey of excavations in Iran during 1970–1971. *Iran* 10:165–168.

1975   Ganj Dareh Tepe. *Iran* 13:178–180.

Smith, Philip E. L., and T. Cuyler Young, Jr.

1972   The evolution of early agriculture and culture in greater Mesopotamia: A trial model. In *Population growth: Anthropological implications*, edited by B. J. Spooner. M.I.T. Press, Cambridge, Massachusetts.

Smith, William Stevenson

1965   *Interconnections in the ancient Near East.* Yale University Press, New Haven.

Solecki, Ralph S.

1959   Early man in cave and village at Shanidar, Kurdistan, Iraq. *Transactions of the New York Academy of Science* 21:712.

1960   Clue to the emergence of food production in the Near East from evidence at Shanidar, northern Iraq. Paper prepared for the Iranian Congress, New York.

1961   Prehistory in Shanidar Valley, northern Iraq. *Science* 129(1551):179–193.

1971   *Shanidar: The first flower people.* Knopf, New York.

Solecki, Ralph S., and Rose L. Solecki

1970   Grooved stones from Zawi Chemi Shanidar, a Proto-Neolithic site in northern Iraq. *American Anthropologist* 72:831–841.

Solecki, Rose L.

   1964   Zawi Chemi Shanidar, a Post-Pleistocene village site in northern Iraq. *Report of the Sixth International Congress on Quaternary, Warsaw, 1961*, pp. 405–412.

de Sonneville-Bordes, Denise

   1960   *Le Paléolithique supérieur en Perigord.* Imprimeries Delmas, Bordeaux, France.

   1965   Review of *Excavaciones en la terraza de "El Khiam" (Jordania)* by J. G. Echegaray. *L'Anthropologie* 69:115–117.

Speiser, E. A.

   1935   *Excavations at Tepe Gawra*, vol. 1. University of Pennsylvania Press, Philadelphia.

Spengler, Oswald

   1926–28 *Decline of the West.* Allen & Unwin, London.

Spooner, Brian

   1973   *The cultural ecology of pastoral nomads.* Addison-Wesley Module in Anthropology, no. 45. Addison-Wesley, Reading, Massachusetts.

Spooner, Brian, ed.

   1972   Population growth: Anthropological implications. M.I.T. Press, Cambridge, Massachusetts.

Starr, Chester G.

   1973   *Early man: Prehistory and the civilizations of the ancient Near East.* Oxford University Press, New York.

Stekelis, M.

   1966   *Archaeological excavations at 'Ubeidiya, 1960–1963.* The Israel Academy of Sciences and Humanities, Jerusalem.

Stekelis, M., O. Bar-Yosef, and Tamar Schick

   1969   *Archaeological excavations at 'Ubeidiya, 1964–1966.* The Israel Academy of Sciences and Humanities, Jerusalem.

Stekelis, M., and Tamar Yizraely

   1963   Excavations at Nahal Oren: Preliminary report. *Israel Exploration Journal* 13(1):1–12.

Stewart, J. Dale

   1960   Form of the pubic bone in Neanderthal man. *Science* 131(3411):1437–1438.

Steward, Julian H.

   1949   Cultural causality and law: A trial formulation of the development of early civilization. *American Anthropologist* 51:1–27.

Steward, Julian H., ed.

   1955   *Irrigation civilizations: A comparative study.* Pan American Union, Washington, D.C.

Stronach, David

   1961   Excavations at Ral al' Amiya. *Iraq* 23:95–105.

Struever, Stuart

1968   Flotation techniques for the recovery of small-scale archaeological remains. *American Antiquity* 33:353–362.

1971   Comments on archeological data requirements and research strategies. *American Antiquity* 35:9–19.

Struever, Stuart, ed.

1971   *Prehistoric agriculture.* Natural History Press, New York.

Suess, H. E.

1970   Bristle-cone pine calibration of the radiocarbon time-space 5200 B.C. to the present. In *Radiocarbon variations and absolute chronology,* edited by Ingrid Olsson. Wiley, New York.

Sumner, William M.

1973   Tall-i Malyan and the chronology of the Kur River basin, Iran. *American Journal of Archaeology* 77:288–291.

Tobler, Arthur J.

1950   *Excavations at Tepe Gawra, 2.* University of Pennsylvania Press, Philadelphia.

Todd, Ian A.

1966   Aşikli Hüyük: A Proto-Neolithic site in central Anatolia. *Anatolian Studies* 16:139–163.

1968a   The dating of Aşikli Hüyük in central Anatolia. *American Journal of Archaeology* 72:157–158.

1968b   Preliminary report on a survey of Neolithic sites in central Anatolia. *Türk Tarih Kurumu Basimevi* 15(2):103–107.

1971   The Neolithic period in Central Anatolia. Paper presented at the 1971 meeting of the Huitième Congres International des Sciences Pré-et Proto-historiques, Belgrade.

Tosi, Maurizio

1969   Excavations at Shar-i Sokhta: Preliminary report on the second campaign, September–December 1968. *East and West* 19(3-4):283–386.

1971   Dilmun. *Antiquity* 45:21–25.

1973   Early urban evolution and settlement patterns in the Indo-Iranian borderland. In *The explanation of culture change: Models in prehistory,* edited by Colin Renfrew. Duckworth, London.

Toynbee, Arnold J.

1934   *A study of history,* 3 vols. Oxford University Press, London.

Tringham, Ruth

1971   *Hunters, fishers, and farmers of eastern Europe 6000–3000* B.C. Hutchinson University Library, London.

Tringham, Ruth, ed.

1973   *Urban settlements: The process of urbanization in archaeological settlements.* Warner Modular, Andover, Massachusetts.

Turnbull, Priscilla F., and Charles A. Reed

1974   The fauna from the terminal Pleistocene of Palegawra Cave, a Zarzian occupation site in northeastern Iraq. *Fieldiana—Anthropology* 63:81–146.

Turville-Petre, F., and A. Keith

1927   *Researchers in prehistoric Galilee, 1925–1926.* British School of Archaeology in Jerusalem.

Ucko, Peter J.

1968   *Anthropomorphic figurines of Pre-Dynastic Egypt and Neolithic Crete with comparative material from the prehistoric Near East and mainland Greece.* Royal Anthropological Institute Occasional Paper, no. 24. Andrew Szmidla, London.

1969   Ethnography and archaeological interpretation of funerary remains. *World Archaeology* 1(2): 262–280.

Ucko, Peter J., and G. W. Dimbleby, eds.

1969   *The domestication and exploitation of plants and animals.* Aldine, Chicago.

Van Liere, Willem J., and Henri de Contenson

1963   A note on five early Neolithic sites in inland Syria. *Les Annales archéologiques de Syrie* 13:175–205.

van Loon, Maurits

1966   First results of the 1965 excavations at Tell Mureybat near Meskene. *Les Annales archéologiques arabes syriennes* 16:211–217.

van Loon, Maurits, James H. Skinner, and Willem van Zeist

1968   The Oriental Institute excavations at Mureybit, Syria: Preliminary report on the 1965 campaign. Part 1: Architecture and general finds. *Journal of Near Eastern Studies* 27(4):265–290.

1970   The Oriental Institute excavations at Mureybit, Syria: Preliminary report of the 1965 campaign. Part 3. *The Paleobotany Journal of Near Eastern Studies* 29:167–176.

van Zeist, Willem

1969   Reflections on prehistoric environments in the Near East. In *The domestication and exploitation of plants and animals,* edited by Peter J. Ucko and G. W. Dimbleby. Aldine, Chicago.

1972   Palaeobotanical results of the 1970 season at Çayönü, Turkey. *Helinium* 12:1–19.

1976   On macroscopic traces of food plants in southwestern Asia. *Philosophical Transactions of the Royal Society of London B* 275:27–41.

van Zeist, Willem, and S. Bottema

1966   Palaeobotanical investigations at Ramad. *Les Annales archéologiques arabes syriennes* 16(2):179–180.

van Zeist, Willem, and Herbert E. Wright, Jr.

1963   Preliminary pollen studies at Lake Zeribar, Zagros Mountains, southwestern Iran. *Science* 140(3562):65–69.

de Vaux, R.

1966   Palestine during the Neolithic and Chalcolithic periods. *The Cambridge ancient history,* vol. 1, edited by I. E. S. Edwards, C. J. Gadd, and N. G. L. Hammond. Cambridge University Press, Cambridge.

Vayda, Andrew P., and Roy A. Rappaport

1968   Ecology: Cultural and noncultural. In *Introduction to cultural anthropology,* edited by James Clifton. Houghton Mifflin, New York.

Vercoutter, Jean

1965   The origins of Egypt and archaic Egypt. In *The Near East: The early civilizations,* edited by Jean Bottéro, Elena Cassin, and Jean Vercoutter. Delacorte, New York.

Vignard, E.

1934   La Paléolithique en Egypte. *Memoires de l'institut francais d'archéologie orientale 46 (melanges Maspero 1):* 165–175.

Vita-Finzi, C., and E. S. Higgs

1970   Prehistoric economy in the Mount Carmel area of Palestine: Site catchment analysis. *Proceedings of the Prehistoric Society* (London) 36:1–37.

Wagner, Philip L.

1960   *The human use of the earth.* Free Press, Glencoe, Illinois.

1977   The concept of environmental determinism in cultural evolution. In *Origins of agriculture,* edited by Charles Reed. Mouton, The Hague.

Wagner, Philip L., and Martin W. Mikesell

1962   *Readings in cultural geography.* University of Chicago Press, Chicago.

Walters, Stanley D.

1970   *Water for Larsa: An Old Babylonian archive dealing with irrigation.* Yale University Press, New Haven.

Walton, Kenneth

1969   *The arid zones.* Aldine, Chicago.

Waterbolk, H. T.

1971   Working with radiocarbon dates. *Proceedings of the Prehistoric Society* (London) 37:15–33.

Watson, Patty Jo

1965   The chronology of north Syria and north Mesopotamia from 10,000 B.C. to 2000 B.C. In *Chronologies in Old World archaeology,* edited by Robert Ehrich. University of Chicago Press, Chicago.

1973   Results of excavations at the prehistoric site of Girikihaciyan, Turkey. Paper presented at the Ninth International Congress of Anthropological and Ethnological Sciences, Chicago.

Watson, Patty Jo, and Steven A. LeBlanc

1973   Excavation and analysis of Halafian materials from southeastern Turkey: The Halafian period reexamined. Paper presented at the seventy-second annual meeting of the American Anthropological Association, New Orleans.

Watson, Patty Jo, Steven A. LeBlanc, and Charles L. Redman

1971   *Explanation in archeology: An explicitly scientific approach.* Columbia University Press, New York.

Watt, Bernice K. and Annabel L. Merrill

1963   *Composition of foods.* Agriculture handbook no. 8, United States Department of Agriculture, Washington, D.C.

Weaver, M. E.

1971   A new water separation process for soil from archeological excavations *Anatolian Studies* 21:65–68.

Weber, Max

1958   *The city.* Free Press, New York.

Weinberg, Saul S.

1965   The Stone Age in the Aegean. *The Cambrige ancient history,* vol. 1, edited by I. E. S. Edwards, C. J. Gadd, and N. G. L. Hammond. Cambridge University Press, Cambridge.

Weiss, Harvey

1975   Kish, Akkad, and Aqade. *Journal of the American Oriental Society* 95:434–453.

Wendorf, Fred, ed.

1968   *The prehistory of Nubia.* Southern Methodist University Press, Dallas.

Wendorf, Fred, Rushdi Said, and Romuaid Schild

1970   Egyptian prehistory: Some new concepts. *Science* 169(3951):1161–1171.

Wertime, Theodore A.

1968   A metallurgical expedition through the Persian desert. *Science* 159(3818):927–936.

1973   The beginnings of metallurgy: A new look. *Science* 182(4115):875–887.

Whallon, Robert J.

1973   Spatial analysis of occupation floors: Part 1, Application of dimensional analysis of variance. *American Antiquity* 38(3):266–278.

Wheeler, Sir Mortimer

1954   *Archaeology from the earth.* Clarendon Press, Oxford. (Pelican printing, 1956).

1956   The first towns? *Antiquity* 30:132–136.

1968   *The Indus civilization,* 3d. ed. Cambridge University Press, Cambridge.

White, Leslie A.

1945   History, evolutionism, and functionalism: Three types of interpretation of culture. *Southwestern Journal of Anthropology* 1:221–248.

Wilke, Philip J., Robert Bettinger, Thomas F. King, and James F. O'Connell

1971   Harvest selection and domestication in seed plants. Paper presented at the 1971 meeting of the Society for American Archaeology, Norman, Oklahoma.

Wilmsen, Edwin N.

1972   *Social exchange and interaction.* The University of Michigan Museum of Anthropology, Anthropological Papers, no. 46. Ann Arbor.

Wilson, John A.

1951   *The culture of ancient Egypt.* University of Chicago Press, Chicago.

1964   *Signs and wonders upon Pharaoh: A history of American Egyptology.* University of Chicago Press, Chicago.

Wittfogel, Karl A.

1956   The hydraulic civilizations. In *Man's role in changing the face of the earth,* edited by William R. Thomas. University of Chicago Press, Chicago.

1957   *Oriental despotism: A comparative study of total power.* Yale University Press, New Haven.

Wittfogel, Karl A. (*continued*)

1967   Review of *The evolution of urban society: Early Mesopotamian and Prehispanic Mexico* by Robert McC. Adams. *American Anthropologist* 69(1):90–93.

Woolley, Sir Leonard

1950   *Ur of the Chaldees.* Penguin, Baltimore.

1955   *Excavations at Ur.* Crowell, New York.

1965   *The beginnings of civilization.* New American Library, New York.

Wright, G. Ernest

1965   The archaeology of Palestine. In *The Bible and the ancient Near East,* edited by G. Ernest Wright. Doubleday, New York.

1974   The Tell: Basic unit for reconstructing complex societies of the Near East. In *Reconstructing complex society,* edited by Charlotte Moore. American Schools of Oriental Research.

Wright, G. Ernest, ed.

1965   *The Bible and the ancient Near East.* Doubleday, New York.

Wright, Gary A.

1969   *Obsidian analysis and prehistoric Near Eastern trade: 7500 to 3500 B.C.* The University of Michigan Museum of Anthropology, Anthropological Papers, no. 37. Ann Arbor.

1971   Origins of food production in southwestern Asia: A survey of ideas. *Current Anthropology* 12(4-5): 447–477.

1974   *Archaeology and trade.* Addison-Wesley Module in Anthropology, no. 49. Addison-Wesley, Reading, Massachusetts.

Wright, Gary A., and Adon A. Gordus

1969   Distribution and utilization of obsidian from Lake Van sources between 7500 and 3500 B.C. *American Journal of Archaeology* 73:75–77.

Wright, Henry T.

1969   *The administration of rural production in an early Mesopotamian town.* The University of Michigan Museum of Anthropology, Anthropological Papers, no. 38. Ann Arbor.

1970   Toward an explanation of the origin of the state. Manuscript.

1972   A consideration of interregional exchange in greater Mesopotamia: 4000–3000 B.C. In *Social exchange and interaction,* edited by Edwin N. Wilmsen. The University of Michigan Museum of Anthropology, Anthropological Papers, no. 46. Ann Arbor.

1977   Recent research on the origin of the state. *Annual Review of Anthropology* 6:379–398.

Wright, Henry T., and Greg A. Johnson

1975   Population, exchange, and early state formation in southwestern Iran. *American Anthropologist* 77:267–289.

Wright, Henry T., J. A. Neely, Greg A. Johnson, and John Speth

1975   Early fourth millennium developments in southwestern Iran. *Iran* 13:103–121.

Wright, Herbert E., Jr.

1960   Climate and prehistoric man in the eastern Mediterranean. In *Prehistoric investigations in Iraqi Kurdistan,* edited by Robert J. Braidwood and Bruce Howe. Studies in Ancient Oriental Civilization, no. 31. University of Chicago Press, Chicago.

1968   Natural environment of early food production north of Mesopotamia, *Science* 161:334–339.

1976   The environmental setting for plant domestication in the Near East. *Science* 194(4263):385–389.

1977   Environmental change and the origin of agriculture in the Old and New Worlds. In *Origins of agriculture,* edited by Charles Reed. Mouton, The Hague.

Young, T. Cuyler, Jr.

1966   Survey in western Iran, 1961. *Journal of Near Eastern Studies* 25:228–239.

Zeuner, Frederick E.

1963   *A history of domesticated animals.* Hutchinson, London.

Zohary, Daniel

1969   The progenitors of wheat and barley in relation to domestication and agricultural dispersal in the Old World. In *The domestication and exploitation of plants and animals,* edited by Peter Ucko and G. W. Dimbleby. Aldine, Chicago.

Zohary, Daniel, and Maria Hopf

1973   Domestication of pulses in the Old World. *Science* 182(4115):887–894.

Zohary, Daniel, and Pinhas Spiegel-Roy

1975   Beginnings of fruit growing in the Old World. *Science* 187(4174):319–327.

Zubrow, Ezra B. W.

1973   Agricultural patterning. Paper presented at 1973 meeting of Society for American Archaeology, San Francisco.

INDEX

INDEX